Eating Disorders and Obesity

Eating Disorders and Obesity

The Challenge for Our Times

Special Issue Editors

Phillipa Hay

Deborah Mitchison

MDPI • Basel • Beijing • Wuhan • Barcelona • Belgrade

Special Issue Editors
Phillipa Hay
School of Medicine Western Sydney University
Australia

Deborah Mitchison
Macquarie University
Australia

Editorial Office
MDPI
St. Alban-Anlage 66
4052 Basel, Switzerland

This is a reprint of articles from the Special Issue published online in the open access journal *Nutrients* (ISSN 2072-6643) from 2018 to 2019 (available at: https://www.mdpi.com/journal/nutrients/special_issues/Eating_Disorders_Obesity)

For citation purposes, cite each article independently as indicated on the article page online and as indicated below:

LastName, A.A.; LastName, B.B.; LastName, C.C. Article Title. *Journal Name* **Year**, *Article Number*, Page Range.

ISBN 978-3-03897-998-2 (Pbk)
ISBN 978-3-03897-999-9 (PDF)

Contents

About the Special Issue Editors

Phillipa Hay, MBCHB (1983), MD (1993), FRANZCP (1991) DPhil (1995) FAED (2013) is Chair of Mental Health at the Translational Health Research Institute, Western Sydney University, Director Eating Disorders Unit Wesley Hospital Ashfield, and Senior Consultant in Psychiatry at Campbelltown Hospital, SWSLHD. She has lead major international clinical trials, meta-analyses and epidemiological studies in the field of Eating Disorders. In 2015 she received the Lifetime Leadership Award from the ANZ Academy for Eating Disorders and in 2013 she was elected Fellow of the (international) Academy for Eating Disorders. In 2014 she was awarded a "Science Without Borders" Visiting Professorship from the CAPES research foundation in Brazil.

Deborah Mitchison, PhD, MClinPsych is NHMRC Early Career Research Fellow at the Translational Health Research Institute, Western Sydney University and immediate past Macquarie University Research Fellow, and Clinical Psychologist, specialising in eating disorders epidemiological research and treatment. She completed her PhD in 2015 temporal changes in eating disorder health burden, and has since developed a strong independent track record leading a research team that is conducting large community and clinical cohort studies. She is a member of the bi-national ANZ Academy for Eating Disorders Executive and an Australian Psychological Society Early Career Researcher Awardee..

nutrients

Editorial

Eating Disorders and Obesity: The Challenge for Our Times

Phillipa Hay [1,*] and Deborah Mitchison [1,2]

1 Translational Health Research Institute (THRI), School of Medicine, Western Sydney University, Locked Bag 1797, Penrith, NSW 2751, Australia
2 Department of Psychology, Macquarie University, Sydney, NSW 2109, Australia; d.mitchison@westernsydney.edu.au
* Correspondence: p.hay@westernsydney.edu.au; Tel.: +61-41-233-0428

Received: 1 May 2019; Accepted: 8 May 2019; Published: 11 May 2019

Abstract: Public health concerns largely have disregarded the important overlap between eating disorders and obesity. This Special Issue addresses this neglect and points to how progress can be made in preventing and treating both. Thirteen primary research papers, three reviews, and two commentaries comprise this Special Issue. Two commentaries set the scene, noting the need for an integrated approach to prevention and treatment. The empirical papers and reviews fall into four broad areas of research: first, an understanding of the neuroscience of eating behaviours and body weight; second, relationships between disordered eating and obesity risk; third, new and integrated approaches in treatment; and fourth, assessment. Collectively, the papers highlight progress in science, translational research, and future research directions.

Keywords: bulimia nervosa; binge eating disorder; weight; dieting; treatment

---

1. Introduction

Public health concerns over the rising health toll resulting from weight disorders have become increasingly strident. However, as outlined in the two commentaries of this Special Issue [1,2], the concomitant mental health toll is largely ignored despite well-researched links between the physical and mental health of people living with larger bodies. Disordered eating is both an important risk and a perpetuating factor for obesity, often mediated through psychological states such as low mood or negative affect. Likewise, psychological concomitants of high Body Mass Iindex (kg/m^2; BMI) such as body dissatisfaction and weight stigma contribute to the increasing burden of eating disorders worldwide.

Thirteen primary research papers, three reviews, and two commentaries comprise this Special Issue. The two commentaries set the scene, calling for an integrated approach to the prevention [1] and treatment [2] of both problems. The primary papers and reviews fall into four broad areas of research: first, an understanding of the neuroscience of eating behaviours and body weight across the biopsychosocial and cultural spectrum; second, an exploration of relationships between disordered eating and obesity risk; third, new and integrated approaches in the treatment of obesity and eating disorders; and fourth, assessment in research and clinical domains.

2. Understanding the Neuroscience of Eating Behaviors and Body Weight

In this Special Issue, the complexity of eating and its sociodemographic and cultural contexts is highlighted in papers ranging from investigating the impact of lifestyle and health literacy in the Roma peoples of the Czech Republic [3] to demonstrating the relationships between family functioning and obesogenic nutrient consumption [4]. In a systematic review of 20 papers [5], there was suggestive but inconclusive support for associations among some food-related parenting practices and parental high BMI.

In neurocognitive research, Edwards et al. [6] found longer electroencephalographic (EEG) measured reaction times are associated with eating disorder symptoms in individuals with a high BMI. In a preliminary study, Schmidt et al. [7] reported associations between weight status and changes in EEG patterns, which correlated with general impulsivity and food approach behaviors. Smith et al. [8] reported a differential neuronal regulation of binge type eating by a novel mechanism, neuromedin U Receptor 2 (NMUR2), which points to future treatment research. The systematic review by Imperatori et al. [9] supported a future role for neural and bio-feedback-based approaches for disordered eating behaviors, such as food craving or rumination, with a neurocognitive rationale (modulation of brain reward mechanisms) supported by empirical research.

3. Exploring Relationships between Disordered Eating and Obesity Risk

Several papers investigated how disordered eating may be related to obesity risk. In addition to socio-demographic factors, Martin-Biggers et al. [10] found higher weight-related teasing, higher body dissatisfaction, and concern about a child's weight status significantly explained maternal obesity risk, which was also associated with food insecurity and poor family food quality. The findings of Blume et al. [11] support distinct neurocognitive profiles for people with binge eating disorders (BED) in comparison with people with a high BMI without BED. In addition, they explored the impacts of food addiction symptoms which are associated with higher levels of depression in individuals with BED.

The study of special populations and people with problems across the weight spectrum can inform understanding of mechanisms of weight loss/gain and under/over-eating. Two papers in this Special Issue highlight such areas for further research. First, the Figel review [12] suggested that athletes who have suffered spinal cord injuries, who have become sedentary and are at risk of becoming overweight, may have a higher risk of poor nutrition or becoming undernourished, as seen in people with eating disorders characterized by weight loss and dietary restriction such as anorexia nervosa. Plichta et al. [13] investigated body satisfaction and nutrition in students with and without orthorexic (rigid healthy eating) tendencies. Although orthorexia may represent a new eating disorder, people with the disorder differ from people with established eating disorders in key ways, particularly in their relationship with nutrition and attitudes towards their body weight, as exemplified in this study.

4. Treatments Addressing Co-Morbidity and Integrated Care

Bariatric surgery is the leading evidence-based approach in the treatment of obesity, but can it cause or exacerbate eating disorders through the inevitable state of imposed dietary restriction? In this Special Issue, Subramaniam et al. [14] reported overall improvement in mental health and eating status six months post-surgery. However, poor mental health and eating prompted by external cues prior to surgery were associated with poorer outcomes post-surgery, highlighting the need to actively address mental health and eating behavior prior to surgery. On the other hand, an effective treatment for bulimia nervosa or BED, such as cognitive behavior therapy, did little to improve metabolic physical health status in a randomized controlled trial by Mathisen et al. [15]. Nitsch et al. [16] concluded the Special Issue with a report on how to improve engagement in a new, online, integrated prevention program that addresses eating, weight, and mental health of adolescents called "Healthy Teens @ School".

5. Assessment and Diagnosis

Assessment instruments and clinically relevant diagnostic schemes are important in any field. Burton et al. [17] evaluated a useful tool, the Eating Beliefs Questionnaire (EBQ), which assesses negative, positive, and permissive beliefs about eating that can contribute to eating behaviors such as binge eating. The validated EBQ can now be used in research investigations; for example, the role of potentially remedial beliefs and behaviors as indicators of obesity and eating disorder risk. Amorim

Palavaras et al. [18] found that the broader definition of binge eating (with emphasis on loss of control over eating rather than quantity consumed) in the ICD-11 proved of greater utility without loss of validity in a clinical population of individuals with high BMI.

6. Conclusions

Collectively, these papers advance the understanding of the complex relationships between weight and eating problems, from scientific reports to translational research papers. The papers also point to the urgent need for additional research and collaboration between the two fields, which for too long have worked in parallel, rarely crossing or meeting. The papers also highlight the ways each field can learn from the other. To this end, we have initiated a collaborative University White Paper to support a new national direction, a Centre of Translational Research and Action for Eating and Weight Disorders (ASTRA—[19]). This White Paper also highlights the need for guidelines on optimal care for people with both problems. Only with such integrated endeavors can these fields jointly progress.

Author Contributions: P.H. co-conceived and co-wrote the paper, D.M. co-conceived and co-wrote this paper.

Funding: This research received no external funding.

Conflicts of Interest: Phillipa Hay receives sessional fees and lecture fees from the Australian Medical Council, Therapeutic Guidelines publication, and New South Wales Institute of Psychiatry and royalties from Hogrefe and Huber, McGraw Hill Education, and Blackwell Scientific Publications, and she has received research grants from the NHMRC and ARC. She is Chair of the National Eating Disorders Collaboration Steering Committee in Australia (2019–) and was a Member of the ICD-11 Working Group for Eating Disorders (2012–2018) and was Chair Clinical Practice Guidelines Project Working Group (Eating Disorders) of RANZCP (2012–2015). She has prepared a report under contract for Shire Pharmaceuticals (July 2017) and conducts educational activities for Shire Pharmaceuticals. All views in this paper are her own. Deborah Mitchison is funded on a research fellowship by the NHMRC.

References

1. Sonneville, K.; Rodgers, R. Shared Concerns and Opportunity for Joint Action in Creating a Food Environment That Supports Health. *Nutrients* **2019**, *11*, 41. [CrossRef] [PubMed]
2. da Luz, F.; Hay, P.; Touyz, S.; Sainsbury, A. Obesity with comorbid eating disorders: Associated health risks and treatment approaches. *Nutrients* **2018**, *10*, 829. [CrossRef] [PubMed]
3. Olišarová, V.; Tóthová, V.; Bártlová, S.; Dolák, F.; Kajanová, A.; Nováková, D.; Prokešová, R.; Šedová, L. Cultural Features Influencing Eating, Overweight, and Obesity in the Roma People of South Bohemia. *Nutrients* **2018**, *10*, 838.
4. Jaramillo, M.; Burke, N.; Shomaker, L.; Brady, S.; Kozlosky, M.; Yanovski, J.; Tanofsky-Kraff, M. Perceived Family Functioning in Relation to Energy Intake in Adolescent Girls with Loss of Control Eating. *Nutrients* **2018**, *10*, 1869. [CrossRef] [PubMed]
5. Patel, C.; Karasouli, E.; Shuttlewood, E.; Meyer, C. Food Parenting Practices among Parents with Overweight and Obesity: A Systematic Review. *Nutrients* **2018**, *10*, 1966. [CrossRef] [PubMed]
6. Edwards, C.; Walk, A.; Thompson, S.; Mullen, S.; Holscher, H.; Khan, N. Disordered Eating Attitudes and Behavioral and Neuroelectric Indices of Cognitive Flexibility in Individuals with Overweight and Obesity. *Nutrients* **2018**, *10*, 1902. [CrossRef] [PubMed]
7. Schmidt, R.; Sebert, C.; Kösling, C.; Grunwald, M.; Hilbert, A.; Hübner, C.; Schäfer, L. Neuropsychological and Neurophysiological Indicators of General and Food-Specific Impulsivity in Children with Overweight and Obesity: A Pilot Study. *Nutrients* **2018**, *10*, 1983. [CrossRef] [PubMed]
8. Smith, A.E.; Kasper, J.M.; Anastasio, N.C.; Hommel, J.D. Binge-Type Eating in Rats is Facilitated by Neuromedin U Receptor 2 in the Nucleus Accumbens and Ventral Tegmental Area. *Nutrients* **2019**, *11*, 327. [CrossRef] [PubMed]
9. Imperatori, C.; Mancini, M.; Della Marca, G.; Valenti, E.; Farina, B. Feedback-based treatments for eating disorders and related symptoms: a systematic review of the literature. *Nutrients* **2018**, *10*, 1806. [CrossRef] [PubMed]

10. Martin-Biggers, J.; Quick, V.; Spaccarotella, K.; Byrd-Bredbenner, C. An Exploratory Study Examining Obesity Risk in Non-Obese Mothers of Young Children Using a Socioecological Approach. *Nutrients* **2018**, *10*, 781. [CrossRef] [PubMed]
11. Blume, M.; Schmidt, R.; Hilbert, A. Executive Functioning in Obesity; Food Addiction, and Binge-Eating Disorder. *Nutrients* **2018**, *11*, 54. [CrossRef] [PubMed]
12. Figel, K.; Pritchett, K.; Pritchett, R.; Broad, E. Energy and Nutrient Issues in Athletes with Spinal Cord Injury: Are They at Risk for Low Energy Availability? *Nutrients* **2018**, *10*, 1078. [CrossRef] [PubMed]
13. Plichta, M.; Jezewska-Zychowicz, M.; Gębski, J. Orthorexic Tendency in Polish Students: Exploring Association with Dietary Patterns, Body Satisfaction and Weight. *Nutrients* **2019**, *11*, 100. [CrossRef] [PubMed]
14. Subramaniam, K.; Low, W.Y.; Lau, P.C.; Chin, K.F.; Chinna, K.; Kosai, N.; Taher, M.; Rajan, R. Eating Behaviour Predicts Weight Loss Six Months after Bariatric Surgery: A Longitudinal Study. *Nutrients* **2018**, *10*, 1616. [CrossRef] [PubMed]
15. Mathisen, T.; Sundgot-Borgen, J.; Rosenvinge, J.; Bratland-Sanda, S. Managing Risk of Non-Communicable Diseases in Women with Bulimia Nervosa or Binge Eating Disorders: A Randomized Trial with 12 Months Follow-Up. *Nutrients* **2018**, *10*, 1887. [CrossRef] [PubMed]
16. Nitsch, M.; Adamcik, T.; Kuso, S.; Zeiler, M.; Waldherr, K. Usability and Engagement Evaluation of an Unguided Online Program for Promoting a Healthy Lifestyle and Reducing the Risk for Eating Disorders and Obesity in the School Setting. *Nutrients* **2019**, *11*, 713. [CrossRef] [PubMed]
17. Burton, A.; Mitchison, D.; Hay, P.; Donnelly, B.; Thornton, C.; Russell, J.; Swinbourne, J.; Basten, C.; Goldstein, M.; Touyz, S.; et al. Beliefs about binge eating: psychometric properties of the eating beliefs questionnaire (EBQ-18) in eating disorder, obese, and community samples. *Nutrients* **2018**, *10*, 1306. [CrossRef] [PubMed]
18. Amorim Palavras, M.; Hay, P.; Claudino, A. An Investigation of the Clinical Utility of the Proposed ICD-11 and DSM-5 Diagnostic Schemes for Eating Disorders Characterized by Recurrent Binge Eating in People with a High BMI. *Nutrients* **2018**, *10*, 1751. [CrossRef] [PubMed]
19. ASTRA: A Centre for Translational Research and Action for Eating and Weight Disorders. Available online: https://www.westernsydney.edu.au/__data/assets/pdf_file/0007/1466377/Eating-Disorders_ICAS3065_White_Paper.pdf (accessed on 1 May 2019).

nutrients

MDPI

Article

An Exploratory Study Examining Obesity Risk in Non-Obese Mothers of Young Children Using a Socioecological Approach

Jennifer Martin-Biggers [1], Virginia Quick [1,*], Kim Spaccarotella [2] and Carol Byrd-Bredbenner [1]

[1] Department of Nutritional Sciences, Rutgers University, 26 Nichol Avenue, New Brunswick, NJ 08901, USA; jmartinbiggers@rutgers.edu (J.M.-B.); bredbenner@sebs.rutgers.edu (C.B.-B.)

[2] Department of Biological Sciences, Kean University, 1000 Morris Avenue, Union, NJ 07082, USA; kspaccar@kean.edu

* Correspondence: vquick@njaes.rutgers.edu; Tel.: +01-848-932-0965

Received: 26 March 2018; Accepted: 15 June 2018; Published: 17 June 2018

Abstract: This cross-sectional, exploratory study aimed to (1) develop an obesity risk score using a comprehensive set of variables assessing mothers' intrapersonal weight-related characteristics and those of their homes' interpersonal and physical environments, and (2) determine how weight-related characteristics differ by obesity risk level. U.S. mothers (N = 550) of preschool-aged children completed an online survey that assessed maternal self-report weight status, sociodemographics, health-related characteristics, and maternal intrapersonal and their homes' interpersonal and physical environment weight-related characteristics. Binomial logistic regression analysis identified variables significantly associated with obesity. Scores for all obesity risk variables were summed to create a weighted obesity risk score for non-obese participants (n = 386). Analysis of variance and Tukey post-hoc tests determined how non-obese mothers' sociodemographic, health-related, and intrapersonal and their homes' interpersonal and physical environment characteristics differed among obesity risk score tertiles. Results revealed that eight variables explained 53 percent of maternal obesity risk, including African American race, lower education level, more children in household, poorer maternal health, higher weight teasing history, higher body dissatisfaction, primary relative with obesity, and greater concern about children's overweight risk. Non-obese mothers in the highest obesity risk tertile had greater food insecurity risk, lower family affluence, worse sleep quality, less fruit/vegetable availability, and reported less frequent modeling of healthy behaviors and more family conflict. In conclusion, eight characteristics that explained more than half of the risk for obesity in non-obese mothers of young children, may help healthcare professionals identify mothers at increased risk of obesity and offer preventive care early.

Keywords: obesity risk; mothers; women; young children; socioecological

1. Introduction

Recent data from the National Health and Nutrition Examination Survey (NHANES) indicate that nearly 34.9 percent of U.S. adults are obese [1]. It is no longer debated that obesity and its comorbidities are significantly impacting Americans both in financial and quality of life costs. A systematic review of 33 studies found that the overall estimated medical costs of obesity accounted for approximately 10 percent of all medical spending in the United States [2]. The physical health consequences of obesity are numerous and include effects on the pulmonary, orthopedic, neurological, gastroenterological, endocrine, and cardiovascular systems, as well as causing systemic inflammation, thereby greatly impacting quality of life [3–6].

The increase in obesity rates in the U.S. likely reflects changes in environmental factors and lifestyle choices related to increased energy intake and inadequate energy expenditure, rather than genetic changes because of the slow rate at which population-wide genetic changes occur [7–9]. Changes in lifestyles and the environment that have occurred in tandem with the increase in obesity include ready availability of food and shifting dietary patterns, which have led to an increase in calorie intake [10,11], combined with a decline in energy expenditure associated with a sedentary lifestyle [12]. Macro-level factors have a more indirect (yet important) role in influencing behaviors and include social norms, agriculture policies, economic policies, advertising, and more. Factors that are more directly influenced by an individual include his or her physical and social environments and personal factors (e.g., home environment, skills, behaviors).

In recent years, health behavior change experts have recognized the influence of factors in the physical environment, as well as in the social environment, on obesity and health outcomes [13]. This ecological approach to public health issues posits that an individual's motivation and skills alone are not adequate to facilitate behavior change; environments also need to support and facilitate the practice of healthful behaviors [14–16]. Reciprocal determinism, a construct of the Social Cognitive Theory, describes how a person's characteristics and behaviors, as well as the physical and social environment where behaviors occur, mutually affect each other [17]. Environments not supportive of weight-management behaviors make it difficult to engage in practices that prevent unhealthy weight gain. Research has increasingly provided evidence that environmental factors significantly influence diet, physical activity, and obesity in adults [15,18,19] and children [16,20–22], yet their relative contribution to obesity risk remains unknown.

The home environment deserves in-depth study given its potential influence on health behaviors [23]. An understanding of factors in the home environment associated with obesity could assist healthcare providers, researchers, parents, and caregivers in creating home environments that support healthy weights for the whole family. Mothers tend to be food gatekeepers in the home and, thus, are well suited to providing an appraisal of their homes' social (interpersonal) and physical environment characteristics [23,24]. Mothers also are children's role models and often the household food decision-maker, thus mothers' own intrapersonal cognitions, behaviors, and weight status play a role in weight-related decisions affecting the entire family [23,24]. Moreover, behaviors directly affecting weight are developed during childhood and track into adulthood [25–28], thereby making it vital to identify factors affecting maternal obesity risk and address them in obesity prevention interventions. A deeper understanding of the full interplay of intrapersonal and interpersonal characteristics and behaviors along with environments could provide a more complete picture of the aspects of the home environment that may place mothers of young children at risk for weight gain. A method for assessing risk for weight gain could enable health care providers and researchers to tailor and design more effective nutrition education.

Health experts acknowledge that lifestyles and the environment play a role in obesity risk [29]; however, few studies have considered these factors when examining obesity risk and none could be located that examined a comprehensive array of factors. Thus, the aims of this exploratory study were to (1) develop an obesity risk score using a comprehensive set of variables assessing mothers' own intrapersonal weight-related characteristics as well as the weight-related characteristics of their homes' interpersonal and physical environments, and (2) determine how these weight-related characteristics differ among levels of obesity risk.

2. Materials and Methods

This research was approved by the Institutional Review Board at Rutgers University. All participants gave informed consent.

2.1. Sample

Survey Sampling International (SSI), a global research company whose services include survey sample participant recruitment (www.surveysampling.com), was utilized. SSI panel members received invitations to participate in an online survey that would help researchers create "a program to help parents to build healthier kids". The goal was to recruit mothers of children in the target age range who had most of the food decision-making authority in their households to adequately capture the most representative responses. To meet eligibility requirements, panel members had to be female, between 18- and 45-years-old, have one or more children 2- to 5-years-old, and be the household's primary food gatekeeper (i.e., made most or all food purchasing and preparation decisions). As an incentive to complete the cross-sectional online survey, participating mothers accrued points from SSI that were redeemable for gifts. A total sample size of 384 was estimated based on a 95% confidence interval, and total population of women in the U.S. that are 20–45 years old using 2010 U.S. Census data [30].

2.2. Instrument

Development and content of the online Home Obesogenicity Measure of EnvironmentS (HOMES) survey is described in detail elsewhere [31–33]. In summary, development began with a comprehensive literature review to identify salient weight-related demographic, environmental, behavioral, and psychographic characteristics. Self-report scales assessing these characteristics, preferably those previously used and validated with a diverse sample of U.S. adults, also were identified. When multiple scales for assessing a characteristic were found, each was reviewed to determine which was most relevant to the study sample, easy to administer and score, and had good reliability and validity. If an instrument assessing a characteristic of interest or fitting the needs of the study could not be located in the literature, items were developed *de novo*. For scales with items substantially modified from their original form or developed *de novo*, standard processes for developing and refining scales were applied [34]. That is, experts (n = 5) in subject matter areas appropriate to the scale content (e.g., nutrition, physical activity, psychology, child development, obesogenic environment), psychometrics, and survey design iteratively reviewed and refined them to ensure scale clarity and content validity [34,35]. The items then underwent cognitive testing with participants who were similar to the study population to assess whether the items were interpreted as intended [35] and to determine ways to reduce participant burden and increase understandability and acceptability [36].

After refinement, the scales were consolidated into a single survey that was posted online (using Qualtrics®). The survey was pilot-tested with 48 participants whose characteristics were the same as those of the target audience for the final study (but were not participants in the final sample) to gauge completion time, identify further refinements needed to improve clarity and ease of completion, ensure protocols for scoring of scales were accurate, and conduct preliminary psychometric analyses. The survey was administered online for ease of data collection and convenience to participants, to help reduce the potential for social desirability bias that can occur during in-person administration, and to increase researcher ability to reach individuals who would be otherwise difficult to access (i.e., distance from researchers or limited time to meet in-person) [37,38].

The HOMES survey included an array of measures that focused on mother's intrapersonal weight-related characteristics and their homes' interpersonal and physical environment characteristics and yielded 79 variables. Table 1 lists the variables in the HOMES survey considered in the creation of the obesity risk score, including number of items, possible score range, and Cronbach's alpha (when applicable).

Table 1. Description of Sociodemographic, Intrapersonal, Interpersonal and Home Environment Characteristics of Participants (N = 550).

Measure	# Items	Possible Score Range	Scale Type	Cronbach's α	Mean ± SD or N (%)
Sociodemographic Characteristics					
Race/Ethnicity	1	n/a	categorical response	*	
White					396 (72.0)
Black or African American					52 (9.5)
Hispanic					25 (4.5)
Multi-racial					43 (7.8)
Asian					31 (5.6)
Other					3 (0.6)
Education Level	1	n/a	categorical response	*	
High School or less					99 (18.0)
Some college or technical/Associate's degree					245 (44.5)
Bachelor's degree or higher					206 (37.5)
Maternal Employment	1	n/a	categorical response	*	
Do not work					303 (55.1)
Part-time (less than 30 h/week)					103 (18.7)
Full-time (30 or more h/week)					143 (26.0)
Number of Children in Household	1	0 to more than 6	Total #	*	2.20 ± 1.01
Family Affluence Score [39,40]	3	0 to 7	varies per item [A]	*	5.61 ± 1.56
Food Insecurity Risk [41]	2	1 to 4	4-point agreement rating [B]	0.84	2.04 ± 1.91
Weight Status					
Mother's BMI	1	n/a	Self-reported height/weight	*	27.69 ± 7.90
Child's BMI percentile (n = 339)	1	n/a	Self-reported height/weight/sex/age	*	63.93 ± 34.93
Health-Related Assessments					
General Health Rating [42,43]	1	1 to 5	5-point excellence rating [C]	*	3.52 ± 0.87
Health-related Quality of Life (# of unhealthy days) [42,43]	1	0 to 30	days/month	*	2.89 ± 4.56
Depression Severity [44]	2	1 to 4	4-point occurrence rating [D]	0.81	1.05 ± 1.44
Age at Birth of First Child (years)	1	n/a	years	*	24.46 ± 5.39
Perception of Weight Teasing History [45]	3	1 to 5	5-point frequency rating [E]	0.95	1.84 ± 1.15
Body Dissatisfaction [46]	1	1 to 4	4-point frequency rating [F]	*	2.58 ± 1.10
Primary Relative with History of Obesity (% yes)	1	0 or 1	yes/no	*	207 (37.6)
Primary Relative with History of Diabetes (% yes)	1	0 or 1	yes/no	*	140 (25.5)

Table 1. *Cont.*

Measure	# Items	Possible Score Range	Scale Type	Cronbach's α	Mean ± SD or *N* (%)
Intrapersonal Characteristics					
Maternal Weight-Related Behaviors					
Physical Activity Level [47–49]	3	0 to 42	8-point exercise scale [G]	*	15.44 ± 9.98
Screentime	1	0 to 1440	minutes/day	*	273.52 ± 253.99
Sleep Duration	1	0 to 24	hours/day	*	7.11 ± 1.84
Sleep Quality [50,51]	1	1 to 5	5-point rating [H]	*	3.24 ± 0.89
Fruit and Vegetable Intake [52–54]	10	0 to 12.17	6-point servings [I] eaten per day scale	*	4.56 ± 2.22
% Calories from Total Fat [52–54]	17	0 to 100	5-point servings eaten scale [J]	*	37.4 ± 5.91
Milk [55,56]	1	0 to 8	9-point servings drank per day scale [K]	*	3.95 ± 3.08
Sugar-Sweetened Beverage [55,56]	4	0 to 4.6	9-point servings drank per day scale [K]	*	0.89 ± 0.88
Maternal Eating Styles					
Disinhibited Eating [57,58]	3	1 to 4	4-point agreement rating [B]	0.81	1.96 ± 0.76
Emotional Eating [57,58]	3	1 to 4	4-point agreement rating [B]	0.75	2.07 ± 0.88
Dietary Restraint Eating [57,58]	4	1 to 4	4-point agreement rating [B]	0.74	2.42 ± 0.74
Adventurous Eating [59–61]	2	1 to 4	4-point agreement rating [B]	0.72	3.16 ± 0.68
Maternal Self-Perceptions					
Personal Organization [62]	4	1 to 5	5-point agreement rating [L]	0.69	3.68 ± 0.82
Need for Cognition [63,64]	1	1 to 5	5-point agreement rating [L]	*	3.49 ± 0.98
Parenting Self-Efficacy [65,66]	1	1 to 5	5-point agreement rating [L]	*	4.1 ± 0.81
Stress Management [67]	2	1 to 4	4-point agreement rating [D]	0.84	3.94 ± 0.76
Stress Management Self-Efficacy	2	1 to 4	4-point agreement rating [D]	0.79	2.63 ± 1.01
Child Weight Cognitions		1 to 5			
Belief that Chubby Kids are Healthy	2	1 to 5	5-point agreement rating [L]	0.65	2.70 ± 0.74
Concern for Child's Overweight Risk [68]	3	1 to 5	5-point agreement rating [L]	0.91	1.91 ± 1.03
Health Behavior Values [31,69–72]					
Importance of Physical Activity for Self	3	1 to 5	5-point agreement rating [L]	0.82	3.49 ± 0.97
Importance of Physical Activity for Child	3	1 to 5	5-point agreement rating [L]	0.68	3.83 ± 0.87
Encourages/Facilitates Child Physical Activity	5	1 to 5	5-point agreement rating [L]	0.88	4.23 ± 0.66
Importance of Modeling Physical Activity to Child	2	1 to 5	5-point agreement rating [L]	0.79	4.13 ± 0.82
Engages in Physical Activity with Child Frequently	2	0 to 7	8-point frequency scale [M]	*	3.67 ± 1.85
Models Physical Activity to Child Frequently	2	0 to 7	8-point frequency scale [M]	*	3.08 ± 1.22
Models Sedentary Behaviors Infrequently	2	0 to 7	8-point frequency scale [M]	*	2.79 ± 2.18
Models Healthy Eating to Child	4	1 to 5	5-point agreement rating [L]	0.56	3.51 ± 0.73
Belief that TV Positively Affects Child Learning	2	1 to 5	5-point agreement rating [L]	0.85	3.89 ± 0.76
Talks Often with Child about TV	2	1 to 5	5-point agreement rating [L]	0.50	3.24 ± 0.97
Limits Child Exposure to TV Commercials and Inappropriate Programs Shows	2	1 to 5	5-point agreement rating [L]	0.50	3.67 ± 0.93
Limits Child to Educational TV	1	1 to 5	5-point agreement rating [L]	*	3.52 ± 1.09

Table 1. *Cont.*

Measure	# Items	Possible Score Range	Scale Type	Cronbach's α	Mean ± SD or N (%)
Home Interpersonal Characteristics					
Child Feeding Practices [68–71,73–75]					
Restricts Child Food Intake	2	1 to 5	5-point agreement rating ^{L}	0.63	3.84 ± 0.86
Pressures Child to Eat	3	1 to 5	5-point agreement rating ^{L}	0.69	2.17 ± 0.96
Maternal Control Over Child Food Access and Choices	7	1 to 5	5-point agreement rating ^{L}	0.65	3.33 ± 0.52
Non-Acceptance of Food Waste	2	1 to 5	5-point agreement rating ^{L}	0.61	3.05 ± 0.97
Instrumental Feeding Practices (uses food to reward children for eating a healthy food)	3	1 to 5	5-point agreement rating ^{L}	0.73	2.63 ± 0.91
Non-Food Rewards (uses non-food (e.g., extra playtime) to reward children for eating a healthy food)	2	1 to 5	5-point agreement rating ^{L}	0.65	2.90 ± 0.95
Allows Child to Independently Access Nutrient Dense Foods	5	0 to 5	yes/no	*	1.82 ± 1.74
Allows Child to Independently Access Low Nutrient Density Foods	6	0 to 6	yes/no	*	0.68 ± 1.32
Nutrient Dense Foods Stored in Locations Visible to Child	5	0 to 5	yes/no	*	2.44 ± 1.71
Low Nutrient Dense Foods Stored in Locations Visible to Child	6	0 to 6	yes/no	*	0.82 ± 1.35
Family Meal Patterns [70,76–80]					
Family Meal Frequency	3	0 to 21	0–7 days for breakfast, lunch, dinner; score is sum of 3 meals	*	13.64 ± 5.05
Importance of Family Meals	3	1 to 5	5-point agreement rating ^{L}	0.70	4.52 ± 0.64
Positive Family Meal Atmosphere	3	1 to 5	5-point agreement rating ^{L}	0.70	4.12 ± 0.85
Fast Food Eaten at Family Meals	1	0 to 7	days/week	*	0.93 ± 1.18
TV on During Family Meals	1	0 to 7	days/week	*	2.24 ± 2.48
Family Meals Eaten at Kitchen or Dining Table	1	0 to 7	days/week	*	4.69 ± 2.51
Family Meals Eaten in the Car	1	0 to 7	days/week	*	0.43 ± 1.16
Family Meal Planning	2	1 to 5	5-point agreement rating ^{L}	0.70	3.40 ± 0.88
Time and Energy for Family Meals	2	1 to 5	5-point agreement rating ^{L}	0.78	4.34 ± 0.85
Family Functioning and Maternal Engagement					
Family Support for Healthy Behaviors [81–83]	4	1 to 5	5-point agreement rating ^{L}	0.81	4.40 ± 0.73
Family Conflict and Lack of Cohesion [84–86]	5	1 to 5	5-point agreement rating ^{L}	0.84	1.83 ± 0.70
Household Disorganization [87,88]	3	1 to 5	5-point agreement rating ^{L}	0.76	2.47 ± 0.92
Verbal Engagement with Children	1	1 to 5	5-point agreement rating ^{L}	*	4.17 ± 0.93
Physical Engagement with Children	1	1 to 5	5-point agreement rating ^{L}	*	4.74 ± 0.51

Table 1. *Cont.*

Measure	# Items	Possible Score Range	Scale Type	Cronbach's α	Mean ± SD or *N* (%)
Home Physical Environment Characteristics					
Physical Activity [69–72,82,89]					
Physical Activity Availability	12	1 to 5	5-point agreement rating [L]	0.72	3.78 ± 0.67
Physical Activity Accessibility †	2	1 to 5	5-point agreement rating [L]	0.90	4.21 ± 1.14
Media Devices in the Home	6	0 to more than 10	Total devices [N]	*	11.57 ± 4.21
Media Devices in Child's Bedroom	7	0 to 7	Total # of media device types [O]	*	1.39 ± 1.62
Daily Screentime Child Allowed	1	0 to 1440	minutes/day	*	495.14 ± 714.22
Food Availability					
Household Fruit and Vegetable Availability (serving/person/day) [52,90]	10	0 to 19.94	9-point servings scale [P]	*	6.41 ± 2.53
Household Fatty/Salty Snack Availability (serving/person/day) [52,90]	4	0 to 32	9-point servings scale [P]	*	8.37 ± 7.22
Household Sugar-Sweetened Beverage Availability (serving/person/day) [55,56]	4	0 to 4.57	9-point servings scale [P]	*	1.87 ± 1.79
Household Breakfast Cereal Availability (serving/person/day) [52,90]	1	0 to 8	9-point servings scale [P]	*	5.35 ± 2.72

Note: n/a = not applicable. * Cronbach's alpha is not appropriate for the scale type or because the scale has <2 items. † n = 524. [A] Family affluence assessed by three questions asking the total number of cars, vans, or trucks the family owns (0 = none, 1 = 1 vehicle, 2 = 2 or more vehicles), # of times family traveled on vacation in past year (0 = never, 1 = 1 time, 2 = 2 times, 3 = 3 or more times), and whether participant had their own bedroom (1 = yes, 0 = no); items are summed. [B] 4-point Agreement Rating: definitely false, mostly false, mostly true, definitely true; scored 1 to 4, respectively. Items averaged with higher scores indicating greater expression of the trait. [C] 5-point Excellence Rating: poor, fair, good, very good, excellent; scored 1 to 5 respectively; higher score indicates better health. [D] 4-point Occurrence Rating: not at all, several days, more than half the days, nearly every day; scored 1 to 4, respectively; scale scores equals average of items with higher scores indicating greater expression of the behavior. [E] 5-point Frequency Rating: never, rarely, sometimes, often, very often; scored 1 to 5 respectively; scale score equals average of item scores with higher scores indicating greater weight teasing history. [F] 4-point Frequency Rating: not at all, slightly, moderately, a lot; scored 1 to 4 respectively; higher scores indicate greater body dissatisfaction. [G] 8-point Exercise Days/week: 0, 1, 2, 3, 4, 5, 6, and 7; days/week weighted by exercise intensity (weights of 1, 2, 3 for walking, moderate, and vigorous activity, respectively) and summed to create scale score; higher scale score indicates greater activity level. [H] 5-point rating scale: very good, good, okay, bad, and very bad; scored 1 to 5 respectively with higher scores indicate poorer sleep quality. [I] 6-point Fruit/Vegetable Servings Rating: <1 serving/week, 1 serving /week, 2 to 3 servings/week, 4 to 6 servings/week, 1 serving/day, 2 or more servings/day; scored 0 to 5 respectively; scale scoring algorithm is protected by copyright and described in detail elsewhere. Possible score range = 0 to 12.17. [J] 5-point Fatty Food Servings Rating: 1 time/month or less, 2 to 3 times/month, 1 to 2 times/week, 3 to 4 times/week, 5 or more times/week; scored 0 to 4 respectively; scale scoring algorithm is protected by copyright and described in detail elsewhere. [K] 9-point Beverage Servings Rating: <1 time/week, 1 day/week, 2 days/week, 3 days/week, 4 days/week, 5 days/week, 6 days/week, 7 days/week, >1 time/day; scored 0 to 8 respectively. Possible score ranges for Sugar-Sweetened Beverages = 0 to 4.6; Milk = 0 to 8. [L] 5-point Agreement Rating: strongly disagree, disagree, neither agree nor disagree, agree, strongly agree; scored 1 to 5 respectively; scale score equals average of item scores with higher scale score indicating greater expression of the trait. [M] 8-point Modeling Days/week: 0 (almost never), 1, 2, 3, 4, 5, 6, and 7; days averaged to create scale score with higher score indicating more frequent modeling. [N] 11-point Media Device Count: 1 = 1 to 10 = 10, 11 = more than 10; scale score equals sum of items; higher score indicates greater number of media devices. Possible score range = 0 to 66. [O] Sum of 7 media devices found in child's bedroom (i.e., TV, DVD player, Computer/Laptop, Smarphone/Tablet/LeapPad, video game devices (Nintendo DS, XBoxKinect), and Internet access). [P] 9-point Household Servings Rating: <1 time/week, 1 day/week, 2 days/week, 3 days/week, 4 days/week, 5 days/week, 6 days/week, 7 days/week, >1 time/day; scored 0 to 8 respectively. Possible score ranges for fruits/vegetables (0 to 19.94), salty/fatty snacks (0 to 32), sugar-sweetened beverages (0 to 4.57), and breakfast cereal (0 to 8) servings/household/member/day.

2.3. Sociodemographics and Health-Related Characteristics

Variables addressing maternal sociodemographic data included race/ethnicity, education level, number of children in the household, family affluence [39,40], maternal employment, and food insecurity risk [41]. There were eight variables examining health-related characteristics (e.g., general health status [42,43], health-related quality of life [42,43], depression severity [44], age at birth of first child, perception of weight teasing history [45], body dissatisfaction [46], primary relative with obesity and/or obesity.

2.3.1. Weight Status

Self-reported heights and weights of participants were used to calculate body mass index (BMI) (weight (kg)/(height (m^2)). Participants also reported their children's height, weight, sex, and age which were used to calculated their children's BMI percentile [91].

2.3.2. Intrapersonal Characteristics

Mothers' personal weight-related behaviors (e.g., physical activity level and screentime [47–49], sleep quality and duration [50,51], fruit/vegetable intake [52–54], percent calories from fat [52–54], milk intake [55,56], sugar-sweetened beverage intake [55,56]) accounted for eight variables. Scales evaluating maternal eating styles (e.g., disinhibited eating [57,58], emotional eating [57,58], dietary restraint eating [57,58], adventurous eating [59–61]) generated four variables. Five variables were produced from measures of mothers' self-perceptions (i.e., personal organization [62], need for cognition [63,64], parenting self-efficacy [65,66], stress management [67], stress management self-efficacy). Cognitions related to children's weight (i.e., belief that chubby kids are healthy, concern about own children's overweight risk [68]) were assessed with two scales. The value of engaging in healthy behaviors for self and child (i.e., importance placed on physical activity, encouragement and facilitation of children's physical activity, importance of modeling physical activity to children, frequency of engaging in active play with children, parent modeling of healthy eating, parenting cognitions and behaviors associated with children's television viewing) [31,69–72] was examined with 12 measures, each generating a variable.

2.3.3. Home Interpersonal Characteristics

Assessments of mothers' child feeding behaviors (e.g., food restriction, pressuring, rewarding) [68–71,73–75] yielded 10 variables. Family meal patterns (e.g., frequency and location of meals) [70,76–80] resulted in nine variables. Scales assessing family functioning and engagement (e.g., family support for healthy behaviors [81–83], family conflict and lack of cohesion [84–86], household organization [87,88]) included five variables.

2.3.4. Home Physical Environment

Appraisal of the home physical environment's accessibility to and availability of physical activity and sedentary activity opportunities (e.g., physical activity supports, media devices in the home, children's TV accessibility) [69–72,82,89] contributed five variables. Measures of household food availability (e.g., fruit/vegetables, sugar-sweetened beverages) [52,55,56,90] generated 4 variables.

2.4. Data Analysis

Internal consistencies of all measures, when applicable, were calculated using Cronbach's alpha. Descriptive statistics of all variables in the total sample were evaluated in four steps before further development of the obesity risk score. First, Spearman rank order correlations of all variables, except mothers' and children's weight status, were examined for multicollinearity. In the correlation matrix, race/ethnicity was categorized into two dichotomous variables (i.e., white or non-white, black or non-black) and education level was dichotomized into low (some college or less) or high (baccalaureate degree or higher). Variables that were intercorrelated (i.e., $r > 0.50$) were reviewed to select a single variable from among them to use in further analyses. The criterion for selecting a single variable from among those that were intercorrelated was that the variable under consideration had to be significantly correlated ($p < 0.05$) with maternal BMI. If none of the intercorrelated variables met this criterion, none were considered in further analyses. If more than one variable met this criterion, the variable with the highest correlation (absolute value) with maternal BMI was selected. In the second step of data analysis, binomial logistic regression was conducted to identify variables significantly associated with obesity. Variables remaining after the first step of the data analysis served as independent variables. The dependent variable was maternal weight status of obese (i.e., BMI $\geq$ 30) vs. non-obese (i.e., BMI $\leq$ 30). In step three of data analysis, the significant obesity risk variables identified in step two were again entered into the binomial logistic regression analysis to determine the best model fit and confirm results. In step four, data for non-obese mothers' were extracted from the data set and median scores were calculated for all variables found to be significantly associated with obesity.

To create the weighted obesity risk score, each non-obese mother was assigned a score for each obesity risk variable found in the regression model, as stated above, to be significantly associated with obesity. If a participant's score for an obesity risk variable was above the median for continuous variables or mothers had the characteristic for dichotomous variables, the score assigned for the variable was the beta coefficient value generated by the binomial logistic regression (reflecting an increased risk for obesity); if a particiapant's score was below the median for continuous variables or mothers did not have the characteristic for dichotomous variables, thereby indicating reduced obesity risk, a score of 0 was awarded for that variable. Scores for all obesity risk variables were then summed to yield a participant's total weighted obesity risk score.

To determine how non-obese mothers differed by obesity risk level, they were assigned to groups based on their obesity risk score tertile (i.e., low, moderate, and high risk). ANOVA and Tukey post-hoc tests were conducted to determine how maternal sociodemographic, health-related, and intrapersonal and their homes' interpersonal and physical environment characteristics differed among and between obesity risk score tertiles. For variables that were statically significant ($p < 0.05$), effect sizes were estimated by examining partial Eta squared, Analyses were performed with SPSS software version 24.0 (IBM corporation, Chicago, IL, USA). Given the number of variables investigated, significance level for main effects was set at 0.01 to reduce the risk of type 1 errors while maintaining sufficient power. Significance level for post-hoc procedures was set at $p < 0.05$.

3. Results

Out of 910 participants who responded to the online survey, only 550 participants were eligible and completed the survey (i.e., 188 did not complete the survey, 96 did not meet inclusion criteria, and 76 had implausible responses (e.g., multiple items had the same answers)) with a survey response rate of 60%. Most participants (n = 550; mean age 32.25 $\pm$ 5.81 SD years) were white (72%) with some post-secondary education (82%). Nearly all measures had good to excellent internal consistency as determined by Cronbach's alpha (see Table 1). Spearman rank order correlation coefficients of the study variables revealed that several variables were multicollinear. Table 2 lists each group of multicollinear variables and the variable selected from each group based on the criteria previously described in the Data Analysis section.

Table 2. Selection Rationale for Single Variable from Multicollinear Variable Groups.

Multicollinear Variable Group	Variable Most Highly and Significantly Correlated with BMI Was Retained in Further Analysis
Depression Severity, Health-related Quality of Life, and Stress Management	Health-Related Quality of Life
Disinhibited Eating and Emotional Eating	Emotional Eating
Importance of Physical Activity for Self with (1) Maternal Physical Activity Level and (2) Importance of Modeling Physical Activity to Child	Importance of Physical Activity for Self
Encourages/Facilitates Child Physical Activity with (1) Importance of Physical Activity for Child and (2) Importance of Modeling Physical Activity to Child	Encourages/Facilitate Child Physical Activity (Note: Importance of Modeling Physical Activity to Child had a higher correlation with BMI; however, it could not be selected because it is intercorrelated with Importance of Physical Activity for Self; see above)
Models Physical Activity to Child Frequently with (1) Maternal Physical Activity Level and (2) Mother: Child Co-Physical Activity	Models Physical Activity to Child Frequently
Instrumental Feeding Practices and Non-Food Rewards	Instrumental Feeding Practices
Allows Child to Independently Access Nutrient Dense Foods and Nutrient Dense Foods Stored in Locations Visible to Child	Neither variable was significantly correlated with BMI (none included)
Allows Child to Independently Access Low Nutrient Density Foods and Low Nutrient Dense Foods Stored in Locations Visible to Child	Low Nutrient Dense Foods Stored in Locations Visible to Child
Family Meals Eaten at Kitchen or Dining Table and TV on During Family Meals	Family Meals Eaten at Kitchen or Dining Table
Positive Family Meal Atmosphere and Household Disorganization	Neither variable was significantly correlated with BMI (none included)
Importance of Family Meals and Time and Energy for Family Meals	Importance of Family Meals
Household Fruit and Vegetable Availability with (1) Fruit and Vegetable Intake and (2) Household Sugar-sweetened Beverage Availability	Household Fruit and Vegetable Availability

Of the original 79 variables examined, scores for the 62 variables that were not highly intercorrelated were retained for further analysis. Binomial logistic regression on the dichotomous dependent variable of non-obese (n = 386) vs obese (n = 164) weight status revealed that all of the variables combined explained 64 percent of maternal obesity risk, with 12 of the variables being significantly associated with obesity risk. The 12 significant obesity risk variables were retained and again subjected to binomial logistic regression resulting in a final model with 8 variables explaining 53 percent of maternal risk for obesity (Table 3). Three of the obesity risk variables were dichotomous variables (i.e., being black or African American, having lower education level, having a primary relative with a history of obesity) and five were continuous variables (i.e., larger number of children in household, poorer general health rating, higher perceived weight teasing history, greater body dissatisfaction, more concern about their children's overweight risk). Using the variable scoring procedure described in the Data Analysis section, the weighted obesity risk score averaged 1.66 ± 0.98 SD and ranged from 0 to 5.49.

Table 3. Binomial Logistic Regression of Variables Associated with Maternal Obesity (n = 550).

Dependent Variable: Maternal Obesity †					
Independent Variables	**B ‡**	**SE #**	**Odds Ratio**	**95% CI**	***p*-value**
Race (black or African American)	1.25	0.41	3.48	(1.56, 7.70)	0.002
Education Level (some college or less)	0.61	0.26	1.83	(1.09, 3.07)	0.021
Number of Children in Household	0.32	0.12	1.38	(1.08, 1.75)	0.010
General Health Rating [a]	0.89	0.17	2.43	(1.73, 3.41)	<0.001
Perception of Weight Teasing History	0.52	0.11	1.69	(1.35, 2.11)	<0.001
Body Dissatisfaction	0.91	0.14	2.29	(1.91, 3.25)	<0.001
Primary Relative with History of Obesity	0.71	0.25	2.04	(1.25, 3.23)	0.004
Concern for Child's Overweight Risk	0.28	0.13	1.32	(1.03, 1.69)	0.026
R					
Cox and Snell R Square	0.374				
Nagelkerke R Square	0.531				
Tests of Model Coefficients	**DF ***	χ^2	***p*-value**		
	8	257.92	<0.001		

‡ Beta coefficient. * DF = Degrees of Freedom. # Standard Error. † Maternal obesity defined at body mass index ≥ 30.
[a] Higher scores indicate poorer perceptions of health status.

ANOVA and Tukey post-hoc tests comparing obesity risk scores by tertiles, as shown in Table 4, revealed significant differences ($p < 0.001$) among low-, moderate-, and high risk groups with a large effect size (i.e., $\eta^2 = 0.833$) for the obesity risk score, as estimated by partial Eta squared. A review of the characteristics related to sociodemographic variables, weight status, and health showed that non-obese mothers in the low obesity risk tertile had significantly higher family affluence ($p < 0.001$), lower food security risk ($p = 0.006$), and higher BMIs ($p < 0.001$) than those in the high obesity risk tertile. Additionally, the high obesity risk tertile reported significantly more days of "not good" health in the past month ($p < 0.001$), younger age at birth of first child ($p = 0.007$), and higher depression severity ($p < 0.001$) compared with those in lower obesity risk tertiles. There were no significant child BMI percentile differences among obesity risk tertiles although there was an increasing trend.

An examination of maternal intrapersonal characteristics showed that those in the high obesity risk tertile were significantly more likely to report worse sleep quality ($p < 0.001$), greater emotional eating ($p < 0.001$), perceive themselves as having less personal organization ($p < 0.001$), lower confidence in parenting ($p = 0.004$), and poorer stress management skills ($p < 0.001$) than those in the lower obesity risk tertiles. Compared to the high obesity risk tertile, mothers in the low obesity risk tertile were significantly more likely to value the importance of physical activity for self ($p < 0.001$) and child ($p = 0.006$), value the importance of modeling physical activity ($p = 0.01$), frequently model physical activity ($p < 0.001$) and less frequently model sedentary activity ($p = 0.007$), model healthy eating ($p = 0.003$), and place more child limits on children's TV program choices ($p = 0.01$). None of the other intrapersonal characteristics differed significantly among obesity risk tertile groups.

The only interpersonal characteristics that differed significantly among obesity risk tertile groups were the frequency of family meals eaten at the kitchen or dining table and family conflict and lack of cohesion. That is, mothers in the high obesity risk tertile reported eating significantly ($p = 0.006$) fewer family meals at a kitchen or dining table and had more family conflict and less cohesion ($p = 0.005$) compared with those in the low obesity risk tertile.

Household fruit and vegetable availability was the only home physical environment characteristic that differed significantly among obesity risk tertiles. That is, mothers in the low obesity risk tertile had greater household availability of fruits and vegetables ($p = 0.013$) than those in the high obesity risk tertile. Estimated effect sizes, as determined by partial Eta squared, for the significantly different intrapersonal, interpersonal, and home environment characteristics were low.

Table 4. ANOVA of Sociodemographic, Intrapersonal, Interpersonal and Home Environment Characteristics among Obesity Risk Score Tertiles of Non-Obese Participants.

	Obesity Risk Score Tertiles of Non-Obese Participants (N = 386)				
	Low Risk (n = 120)	**Moderate Risk (n = 135)**	**High Risk (n = 131)**		
Weighted Score Cut-offs	**0 to 1.12**	**1.13 to 2.07**	**≥2.08**	**ANOVA ***	
	Mean ± SD or N (%)	**Mean ± SD or N (%)**	**Mean ± SD or N (%)**	**F or χ^2**	**p-value**
Obesity risk score (possible score range 0–5.49)	0.58 ± 0.36 †[a]	1.52 ± 0.27 [b]	2.78 ± 0.53 [c]	953.53	<0.001
Sociodemographic Characteristics					
Maternal Employment				5.03	0.284
Do not work	56 (46.7)	73 (54.1)	78 (59.5)		
Part-time (less than 30 h/week)	24 (20.0)	28 (20.7)	21 (16.0)		
Full-time (30 or more h/week)	40 (33.3)	34 (25.2)	32 (24.4)		
Number of Children in Household	2.07 ± 0.97	2.21 ± 1.02	2.22 ± 0.96	0.94	0.392
Family Affluence Score	6.09 ± 1.49 [a]	5.63 ± 1.61 [b]	5.49 ± 1.53 [b]	5.16	0.006
Food Insecurity Risk	1.38 ± 1.76 [a]	1.78 ± 1.80	2.27 ± 1.82 [b]	7.81	<0.001
Weight Status					
Mother's BMI	22.15 ± 2.64 [a]	22.93 ± 3.03 [a]	25.19 ± 3.05 [b]	37.36	<0.001
Child's BMI percentile (n = 339)	59.85 ± 34.58	62.07 ± 34.76	65.45 ± 35.45	0.89	0.413
Health-Related Assessments					
Health-Related Quality of Life (# of unhealthy days)	0.94 ± 1.57 [a]	1.61 ± 2.51 [a]	4.16 ± 5.49 [b]	27.97	<0.001
Depression Severity	0.57 ± 1.02 [a]	0.85 ± 1.41 [a]	1.33 ± 1.48 [b]	10.68	<0.001
Age at Birth of First Child (years)	25.92 ± 4.72 [a]	24.30 ± 5.12 [a]	23.92 ± 5.59 [b]	5.08	0.007
Primary Relative with History of Diabetes (% yes)	23 (19.2)	21 (15.6)	38 (29.0)	7.64	0.022
Intrapersonal Characteristics					
Maternal Weight-Related Behaviors					
Physical Activity Level	17.43 ± 9.78	15.93 ± 9.49	14.65 ± 10.50	2.46	0.087
Screentime (minutes/day)	216.25 ± 214.87	270.78 ± 249.99	277.67 ± 251.36	2.43	0.089
Sleep Duration (hours/day)	7.49 ± 1.97	7.22 ± 1.85	6.87 ± 1.89	3.31	0.038
Sleep Quality	3.58 ± 0.87 [a]	3.46 ± 0.82 [a]	3.03 ± 0.83 [b]	15.00	<0.001
Fruit and Vegetable (servings/day)	4.98 ± 2.37	4.84 ± 2.30	4.24 ± 2.29	3.65	0.027
% Calories from Total Fat	36.83 ± 5.36	37.61 ± 6.55	36.98 ± 5.87	0.64	0.530
Milk (servings/day)	4.18 ± 3.19	4.31 ± 2.95	3.33 ± 3.11	3.79	0.023
Sugar-Sweetened Beverage (servings/day)	0.70 ± 0.78	0.95 ± 1.06	0.93 ± 0.86	2.83	0.060
Maternal Eating Styles					
Disinhibited Eating	1.77 ± 0.77	1.95 ± 0.76	2.00 ± 0.73	2.25	0.040
Emotional Eating	1.73 ± 0.74 [a]	1.87 ± 0.80 [a]	2.19 ± 0.88 [b]	10.95	<0.001
Dietary Restraint Eating	2.31 ± 0.79	2.47 ± 0.79	2.49 ± 0.69	2.27	0.105

Table 4. *Cont.*

	Obesity Risk Score Tertiles of Non-Obese Participants (N = 386)				
	Low Risk (n = 120)	**Moderate Risk (n = 135)**	**High Risk (n = 131)**		
Weighted Score Cut-offs	**0 to 1.12**	**1.13 to 2.07**	**≥2.08**	**ANOVA ***	
	Mean ± SD or N (%)	**Mean ± SD or N (%)**	**Mean ± SD or N (%)**	**F or χ^2**	**p-value**
Adventurous Eating	3.21 ± 0.69	3.16 ± 0.66	3.12 ± 0.67	0.52	0.597
Maternal Self-Perceptions					
Personal Organization (self-effectiveness)	3.91 ± 0.75 ^{a}	3.79 ± 0.79 ^{a}	3.49 ± 0.83 ^{b}	9.31	<0.001
Need for Cognition	3.66 ± 1.01	3.47 ± 0.94	3.37 ± 0.98	2.76	0.065
Parenting Self-Efficacy	4.23 ± 0.71 ^{a}	4.23 ± 0.75 ^{a}	3.95 ± 0.82 ^{b}	5.71	0.004
Stress Management	4.19 ± 0.54 ^{a}	4.02 ± 0.71 ^{a}	3.79 ± 0.83 ^{b}	10.41	<0.001
Stress Management Self-Efficacy	2.88 ± 1.01	2.51 ± 1.05	2.64 ± 0.99	1.43	0.242
Child Weight Cognitions					
Belief that Chubby Kids are Healthy	2.72 ± 0.75	2.79 ± 0.68	2.61 ± 0.72	1.95	0.143
Health Behavior Values					
Importance of Physical Activity for Self	3.90 ± 0.92 ^{a}	3.75 ± 0.81 ^{a}	3.34 ± 0.92 ^{b}	13.94	<0.001
Importance of Physical Activity for Child	4.03 ± 0.78 ^{a}	3.85 ± 0.85	3.69 ± 0.87 ^{b}	5.12	0.006
Encourages/Facilitates Child Physical Activity	4.37 ± 0.67	4.29 ± 0.61	4.16 ± 0.64	3.44	0.033
Importance of Modeling Physical Activity to Child	4.35 ± 0.82 ^{a}	4.26 ± 0.71	4.07 ± 0.76 ^{b}	4.61	0.010
Engages in Physical Activity with Child Frequently	3.92 ± 1.90	3.61 ± 1.91	3.44 ± 1.80	2.11	0.123
Models Physical Activity to Child Frequently	3.55 ± 1.10 ^{a}	3.13 ± 1.21 ^{b}	2.93 ± 1.18 ^{b}	9.14	<0.001
Models Sedentary Behaviors Infrequently	3.54 ± 2.11 ^{a}	2.84 ± 2.08 ^{b}	2.75 ± 2.27 ^{b}	5.00	0.007
Models Healthy Eating to Child	3.72 ± 0.75 ^{a}	3.62 ± 0.63	3.43 ± 0.69 ^{b}	5.74	0.003
Belief that TV Positively Affects Child Learning	3.91 ± 0.68	3.91 ± 0.8	3.78 ± 0.78	1.30	0.274
Talks Often with Child about TV	3.38 ± 1.01	3.27 ± 0.94	3.26 ± 0.94	0.60	0.548
Limits Child Exposure to TV Commercials and Inappropriate Programs Shows	3.77 ± 0.90	3.71 ± 0.86	3.66 ± 0.93	0.48	0.621
Limits Child to Educational TV	3.68 ± 1.03 ^{a}	3.64 ± 1.02 ^{a}	3.31 ± 1.09 ^{b}	4.66	0.010
Home Interpersonal Characteristics					
Child Feeding Practices					
Restricts Child Food Intake	3.85 ± 0.88	3.91 ± 0.84	3.83 ± 0.83	0.31	0.737
Pressures Child to Eat	2.22 ± 1.04	2.18 ± 0.95	2.15 ± 0.89	0.18	0.837
Maternal Control Over Child Food Access and Choices	3.44 ± 0.49	3.38 ± 0.55	3.30 ± 0.48	2.40	0.092
Non-Acceptance of Food Waste	3.12 ± 0.96	3.26 ± 0.94	3.05 ± 0.89	1.75	0.175
Instrumental Feeding Practices (uses food to reward children for eating a healthy food)	2.74 ± 0.97	2.77 ± 0.93	2.55 ± 0.87	2.01	0.136
Non-Food Rewards (uses non-food [e.g., extra playtime] to reward children for eating a healthy food)	2.93 ± 1.00	2.95 ± 0.98	2.89 ± 0.86	0.16	0.854
Allows Child to Independently Access Nutrient Dense Foods	1.74 ± 1.74	1.96 ± 1.68	1.73 ± 1.78	0.75	0.475
Allows Child to Independently Access Low Nutrient Density Foods	0.48 ± 1.04	0.78 ± 1.43	0.70 ± 1.40	1.81	0.166
Nutrient Dense Foods Stored in Locations Visible to Child	2.30 ± 1.72	2.42 ± 1.71	2.61 ± 1.78	1.03	0.360
Low Nutrient Dense Foods Stored in Locations Visible to Child	0.58 ± 1.21	0.79 ± 1.39	0.94 ± 1.36	2.26	0.106

Table 4. *Cont.*

	Obesity Risk Score Tertiles of Non-Obese Participants (N = 386)				
	Low Risk (n = 120)	Moderate Risk (n = 135)	High Risk (n = 131)		
Weighted Score Cut-offs	0 to 1.12	1.13 to 2.07	≥2.08	ANOVA *	
	Mean ± SD or N (%)	Mean ± SD or N (%)	Mean ± SD or N (%)	F or χ^2	p-value
Family Meal Patterns					
Family Meal Frequency (per week)	14.25 ± 5.00	13.92 ± 4.49	12.97 ± 5.09	2.39	0.093
Importance of Family Meals	4.64 ± 0.57	4.53 ± 0.64	4.42 ± 0.65	3.69	0.026
Positive Family Meal Atmosphere	4.18 ± 0.86	4.09 ± 0.88	4.08 ± 0.79	0.57	0.569
Fast Food Eaten at Family Meals					
TV on During Family Meals (days/week)	1.53 ± 2.17	2.22 ± 2.53	2.24 ± 2.43	3.55	0.030
Family Meals Eaten at Kitchen or Dining Table (days/week)	5.38 ± 2.23 [a]	4.82 ± 2.48	4.42 ± 2.42 [b]	5.13	0.006
Family Meals Eaten in the Car	0.51 ± 1.29	0.54 ± 1.39	0.35 ± 0.90	0.92	0.401
Family Meal Planning	3.53 ± 0.93	3.46 ± 0.9	3.4 ± 0.80	0.70	0.496
Time and Energy for Family Meals	4.46 ± 0.78	4.33 ± 0.85	4.22 ± 0.92	2.57	0.078
Family Functioning and Maternal Engagement					
Family Support for Healthy Behaviors	4.54 ± 0.74	4.34 ± 0.86	4.37 ± 0.65	2.56	0.079
Family Conflict and Lack of Cohesion	1.65 ± 0.62 [a]	1.76 ± 0.64	1.91 ± 0.66 [b]	5.29	0.005
Household Disorganization	2.32 ± 0.96	2.48 ± 0.92	2.55 ± 0.87	2.03	0.133
Verbal Engagement with Children	4.33 ± 0.84	4.15 ± 0.91	4.05 ± 1.01	2.91	0.056
Physical Engagement with Children	4.81 ± 0.44	4.67 ± 0.6	4.73 ± 0.51	2.11	0.122
Home Physical Environment Characteristics					
Physical Activity					
Physical Activity Availability	3.90 ± 0.68	3.82 ± 0.62	3.78 ± 0.64	1.12	0.327
Physical Activity Accessibility	4.42 ± 0.98	4.39 ± 1.16	4.12 ± 1.15	2.84	0.060
Media Devices in the Home (total number)	11.53 ± 4.29	11.09 ± 4.19	11.5 ± 3.71	0.49	0.613
Media Devices in Child's Bedroom (total number)	1.05 ± 1.55	1.37 ± 1.70	1.63 ± 1.75	3.71	0.025
Daily Screentime Child Allowed (minutes/day)	342.00 ± 413.14	433.78 ± 642.76	509.54 ± 710.46	2.39	0.093
Food Availability					
Household Fruit and Vegetable Availability (serving/person/day)	6.96 ± 2.41 [a]	6.80 ± 2.62	6.09 ± 2.44 [b]	4.40	0.013
Household Fatty/Salty Snack Availability (serving/person/day)	9.21 ± 7.81	8.67 ± 7.73	8.07 ± 6.81	0.73	0.481
Household Sugar-Sweetened Beverage Availability (serving/person/day)	1.70 ± 2.02	2.21 ± 2.02	1.72 ± 1.51	3.15	0.044
Household Breakfast Cereal Availability (servings/person/day)	5.67 ± 2.78	5.39 ± 2.70	5.49 ± 2.52	0.36	0.698

* Analysis of Variance (ANOVA) for continuous variables and Chi-square analysis for categorical variables examined characteristic differences among the Obesity Risk Score Tertile groups (low risk, moderate risk, and high risk). Tukey post-hoc tests were conducted for characteristics that were statistically significant ($p < 0.01$) in the ANOVA to determine significant between group differences. † Differing superscript lowercase letters in the same row indicate significant ($p < 0.05$) between group differences as determined by Tukey post-hoc tests.

4. Discussion

This study developed an obesity risk score for non-obese mothers of young children using a comprehensive array of sociodemographic and weight-related intrapersonal, interpersonal, and home environmental characteristics. The eight characteristics comprising the obesity risk score may help health professionals identify non-obese mothers with young children at increased risk for obesity and provide early obesity prevention intervention.

The eight independent variables identified in this study explained over half of maternal risk for obesity have been shown in other studies to be strongly associated with obesity. That is, women of African American race are more likely to be overweight or obese than other racial and ethnic groups [1]; lower education attainment is associated with overweight and obesity [1,83]; obese adults have more chronic disease [92,93] and report poorer health [94]; obese women are more likely to report being teased growing up [95,96]; and body shape dissatisfaction is associated with overweight and obesity [97,98]. The study reported here also provides insight into variables that are associated with obesity which are not changeable through nutrition and health promotion programs (e.g., race, family history, affluence), and those which are, yet are rarely targeted in nutrition education interventions (e.g., family conflict, body dissatisfaction).

Examining non-obese mothers by high, moderate, and low obesity risk tertiles provided an efficient means for exploring how risk level was associated with interpersonal, intrapersonal, and environmental characteristics. Several sociodemographic variables, health-related assessments, and intrapersonal, and interpersonal characteristics were associated with high obesity risk score among non-obese mothers whereas home physical environment factors tended to not be associated with obesity risk. Trends in sociodemographic and health-related characteristics noted among participants at high risk for obesity (e.g., food insecurity, lower family affluence, more unhealthy days in past month, and greater depression severity) mirror national data [1,83]. For instance, mothers in the high obesity risk group reported less family affluence and greater depression severity, which is consistent with literature indicating obesity rates are higher among adult women with low socio-economic status [99] and obese women are more likely to suffer from depression (although this association may be bi-directional) [100,101].

High obesity risk mothers did not significantly differ from lower obesity risk moms in their physical activity and screentime behaviors possibly because at risk, but not obese, women are not yet hindered by their weight interfering with their activity level. These findings suggest that activity level may not be a significant risk factor for maternal obesity but is associated with obesity weight status, raising the question of reverse causality. That is, are obese mothers inactive and more sedentary [102] because their weight inhibits physical activity instead of inactivity causing weight gain; or, are there other factors contributing to these relationships, such as the environmental supports for physical activity? Environments that promote access to and availability of physical activity are associated with more physical activity behaviors [103–107]. However, a recent systematic review has found inconsistent results in the associations between the built physical environment and obesity in adults [108], perhaps due to the great variation in metrics used and differing contexts of prior studies [108].

There is growing interest in the associations of sleep duration and quality with weight [109]. In the present study, poor sleep quality was significantly more prevalent in high obesity risk mothers. Although non-significant, the number of total hours slept each night linearly decreased as obesity risk increased, with those in the high obesity risk group receiving less than the recommended total sleep hours per night for adults of 7 to 9 h [110]. These findings suggest the need for continued investigation of the mechanisms of how sleep may be related to weight gain, and indicate the importance of including sleep management in weight-management interventions.

A linear trend showed that high obesity risk mothers were less active with their children and allowed children to have more minutes of screentime daily than lower obesity risk mothers. This finding is similar to reports of associations between maternal characteristics, child activity, and sedentary behaviors [111,112], and further highlights the importance of maternal modeling, encouraging, and facilitating physical activity for their children [69]. Not surprisingly, low obesity risk mothers engaged in significantly more modeling of both physical activity and less sedentary behaviors. Additionally, mothers at low obesity risk were less likely to model unhealthy emotional eating behaviors for their children. Parents and caregivers act as powerful socialization agents and serve as models of eating that children learn to emulate [113]. Future work should explore how low obesity risk mothers' modeling of healthy behaviors affects the health and weight status of their children.

Home food availability, parental diet, and family eating habits are associated with diet quality of children [114,115]. In this study, high obesity risk moms had less household availability of fruits and vegetables and ate fewer family meals at a kitchen or dining room table which may have influenced their child's diet quality and weight status. Although non-significant, there was a positive linear trend in child BMI percentile and maternal obesity risk score. Studies on weight-resilience (i.e., maintaining a healthy weight despite living in an obesogenic environment) suggest that homes with healthy weight children and teens are more likely to have healthier food options available and limit access to unhealthy foods [116,117]. In the study reported here, only a non-significant linear trend occurred, with mothers at low obesity risk limiting children's access to low nutrient dense foods and storing nutrient dense foods in a manner that was clearly visible to children. Thus, future interventions should consider targeting family nutrition education that encourages positive changes in the home food supply and healthful dietary practices in the home.

This study found a non-significant decreasing trend in the relationships among obesity risk tertiles and family meal frequency. Other studies have found cross-sectional associations of family meal frequency were inversely associated with obesity in adolescents, but longitudinal analyses have not corroborated those results [118–120]. The results of this study contribute to the mixed associations among family meals and weight status [121]. It may be that characteristics of the family meal environment are confounding potential associations. For example, non-obese mothers at high risk for obesity reported significantly more family conflict and lack of cohesion. Having poor family functioning (i.e., more conflict and less cohesion) during mealtimes may lead to less frequent family meals, especially when there is a negative meal atmosphere [122–124]. Further research examining the influences of family dynamics with family meal frequency and weight-related behaviors are warranted [122,125].

The relationships between home food availability and maternal dietary intake are not clear. For instance, sugar-sweetened beverage intake was relatively lower among low obesity risk mothers yet household availability of sugar-sweetened beverages was similar in households across maternal obesity risk tertiles. Mothers at low obesity risk ate relatively more fruits and vegetables and had significantly greater household availability of fruits and vegetables than those of higher obesity risk. Whether foods were eaten from household food stores or outside the home was not investigated; the incongruence of beverage intake and household availability may indicate these beverages were consumed at home as well as outside the home, whereas the relative consistency between fruit and vegetable intake and household food supplies may indicate these foods are typically eaten at home. Further research is needed to understand where food and beverages are typically consumed and the impact of consumption location on household food supplies, overall family dietary intakes, and obesity risk.

A major strength of this study was the use of a socioecological framework to guide the comprehensive selection of constructs obesity risk in mothers of young children. A systematic method [34] was used to examine the potential scales for application to the study population (i.e., mothers and young children of varying races/ethnicities and educational attainment). Use of reliable and valid scales is vital to ensure the most accurate responses. In this survey, previously validated and refined tools were used when possible, and nearly all had good to high internal consistency with the study sample. Despite the strengths of this study, it is important to note its limitations. Inference of causality of observed associations cannot be made due to the cross-sectional study design. In addition, the study sample only included mothers of preschool-aged children in the U.S. with greater educational attainment than the national average, so findings may not be generalizable to mothers with lower education levels or mothers with children of different ages or those residing in other countries. This study also did not evaluate characteristics and behaviors of other family or friends or environments outside of the home environment. Although the estimated effect size for the obesity risk score was high, the significantly different intrapersonal, interpersonal, and home environment characteristics that occurred across obesity risk tertiles had low effect sizes. Lastly, data collected from participants were self-reported and may be subject to both reporting error and bias. However, heights and weights self-reported by adults are highly correlated with measured heights and weights [126] and online data collection offers privacy and relative anonymity that may improve veracity when answering questions [127–129].

5. Conclusions

In conclusion, this exploratory study identified eight characteristics that, together, explain more than half of the risk of obesity in non-obese mothers of young children. These eight characteristics may help healthcare professionals identify mothers at increased risk of obesity and offer preventive care early and more specifically tailor care (e.g., psychological assistance for those with body dissatisfaction). Many of the eight characteristics are not usually assessed in clinical practice, but are simple to assess and may yield valuable obesity risk information to healthcare providers. In addition, nutrition communication and health promotion professionals can apply the findings by targeting intervention efforts to those at increased risk and expanding intervention content to address topics not typically addressed in obesity prevention programs, such as strategies for managing family conflicts and changing the home food environment. Further research with larger, more diverse samples who are longitudinally assessed is needed to confirm the results of this study. Additional research to clarify the contribution of early identification of those at high risk for obesity and inclusion of new topics in obesity prevention programs also is warranted.

Author Contributions: C.B.-B. and J.M.-B. conceived and designed the study. J.M.-B. and C.B.-B. collected data. J.M.-B., V.Q., and C.B.-B. analyzed the data. J.M.-B., V.Q., K.S., and C.B.-B. were involved in manuscript preparation and revision and approved the final manuscript.

Funding: This research was funded by United States Department of Agriculture, National Institute of Food and Agriculture, Grant Number 2011-68001-30170.

Acknowledgments: This study was funded by USDA NIFA #2011-68001-30170. An earlier draft of parts of this manuscript were from J. Martin-Biggers (2016) Home Environment Characteristics Associated with Obesity Risk In Preschool-Aged Children and Their Mothers, doctoral dissertation, Rutgers, The State University of New Jersey, New Brunswick, NJ.

Conflicts of Interest: The authors declare no conflict of interest.

References

1. Ogden, C.; Carroll, M.; Kit, B.; Flegal, K. Prevalence of childhood and adult obesity in the United States, 2011–2012. *JAMA* **2014**, *311*, 806–814. [CrossRef] [PubMed]
2. Tsai, A.; Williamson, D.; Glick, H. Direct medical cost of overweight and obesity in the United States: A qunatitative systematic review. *Obes. Rev.* **2012**, *12*, 50–61. [CrossRef] [PubMed]
3. Pi-Sunyer, F.X. The Obesity Epidemic: Pathophysiology and Consequences of Obesity. *Obesity* **2002**, *10* (Suppl. 12), 97S–104S. [CrossRef] [PubMed]
4. Organization, W.H. *Obesity: Preventing and Managing the Global Epidemic*; World Health Organization: Geneva, Switzerland, 2000.
5. Lobstein, T.; Baur, L.; Uauy, R. Obesity in children and young people: A crisis in public health. *Obes. Rev.* **2004**, *5*, 4–85. [CrossRef] [PubMed]
6. Hassan, M.K.; Joshi, A.V.; Madhavan, S.S.; Amonkar, M.M. Obesity and health-related quality of life: A cross-sectional analysis of the US population. *Int. J. Obes. Relat. Metab. Disord.* **2003**, *27*, 1227–1232. [CrossRef] [PubMed]

7. Brinkley, J.; Eales, J.; Jekanowski, M. The relation between dietary change and rising US obesity. *Int. J. Obes. Relat. Metab. Disord.* **2000**, *24*, 1032–1039. [CrossRef]
8. Golan, M.; Crow, S. Parents are key players in the prevention and treatment of weight-related problems. *Nutr. Rev.* **2004**, *62*, 39–50. [CrossRef] [PubMed]
9. Hill, J.; Wyatt, H.; Reed, G.; Peters, J. Obesity and the environment: Where do we go from here? *Science* **2003**, *203*, 853–856.
10. Wang, Y.C.; Bleich, S.N.; Gortmaker, S.L. Increasing caloric contribution from sugar-sweetened beverages and 100% fruit juices among US children and adolescents, 1988–2004. *Pediatrics* **2008**, *121*, e1604–e1614. [PubMed]
11. Wang, Y.C.; Orleans, C.T.; Gortmaker, S.L. Reaching the healthy people goals for reducing childhood obesity: Closing the energy gap. *Am. J. Prev. Med.* **2012**, *42*, 437–444. [PubMed]
12. *Diet, Nutrition and the Prevention of Chronic Diseases*; World Health Organization Technical Report Series 916, backcover; World Health Organization: Geneva, Switzerland, 2003; Volume i–viii, pp. 1–149.
13. Richard, L.; Gauvin, L.; Raine, K. Ecological Models Revisited: Their Uses and Evolution in Health Promotion Over Two Decades. *Annu. Rev. Public Health* **2011**, *32*, 307–326. [CrossRef] [PubMed]
14. Sallis, J.; Owen, N. *Ecological Models of Health Behavior*, 5th ed.; Jossey-Bass: San Francisco, CA, USA, 2015.
15. Giskes, K.; van Lenthe, F.; Avendano-Pabon, M.; Brug, J. A systematic review of environmental factors and obesogenic dietary intakes among adults: Are we getting closer to understanding obesogenic environments? *Obes. Rev.* **2011**, *12*, e95–e106. [CrossRef] [PubMed]
16. Van der Horst, K.; Oenema, A.; Ferreira, I.; Wendel-Vos, W.; Giskes, K.; van Lenthe, F.; Brug, J. A systematic review of environmental correlates of obesity-related dietary behaviors in youth. *Health Educ. Res.* **2007**, *22*, 203–226. [CrossRef] [PubMed]
17. Kelder, S.; Hoelscher, D.; Perry, C. How individuals, environments, and health behavior interact; Social Cognitive Theory. In *Health Behavior: Theory, Research, and Practice*, 5th ed.; Glanz, K., Rimer, B., Viswanath, K., Eds.; Jossey-Bass: San Francisco, CA, USA, 2015; pp. 159–182.
18. Saelens, B.; Sallis, J.; Frank, L. Environmental correlates of walking and cycling: Findings from the transportation, urban design, and planning literatures. *Ann. Behav. Med.* **2003**, *25*, 80–91. [CrossRef] [PubMed]
19. Humpel, N.; Owen, N.; Leslie, E. Environmental factors associated with adults' participation in physical activity: A review. *Am. J. Prev. Med.* **2002**, *22*, 188–199. [CrossRef]
20. Berge, J.M.; Larson, N.; Bauer, K.W.; Neumark-Sztainer, D. Are parents of young children practicing healthy nutrition and physical activity behaviors? *Pediatrics* **2011**, *127*, 881–887. [CrossRef] [PubMed]
21. Evans, A.E.; Dave, J.; Tanner, A.; Duhe, S.; Condrasky, M.; Wilson, D.; Griffin, S.; Palmer, M.; Evans, M. Changing the home nutrition environment: Effects of a nutrition and media literacy pilot intervention. *Fam. Community Health* **2006**, *29*, 43–54. [CrossRef] [PubMed]
22. *Children's Food Environment State Indicator Report*; Centers for Disease Control and Prevention: Atlanta, GA, USA, 2011.
23. Vaughn, A.; Ward, D.; Fisher, J.; Faith, M.; Hughes, S.; Kremers, S.; Musher-Eizenman, D.; O'Connor, T.; Patrick, H.; Power, T. Fundamental constructs in food parenting practices: A content map to guide future research. *Nutr. Rev.* **2016**, *74*, 98–117. [CrossRef] [PubMed]
24. Reid, M.; Worsley, A.; Mavondo, F. The obesogenic household: Factors influencing dietary gatekeeper satisfaction with family diet. *Psychol. Mark.* **2015**, *32*, 544–557. [CrossRef]
25. Mamun, A.; O'Callaghan, M.; Callaway, L.; Williams, G.; Najman, J.; Lawlor, D. Associations of Gestational Weight Gain with Offspring Body Mass Index and Blood Pressure at 21 Years of Age Evidence from a Birth Cohort Study. *Circulation* **2009**, *119*, 1720–1727. [CrossRef] [PubMed]
26. Lagström, H.; Hakanen, M.; Niinikoski, H.; Viikari, J.; Rönnemaa, T.; Saarinen, M.; Pahkala, K.; Simell, O. Growth Patterns and Obesity Development in Overweight or Normal-Weight 13-Year-Old Adolescents: The STRIP Study. *Pediatrics* **2008**, *122*, e876–e883. [CrossRef] [PubMed]
27. Shibli, R.; Rubin, L.; Akons, H.; Shaoul, R. Morbidity of overweight (85th percentile) in the first 2 years of life. *Pediatrics* **2008**, *122*, 267–272. [CrossRef] [PubMed]
28. Ogata, B.; Hayes, D. Position of the Academy of Nutrition and Dietetics: Nutrition guidance for healthy children ages 2 to 11 years. *J. Acad. Nutr. Diet.* **2014**, *114*, 1257–1276. [CrossRef] [PubMed]

29. Centers for Disease Control and Prevention Adult Obesity Causes & Consequences. Available online: https://www.cdc.gov/obesity/adult/causes.html (accessed on 1 November 2017).
30. U.S. Census Bureau Age and Sex Composition: 2010. Available online: https://www.census.gov/prod/cen2010/briefs/c2010br-03.pdf (accessed on 1 May 2017).
31. Martin-Biggers, J. Home Environment Characteristics Associated with Obesity Risk in Preschool-Aged Children and THEIR mothers. Ph.D. Dissertation, Rutgers, The State University of New Jersey, New Brunswick, NJ, USA, 2016.
32. Martin-Biggers, J.; Cheng, C.; Spaccarotella, K.; Byrd-Bredbenner, C. The Physical Activity Environment in Homes and Neighborhoods. In *Recent Advances in Obesity in Children*; Avid Science Publications: Berlin, Germany, 2016; Available online: www.avidscience.com/wp-content/uploads/2016/05/OIC-15-04_May-06-2016.pdf (accessed on 1 November 2017).
33. Martin-Biggers, J.M.; Worobey, J.; Byrd-Bredbenner, C. Interpersonal Characteristics in the Home Environment Associated with Childhood Obesity. In *Recent Advances in Obesity in Children*; Avid Science Publications: Berlin, Germany, 2016; Chapter 3.
34. Redding, C.A.; Maddock, J.E.; Rossi, J.S. The sequential approach to measurement of health behavior constructs: Issues in selecting and developing measures. *Calif. J. Health Promot.* **2006**, *4*, 83–101.
35. Linn, R.; Gronlund, N. *Measuring and Assessment in Teaching*, 8th ed.; Prentice-Hall: Englewood Cliffs, NJ, USA, 2000.
36. Carbone, E.T.; Campbell, M.K.; Honess-Morreale, L. Use of cognitive interview techniques in the development of nutrition surveys and interactive nutrition messages for low-income populations. *J. Am. Diet. Assoc.* **2002**, *102*, 690–696. [CrossRef]
37. Wright, K.B. Researching Internet-Based Populations: Advantages and Disadvantages of Online Survey Research, Online Questionnaire Authoring Software Packages, and Web Survey Services. *J. Comput.-Med. Commun.* **2005**, *10*. [CrossRef]
38. Masse, L. Innovations in Measurement of Parenting Constructs, Parenting Meausurement: Current Status and Consensus Reports. In Proceedings of the International Society for Behavioral Nutrition and Physical Activity, Houston, TX, USA, 20 May 2012.
39. Hartley, J.; Levin, K.; Currie, C. A new version of the HBSC Family Affluence Scale—FAS III: Scottish qualitative findings from the international FAS developments study. *Child Indic. Res.* **2016**, *9*, 233–245. [CrossRef] [PubMed]
40. Currie, C.; Mollcho, M.; Boyce, W.; Holstein, B.; Torsheim, T.; Richter, M. Researching health inequalities in adolescents: The development of the health behavior in school-aged children (HBSC) family affluence scale. *Soc. Sci. Med.* **2008**, *66*, 1429–1436. [CrossRef] [PubMed]
41. Hager, E.; Quigg, A.; Black, M.; Coleman, S.; Heeren, T.; Rose-Jacobs, R.; Cook, J.; Ettinger de Cuba, S.; Casey, P.; Chilton, M.; et al. Development and validity of a 2-Item screen to identify families at risk for food insecurity. *Pediatrics* **2010**, *126*, e26–e32. [CrossRef] [PubMed]
42. Centers for Disease Control and Prevention HRQOL Concepts. Why Is Quality of Life Important? Available online: www.cdc.gov/hrqol/concept.htm (accessed on 9 May 2016).
43. Centers for Disease Control and Prevention CDC HRQOL-14 Healthy Days Measure. Available online: www.cdc.gov/hrqol/hrqol14_measure.htm (accessed on 9 May 2016).
44. Kroenke, K.; Spitzer, R.L.; Williams, J.B.W. The Patient Health Questionnaire-2: Validity of a two-item depression screener. *Med. Care* **2003**, *41*, 1284–1292. [CrossRef] [PubMed]
45. Thompson, J.; Cattarin, J.; Fowler, B.; Fisher, E. The Perception of Teasing Scale (POTS): A revision and extension of the Physical Appearance Related Teasing Scale (PARTS). *J. Personal. Assess.* **1995**, *65*, 146–157. [CrossRef] [PubMed]
46. Fairburn, C.; Beglin, S. Assessment of eating disorders: Interview or self-report questionnaire? *Int. J. Eat. Disord.* **1994**, *16*, 363–370. [PubMed]
47. Quick, V.; Byrd-Bredbenner, C.; Shoff, S.; White, A.; Lohse, B.; Horacek, T.; Kattlemann, K.; Phillips, B.; Hoerr, S.; Greene, G. A streamlined, enhanced self-report physical activity measure for young adults. *Int. J. Health Promot. Educ.* **2016**. [CrossRef]
48. Lee, P.; Macfarlane, D.; Lam, T.; Stewart, S. Validity of the international physical activity questionnaire short form (IPAQ-SF): A systematic review. *Int. J. Behav. Nutr. Phys. Act.* **2011**, *8*, 115. [CrossRef] [PubMed]

49. Craig, C.L.; Marshall, A.L.; Sjorstrom, M.; Bauman, A.E.; Booth, M.L.; Ainsworth, B.E.; Pratt, M.; Ekelund, U.L.; Yngve, A.; Sallis, J.F.; et al. International Physical Activity Questionnaire: 12-country reliability and validity. *Med. Sci. Sports Exerc.* **2003**, *35*, 1381–1395. [CrossRef] [PubMed]
50. Buysse, D.; Reynolds, C.; Monk, T.; Berman, S.; Kupfer, D. The Pittsburgh Sleep Quality Index: A new instrument for psychiatric practice and research. *Psychiatr. Res.* **1989**, *28*, 193–213. [CrossRef]
51. Carpenter, J.; Andrykowski, M. Psychometric evaluation of the Pittsburgh Sleep Quality Index. *J. Psychosom. Res.* **1998**, *45*, 5–13. [CrossRef]
52. Block, G.; Gillespie, C.; Rosenbaum, E.H.; Jenson, C. A rapid food screener to assess fat and fruit and vegetable intake. *Am. J. Prev. Med.* **2000**, *18*, 284–288. [CrossRef]
53. Block, G.; Hartman, A.; Naughton, D. A reduced dietary questionnaire: Development and validation. *Epidemiology* **1990**, *1*, 58–64. [CrossRef] [PubMed]
54. Block, G.; Thompson, F.; Hartman, A.; Larkin, F.; Guire, K. Comparison of two dietary questionnaires validated against multiple dietary records collected during a 1-year period. *J. Am. Diet. Assoc.* **1992**, *92*, 686–693. [PubMed]
55. Nelson, M.; Lytle, L. Development and evaluation of a brief screener to estimate fast-food and beverage consumption among adolescents. *J. Am. Diet. Assoc.* **2009**, *109*, 730–734. [CrossRef] [PubMed]
56. West, D.; Bursac, Z.; Quimby, D.; Prewit, T.; Spatz, T.; Nash, C.; Mays, G.; Eddings, K. Self-reported sugar-sweetened beverage intake among college students. *Obesity* **2006**, *14*, 1825–1831. [CrossRef] [PubMed]
57. Stunkard, A.; Messick, S. The three-factor eating questionnaire to measure dietary restraint, disinhibition and hunger. *J. Psychosom. Res.* **1985**, *29*, 71–83. [CrossRef]
58. Karlsson, J.; Persson, L.-O.; Sjostrom, L.; Sullivan, M. Psychometric properties and factor structure of the Three-Factor Eating (TFEQ) in obese men and women. Results from the Swedish Obese Subjects (SOS) study. *Int. J. Obes.* **2000**, *24*, 1715–1725. [CrossRef]
59. Pliner, P.; Hobden, K. Development of a scale to measure the trait of food neophobia in humans. *Appetite* **1992**, *19*, 105–120. [CrossRef]
60. Ullrich, N.V.; Touger-Decker, R.; O'Sullivan-Maillet, J.; Tepper, B.J. PROP taster status and self-perceived food adventurousness influence food preferences. *J. Am. Diet. Assoc.* **2004**, *104*, 543–550. [CrossRef] [PubMed]
61. Pliner, P.; Loewen, E. Temperament and food neophobia in children and their mothers. *Appetite* **1997**, *28*, 239–254. [CrossRef] [PubMed]
62. Matheny, A.; Wachs, T.; Ludwig, J.; Phillips, K. Bringing order out of chaos: Psychometric characteristics of the confusion, hubbub, and order scale. *J. Appl. Dev. Psychol.* **1995**, *16*, 429–444. [CrossRef]
63. Cacioppo, J.; Petty, R. The need for cognition. *J. Personal. Soc. Psychol.* **1982**, *42*, 116–131. [CrossRef]
64. Cacioppo, J.; Petty, R.; Kao, C.F. The efficient assessment of need for cognition. *J. Personal. Assess.* **1984**, *48*, 306–307. [CrossRef] [PubMed]
65. Johnston, C.; Mash, E. A measure of parenting satisfaction and efficacy. *J. Clin. Child Psychol.* **1989**, *18*, 167–175. [CrossRef]
66. Gibaud-Wallston, J.; Wandersmann, L. *Development and Utility of the Parenting Sense of Competence Scale*; John F. Kennedy Center for Research on Education and Human Development: Washington, DC, USA, 1978.
67. Cohen, S.; Kamarck, T.; Mermelstein, R. A global measure of perceived stress. *J. Health Soc. Behav.* **1983**, *24*, 385–396. [CrossRef] [PubMed]
68. Birch, L.; Fisher, J.; Grimm-Thomas, K.; Markey, C.; Sawyer, R.; Johnson, S. Confirmatory factor analysis of the Child Feeding Questionnaire: A measure of parental attitudes, belief and practices about child feeding and obesity proneness. *Appetite* **2001**, *36*, 202–210. [CrossRef] [PubMed]
69. Gattshall, M.; Shoup, J.; Marshall, J.; Crane, L.; Estabrooks, P. Validation of a survey instrument to assess home environments for physical activity and healthy eating in overweight children. *Int. J. Behav. Nutr. Phys. Act.* **2008**, *5*, 3. [CrossRef] [PubMed]
70. Spurrier, N.; Magarey, A.; Golley, R.; Curnow, F.; Sawyer, M. Relationships between the home environment and physical activity and dietary patterns of preschool children: A cross-sectional study. *Int. J. Behav. Nutr. Phys. Act.* **2008**, *5*, 31. [CrossRef] [PubMed]
71. Bryant, M.; Ward, D.; Hales, D.; Vaughn, A.; Tabak, R.; Stevens, J. Reliability and validity of the Healthy Home Survey: A tool to measure factors within homes hypothesized to relate to overweight in children. *Int. J. Behav. Nutr. Phys. Act.* **2008**, *5*, 23. [CrossRef] [PubMed]

72. Earls, F.; Brooks-Gunn, J.; Raudenbush, S.; Sampson, R. *Project on human development in Chicago neighborhoods (PHDCN): Home and life interview, wave 2, 1997–2000. Instruments for ICPSR 13630*; Inter-University Consortium for Political and Social Research: Ann Arbor, MI, USA, undated.
73. Hughes, S.; Cross, M.; Hennessy, E.; Tovar, A.; Economos, C.; Power, T. Caregiver's Feeding Styles Questionnaire. Establishing cutoff points. *Appetite* **2012**, *58*, 393–395. [CrossRef] [PubMed]
74. Wardle, J.; Sanderson, S.; Guthrie, C.A.; Rapoport, L.; Plomin, R. Parental feeding style and the inter-generational transmission of obesity risk. *Obes. Res.* **2002**, *10*, 453–462. [CrossRef] [PubMed]
75. Ogden, J.; Reynolds, R.; Smith, A. Expanding the concept of parental control: A role for overt and covert control in children's snacking behaviour? *Appetite* **2006**, *47*, 100–106. [CrossRef] [PubMed]
76. Neumark-Sztainer, D.; Story, M.; Hannan, P.; Perry, C.; Irving, L. Weight-related concerns and behaviors among overweight and nonoverweight adolescents implications for preventing weight-related disorders. *Arch. Pediatr. Adol. Med.* **2002**, *156*, 171–178. [CrossRef]
77. Neumark-Sztainer, D.; Larson, N.; Fulkerson, J.; Eisenberg, M.; Story, M. Family meals and adolescents: What have we learned from Project EAT (Eating Among Teens)? *Public Health Nutr.* **2010**, *13*, 1113–1121. [CrossRef] [PubMed]
78. Koszewski, W.; Behrends, D.; Nichols, M.; Sehi, N.; Jones, G. Patterns of family meals and food and nutrition intake in limited resource families. *Fam. Consum. Sci. Res. J.* **2011**, *39*, 431–441. [CrossRef]
79. Neumark-Sztainer, D.; Wall, M.; Story, M.; Perry, C. Correlates of unhealthy weight-control behaviors among adolescents: Implications for prevention programs. *Health Psychol.* **2003**, *22*, 88–98. [CrossRef] [PubMed]
80. Storfer-Isser, A. *Association of Maternal Employment with Attitudes, Subjective Norms, and Perceived Behavioral Control Regarding Meal Preparation Among Mothers of 4–5 Years Old Children*; Bowling Green State University: Bowling Green, OH, USA, 2013.
81. Trost, S.G.; Sallis, J.F.; Pate, R.R.; Freedson, P.S.; Taylor, W.C.; Dowda, M. Evaluating a model of parental influence on youth physical activity. *Am. J. Prev. Med.* **2003**, *25*, 277–282. [CrossRef]
82. Sallis, J.F.; Prochaska, J.J.; Taylor, W.C.; Hill, J.O.; Geraci, J.C. Correlates of physical activity in a national sample of girls and boys in Grades 4 through 12. *Health Psychol.* **1999**, *18*, 410–415. [CrossRef] [PubMed]
83. Ball, K.; Crawford, D. An investigation of psychological, social and environmental correlates of obesity and weight gain in young women. *Int. J. Obes.* **2006**, *30*, 1240–1249. [CrossRef] [PubMed]
84. Moos RH, M.B. *Family Environment Scale Manual: Development, Applications, Research*, 3rd ed.; Consulting Psychologists Press: Palo Alto, CA, USA, 1994.
85. Saucier, G.; Wilson, K.; Warka, J. The structure of retrospective accounts of family environments: Related to the structure of personality attributes. *J. Personal. Assess.* **2007**, *88*, 295–308. [CrossRef] [PubMed]
86. Greene, R.; Plank, R. The short-form family environment scale: Testing a different response format. *Psychol. Rep.* **1994**, *74*, 451–464. [CrossRef]
87. Coldwell, J.; Pike, A.; Dunn, J. Household chaos—Links with parenting and child behaviour. *J. Child. Psychol. Psychiatry* **2006**, *47*, 1116–1122. [CrossRef] [PubMed]
88. Matheny, A.W.T., Jr.; Ludwig, J.L.; Phillips, K. Bringing order out of chaos: Psychometric characteristics of the confusion, hubbub, and order scale. *J. Appl. Dev. Psychol.* **1995**, *16*, 319–429. [CrossRef]
89. Crawford, D.; Telford, A.; Salmon, J. Perceptions about the local neighborhood and walking and cycling among children. *Prev. Med.* **2004**, *38*, 39–47.
90. Byrd-Bredbenner, C.; Maurer Abbot, J.; Cussler, E. Nutrient Profile of Household Food Supplies of Families with Young Children. *J. Am. Diet. Assoc.* **2009**, *109*, 2057–2062. [CrossRef] [PubMed]
91. Centers for Disease Control and Prevention CDC Growth Charts: United States. Available online: http://www.cdc.gov/nchs/about/major/nhanes/growthcharts/charts.htm (accessed on 2 June 2004).
92. Chu, S.Y.; Callaghan, W.M.; Kim, S.Y.; Schmid, C.H.; Lau, J.; England, L.J.; Dietz, P.M. Maternal obesity and risk of gestational diabetes mellitus. *Diabetes Care* **2007**, *30*, 2070–2076. [CrossRef] [PubMed]
93. Metzger, B.E.; Coustan, D.R.; Committee, O. Summary and recommendations of the fourth international workshop-conference on gestational diabetes mellitus. *Diabetes Care* **1998**, *21*, B161–B167. [PubMed]
94. Propser, M.-H.; Moczulski, V.; Qureshi, A. Obesity as a predictor of self-rated health. *Am. J. Health Behav.* **2009**, *33*, 319–329.
95. Jackson, T.D.; Grilo, C.M.; Masheb, R.M. Teasing history, onset of obesity, current eating disorder psychopathology, body dissatisfaction, and psychological functioning in binge eating disorder. *Obes. Res.* **2000**, *8*, 451–458. [CrossRef] [PubMed]

96. Quick, V.; McWilliams, R.; Byrd-Bredbenner, C. Fatty, Fatty, Two-By-Four: Weight teasing history and disturbed eating in young adult women. *Am. J. Public Health* **2013**, *103*, 508–515. [CrossRef] [PubMed]
97. Schwartz, M.B.; Brownell, K.D. Obesity and body image. *Body Image* **2004**, *1*, 43–56. [CrossRef]
98. Quick, V.; Eisenberg, M.; Bucchianeri, M.; Neumark-Sztainer, D. Prospective predictors of body dissatifaction in young adults: 10-year longitudinal findings. *Emerg. Adulthood* **2013**, *1*, 271–282. [CrossRef] [PubMed]
99. Newton, S.; Braithwaite, D.; Akinyemiju, T. Socio-economic status over the life course and obesity: Systematic review and meta-analysis. *PLoS ONE* **2017**, *12*, e0177151. [CrossRef] [PubMed]
100. Stunkard, A.J.; Faith, M.S.; Allison, K.C. Depression and obesity. *Biol. Psychiatry* **2003**, *54*, 330–337. [CrossRef]
101. Carey, M.; Small, H.; Yoong, S.; Boyes, A.; Bisquera, A.; Sanson-Fisher, R. Prevalence of comorbid depression and obesity in general practice: A cross-sectional survey. *Br. J. Gen. Pract.* **2014**, *64*, e122–e127. [CrossRef] [PubMed]
102. Thorp, A.; Owen, N.; Neuhas, M.; Dunstan, D. Sedentary behaviors and subsequent health outcomes in adults a systematic review of longitudinal studies, 1996–2011. *Am. J. Prev. Med.* **2011**, *41*, 207–215. [CrossRef] [PubMed]
103. Stronegger, W.; Titze, S.; Oja, P. Perceived characteristics of the neighborhood and its association with physical activiy behavior and self-rated health. *Health Place* **2010**, *16*, 736–743. [CrossRef] [PubMed]
104. Miller, W.D.; Pollack, C.E.; Williams, D.R. Healthy homes and communities: Putting the pieces together. *Am. J. Prev. Med.* **2011**, *40* (Suppl. 1), S48–S57. [CrossRef] [PubMed]
105. Davison, K.; Lawson, C. Do attributes in the physical environment influence children's physical activity? A review of the literature. *Int. J. Behav. Nutr. Phys. Act.* **2006**, *3*, 19. [CrossRef] [PubMed]
106. Kumanyika, S.K.; Parker, L.; Sim, L.J. *Bridging the Evidence Gap in Obesity Prevention: A Framework to Inform Decision Making*; Institute of Medicine of the National Academies: Washington, DC, USA, 2010.
107. Trost, S.G.; Owen, N.; Bauman, A.E.; Sallis, J.F.; Brown, W. Correlates of adults' participation in physical activity: Review and update. *Med. Sci. Sports Exerc.* **2002**, *34*, 1996–2001. [CrossRef] [PubMed]
108. Mackenbach, J.; Rutter, H.; Compernolle, S.; Glonti, K.; Oppert, J.; Charreire, H.; Bourdeaudhuij, I.; Brug, J.; Nijpels, G.; Lakerveld, J. Obesogenic environments: A systematic review of the association between the physical environment and adult weight status, the SPOTLIGHT project. *BMC Public Health* **2014**, *14*, 233. [CrossRef] [PubMed]
109. Golem, D.L.; Martin-Biggers, J.T.; Koenings, M.M.; Davis, K.F.; Byrd-Bredbenner, C. An integrative review of sleep for nutrition professionals. *Adv. Nut. Int. Rev. J.* **2014**, *5*, 742–759. [CrossRef] [PubMed]
110. Hirshkowitz, M.; Whiton, K.; Albert, S.; Alessi, C.; Bruni, O.; DonCarlos, L.; Hazen, N.; Herman, J.; Katz, E.; Kheirandish-Gozal, L.; et al. National Sleep Foundation's sleep time duration recommedations: Methodology and results summary. *Sleep Health* **2015**, *1*, 40–43. [CrossRef] [PubMed]
111. Sallis, J.; Prochaska, J.; Taylor, W. A review of correlates of physical activity of children and adolescents. *Med. Sci. Sports Exerc.* **2000**, *32*, 963–975. [CrossRef] [PubMed]
112. Sonneville, K.; Rifas-Shiman, S.; Kleinman, K.; Gortmaker, S.; Gillman, M.; Taveras, E. Associations of obesogenic behaviors in mothers and obese children participating in a randomized trial. *Obesity* **2012**, *20*, 1449–1454. [CrossRef] [PubMed]
113. Savage, J.; Fisher, J.; Birch, L. Parental influence on eating behavior: Conception to adolescence. *J. Law Med. Ethics* **2007**, *35*, 22–34. [CrossRef] [PubMed]
114. Santiago-Torres, M.; Adams, A.; Carrel, A.; LaRowe, T. Home food availability, parental dietary intake, and familial eating habits influence diet quality of urban Hispanic children. *Child. Obes.* **2014**, *10*, 408–415. [CrossRef] [PubMed]
115. Couch, S.; Glanz, K.; Zhou, C.; Sallis, J.; Saelens, B. Home food environment in relation to children's diet quality and weight status. *J. Acad. Nutr. Diet.* **2014**, *114*, 1569–1579. [CrossRef] [PubMed]
116. Brogan, K.; Idalski Carone, A.; Jen, K.; Ellis, D.; Marshall, S.; Naar-King, S. Factors associated with weight resilience in obesogenic environments in female African-American adolescents. *J. Acad. Nutr. Diet.* **2012**, *112*, 718–724. [CrossRef] [PubMed]
117. Williams, L.; Veitch, J.; Ball, K. What helps children eat well? A qualitative exploration of resilience among disadvantages families. *Health Educ. Res.* **2011**, *26*, 296–307. [CrossRef] [PubMed]
118. Fulkerson, J.A.; Neumark-Sztainer, D.; Hannan, P.J.; Story, M. Family meal frequency and weight status among adolescents: Cross-sectional and 5-year longitudinal associations. *Obesity* **2008**, *16*, 2529–2534. [CrossRef] [PubMed]

119. Sen, B. Frequency of family dinner and adolescent body weight status: Evidence from the national longitudinal survey of youth, 1997. *Obesity* **2006**, *14*, 2266–2276. [CrossRef] [PubMed]
120. Chan, J.C.; Sobal, J. Family meals and body weight. Analysis of multiple family members in family units. *Appetite* **2011**, *57*, 517–524. [CrossRef] [PubMed]
121. Martin-Biggers, J.; Spaccarotella, K.; Berhaupt-Glickstein, A.; Hongu, N.; Worobey, J.; Byrd-Bredbenner, C. Come and get it! A discussion of family mealtime literature and factors affecting obesity risk. *Adv. Nutr.* **2014**, *5*, 235–247. [CrossRef] [PubMed]
122. Halliday, J.; Palma, C.; Mellor, D.; Green, J.; Renzaho, A. The relationship between family functioning and child and adolescent overweight and obesity: A systematic review. *Int. J. Obes.* **2014**, *38*, 480–493. [CrossRef] [PubMed]
123. Cyril, S.; Halliday, J.; Green, J.; Renzaho, A.M. Relationship between body mass index and family functioning, family communication, family type and parenting style among African migrant parents and children in Victoria, Australia: A parent-child dyad study. *BMC Public Health* **2015**, *15*, 707. [CrossRef] [PubMed]
124. Zeller, M.; Reiter-Purtill, J.; Modi, A.; Gutzwiller, J.; Vannatta, K.; Davies, W. Controlled study of critical parent and family factors in the obesigenic environment. *Obesity* **2007**, *15*, 126–136. [CrossRef] [PubMed]
125. Sigman-Grant, M.; Hayes, J.; VanBrackle, A.; Fiese, B. Childhood obesity: Family Resiliency: A Neglected Perspective in Addressing Obesity in Young Children. *Child. Obes.* **2015**, *11*, 664–673. [CrossRef] [PubMed]
126. Pursey, K.; Burrows, T.; Stanwell, P.; Collins, C. How accurate is web-based self-reported height, weight and body mass index in young adults? *J. Med. Internet Res.* **2014**, *16*, e4. [CrossRef] [PubMed]
127. Chang, L.; Krosnick, J. National surveys via RDD elephone interviewing versus the internet comparing sample representativeness and response quality. *Public Opin. Q.* **2009**, *73*, 641–678. [CrossRef]
128. Sheehan, K.B. Crowdsourcing research: Data collection with Amazon's Mechanical Turk. *Commun. Monogr.* **2018**, *85*, 140–156. [CrossRef]
129. Lefever, S.; Dal, M. Online data collection in academic research: Advantages and limitations. *Br. J. Educ. Technol.* **2007**, *38*, 574–582. [CrossRef]

nutrients

MDPI

Commentary

Obesity with Comorbid Eating Disorders: Associated Health Risks and Treatment Approaches

Felipe Q. da Luz [1,2,3,*], Phillipa Hay [4], Stephen Touyz [2] and Amanda Sainsbury [1,2]

1 The Boden Institute of Obesity, Nutrition, Exercise & Eating Disorders, Faculty of Medicine and Health, Charles Perkins Centre, The University of Sydney, Camperdown, NSW 2006, Australia; Amanda.salis@sydney.edu.au

2 Faculty of Science, School of Psychology, the University of Sydney, Camperdown, NSW 2006, Australia; Stephen.touyz@sydney.edu.au

3 CAPES Foundation, Ministry of Education of Brazil, Brasília, DF 70040-020, Brazil

4 Translational Health Research Institute (THRI), School of Medicine, Western Sydney University, Locked Bag 1797, Penrith, NSW 2751, Australia; P.hay@westernsydney.edu.au

* Correspondence: Felipe.quintodaluz@sydney.edu.au; Tel.: +61-02-8627-1961

Received: 11 May 2018; Accepted: 25 June 2018; Published: 27 June 2018

Abstract: Obesity and eating disorders are each associated with severe physical and mental health consequences, and individuals with obesity as well as comorbid eating disorders are at higher risk of these than individuals with either condition alone. Moreover, obesity can contribute to eating disorder behaviors and vice-versa. Here, we comment on the health complications and treatment options for individuals with obesity and comorbid eating disorder behaviors. It appears that in order to improve the healthcare provided to these individuals, there is a need for greater exchange of experiences and specialized knowledge between healthcare professionals working in the obesity field with those working in the field of eating disorders, and vice-versa. Additionally, nutritional and/or behavioral interventions simultaneously addressing weight management and reduction of eating disorder behaviors in individuals with obesity and comorbid eating disorders may be required. Future research investigating the effects of integrated medical, psychological and nutritional treatment programs addressing weight management and eating disorder psychopathology in individuals with obesity and comorbid eating disorder behaviors—such as binge eating—is necessary.

Keywords: obesity; eating disorders; binge eating; dieting; treatment

---

1. Introduction

Obesity is commonly associated with health complications. Individuals with obesity are at high risk of several physical diseases, such as certain cancers, diabetes, hypertension, heart disease, stroke, as well as being at increased risk of mortality [1–7]. Obesity is also often associated with mental health problems and psychosocial difficulties. Indeed, women with obesity tend to report worse mental health than women without obesity [8]. Moreover, women tend to experience more mental health complications associated with obesity than men [9], albeit mental health problems associated with obesity (e.g., anxiety) occur in both women and men [9]. One factor that can be detrimental to the mental health of individuals with obesity is exposure to well-documented discriminatory attitudes and behaviors in different areas, such as employment, education and healthcare [10]. Additionally, discrimination against individuals with higher body mass index (BMI) can be particularly problematic because it can induce strong dissatisfaction with one's body weight and/or shape, which is a risk factor for the development of comorbid eating disorder behaviors [11].

The eating disorders that have been most frequently studied in individuals with obesity are binge eating disorder and bulimia nervosa. Binge eating disorder is defined in the current Diagnostic and Statistical Manual of Mental Disorders (DSM-5) by recurrent binge eating episodes occurring at least once a week for the past 3 months, and associated with marked distress [12]. The DSM-5 criteria for binge eating disorder also require that individuals experience at least three of the following five features: eating much more quickly than normal; eating until feeling excessively full; overeating when not feeling physically hungry; eating alone because of embarrassment related to the amount of food consumed; and feeling disgusted, depressed, or very guilty after the binge eating episodes [12]. Bulimia nervosa is characterized by self-evaluation that is excessively influenced by body weight and shape, recurrent binge eating, and recurrent unhealthy compensatory behaviors to prevent weight gain (i.e., self-induced vomiting; misuse of laxatives, diuretics or other medications; fasting; excessive exercise) [12]. The DSM-5 criteria for bulimia nervosa require that the binge eating episodes and compensatory unhealthy behaviors have occurred at least once per week for the past 3 months [12]. In addition to binge eating disorder and bulimia nervosa, individuals with obesity can also experience "other specified feeding or eating disorder" when presentations cause significant distress or impairment but do not completely meet the DSM-5 criteria for a specific eating disorder [12]. For example, according to the DSM-5, a person may have binge eating disorder of low frequency and/or limited duration. In this case, the person meets the DSM-5 criteria for binge eating disorder, except that binge eating has occurred less than once a week and/or for less than 3 months [12].

There is a significant co-occurrence of eating disorders, particularly binge eating disorder, in individuals with higher BMI. In Latin America, for example, the prevalence of binge eating disorder was 16–52% in individuals with obesity (BMI $\geq$ 30 kg/m^2) attending weight loss programs [13]. In the United States, a study with a nationally-representative sample of 9282 people assessed in 2001–2003 found that 42% of individuals that had had a binge eating disorder at any stage in their life had obesity at the time of the survey [14]. A more recent study in the United States, with a sample of 36,306 participants assessed in 2012–2013, found that relative to those with no history of eating disorders, participants who met criteria for binge eating disorder in the last 12 months, or at any time in their lives, had significantly increased odds of having obesity or extreme obesity [15]. On the flip side, a study with a clinical sample of 1383 individuals with current eating disorders, including 123 with binge eating disorder and 551 with bulimia nervosa, found that 87% of individuals with binge eating disorder, and 33% of individuals with bulimia nervosa, had also had obesity at some point in their lives [16]. These studies show a significant co-occurrence of obesity and eating disorders, and are consistent with the hypothesis that these conditions can potentially contribute to and/or exacerbate each other. Additionally, obesity with comorbid eating disorder behaviors, such as binge eating, may be a growing problem. In a population-representative sample of 9053 people in Australia between the years of 1995 to 2015, there were significant increases in the prevalence of obesity and eating disorder behaviors independently; however, the greatest increases were in the prevalence of individuals with obesity and comorbid binge eating or very strict dieting (7.3 fold and 11.5 fold, respectively) [17]. The increases in the prevalence of obesity and comorbid eating disorder behaviors mentioned above may be related to a potential contribution of binge eating to obesity [14,18,19], as well as to the social expectancy for people with obesity to lose excess weight [17]. The potentially growing prevalence of individuals with obesity and comorbid eating disorder behaviors is concerning due to the medical and psychosocial risks that these individuals are exposed to.

2. Health Risks of Obesity with Comorbid Eating Disorders

Individuals with obesity and comorbid eating disorders are at high risk of several medical and psychosocial complications. A study with 152 treatment-seeking individuals with obesity found that those with binge eating disorder had higher BMIs, more severe levels of depression and obsessive-compulsive symptoms, and stronger feelings of inadequacy and inferiority than those without binge eating disorder [20]. Similarly, bariatric surgery candidates with comorbid binge eating disorder had significantly more mood and anxiety disorders than bariatric surgery candidates without binge eating disorder (27% versus 5% for mood disorders, and 27% versus 8% for anxiety disorders, respectively) [21]. Indeed, 40% of bariatric surgery candidates with comorbid binge eating disorder had a mood or anxiety disorder, with some participants having both a mood and an anxiety disorder [21]. Similarly, gastric bypass surgery candidates with binge eating disorder had more disordered eating attitudes and behaviors, as well as worse physical, emotional and social quality of life, than gastric bypass surgery candidates without binge eating disorder [22]. Not only is binge eating in individuals with obesity associated with poor mental health and poor quality of life, but binge eating can also hinder weight loss in individuals with morbid obesity. For instance, a systematic review found that individuals submitted to bariatric surgery that had clinically significant binge eating before and after the surgery had worse weight loss outcomes than those without pre-surgical binge eating, or than those who stopped binge eating after the surgery [23]. The occurrence of obesity in individuals with eating disorders is also associated with greater mental health complications. For instance, individuals with eating disorders that had had obesity at any stage in their lives had higher eating disorder severity and greater general psychopathology than those with eating disorders that had never had obesity [16]. Finally, obesity with comorbid binge eating can be functionally detrimental. For example, individuals with obesity and comorbid binge eating had greater work-related impairment in productivity than those with obesity only, or binge eating only, or than those of normal weight without binge eating [24]. Thus, individuals with obesity and comorbid eating disorders are at higher risk of medical and psychosocial complications than individuals with only one or the other condition. However, the most appropriate treatment approaches for individuals experiencing these combined conditions is a controversial topic amongst healthcare professionals.

3. The Potential Benefits and Harms of Dieting to Lose Weight

There are often theoretical and clinical debates amongst healthcare professionals regarding the most appropriate treatment approaches for individuals with obesity and comorbid eating disorders. The most controversial aspect of this debate relates to potential benefits and harms of dieting to lose weight. Healthcare professionals specializing in obesity often recommend dieting to their patients or clients with overweight or obesity, encouraging them to reduce and then maintain a healthy weight. Conversely, healthcare professionals specializing in eating disorders, especially those working mainly with individuals with anorexia nervosa and bulimia nervosa, are often concerned about the use of diets driven by idealization of thinness [25].

The negative perception that some healthcare professionals may sustain regarding dieting is understandable when one considers that strict dieting is often a core symptom of eating disorders such as anorexia nervosa and bulimia nervosa [11]. For example, the trans-diagnostic cognitive-behavioral model of eating disorders, which is used to guide the "gold standard" treatment for binge eating disorder and bulimia nervosa, namely cognitive behavior therapy—enhanced (CBT-E), shows strict dieting as a central behavioral component in the maintenance of eating disorders [11]. Furthermore, concerns regarding dieting are derived from studies that found relationships between dieting and eating disorder symptoms [26–28]. A classic study in this field, namely the Keys' study, found that young healthy men submitted to prolonged periods of semi-starvation experienced symptoms that were similar to those experienced by people with eating disorders, such as preoccupation with food, binge eating, distress and depression [26]. Additionally, literature reviews of studies including clinical and non-clinical samples suggest that cognitive restraint can make dieters vulnerable to disinhibition and consequent binge eating [27], and that dietary restriction can lead to binge eating, emotional alterations, distractibility and preoccupation with food and eating [28]. Notwithstanding that dieting can be associated with these negative consequences, one literature review concluded that some dietary restriction (i.e., the consumption of certain foods in moderation) may be necessary for individuals with obesity or for those at risk of developing weight-related health problems in order to reduce the health consequences of overweight [28].

Although there are some important concerns regarding the safety of dieting, the relationship between dieting and binge eating is not clear-cut and needs to be further examined. For instance, a study with 166 patients with bulimia nervosa at admission for residential treatment found that a significant proportion of them (43%) were *not* currently dieting to lose weight or to avoid weight gain [29]. Additionally, this study also found that those who were dieting to lose weight reported lower binge eating frequency in comparison to non-dieters [29]. In line with this, a literature review of studies on different levels of dietary restraint, and retrospective and prospective studies examining the effects of dieting on eating behavior, did not find consistent evidence supporting the view that medically supervised dietary restriction exacerbates binge eating disorder [30]. It is possible that other factors besides dieting need to be present in order to increase the risk for eating disorder behaviors. For example, a prospective study with a population-based sample of 1827 adolescents and young adults and a 10-year follow-up period, found that symptoms of depression and low self-esteem in dieters were important elements increasing the risk of binge eating [31]. Moreover, a narrative review concluded that while dieting may contribute to eating disorders, other factors mediate this relationship, namely a family history of eating disorders, mood disorders, problems with substance/alcohol use, personality characteristics, problematic family interactions, and biological vulnerability [32]. Finally, a systematic review showed that clinically supervised severe energy restriction to treat obesity—as in that used with total meal replacement diets such as very low energy diets—mostly did not cause binge eating, and even reduced binge eating in those with pre-treatment binge eating behaviors [33]. These findings are in line with a previous literature review which showed that moderate dietary energy restriction in combination with behavioral weight loss therapy does not seem to induce binge eating in overweight adults without pre-treatment binge eating, and can reduce binge eating in those with pre-treatment binge eating behaviors [34]. Taken together, these findings suggest that the relationship between dieting and binge eating may be significantly influenced by several other variables, e.g., degree of psychological support and medical need for weight loss. Notably, the young men in the Key's experiment (see above) were not in medical need of weight loss. Whilst they considered themselves extremely well supervised from a medical perspective [26], psychological effects were less well understood and they would go to great lengths to avoid the shame of dismissal from the trial and the stigma of being a "cheater" when they had broken the diet [29]. The complexity of the relationship between dieting to lose weight and eating disorder behaviors and weight stigma potentially contributes to disagreements amongst healthcare professionals regarding the most appropriate treatment approaches for individuals with obesity and comorbid eating disorders.

4. Treatments for Obesity with Comorbid Eating Disorders

Previous studies have examined the effects of treating individuals with obesity and comorbid eating disorders with weight loss or eating disorder treatments, alone or in combination [35–38]. One study investigated the effects of cognitive behavior therapy (CBT), behavioral weight loss therapy, or a sequential approach of CBT followed by behavioral weight loss therapy on body weight and binge eating [38]. This study showed that at 12-month follow-up, 51% of participants submitted to CBT, 36% of those submitted to behavioral weight loss therapy, and 40% of those submitted to CBT followed by behavioral weight loss therapy, had achieved binge eating remission [39]. It also showed that at 12 months, CBT induced significantly greater reduction in binge eating than behavioral weight loss therapy, and that behavioral weight loss therapy induced significantly greater weight loss than CBT [38]. Moreover, participants who exhibited remission from binge eating had significantly greater reductions in BMI compared to participants who did not [38]. Nonetheless, the reduction in BMI induced by behavioral weight loss therapy was relatively small (i.e., -2.1 kg/m^2) [38], and the combination of CBT with other obesity treatments could potentially induce greater weight loss. In line with this, another study found significant reductions in body weight (average loss of 12 kg) and binge eating at 6 months from treatment commencement in individuals submitted to a diet allowing 7100 kJ (1700 kcal) per day, combined with CBT, sertraline (a serotonin reuptake inhibitor) and topiramate (an anti-convulsant sometimes used in the treatment of obesity) [35].This same study did not show any significant change in body weight or binge eating in the comparison groups of individuals submitted to a 7100 kJ (1700 kcal) per day diet, CBT and sertraline (without topiramate), or in those submitted to nutritional counselling and CBT [35]. We could thus conclude from this study that complex treatments including dietary intervention, CBT and a combination of pharmaceuticals can induce substantial reductions in body weight and binge eating. Another study assessed the addition of CBT to 16 sessions of group behavioral weight loss therapy in 116 women with overweight/obesity and comorbid binge eating disorder [36]. In this study, the serotonin reuptake inhibitor fluoxetine (or placebo) was also investigated. Thus, participants were randomized to one of the following four groups, with all groups receiving the same behavioral weight loss therapy: (1) CBT + fluoxetine; (2) CBT + placebo; (3) fluoxetine; or (4) placebo [36]. This study showed that participants in the groups that included CBT had significantly greater reductions in binge eating frequency, and greater abstinence from binge eating, than participants in groups that did not include CBT [36]. Additionally, this study found that participants reporting abstinence from binge eating at the end of treatment ($n = 54$) exhibited greater weight loss in comparison to those who did not report abstinence from binge eating ($n = 62$) (i.e., a weight loss of 6.2 kg versus weight gain of 0.7 kg, respectively) [36]. From these findings it thus seems that CBT is particularly important for binge eating reduction and abstinence, and that binge eating abstinence may be necessary for successful weight loss. While CBT appears to be an essential element of treatment, another study suggests that there is some flexibility in the types of dietary interventions that can be combined with CBT in order to reduce body weight and binge eating. Indeed, in another study involving 50 individuals with obesity and comorbid binge eating disorder, participants were randomized to CBT + a diet of low energy density, or CBT + general nutrition counselling [37]. This study found that 13 out of the 43 participants that completed their assigned intervention lost at least 5% of their initial body weight, and reduced binge eating episodes by 55–75%, with no significant differences in outcomes between participants in the two groups [37]. Overall, the above-mentioned studies showed that certain combinations of obesity treatments with CBT for eating disorders can induce significant reduction of binge eating and weight loss in individuals with obesity and comorbid eating disorders.

While some scientific studies have examined the effects of combining obesity treatments with eating disorder treatments [35–37], most of the current treatment programs for obesity or eating disorders still target only one or the other condition. For example, CBT-E is suitable for use in binge eating disorder, however, it does not encourage weight loss for those with overweight or obesity and comorbid binge eating disorder [11], nor does it result in substantial weight loss [38,39]. In the same way, a recent systematic review and meta-analysis on the effectiveness of treatments for binge eating disorder found that therapist-led CBT induced greater reduction of binge eating frequency in comparison to behavioral weight loss therapy; however, greater body weight reduction was achieved with behavioral weight loss therapy in comparison to CBT [39]. According to this systematic review, at the end of treatment, participants submitted to CBT reduced BMI by an average of 0.41 kg/m^2 (which is not clinically significant), whereas participants submitted to behavioral weight loss therapy reduced BMI by an average of 2.2 kg/m^2 (which is clinically significant) [39]. Furthermore, another review of treatments for binge eating disorder concluded that weight loss treatments should be offered only to individuals with obesity that do not engage in binge eating [40]. This contrasts with a study which found that behavioral weight loss therapy, although not designed to thoroughly address eating disorder psychopathology, concomitantly reduced binge eating and body weight in individuals with obesity and comorbid binge eating disorder [38]. Additionally, a systematic review and meta-analyses found a lack of treatments aiming to simultaneously assist weight management and reduce eating disorder behaviors in individuals with obesity and comorbid bulimia nervosa [41]. According to that systematic review and meta-analysis, it is necessary to develop and test integrated treatments for obesity with bulimia nervosa due to the rise in prevalence of individuals with obesity and comorbid bulimia nervosa [41]. In line with this, we have been involved with the development of a new integrated treatment, named HAPIFED (a **H**ealthy **AP**proach to we**I**ght management and **F**ood in **E**ating **D**isorders), which aims to simultaneously aid weight management (i.e., via a moderate to slow rate of weight loss) and to reduce eating disorder behaviors in individuals with obesity and comorbid eating disorders [42]. The feasibility and acceptability of this intervention was shown in a pilot study that used 20 sessions of group multidisciplinary therapy [42], and this treatment is currently under examination in a randomized controlled trial comparing 30 sessions of group therapy of either HAPIFED or CBT-E [43]. Moreover, the effectiveness of HAPIFED in "real world" clinics is also currently been investigated [44].

Integrated treatments, such as HAPIFED, may be particularly attractive to individuals with obesity and comorbid eating disorders. For instance, a systematic review found that only an estimated 23% of individuals with eating disorders sought treatment for their eating disorder, whereas 30–73% of individuals with eating disorders sought treatments for their overweight or obesity (13). This tendency for individuals with eating disorders to seek weight loss treatments instead of eating disorder treatments could potentially be used to facilitate treatment of a significant proportion of individuals with eating disorders that are overweight or have obesity. In addition to potentially improving treatment adherence, integrated treatments for obesity with comorbid eating disorders may also promote greater physical and mental health benefits than treatments focused on only one or the other condition. For instance, individuals with clinically significant binge eating are more susceptible to difficulties achieving a healthy body weight after undergoing a weight loss treatment (i.e., bariatric surgery) in comparison to those without clinically significant binge eating [23]. Therefore, it is important to further investigate integrated treatment options aiming to simultaneously reduce body weight and eating disorder behaviors and to discuss these studies with healthcare professionals working with clients with obesity or eating disorders. This is especially important given that healthcare professionals working in the fields of obesity or eating disorders frequently have different professional backgrounds (i.e., psychological versus medical versus nutritional).

5. Conclusions

Individuals with obesity and comorbid eating disorders are at higher risk for several medical and psychosocial complications than individuals with either condition alone. The co-occurrence of obesity with comorbid eating disorders, particularly binge eating disorder, requires attention of healthcare professionals working with clients with either of these conditions. Healthcare professionals specialized in obesity treatment and not addressing eating disorder behaviors of their clients—when these are present—will likely see unsuccessful weight loss interventions in the long-term due to continued binge eating. On the flip side, healthcare professionals specialized in eating disorders and not addressing weight management with their clients with comorbid overweight or obesity may see a reduced interest from their clients, potentially resulting in disengagement from (or lack of engagement at all in) the eating disorder treatment, seeking instead weight loss treatments that do not address their eating disorder behaviors. While these healthcare professionals may sometimes disagree on the potential benefits and harms of recommending weight loss diets to their clients, healthcare professionals working in either of these fields of obesity or eating disorders can acknowledge the common goal of promoting healthy eating behaviors, healthy relationships of their clients with their bodies, and positive personal health goals of weight loss. We contend, it is vital to develop and test innovative medical, psychological, and nutritional treatment options that simultaneously address obesity as well as comorbid eating disorders. Such integrated treatments can potentially induce greater improvements in health—and in more people—than treatments targeting only one or the other condition.

Author Contributions: F.Q.d.L. conceived, reviewed the literature discussed in the paper and wrote his paper P.H. co-conceived and co-wrote the paper and contributed additional literature, S.T. co-conceived and co-wrote the paper and A.S. co-conceived and c0-wrote this paper.

Funding: This work was supported by the CAPES Foundation, Ministry of Education of Brazil, via a postgraduate scholarship to Felipe Q. da Luz, the National Health and Medical Research Council (NHMRC) of Australia via a Senior Research Fellowship to Amanda Sainsbury.

Conflicts of Interest: Amanda Sainsbury has received payment from Eli Lilly, the Pharmacy Guild of Australia, Novo Nordisk and the Dietitians Association of Australia for seminar presentation at conferences, and from Nestlé Nutrition for consulting services. Amanda Sainsbury is also the author of The Don't Go Hungry Diet (Bantam, Australia and New Zealand, 2007) and Don't Go Hungry For Life (Bantam, Australia and New Zealand, 2011). Stephen Touyz receives royalties from Hogrefe and Huber, Routledge and McGraw-Hill Publishers. He has also been the recipient of honoraria and travel and research grants from Shire Pharmaceuticals. He has chaired their Australian Binge Eating Disorder Advisory Board and has been the author of commissioned reports. All views expressed in these reports have been his own. Phillipa Hay receives sessional fees and lecture fees from the Australian Medical Council, Therapeutic Guidelines publication, and New South Wales Institute of Psychiatry and royalties from Hogrefe and Huber, McGraw Hill Education, and Blackwell Scientific Publications, and she has received research grants from the NHMRC and ARC. She is Deputy Chair of the National Eating Disorders Collaboration Steering Committee in Australia (2012–) and Member of the ICD-11 Working Group for Eating Disorders (2012–) and was Chair Clinical Practice Guidelines Project Working Group (Eating Disorders) of RANZCP (2012–2015). She has prepared a report under contract for Shire Pharmaceuticals (July 2017) and conducts educational activities for Shire Pharmaceuticals. All views in this paper are her own.

References

1. Wang, Y.C.; McPherson, K.; Marsh, T.; Gortmaker, S.L.; Brown, M. Health and economic burden of the projected obesity trends in the USA and the UK. *Lancet* **2011**, *378*, 815–825. [CrossRef]
2. Zhang, H.; Rodriguez-Monguio, R. Racial disparities in the risk of developing obesity-related diseases: A cross-sectional study. *Ethn. Dis.* **2012**, *22*, 308–316. [PubMed]
3. Dehal, A.; Garrett, T.; Tedders, S.H.; Arroyo, C.; Afriyie-Gyawu, E.; Zhang, J. Body mass index and death rate of colorectal cancer among a national cohort of U.S. Adults. *Nutr. Cancer* **2011**, *63*, 1218–1225. [CrossRef] [PubMed]
4. Vranian, M.; Blaha, M.; Silverman, M.; Michos, E.; Minder, C.; Blumenthal, R.; Nasir, K.; de Carvalho, J.M.; Santos, R. The interaction of fitness, fatness, and cardiometabolic risk. *J. Am. Coll. Cardiol.* **2012**, *59*, E1754. [CrossRef]
5. Ma, Y.; Hébert, J.R.; Manson, J.E.; Balasubramanian, R.; Liu, S.; Lamonte, M.J.; Bird, C.E.; Ockene, J.K.; Qiao, Y.; Olendzki, B.; et al. Determinants of racial/ethnic disparities in incidence of diabetes in postmenopausal women in the U.S.: The Women's Health Initiative 1993–2009. *Diabetes Care* **2012**, *35*, 2226–2234. [CrossRef] [PubMed]
6. Kitahara, C.M.; Flint, A.J.; de Gonzalez, A.B.; Bernstein, L.; Brotzman, M.; MacInnis, R.J.; Moore, S.C.; Robien, K.; Rosenberg, P.S.; Singh, P.N.; et al. Association between class iii obesity (bmi of 40–59 kg/m^2) and mortality: A pooled analysis of 20 prospective studies. *PLoS Med.* **2014**, *11*, e1001673. [CrossRef] [PubMed]
7. Tanamas, S.K.; Ng, W.L.; Backholer, K.; Hodge, A.; Zimmet, P.Z.; Peeters, A. Quantifying the proportion of deaths due to body mass index- and waist circumference-defined obesity: Mortality attributable to obesity. *Obesity* **2016**, *24*, 735–742. [CrossRef] [PubMed]
8. Magallares, A.; Pais-Ribeiro, J.L. Mental health and obesity: A meta-analysis. *Appl. Res. Qual. Life* **2014**, *9*, 295–308. [CrossRef]
9. Tronieri, J.S.; Wurst, C.M.; Pearl, R.L.; Allison, K.C. Sex differences in obesity and mental health. *Curr. Psychiatry Rep.* **2017**, *19*, 29. [CrossRef] [PubMed]
10. Puhl, R.; Brownell, K.D. Bias, discrimination, and obesity. *Obes. Res.* **2001**, *9*, 788–805. [CrossRef] [PubMed]
11. Fairburn, C. *Cognitive Behavior Therapy and Eating Disorders*; Guilford: New York, NY, USA, 2008.
12. American Psychiatric Association. *Diagnostic and Statistical Manual of Mental Disorders*, 5th ed.; American Psychiatric Association: Washington, DC, USA, 2013.
13. Palavras, M.A.; Kaio, G.H.; Mari, J.; Claudino, A.M. A review of latin american studies on binge eating disorder. *Rev. Bras. Psiquiatr.* **2011**, *33*, s81–s94. [CrossRef] [PubMed]
14. Hudson, J.I.; Hiripi, E.; Pope, H.G., Jr.; Kessler, R.C. The prevalence and correlates of eating disorders in the national comorbidity survey replication. *Biol. Psychiatry* **2007**, *61*, 348–358. [CrossRef] [PubMed]
15. Udo, T.; Grilo, C.M. Prevalence and correlates of dsm-5 eating disorders in nationally representative sample of united states adults. *Biol. Psychiatry* **2018**. [CrossRef] [PubMed]
16. Villarejo, C.; Fernandez-Aranda, F.; Jimenez-Murcia, S.; Penas-Lledo, E.; Granero, R.; Penelo, E. Lifetime obesity in patients with eating disorders: Increasing prevalence, clinical and personality correlates. *Eur. Eat. Disord. Rev.* **2012**, *20*, 250–254. [CrossRef] [PubMed]

17. Da Luz, F.Q.; Sainsbury, A.; Mannan, H.; Touyz, S.; Mitchison, D.; Hay, P. Prevalence of obesity and comorbid eating disorder behaviors in south australia from 1995 to 2015. *Int. J. Obes.* **2017**, *41*, 1148–1153. [CrossRef] [PubMed]
18. Fairburn, C.G.; Doll, H.A.; Welch, S.L.; Hay, P.J.; Davies, B.A.; O'Connor, M.E. Risk factors for binge eating disorder: A community-based, case-control study. *Arch. Gen. Psychiatry* **1998**, *55*, 425–432. [CrossRef] [PubMed]
19. Raman, J.; Smith, E.; Hay, P. The clinical obesity maintenance model: An integration of psychological constructs including mood, emotional regulation, disordered overeating, habitual cluster behaviours, health literacy and cognitive function. *J. Obes.* **2013**, *2013*, 240128. [CrossRef] [PubMed]
20. Poli, R.; Maninetti, L.; Bodini, P.; Agrimi, E. Obesity, binge eating, obstruction sleep apnea and psychopathological features. *Clin. Neuropsychiatry* **2012**, *9*, 166–170.
21. Jones-Corneille, L.; Wadden, T.; Sarwer, D.; Faulconbridge, L.; Fabricatore, A.; Stack, R.; Cottrell, F.; Pulcini, M.; Webb, V.; Williams, N. Axis i psychopathology in bariatric surgery candidates with and without binge eating disorder: Results of structured clinical interviews. *Obes. Surg.* **2012**, *22*, 389–397. [CrossRef] [PubMed]
22. Hsu, L.K.G.; Mulliken, B.; McDonagh, B.; Krupa Das, S.; Rand, W.; Fairburn, C.G.; Rolls, B.; McCrory, M.A.; Saltzman, E.; Shikora, S.; et al. Binge eating disorder in extreme obesity. *Int. J. Obes. Relat. Metab. Disord.* **2002**, *26*, 1398–1403. [CrossRef] [PubMed]
23. Niego, S.H.; Kofman, M.D.; Weiss, J.J.; Geliebter, A. Binge eating in the bariatric surgery population: A review of the literature. *Int. J. Eat. Disord.* **2007**, *40*, 349–359. [CrossRef] [PubMed]
24. Striegel, R.H.; Bedrosian, R.; Wang, C. Comparing work productivity in obesity and binge eating. *Int. J. Eat. Disord.* **2012**, *45*, 995–998. [CrossRef] [PubMed]
25. Sainsbury, A.; Hay, P. Call for an urgent rethink of the 'health at every size' concept. *J. Eat. Disord.* **2014**, *2*, 8. [CrossRef] [PubMed]
26. Keys, A.; Brozek, J.; Henschel, A. *The Biology of Human Starvation*; University of Minnessota Press: Minneapolis, MN, USA, 1950; Volume 2.
27. Polivy, J.; Herman, C.P. Dieting and binging. A causal analysis. *Am. Psychol.* **1985**, *40*, 193–201. [CrossRef] [PubMed]
28. Polivy, J. Psychological consequences of food restriction. *J. Am. Diet. Assoc.* **1996**, *96*, 589–592. [CrossRef]
29. Lowe, M.R.; Witt, A.A.; Grossman, S.L. Dieting in bulimia nervosa is associated with increased food restriction and psychopathology but decreased binge eating. *Eat. Behav.* **2013**, *14*, 342–347. [CrossRef] [PubMed]
30. Howard, C.E.; Porzelius, L.K. The role of dieting in binge eating disorder: Etiology and treatment implications. *Clin. Psychol. Rev.* **1999**, *19*, 25–44. [CrossRef]
31. Goldschmidt, A.B.; Wall, M.; Loth, K.A.; Le Grange, D.; Neumark-Sztainer, D. Which dieters are at risk for the onset of binge eating? A prospective study of adolescents and young adults. *J. Adolesc. Health* **2012**, *51*, 86–92. [CrossRef] [PubMed]
32. Hsu, L.K. Can dieting cause an eating disorder? *Psychol. Med.* **1997**, *27*, 509–513. [CrossRef] [PubMed]
33. Da Luz, F.Q.; Hay, P.; Gibson, A.A.; Touyz, S.W.; Swinbourne, J.M.; Roekenes, J.A.; Sainsbury, A. Does severe dietary energy restriction increase binge eating in overweight or obese individuals? A systematic review. *Obes. Rev.* **2015**, *16*, 652–665. [CrossRef] [PubMed]
34. Yanovski, S.Z.; Billington, C.J.; Epstein, L.H.; Goodwin, N.J.; Hill, J.O.; Pi-Sunyer, F.X.; Rolls, B.J.; Stern, J.S.; Wadden, T.A.; Weinsier, R.L.; et al. Dieting and the development of eating disorders in overweight and obese adults. *Arch. Intern. Med.* **2000**, *160*, 2581–2589.
35. Brambilla, F.; Samek, L.; Company, M.; Lovo, F.; Cioni, L.; Mellado, C. Multivariate therapeutic approach to binge-eating disorder: Combined nutritional, psychological and pharmacological treatment. *Int. Clin. Psychopharmacol.* **2009**, *24*, 312–317. [CrossRef] [PubMed]
36. Devlin, M.J.; Goldfein, J.A.; Petkova, E.; Jiang, H.; Raizman, P.S.; Walk, S.; Mayer, L.; Carino, J.; Bellace, D.; Kamenetz, C.; et al. Cognitive behavioral therapy and fluoxetine as adjuncts to group behavioral therapy for binge eating disorder. *Obesity* **2005**, *13*, 1077–1088. [CrossRef] [PubMed]
37. Masheb, R.M.; Grilo, C.M.; Rolls, B.J. A randomized controlled trial for obesity and binge eating disorder: Low-energy-density dietary counseling and cognitive-behavioral therapy. *Behav. Res. Ther.* **2011**, *49*, 821–829. [CrossRef] [PubMed]

38. Grilo, C.M.; Masheb, R.M.; Wilson, G.T.; Gueorguieva, R.; White, M.A. Cognitive-behavioral therapy, behavioral weight loss, and sequential treatment for obese patients with binge-eating disorder: A randomized controlled trial. *J. Consult. Clin. Psychol.* **2011**, *79*, 675–685. [CrossRef] [PubMed]
39. Peat, C.M.; Berkman, N.D.; Lohr, K.N.; Brownley, K.A.; Bann, C.M.; Cullen, K.; Quattlebaum, M.J.; Bulik, C.M. Comparative effectiveness of treatments for binge-eating disorder: Systematic review and network meta-analysis. *Eur. Eat. Disord. Rev.* **2017**, *25*, 317–328. [CrossRef] [PubMed]
40. Dingemans, A.E.; Bruna, M.J.; Van Furth, E.F. Binge eating disorder: A review. *Int. J. Obes.* **2002**, *26*, 299–307. [CrossRef] [PubMed]
41. Palavras, M.A.; Hay, P.; Dos Santos, C.A.; Claudino, A. The efficacy of psychological therapies in reducing weight and binge eating in people with bulimia nervosa and binge eating disorder who are overweight or obese-a critical synthesis and meta-analyses. *Nutrients* **2017**, *9*, 299. [CrossRef] [PubMed]
42. Da Luz, F.Q.; Swinbourne, J.; Sainsbury, A.; Touyz, S.; Palavras, M.; Claudino, A.; Hay, P. Hapifed: A healthy approach to weight management and food in eating disorders: A case series and manual development. *J. Eat. Disord.* **2017**, *5*, 29. [CrossRef] [PubMed]
43. Palavras, M.A.; Hay, P.; Touyz, S.; Sainsbury, A.; da Luz, F.; Swinbourne, J.; Estella, N.M.; Claudino, A. Comparing cognitive behavioural therapy for eating disorders integrated with behavioural weight loss therapy to cognitive behavioural therapy-enhanced alone in overweight or obese people with bulimia nervosa or binge eating disorder: Study protocol for a randomised controlled trial. *Trials* **2015**, *16*, 578. [PubMed]
44. Australian New Zealand Clinical Trials Regisitry. *The Real Happy Trial: A Multi-Centre, Prospective, Open-Label, Non-Comparative Assessment of the Real-World Effectiveness of Hapifed (A Healthy Approach to Weight Management and Food in Eating Disorders) in Reducing Weight and Treating the Symptoms of Binge Eating in Participants with Overweight/Obesity and Binge Eating Disorder, Bulimia Nervosa or Other Specified Feeding and Eating Disorders*; ACTRN12617001020370; ANZCTR: Camperdown, Australia, 2017.

nutrients

MDPI

Article

Cultural Features Influencing Eating, Overweight, and Obesity in the Roma People of South Bohemia

Věra Olišarová [1,*], Valérie Tóthová [1], Sylva Bártlová [1], František Dolák [1], Alena Kajanová [2], Dita Nováková [1], Radka Prokešová [3] and Lenka Šedová [1]

1 Institute of Nursing, Midwifery and Emergency Care, Faculty of Health and Social Sciences, University of South Bohemia in Ceske Budejovice, J. Boreckeho 1167/27, 370 05 Ceske Budejovice, Czech Republic; tothova@zsf.jcu.cz (V.T.); sbartlova@zsf.jcu.cz (S.B.); fdolak@zsf.jcu.cz (F.D.); novakovad@zsf.jcu.cz (D.N.); lsedova@zsf.jcu.cz (L.Š.)

2 Institute of Social and Special-paedagogical Sciences, Faculty of Health and Social Sciences, University of South Bohemia in Ceske Budejovice, J. Boreckeho 1167/27, 370 05 Ceske Budejovice, Czech Republic; kajanova@zsf.jcu.cz

3 Institute of Legal Branches, Management and Economics, Faculty of Health and Social Sciences, University of South Bohemia in Ceske Budejovice, J. Boreckeho 1167/27, 370 05 Ceske Budejovice, Czech Republic; rprokes@zsf.jcu.cz

* Correspondence: volisarova@zsf.jcu.cz; Tel.: +420-389-037-501

Received: 22 March 2018; Accepted: 19 June 2018; Published: 28 June 2018

Abstract: This article describes the important cultural specifics that impact on treatment of overweight and obesity for the Roma people of South Bohemia. Methods: Data on health and nutrition were collected using a semi-structured interview of 302 Roma adults (quantitative phase). A further 25 participants received in-depth interviews regarding their eating and lifestyle habits and perceptions about obesity and overweight (qualitative phase). Height and weight were measured with calibrated scales and stadiometer. Qualitative data were analyzed with the "grounded theory" method. Results: The participants reported a relatively high consumption of high-sugar drinks and foods compared to fruits and vegetables. Lifestyle factors increasing risk of overweight identified from the qualitative interview included unemployment, socially isolating housing, poor transport, poverty, inactivity, tobacco smoking, and for women weight gain after childbirth. Also identified was the need for better health literacy. Conclusions: Effective health education may help to address risk factors for overweight and obesity in Roma peoples. Other measures include improved socioeconomic status and housing security, and improved health literacy of the Roma people.

Keywords: the Roma; nurse; overweight; obesity; health education; lifestyle factors; nutrition; cultural features

1. Introduction

Determinants of obesity include genetic predisposition, environmental factors, and the social-cultural environment [1–3].

Overweight and obesity date perhaps as far back as prehistoric times, i.e., as long as people have dealt with both an excess and a scarcity of food. However, over the course of societal development and with advances in scientific and medical knowledge, the social and cultural interpretations of diagnoses of overweight and obesity have changed as well. Although they are symbols of affluence in some societies, they also indisputably impact on health. According to available data, more than half of the population (52%) of the European Union are overweight or obese, and in the Czech Republic, 61.7% of the population have a body mass index (BMI) ≥ 25 kg/m^2 [4]. Although the number of adult individuals with a BMI ≥ 25 kg/m^2 seems to have levelled off, the proportion of people suffering from obesity is still rising [5].

The high rates of overweight are also evident in minority groups such as the Roma, who are one of the largest minorities of the Czech Republic [6,7]. Their number is estimated at 250–280,000 persons [8]. Studies designed to monitor the health status of the Roma show that, in spite of government efforts across Europe, they suffer from poorer access to health care and are often discriminated against [9]. Vazarova de Courten et al. [10] confirmed a potential link between the high prevalence of obesity with unhealthy lifestyles and improper eating habits. One study that looked at the incidence of overweight and obesity in Roma women in Slovakia found similar results. It was found that Roma suffer from extreme degrees of obesity much more often than the rest of the population. In these cases, the genetic predispositions of susceptible individuals are also supported by unhealthy lifestyles [11].

Together with external determinants, persistent cultural characteristics of the Roma can notably influence the efficiency of the public and other health interventions [12,13]. The Roma are a distinctive group with distinctive cultural features, language, and a singular cultural identity, setting them apart from the majority of the population [14]. Over the course of the centuries, they spread all over the world thanks to their nomadic lifestyle. Due to encounters with the dominant culture, there have been changes in their traditional way of life, but some particularities persist [15,16]. These particularities are evident primarily in the way of life, eating habits, experiences and perceptions of time, socio-economic status, and poorer access to services or health [14]. Preventive programs, in order to be effective, need to consider diverse cultural determinants of health and, above all, the individual needs of the target group [17]. At the same time, the level of nutritional acculturation or the level of adoption of the nutritional habits of the majority population by immigrants or other minority groups should be taken into account [18]. The preventive programs implemented at present with focus on overweight and obesity is developed for the dominant population in the Czech Republic. Their effectiveness for the Roma appears to be very low.

This article aims at to explore cultural features of the Roma that could be associated with their high prevalence of overweight and obesity and the inefficiency of currently implemented interventions. First, the anthropometrics status, nutritional intake, and eating patterns of a group of Roma participants were investigated. This was followed by exploratory interviews investigating lifestyle, intake, and sociodemographic features of a subsample of respondents.

2. Materials and Methods

2.1. Quantitative Phase

Participants were sourced from the Roma population in the South Bohemian Region between 1 June 2014 and 31 March 2015. General nurses from the Centre for Prevention of Life Style Diseases in České Budějovice recruited participants at community events and in the respondents' natural environment with the assistance of contact persons. Because census data is not available for the Roma minority in the Czech Republic, respondents were selected using the snowball method aiming to ensure an equal representation of men and women (as in the general population in the Czech Republic). Further, the respondents from the Roma minority were selected based on their subjectively perceived Roma identity.

Face-to-face semi-structured interviews were conducted using a prepared non-standardized questionnaire. The communication with the respondents was performed in Czech. The respondents were given primarily close-ended questions with employment of scaled answers. Further, the following anthropometric values were obtained: weight (determined with electronic flat scale SECA 813); height (determined with a SECA 213 folding height meter); waist and hip circumference (measured with tape measure); and body fat content (measured with OMRON BF306 Body Composition Monitor). Body mass index (BMI; kg/m^2) was subsequently calculated.

BMI reference values for obesity were applied according to those of the World Health Organization (WHO), i.e., BMI 18.5–24.9 kg/m^2 normal, BMI 25–29.9 kg/m^2 overweight, and $\geq$30 kg/m^2 obese [19]. Reference values suggesting risk metabolic complications were applied for waist circumference:

men, ≥94 cm, suggesting increased risk, and ≥102 cm, suggesting very high risk; women, ≥80 cm, suggesting increased risk, and ≥88 cm, suggesting very high risk [19].

Three hundred and two Roma individuals over 18 years of age participated; males and females were equally represented. Most were aged 18–29 years (132, i.e., 43.8%); 56 (18.6%) were aged 40–49 years, 49 (16.3%) were aged 30–39 years, 39 (13%) were aged 50–59 years, 20 (6.6%) were aged 60–69 years (20, i.e., 6.6%), and only 5 (1.7%) were aged ≥70 years. There were more respondents who had three or more children (n = 134, 44.3%) than those who had no children (n = 77, 25.6%). One hundred and forty-nine (50.1%) persons were unemployed and only 51 (17.2%) were practicing a profession. The others received a disability or old age pension or were on maternity leave.

2.2. Analyses

Data analysis was carried out with using the SASD (Statistical Analysis of 129 Social Data) program and SPSS program (in version 13.1). Statistical associations were tested with the Pearson Chi-square test—X^2) and significance levels of $\alpha < 0.05$, $\alpha < 0.01$ and $\alpha < 0.001$. In case of insufficient observations, Yates correction was applied.

2.3. Qualitative Phase

The qualitative research was aimed at acquiring more in-depth information regarding attitudes the Roma minority to overweight and obesity. It was also aimed at mapping the nutritional habits and describing the risk factors with respect to culturally conditioned behavior patterns occurring in the natural environment (Roma households and communities). The qualitative research set consisted of 25 Roma respondents over 18 years of age (8 males and 17 females). The male sample included six overweight individuals (BMI ≥ 25 kg/m^2) and two obese ones (BMI ≥ 30 kg/m^2); ages ranged from 19 to 64 years. The female sample included eight overweight individuals and nine obese individuals; ages ranged from 29 to 64 years.

Participants received a semi-structured interview; this comprised a circle of 35 basic questions with 90 sub questions in advance, and their order could be changed to achieve the highest possible interview efficiency. The interview scheme prepared in this manner included 35 basic questions divided into four circles: eating habits, physical and leisure-time activities (lifestyle), and self-perception and perceptions of overweight and obesity. The interviews took place from April 2014 to April 2015 in the community, primarily in individual's homes. They were conducted in Czech and complemented by anthropometric measurement (height, weight, calculation of BMI, waistline and body fat measurements as above). The interviews made particular use of open-ended questions. The interviews were subsequently digitalized and transcribed verbatim. The MAXQDA 11 (Software for Qualitative and Mixed Methods Research) program was chosen for the text analysis. One thousand and eight-two segments in total were marked in the transcribed interviews, subsequently exported, and further processed. To analyze the data, we used "grounded theory" including open, axial, and selective coding. Finally, we identified the central category—lifestyle. From among other categories, we identified eating habits, motivation, attitude and body image. To ensure anonymity, the respondents were given randomly selected names when processing the data.

3. Results

3.1. Quantitative Phase

The analysis of the data related to the assessment of the basic health indicators suggests that in the research set including 302 Roma from the South Bohemian Region, 61.8% persons had BMI ≥ 25 kg/m^2. Overweight (BMI 25.0–29.9 kg/m^2) was found in 29.7% of participants and obesity (BMI ≥ 30 kg/m^2) in 32.1% of respondents. It was proved that there were statistically significant differences between males and females in terms of BMI index ($p < 0.01$; $X^2 = 11.17$; df = 2). The males had lower

BMI index significantly more often, while the females were overweight (BMI 25.0–29.9 kg/m^2) and obese (BMI $\geq$ 30 kg/m^2) more often.

From among further indicators of overweight and obesity, the waistline values were observed. Increased values were recorded. One-third of the examined Roma (n = 152) had a waistline exceeding 102 cm. It should be stated here that males' waistline values over 102 cm are related with noticeable metabolic complications. Waistline values related to noticeable metabolic complications (over 88 cm for females) were also found in Roma women (63.3%, n = 150). Also, the measured values of body fat correspond to the above stated indicators. The difference between genders was minimal, but the higher values of body fat of the Roma (found in 67.55% of respondents) in the South Bohemian Region were measured.

From the perspective of prevention of overweight and obesity, the information related to consumption, selection, preparation and intake frequency of foodstuffs is important. We show the preference of selected foodstuff types in the Roma minority (Table 1) below.

Table 1. Preference of selected foodstuffs in the Roma minority per week (n = 302).

	Intake Frequency, n (%)						
Selected Foodstuff	**Not at All**	**1–2 Times a Week**	**3–4 Times a Week**	**5–6 Times a Week**	**Every Day**	**Several Times a Day**	**Did Not Answer**
Pork	28 (10.3%)	112 (41.3%)	96 (35.5%)	21 (7.7%)	10 (3.7%)	4 (1.5%)	31 (10.3%)
Beef	82 (32.0%)	148 (57.8%)	19 (7.4%)	5 (2.0%)	1 (0.4%)	1 (0.4%)	46 (15.23%)
Fish	158 (56.2%)	106 (37.7%)	10 (3.6%)	2 (0.7%)	3 (1.1%)	2 (0.7%)	21 (6.95%)
Chicken	16 (5.8%)	125 (45.3%)	98 (35.5%)	25 (9.1%)	7 (2.5%)	5 (1.8%)	26 (8.61%)
Potatoes	14 (5.0%)	157 (56.4%)	79 (28.3%)	14 (5.0%)	11 (3.9%)	4 (1.4%)	23 (7.62%)
Pasta	17 (6.3%)	191 (70.4%)	40 (14.8%)	15 (5.5%)	7 (2.6%)	1 (0.4%)	31 (10.26)
Rice	24 (8.9%)	186 (68.9%)	42 (15.6%)	12 (4.4%)	4 (1.5%)	2 (0.7%)	32 (10.6%)
Dumplings	22 (8.1%)	181 (67.1%)	49 (18.1%)	11 (4.1%)	6 (2.2%)	1 (0.4%)	32 (10.6%)
Sweet baked goods	53 (18.5%)	126 (44.2%)	57 (19.9%)	8 (2.8%)	39 (13.6%)	3 (1.0%)	16 (5.3%)
Sweets	46 (15.9%)	125 (43.3%)	46 (15.9%)	15 (5.2%)	50 (17.3%)	7 (2.4%)	13 (4.3%)
Sweet drinks	52 (18.1%)	80 (27.8%)	53 (18.4%)	19 (6.6%)	75 (26.0%)	9 (3.1%)	14 (4.64%)
Fruits	38 (13.5%)	122 (43.4%)	61 (21.7%)	9 (3.2%)	37 (13.2%)	14 (5.0%)	21 (7.95%)
Vegetables	30 (10.8%)	96 (34.7%)	64 (23.1%)	23 (8.3%)	53 (19.1%)	11 (4.0%)	25 (8.27%)

As shown on Table 1, chicken was the most frequently consumed meat, followed by pork and then beef. More than half of the respondents (56.2% persons) did not eat fish. "Side dishes" of potatoes, pasta, rice and dumplings were most commonly eaten 1–2 times a week, followed by 3–4 times a week. Fruits and vegetables were consumed at a lower frequency: most often either not at all or only 1–2 times a week. With respect to sweet baked goods, those most frequently consumed were cakes and doughnuts, but also pies, and cakes. Sweets included different types of wafers, ice cream, biscuits, chocolate and candies.

In relation to the energy balance, we also consider significant the findings related to consumption of sweet drinks (like cola, juices, water with squash, energy drinks, etc.). In this case, analysis showed that the members of the Roma minority drink soft drinks in higher frequency.

3.2. Qualitative Phase

The qualitative phase was implemented to explore motivational factors and culturally conditioned behavior patterns with respect to prevention and treatment of overweight and obesity. The qualitative data were analyzed by the MAXQDA 11 program. We worked with transcribed interviews. In this study, 1082 interview segments were marked in total, exported and analyzed. The analysis was made using "grounded theory" use of open, axial and selective coding [20]. The terms found were grouped by their potential belonging to categories (open coding). However, at that point, the categories could not be considered final, as their belonging to any given phenomenon was only apparent. The conceptual range of the categories gave base to their contents. We show an example in the table (Table 2).

Table 2. Open coding.

Category	Subcategory	Characteristic
Food intake	Motivation for foodstuff selection Preferred foodstuff preparation Place of alimentation Number of meals a day Frequency of alimentation	
	Regularity	Breakfast Morning snack Lunch Afternoon snack Dinner

The open coding allowed us to divide the acquired data and to determine some categories and their characteristics. Axial coding allowed us to put the data together in a new way by creating links between the categories and their subcategories. As an example, we show the embedding of the "body image" category into the paradigmatic model (Table 3).

Table 3. Application of paradigmatic model.

Causal Conditions	Phenomenon	Context	Intervening Conditions	Action Strategy	Consequences
Weight Health condition Self-perception Subjective assessment of own figure Life satisfaction	Body image	Feeling Body proportions Health complications Weight deviations Nature Family Housing	Unemployment Housing conditions Culturally conditioned behavior patterns Insufficient health literacy Number of children	Exercise Dietary measures	Temporary weight reduction Improvement of health complications Better self-feeling

Visual inspection of the paradigmatic model showed that the circular dimension best explains phenomena, as consequences sometimes may mingle with causal conditions.

Based on the acquired overview of the relations among individual categories and subcategories, the codes found were subjected to a deeper analysis. The analysis helped to identify the central category of "lifestyle", to which all other categories are related. Lifestyle constitutes the phenomenon that is closely related to eating habits, motivation, and attitude to overweight and obesity, as well as to body image. It is connected not only with the way of spending leisure time, risk behaviors, and the way of spending weekdays, but it also reflects the cultural perspective. Its characteristics influence individual areas of eating habits (e.g., choice of foodstuffs, regularity of eating, etc.). The factors resulting from it are reflected in the motivation to reduce weight, and in the individual's attitude to overweight and obesity. In this point, they are closely related to self-perception and to body image, as well as to life satisfaction.

To achieve integration of the findings, the story skeleton was interpreted, and, upon this basis, a scheme of the relations found was created (Supplementary Figure S1).

3.2.1. Story Skeleton

Remedial risk factors for overweight and obesity are related to lifestyle in the Roma population. The vast majority of the respondents were unemployed, women who were at home with children, and some men receiving the disability or old-age pension. This factor undoubtedly plays a role in the distribution of activities during the day. Their weekdays are related primarily to cleaning, eating, caring for children, and community life. Most of those Roma live in socially excluded localities, in residence halls far from the town center. They have poor transport access. Their life is noted for risk behaviors like heavy smoking and inactivity. Consumption of alcohol is rather occasional, although there are exceptions too. Poor access to transport influences their eating habits, primarily due to the accessibility of groceries.

The above-stated distribution of daily activities, normal times of getting up, and factors of social life in broader family living in the given community influence eating habits such as frequency and regularity of eating. The Roma report eating at home and in the homes of relatives whom they visit. Some of them have even multiple main dishes. Nevertheless, they have problems with describing their meals. It is difficult for them to tell how many times a day they eat. Great differences can be seen when they describe their meals of the previous day. It is effective to make use of the opportunity to describe the course of the day and to encourage them to recount what they did from the time they woke up in the morning. Then they are able to approximately describe the foodstuffs and liquids they took in. As for foodstuffs and liquids, they use illustrative comparison and examples, which they can grasp better. Their composition of foodstuffs does not essentially differ. They show a tendency to give more healthy foodstuffs (fruits and vegetables) to their children. The socioeconomic perspective is often mentioned here. We can see the financial issue. They prefer to buy something for the children, and if some money is left, they buy something for themselves too. They agree in the traditional Roma meals. However, they report their intake in a frequency of several times a month.

They are aware of the causal relation between eating and increasing weight. The women often restrict food intake to decrease their weight. However, they do not show long-lasting eating changes or dietary measures related to other diseases they suffer from. They observe regime recommendations only until the acute symptoms subside; as for medicines, they take them only until they finish the package. They do not go to the physician to ask for more. Women do not include significant amounts of exercise in their lifestyle; they exercise primarily if the physician has suggested so because of backache. On the contrary, men make use of short-term exercise in fitness centers, trying to improve their physical condition. Some of them are aware of the positive effect of exercise and sports. The increased weight of women is primarily related to childbirths after which they did not succeed in reducing their weight, although many desire to lose weight. When assessing their own figure, particularly the women tend to be undervalue their weight; they perceive themselves slimmer than they actually are. On the contrary, men are usually more objective.

The self-perception is related to life satisfaction that is reflected also in the lifestyle and affects motivation. The Roma are rather satisfied with their family lives; they perceive themselves as cheerful and quick-tempered persons. However, their life satisfaction is affected by housing, primarily by the life in communities and socially excluded localities. Many of them are not satisfied with such a lifestyle. They do not perceive the difference between overweight and obesity, they relate them rather to a disease or overeating. Most of them do not take any attitude do such people; they do not criticize them, but some feel sorry for them. Some motivation to reduce the weight consists primarily in weight reduction recommended by physicians, and women also consider the aesthetic side, if they cannot dress what they like or if they feel they compare poorly next to their partner.

3.2.2. Diagram 1 Visualization of Relations

The visualized relations helped us to create the following categories: lifestyle, eating habits, motivation, attitude, and body image. Lifestyle was identified as the central category (Table 4). Based on the connections found, we came to the conclusion that the prevention and treatment of Roma overweight and obesity are influenced by culturally conditioned influenceable risk factors resulting from their lifestyle. To eliminate them, adequate motivation and efficient education should be used. Indispensable measures include motivation to long-lasting changes, to increasing health literacy of the Roma and regular monitoring of basic health indicators. However, the impact of the other risk factors cannot be omitted in the given context. The risk factors include primarily lack of exercise, risk behaviors (smoking), socioeconomic factors related to financial security, and housing and life in socially excluded localities.

Table 4. Resulting categories.

Category	Subcategory
Life style	Weekday Leisure time activities Prevention Risky behavior
Eating habits	Food components Traditional cuisine Food intake
Motivation	Reduction efforts Consequences
Attitude	Perception of overweight and obesity Preference of figures
Body image	Weight Life satisfaction

4. Discussion

The prevalence of obesity in Europe is regularly confirmed in a range of 10–40% of the population. In addition to a genetic predisposition, the main causes include lifestyle and underestimation of the seriousness of the complications related to this disease [21]. Further determinants are: influence of the environment, improved economic situation of individuals or ethnic differentiation. The economic situation is closely related to education and income level of the population. Thus, it can be stated that the obesity in highly developed countries, including the Czech Republic, is more frequent in inhabitants with lower education and lower income, as well as in rural populations. On the contrary, the obesity in developing countries is rather related with higher social status and social prestige [5,22]. With regards to ethnicity, it is assumed that ethnicity is often a more significant predictor for overweight and obesity in children than social class or other socio-economic variables [23–26]. The results of the present study clearly suggest that, according to the above stated indicators, the Roma are at increased risk of obesity.

Normal waistline values were found in 21.4% of Roma females in the examination. In the present study the majority of the Roma participants had increased waist measurements and high BMI. Reported lifestyle factors such as unemployment and late rising (often at 10–11 a.m.) likely also contribute to obesity risk. Similarly, the qualitative findings found Roma to be underemployed with a lifestyle of sedentary activities (sitting at the computer, watching TV, contact with friends and relatives, or sleeping). However, some were aware of the positive effect of exercise and reported that when they exercised, they had less backache or pains of legs and arms.

Risk behaviors—primarily smoking—are determined by lifestyle to some degree. The respondents of the qualitative phase included more than one half of smokers; the smokers could be divided into two groups. The first group included persons who smoked less than 10 cigarettes a day; the second (comparably large) group would include person who smoke more than a pack of cigarettes a day. A distinct representation of smokers among the Roma is reported also by Urban and Kajanová [27]. They examined a sample of 164 Czech Roma and found 63.5% of males were smokers, and 58% of females. They add that the respondents started smoking at 14 years of age on average. The results related to consumption of alcohol were a little more positive. Occasional or no consumption prevailed among the respondents.

The area of nutrition of the Roma minority is described well in the following quotation [28]: "The Roma may be as poor as a church mouse, but must have enough food, even if there may be nothing left for tomorrow." These words suggest the usual eating habits. Eating is not a regular ritual, but it is closely related to the status of the family [12,29]. At present, the Roma families cook a lot, particularly after the payment of wages of social or other benefits. The parents often try to give their children everything they were deprived of. Children's food is usually not distinguished from the adults' food; meat, smoked meat products, and sweets are mostly consumed. Fruits and vegetables are not frequently consumed [30]. A very low intake of fruits and vegetables is confirmed also by Stávková and Derflerová Brázdová [31]. They also reflect on the issue of nutrition literacy, as their study showed that only 15.7% of the Roma respondents (n = 102) knew the recommendations with respect to minimum fruit and vegetable intake. Consumption of fruits and vegetables was also low, and most were cooked: "Well, yes, I eat them. We always have them. Raw, no. Not even salad, nothing. Only in meals. No, not every day, about twice a week" (Jolana). The most frequently consumed vegetables included tomatoes, peppers, cucumbers and carrots. In contrast, the traditional Roma meals constitute an integral part of the Roma diet. Oláhová [28] includes goja and flour pancakes among them. Very thick soups are reported by Davidová [30]. Our respondents reported, additionally to goja, also halusky, filled cabbage, pork with dumplings and fasulja, a traditional thick soup. They also reported eating such meals only several times a month, i.e., they did not perceive their consumption as too frequent. One of the female respondents characterized the Roma cuisine as follows: "The Gypsies have the marikl'a, halušky, fasulja (that is bean soup). We love meat. You can see meat, schnitzel, pork on Gypsy tables. Just meat, fatback, dumplings, pork, yeah. Meals of that kind. Pishot is a Gypsy meal too. Sweet triangles with cream cheese and marmalade. And the Gypsies have four to five meals, just a lot of food. And the Gypsies are used to put food on the table, if they have it. You know, we like eating. But attention, the Gypsies love oil, fat." (Irena). The above stated characteristics of traditional Roma cuisine may explain, to some degree, the preference for some side dishes (e.g., potatoes, dumplings, etc.). The analysis of the qualitative data also suggested the importance of attitude to overweight and obesity. This is primarily a result of the respondents' own experiences and health conditions, and is influenced by sociocultural background. A possible relationship between the social pressure directed at the preferred physical appearance across different cultures, and between the determinants like education, degree of acculturation, or BMI is confirmed also by Cachelin et al. [32]. Although our respondents did not perceive the difference between overweight and obesity, many of them had their own experience of the consequences of such conditions. They most frequently reported leg pain, breathlessness (primarily when climbing stairs and running to catch the bus), and backache. Some women mentioned also the impact on the individual's appearance, which is, however, not necessarily sufficient motivation for change: "Well, great. Primarily appearance. Health impact not much, well, the legs, nothing. But only when I looked at the mirror, nothing suited me. I took it off." (Irma), "Well, you cannot dress everything; although now I have lost some weight." (Irena).

The Roma may be at increased risk of eating disorders as well as higher weight through factors such as less regular eating and a culture of moderate overconsumption. Culturally-based behavior patterns appear to be very important determinants of eating habits. Also evident is the impact of perception of overweight and obesity, body image, lifestyle, and in living in socially excluded localities. On the other hand, the decreased regard for health benefits of weight loss may be protective. Further studies are needed to examine disordered eating behaviors such as binge eating in Roma and whether increased exposure to the 'mainstream' attitudes to weight and shape may result in an increase in eating disorders.

5. Conclusions

Remedial risk factors for overweight and obesity in the Roma respondents we approached included primarily inactivity, lifestyle, and inappropriate structure of food together with eating habits and, to some degree, socioeconomic factors such as living in socially excluded localities. It has also been found that the Roma do not differentiate between overweight and obesity. They call both conditions "fat" and they often related increased weight primarily to a disease or to overeating. It is unknown to what degree these attitudes may however protect them from eating disorders common in the other European populations.

Supplementary Materials: The following are available online at http://www.mdpi.com/2072-6643/10/7/838/s1, Figure S1: Visualization of relations.

Author Contributions: V.O. performed the experiments, analyzed the data and wrote the paper; V.T. conceived and designed the experiments, analyzed data, and wrote the paper; S.B. conceived and designed the experiments, analyzed data and wrote the paper; F.D. performed the experiments, analyzed the data; A.K. performed the experiments, analyzed the data; D.N. performed the experiments, analyzed the data; R.P. analyzed the data, contributed analysis tools; L.Š. performed the experiments, analyzed the data and wrote the paper.

Acknowledgments: The article is related to research grant project No. LD14114, implemented with financial support from the Ministry of Education, Youth and Physical Education within COST (Cooperation on Scientific and Technical Research) and designated for the study of Obesity and Overweight in the Roma Minority in South Bohemian Region.

Conflicts of Interest: The authors declare no conflict of interest.

References

1. Kasalický, M. Tabulizace Žaludku. In *Chirurgická Léčba Obezity*; Triton: Praha, Czech Republic, 2007.
2. World Health Organization (WHO). Obesity and Overweight. Key Fact. 2017. Available online: http://www.who.int/en/news-room/fact-sheets/detail/obesity-and-overweight (accessed on 30 April 2018).
3. OECD/European Union. Health at a Glance: Europe. 2012. Available online: http://www.oecd-ilibrary.org/sites/9789264183896-en/02/07/index.html?itemId=/content/chapter/9789264183896-26-en (accessed on 11 January 2017).
4. World Health Organization (WHO). Global Health Observatory Data Repository. Overweight (Body Mass Index >= 25). Data by Country. 2008. Available online: http://apps.who.int/gho/data/node.main.A897 (accessed on 11 January 2017).
5. Kasalický, M. *Chirurgická Léčba Obezity*; Ottova Tiskárna: Praha, Czech Republic, 2011.
6. Vláda České Republiky. Koncepce Romské Integrace na Období 2010–2013. Available online: http://www.romadecade.org/cms/upload/file/9323_file8_roma_czech_republic_strategy_cs.pdf (accessed on 11 January 2017).
7. Mačeková, S.; Bernasovský, I.; Gabriková, D.; Bôžiková, A.; Bernasovská, J.; Boroňová, I.; Behulová, R.; Svíčková, P.; Petrejčíková, E.; Soták, M.; et al. Association of the FTO rs9939609 polymorphism with obesity in Roma/Gypsy population. *Am. J. Phys. Anthropol.* **2012**, *1*, 30–34. [CrossRef] [PubMed]
8. Kalibová, K. Kolik Romů žije v Česku? *Geogr. Rozhl.* **2008**, *17*, 8–9.
9. Šedová, L.; Olišarová, V.; Tóthová, V. Romové a specifika zdravotní edukace. *Stud. Kinanthropol.* **2014**, *15*, 259–267.
10. Vazarova de Courten, B.; de Courten, M.; Hanson, R.L.; Zahorakova, A.; Egyenes, H.P.; Tataranni, P.A.; Bennett, P.H.; Vozar, J. Higher prevalence of type 2 diabetes, metabolit syndrome and cardiovascular diseases in gypsies that in non-gypsies in Slovakia. *Diabetes Res. Clin. Pract.* **2003**, *62*, 95–103. [CrossRef]
11. Dolinska, S.; Kudlackova, M.; Ginter, E. The prevalence of female obesity in the world and in the Slovak Gypsy women. *Bratisl. Lek. Listy* **2007**, *108*, 207–211. [PubMed]
12. Prokešová, M. Romové. In *Otázky a Hledání Odpovědí*; Repronis: Ostrava, Czech Republic, 2010.
13. Šlechtová, D.; Bürgerová, O. Specifika romského etnika ve vztahu k poskytování zdravotní a ošetřovatelské péče. *Kontakt* **2009**, *11*, 189–192.
14. Ippolito, F.; Sánchez, S.I. *Protecting Vulnerable Groups: The European Human Rights Framework*; Modern Studies in European Law; Bloomsbury Publishing: London, UK, 2015.
15. O'Nions, H. *Minority Rights Protection in International Law: The Roma of Europe*; Research in Migration and Ethnic Relations Series; Ashgate Publishing: Farnham, UK, 2012.
16. Strielkowski, W. *Roma Migrations*; Faculty of Social Science, Charles University in Prague: Prague, Czech Republic, 2012.
17. Crawford, P.B.; Story, M.; Wang, M.C.; Ritchie, L.D.; Sabry, Z.I. Ethnic issues in the epidemiology of childhood obesity. *Pediatr. Clin. N. Am.* **2001**, *48*, 855–878. [CrossRef]

18. Satia-Abouta, J.; Patterson, R.E.; Kristal, A.R.; Teh, C.; Tu, S.P. Psychosocial predictors of diet and acculturation in Chinese American and Chinese Canadian women. *Ethn. Health* **2002**, *7*, 21–39. [CrossRef] [PubMed]
19. World Health Organization (WHO). *Obesity: Preventing and Managing the Global Epidemic: Report of a WHO Consultation on Obesity, Geneva, 3–5 June 1997*; WHO: Geneva, Switzerland, 1998. Available online: http://apps.who.int/iris/handle/10665/63854 (accessed on 11 January 2018).
20. Strauss, A.; Corbinová, J. Základy kvalitativního výzkumu. In *Postupy a Techniky Metody Zakotvené Teorie*; Albert: Brno, Czech Republic, 1999.
21. Adámková, V. Obezita a nadváha jako celospolečenský problem. In *Prevence Obesity a Nadváhy u Romské Minority v Komunitním Ošetřovatelství*; Tóthová, V., Ed.; NLN, s.r.o.: Praha, Czech Republic, 2016; pp. 16–25.
22. Brewiss, A.A. *Obesity: Cultural and Biocultural Perspectives*; Rutgers University Press: New Brunswick, NJ, USA, 2011.
23. Saxena, S.; Ambler, G.; Cole, T.J.; Majeed, A. Ethnic group differences in overweight and obese children and young people in England: Cross sectional survey. *Arch. Dis. Child.* **2004**, *89*, 30–36. [PubMed]
24. Robertson, A.; Lobstein, T.; Knai, C. Obesity and Socio-Economic Groups in Europe: Evidence Review and Implications for Action. 2007. Available online: http://ec.europa.eu/health/ph_determinants/life_style/nutrition/documents/ev20081028_rep_en.pdf (accessed on 11 January 2017).
25. Higgins, V.; Dale, A. *Ethnic Differences in Overweight and Obese Children in England*; The University of Manchester: Manchester, UK, 2010. Available online: http://www.cmist.manchester.ac.uk/medialibrary/archive-publications/working-papers/2010/2010-07-ethnic-differences.pdf (accessed on 11 January 2017).
26. Karlsen, S.; Morris, S.; Kinra, S.; Vallejo-Torres, L.; Viner, R.M. Ethnic variations in overweight and obesity among children over time: Findings from analyses of the Health Surveys for England 1998–2009. *Pediatr. Obes.* **2013**, *9*, 186–196. [CrossRef] [PubMed]
27. Urban, D.; Kajanová, A. Kouření a konzumace alkoholu u romských komunit v České a Slovenské republice. *Kontakt* **2011**, *13*, 328–335.
28. Oláhová, L. *Nejen Romská Kuchařka*; Fortuna: Praha, Czech Republic, 2000.
29. Šišková, T. *Menšiny a Migranti v České Republice: My a Oni v Multikulturní Společnosti 21. Století*; Portál: Praha, Czech Republic, 2001.
30. Davidová, E. Způsob života a kultura: Změny ve hmotné kultuře Romů—Bydlení, strava. In *Černobílý Život*; Černá, M., Ed.; Gallery: Praha, Czech Republic, 2000; pp. 80–89.
31. Stávková, J.; Derflerová Brázdová, Z. Konzumace ovoce a zeleniny a jiné stravovací zvyklosti Romské populace. *Hygiena* **2014**, *59*, 179–183. [CrossRef]
32. Cachelin, F.M.; Rebeck, R.M.; Chung, G.H.; Pelayo, E. Does ethnicity influence body-size preference? A comparison of body image and body size. *Obes. Res.* **2002**, *10*, 158–166. [CrossRef] [PubMed]

nutrients

MDPI

Review

Energy and Nutrient Issues in Athletes with Spinal Cord Injury: Are They at Risk for Low Energy Availability?

Katherine Figel [1,*], Kelly Pritchett [1], Robert Pritchett [1] and Elizabeth Broad [2]

[1] Central Washington University, Ellensburg, WA 98926, USA; Kelly.pritchett@cwu.edu (K.P.); Robert.pritchett@cwu.edu (R.P.)

[2] United States Olympic Committee, Chula Vista, CA 91915, USA; Elizabeth.broad@usoc.org

* Correspondence: Katherine.figel@cwu.edu; Tel.: +1-206-755-1001

Received: 8 June 2018; Accepted: 6 August 2018; Published: 13 August 2018

Abstract: Low energy availability (LEA) and nutrient intake have been well studied in able-bodied athletes, but there is a lack of research examining these issues amongst athletes with spinal cord injury (SCI). To date, there have been no studies that have examined energy availability (EA) amongst this population. Furthermore, athletes with SCI may experience unique challenges around nutrition that may increase their risk of LEA. This review will evaluate the literature and assess whether this population is at risk for LEA. Due to the limited research on this topic, sedentary individuals with SCI and para athletes were also included in this review. Review of the current literature suggests that athletes with SCI may be at an increased risk for LEA. While research examining EA and risk of LEA in athletes with SCI is lacking, the number of athletes with SCI continues to increase; therefore, further research is warranted to assess nutrient and energy needs and their risk to this population.

Keywords: spinal cord injury; athlete; energy availability; nutrient deficiency; low energy availability; bone mineral density; para athlete; menstrual dysfunction; Female Athlete Triad; Relative Energy Deficiency in Sports (RED-S)

---

1. Introduction

Energy and nutrient availability have been widely studied in able-bodied athletes; however, there is a lack of research examining energy availability (EA) and nutrient intake in para athletes, including athletes with a spinal cord injury (SCI). Para athletes are defined as athletes with physical disabilities [1–3]. Athletes who experience an SCI are a specific group within the para athlete group. While there is no research specially looking at EA amongst athletes with SCI, some studies assessing energy intake and expenditure have suggested that this population may be at increased risk for LEA.

Low energy availability (LEA) can lead to menstrual dysfunction and low bone mineral density (BMD) in able-bodied athletes. These conditions are included in the Female Athlete Triad (Triad) and are characterized on a spectrum ranging from optimal health to a disease state. The Triad fits within the more recent, broader, and more comprehensive term for the condition called Relative Energy Deficiency in Sport (RED-S) [4,5]. LEA and components of the Triad and RED-S can lead to decreased athletic performance and serious short and long-term health consequences. This highlights the need for early detection, diagnosis, and treatment of these medical conditions amongst male and female athletes [4,5].

Athletes with SCI have differing energy requirements and bone densities compared to the able-bodied population. This makes it more challenging to identify whether this group is at risk for LEA, and yet this research is even more vital given this lack of knowledge and growing number of athletes with SCI [1]. While menstrual dysfunction and low BMD may be caused by LEA in the able-bodied population, these conditions may be related to the athlete's disability rather than LEA in the para athlete population, including athletes with SCI [1,2].

Health issues associated with SCI may also put these athletes at a greater risk for LEA. Pain associated with the injury may decrease appetite, while medications used to manage pain may cause constipation or nausea. Kidney and bladder infections are more common amongst athletes with SCI compared to able-bodied athletes. The use of antibiotics to treat or prevent these infections may cause diarrhea or a decrease in gut bacteria, which could result in compromised gut health and nutrient absorption. Challenges around grocery shopping and preparing food due to physical limitations may also influence energy intake. In addition, athletes with SCI may experience difficulties swallowing, leading to decreased food intake. Finally, individuals with SCI may increase fiber intake to regulate bowels, although excessive fiber intake may decrease overall energy intake, since it has a slower gastric emptying time.

Oftentimes, when an individual experiences an SCI, they receive nutrition counseling focusing on weight management, since their energy needs are decreased compared to those of an able-bodied individual. When they become an athlete however, their energy needs increase compared to sedentary individuals with SCI. Given that there is a paucity of research around the nutritional needs of athletes with SCI, these athletes may not receive proper education or guidance around their adjusted calorie needs and thus may be at increased risk for LEA.

The number of athletes participating in para sport is increasing with a record number of athletes participating in the 2018 Winter Paralympics in PyeongChang [6]. In addition, the number of athletes participating in the 2016 Summer Paralympics in Rio was over 4300 [7]. Para athletes, including athletes with SCI, may be at risk for inadequate dietary intakes, and thus more research is needed amongst this population [1–3,8–11]. This review evaluates the literature examining EA, LEA, and related conditions among athletes with SCI.

2. Materials and Methods

A review of literature was conducted between January and May of 2018 using PubMed. Search terms included BMD, EA, nutrient intake, SCI, para athlete, total energy expenditure (TEE), energy intake (EI), exercise energy expenditure (EEE), LEA, and menstrual function in reference to athletes with SCI. Persons with an SCI include people with full or partial paralysis to parts of their body due to an injury to the spinal cord. Paraplegia and tetraplegia are the result of a complete or incomplete injury to the spine. Original research, reviews, and relevant books published in 1985 or later were included in the search. To date, we have been unable to find any research studies examining EA in athletes with SCI. In addition, there was limited data specifically related to athletes with SCI (who are defined as someone who has experienced an injury to their spinal cord and now participates in sports). Therefore, research using sedentary individuals with SCI and para athletes (who are defined as athletes with a disability that may be SCI but could also include amputation, spina bifida, visual impairment, cerebral palsy, or acquired brain injury) was also included.

3. Results

3.1. Energy

3.1.1. Energy Intake

Collection tools such as food journals and food frequency questionnaires have limitations and great difficulties in accurately capturing energy intake and thus create challenges around accurate assessment and data collection [12]. Participant-recorded food journals may reflect underreporting of energy and nutrient intake, as subjects tend to underestimate portion sizes or fail to include all food consumed during the collection timeframe. It is estimated that amongst athletes, underreporting accounts for 10–45% of total energy expenditure [13]. Most studies included in this review paper used a 24 h or 3-day food record as their collection method and did not correct for underreporting amongst subjects. Disadvantages to this method include high subject burden and cooperation, and may cause altered diet behaviors due to act of recording food intake [14]. While short term food journals are primarily used, it is estimated that a diet record may need to be kept for 27–35 days in order to accurately assess energy intake in male and female subjects [14]. In addition, many studies assessing energy intake amongst para athletes, including athletes with SCI, use food journals while athletes are at training camp facilities where meals are provided. While this may enable more accurate estimation of nutrient intake, it may provide an inaccurate picture of what the athlete is consuming at home when food choices may be different, although Krempien et al. [9] found no difference in overall energy intake when athletes kept a 3-day food journal at home versus at training camp. Obstacles associated with grocery shopping, food preparation, and cooking may provide additional challenges amongst athletes with SCI who have limited accessibility. These obstacles may greatly impact athletes' food choices and may put them at greater risk of experiencing inadequate food and nutrient intake and thus LEA. Dysphagia (difficulty swallowing) and slower gastric emptying are conditions some athletes with SCI experience; they can also increase the risk of inadequate energy and fluid intake [3]. Medications commonly used by individuals with SCI may cause unwanted side effects such as nausea, gastrointestinal upset, poor sleep patterns, and changes in gut bacteria and appetite. These side effects may influence diet, energy intake, and nutrient absorption of athletes with SCI [3].

Studies have found that energy intakes amongst male para athletes vary greatly, ranging from 23–64 kcal/kg/day [11]. Despite lower energy needs, athletes with SCI may still be consuming too few calories [15,16]. Madden et al. [16] found that elite male and female wheelchair athletes consumed on average 2092 kcal/day and 1602 kcal/day, respectively. Similar trends were observed in male and female athletes with SCI with average energy intake found to be comparable to or lower than the energy intake recommendations of sedentary, able-bodied individuals [8–10].

While Grams et al. [11] found a higher average energy intake amongst male wheelchair basketball players (2673 kcal/day) compared with other studies, energy intakes ranged considerably between individuals from 1597 to 3651 kcal/day. This suggests that there is a wide variation in energy intake amongst this population even within the same sport [11]. This variation is likely due to differences in body weight, disability, and injury level. While more research needs to be done, actual energy intake amongst athletes with SCI is considerably lower compared to recommendations for able-bodied athletes. Given that male and female athletes with SCI have increased physical activity levels, their energy needs are likely greater than able-bodied sedentary individuals and thus their intake may be too low [11,17].

3.1.2. Total Energy Expenditure (TEE)

Total energy includes resting metabolic rate (RMR), thermic effect of feeding (TEF), and physical activity. RMR measures the energy that your body burns while at rest. Male and female athletes with SCI have lower energy requirements compared to able bodied athletes [3,17–19]. In addition to the amount of physical activity, level and severity of spinal cord lesion also play a role in determining overall energy expenditure of an individual. TEE studies have primarily been conducted in able-bodied persons and athletes, while limited studies have assessed energy expenditure in the SCI population. Furthermore, most work has been done in clinical settings on sedentary individuals with SCI, therefore little is known regarding the energy cost of wheelchair-based activities. Table 1 shows studies that have examined energy expenditure in para athletes including athletes with SCI. It should be noted that in order to measure TEE, fat free mass (FFM) needs to be assessed. Most studies used dual-energy x-ray absorptiometry to assess body composition.

Table 1. Overview of studies that have examined energy expenditure amongst para athletes including athletes with SCI.

Reference	Subjects	Methods	Results
Buchholtz et al. [18]	34 control 28 paraplegics with SCI	indirect calorimetry following 12-h fast	RMR C: 1676 ± 223 kcal/day RMR SCI: 1472 ± 228 kcal/day (No diff. when adjusted for FFM) TEF C: 6.25 ± 2.2% TEF SCI: 5.53 ± 1.8%
Pelly et al. [20]	7 M WC athletes with SCI and 6 able-bodied controls	indirect calorimetry following 12-h fast	RMR no difference found between groups When adjusted for LTM: SCI: 35 ± 7 kcal/kg LTM C: 30 ± 2 kcal/kg LTM Prediction equations—not warranted for SCI population

SCI = spinal cord inury, RMR = resting metabolic rate, C = control subjects, FFM fat free mass, TEF = thermic effect of feeding, WC = wheelchair, LTM = lean tissue mass.

3.1.3. Resting Metabolic Rate (RMR)/Basal Metabolic Rate (BMR)

It has been suggested by Mollinger et al. [21] that individuals with SCI may have a 12–27% lower basal metabolic rate (BMR) when compared to able-bodied individuals [21]. In Mollinger's study, BMR was measured on three consecutive days using 10-min samples of expired air shortly after the subject was awakened in the morning. The variance in BMR in individuals with SCI is correlated with the level of lesion and whether the injury is a complete or incomplete lesion [21]. A lower BMR is associated with a higher level of lesion. A complete injury is also associated with a lower BMR compared to an incomplete SCI, which allows for limited nerve signaling from the spinal cord to brain and possible limited movement and sensation below the injury site. The greatest difference in BMR compared to the able-bodied population is believed to be due to decreased muscle mass and increased adipose tissue in individuals with SCI. Furthermore, studies have suggested that when adjusted for lean body tissue, there is no difference or possibly even a greater RMR in individuals with SCI compared with a control group of able-bodied individuals [17,18,20]. Interestingly, Pelly et al. [20] found that when adjusted for lean tissue mass (LTM), RMR was actually higher in athletes with SCI compared to controls. This suggests that athletes with SCI were using more calories per kg of LTM. These results may be due to the greater metabolic activity of the viscera compared to skeletal muscles at rest [20]. Both Pelly et al. [20] and Buchholz et al. [18] measured RMR with subjects in a reclined position, refraining from caffeine and exercise for 24 h prior to testing and following a 12 h fast. Females were self-reported to be in the follicular phase of their menstrual cycle. Buchholz et al. [18] used male and female wheelchair athletes, while Pelly et al. [20] used male athletes with SCI as subjects.

Accurately measuring TEF is very challenging. This review looked at two studies examining differences in TEF in the SCI population compared to the able-bodied population. Both Aksnes et al. [22] and Buchholz et al. [18] found no significant difference in TEF between individuals with SCI and able-bodied controls. Aksnes et al. [22] measured TEF in the morning after subjects had gone through an overnight fast of 12–14 h. Expired gas was collected from subjects using a mouth piece for measurements of ventilation. Respiratory gas exchanges were measured using a pneumotachograph and paramagnetic and infrared analyzers for oxygen and carbon dioxide, respectively. Expired gas was collected for 30 min in the resting state and for 7 min at the end of each 15-min time segment for 2 h post prandial. Venous blood samples were taken before and every 15 min post prandial to determine plasma concentrations of glucose and insulin. The meal was in a liquid form and was comprised of 52% carbohydrate, 37% fat, and 11% protein. The control group received only water in the same corresponding volume of the liquid meal provided to the other group.

Buchholz et al. [18] also measured TEF using indirect calorimetry for 2 h post prandial. Subjects reported for the study following a 12 h fast. Expired air was measured using a ventilated canopy for 60 min with the last 40 min of the data used. TEF was then measured with indirect calorimetry for 120 min after the plateau blood sample and following consumption of a mixed liquid meal consisting of 55% carbohydrate, 30% fat, and 15% protein. The dose of the meal was calculated to be 30% of RMR for each subject.

3.1.4. Exercise Energy Expenditure (EEE)

It is estimated that male and female athletes with SCI have 25–75% lower energy needs compared to able-bodied athletes [17]. Expended energy depends on the sport and level of injury. For example, male wheelchair basketball players are estimated to expend 75% of the calories expended by able bodied basketball players. An even greater energy discrepancy is found in men's rugby, where it's estimated that wheelchair rugby players expend only 26% of the calories expended by able bodied male rugby players [17].

Numerous tools have been used to assess energy expenditure amongst individuals with SCI, including indirect calorimetry, heart rate monitoring, accelerometers, and energy expenditure questionnaires including the Physical Activity Recall Assessment for People with Spinal Cord Injury (PARA-SCI) and the Leisure Time Physical Activity Questionnaire for People with Spinal Cord Injury LTPAQ-SCI [23,24]. However, there are limitations surrounding these methods when applying them to athletes with SCI [2]. As a result, there is insufficient research to determine a validated gold standard for assessing energy expenditure in athletes with SCI [20,23].

In addition, individuals with SCI, particularly those with a high level spinal lesion, may have reduced sympathetic nervous system (SNS) availability compared to able-bodied individuals. The SNS is involved with hepatic glycogenolysis and gluconeogenesis, and thus may impact the metabolism of athletes with SCI [17]. Individuals with SCI also have reduced muscle mass available for exercise capacity [17,19]. This, combined with a decrease in SNS activity and lower VO_{2peak} and peak power output, can result in reduced exercise capacity compared with able-bodied controls, suggesting that these athletes may expend less energy compared to able-bodied athletes doing the same activity [19].

Some studies have measured energy expenditure while athletes are living at training camps. Distances between living and training quarters, as well as terrain, can all significantly impact the energy expenditures of these athletes, since the calories expended getting to these locations may be greater compared to that of able-bodied individuals. Thus, energy expenditure may differ drastically depending on the athlete's setting. Mode of ambulation and completeness of injury may also differ, which influences energy expenditure and makes it harder to assess energy expenditure in athletes with SCI. Although further research is warranted, non-exercise activity thermogenesis (NEAT) may be greater in people with SCI given that it may be more challenging to accomplish daily activities, while energy cost during structured exercise may be lower than what is observed in able bodied athletes.

3.1.5. Energy Availability

Research has yet to examine EA in athletes with SCI. However, some literature looking at energy intake or energy expenditure suggests that both male and female athletes with SCI may demonstrate risk factors for LEA [1,3,25]. EA is calculated as total energy intake (kcals) minus exercise energy expenditure (kcals) divided by kilograms (kg) of fat free mass (FFM). Optimal energy availability in female athletes is believed to be >45 calories per kilogram of FFM. Reduced energy availability in this population is defined in the literature as <45 kcals/kg/FFM, and LEA is defined as less than 30 calories per kilogram of FFM per day, although may be lower amongst males [4,5,26–28]. These cutoffs may not predict associated consequences amongst all athletes, including males, and have yet to be validated in athletes with SCI [5]. Thus, this equation and reference ranges may be inappropriately applied to athletes with SCI due to their lower active muscle mass, decreased mobility, and reductions in the sympathetic nervous system due to paralysis [17,18].

When an athlete experiences reduced EA, subclinical menstrual disorders and low BMD may occur [29]. Identifying whether an athlete with SCI has LEA is challenging, since these conditions may be present regardless of EA. Melin et al. [26] estimated that 63% of elite, able-bodied female endurance athletes were found to have either low (<30 kcal/kg FFM/day) or reduced EA (<45 kcal/kg) over a 7-day study period [26]. However, the incidence of LEA amongst male and female athletes with SCI has yet to be determined.

LEA can be acute, chronic, or intermittent. There is currently no established guideline pertaining to the length of time an athlete must be experiencing LEA in order to be considered at "chronic" LEA. For example, many research studies use short term/acute tools such as 24 h or 7-day food journals to collect data, which may over or under estimate energy intake and result in inaccurate conclusions around long term energy availability amongst athletes. However, even a short timeframe of LEA is believed to be disruptive to metabolic substrate and hormone function. Loucks and Thuma [30] found that after only 5 days of LEA (<30 kcal/kg FFM/day), adult females experienced reductions in blood glucose levels and hypothalamic pituitary-axis hormones [30].

Gorgey et al. [15], using indirect calorimetry and four 5-day participant recorded food diaries, suggested that calorie intake amongst sedentary males with SCI using either a manual or power wheelchair was significantly lower than estimated total energy expenditure (TEE).

3.1.6. Nutrition Knowledge and Behaviors

Poor nutrition knowledge has been suggested to be a risk factor for inadequate energy intake amongst able-bodied athletes [31,32]. Zawila et al. [31] found that 83.3% of abled bodied female cross-country runners responded yes to the statement "Does your knowledge of nutrition affect how you eat?". While it is unknown what effect this has on their nutrition, 91.7% of subjects in the same study strongly agreed or agreed with the statement "Learning facts about nutrition is the best way to achieve favorable changes in food habits". Nutrition knowledge amongst athletes with SCI may be lacking. Research suggests that para athletes may be lacking in nutrition knowledge [25,33]. Eskici and Ersoy [25], using a 76-question nutrition knowledge questionnaire, found that the majority of female wheelchair basketball players in their study had inadequate nutrition knowledge, particularly pertaining to sport nutrition-specific information such as nutrition recommendations to support recovery and hydration of athletes.

Nutrition support provided to para athletes varies between countries and is still relatively new, although it is increasing across the globe. In the USA, para athletes and many able-bodied sports are not supported by the National Collegiate Athletic Association (NCAA), and hence these teams and athletes may not receive the nutritional resources and support that other athletes receive [2]. The lack of knowledge amongst the population highlights the need for access to a registered sports dietitian to improve nutrition and decrease the risk for LEA.

3.2. Risk for Disordered Eating

3.2.1. Attitudes about Eating

More research is needed regarding the eating attitudes and behaviors of athletes with disabilities, as there is no research looking at the prevalence of eating disorders amongst athletes with SCI. However, because athletes with SCI may have lower energy needs, this population may be at risk for disordered eating [1,34]. Krempien et al. [34] found that male athletes with SCI exhibited strong tendencies towards cognitive dietary restraint, while female athletes with SCI exhibited similar scores to able-bodied populations. Both male and female athletes with SCI showed lower scores for disinhibition and hunger compared to able-bodied individuals, suggesting that they may monitor body weight for sport. While the reason for this is not currently understood, it should be noted that this characteristic could put this population at risk for LEA [34].

3.2.2. Leanness in Sports

In the able-bodied population, athletes competing in a sport emphasizing leanness may be at increased risk of LEA compared with athletes competing in other sports. However, this correlation is not a well-established risk factor amongst para athletes. Krempien et al. [34] suggested that elite athletes with SCI display behaviors that may be associated with LEA, such as strong tendencies towards dietary restraint and restriction of energy intake (Table 2). Blauwet et al. [35] found that there was no difference around risk for low energy intake amongst male and female para athletes who competed in sports emphasizing leanness compared to other sports. This suggests that para athletes may be at risk for LEA regardless of sport. In addition, 40% of subjects reported currently trying to lose weight, and 61% reported attempting to change their body composition to improve their performance [35]. While more research is warranted, the responses show that athletes with SCI may be at an increased risk for LEA.

Table 2. Research examining risk of disordered eating and eating behaviors amongst para athletes, including athletes with SCI.

Reference	Subjects	Methods	Results
Krempien et al. [34]	32 M/F athletes w/SCI	TFEQ	M—strong tendency towards cognitive restraint M/F—lower scores for disinhibition and hunger
Blauwet et al. [35]	248 M/F para athletes	Online questionnaire	40% reported currently trying to lose wt 61% reported attempting to change body composition

Male = male, F = female, SCI = spinal cord injury, TFEQ = Three Factor Eating Questionnaire, Wt = weight.

3.3. Nutrients

3.3.1. Macronutrient Intake

Based on the recommendation used for able-bodied athletes, athletes should consume between 3.0–12.0 g of carbohydrate (CHO)/kg of body weight (BW) and 1.2–2.0 g of protein/kg BW [36]. These ranges accommodate variances due to sport, intensity, duration, etc. The literature review found limited studies examining the macronutrient intake of para athletes, and most studies used 24-h food journals (Table 3). Madden et al. [16] found that male and female elite wheelchair athletes had a mean intake of 3.5 g CHO/kg BW. Females consumed less protein at 1.4 g protein/kg BW, while males consumed 1.6 g protein/kg BW. Gerrish et al. [8] and Goosey-Tolfrey et al. [10] found similar results, with wheelchair athletes consuming between 3.1–4.3 g CHO/kg BW, females consuming 1.0–1.1 g protein/kg BW, and males consuming 1.4–1.7 g protein/kg BW. While these technically fall within the appropriate range, carbohydrate intakes for both sexes and protein intake for females are at the lower end of recommendations, which may suggest increased risk of low energy intake.

Table 3. Overview of studies examining macronutrient intake of para athletes.

Reference	Subjects	Methods	Results-Macronutrients
Gerrish et al. [8]	39 M/F SCI athletes	Self-reported, single 24-h food journal in autumn and winter	Fall: Energy (M): 1893 ± 725 kcal/day Energy (F): 1602 ± 718 kcal/day CHO (M/F): 3.5 ± 1.17 g/kg Pro (M/F): 1.4 ± 0.2 g/kg Winter: Energy (M): 1,669 ± 683 kcal/day Energy (F):1463 ± 844 kcal/day CHO (M/F): 3.1 ± 0.8 g/kg Pro (M):1.2 ± 0.4 g/kg
Krempien et al. [9]	32 M/F SCI athletes	3-day self-reported food journal kept at home and training camp	Energy (M): 2156 ± 431 kcal/day Energy (F): 1991 ± 510 kcal/day CHO (M/F): 4.4 ± 1.1 g/kg Pro (M/F):1.4 ± 0.4 g/kg
Grams et al. [11]	17 M WC BB athletes	3-day weighted food journal over 3 consecutive days during 3 training camps over 2 consecutive years.	Energy: 2673 ± 485 kcal/day CHO: 3.9 (1.8; 8.1) g/kg Pro: 1.7 ± 0.6 g/kg
Eskiki and Ersoy [25]	22 F WC athletes	24-h retrospective diet recall	Energy: 2867.8 ± 23.6 kcal/day CHO: 5.3 ± 1.5 g/kg Pro: 1.6 ± 0.3 g/kg
Madden et al. [16]	40 M/F Paralympic athletes	3-day, consecutive self-reported food journal	Energy (M): 2092 (1695–2690) kcal/day Energy (F): 1602 (1439–2059) kcal/day CHO (M/F): 3.5 ± 1.1 g/kg Pro (M/F): 1.5 (1.3–1.7) g/kg

Intakes are presented as mean and standard deviation or mean and range. M = males, F = females, SCI = spinal cord injury, Energy = energy intake, CHO = carbohydrate, Pro = protein, WC = wheelchair, BB = basketball, TEE = total energy expenditure.

3.3.2. Micronutrient Intake

Inadequate macronutrient intake may cause athletes with SCI to experience low micronutrient intake [3,8–11,25]. To the best of our knowledge, with the exception of vitamin D, there is no data looking at actual micronutrient status amongst individuals with SCI. It is, however, well documented that athletes with SCI are at increased risk for vitamin D deficiency [37], and they may be lacking in additional nutrients. The prevalence of vitamin D deficiency or insufficiency ranges from 32–93%, which is high compared to the able-bodied population. Some factors influencing deficiency include immobility, lesion level, the presence of pressure ulcers, and whether the person practices their sport indoors or outdoors [37]. Table 4 includes studies found in the literature review that examined micronutrient intake of para athletes. Krempien et al. [9] found that over 25% of male and female athletes with SCI had micronutrient intakes below the Estimated Average Requirement (EAR) for calcium, magnesium, folate, and vitamin D. Vitamin and mineral supplementation increased overall micronutrient intake amongst men, while supplement use amongst women did not significantly change their nutrient intake. Even when factoring in supplement use, athletes still did not consume adequate amounts of these nutrients [9]. Gerrish et al. [8] found that during winter training camp, over 60% of female athletes with SCI failed to meet the EAR of many micronutrients including vitamin D, vitamin B6, vitamin B12, vitamin C, folate, calcium, iron, magnesium, and zinc. Male athletes displayed similar trends around micronutrient insufficiencies [9,11]. Madden et al. [16] suggested that while para athletes met most of their micronutrient RDAs, females fell short for iron and calcium, while males did not meet the RDA for vitamin A and folate. In addition to deficiencies related to diet, impairments and altered GI function associated with SCI may also put an athlete at greater risk for micronutrient deficiencies compared to able-bodied athletes [3]. Lastly, there are challenges around accurately assessing true micronutrient intake. Studies that use food journals as a collection method may have underreporting issues. The studies that we included in our review utilized this collection method, so it should be noted that this is a limitation to the data presented.

Table 4. Overview of studies examining micronutrient intake of para athletes, including athletes with SCI.

Reference	Subjects	Methods	Reference Tool	Results-Micronutrients
Gerrish et al. [8]	39 M/F SCI athletes	Self-reported, single 24-h food journal in autumn and winter	EAR	Low: vitamin B6, vitamin B12, vitamin C, folate, calcium, iron, magnesium, zinc
Krempien et al. [9]	32 M/F para athletes	3-day, self-reported food journal kept at home and training camp	EAR	Low: (M)-calcium, magnesium, zinc, riboflavin, folate, vitamin B12, vitamin D (F)-calcium, magnesium, folate, vitamin D
Goosey-Tolfrey [10]	23 M/F WC para athletes	7-day consecutive, participant-reported weighed food journal	UK DRV	Low: iron, fiber
Grams et al. [11]	17 M WC BB para athletes	3-day food weighed journal over 3 consecutive days during 3 training camps in 2 consecutive years	RDA	Low: vitamin E, calcium
Eskiki and Ersoy [25]	22 F WC para athletes	24-h retrospective diet recall	RDA	Low: vitamin B1, folic acid, magnesium, iron, fiber
Madden et al. [16]	40 M/F Paralympic athletes	3-day consecutive, self-reported food journal	RDA	Low: (M): vitamin A, folate (F): iron, calcium

M = male, F = female, SCI = spinal cord injury, EAR = Estimated Average Requirement, DRI = Dietary Reference Intake, UK DRV = UK Dietary Reference Value, WC = wheelchair, BB = basketball, RDA = Recommended Dietary Allowance.

These studies suggest that regardless of whether energy and macronutrient intakes are adequate, athletes with SCI must maximize their diet with high nutrient-dense foods, given their lower energy "budget" compared to able-bodied athletes [2]. However, nutrient-dense foods may be perceived as expensive. Athletes with SCI are not supported by the NCAA, and very few are professional athletes;

thus, financial restrictions may also influence food choices and increase the intake of low nutrient-dense foods by athletes with SCI. Inadequate consumption of these nutrients may put an athlete at risk for poor bone health, low energy levels, compromised immunity, and other health concerns associated with these nutrient deficiencies.

3.4. Menstrual Dysfunction

Menstrual dysfunction refers to various irregularities including oligomenorrhea, which is defined as experiencing nine or fewer menstrual periods over a 12 month timeframe, or secondary amenorrhea, which is defined as cessation of menses for at least three consecutive months [38]. These definitions are once again used for both the female able-bodied population and those with disabilities.

Menstrual dysfunction can occur when an athlete has LEA (<30 kcal/kg FFM). It is well documented that menstrual dysfunction not only has an impact on reproductive health but can also lead to negative health consequences, including increased risk around the number of cardiovascular risk factors and premature osteopenia and osteoporosis [26,39]. BMD may decrease as the frequency of missed menstrual cycles increases. Menstrual dysfunction was identified as an independent predictor of bone stress injuries (BSI) when using the 2014 Female Athlete Triad Cumulative Risk Assessment [40]. Furthermore, prevalence of stress fractures is 2–4 times greater in amenorrheic athletes than eumenorrheic athletes [40].

The majority of research suggests that while changes in menstruation may occur after the acute phase post SCI, no chronic disruptions in menstrual function have been noted amongst females with SCI [1,38,41,42]. Stress experienced from the trauma of the injury and dysfunction of the hypothalamic-pituitary axis as a result of the injury may occur. In turn, acute low levels of sex hormones can temporarily stop menses [1]. Females with SCI typically resume menstruation 5 or 6 months following their injury (on average), while many athletes experience no disruptions in menstruation whatsoever [1,38,42]. Adolescent females who sustained a SCI prior to menarche experience the onset of menses at an age similar to that of their mothers and to individuals with SCI who were injured after menarche [38]. In addition, the level of lesion amongst females with SCI does not seem to influence length or duration of menses, and fertility is believed to be unimpaired in individuals with SCI [38,42].

There is currently limited research examining low energy availability and menstrual health amongst athletes with SCI. However, Blauwet et al. [35] found that 32% of pre-menopausal female para athletes (including athletes with SCI and other conditions) reported oligomenorrhea. While more research is warranted, this suggests that female para athletes, including athletes with SCI, may have a high prevalence of menstrual dysfunction. Whether this is due to LEA or other reasons is yet to be determined.

Recent data suggests that 27.6% of US and 30.0% of UK women of reproductive age use hormonal contraceptives [43,44]. Contraceptive use to manipulate or delay menstruation may be a tool implemented by female athletes, since menstruation and menstrual symptoms may be perceived as barriers to physical activity [45]. In a recent study, 50% of elite female athletes believed that their menstrual cycle affected training and performance [46]. Martin et al. [47] found that 50% of elite able-bodied athletes were currently using hormonal contraceptives. The use of hormonal contraceptives may be higher amongst elite athletes compared to that of the general population [48]. The use of contraceptives amongst athletes with SCI is unknown.

Martin et al. [47] found that of the elite athletes using hormonal contraceptives, many reported benefits around the ability to predict and/or manipulate their menses [47]. Schaumberg [45] found that 73% of competitive female athletes reported manipulating their menstrual cycle at least once over the past year. Of that group, 54% reported doing so for sports-related training or competition [45]. While there is no research pertaining to contraceptive use or manipulation of menses amongst athletes with SCI, this rate may be equal or even greater given that menstruation management may be perceived as more challenging or difficult amongst this population. Practitioners should be aware that contraceptive use may mask menstrual dysfunction and make it harder to assess risk of LEA and the Triad amongst athletes with SCI.

3.5. Bone Mineral Density

Low BMD places an athlete at increased risk for osteoporosis, in which bones become fragile and brittle [49]. While osteoporosis cannot be diagnosed by z-score alone, a BMD z-score ≤ -2.0 is defined as "below the expected range for age" for males and females [29,50], while a z-score < -1.0 defines low BMD in female athletes in weight-bearing sports [29,39]. However, it is unclear whether these are appropriate diagnostic criteria for people with SCI [1]. In addition, low BMD can increase the risk of bone-related injuries such as bone and stress fractures. While research varies around frequency, it is estimated that the prevalence of osteopenia is between 22 and 50%, while the prevalence of osteoporosis is between 0 and 13% in able-bodied female athletes [39].

BMD declines drastically during acute phase post SCI and then continues to decline at a slower rate long-term. Osteoporosis is common amongst individuals with SCI due to reduced skeletal loading experienced over time [51]. Compared with males, females with SCI are at an even greater risk of developing osteoporosis due to progressive decline in bone mass associated with estrogen loss with aging in addition to the decline in BMD related to SCI [52]. Loss of BMD in the proximal femur occurs within 1-year post injury and can reach a fracture threshold, thus increasing risk of fracture by year 1–5 [1]. Fractures most often occur in the distal femur and proximal tibia. While the length of time post injury can greatly influence BMD, it can also be impacted by other factors such as individuals' bone health prior to injury, weight-bearing status after the onset of injury, and region of the body. Dauty et al. found that individuals who had experienced an SCI at least one year ago experienced a decrease in distal femur BMD of 52% and proximal tibia BMD of 70% [53]. While it is well known that individuals with SCI experience significant loss of overall BMD [35,51,54,55], there is little research looking more specifically at BMD amongst athletes with SCI (Table 5).

Table 5. Overview of studies examining BMD in para athletes.

Reference	Subjects	Methods	Results
Miyahara et al. [54]	28 M WC athletes w/SCI 25 M AB athletes	DXA	-No significant difference in BMD based on level of injury, sport, age amongst SCI. -BMD in trunk, legs, & whole body negatively associated w/time since injury. -Sooner SCI returned to sport post injury, greater the BMD in trunk, legs, and whole body. -Greater BMD in arms and lower BMD in legs and whole body of SCI compared with AB.
Goktepe et al. [56]	17 M WC BB athletes w/SCI 17 sedentary WC w/SCI	DXA	-Greater radial density in WC BB compared to sedentary WC. -No diff in lumbar and hip BMD between WC BB and sedentary WC.

M = male, WC = wheelchair, SCI = spinal cord injury, AB = able-bodied, DXA = dual-energy X-ray absorptiometry, BMD = bone mineral density, BB = basketball.

While overall BMD is generally lower, some early research suggests that individuals with SCI may have equal or greater lumbar BMD compared to the able-bodied population [51,56]. While the exact mechanism for this is still debated, it is thought to be due to continued loading on this region and effects of extended duration in a seated posture on the spine [56]. However, more recent research has challenged this idea and actually suggests that the use of DXA in this population may overestimate BMD in the spine due to the calcification associated with moderate to high degenerative joint disease (DJD) [55,57]. Bauman et al. [55] measured BMD using two assessment tools: DXA and quantitative computerized tomography (qCT). They found that subjects with moderate/high DJD had significantly higher *T*-scores using DXA compared to qCT. There was no difference found in individuals with mild DJD [55]. Therefore, individuals with SCI with moderate to high DJD may be at a greater risk for fracture and have a lower lumbar BMD than initially assumed.

It is widely accepted that regular physical activity can help to maintain and potentially improve bone density in able-bodied persons. However, this research has primarily been done in able-bodied individuals versus para athletes. Miyahara et al. [54] observed 28 male wheelchair athletes with SCI and found that while BMD in the legs, trunk, and entire body was negatively associated with the time period since injury, the sooner that the para athlete returned to a sport post injury, the higher the BMD in those regions. Compared to able-bodied athletes, the para athletes with SCI were found to have lower BMD in their legs and whole body, although they were found to have greater BMD in their arms. The greater BMD in the arm region suggests that increased loading to the arms through physical activity may help to preserve bone mass in the radial density in athletes with SCI [54,56], although overall BMD continues to be lower in para athletes compared to able bodied athletes.

Another study examining male paraplegic wheelchair basketball players with SCI found a greater distal radial density in the athletes compared with sedentary paraplegic individuals with SCI [56]. There was no difference found in lumbar and hip densities between groups, which suggests that while the athletes experienced a change in BMD above the level of injury, there was no change experienced below the site of injury amongst this population. While this research is limited, it suggests that athletes with SCI may have improved BMD in the distal radius compared to sedentary individuals with SCI. However, the BMD of athletes with SCI was not compared to that of able-bodied athletes, and thus it is unknown how these results compare.

This preliminary research suggests that engaging in physical activity may be extremely beneficial in helping to slow the acceleration of bone loss in people with SCI. Athletes with SCI have a lower total body BMD compared to able-bodied athletes; however, they may have greater BMD above the level of lesion compared with sedentary individuals with SCI [56]. To date, no research has been conducted around BMD amongst female athletes, and thus more research is warranted in order to make this conclusion, particularly amongst female athletes with a SCI.

Athletes with SCI may also be at increased risk of low BMD due to low micronutrient intake and nutrient deficiencies [37,58]. Krempien and Barr [9] found that athletes with SCI tended to have inadequate intake of certain micronutrients associated with bone health including calcium and vitamin D. The inclusion of supplements increased the overall intake of these nutrients; however, athletes still fell below the recommended dietary intake for both of these micronutrients [9]. Other studies have found similar results in that athletes with SCI failed to meet the Estimated Average Requirement (EAR) for calcium, magnesium, and vitamin D [8,11]. This is of particular concern given that athletes with SCI have a greater risk of low BMD, and these specific nutrients play a key role in bone health [58]. Finally, given that low BMD is common in most individuals with SCI, regardless of energy intake, diagnostic criteria may need to be altered for assessing risk of LEA in athletes with SCI.

4. Discussion

Much of the current research around EA, nutrient issues, and the prevalence of LEA has been conducted in able-bodied athletes. However, athletes with SCI have unique physical challenges and health issues, which may put them at increased risk for low nutrient intake and LEA. With the exception of vitamin D, the risk of nutrient deficiencies is unknown in this population. In addition, no research has been done around EA in athletes with SCI. Thus, recommendations around energy needs and risk for LEA amongst athletes with disabilities is unknown. Furthermore, the criteria used to assess LEA among athletes with SCI may need to be altered given that low BMD is common in most individuals with SCI, regardless of energy intake. Despite these challenges, as the number of US Paralympic athletes continues to grow, research is warranted for supporting this population of athletes in providing assessment and treatment recommendations for the sports medicine team (physicians, trainers, coaches, dietitians, and other personnel) and coaches.

5. Conclusions

In conclusion, athletes with SCI may be at increased risk around inadequate nutrient intake and LEA. However, the findings of this review should be weighed with limitations as there are no current studies which assess EA amongst this population. Due to this limitation, the authors used research which assessed nutrient and energy intake amongst para athletes and sedentary individuals. As the number of para athletes continues to grow, research and understanding around the risk of low nutrient intake and LEA in this population is necessary.

Author Contributions: Conceptualization, K.F. and K.P.; Writing-Original Draft Preparation, K.F., K.P. and E.B.; Writing-Review & Editing, K.F., K.P., R.P., and E.B.; Supervision, K.P.

Funding: This research received no external funding.

Conflicts of Interest: The authors declare no conflict of interest.

References

1. Blauwet, C.A.; Brook, E.M.; Tenforde, A.S.; Broad, E.; Hu, C.H.; Abdu-Glass, E.; Matzkin, E.G. Low Energy Availability, Menstrual Dysfunction, and Low Bone Mineral Density in Individuals with a Disability: Implications for the Para Athlete Population. *Sports Med.* **2017**, *47*, 1697–1708. [CrossRef] [PubMed]
2. Broad, E. Let her play! Sports nutrition and energy availability–Unique variability amongst Olympic and paralympic female athletes. In Proceedings of the American Collge of Sports Medicine Annual Meeting, Boston, MA, USA, 31 May–4 June 2016.
3. Scaramella, J.; Kirihennedige, N.; Broad, E. Key Nutritional Strategies to Optimize Performance in Para Athletes. *Phys. Med. Rehabil. Clin. N. Am.* **2018**, *29*, 283–298. [CrossRef] [PubMed]
4. Mountjoy, M.; Sundgot-Borgen, J.; Burke, L.; Carter, S.; Constantini, N.; Lebrun, C.; Meyer, N.; Sherman, R.; Steffen, K.; Budgett, R.; et al. The IOC consensus statement: Beyond the Female Athlete Triad—Relative Energy Deficiency in Sport (RED-S). *Br. J. Sports Med.* **2014**, *48*, 491–497. [CrossRef] [PubMed]
5. Mountjoy, M. International Olympic Committee (IOC) Consensus Statement on Relative Energy Deficiency in Sport (RED-S): 2018 Update. *Int. J. Sport Nutr. Exerc. Metab.* **2018**, 1–19. [CrossRef] [PubMed]
6. International Paralympic Committee about the PyeongChang 2018 Paralympics 2018. Available online: https://www.paralympic.org/pyeongchang-2018/about (accessed on 16 March 2018).
7. International Paralympic Committee Paralympics: Rio 2016. 2018. Available online: https://www.paralympic.org/rio-2016 (accessed on 16 March 2018).
8. Gerrish, H.R.; Broad, E.; LaCroix, M.; Ogan, D.; Pritchett, R.C.; Pritchett, K. Nutrient intake of elite Canadian and American athletes with spinal cord injury. *Int. J. Exerc. Sci.* **2017**, *10*, 1018. [PubMed]
9. Krempien, J.L.; Barr, S.I. Risk of nutrient inadequacies in elite Canadian athletes with spinal cord injury. *Int. J. Sport Nutr. Exerc. Metab.* **2011**, *21*, 417–425. [CrossRef] [PubMed]
10. Goosey-Tolfrey, V.L.; Crosland, J. Nutritional practices of competitive British wheelchair games players. *Adapt. Phys. Act. Q.* **2010**, *27*, 47–59. [CrossRef]
11. Grams, L.; Garrido, G.; Villacieros, J.; Ferro, A. Marginal Micronutrient Intake in High-Performance Male Wheelchair Basketball Players: A Dietary Evaluation and the Effects of Nutritional Advice. *PLoS ONE* **2016**, *11*, e0157931. [CrossRef] [PubMed]
12. Burke, L.M.; Melin, A.; Lundy, B. Pitfalls and problems with measuring energy availability. *Int. J. Sports Nutr. Exerc. Metab.*. in press.
13. Magkos, F.; Yannakoulia, M. Methodology of dietary assessment in athletes: Concepts and pitfalls. *Curr. Opin. Clin. Nutr. Metab. Care* **2003**, *6*, 539–549. [CrossRef] [PubMed]
14. Larson-Meyer, D.E.; Woolf, K.; Burke, L. Assessment of Nutrient Status in Athletes and the Need for Supplementation. *Int. J. Sport Nutr. Exerc. Metab.* **2018**, *28*, 139–158. [CrossRef] [PubMed]
15. Gorgey, A.S.; Caudill, C.; Sistrun, S.; Khalil, R.E.; Gill, R.; Castillo, T.; Lavis, T.; Gater, D.R. Frequency of Dietary Recalls, Nutritional Assessment, and Body Composition Assessment in Men With Chronic Spinal Cord Injury. *Arch. Phys. Med. Rehabil.* **2015**, *96*, 1646–1653. [CrossRef] [PubMed]
16. Madden, R.; Shearer, J.; Parnell, J. Evaluation of Dietary Intakes and Supplement Use in Paralympic Athletes. *Nutrients* **2017**, *9*, 1266. [CrossRef] [PubMed]
17. Price, M. Energy expenditure and metabolism during exercise in persons with a spinal cord injury. *Sports Med.* **2010**, *40*, 681–696. [CrossRef] [PubMed]
18. Buchholz, A.C.; Pencharz, P.B. Energy expenditure in chronic spinal cord injury. *Curr. Opin. Clin. Nutr. Metab. Care* **2004**, *7*, 635–639. [CrossRef] [PubMed]
19. Price, M.; Campbell, I. Effects of spinal cord lesion level upon thermoregulation during exercise in the heat. *Med. Sci. Sports Exerc.* **2003**, *35*, 1100–1107. [CrossRef] [PubMed]

20. Pelly, F.E.; Broad, E.M.; Stuart, N.; Holmes, M.A. Resting energy expenditure in male athletes with a spinal cord injury. *J. Spinal Cord Med.* **2017**, 1–8. [CrossRef] [PubMed]
21. Mollinger, M.; Mollinger, L.A.; Spurr, G.B.; el Ghatit, A.Z.; Barboriak, J.J.; Rooney, C.B.; Davidoff, D.D.; Bongard, R.D. Daily energy expenditure and basal metabolic rates of patients with spinal cord injury. *Arch. Phys. Med. Rehabil.* **1985**, *66*, 420–426. [PubMed]
22. Scient, A.A.C.; Brundin, T.; Hjeltnes, N.; Maehlum, S.; Wahren, J. Meal-induced rise in resting energy expenditure in patients with complete cervical spinal cord lesions. *Spinal Cord* **1993**, *31*, 462. [CrossRef] [PubMed]
23. Nightingale, T.E.; Rouse, P.C.; Thompson, D.; Bilzon, J.L.J. Measurement of Physical Activity and Energy Expenditure in Wheelchair Users: Methods, Considerations and Future Directions. *Sports Med. Open* **2017**, *3*. [CrossRef] [PubMed]
24. Tanhoffer, R.A.; Tanhoffer, A.I.P.; Raymond, J.; Johnson, N.A.; Hills, A.P.; Davis, G.M. Energy Expenditure in Individuals with Spinal Cord Injury Quantified by Doubly Labeled Water and a Multi-Sensor Armband. *J. Phys. Act. Health* **2015**, *12*, 163–170. [CrossRef] [PubMed]
25. Eskici, G.; Ersoy, G. An evaluation of wheelchair basketball players' nutritional status and nutritional knowledge levels. *J. Sports Med. Phys. Fitness* **2016**, *56*, 259–268. [PubMed]
26. Melin, A.; Tornberg, Å.B.; Skouby, S.; Møller, S.S.; Sundgot-Borgen, J.; Faber, J.; Sidelmann, J.J.; Aziz, M.; Sjödin, A. Energy availability and the female athlete triad in elite endurance athletes: Energy availability in female athletes. *Scand. J. Med. Sci. Sports* **2015**, *25*, 610–622. [CrossRef] [PubMed]
27. Koehler, K.; Hoerner, N.R.; Gibbs, J.C.; Zinner, C.; Braun, H.; De Souza, M.J.; Schaenzer, W. Low energy availability in exercising men is associated with reduced leptin and insulin but not with changes in other metabolic hormones. *J. Sports Sci.* **2016**, *34*, 1921–1929. [CrossRef] [PubMed]
28. Koehler, K.; Achtzehn, S.; Braun, H.; Mester, J.; Schaenzer, W. Comparison of self-reported energy availability and metabolic hormones to assess adequacy of dietary energy intake in young elite athletes. *Appl. Physiol. Nutr. Metab.* **2013**, *38*, 725–733. [CrossRef] [PubMed]
29. De Souza, M.J.; Nattiv, A.; Joy, E.; Misra, M.; Williams, N.I.; Mallinson, R.J.; Gibbs, J.C.; Olmsted, M.; Goolsby, M.; Matheson, G. Expert Panel 2014 Female Athlete Triad Coalition Consensus Statement on Treatment and Return to Play of the Female Athlete Triad: 1st International Conference held in San Francisco, California, May 2012 and 2nd International Conference held in Indianapolis, Indiana, May 2013. *Br. J. Sports Med.* **2014**, *48*, 289. [PubMed]
30. Loucks, A.B.; Thuma, J.R. Luteinizing Hormone Pulsatility Is Disrupted at a Threshold of Energy Availability in Regularly Menstruating Women. *J. Clin. Endocrinol. Metab.* **2003**, *88*, 297–311. [CrossRef] [PubMed]
31. Zawila, L.G.; Steib, C.-S.M.; Hoogenboom, B. The female collegiate cross-country runner: Nutritional knowledge and attitudes. *J. Athl. Train.* **2003**, *38*, 67. [PubMed]
32. Torres-McGehee, T.M.; Pritchett, K.L.; Zippel, D.; Minton, D.M.; Cellamare, A.; Sibilia, M. Sports nutrition knowledge among collegiate athletes, coaches, athletic trainers, and strength and conditioning specialists. *J. Athl. Train.* **2012**, *47*, 205–211. [CrossRef] [PubMed]
33. Rastmanesh, R.; Taleban, F.A.; Kimiagar, M.; Mehrabi, Y.; Salehi, M. Nutritional knowledge and attitudes in athletes with physical disabilities. *J. Athl. Train.* **2007**, *42*, 99. [PubMed]
34. Krempien, J.L.; Barr, S.I. Eating attitudes and behaviours in elite Canadian athletes with a spinal cord injury. *Eat. Behav.* **2012**, *13*, 36–41. [CrossRef] [PubMed]
35. Blauwet, C.A.; Brook, E.M.; Broad, E.; Tenforde, A.S.; Matzkin, E.G. An analysis of female athlete triad risk in elite para athletes. In Proceedings of the Academy of College and Sports Medicine Annual Meeting, Boston, MA, USA, 31 May–4 June 2016.
36. Thomas, D.T.; Erdman, K.A.; Burke, L.M. Position of the Academy of Nutrition and Dietetics, Dietitians of Canada, and the American College of Sports Medicine: Nutrition and Athletic Performance. *J. Acad. Nutr. Diet.* **2016**, *116*, 501–528. [CrossRef] [PubMed]
37. Flueck, J.; Perret, C. Vitamin D deficiency in inidividuals with a spinal cord injury: A literature review. *Spinal Cord* **2017**, *55*, 428–434. [CrossRef] [PubMed]
38. Anderson, C.; Mulcahey, M.S.; Vogel, L.C. Menstruation and pediatric spinal cord injury. *J. Spinal Cord Med.* **1997**, *20*, 56–59. [CrossRef] [PubMed]
39. Nattiv, A.; Loucks, A.B.; Manore, M.M.; Sanborn, C.F.; Sundgot-Borgen, J.; Warren, M.P. The Female Athlete Triad. *Med. Sci. Sports Exerc.* **2007**, *39*, 1867–1882. [CrossRef] [PubMed]

40. Tenforde, A.S.; Carlson, J.L.; Chang, A.; Sainani, K.L.; Shultz, R.; Kim, J.H.; Cutti, P.; Golden, N.H.; Fredericson, M. Association of the Female Athlete Triad Risk Assessment Stratification to the Development of Bone Stress Injuries in Collegiate Athletes. *Am. J. Sports Med.* **2017**, *45*, 302–310. [CrossRef] [PubMed]
41. Reame, N. A prospective study of the menstrual cycle and spinal cord injury. *Am. J. Phys. Med. Rehabil.* **1992**, 15–21. [CrossRef]
42. Castro, J.S.; Lourenço, C.; Carrilho, M. Successful pregnancy in a woman with paraplegia. *BMJ Case Rep.* **2014**, *2014*, bcr2013202479. [CrossRef] [PubMed]
43. Daniels, K.; Daugherty, J.D.; Jones, J. Current contraceptive status among women aged 15–44: United States, 2011–2013. *NCHS Data Brie* **2014**, *173*, 1–8.
44. Cea-Soriano, L.; García Rodríguez, L.; Machlitt, A.; Wallander, M.-A. Use of prescription contraceptive methods in the UK general population: A primary care study. *BJOG Int. J. Obstet. Gynaecol.* **2014**, *121*, 53–61. [CrossRef] [PubMed]
45. Schaumberg, M.A.; Emmerton, L.M.; Jenkins, D.G.; Burton, N.W.; Janse de Jonge, X.A.K.; Skinner, T.L. Use of Oral Contraceptives to Manipulate Menstruation in Young, Physically Active Women. *Int. J. Sports Physiol. Perform.* **2018**, *13*, 82–87. [CrossRef] [PubMed]
46. Bruinvels, G.; Burden, R.; Brown, N.; Richards, T.; Pedlar, C. The Prevalence and Impact of Heavy Menstrual Bleeding (Menorrhagia) in Elite and Non-Elite Athletes. *PLoS ONE* **2016**, *11*, e0149881. [CrossRef] [PubMed]
47. Martin, D.; Sale, C.; Cooper, S.B.; Elliott-Sale, K.J. Period Prevalence and Perceived Side Effects of Hormonal Contraceptive Use and the Menstrual Cycle in Elite Athletes. *Int. J. Sports Physiol. Perform.* **2017**, 1–22. [CrossRef] [PubMed]
48. Torstveit, M.K. Participation in leanness sports but not training volume is associated with menstrual dysfunction: A national survey of 1276 elite athletes and controls. *Br. J. Sports Med.* **2005**, *39*, 141–147. [CrossRef] [PubMed]
49. National Institute of Health NIH. *Osteoporosis Overview 2018*; NIH: Bethesda, MD, USA, 2018.
50. American Bone Health Understanding Bone Density Results. Available online: https://americanbonehealth.org/about-bone-density/understanding-the-bone-density-t-score-and-z-score/ (accessed on 30 April 2018).
51. Jiang, S.-D.; Dai, L.-Y.; Jiang, L.-S. Osteoporosis after spinal cord injury. *Osteoporos. Int.* **2006**, *17*, 180–192. [CrossRef] [PubMed]
52. Slade, J.M.; Bickel, C.S.; Dudley, G.A. The effect of a repeat bout of exercise on muscle injury in persons with spinal cord injury. *Eur. J. Appl. Physiol.* **2004**, *92*. [CrossRef] [PubMed]
53. Dauty, M.; Verbe, B.P.; Maugars, Y.; Dubois, C.; Mathe, J.F. Supralesional and sublesional bone mineral density in spinal cord-injured patients. *Bone* **2000**, *27*, 305–309. [CrossRef]
54. Miyahara, K.; Wang, D.-H.; Mori, K.; Takahashi, K.; Miyatake, N.; Wang, B.-L.; Takigawa, T.; Takaki, J.; Ogino, K. Effect of sports activity on bone mineral density in wheelchair athletes. *J. Bone Miner. Metab.* **2008**, *26*, 101–106. [CrossRef] [PubMed]
55. Bauman, W.A.; Schwartz, E.; Song, I.S.Y.; Kirshblum, S.; Cirnigliaro, C.; Morrison, N.; Spungen, A.M. Dual-energy X-ray absorptiometry overestimates bone mineral density of the lumbar spine in persons with spinal cord injury. *Spinal Cord* **2009**, *47*, 628. [CrossRef] [PubMed]
56. Goktepe, A.S.; Yilmaz, B.; Alaca, R.; Yazicioglu, K.; Mohur, H.; Gunduz, S. Bone Density Loss After Spinal Cord Injury: Elite Paraplegic Basketball Players vs. Paraplegic Sedentary Persons. *Am. J. Phys. Med. Rehabil.* **2004**, *83*, 279–283. [CrossRef] [PubMed]
57. Liu, C.C.; Theodorou, D.J.; Theodorou, S.J.; Andre, M.P.; Sartoris, D.J.; Szollar, S.M.; Martin, E.M.; Deftos, L.J. Quantitative computed tomography in the evaluation of spinal osteoporosis following spinal cord injury. *Osteoporos. Int.* **2000**, *11*, 889–896. [CrossRef] [PubMed]
58. Broad, E. *Sports Nutrition for Paralympic Athletes*; CRC Press: Boca Raton, FL, USA, 2014.

nutrients

MDPI

Article

Beliefs about Binge Eating: Psychometric Properties of the Eating Beliefs Questionnaire (EBQ-18) in Eating Disorder, Obese, and Community Samples

Amy L. Burton [1], Deborah Mitchison [2,3,*], Phillipa Hay [3], Brooke Donnelly [1,4], Christopher Thornton [5], Janice Russell [1,4], Jessica Swinbourne [1], Christopher Basten [2], Mandy Goldstein [6], Stephen Touyz [1] and Maree J. Abbott [1]

1 School of Psychology, The University of Sydney, Sydney, NSW 2006, Australia; amy.burton@sydney.edu.au (A.L.B.); brooke.donnelly@health.nsw.gov.au (B.D.); janice.russell@sydney.edu.au (J.R.); drjessicaswinbourne@gmail.com (J.S.); stephen.touyz@sydney.edu.au (S.T.); maree.abbott@sydney.edu.au (M.J.A.)
2 Centre for Emotional Health, Department of Psychology, Macquarie University, North Ryde, NSW 2109, Australia; chrisb@bastenpsychology.com.au
3 School of Medicine, Western Sydney University, Campbelltown, NSW 2560, Australia; p.hay@westernsydney.edu.au
4 The Peter Beumont Eating Disorder Service, Royal Prince Alfred Hospital, Sydney, NSW 2006, Australia
5 The Redleaf Practice, Wahroonga, NSW 2076, Australia; chris.thornton@theredleafpractice.com
6 Mandy Goldstein Psychology, Bondi Junction, NSW 2022, Australia; mandy.goldstein@mgpsych.com
* Correspondence: deborah.mitchison@mq.edu.au

Received: 30 August 2018; Accepted: 12 September 2018; Published: 14 September 2018

Abstract: Binge eating is a core diagnostic feature of bulimia nervosa, binge eating disorder, anorexia nervosa binge/purge type, and is a common feature of "other specified" and "unspecified" feeding and eating disorders. It has been suggested that specific metacognitive beliefs about food, eating, and binge eating may play a key role in the maintenance of binge eating behaviour. The Eating Beliefs Questionnaire (EBQ-18) provides a brief self-report assessment tool measuring three types of metacognitive beliefs: negative, positive, and permissive beliefs about food and eating. This study aimed to build on past research by validating the factor structure and psychometric properties of the EBQ-18 using both a clinical and non-clinical sample. A sample of 688 participants ($n = 498$ non-clinical participants, $n = 161$ participants seeking treatment for an eating disorder, and $n = 29$ participants seeking treatment for obesity) completed a battery of questionnaires, including the EBQ-18 and other measures of eating disorder symptoms and relevant constructs. A subset of 100 non-clinical participants completed the test battery again after an interval of two-weeks, and 38 clinical participants completed the EBQ-18 before and after receiving psychological treatment for their eating disorder. A confirmatory factor analysis (CFA) was conducted and psychometric properties of this measure were assessed. The results of this study provide support for the three-factor model of the EBQ-18. In addition, the EBQ-18 was found to be a valid and reliable measure, with excellent internal consistency, good test-retest reliability in the non-clinical sample, and also demonstrated evidence of sensitivity to treatment in clinical samples with binge eating pathology. Receiver operating characteristic (ROC) curve analyses were used to identify optimal cut-off scores for the EBQ-18. This study provides valuable information about the utility of the EBQ-18 as a measure for use in both clinical and research settings.

Keywords: binge eating; questionnaire; psychometric; eating disorders; obesity

1. Introduction

Recurrent binge eating is a core diagnostic feature of binge eating disorder (BED), bulimia nervosa (BN), anorexia nervosa binge-purge type (AN-BP), and it is a common feature of "other specified" and "unspecified" feeding and eating disorders (OSFED; UFED [1]). A binge eating episode is defined as eating an objectively large amount of food in a discrete time period, accompanied by a sense of loss of control [1]. In BED, and often in other eating disorders, binge eating episodes are paired with feelings of guilt, disgust, marked distress, and/or low mood. To meet criteria for BED or BN, individuals need to have been engaging in binge eating episodes one or more times per week for a period of at least three months [1]. Population studies from the USA and Australia have found prevalence of approximately 1–1.5% for BN, 1.5–1.6% for BED, 0.4–0.5% for Anorexia Nervosa (AN), and 3.2% for OSFED [1,2]. The prevalence of recurrent binge eating in the general community has been found to range between 7.2% to 13%, with reports indicating that this prevalence is increasing over time [3,4]. This is a health behaviour of significant public interest due to its association with obesity [5], eating disorders [2] and other significant social, physical, and mental health concerns [6–8]. Known comorbidities of binge eating include anxiety, depression, substance abuse, chronic pain, diabetes, and obesity [9,10]. Furthermore, the presence of binge eating has been found to complicate obesity management and negatively impact the efficacy of obesity treatments [11–13].

In an attempt to understand the complex eating disorder symptom of binge eating better, a number of psychological models for BN and binge eating have been proposed in the literature, with many focusing on the role of restrained eating practices, poor self-esteem, poor distress tolerance, an overvaluation of body weight and shape, and specific unhelpful beliefs about binge eating (for a review of psychological models of binge eating see Burton & Abbott, 2017 [14]). In order to develop and evaluate effective psychological treatments for binge eating, it is important to be able to reliably measure the features underlying the development and maintenance of binge eating. Validated measures exist for the measurement of poor self-esteem (e.g., Rosenberg's Self-Esteem Scale), poor distress tolerance (e.g., Difficulty with Emotional Regulation Scale and Distress Tolerance Scale), as well as the frequency of binge eating itself, restrained eating, the overvaluation of body shape and weight (e.g., Eating Disorders Examination), and others features that are relevant to binge eating [15]. However, to our knowledge there are only three measures available for the assessment of beliefs about binge eating predicted to maintain binge eating in individuals with eating disorders: the Eating Disorders Thought Questionnaire, Eating Disorders Core Belief Questionnaire, and the Eating Beliefs Questionnaire (EBQ). Of these, only the EBQ has been validated with a clinical sample [15].

The eighteen-item self-report Eating Beliefs Questionnaire (EBQ-18) consists of three subscales (negative, positive, and permissive beliefs about eating) with each subscale measuring a specific type of belief about eating that is believed to maintain binge eating in individuals with eating disorders [16,17]. Based on metacognitive theory [18,19] and the cognitive model of BN [17], the EBQ-18 measures negative beliefs about eating (beliefs that relate to a perception of having no control in relation to food and eating, for example, difficulty with resisting urges to eat and/or stopping eating once an episode of binge eating has started), positive beliefs about eating (beliefs that relate to the perceived benefits of binge eating, such as reducing emotional distress), and permissive beliefs about binge eating (beliefs that one should allow oneself to commence or continue to binge eat). Items for the three EBQ-18 subscales were developed with input from a number of experts in the area of eating disorders and cognitive therapy, for example, clinical psychologists and psychiatrists with training and experience in the assessment and treatment of eating disorders and/or the delivery of cognitive therapy [16,20]. Subscales were refined while using exploratory and confirmatory factor analysis such that the current EBQ-18 contains the six best items from each of the three subscales [15,16,20]. The EBQ-18 can be used to assess for the presence and severity of binge eating related cognitions in both clinical and community samples. The results of a recent study using a large non-clinical sample found that the EBQ-18 demonstrates promising measurement properties, such as good internal consistency, convergent validity, and interpretability with a large non-clinical sample [20]. The factor structure of the EBQ-18 has not yet been verified with a clinical or binge eating sample. An earlier two-subscale version of the EBQ demonstrated evidence of clinical utility and responsiveness to treatment [15], with EBQ scores successfully differentiating individuals with BN or BED from non-clinical control participants, and optimal clinical cut-off scores were identified [21]. In its current three-factor form, the clinical utility of EBQ-18 has yet to be assessed with an eating disorder sample.

According to specific criteria for the assessment of a measure's methodological quality [22,23], a measure should be able to demonstrate adequacy across a number of important measurement properties, including content validity, internal consistency, criterion validity, construct validity, structural validity, agreement, reliability, responsiveness, floor and ceiling effect, and interpretability. In this paper, we seek to provide a thorough assessment of the EBQ-18's methodological quality according to the principles described in by Terwee et al. [22] and Mokkink et al. [23] to determine whether the EBQ-18 provides a valid, reliable, and clinically useful measure of eating beliefs within the clinical target population.

Using both a clinical and non-clinical sample, this study aimed to provide a comprehensive assessment of psychometric properties and clinical utility of the EBQ-18 and to identify optimal clinical cut-off scores while using receiver operating characteristics (ROC) curve analysis. We predicted that the confirmatory factor analysis would provide support for the three-factor solution that was identified in the initial exploratory factor analysis [20]: negative beliefs, positive beliefs, and permissive beliefs about eating. In line with previous findings, we hypothesised that the EBQ-18 scores would positively correlate with binge eating frequency, measures of eating disorder symptoms and psychopathology, and other measures of eating-related beliefs, thereby demonstrating convergent validity. We further hypothesised that the EBQ-18 would demonstrate evidence of adequate internal consistency, test-retest reliability over a two-week interval, and sensitivity to treatment following a psychological intervention. It was predicted that the EBQ-18 scores would differ significantly depending on binge eating status, such that those individuals engaging in regular binge eating would score significantly higher on the EBQ-18 and its subscales than those not engaging in binge eating, and those individuals that were diagnosed with a binge-related eating disorder (e.g., BN or BED) would score significantly higher on the EBQ-18 than those individuals with a restrictive eating disorder (e.g., AN).

2. Materials and Methods

2.1. Participants

In total, data from 688 participants were included in this study (63.1% female, mean age = 25.38, standard deviation (SD) = 11.82 years, mean body mass index (BMI) = 24.30, SD = 8.40). This sample consisted of both non-clinical participants (n = 498) and treatment-seeking participants (n = 190).

Non-clinical samples: First year psychology students from The University of Sydney (n = 308) completed the research test battery in exchange for course credit. In addition, participants from the general community (n = 190) responded to an advert that was placed on internet-based community classifieds asking for interested volunteers for research.

Treatment-seeking samples: Participants were recruited from a number of different metropolitan treatment sites, including hospital-based eating disorder treatment services, private eating disorder treatment services, and hospital-based obesity services. These numbers reflect the total number of consenting participants that were recruited from these sites who provided complete EBQ-18 data and were therefore eligible to be included in the study. Refer to Table 1 for demographic information for these samples.

Clinical subgroups: Two subgroups of participants were created based on self-reported binge eating status. Items of the Eating Disorder Examination Questionnaire (EDE-Q) were used to assess self-reported binge eating status of participants (refer to Measures section for more information on this questionnaire). From the total sample of 688,343 participants (52.9%) reported that they had not engaged in any episodes of overeating over the previous 28 days, these 343 participants were grouped for the purposes of providing a non-binge eating comparison sample (referred to as the Non-BE subgroup) for subsequent analyses. Of the total sample of 688,190 participants, (27.9%) self-reported that they engaged in at least four episodes of objective binge eating (objective overeating with a sense of loss of control; OBE) over the previous 28 days and were grouped together for the purpose of providing a binge eating sample (referred to as the BE subgroup). In addition, seven diagnostic subgroups from the treatment-seeking sample were also identified; AN restrictive type (AN-R), AN binge eating/purging type (AN-BP), BN, BED and OSFED atypical AN (OSFED AN), BN of low frequency or limited duration (OSFED BN), and BED of low frequency or limited duration (OSFED BED). Clinical diagnoses were provided by a clinical psychologist or psychiatrist with expertise and training in eating disorder assessment and treatment. Demographics for these subgroups are also reported in Table 1.

Table 1. Demographic Information for participant samples.

Sample	*n*	Mean Age (SD)	Mean BMI (SD)	% Female	Mean OBEs in Past 28 Days (SD)
Non-clinical samples:					
First Year University Students	308	19.66 (4.54)	22.08 (3.81)	80.8	2.18 (4.32)
General Community	190	31.22 (12.83)	25.10 (6.08)	62.6	3.19 (6.21)
Treatment-seeking samples:					
Hospital-based Obesity Treatment Service	29	50.97 (14.23)	46.53 (12.56)	55.2	2.32 (3.29)
Hospital-based Outpatient Eating Disorder Treatment Service	19	30.29 (8.86)	26.59 (13.24)	100	7.06 (9.90)
Hospital-based Outpatient Binge Eating Group Treatment Program	31	28.00 (11.72)	25.85 (5.68)	100	20.43 (18.65)
Private Eating Disorder Treatment Services	111	23.57 (9.92)	23.20 (11.20)	91.9	7.15 (10.20)
Subgroup based on self-reported binge eating status:					
Non-BE	343	25.30 (12.62)	23.53 (7.40)	73.2	0
BE	190	25.39 (10.38)	24.98 (7.97)	87.3	13.14 (11.00)
Eating Disorder Subgroups:					
AN-R	24	22.00 (9.27)	18.82 (3.67)	91.7	1.70 (4.97)
AN-BP	10	21.20 (4.94)	17.39 (3.07)	100	12.00 (14.52)
BN	35	25.81 (6.96)	25.06 (7.94)	97.1	18.03 (14.28)
BED	19	31.85 (13.69)	34.57 (13.41)	89.5	19.24 (19.10)
OSFED AN	12	24.25 (10.82)	21.76 (4.38)	100	5.00 (6.15)
OSFED BN	4	23.00 (5.77)	25.42 (3.87)	100	6.50 (5.97)
OSFED BED	4	34.67 (4.16)	25.56 (5.03)	75.0	19.75 (21.48)

SD = standard deviation, BMI = body mass index, OBE = objective binge eating episodes, Non-BE = participants who self-reported 0 incidents of objective binge episodes in 28 days prior to completing the test battery; BE = participants who self-reported engaging in 4 or more incidents of objective binge eating episodes in the 28 days prior to completing the test battery, AN-R = anorexia nervosa restrictive type, AN-BP = anorexia nervosa binge/purge type, BN = bulimia nervosa, BED = binge eating disorder, OSFED = other specified feeding or eating disorder.

2.2. Measures

The Eating Beliefs Questionnaire (EBQ-18; included in supplementary materials as S1) [20]. The EBQ-18 is an 18-item self-report questionnaire that measures negative, positive, and permissive beliefs about eating and urges to eat in the absence of hunger. Respondents rate how much they agree with 18 statements from 1 (strongly disagree) to 5 (strongly agree). It has demonstrated psychometric properties, as reported in the Introduction.

The Eating Disorder Examination Questionnaire (EDE-Q) [24]. Based on the Eating Disorder Examination interview (EDE; Fairburn, Wilson [25]), the EDE-Q is a self-report questionnaire that assesses of the severity and frequency of eating disorder symptoms (including binge eating) experienced over the 28 days prior. Respondents provide a rating between 0 and 6 for 28 items, where higher scores are indicative of an increased frequency or severity of symptoms. Respondents also provided frequencies for eating disorder behaviours (e.g., overeating, binge eating, purging, driven exercise). The EDE-Q global score provides an indication of the severity of eating disorder symptoms, and four subscales assess severity of dietary restraint, eating concern, weight concern, and shape concern. The EDE-Q has demonstrated evidence of its reliability and validity [26]. Cronbach's alpha of 0.94 for the EDE-Q global score for the sample in this study.

Depression Anxiety Stress Scale (DASS-21) [27]. The DASS-21 is a self-administered screening tool and it was used here to measure symptoms of depression, anxiety, and stress that were experienced over the previous week. The DASS-21 has demonstrated evidence of its reliability and validity [28]. Cronbach's alpha of 0.95 for the total score in the current study.

Dutch Eating Behaviour Questionnaire (DEBQ) [29]. The DEBQ is a self-report scale that measures the presence of particular eating behaviours and attitudes. The current study used the DEBQ emotional eating scale and the DEBQ external eating scale. The third scale of the DEBQ measures restrained eating, as the EDE-Q provides a measure of dietary restraint we did not include the restrained eating scale in our test battery in the interest of reducing repetition and participant burden as much as possible. The emotional eating scale provides a 13-item measure of the influence of emotional or internal cues on eating behaviour, and the external eating scale is a 10-item measure of the influence of environmental or external cues on eating behaviour. Both DEBQ scales have demonstrated adequate internal consistency [29]. Cronbach's alpha of 0.94 for the emotional eating subscale and Cronbach's alpha of 0.81 for the external eating subscale were obtained in the current study.

Eating Disorder Thoughts Questionnaire (EDTQ) [30]. The EDTQ is a 26-item self-report questionnaire measuring the presence of beliefs about the positive and negative consequences of eating, permissive thoughts and thoughts of no control over eating. The EDTQ has demonstrated evidence of good internal consistency and validity [30]. Cronbach's alpha of 0.95 was obtained for the whole measure in the current study.

2.3. Procedure

Non-clinical: Participants completed a battery of questionnaires online using Qualtrics Survey Software. First year university participants (n = 308) completed a larger test battery that consisted of all measures that were described in the Materials section. At recruitment, participants could choose to sign up for the standard or two-part version of the study. A sample of 100 participants from the university sample completed the two-part version of the study, which involved completing the EBQ-18 a second time following an interval of two weeks (84% female, mean age = 20.69 years, SD = 7.06 years, mean BMI = 21.63, SD = 2.96). Community participants (n = 190) completed a briefer test battery that consisted of demographics items, the EBQ-18, the DASS-21, and the EDE-Q.

Treatment-seeking: Participants recruited from clinical settings were offered the opportunity to take part in a questionnaire-based research study by a member of administrative staff. Those who consented to participate then completed a test battery including demographic items, EBQ-18, DASS-21, and the EDE-Q. Diagnoses were recorded by the treating clinician; a clinical psychologist or psychiatrist with expertise and training in the assessment and treatment of eating disorders. The EBQ-18 was administered to clinical participants before and after receiving psychological treatment; in total, thirty-eight participants who received psychological treatment for an eating disorder provided both pre- and post-treatment EBQ-18 scores.

All the procedures performed in studies involving human participants were in accordance with the ethical standards of the University of Sydney Human Research Ethics Committee (Project Code: 2014_082) and with the 1964 Helsinki Declaration and its later amendments.

2.4. Missing Data

For the purposes of the analyses that were reported in this paper, complete EBQ-18 data was required. Where participants were missing one item per EBQ-18 subscale (i.e., 83.3% of items were completed), the missing item was replaced with the mean of the remaining items in that subscale. If more than one item per subscale was missing, then that participant's data was considered incomplete and excluded from analysis. For other measures, the same approach was taken whereby if one item was missing on a scale or subscale, the missing item was replaced with the mean score, and if more than one item was missing, the data for that measure was considered to be incomplete and excluded from the analysis.

2.5. Analyses

Descriptive statistics and analyses of the validity and reliability of the EBQ-18 were conducted using the SPSS v22 program (IBM, New York, NY, USA). Internal consistency was examined with Cronbach's alpha. Test-retest reliability and construct validity were assessed with Pearson correlations and intraclass correlations (ICC). Between group differences were tested with one-way ANOVAs. Treatment sensitivity was assessed using repeated measures ANOVAs, Cohen's d was used to calculate effect size and cut-off points for clinically significant change were calculated while using ROC Curve analyses. Using a Maximum Likelihood method, the AMOS v12 program [31] was used to conduct the CFA on the EBQ-18 items to evaluate the fit of the data to the three-factor model reflective of the three subscales of negative, positive, and permissive beliefs. The MedCalc program (MedCalc Software, Mariakerke, Belgium) was used to conduct ROC curve analyses to determine optimal clinical cut-off scores and the associated indicators of test performance: area under the curve (AUC), sensitivity, specificity, and positive and negative predictive values.

3. Results

3.1. Confirmatory Factor Analysis (CFA)

A CFA was conducted in AMOS (IBM, New York, NY, USA) while using a Maximum Likelihood method. The three-factor solution (negative beliefs, positive beliefs and permissive beliefs) was fitted to the data (non–clinical sample, $n = 498$, providing a sample of adequate size with 27.6 participants per item on the scale) and demonstrated good fit [32,33]: $\chi^2/\text{df} = 2.16$, Goodness of Fit Index (GFI) = 0.94, Incremental Fit Index (IFI) = 0.96, Tucker Lewis Index (TLo) = 0.96, Comparative Fit Index (CFI) = 0.96, and the Root Mean Square Error of Approximation (RMSEA) = 0.048 with its 90% confidence intervals (CI) 0.041 to 0.056. This supports the findings of previous research [20]. The three-factor model was also fitted to the binge eating subgroup data (BE, $n = 190$, providing a sample with 10.5 participants per item on the scale) and demonstrated adequate fit [32,33]: $\chi^2/\text{df} = 2.37$, GFI = 0.85, IFI = 0.89, TLo = 0.87, CFI = 0.89, and the RMSEA = 0.085 with its 90% CI 0.073 to 0.097. Refer to Table 2 for standardised regression weights and communalities of the three-factor solution for the EBQ-18 with a binge eating sample.

Table 2. Results of a Confirmatory Factor Analysis of the Eating Beliefs Questionnaire (EBQ-18) with the binge eating sample ($n = 190$) Standardised Regression Weights & Communalities.

EBQ-18 Items	F1: Negative Beliefs	F2: Positive Beliefs	F3: Permissive Beliefs	Communality (h^2)
I'm not able to control my urges to eat	0.71			0.51
Once I start eating I can't stop	0.78			0.61
I have no willpower in relation to food	0.79			0.63
I can't control my eating because I am weak	0.82			0.67
If I don't control myself I would never stop eating	0.62			0.38
There is nothing I can do to stop eating	0.66			0.44
Eating means I don't have to think about negative things		0.70		0.49
Eating helps to control my emotions		0.77		0.59
Eating keeps my feelings at a tolerable level		0.76		0.57
Eating helps me to cope with negative thoughts		0.83		0.69
Eating helps me cope with negative feelings		0.85		0.73
Eating is my best way of coping with unwanted feelings		0.73		0.54
Bingeing is something that I can have for myself			0.48	0.24
I deserve to have a pleasure like binge eating			0.61	0.37
It's okay to have the nice experience of binge eating			0.62	0.38
Bingeing allows me to have something nice for myself			0.82	0.68
It won't make a difference if I eat more			0.26	0.07
I like to binge			0.57	0.33

F1 = Factor 1, F2 = Factor 2, F3 = Factor 3.

3.2. Psychometric Properties

The EBQ-18 subscales were found to correlate significantly ($n = 688$): positive and negative, $r = 0.64$, $p < 0.01$; negative and permissive, $r = 0.52$, $p < 0.01$; and, positive and permissive, $r = 0.46$, $p < 0.01$. Across all 688 participants, scores on the EBQ-18 total ranged from the minimum score of 18 and highest score of 85. With regard to the floor and ceiling effects, only 2.6% of participants achieved the lowest possible score, and 0% of participants achieved the highest possible score of 90. Scores on the EBQ-18 subscales ranged from the lowest possible score of 6 (negative scale, 9.2%; positive scale 9.2%; permissive scale 10.2%) to the highest score of 30 (negative scale, 1.2%; positive scale 0.6%) or 29 (permissive scale 0.1%).

3.3. Internal Consistency

Cronbach's alphas were calculated with the full sample ($n = 688$), and for the different sample groups, see Table 3. EBQ-18 subscales were found to have good internal consistency with Cronbach's alphas ranging between 0.88 and 0.96 for the EBQ-18 total score, Cronbach's alphas (α) between 0.84 and 0.94 for the negative beliefs scale, Cronbach's alphas between 0.84 and 0.95 for the Positive Beliefs scale, and Cronbach's alphas between 0.72 and 0.84 for the Permissive Beliefs scale.

Table 3. Internal Consistency of EBQ Scales across Different Sample Groups.

Sample	EBQ-18 Total (α)	Negative Beliefs Scale (α)	Positive Beliefs Scale (α)	Permissive Beliefs Scale (α)
Full Sample ($n = 688$)	0.92	0.90	0.91	0.83
Sample Groups:				
Community Sample ($n = 190$)	0.90	0.88	0.90	0.83
University Sample ($n = 308$)	0.90	0.84	0.88	0.84
Binge Eating Group Sample ($n = 31$)	0.88	0.88	0.92	0.74
Obesity Sample ($n = 29$)	0.94	0.87	0.85	0.82
Hospital Eating Disorder Treatment Sample ($n = 19$)	0.92	0.84	0.84	0.72
Private Eating Disorder Treatment Sample ($n = 111$)	0.96	0.94	0.95	0.81

3.4. Test-Retest Reliability

Test–retest reliability was calculated for the EBQ-18 total and the three subscales while using a sample of 100 university participants who completed the EBQ-18 a second time after an interval of two weeks. An intraclass correlations (ICC) ≥ 0.70 indicates acceptable reproducibility of a measure [22]. Results showed good test-retest reliability across the EBQ-18 and all three subscales with significant Pearson's r and ICC between Time 1 and Time 2 scores (EBQ-18 Total, $r = 0.83$, ICC = 0.91, p's < 0.001; negative beliefs scale, $r = 0.74$, ICC = 0.85, p's < 0.001; EBQ-18 Positive Beliefs scale, $r = 0.82$, ICC = 0.90, p's < 0.001; Permissive Beliefs scale, $r = 0.77$, ICC = 0.87, p's < 0.001).

3.5. Construct Validity

Convergent validity between EBQ-18 scores and the included measures of specific eating disorder symptoms and related psychopathology was assessed by examining the correlations between the included measures. Correlations between the included measures with the full scale (EBQ Total), Negative Beliefs, and Positive Beliefs scales were all significantly and positively correlated. A number of correlations between the EBQ-18 Permissive Beliefs scale and other measures were not significant, see Table 4. The number of participants included in these correlations differs depending on the total number of the participants that had completed the relevant comparison measures.

Table 4. Correlations between EBQ-18 Scores and other symptom and cognitive measures.

Scale	EBQ-18 Total Score	Negative Beliefs Scale	Positive Beliefs Scale	Permissive Beliefs Scale
DASS-21 Depression (n = 645)	0.24 **	0.22 **	0.24 **	0.14 **
DASS-21 Anxiety (n = 645)	0.16 **	0.15 **	0.12 **	0.15 **
DASS-21 Stress (n = 645)	0.27 **	0.26 **	0.25 **	0.14 **
EDE-Q-Objective Binge Episodes (OBE) (n = 650)	0.48 **	0.45 **	0.50 **	0.25 **
EDE-Q Global Score (n = 650)	0.30 **	0.33 **	0.42 **	−0.03
EDE-Q Restraint (n = 650)	0.12 **	0.17 **	0.23 **	−0.14 **
EDE-Q Eating Concern (n = 650)	0.36 **	0.36 **	0.47 **	0.05
EDE-Q Shape Concern (n = 650)	0.33 **	0.35 **	0.41 **	0.02
EDE-Q Weight Concern (n = 650)	0.29 **	0.32 **	0.41 **	−0.05
DEBQ Emotional Eating (n = 201)	0.62 **	0.62 **	0.52 **	0.34 **
DEBQ External Eating (n = 201)	0.39 **	0.31 **	0.43 **	0.21 **
EDTQ–Negative Thoughts (n = 201)	0.42 **	0.34 **	0.55 **	0.14 *
EDTQ–Positive Thoughts (n = 201)	0.64 **	0.62 **	0.52 **	0.36 **
EDTQ–Permissive Thoughts (n = 201)	0.60 **	0.53 **	0.43 **	0.51 **

** = $p < 0.01$ (two-tailed), * = $p < 0.05$ (two-tailed), EBQ-18 = Eating Beliefs Questionnaire 18-item version, DASS-21 = Depression Anxiety Stress Scales 21-item version, EDE-Q = Eating Disorders Examination Questionnaire, DEBQ = Dutch Eating Behaviours Questionnaire, EDTQ = Eating Disorders Thoughts Questionnaire.

3.6. Group Differences

Table 5 summarises the mean total scores and subscale scores for the different samples and for subgroups of the participants that are based on self-reported binge eating status, as well as based on formal eating disorder diagnosis as recorded by the participants' treating clinician.

Table 5. EBQ-18 Subscale means and SDs for different sample groups.

Sample	Total EBQ-18 Score Mean (SD)	Negative Beliefs Mean (SD)	Positive Beliefs Mean (SD)	Permissive Beliefs Mean (SD)
University Sample (n = 308)	41.50 (11.80)	14.57 (5.27)	12.73 (4.42)	14.20 (4.92)
Community Sample (n = 190)	42.21 (13.14)	14.71 (6.07)	13.20 (5.42)	14.29 (5.38)
Hospital-based Obesity Treatment-seeking Sample (n = 29)	42.76 (17.15)	14.76 (6.13)	14.83 (6.31)	13.17 (5.29)
Hospital-based Outpatient Eating Disorder Treatment-seeking Sample (n = 19)	42.05 (15.97)	14.79 (6.33)	16.05 (6.93)	11.21 (4.45)
Hospital-based Outpatient Binge Eating Group Treatment-seeking Sample (n = 31)	63.06 (12.15)	22.65 (4.88)	20.74 (5.33)	19.67 (4.64)
Private Eating Disorder Treatment-seeking Sample (n = 111)	42.52 (18.59)	16.26 (7.65)	14.90 (7.68)	11.36 (5.17)
Binge Eating Subgroups:				
Non-BE (n = 343)	35.90 (11.29)	12.57 (4.86)	10.85 (3.89)	12.48 (5.21)
BE (n = 190)	53.89 (12.89)	19.32 (6.04)	18.62 (5.74)	15.96 (4.93)
Eating Disorder Subgroups:				
AN-R (n = 24)	26.86 (9.57)	9.17 (3.85)	9.42 (4.18)	8.29 (3.26)
AN-BP (n = 10)	44.20 (18.70)	17.30 (7.21)	15.60 (8.59)	11.30 (5.54)
BN (n = 35)	62.29 (11.43)	23.43 (5.00)	21.17 (5.33)	17.69 (5.17)
BED (n = 19)	64.42 (10.39)	22.47 (4.60)	23.37 (4.54)	18.58 (4.49)
OSFED AN (n = 12)	35.25 (11.04)	13.50 (4.62)	11.50 (4.83)	10.25 (3.67)
OSFED BN (n = 4)	54.50 (9.18)	18.75 (3.77)	21.00 (3.56)	14.75 (4.19)
OSFED BED (n = 4)	50.25 (15.06)	21.25 (7.41)	15.50 (4.36)	13.50 (4.65)

EBQ-18 = Eating Beliefs Questionnaire 18-item version, SD = standard deviation, Non-BE = participants who self-reported 0 incidents of objective binge episodes in 28 days prior to completing the test battery; BE = participants who self-reported engaging in 4 or more incidents of objective binge eating episodes in the 28 days prior to completing the test battery, AN-R = anorexia nervosa restrictive type, AN-BP = anorexia nervosa binge/purge type, BN = bulimia nervosa, BED = binge eating disorder, OSFED = other specified feeding or eating disorder.

Results from one-way ANOVAs identified that participants in the BE subgroup scored significantly higher on the EBQ-18 and its subscales than those in the Non-BE subgroup, with moderate-to-large effect sizes (η_p^2); EBQ-18 total score: $F(1,532) = 280.08$, $p < 0.01$, $\eta_p^2 = 0.35$; Negative Beliefs score: $F(1,532) = 197.18$, $p < 0.01$, $\eta_p^2 = 0.27$; Positive Beliefs score: $F(1,532) = 343.51$, $p < 0.01$, $\eta_p^2 = 0.39$; Permissive Beliefs score: $F(1,532) = 56.51$, $p < 0.01$, $\eta_p^2 = 0.10$.

In addition, participants with a diagnosis of BN scored significantly higher on the EBQ-18 subscales than participants with a diagnosis of AN-R with large effect sizes (EBQ-18 total score: $F(1,58) = 155.46$, $p < 0.01$, $\eta_p^2 = 0.73$; Negative Beliefs score: $F(1,58) = 138.71$, $p < 0.01$, $\eta_p^2 = 0.71$; Positive Beliefs score: $F(1,58) = 81.92$, $p < 0.01$, $\eta_p^2 = 0.59$; Permissive Beliefs score: $F(1,58) = 62.14$, $p < 0.01$, $\eta_p^2 = 0.52$) and significantly higher than those with a diagnosis of AN-BP with moderate-to-large effect sizes (EBQ-18 total score: $F(1,44) = 14.42$, $p < 0.01$, $\eta_p^2 = 0.25$; Negative Beliefs score: $F(1,44) = 9.54$, $p < 0.01$, $\eta_p^2 = 0.18$; Positive Beliefs score: $F(1,44) = 6.36$ $p < 0.05$, $\eta_p^2 = 0.13$; Permissive Beliefs score: $F(1,44) = 11.52$, $p < 0.01$, $\eta_p^2 = 0.21$).

Participants with a diagnosis of BED also scored significantly higher on the EBQ-18 subscales than the participants with a diagnosis of AN-R, with large effect sizes (EBQ-18 total score: $F(1,42) = 151.29$, $p < 0.01$, $\eta_p^2 = 0.79$; Negative Beliefs score: $F(1,42) = 106.63$, $p < 0.01$, $\eta_p^2 = 0.72$; Positive Beliefs score: $F(1,42) = 109.60$, $p < 0.01$, $\eta_p^2 = 0.73$; Permissive Beliefs score: $F(1,42) = 75.73$, $p < 0.01$, $\eta_p^2 = 0.65$), and significantly higher than those with a diagnosis of AN-BP, with moderate-to-large effect sizes (EBQ-18 total score: $F(1,28) = 14.21$, $p < 0.01$, $\eta_p^2 = 0.35$; Negative Beliefs score: $F(1,28) = 5.58$, $p < 0.05$, $\eta_p^2 = 0.17$; Positive Beliefs score: $F(1,28) = 10.32$, $p < 0.01$, $\eta_p^2 = 0.28$; Permissive Beliefs score: $F(1,28) = 14.67$, $p < 0.01$, $\eta_p^2 = 0.35$).

Participants with AN-BP were found to score significantly higher than those with AN-R for the EBQ total score, $F(1,33) = 12.91$, $p < 0.01$, $\eta_p^2 = 0.29$, the Negative Beliefs scale, $F(1,33) = 18.46$, $p < 0.01$, $\eta_p^2 = 0.37$, and the Positive Beliefs scale, $F(1,33) = 8.10$, $p < 0.01$, $\eta_p^2 = 0.20$, but no significant difference was identified between AN-BP and AN-R on the Permissive Belief scale scores, $p > 0.05$. No significant differences found between BN and BED sample on EBQ-18 total or subscale scores, all p's > 0.05.

3.7. Treatment Sensitivity

A total of thirty-eight participants that were seeking treatment for an eating disorder completed the measures both before and after psychological treatment. Ten of these participants had completed an 8 to 10-week hospital-based outpatient binge eating group therapy treatment program ($n = 5$ with a diagnosis of BN and $n = 5$ with a diagnosis of BED). A further twenty-eight of these participants had completed individual psychological treatment at private specialist eating disorder treatment centres ($n = 5$ with a diagnosis of AN-R, $n = 5$ with a diagnosis of AN-BP, $n = 3$ with a diagnosis of BN, $n = 4$ with a diagnosis of BED, $n = 6$ with a diagnosis of OSFED AN, $n = 1$ with a diagnosis of OSFED BN, $n = 3$ with a diagnosis of OSFED BED, and $n = 1$ with a diagnosis of UFED). Treatments, both group and individual, were based on a cognitive-behavioural approach and they were delivered by trained and experienced clinicians. Table 6 summarises the group means, SD, and Cohen's d effect sizes at pre- and post-treatment for the EBQ-18 total score and subscales across the whole treatment sample and the subgroup that includes only those participants with diagnosed eating disorders with binge eating as a core feature (BE).

Results from repeated measures ANOVAs identified that the pre-treatment EBQ-18 scores were significantly higher than post-treatment scores across the total sample of treatment completers ($n = 38$): EBQ-18 total score: $F(1,37) = 17.48$, $p < 0.01$, $\eta_p^2 = 0.32$; Negative Beliefs score: $F(1,37) = 15.67$, $p < 0.01$, $\eta_p^2 = 0.30$, Positive Beliefs score: $F(1,37) = 6.86$, $p < 0.05$, $\eta_p^2 = 0.16$,Permissive Beliefs score: $F(1,37) = 10.42$, $p < 0.01$, $\eta_p^2 = 0.22$.

We also examined the difference in pre and post-treatment EBQ-18 scores for just those participants who were diagnosed with BED ($n = 9$) or BN ($n = 8$). Results from repeated measures ANOVAs identified that, for the BN/BED subgroup ($n = 17$), pre-treatment EBQ-18 scores were significantly higher than post-treatment scores, with large effect sizes: EBQ-18 total score: $F(1,16) = 19.60$, $p < 0.01$,

$\eta_p^2 = 0.55$; Negative Beliefs score: $F(1,16) = 18.82$, $p < 0.01$, $\eta_p^2 = 0.54$, Positive Beliefs score: $F(1,16) = 5.44$, $p < 0.05$, $\eta_p^2 = 0.25$, Permissive Beliefs score: $F(1,16) = 10.86$, $p < 0.01$, $\eta_p^2 = 0.40$.

Table 6. Means, SDs and Cohen's d effect sizes for EBQ-18 scores at pre and post treatment.

Sample	EBQ-18 Total Score Mean (SD)			Negative Beliefs Mean (SD)			Positive Beliefs Mean (SD)			Permissive Beliefs Mean (SD)		
	Pre	Post	*d*	Pre	Post	*d*	Pre	Post	*d*	Pre	Post	*d*
All Treatment (n = 38)	49.24 (18.73)	40.11 (14.76)	0.54	18.21 (7.57)	14.18 (6.27)	0.58	17.50 (7.59)	14.82 (6.46)	0.38	13.53 (5.89)	11.16 (4.43)	0.45
BN/BED (n = 17)	63.47 (10.14)	51.30 (9.48)	1.24	22.88 (5.11)	17.94 (5.30)	0.95	22.41 (5.29)	19.53 (4.17)	0.60	18.17 (4.73)	13.94 (3.47)	1.02

EBQ-18 = Eating Beliefs Questionnaire 18-item version, SD = standard deviation, BN/BED = Combined bulimia nervosa and binge eating disorder subgroup sample, d = Cohen's d effect size.

In order to assess whether the differences between the pre-treatment scores and post-treatment scores were of clinical significance, we applied the formula from Jacobson and Truax [34] to determine the EBQ-18 score for clinically significant change for each group. We used mean normative data for the EBQ-18 from a non-clinical sample of 883 participants that found a mean of 38.25 and standard deviation of 12.87 for the EBQ-18 total score [20]. Therefore, the score of clinically significant change for both the whole treatment sample, c(Trmt), and the BN/BED subgroup, c(BN/BED), were as follows:

$$\mathrm{c(Trmt)} = \frac{\mathrm{S0M1 + S1M0}}{\mathrm{S0 + S1}} = \frac{12.87(49.24) + 18.73(38.25)}{12.87 + 18.73} = \frac{633.72 + 716.42}{31.6} = 42.73 \quad (1)$$

$$\mathrm{c(BN/BED)} = \frac{\mathrm{S0M1 + S1M0}}{S0 + S1} = \frac{12.87(63.47) + 10.14(38.25)}{12.87 + 10.14} = \frac{816.86 + 387.86}{23.01} = 52.36 \quad (2)$$

Applying the Jacobson and Truax's (1991) [34] formula, participants who scored less than 42.73 at post-treatment (and less than 52.36 at post-treatment for those in the BN/BED subgroup) would likely have experienced a clinically significant effect of treatment. Post-treatment means are lower than the identified scores of clinically significant change for the EBQ-18 total score, indicating that meaningful change has occurred as a result of treatment. Of the whole treatment sample, 55.26% scored less than 42.73 at post-treatment, and of the BN/BED subgroup, 64.7% scored less than 52.36 on the EBQ-18 at post-treatment.

3.8. Receiver Operating Characteristic (ROC) Curve Analyses

ROC curve analyses were used to identify the optimal clinical cut-off scores for the EBQ-18 and to assess the associated test performance indicators (sensitivity, specificity, and positive and negative predictive values). Here, we report the associated criterion for the Youden-Index, which provides a cut-off score for which both sensitivity and specificity is maximal [35]. For the purposes of these analyses, a non-binge eating control sample of 61 participants from the community sample who self-reported to engage in 0 episodes of objective binge eating in the past 28 days, and a clinical BN/BED sample of 54 participants, including 35 participants with a clinician confirmed diagnosis of BN and 19 participants with a clinician confirmed diagnosis of BED, were utilised.

Table 7 summarises the cut-off criteria and associated test performance indicators for the EBQ-18 and its subscales for the comparison sample of the combined BN and BED sample versus controls. The cut-off scores that were identified for all of the subscales have significant area under the curve (AUC) values, indicating that the identified cut-off scores perform better than chance in discriminating between clinical cases (those with BN or BED) and non-clinical cases.

Table 7. Results from ROC Curve Analyses for EBQ Total and subscale scores.

Sample	EBQ-18 Scale	Cut-Off Score	Sensitivity (95% CI)	Specificity (95% CI)	PPV (95% CI)	NPV (95% CI)	AUC (95% CI)
BN/BED (n = 54) vs. Control (n = 61)	EBQ-18 Total Score	>45	92.59 (82.1–97.9)	93.44 (84.1–98.2)	92.6 (82.9–97.0)	93.4 (84.7–97.3)	0.98 ** (0.93–0.99)
	Negative Beliefs Scale	>16	88.89 (77.4–95.8)	88.52 (77.8–95.3)	87.3 (77.2–93.3)	90.0 (80.8–95.1)	0.95 ** (0.89–0.98)
	Positive Beliefs Scale	>14	90.74 (79.7–96.9)	93.44 (84.1–98.2)	92.5 (82.6–96.9)	91.9 (83.1–96.3)	0.97 ** (0.92–0.99)
	Permissive Beliefs Scale	>13	81.48 (68.6–90.7)	70.49 (57.4–81.5)	71.0 (61.9–78.6)	81.1 (70.6–88.5)	0.83 ** (0.75–0.89)

EBQ-18 = Eating Beliefs Questionnaire 18-item version, CI = Confidence Intervals, PPV = Positive predictive value, NPV = Negative predictive value, AUC = Area under the curve, BN/BED = Combined bulimia nervosa and binge eating disorder subgroup sample, ** = $p < 0.001$.

Table 8 summarises the cut-off criteria and associated test performance indicators for the EBQ-18 total score across four different comparison samples (1) BN subgroup versus controls; (2) BED subgroup versus controls; (3) AN-BP versus controls; (4) AN-R versus controls. The cut-off scores identified for BN, BED and AN-R have significant AUC values, indicating that the identified cut-off scores perform better than chance in discriminating between clinical cases and non-clinical cases. The AUC value associated with the identified cut-off score for discriminating those with AN-BP from non-clinical cases was not significant, and therefore this cut-off score may not be a reliable indicator for this group.

Table 8. Results from receiver operating characteristics (ROC) Curve Analyses for EBQ-18 total score across different diagnostic groups.

Sample	Cut-off Score	Sensitivity (95% CI)	Specificity (95% CI)	PPV (95% CI)	NPV (95% CI)	AUC (95% CI)
BN (n =35) vs. Control (n = 61)	>50	85.71 (69.4–95.2)	96.72 (88.7–99.6)	93.7 (79.2–98.2)	92.2 (84.0–96.4)	0.97 ** (0.92–0.99)
BED (n =19) vs. Control (n = 61)	>46	100.00 (82.4–100.0)	95.08 (86.3–99.0)	86.4 (67.8–95.0)	100.00	0.99 ** (0.93–1.00)
AN-BP (n = 10) vs. Control (n = 61)	>46	40.00 (12.2–73.8)	95.08 (86.3–99.0)	57.1 (25.9–83.6)	90.6 (85.3–94.1)	0.69 (0.57–0.79)
AN-R (n = 24) vs. Control (n = 61)	≤23	58.33 (36.6–77.9)	78.69 (66.3–88.1)	51.9 (37.4–66.0)	82.8 (74.6–88.7)	0.68 ** (0.57–0.78)

EBQ-18 = Eating Beliefs Questionnaire 18-item version, CI = Confidence Intervals, PPV = Positive predictive value, NPV = Negative predictive value, AUC = Area under the curve, BN = bulimia nervosa, BED = binge eating disorder, AN-BP = anorexia nervosa binge/purge type, AN-R = anorexia nervosa restrictive type, ** = $p < 0.001$.

4. Discussion

This study sought to provide a thorough examination of the validity, reliability, and clinical utility of the EBQ-18 while using both a clinical eating disorder treatment-seeking sample and a non-clinical sample. Overall, the results of this study indicate that the EBQ-18 is a valid, reliable, and clinically useful measure for use in the general population as well as with individuals seeking treatment for binge eating. These findings build upon the previous research that found an earlier, two subscale version of the EBQ to be valid and reliable with clinical and non-clinical samples [15,16,21]. These findings are also consistent with the initial examination of the factor structure, internal consistency, and content validity of the current EBQ-18 with a non-clinical sample [20]. The findings of the present study extend existing research by further assessing the test-retest reliability, comparisons of diagnostic groups, responsiveness to treatment, clinical significance, and identifying clinically useful cut-off scores for the EBQ-18. The results of this study were in keeping with the hypotheses.

4.1. Factor Structure

As predicted, the confirmatory factor analysis provided support for the three-factor solution that was identified in the initial exploratory factor analysis [20]: negative beliefs, positive beliefs, and permissive beliefs about eating. The three-factor solution demonstrated good-fit with the non-clinical sample that provided a homogenous sample of adequate size for CFA. When the three-factor solution was fitted to the self-report binge eating sample, we found adequate fit to the data. Although, we would wish for good fit across all of the fit indices, it is important to note that the BE sample was not homogeneous (participants within this sample were recruited across university, community, and treatment-seeking samples) and the sample (n = 190) was relatively small with regard to CFA, which finds that fit statistics are more accurate when the sample is larger than n = 250 [33]. The CFA with the BE sample also found that one item from the permissive scale did not load as well as other items, "It won't make a difference if I eat more", with a standardised regression weight of less than 0.40 and communality of less than 0.20. This low loading item could be impacting the psychometric properties of the Permissive Beliefs scale as a whole. Conceptually, this item is different from other the permissive items that focus more on the theme that binge eating is a pleasant experience that one deserves, and instead this item assesses a sense of allowing oneself to continue a binge once eating has commenced. Despite having the lowest factor loading, this item was retained for its clinical and theoretical value, as well as because this item has demonstrated improved performances in other larger studies assessing the factor structure of the EBQ. Differences across the samples, including the homogeneity of the present sample, might account for this minor difference.

4.2. Psychometric Properties

In keeping with our hypotheses and with previous findings, the EBQ-18 and its subscales demonstrated good internal consistency across different sample groups, with all the Cronbach's alphas over 0.70, thereby meeting the Terwee criteria for adequacy for internal consistency [22]. The EBQ-18 also demonstrated adequacy for agreement, showing good test-retest reliability over two weeks with a sample of 100 university students with strong, significant correlations between Time 1 and Time 2 for the EBQ-18 and its three subscales.

Adequate content validity was also demonstrated with the EBQ-18 Total, Negative Beliefs and Positive Belief subscale scores positively and significantly correlated with the measures of binge eating frequency and other eating disorder symptoms (EDE-Q), other eating disorder measures (DEBQ; EDTQ), and a measure of depression, anxiety, and stress (DASS-21). The Permissive Beliefs scale did not correlate with EDE-Q Global Score, Eating Concerns, Shape Concerns, and Weight Concerns subscales. However, the Permissive Beliefs scale did negatively correlate with the EDE-Q Restraint subscale. As the EDE-Q Restraint subscale measures the individual's recent attempts at restrictive eating practices, such as dieting and fasting, it is unsurprising to find that it is negatively correlated with the Permissive Beliefs scale, which measures beliefs about allowing for oneself to engage in binge eating. Furthermore, this interesting finding differs from the correlations between the EBQ-18 Permissive Beliefs scale and the EDE-Q subscale in a large non-clinical sample in Burton & Abbott (2018) [20], who found small, significant correlations between the EDE-Q Global Score, Eating Concerns, Shape Concerns, and Weight Concerns subscales and the Permissive Beliefs scale, and a non-significant negative correlation between the Restraint subscale and the Permissive Beliefs scale. This difference in the results can be accounted for by the difference in the samples used in the two different studies with the present study, including a clinical, eating disordered sample and overall a higher proportion of the whole sample self-reporting to be engaging in regular binge eating (28% in the present study compared to 19% in Burton & Abbott, 2018) [20]. It is important to note that, while the correlations between the EBQ-18 and the included measures were significant and in the expected direction, they are relatively small correlations.

4.3. Clinical Utility

As predicted, the EBQ-18 scores were found to differ significantly depending on binge eating status, such that those individuals engaging in regular binge eating scored significantly higher on the EBQ-18 than those not engaging in binge eating, and that those individuals diagnosed with BN, BED, or AN-BP scored significantly higher on the EBQ-18 than those individuals with AN-R. There was no significant difference in EBQ-18 scores between those with a diagnosis of BN and those with BED, further supporting the role of metacognitive beliefs in theoretical models of BN, BED, and transdiagnostic models [17,20].

Furthermore, adequacy for responsiveness to treatment was demonstrated with a significant reduction in EBQ-18 scores following a psychological intervention for eating disorders. The effect of treatment on EBQ-18 scores was especially strong (large Cohen's d) for those with BN or BED. The treatment effect was also found to indicate clinically significant, or meaningful, change with post-treatment means lower than the cut-off for clinically significant change calculated using the formula from Jacobson and Truax [34]. Using ROC Curve Analysis, optimal cut-off scores for the EBQ-18 and its subscales were identified. With significant AUC values, the cut-off scores that were identified can reliably be used to discriminate clinical cases, those with BED and BN, from non-clinical cases [36,37]. That is, respondents scoring higher than 45 on the EBQ-18 total score can be considered to be experiencing a clinically significant level of eating disorder related beliefs about eating. However, it is important to note that the results of the ROC curve analysis did not provide support for the use of the identified cut-off score to be used to discriminate AN-BP cases from non-clinical cases. Interestingly, very low scores on the EBQ-18 can be informative too, with results indicating that a score of 23 or less could discriminate the cases of restrictive type AN from non-clinical cases. The EBQ-18 could therefore provide an informative addition to test batteries assessing for the presence or nature of disordered eating beliefs and behaviours. One potential application of this would be for the EBQ-18 to be administered to candidates for bariatric surgery to assess for the presence of eating disorder related cognitions. Furthermore, the EBQ-18 can be used in research examining the predictors of successful outcomes for obesity treatments, such as bariatric surgery or cognitive and behavioural interventions.

4.4. Limitations and Future Direction

One limitation of this study is that the evaluation of responsiveness to treatment used a mixed sample, including both a group treatment for binge eating and individual treatment for a range of eating disorder presentations from a number of different specialised private and public eating disorder treatment clinics. Furthermore, the treatment used did not explicitly address or challenge the specific unhelpful beliefs about eating that are measured by the EBQ-18. Future research should compare change in eating beliefs over course of treatment between treatment-as-usual (CBT) and a metacognitive therapy approach, such as that outlined in Cooper, Todd, and Wells [38], which explicitly targets the underlying beliefs about eating thought to maintain binge eating. A further potential limitation is the relatively small size of the sample for the treatment sensitivity analyses ($n = 38$), this relatively small n was due to participant attrition following initial assessment and also due to participants not completing the follow-up surveys after completing treatment. However, this clinical sample size is comparable to the clinical sample sizes that were used in eating disorder research [15], and we did not find that this sample size limited our results, obtaining significant findings with regard to the EBQ-18's sensitivity to treatment.

Furthermore, while the EBQ-18 and subscales demonstrated good test-retest reliability over a two-week period, future research should also assess the medium and longer-term temporal stability of the EBQ-18. Future studies could also assess the use of the EBQ-18 in other relevant sample groups that were not included in this study, such as in individuals who are overeating without a sense of loss of control and those who are engaging in subjective binge eating episodes (sense of loss of control over eating, but without objective overeating).

5. Conclusions

Overall, this paper provides new information on the factor structure, validity, reliability, and clinical utility of the EBQ-18 across clinical and non-clinical samples. Notably, the results of this paper add to the existing literature on the relevance of the three types of eating beliefs that were measured by this questionnaire: negative, positive and permissive beliefs about eating. Endorsement of these beliefs have been found to be significantly higher in individuals engaging in binge eating than those who do not report binge eating, as well as endorsement of these beliefs being found to be significantly higher in those individuals experiencing BN and BED as compared to other eating disorder and control groups. We have also found that these beliefs reduce significantly as a result of psychological treatment.

Given the increasing prevalence and seriousness of the associated co-morbid conditions of binge eating, including obesity, other physical and mental health conditions, and poorer quality of life, it is important that clinicians and researchers have access to good quality, informative and easy-to-administer assessment tools that can help to inform clinical formulation and to monitor change over the course of treatment. The EBQ-18 is a valid, reliable, and clinically useful brief self-report assessment of the presence of three types of specific unhelpful beliefs (negative, positive, and permissive beliefs about eating), which are considered to maintain binge eating in individuals with disordered eating. The EBQ-18 demonstrated evidence of good psychometric properties within a clinical treatment-seeking sample, a sample self-reporting to be engaging in regular binge eating, and a non-clinical sample.

Supplementary Materials: The following are available online at http://www.mdpi.com/2072-6643/10/9/1306/s1, S1: EBQ-18—Eating Beliefs Questionnaire.

Author Contributions: A.L.B. prepared the manuscript. M.J.A., A.L.B. and S.T. were involved in the conception and design of the study. A.L.B. collected the non-clinical data. D.M., P.H. and B.D. substantially contributed to the collection of clinical data for this project. C.T., C.B., J.R., J.S., M.G. and S.T. contributed to the collection of clinical data for this project. A.L.B. and M.J.A. analysed and interpreted the data. M.J.A. substantially contributed to the revision of the manuscript. All authors read and approved the final manuscript.

Acknowledgments: The authors would like to acknowledge the participants for their time in completing the questionnaires, the staff at the various clinical data collection sites for their assistance in collecting the questionnaire responses from participants, and Scott Fatt for his assistance in cleaning the clinical data file.

Conflicts of Interest: Author P.H. receives royalties from Hogrefe and Huber, McGraw-Hill, PLOS Medicine and BioMedCentral publishers. Author S.T. has received honoraria, travel grants, research grant funding and consultancy fees from Shire, is a consultant to Weight Watchers, has also received honoraria from Hogrefe and Huber, McGraw-Hill and Taylor and Francis for publication of book chapters. All other authors declare that they have no conflicts of interest.

References

1. American Psychiatric Association. *Diagnostic and Statistical Manual of Mental Disorders (DSM-5)*; American Psychiatric Publishing: Washington, DC, USA, 2013.
2. Hay, P.; Mitchison, D.; Lopez Collado, A.E.; González-Chica, D.A.; Stocks, N.; Touyz, S. Burden and health-related quality of life of eating disorders, including Avoidant/Restrictive Food Intake Disorder (ARFID), in the Australian population. *J. Eat. Disord.* **2017**, *5*. [CrossRef] [PubMed]
3. Hay, P.; Mond, J.; Buttner, P.; Darby, A. Eating disorder behaviors are increasing: Findings from two sequential community surveys in South Australia. *PLoS ONE* **2008**, *3*, e1541. [CrossRef] [PubMed]
4. Mitchison, D.; Touyz, S.; González-Chica, D.A.; Stocks, N.; Hay, P. How abnormal is binge eating? 18-Year time trends in population prevalence and burden. *Acta Psychiatry Scand.* **2017**, *138*. [CrossRef] [PubMed]
5. Da Luz, F.; Sainsbury, A.; Mannan, H.; Touyz, S.; Mitchison, D.; Hay, P. Prevalence of obesity and comorbid eating disorder behaviors in South Australia from 1995 to 2015. *Int. J. Obes.* **2017**, *41*, 1148–1153. [CrossRef] [PubMed]
6. Mitchell, J.E. Medical comorbidity and medical complications associated with binge-eating disorder. *Int. J. Eat. Disord.* **2016**, *49*, 319–323. [CrossRef] [PubMed]

7. Wilfley, D.E.; Friedman, M.A.; Dounchis, J.Z.; Stein, R.I.; Welch, R.R.; Ball, S.A. Comorbid psychopathology in binge eating disorder: Relation to eating disorder severity at baseline and following treatment. *J. Consult. Clin. Psychol.* **2000**, *68*, 641–649. [CrossRef] [PubMed]
8. Olguin, P.; Fuentes, M.; Gabler, G.; Guerdjikova, A.I.; Keck, P.E., Jr.; McElroy, S.L. Medical comorbidity of binge eating disorder. *Eat. Weight Disord.* **2017**, *22*, 13–26. [CrossRef] [PubMed]
9. Kessler, R.C.; Berglund, P.A.; Chiua, W.T.; Deitz, A.C.; Hudson, J.I.; Shahly, V.; Aguilar-Gaxiola, S.; Alonsof, J.; Angermeyer, M.C.; Benjet, C.; et al. The prevalence and correlates of binge eating disorder in the World Health Organization World Mental Health Surveys. *Biol. Psychiatry* **2013**, *73*, 904–914. [CrossRef] [PubMed]
10. Ulfvebrand, S.; Birgegård, A.; Norring, C.; Högdahl, L.; von Hausswolff-Juhlin, Y. Psychiatric comorbidity in women and men with eating disorders results from a large clinical database. *Psychiatry Res.* **2015**, *230*, 294–299. [CrossRef] [PubMed]
11. Beck, N.N.; Mehlsen, M.; Støving, R.K. Psychological characteristics and associations with weight outcomes two years after gastric bypass surgery: Postoperative eating disorder symptoms are associated with weight loss outcomes. *Eat. Behav.* **2012**, *13*, 394–397. [CrossRef] [PubMed]
12. Livhits, M.; Mercado, C.; Yermilov, I.; Parikh, J.A.; Dutson, E.; Mehran, A.; Ko Clifford, Y.; Gibbons, M.M. Behavioral factors associated with successful weight loss after gastric bypass. *Am. Surg.* **2010**, *76*, 1139–1142. [PubMed]
13. Mauro, M.; Taylor, V.; Wharton, S.; Sharma, A.M. Barriers to Obesity Treatment. *Eur. J. Internal Med.* **2008**, *19*, 173–180. [CrossRef] [PubMed]
14. Burton, A.L.; Abbott, M.J. Conceptualising Binge Eating: A Review of the Theoretical and Empirical Literature. *Behav. Chang.* **2017**, *34*, 168–198. [CrossRef]
15. Burton, A.L.; Hay, P.; Kleitman, S.; Smith, E.; Raman, J.; Swinbourne, J.; Touyz, S.W.; Abbott, M.J. Confirmatory factor analysis and examination of the psychometric properties of the eating beliefs questionnaire. *BMC Psychiatry* **2017**, *17*. [CrossRef] [PubMed]
16. Groves, S.J. Macquarie University, Baillie, A.J.; Abbott, M.J. The development and validation of the Eating Beliefs Questionnaire: Positive and negative beliefs about binge-eating. 2018; unpublished work.
17. Cooper, M.J.; Wells, A.; Todd, G. A cognitive model of bulimia nervosa. *Br. J. Clin. Psychol.* **2004**, *43*, 1–16. [CrossRef] [PubMed]
18. Wells, A. *Metacognitive Therapy for Anxiety and Depression*; Guilford press: New York, NY, USA, 2011.
19. Wells, A. *Emotional Disorders and Metacognition: Innovative Cognitive Therapy*; John Wiley & Sons: Hoboken, NJ, USA, 2002.
20. Burton, A.L. (University of Sydney); Abbott, M.J. The revised short-form of the Eating Beliefs Questionnaire: Measuring Positive, Negative and Permissive Beliefs about Binge Eating. Unpublished work, 2018.
21. Burton, A.L.; Smith, E.; Abbott, M.J. Assessing the Clinical Utility of the Eating Beliefs Questionnaire: Results from Receiver Operating Characteristic Curve Analysis with a Clinical Sample. *Eur. J. Psychol. Assess.* in press.
22. Terwee, C.B.; Bot, S.D.M.; de Boer, M.R.; van der Windt, D.A.W.M.; Knol, D.L.; Dekker, J.; Bouter, L.M.; de Vet, H.C.W. Quality criteria were proposed for measurement properties of health status questionnaires. *J. Clin. Epidemiol.* **2007**, *60*, 34–42. [CrossRef] [PubMed]
23. Mokkink, L.B.; Terwee, C.B.; Patrick, D.L.; Alonso, J.; Stratford, P.W.; Knol, D.L.; Bouter, L.M.; de Vet, H.C.W. The COSMIN checklist for assessing the methodological quality of studies on measurement properties of health status measurement instruments: An international Delphi study. *Qual. Life Res.* **2010**, *19*, 539–549. [CrossRef] [PubMed]
24. Fairburn, C.G.; Beglin, S.J. Assessment of eating disorders: Interview or self-report questionnaire? *J. Eat. Disord.* **1994**, *16*, 363–370.
25. Fairburn, C.G.; Wilson, G.T.; Schleimer, K. *Binge Eating: Nature, Assessment, and Treatment*; Guilford Press: New York, NY, USA, 1993.
26. Burton, A.L.; Abbott, M.J.; Psych, M.C.; BPsych, M.M.; Touyz, S. Psychometric evaluation of self-report measures of binge eating symptoms and related psychopathology: A systematic review of the literature. *J. Eat. Disord.* **2016**, *49*, 123–140. [CrossRef] [PubMed]
27. Lovibond, P.F.; Lovibond, S.H. The structure of negative emotional states: Comparison of the Depression Anxiety Stress Scales (DASS) with the Beck Depression and Anxiety Inventories. *Behav. Res. Ther.* **1995**, *33*, 335–343. [CrossRef]

28. Antony, M.M.; Bieling, P.J.; Cox, B.J.; Enns, M.W.; Swinson, R.P. Psychometric properties of the 42-item and 21-item versions of the Depression Anxiety Stress Scales in clinical groups and a community sample. *Psychol. Assess.* **1998**, *10*, 176–181. [CrossRef]
29. Van Strien, T.; Frijters, J.E.R.; Bergers, G.P.A.; Defares, P.B. The Dutch Eating Behavior Questionnaire (DEBQ) for assessment of restrained, emotional, and external eating behavior. *Int. J. Eat. Disord.* **1986**, *5*, 295–315. [CrossRef]
30. Cooper, M.J.; Todd, G.; Woolrich, R.; Somerville, K.; Wells, A. Assessing eating disorder thoughts and behaviors: The development and preliminary evaluation of two questionnaires. *Cognit. Ther. Res.* **2006**, *30*, 551–570. [CrossRef]
31. Arbuckle, J. *AMOS 22 User's Guide*; Small Waters Corporation: Chicago, IL, USA, 2013.
32. Kline, R. Methodology in the social sciences. In *Principles and Practice of Structural Equation Modeling*, 2nd ed.; Guilford Press: New York, NY, USA, 2005.
33. Hu, L.T.; Bentler, P.M. Cutoff criteria for fit indexes in covariance structure analysis: Conventional criteria versus new alternatives. *Struct. Equ. Model.* **1999**, *6*, 1–55. [CrossRef]
34. Jacobson, N.S.; Truax, P. Clinical significance: A statistical approach to defining meaningful change in psychotherapy research. *J. Consult. Clin. Psychol.* **1991**, *59*, 12–19. [CrossRef] [PubMed]
35. Fluss, R.; Faraggi, D.; Reiser, B. Estimation of the Youden Index and its associated cutoff point. *Biom. J.* **2005**, *47*, 458–472. [CrossRef] [PubMed]
36. Hsiao, J.K.; Bartko, J.J.; Potter, W.Z. Diagnosing diagnoses: Receiver operating characteristic methods and psychiatry. *Arch. Gen. Psychiatry* **1989**, *46*, 664–667. [CrossRef] [PubMed]
37. Hanley, J.A.; McNeil, B.J. The meaning and use of the area under a receiver operating characteristic (ROC) curve. *Radiology* **1982**, *143*, 29–36. [CrossRef] [PubMed]
38. Cooper, M.J.; Todd, G.; Wells, A. *Treating Bulimia Nervosa and Binge Eating: An Integrated Metacognitive and Cognitive Therapy Manual*; Routledge: London, UK, 2008.

nutrients

MDPI

Article

Eating Behaviour Predicts Weight Loss Six Months after Bariatric Surgery: A Longitudinal Study

Kavitha Subramaniam [1,2], Wah-Yun Low [3,*], Peng-Choong Lau [4], Kin-Fah Chin [4], Karuthan Chinna [5], Nik Ritza Kosai [6], Mustafa Mohammed Taher [6] and Reynu Rajan [6]

1. Medical Education, Research and Development Unit, Faculty of Medicine, University of Malaya, Kuala Lumpur 50603, Malaysia; eskei13@yahoo.co.uk
2. Department of Physical and Mathematical Science, Faculty of Science, Tunku Abdul Rahman University, Kampar, Perak 31900, Malaysia
3. Faculty of Medicine Dean's Office, University of Malaya, Kuala Lumpur 50603, Malaysia
4. Department of Surgery, Faculty of Medicine, University of Malaya, Kuala Lumpur 50603, Malaysia; laupc@ummc.edu.my (P.-C.L.); mdskfc@gmail.com (K.-F.C.)
5. Department of Social and Preventive Medicine, Faculty of Medicine, University of Malaya, Kuala Lumpur 50603, Malaysia; karuthan@gmail.com
6. Minimally Invasive, Upper Gastrointestinal and Bariatric Surgery unit, Department of surgery, Faculty of Medicine, Universiti Kebangsaan Malaysia Medical Centre (UKMMC), Universiti Kebangsaan Malaysia, Kuala Lumpur 56000, Malaysia; nikkosai@ppukm.ukm.edu.my (N.R.K.); mutafa@ppukm.ukm.edu.my (M.M.T.); dr.reynu@gmail.com (R.R.)

* Correspondence: lowwy@um.edu.my; Tel.: +600379675729 (ext. 39)

Received: 21 September 2018; Accepted: 15 October 2018; Published: 2 November 2018

Abstract: Bariatric surgery is currently the most durable weight loss solution for patients with morbid obesity. The extent of weight loss achieved, however, is subject to variation due to various factors, including patients' behaviour. In this study, we aimed to identify pre- and post-surgical predictors of weight loss following bariatric surgery. This prospective study included 57 participants who went through bariatric surgery (laparoscopic Roux-en-Y gastric bypass: $n = 30$; laparoscopic sleeve gastrectomy: $n = 23$; one anastomosis gastric bypass-mini gastric bypass: $n = 4$) in two tertiary referral hospitals. Consenting participants were assessed prior to surgery (T_0), and three months (T_1) and six months (T_2) after surgery. The assessment included interview and anthropometric measurements. The interview was done with the aid of instruments, including the Hospital Anxiety and Depression Scale (HADS) for anxiety and depression screening and the Dutch Eating Behaviour Questionnaire (DEBQ) for eating behaviour assessment. Baseline comorbidity status was obtained from medical records. A Generalised Estimating Equation (GEE) was developed to determine predictors of weight loss. Participants in the study were mostly women ($n = 37$, 65%) with a mean age of 39.4 (SD = 10.01) years. The mean excess BMI loss (EBMIL) and total weight loss (TWL) at the sixth month was 63.31% and 23.83%, respectively. Anxiety, depression, and external eating scores reduced over time. Advancing age, high BMI, and higher scores for emotional and external eating emerged as significant negative predictors for TWL%. It can be concluded that the patients experienced substantial weight loss after surgery. Continuous monitoring of psychological well-being and eating behaviour are essential for optimal weight loss.

Keywords: obesity; weight loss; bariatric surgery; eating behaviour; psychology

1. Introduction

The global prevalence of obesity has increased greatly over the past four decades [1], with a dramatic rise in the rates of morbid and severe obesity [2]. Currently, bariatric surgery is the most durable weight loss solution for patients with morbid obesity. It enables an average loss of up to

60–70% of excess weight, and long-term maintenance of the loss [3,4]. Despite the impressive average weight loss values, there is individual variation in the rate of weight loss; around 10–30% of the patients have suboptimal weight loss or weight-regain [5,6]. This has motivated research on predictors of successful weight loss, to identify behavioural traits that are important for better weight loss outcome and development of post-surgical interventions.

The existing studies have identified a myriad of pre- and post-surgical predictors of weight loss, which remain inconclusive, until now. The impact of gender is a factor that has been previously addressed, and the findings vary from a favourable outcome among women [7] and suboptimal loss among men [8], to absence variation in the achievement of excess weight loss (EWL) [9] and maintenance of weight loss [6] across gender groups. A study that compared the analyses on surgical outcomes performed using cross-sectional, as well as a longitudinal analytical technique, reported that cross-sectional comparison showed higher EWL values among women, whereas longitudinal regression with weight as outcome showed that women lost less weight, as compared to men, across time [10]. This finding cautions that interpretation of the role of gender should be made by taking into account possibilities, such as women having lower initial weight and, consequently, having achieved higher EWL values. Younger participants were found to have better weight loss outcomes [9,11]. Participants of Black Ethnic group were found to have lower weight loss compared to Caucasians at the 6th and 12th month after surgery [7].

Obesity related co-morbidities were reported to affect weight loss. Patients with diabetes mellitus [12,13] were found to have achieved lower weight loss averages, as compared to those without diabetes and, among those with diabetes, patients who received insulin therapies had poorer outcome [12]. Elevated level of triglycerides and HbA1C were also reported to affect weight loss outcome [9]. The HbA1C level, or the glycaemic control, was found to be a stronger predictor of weight loss than being diagnosed for diabetes [9]. Mixed findings have been reported when psychiatric morbidity is concerned. The combination of the presence of two or more psychiatric disorders, no eating disorders, and having adverse childhood experiences, was found to be associated with low average weight loss [14]. Contradicting evidence was reported in other studies, in which higher depression scores were associated with lesser risk of weight regain [6], and pre-surgical history of mood disorders were associated with better weight loss outcome [15]. In a review study on the impact of psychopathology on weight loss, the authors concluded that post-operative—and not the pre-operative—psychopathology affected weight loss, as the former affects one's flexibility and ability to adapt to post-surgical behavioural changes [16]. This explains the reported favourable association between psychopathology and weight loss. An earlier review study showed that presence of obesity-related psychopathology, such as mild depression and low self-esteem, did not impose a detrimental effect on weight loss, but serious psychiatric morbidities, such as major depression and personality disorders, did, as these conditions impose difficulties in adapting to necessary post-surgical behavioural changes [17]. Recent evidence further supported that negative personality traits were associated with lower weight loss outcome [11].

Adherence to the dietary recommendations provided was shown to be an important predictor of successful weight loss outcome [18]. Presence of disordered eating behaviours, such as grazing [18] and bingeing [19], were associated poorer weight loss outcomes. Interestingly, among those who had low adherence to recommended dietary regiments, those who grazed not more than once per day had a weight loss success rate of 68.3%, as compared to 27.6% among those who grazed more than once [18]. These findings show the interconnectedness of the behavioural traits, that should be noted while monitoring patients. Emotional and uncontrolled eating traits were associated with lower weight loss achievements [20]. In addition to that, behaviours such as frequent clinical visits [18] and regular exercise [21] were associated with better weight loss.

The abovementioned studies provided valuable input on factors that affected weight loss after surgery. The variations in type of surgery, duration of follow-up, time of assessment, and assessment methods, have contributed greatly to the inconsistencies in the findings. Studies of cross-sectional nature do not account for the change in behaviour; regression models for weight loss outcome based on pre-surgical psychological or behavioural parameters do not leave the readers with much clue on the impact of post-surgical factors. Similarly, models based on behaviours at post-surgical timelines do not provide much information on necessary behavioural changes. With regards to those findings, the current study was designed to identify the trends in weight loss and predictors of total weight loss (TWL), six months after surgery, with behavioural predictors assessed over time. The duration of six months was selected to determine if the behavioural variables, especially modifiable variables, have an impact on weight loss at the acute weight loss phase, when a dramatic weight loss is expected. Preventive measures could be drafted to handle such modifiable predictors, in order to optimise weight loss during the period at which rapid weight loss is expected. In addition to that, patients have frequent contacts with healthcare providers during the first six months after surgery and, thus, could be easily monitored.

2. Materials and Methods

2.1. Participants

Participants of the study were patients with obesity who underwent bariatric surgery for weight loss in two tertiary referral hospitals in Kuala Lumpur, Malaysia, between December 2011 to December 2016 in one hospital, and January 2016 to January 2017 in the other. Consenting participants were assessed thrice, before surgery (T_0), and three months (T_1) and six months (T_2) after surgery. Follow-up interviews were mostly conducted during clinical appointments. During the clinical appointment, patients met the surgeons who evaluated their recovery after surgery, dietitians who advised them on dietary plans, and sports medicine specialists who advised them on essential exercises. The follow-up interviews for this study, which evaluated their psychological improvements, were not part of the patient care regime, and were carried out for research purposes only. The participants who had no appointments at a suitable duration were either met elsewhere or interviewed over the telephone. Those who refused both the options were classified as not available for the particular interview. Participants who were not available for any follow-up were excluded.

In total, 80 participants were recruited upon obtaining written consent and, of them, 57 (71.25%) completed at least one follow-up interview, and were included in the study. Forty-five (56.25%) of the 80 participants turned up for the second interview, and 43 (53.75%) turned up for the third interview. A total of 36 (63% of those included in the study) participants had completed all three follow-ups. The surgical interventions given were laparoscopic Roux-en-Y gastric bypass 30 (53%), laparoscopic sleeve gastrectomy 23 (40%), and laparoscopic one anastomosis gastric bypass–mini gastric bypass 4 (7%).

2.2. Measures

The participants of the study were interviewed, and subjected to height and weight measurements during the assessments. Medical records were reviewed to obtain information on co-morbidity and type of surgery. The Hospital Anxiety and Depression Scale [22] was used to screen for anxiety and depression. The recommended cut-off score for the anxiety and depression subscales were 7–8 and above, for possible anxiety and depression; 10–11 and above, for probable anxiety and depression; and a score of 14–15 and above, for severe anxiety and depression. This instrument has shown good validity and reliability for the Malaysian population [23].

Eating behaviour was assessed with the Dutch Eating Behaviour Questionnaire (DEBQ) [24]. This questionnaire contains 33 items that assess three types of eating behaviours: (i) emotional eating—eating in response to emotional cues [25], (ii) external eating—eating in response to external food-related cues [26], and (iii) dietary restraint (restrained eating)—dietary control via cognitive cues with the intention to lose weight [27]. Higher scores for each subscale indicated stronger behavioural traits. The DEBQ instrument had satisfactory structural validity and reliability for our Malaysian samples [28].

Basic sociodemographic information collected include gender, age, ethnicity, marital status, occupation, housing, and mode of transport used. Two items, housing and mode of transport, were included as additional socioeconomic indicators, as a person's socioeconomic status is influenced by the income of the nucleus family, and one's occupation, alone, may not be adequate to depict it. Family history of obesity was also recorded. Information on the presence of obesity-related co-morbidities, including diabetes, hypertension, dyslipidemia, fatty liver disease, sleep apnoea, and conditions that caused difficulty in walking, was obtained from patients' medical records.

Height and weight measurements were taken during follow-ups, where height was measured at the nearest 0.1 cm, and weight to the nearest 0.1 kg, using the standard scales in the hospitals. Body mass index (BMI) was estimated as (weight in kg)/(height in m)^2. Total weight lost (TWL)% was estimated as ((preoperative weight − postoperative weight)/preoperative weight) × 100%. Excess BMI loss, EBMIL, was estimated as follows: ((pre-treatment BMI − current BMI)/(pre-treatment BMI − 25)) × 100%. Ideal weight was the weight that had a BMI of 25.

The EWL and EBMIL are the standard weight matrices reported in almost all bariatric literature. The EBMIL was calculated across timelines to compare the findings with existing literature. TWL was used to study the weight loss pattern and predictors of weight loss instead of the EWL/EBMIL, since the BMI of 25, which is used to estimate EBMIL and EWL, is not the optimal BMI cut-off for an Asian population. That is because, for Asians, a higher risk of chronic diseases was reported at a lower BMI than for Caucasians [29,30]. The World Health Organisation (WHO) Expert Consultation did not suggest a different BMI cut-off for the entire diverse Asian population. The panel of experts, however, suggested BMI 23 kg/m^2 to be considered as high risk, and 27.5 kg/m^2 as very high risk for public health intervention [31]. In line with these, the value of BMI 25 in the EBMIL formula was not amended for the current study. A measure that is non-dependent on any cut-off criteria will be a better option to identify predictors of weight loss in this case. The TWL was least associated with pre-surgical weight [32], an important predictor of post-surgical weight [10,32]. Using TWL, the impact of other modifiable variables could be identified, which will be helpful in patient selection and management, to optimise weight loss after surgery.

2.3. Ethics Clearance

Ethical approval was obtained from the ethics committee of both hospitals (MEC Ref No 732.19; JEP-2016-276). Written informed consent was obtained from all participants during the first interview.

2.4. Statistical Analysis

Friedman's test was used to compare the change of distribution across timelines, and Wilcoxon's sign rank test with Bonferroni's adjustment was used to conduct post hoc comparisons. Kendall's W was used for effect size estimates. Effect size measured by Kendall's W is considered small if the value is 0.1, moderate if 0.3, and strong if 0.5 and above. Mann–Whitney U test was used to compare the cross-sectional difference between groups. Spearman's correlation co-efficient value was used to determine the strength of association between the variables. Factors associated with TWL were studied using a generalised estimating equation (GEE). The GEE was used instead of the linear mixed model, which was used in previous studies, and deemed suitable to study the impact of weight loss [10]. This is because the quasi-likelihood estimation employed by the GEE, unlike the restricted maximum likelihood estimation used in the mixed model, is not stringent on normality assumption [33,34]. The distribution of weight loss and other psychological variables, in this study, were found to deviate from normality. The GEE is a better option for such datasets [34]. Pre-surgical as well as time-varying (from pre to post) variables were included in the model. The pre-surgical factors included were age, gender, ethnicity, marital status, family history of obesity, initial BMI, and baseline co-morbidities. The time-varying factors tested were longitudinal BMI, eating behaviour, anxiety, and depression, across the study duration. Variables that were statistically significant ($p < 0.05$) and improved overall fit of the model were retained.

3. Results

3.1. Demographic and Health Information

The participants in this study (n = 57) formed 71.0% of the total surgical patients recruited. The characteristics of the participants and dropout group were compared. It was found that the two groups were similar in terms of demography and weight distribution (Table 1). The study group was representative of the cohort of patients who went through surgery. The participants in the study were mostly Malay and women, with an average age of 39.40 years (SD = 10.01) and average initial BMI of 45.52 kg/m^2 (SD = 9.94) (Table 1). The Non-Malay group that formed a substantial minority of 25% (n = 15), consisted of Indians (n = 10, 17.5%), Chinese (n = 2, 3.5%), Caucasian (n = 1, 1.75%), and a Pakistani (n = 1, 1.75%). The Caucasian and Pakistani participants had resided in Malaysia for a long time (over three decades for the Caucasian participant; the Pakistani participant was born and brought up in Malaysia) and had Malaysian citizenship. Most participants were living in their own houses and had their own transportation. Most participants (n = 35, 61%) were employed as professionals, associate professionals, or in managerial and executive positions (Table 1).

Table 1. Characteristics of surgical patients who were included and excluded in this study.

Factor	Included in the Study (N = 57) n (%)	Excluded from the Study (N = 23) n (%)	Test Statistics (χ^2, p)
Gender			
Female	37 (64.9)	11 (47.8)	1.993, 0.123
Male	20 (27.0)	12 (52.2)	
Ethnicity			
Malay	43 (75.0)	17 (74.0)	0.000, 0.592
Non-Malays	14 (25.0)	6 (26.0)	
Age (years)			
Mean ± SD	39.40 ± 10.01	39.30 ± 10.98	−0.039. 0.969 [c]
Median ± IQR [a]	38.00 ± 15.00	39.00 ± 12.00	
Educational Qualification			
School [b]	17 (30)	10 (43.5)	1.248, 0.195
College/University	39 (70)	13 (56.5)	
Housing Situation			
Own House	47 (82.5)	17 (74.0)	0.748, 0.387
Rented House/Quarters	10 (17.5)	6 (25.0)	
Mode of Transport			
Own Transport	52 (91.0)	18 (78.3)	2.519, 0.112
Public Transport/Others	5 (9.0)	5 (21.7)	
Occupation			
Professional/Associate Professional	20 (35)	7 (30.4)	
Management and Executive	7 (12)	1 (4.3)	
Clerical Support	8 (14)	3 (13.0)	
Armed Forces	4 (7)	1 (4.3)	NIL [d]
Business Owners	5(9)	2 (9.0)	
Students	3 (5.4)	4 (17.0)	
Retired/At Home/Unemployed	10 (17.5)	5 (22.0)	
Initial BMI			
Mean ± SD	45.52 ± 18.26	49.88 ± 18.29	1.060, 0.299 [c]
Median ± IQR [b]	43.35 ± 12.33	45.52 ± 9.95	
Obesity Classification			
Class I	10 (17.50)	5 (22.00)	
Class II	6 (10.53)	3 (13.00)	0.105, 0.368 [e]
Class III	41 (71.90)	15 (65.00)	

[a] interquartile range; [b] inclusive primary school, secondary school, and religious school, where one participant belonged to the latter category; [c] independent sample t-test value and corresponding p-value is reported; [d] no comparison was made, due to the small sample size in each category; [e] chi-square value is obtained by categorising obesity Class I and II as one group (not-morbid obesity) and Class III (morbid obesity) as one group

3.2. Weight Loss

The mean weight and BMI loss experienced in the first three months after surgery were 20.52 kg (SD = 7.95) and 7.57 kg/m^2 (SD = 2.62), whereas between the fourth to sixth month, they were 9.88 kg (SD = 10.61) and 3.59 kg/m^2 (SD = 3.61). Post hoc comparisons showed that weight and BMI differed significantly across all timelines, and had a large effect size (Table 2). The average EBMIL and TWL achieved at the third month were 40.53% and 22.28%, and at the sixth month, they were 63.33% and 23.83%. The most impactful weight loss occurred during the third month. The participants of the study, who were given different surgical interventions, did not differ in terms of initial BMI (Z = 0.470, $p = 0.638$) and weight (Z = −0.157, $p = 0.876$). Patients who had laparoscopic Roux-en-Y gastric bypass (LRYGB) or one anastomosis gastric bypass–mini gastric bypass (MGB) performed on them had higher EBMIL and TWL at the third and the sixth month, as compared to those who had LSG performed. A significant difference ($p < 0.05$) was only observed in the value of TWL between LRYGB and LSG patients at the sixth month (T_2) (Table 3). The MGB group was not included in the analyses, due to it having a small sample size. Change of TWL across time formed a steep line from 0 to 3 months, that almost flattened from the third to sixth month (Figure 1).

Table 2. Weight changes across study duration.

Measure	Descriptive	Baseline (T_0) (n = 57)	Third Month (T_1) (n = 45)	Sixth Month (T_2) (n = 43)	χ^2	p	W
Weight (kg)	Mean, SD Median, IQR	122.33, 35.11 114.0, 30.3	101.80, 31.74 96.73, 22.70	91.93, 25.41 87.00, 18.50	68.814	<0.001	0.930
BMI (kg/m^2)	Mean, SD Median, IQR	45.48, 10.58 42.453, 12.60	37.75, 9.86 35.70, 8.52	34.11, 8.07 32.39, 7.32	68.814	<0.001	0.930
TWL%	Mean, SD Median, IQR		22.28, 7.82 22.45, 8.88	23.83, 7.40 23.68, 7.71		NA	
EWL%	Mean, SD Median, IQR		40.55, 18.33 37.81, 23.11	63.33, 33.18 57.83, 30.57		NA	
EBMIL%	Mean, SD Median, IQR		40.55, 18.33 37.81, 23.11	63.33, 33.18 57.83, 30.57		NA	

SD—standard deviation; IQR—interquartile range; TWL—total weight loss; NA—not applicable; EWL—excess weight loss; EBMIL—excess BMI loss; Friedman's chi-square, p-value and the effect size, Kendall's W are reported.

Table 3. Weight changes across study duration (by surgery type).

Surgery (mean, SD) (median, IQR)	EBMIL		TWL	
	T_1 (n = 45)	T_2 (n = 43)	T_1 (n = 45)	T_2 (n = 43)
LRYGB (n = 30) (number followed-up)	41.89, 17.59 42.58, 21.05 n = 24	67.01, 36.91 58.13, 26.54 n = 28	17.07, 6.02 17.71, 6.84 n = 24	25.14, 6.98 24.97, 8.2 n = 28
LSG (n = 23)	38.87, 20.84 33.50, 23.44 n = 18	53.96, 28.26 45.97, 48.55 n = 11	15.74, 4.76 16.20, 8.60 n = 18	19.28, 6.33 19.84, 9.79 n = 11
MGB (n = 4)	42.76, 7.72 46.14, NA n = 3	69.98, 13.55 72.66, 25.13 n = 4	18.29, 4.12 16.15, NA n = 3	29.40, 7.52 27.99, 13.98 n = 4
Z, p^a	−0.966, 0.334	−1.373, 0.170	−0.872, 0.383	−2.269, 0.023

LRYGB—laparoscopic Roux-en-Y gastric bypass; LSG—laparoscopic sleeve gastrectomy; MGB—one anastomosis gastric bypass–mini gastric bypass; SD—standard deviation; IQR—interquartile range; TWL—total weight loss; NA—not applicable; EWL—excess weight loss; EBMIL—excess BMI loss; [a] Mann–Whitney's U test was conducted to compare the difference in EBMIL and TWL at the third and sixth month between surgical groups. The MGB group was not included, due to small sample size.

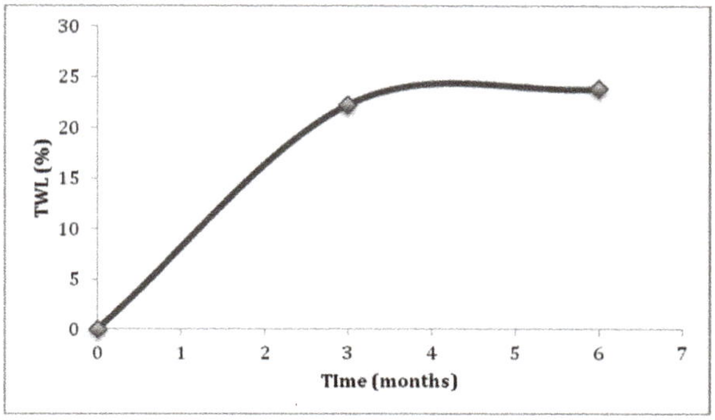

Figure 1. Total weight loss (TWL) experienced across the study duration.

3.3. Psychological Factors and Eating Behaviour

Changes in psychological variables across time are shown in Table 4. Anxiety scores decreased over time, with a significant reduction between baseline and the sixth month. The prevalence rate of anxiety was 21% at T_0, and dropped to 7% at T_1 and 3.5% at T_2. Depression scores reduced significantly between baseline and the third month, as well as between baseline and the sixth month. The prevalence rate of depression at baseline was 7%, and was reduced to 5.3% at T_1 and 1.8% at T_2. Changes in anxiety and depression had a moderate effect size (Table 4).

External eating was the only eating behaviour that changed over time, with a significant reduction between baseline and the third month, as well as between baseline and the sixth month. The change had a moderate effect size (Table 4). The emotional eating scores across time were positively correlated. A similar observation was obtained for the external eating scores. There was also a positive correlation between the emotional and external eating scores. Restrained eating at T_2 correlated with emotional eating across all timelines (Table 5). The emotional and external eating scores at T_2 were correlated with anxiety and depression across almost all timelines (Table 6). The external and emotional eating scores, due to the correlation between them, could not be regressed together. Two separate GEE models were developed to explain the impact of the variables on TWL.

Table 4. Changes in psychological factors following surgery.

Measure Mean (SD)	T_0	T_1	T_2	Test Statistics (χ^2, p)	Effect Size (W)
Anxiety	4.88 (3.23)	3.43 (2.94)	2.40 (2.47)	32.53 ^{**,b}	0.465
Depression	3.72 (2.89)	2.02 (2.59)	1.60 (2.13)	28.82 ^{**,a,b}	0.412
Emotional eating	2.06 (0.94)	1.64 (0.80)	1.81 (0.81)	4.12 ^{ns}	0.082
External eating	2.86 (0.68)	2.25 (0.79)	2.38 (0.64)	19.29 ^{**,a,b}	0.386
Restraint	2.65 (0.73)	2.93 (0.86)	2.75 (0.80)	3.49 ^{ns}	0.070

** $p < 0.01$, ns—not significant, a—significant difference between T_0 and T_1, b—significant difference between T_0 and T_2.

Table 5. Correlation between the eating behaviour traits across time.

	Emotional T_0	Emotional T_1	Emotional T_2	External T_0	External T_1	External T_2	Restrained T_0	Restrained T_1	Restrained T_2
Emotional T_0	1.00	0.452 **	0.787 **	0.484 **	0.302	0.623 **	−0.045	0.264	0.425 **
Emotional T_1		1.00	0.808 **	0.312	0.763 **	0.709 **	0.277	0.239	0.489 *
Emotional T_2			1.00	0.452 **	0.653 **	0.774 **	0.190	0.291	0.489 **

Table 5. *Cont.*

	Emotional T_0	Emotional T_1	Emotional T_2	External T_0	External T_1	External T_2	Restrained T_0	Restrained T_1	Restrained T_2
External T_0				1.00	0.389 *	0.667 *	0.031	0.356 *	0.348
External T_1					1.00	0.781 *	0.080	0.146	0.389
External T_2						1.00	0.117	0.298	0.241
Restrained T_0							1.00	0.304	0.381 *
Restrained T_1								1.00	0.450
Restrained T_2									1.00

* $p < 0.05$, ** $p < 0.01$.

Table 6. Correlation between anxiety, depression, and eating behaviour.

	Emotional T_0	Emotional T_1	Emotional T_2	External T_0	External T_1	External T_2	Restrained T_0	Restrained T_1	Restrained T_2
Anxiety T_0	0.078	0.343 *	0.484 **	0.180	0.104	0.325 *	0.230	0.357 *	0.430 **
Anxiety T_1	0.210	0.382 *	0.473 **	0.009	0.232	0.347 *	0.500 **	0.254	0.390 *
Anxiety T_2	0.345 *	0.575 *	0.569 **	0.291	0.414 *	0.573 **	0.157	0.457 *	0.216
Depression T_0	0.102	0.169	0.377 **	0.234	0.092	0.341 *	0.309 *	0.189	0.387 *
Depression T_1	−0.067	0.112	0.225	0.134	0.097	0.207	0.211	−0.071	0.234
Depression T_2	0.355 *	0.3361	0.559 **	0.165	0.193	0.359 *	0.198	−0.017	0.277

Emotional—emotional eating, External—external eating, Restrained—restrained eating, Anxiety—anxiety score, Depression—depression score. T_0—before surgery, T_1—three months after surgery, T_2—six months after surgery. * $p < 0.05$, ** $p < 0.01$.

3.4. Predictors of Weight Loss Following Surgery

The GEE models show that the average monthly TWL experienced was 5.7% ($6.12t - 0.42t^2$) (Table 6) and 5.3% ($5.68t - 0.38t^2$) (Table 7). The squared term for time had a negative value, indicating a quadratic equation with an increasing trend (inverted *U* pattern). In the first model, increased age, higher BMI, and higher emotional eating scores were found to be associated with lower TWL percentages (Table 7). The second model showed that increased age, higher BMI, and higher external eating scores were associated with lower TWL percentages (Table 8). All other predictors (except eating behaviours) in both the models were similar, and had slope values that were almost similar.

Depression, which was found to be a significant predictor of TWL after controlling for age, BMI and time, became insignificant upon inclusion of emotional and external eating in the equations. Eating behaviours were found to be stronger psychological predictors than depression. Anxiety, initial weight, initial BMI, comorbidities, family history of obesity, and other sociodemographic factors, were not significantly associated with change in TWL%.

Table 7. Predictors of total weight loss (TWL) following bariatric surgery.

Factor	Regression Coefficient, β	95% Confidence Interval of β	df
Intercept	12.67 **	(7.34, 18.00)	1
Time (month)	6.19 **	(5.15, 7.23)	1
Time^2	−0.42 **	(−0.60, −2.34)	1
Age	−0.10 **	(−0.19, −0.02)	1
Emotional Eating	−0.32 **	(−0.57, −0.06)	1
BMI	−0.18 **	(−0.25, −0.10)	1

df—degrees of freedom. ** $p < 0.01$.

Table 8. Predictors of total weight loss (TWL) following bariatric surgery.

Parameter	Regression Coefficient, β	95% Confidence Interval	df
(Intercept)	19.196 **	(11.67, 26.73)	1
Time	5.688 **	(4.66, 6.73)	1
Time^2	−0.376 **	(−0.55, −0.20)	1
Age	−0.122 **	(−0.21, −0.03)	1
BMI	−0.291 **	(−0.42, −0.16)	1
External	−0.344 *	(−0.62, −0.07)	1

df—degrees of freedom. * $p < 0.05$, ** $p < 0.01$.

4. Discussion

This study examined the weight loss and predictors of weight loss at six months post-surgery. The mean EBMIL experienced in the six months was 63.33%, which was around the values reported for the same duration in previous studies, 56.4% [7] and 65% [13]. The mean TWL at the sixth month, 23.83%, was also around the value reported for six months in another study, 25.7% [7]. The weight loss achieved by the participants in this study is comparable to what is reported elsewhere.

Initial weight is a predictor for weight loss that has been replicated in many studies. Models with EWL/EBMIL as the outcome showed that higher initial weight (or BMI) were negative predictors of weight loss outcome [7,9,13,35], and the impact was seen at the sixth month post-surgery [7,13]. It has been shown that initial weight was the most important predictor that explained over 93% of the variation in weight [36]. In this study, initial BMI was not a significant predictor of TWL. A previous study that used TWL as the outcome also reported an absence of association between initial weight and TWL [37]. The negative slope obtained for the continuous BMI variable, however, still leads to a similar conclusion of an inverse association with higher weight and percentage of weight loss. The negative relationship could be due to a lower level of physical activities among heavier patients [36]. In addition, large absolute values of weight loss experienced by these patients, when converted to percentage of total body weight lost, could be projected as a smaller value, as compared to a person with lower body weight.

The inverse association between increased age and weight loss, found in this study, is in coherence with previous findings [9,11]. Lower rates of co-morbidities among younger patients [16], decreased physically activity among older adults [38], and slower recovery with increasing age, could contribute to the age effect. The slope value of $\beta = -0.10$ and $\beta = -0.12$ for age shows that TWL is reduced by 0.1 or 0.12 units, with the increase in age by one unit. A patient who is 60 years old is expected to experience between 6% and 7.2% less weight loss due to age, whereas a 40-year-old person experienced between 4% and 4.8% less weight loss. A difference of 2% and 2.4%, for a 20-year age gap, is not a formidable amount. Age should not be a reason for older patients being denied this surgical option, considering the many improvements in co-morbidity and metabolism that followed [39].

The observed positive correlations between emotional eating scores across time indicate that higher scores at pre-surgical time-line were indicative of higher score post-surgically. A similar trend was seen for external eating. These findings show that the eating behaviour traits do not disappear during the early stages after surgery and affect weight loss during the rapid weight loss period. The findings could be related to a previous study which showed that emotional eating was associated with suboptimal weight loss (failure to achieve EWL > 50%) two years post-surgery [20]. A study with a 10-year follow-up showed that those who had lost <10% EWL, or regained weight, had higher uncontrolled eating and hunger scores [40]. The uncontrolled eating or disinhibition was described as eating opportunistically, or in relation to external food-related cues [41], and overlaps, to an extent, with the concept of external eating. The previous findings could, thus, be related to the current finding that eating in response to external stimuli, be it emotional or food-related cues, has an adverse effect on weight loss outcome post-surgery. The observed correlation between restrained eating at T_2, and emotional eating at all time lines, could potentially refer to the effort that the patients with emotional eating take to control their diet, probably due to the unsatisfactory weight loss percentages achieved.

A review showed that emotional eating, in addition to having a direct negative impact on weight loss, was also found to be the underlying reason for various disordered eating behaviours; such as uncontrolled eating, grazing, and binge eating [42]. Those behaviours were found to be induced by a variety of emotional triggers [42]. A recent finding showed that the emotional and external eating behaviours were associated with depression [43]. These lines of evidence, that showed the existence of a complex relationship between eating behaviour and psychopathology, are further supported by our findings, which show that emotional and external eating, six months after surgery, were correlated with anxiety and depression scores.

The clinical implication of the current finding is that eating behaviours affect weight loss during the acute weight loss period. It is a stronger negative predictor than depression scores at the early stage. However, it is of note that psychopathology was low among the participants, due to the patient selection process for surgery, where patients with severe psychiatric morbidity were excluded. Patients with tendencies to eat in response to external cues, be it emotion or food-related stimuli, should be identified and subjected to counselling and behavioural therapy, and given continuous support to curb the behaviours which are detrimental to weight loss. Acceptance-based behavioural treatments, which have been shown to be effective in improving negative eating behaviours and causing better weight loss or maintenance [44], could be adapted for such surgery candidates. It is of utmost importance to note that the eating behaviour traits were self-reported measures made using screening instruments and, thus, should not be used as a patient selection tool but, rather, an additional way of guiding the patients towards better weight loss outcome.

There are some limitations to the study. Firstly, the limited sample size has an inhibitive effect on the power to identify predictors with smaller impacts. The follow-up duration of six months was selected to study the impact of behavioural variables at an early stage. A longer follow-up duration is essential to observe the impact of behavioural factors on weight loss. The psychological factors and eating behaviour variables were self-reported by patients and, thus, the risks of under- or overreporting are undeniable. Future studies, with larger sample sizes, longer follow-up durations, and psychological and eating behaviour assessments by experts, are warranted. Despite these limitations, the current finding shows that the impact of psychobehavioural factors, at the early stage after surgery, is of importance for clinical management of patients and, thus, warrants attention.

5. Conclusions

The findings show that patients experienced significant weight loss and improvements in psychological factors after surgery. Eating behaviours were important predictors of weight loss six months post-surgery. Continuous assessment of eating behaviour during pre- and post-surgical follow-up is essential to achieve good weight loss outcomes.

Author Contributions: Contribution of each authors is as follows: conceptualization, K.S., W.-Y.L., P.-C.L., N.R.K., M.M.T., R.R., and K.-F.C.; methodology, K.S., W.-Y.L., and K.C.; software, K.S. and K.C.; formal analysis, K.S.; resources, K.S.; writing—original draft preparation, K.S.; writing—review and editing, P.-C.L. and W.-Y.L.; supervision, W.-Y.L., P.-C.L., K.-F.C., N.R.K., M.M.T., and R.R.; project administration, K.S. and W.-Y.L.; funding acquisition, K.-F.C and W.-Y.L.

Funding: This research was funded by University of Malaya Postgraduate Research Fund, grant number: PV122/2012A.

Acknowledgments: We would like to thank University of Malaya for supporting this study via Postgraduate Research Fund. We also would like to thank University of Malaya Medical Centre (UMMC) and Universiti Kebangsaan Malaysia Medical Centre (UKMMC) for all the support rendered.

Conflicts of Interest: The authors declare no conflict of interest.

References

1. Cesare, M.D.; Bentham, J.; Stevens, G.A.; Zhou, B.; Danaei, G.; Lu, Y.; Bixby, H.; Cowan, M.J.; Riley, L.M.; Hajifathalian, K.; et al. Trends in adult body-mass index in 200 countries from 1975 to 2014: A pooled analysis of 1698 population-based measurement studies with 19.2 million participants. *Lancet* **2016**, *387*, 1377–1396.
2. Sturm, R.; Hattori, A. Morbid obesity rates continue to rise rapidly in the United States. *Int. J. Obes.* **2013**, *37*, 889–891. [CrossRef] [PubMed]
3. Carter, P.L. The evolution of bariatric surgery. *Am. J. Surg.* **2015**, *209*, 779–782. [CrossRef] [PubMed]
4. Madura, J.A.; Dibaise, J.K. Quick fix or long-term cure? Pros and cons of bariatric surgery. *F 1000 Med. Rep.* **2012**, *9*, 1–9. [CrossRef] [PubMed]
5. Karlsson, J.; Taft, C.; Rydén, A.; Sjöström, L.; Sullivan, M. Ten-year trends in health-related quality of life after surgical and conventional treatment for severe obesity: The SOS intervention study. *Int. J. Obes.* **2007**, *31*, 1248–1261. [CrossRef] [PubMed]
6. Odom, J.; Zalesin, K.C.; Washington, T.L.; Miller, W.W.; Hakmeh, B.; Zaremba, D.L.; Altattan, M.; Balasubramaniam, M.; Gibbs, D.S.; Krause, K.R.; et al. Behavioral predictors of weight regain after bariatric surgery. *Obes. Surg.* **2010**, *20*, 349–356. [CrossRef] [PubMed]
7. Wise, E.; Hocking, K.M.; Kavic, S.M. Predictors of excess weight loss after laparoscopic Roux-en-Y gastric bypass: Data from an artifical neural network. *Surg. Endosc.* **2016**, *30*, 480–488. [CrossRef] [PubMed]
8. Melton, G.B.; Steele, K.E.; Schweitzer, M.A.; Lidor, A.O.; Magnusin, T.H. Suboptimal weight loss after gastric bypass surgery: Correlation of demographics, comorbidities, and insurance status with outcomes. *J. Gastrointest. Surg.* **2008**, *12*, 250–255. [CrossRef] [PubMed]
9. Ortega, E.; Morı, R.; Flores, L.; Moizem, V.; Rios, M.; Lacy, A.M.; Vidal, J. Predictive factors of excess body weight loss 1 year after laparoscopic bariatric surgery. *Surg. Endosc.* **2012**, *26*, 1744–1750. [CrossRef] [PubMed]
10. Dallal, R.M.; Quebbemann, B.B.; Hunt, L.H.; Braitman, L.E. Analysis of weight loss after bariatric surgery using mixed-effects linear modeling. *Obes Surg.* **2009**, *19*, 732–737. [CrossRef] [PubMed]
11. Piaggi, P.; Lippi, C.; Fierabracci, P.; Maffei, M.; Calderone, A.; Mauri, M.; Anselmino, M.; Cassano, G.B.; Vitti, P.; Pinchera, A.; et al. Artificial neural networks in the outcome prediction of adjustable gastric banding in obese women. *PLoS ONE.* **2010**, *5*, 1–12. [CrossRef] [PubMed]
12. Campos, G.M.; Rabl, C.; Mulligan, K.; Posselt, A.; Rogers, S.J.; Westphalen, A.C.; Lin, F.; Vittinghoff, E. Factors associated with weight loss after gastric bypass. *Arch Surg.* **2008**, *143*, 877–884. [CrossRef] [PubMed]
13. Still, C.D.; Wood, G.C.; Chu, X.; Manney, C.; Strodel, W.; Petrick, A.; Gabrielsen, J.; Mirshahi, T.; Argyropoulos, G.; Seiler, J.; et al. Clinical factors associated with weight loss outcomes after Roux-en-Y gastric bypass surgery. *Obesity.* **2014**, *22*, 888–894. [CrossRef] [PubMed]
14. Kinzl, J.F.; Schrattenecker, M.; Traweger, C.; Mattesich, M.; Fiala, M.; Biebl, W. Psychosocial predictors of weight loss after bariatric surgery. *Obes. Surg.* **2006**, *16*, 1609–1614. [CrossRef] [PubMed]
15. Sockalingam, S.; Hawa, R.; Wnuk, S.; Santiago, V.; Kowgier, M.; Jackson, T.; Okrainec, A.; Cassin, S. Psychosocial predictors of quality of life and weight loss two years after bariatric surgery: Results from the Toronto Bari-PSYCH study. *Gen. Hosp. Psychiatry* **2017**, *47*, 7–13. [CrossRef] [PubMed]
16. Wimmelmann, C.L.; Dela, F.; Mortensen, E.L. Psychological predictors of weight loss after bariatric surgery: A review of the recent research. *Obes. Res. Clin. Pract.* **2014**, *8*, e299–e313. [CrossRef] [PubMed]
17. Herpertz, S.; Keilmann, R.; Wolf, A.M.; Hebebrand, J.; Senf, W. Do psychosocial variables predict weight loss or mental health after obesity surgery? A systematic review. *Obes. Res.* **2004**, *12*, 1554–1569. [CrossRef] [PubMed]
18. Robinson, A.H.; Adler, S.; Stevens, H.B.; Darcy, A.M.; Morton, J.M.; Safer, D.L. What variables are associated with successful weight loss outcomes for bariatric surgery after 1 year? *Surg. Obes. Relat. Dis.* **2014**, *10*, 697–704. [CrossRef] [PubMed]
19. Luiz, L.B.; Brito, D.S.; Debon, M.; Brandalise, N.; Azevodo, J.T.; Monbach, K.D.; Herberie, S.; Mottin, C.C. Variation of beinge eating one year after Roux-en-Y gastric bypass and its relationship with excess weight loss. *PLoS ONE* **2016**, *11*, e0167577. [CrossRef] [PubMed]

20. Novelli, I.R.; Fonseca, L.G.; Lopes, D.G.; Dutra, E.S.; Baiocchi de Carvalho, K.M. Emotional eating behavior hinders body weight loss in women after roux-en-Y gastric bypass surgery. *Nutrition* **2018**, *49*, 13–16. [CrossRef] [PubMed]
21. Egberts, K.; Brown, W.A.; Brennan, L.; O'Brien, P.E. Does Exercise improve weight loss after bariatric surgery? A systematic review. *Obes. Surg.* **2012**, *22*, 335–341. [CrossRef] [PubMed]
22. Zigmond, A.S.; Snaith, R.P. The Hospital Anxiety and Depression Scale. *Acta. Psychiatr. Scand.* **1983**, *67*, 361–370. [CrossRef] [PubMed]
23. Fatt, Q.K.; Atiya, A.S.; Heng, N.G.C.; Beng, C.C. Validation of the hospital anxiety and depression scale and the psychological disorder among premature ejaculation subjects. *Int. J. Impot. Res.* **2007**, *19*, 321–325. [CrossRef] [PubMed]
24. Van Strien, T.; Frijters, J.E.R.; Bergers, G.P.; Defares, P.B. The Dutch Eating Behaviour Questionnaire (DEBQ) for assessment of restrained, emotional and external eating behaviour. *Int. J. Eat Disord.* **1986**, *5*, 295–315. [CrossRef]
25. Bruch, H. Obesity in childhood and personality development. *Obes. Res.* **1997**, *5*, 157–161. [CrossRef] [PubMed]
26. Schacter, S.; Goldman, R.; Gordon, A. Effects of fear, food deprivation, and obesity on eating. *J. Pers. Soc. Psychol.* **1968**, *10*, 91–97. [CrossRef]
27. Herman, C.; Polivy, J. *Obesity*; Restrained Eating; Saunders: Philadelphia, PA, USA, 1980; pp. 208–225.
28. Subramaniam, K.; Low, W.Y.; Chinna, K.; Chin, K.; Krishnaswamy, S. Psychometric properties of the Malay version of the Dutch Eating Behaviour Questionnaire (DEBQ) in a Sample of Malaysian Adults Attending a Health Care Facility. *Malaysian J. Med. Sci.* **2017**, *24*, 64–73. [CrossRef] [PubMed]
29. Chiu, M.; Austin, P.C.; Manuel, D.G.; Shah, B.R.; Tu, J.V. Deriving ethnic-specific BMI cutoff points for assessing diabetes risk. *Diabetes Care.* **2011**, *34*, 1741–1748. [CrossRef] [PubMed]
30. He, W.; Li, Q.; Yang, M.; Jiao, J.; Ma, X.; Zhou, Y.; Song, A.; Heymsfield, S.B.; Zhang, S.; Zhu, S. Lower BMI cutoffs to define overweight and obesity in China. *Obesity.* **2015**, *23*, 684–691. [CrossRef] [PubMed]
31. World Health Organization (WHO) Expert Consultations. Appropriate body-mass index for Asian populations and its implication for policy and intervention strategies. *Lancet.* **2004**, *363*, 157–163. [CrossRef]
32. Hatoum, I.J.; Kaplan, L. Advantage of percent weight loss as a method for reporting weight loss after Roux-en-Y gastric bypass. *Obesity.* **2013**, *21*, 1519–1525. [CrossRef] [PubMed]
33. Hedeker, D.; Gibbons, R.D. *Longitudinal Data Analysis*, 6th ed.; Wiley-Interscience: Hoboken, NJ, USA, 2006.
34. Naseri, P.; Majd, H.A.; Kariman, N.; Sourtiji, A. Comparison of generalised estimating equation (GEE), mixed effects models (MEM) and repeated measure ANOVA in analysis of menorrhagia data. *J. Paramed. Sci.* **2016**, *7*, 32–40.
35. Sillén, L.; Andersson, E.; Andersson, E. Patient factors predicting weight loss after Roux-en-Y gastric bypass. *J. Obes.* **2017**. [CrossRef] [PubMed]
36. Sczepaniak, J.P.; Owens, M.L.; Garner, W.; Dako, F.; Masukawa, K.; Wilson, S.E. A simpler method for predicting weight loss in the first year after Roux-en-Y gastric bypass. *J. Obes.* **2012**, *2012*, 1–5. [CrossRef] [PubMed]
37. Lai, C.; Aceto, P.; Petrucci, I.; Castelnuovo, G.; Callari, C.; Giustacchini, P.; Sollazzi, L.; Mingrone, G.; Bellantone, R.; Raffaelli, M. The influence of preoperative psychological factors on weight loss after bariatric surgery: A preliminary report. *J. Health Psychol.* **2016**. [CrossRef] [PubMed]
38. Hallal, P.C.; Andersen, L.B.; Bull, F.C.; Guthold, R.; Haskell, W.; Ekelund, U. Global physical activity levels: Surveillance progress, pitfalls, and prospects. *Lancet.* **2012**, *380*, 247–257. [CrossRef]
39. Sjostrom, L. Review of the key results from the Swedish Obese Subjects (SOS) trial—A prospective controlled intervention study of bariatric surgery. *J Intern Med.* **2013**, *273*, 219–234. [CrossRef] [PubMed]
40. Konttinen, H.; Peltonen, M.; Sjöström, L.; Carlsson, L.; Karlsson, J. Psychological aspects of eating behavior as predictors of 10-y weight changes after surgical and conventional treatment of severe obesity: Results from the Swedish. *Am. J. Clin. Nutr.* **2015**, *101*, 16–24. [CrossRef] [PubMed]
41. Bryant, E.J.; King, N.A.; Blundell, J.E. Disinhibition: Its effects on appetite and weight regulation. *Obes. Rev.* **2008**, *9*, 409–419. [CrossRef] [PubMed]
42. Chesler, B.E. Emotional eating: A virtually untreated risk factor for outcome following bariatric surgery. *Sci. World J.* **2012**, *2012*, 365961. [CrossRef] [PubMed]

43. Sevinçer, G.M.; Konuk, N.; İpekçioğlu, D.; Crosby, R.D.; Cao, L.; Coskun, H.; Mitchell, J.E. Association between depression and eating behaviors among bariatric surgery candidates in a Turkish sample. *Eat Weight Disord.* **2016**, *22*, 117–123. [CrossRef] [PubMed]
44. Forman, E.M.; Butryn, M.L.; Juarascio, A.S.; Bradley, L.E.; Lowe, M.R.; Herbert, J.D.; Shaw, J.A. The Mind Your Health Project: A randomized controlled trial of an innovative behavioral treatment for obesity. *Obesity* **2013**, *21*, 1119–1126. [CrossRef] [PubMed]

nutrients

MDPI

Article

An Investigation of the Clinical Utility of the Proposed ICD-11 and DSM-5 Diagnostic Schemes for Eating Disorders Characterized by Recurrent Binge Eating in People with a High BMI

Marly Amorim Palavras [1,2], Phillipa Hay [2] and Angélica Claudino [1,*]

[1] Eating Disorders Program (PROATA), Department of Psychiatry, Universidade Federal de São Paulo (UNIFESP), São Paulo 04017030, Brazil; marlypalavras@gmail.com

[2] Translational Health Research Institute, School of Medicine, Western Sydney University, Sydney 2751, Australia; p.hay@westernsydney.edu.au

* Correspondence: amclaudino@gmail.com; Tel.: +55-11-991825552

Received: 17 October 2018; Accepted: 8 November 2018; Published: 13 November 2018

Abstract: The aims of this paper were to compare (1) the proportion of participants diagnosed with threshold or subthreshold Bulimia Nervosa (BN) and Binge Eating Disorder (BED) (clinical utility), and (2) the severity of participants' clinical features and mental Health-Related Quality of Life (HRQoL) (convergent validity), when diagnosed according to either the Diagnostic and Statistical Manual of Mental Disorders—5th edition (DSM-5) or the proposed International Classification of Diseases 11th edition (ICD-11) schemes. One hundred and seven adult men and women, with a high Body Mass Index (BMI) were evaluated by interview to confirm their eating disorder diagnoses. All participants completed self-report assessments of current symptoms and mental HRQoL. The majority of participants in either diagnostic scheme were included in the main categories of BN or BED (102/107, 95% in the ICD-11 and 85/107, 79% in the DSM-5). Fewer individuals received a subthreshold other or unspecified diagnosis with the ICD-11 compared to the DSM-5 scheme (5% vs. 21%). No significant differences in demographic, clinical features or mental HRQoL of participants with complete or partial BN or BED were found between diagnostic categories. Compared to the DSM-5, the proposed ICD-11 was not over inclusive, i.e., it did not appear to include people with less severe and potentially less clinically relevant symptoms. These results support the greater clinical utility of the ICD-11 whilst both schemes showed convergent validity.

Keywords: Bulimia Nervosa; binge-eating disorder; Diagnostic and Statistical Manual of Mental Disorders; International Classification of Diseases

1. Introduction

Currently two diagnostic classification systems guide the field of mental disorders, the Diagnostic and Statistical Manual of Mental Disorders in its 5th edition (DSM-5) [1] and the International Classification of Diseases, now in its 10th edition (ICD-10) [2]. The 11th edition of the ICD- is in preparation [3,4]. A World Psychiatric Association Global Survey (WPA-WHO) involving 4887 psychiatrists in 44 countries indicated that 79.2% of the sample often or almost always/always used one of these formal classification systems as part of their day-to-day clinical work [5]. The DSM-5, which covers mental health exclusively, is very commonly used in the United States, United Kingdom, Australasia, and in international research. The ICD-10 is more extensive, as it includes all medical diagnoses, and it is the official government classification scheme in the majority of countries worldwide [2,5]. Further, the two schemes differ substantively in their structure, definitions and diagnostic guidelines, particularly concerning disorders characterized by recurrent binge eating such as Binge Eating Disorder (BED) and Bulimia Nervosa (BN) [6,7].

In both schemes, BED is now included as the third major eating disorder after BN and anorexia nervosa (AN). Both systems also became more inclusive aiming to reduce the formerly very high number of cases (around 60%) diagnosed within the residual poorly specified categories. DSM-5 now has two such categories—Other Specified Feeding or Eating Disorder (OSFED) and Unspecified Feeding or Eating Disorder (UFED), respectively. OSFED has five diagnostic groups: (1) atypical anorexia nervosa; (2) BN of low frequency and/or limited duration; (3) BED of low frequency and/or duration; (4) purging disorder; and (5) night eating syndrome. UFED is the residual category with no specific criteria [1]. The proposed ICD-11 guidelines [8,9] have such category—Other Feeding or Eating Disorder (OFED). The proposed OFED is closer to the DSM-5 UFED, in being a more general, nonspecific category of people who fall outside diagnostic criteria for a main eating disorder. The main features of OFED are the inclusion of atypical eating behaviors; symptoms that do not fulfill criteria for other Feeding and Eating Disorder (FED), for another mental and behavioral disorder, for another health condition, or that are not secondary to the use of substance or medication interfering on the central nervous system; symptoms and behaviors that are not sanctioned by cultural aspects; and finally, symptoms that impact on the person's personal, social, or work life.

In the DSM-5 [1] and the provisional ICD-11 guidelines [9], the essential features of binge eating are: (1) frequency of once weekly or more; (2) loss of control over the binge eating episode; and (3) marked distress. ICD-11 differs in the inclusion of subjective binge eating episodes (SBEs), where the amount consumed is normal or small although subjectively considered as large by the individual. This is supported by a large body of research [10–13]. A second point of difference between the DSM-5 and proposed ICD-11 criteria for BN and BED is the duration of binge eating episodes. In the DSM-5 this is at least 3 months for both disorders. In the proposed ICD-11 the recommendation is at least one month for BN and three months for BED except where the binge eating episodes are very frequent and the diagnosis of BED may be made for shorter period, such as one month. Third, the presence of diagnostic specifiers are required as diagnostic criteria for BED in DSM-5, while these are not essential in the provisional ICD-11.

In the DSM-5, a mental disorder is defined as "associated with significant distress or disability in social, occupational, or other important activities" (p. 20, [1]) and the proposed ICD-11 states the same [2]. Whilst functional disability is not further specified for either BN or BED, many studies do attest to the poor mental Health-Related Quality of Life (HRQoL) and role impairment, defined as "days in which the person was unable to perform the usual work or other activities, e.g., caring for children in the home" [14]. As the ICD-11 proposes broader symptomatic criteria, it is important to know if these define a syndrome of individuals with less impairment or poorer HRQoL than would be found using the DSM-5 scheme, and who may not meet the over-arching requirement for social or functional impairment as suggested in recent epidemiological studies [15,16].

Thus, the aims of this study were to compare (1) the proportion of participants diagnosed with threshold or subthreshold BN and BED (clinical utility); and (2) the severity of clinical features and mental HRQoL of these categories (convergent validity), in either scheme. We hypothesized that the broader criteria proposed in the ICD-11 would decrease the number of diagnoses of unspecified or not otherwise specified categories to a greater degree than in the DSM-5.

2. Materials and Methods

2.1. Procedures

Data were collected in a sample of 107 individuals of both genders, with threshold and subthreshold BN or BED, who attended the second phase of assessment for eligibility to participate in a randomized controlled trial (RCT) testing the efficacy of a new psychological intervention to treat overweight or obese people with BN or BED [17]. Participants were recruited from the waiting list of a Brazilian university center specialized in the treatment of eating disorders and advertisements in printed, internet and oral media. Assessment started with a brief screening interview by telephone. Volunteers were then assessed in person with the Mini International Neuropsychiatric Interview (MINI) [18,19], administered by psychiatrists, and height and weight measured with calibrated scales and a stadiometer.

A third assessment phase involved the administration of a semi-structured interview named the Eating Disorder Examination Edition 17.0 D (EDE) [20]. This interview was used both to confirm the eating disorder diagnoses of participants and to collect detailed data on overall eating disorder symptoms and behaviors. One author (MAP), who had been trained at the Centre for Research on Eating Disorders at Oxford, administered the EDE and made the diagnoses of each patient based on DSM-5 criteria [1] and the provisional ICD-11 diagnostic guidelines [8,9]. For the purpose of this secondary study, inclusion criteria were: participants that met DSM-5 diagnostic criteria for BN, BED, OSFED–BN, OSFED-BED, or UFED, were aged ≥18 years and had a Body Mass Index (BMI) between 27 and 39.9 kg/m^2. Thus, in this secondary study, 107 participants were selected, including 98 people who enrolled in the RCT and 9 participants who participated in all selection and recruitment assessments, but declined to enter the treatment intervention. Figure 1 shows the participant flow and reasons for exclusion during recruitment phases.

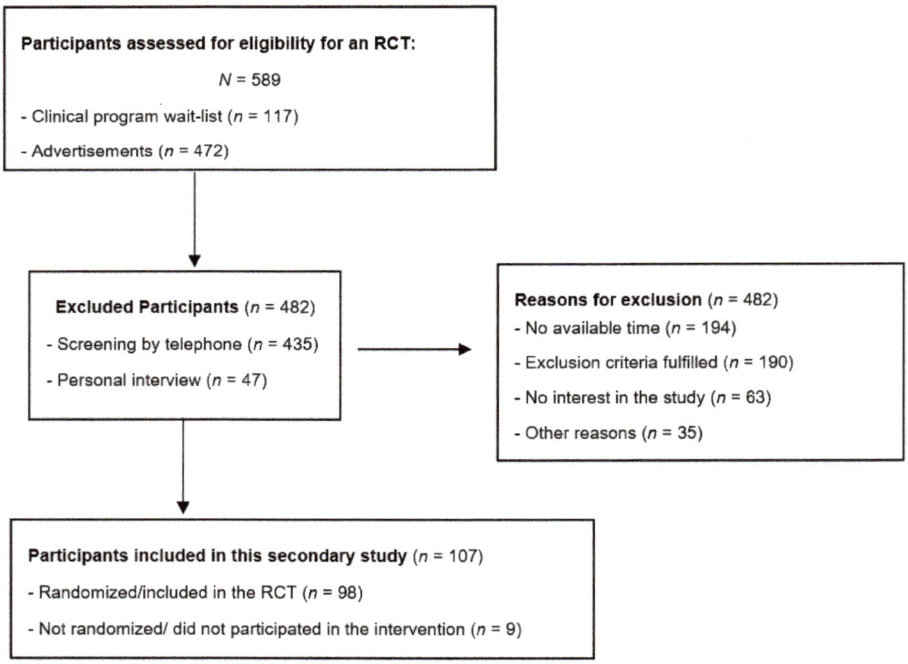

Figure 1. Flow chart of patient selection.

2.2. Measures

The assessment measures used for the study are detailed below:

1. Mini International Neuropsychiatric Interview (MINI) [18,19]: this structured interview is reliable and validated for diagnoses according to the DSM-5 [1]. The MINI version 5 [21] assessing DSM-IV diagnoses [22] has been translated into Portuguese. Thus, the MINI-5 was used in this study, with modifications to coding according to DSM-5 criteria, as in the MINI-7 [19].

2. Eating Disorder Examination (EDE) Edition 17.0D [20]: the EDE is a semi-structured interview. It assesses eating disorder features. It has four subscales measuring levels of dietary restraint, eating, shape and weight concerns. The global score is a mean of subscale scores. In this study, the new Version 17.0D item scoring, that included "being in control" as a reason for the behavior or cognition, was used. EDE version 16.0 [23] has been translated to Brazilian/Portuguese by researchers from the Universidade Federal do Rio de Janeiro (Silvia Freitas, José Carlos Appolinario), by authors of this paper (MAP, AC) and by an eating disorder specialist and member of the Eating Disorder Program (Christina Morgan—CM). A certified translator then back translated it into English. An author of the EDE (O'Connor, M) approved the final version. The translated EDE interrater reliability and concurrent validity were tested and found to be satisfactory. In the validity study, the diagnoses were made according to the eating disorder module of the SCID-I/P interview [24] (Portuguese version) [25]. Diagnostic agreement between the Portuguese EDE version 16.0 and the SCID I/P (both testing DSM-IV diagnoses) was found to be moderate (Kappa = 0.66; n = 149), with a Cronbach α of 0.91 (95% CI: 0.88 0.92) (unpublished data provided by AC). For the purpose of the present study, small adjustments were made by MAP, so that the Portuguese version used was consistent with the 17th version of the EDE [20], in order to derive DSM-5 categories. Cronbach α in this sample was 0.66, n = 107.
3. Binge Eating Scale (BES) [26]: the BES is a 16-item self-report instrument that was translated and validated in a Brazilian sample [27]. The BES measures frequency and severity of binge eating. The Brazilian version has undergone psychometric assessment and has a cut-off point for normality of 17 for the screening of eating disorders in obese individuals seeking treatment for weight loss. Cronbach α in this sample was 0.83, n = 106.
4. Loss of Control over Eating Scale (LOCES) [28]. This 24-item self-report scale measures loss of control during binge eating episodes in the last 4 weeks, with a mean score of 1.70 (SD = 5.72). It has been translated into Brazilian/Portuguese. This translated version has adequate psychometric properties (factor analysis and convergent validity) [29]. Cronbach α in this sample was 0.91, n = 107.
5. Depression, Anxiety and Stress Scale (DASS-21) [30,31] was used in its translated and validated Brazilian/Portuguese version [32]. The DASS is a 21-item self-report instrument that measures the presence and severity of depressive symptoms, anxiety and stress with a cut-off point for normality of 9 for depression, 7 for anxiety and 14 for stress. Cronbach α in this sample was 0.92, and for each subscale was: stress 0.85, depression 0.89, and anxiety 0.77, n = 107.
6. Health-related quality of life was assessed with the 12-item Short Form Health Survey (SF-12) [33]: a self-report questionnaire. It has two scales, the Physical Health Component Summary scale (PCS) and Mental Health Component Summary scale (MCS). The English language version has sound psychometric properties and it has been translated into Brazilian/Portuguese [34]. Cronbach α in this sample was 0.79, n = 106.
7. Disability was asked with a question closely similar to the 'days out of role' questions employed in the Australian National Survey of Mental Health and Well-Being [35]. Participants were asked to write for the past 4 weeks a response to, *"on how many days, if any, were you unable to complete your work, study or household responsibilities because of any problem with your (physical or emotional) health"?* An author (MAP) translated this text.

2.3. Statistical Analyses

Frequency and percentage statistics were used to report the distribution of diagnoses including OSFED, UFED and OFED categories for each scheme. Chi square statistic (χ^2) and Fisher's Exact Test were used to compare the frequency distributions of BN, BED, and OSFED/UFED or OFED for each scheme. The t-test or the Mann-Whitney U test were employed for parametric or non-parametric data and/or very small group sizes respectively, with correction of p to < 0.01 for multiple testing. SPSS v.23 was used for analyses [36].

2.4. Ethics

The RCT study was approved by the Human Research Ethics Committee of the Universidade Federal de São Paulo (UNIFESP), Brazil (CAAE 43874315.4.0000.5505). All participants provided written informed consent. Access to the data was limited to investigators and authorized researchers. The trial was formally registered in the U.S. National Institutes of Health Clinical, trial registration number NCT02464345, on 1 June 2015.

3. Results

One hundred and seven participants were included in this study. The majority of the participants were women (96%), and white (75%). A large minority were married (44%), and completed an under-graduate level of education (43%). The mean age was 40.07 years (SD 11.67), and mean BMI was 33.69 (SD 3.32). The sample included 50 (47%) participants with twice weekly Objective Binge Eating Episodes (OBEs) and 36 (34%) with weekly OBEs in the past 3 months. The remainder had a mix of OBEs and SBEs with the exception of one participant who had only SBEs.

Diagnostic evaluation using DSM-5 criteria resulted in 15/107 (14%) participants with BN, 70/107 (65.4%) with BED, 8/107 (7.5%) with OSFED-BN, 5/107 (4.7%) with OSFED-BED, and 9/107 (8.4%) participants with UFED. Applying the proposed ICD-11 criteria, there were 20/107 (18.7%) with BN, 82/107 (76.6%) with BED and 5/107 (4.7%) participants with OFED. The provisional ICD-11 diagnostic guidelines included 102/107 participants (95%) in the main categories of BN or BED compared to DSM-5 with 85/107 (79%), and 5/107 (5%) versus 22/107 (21%) with other or unspecified diagnosis ($\chi^2 = 20.265$, df = 1, $p < 0.001$, Fisher's Exact Test).

Comparative clinical features of the participants diagnosed according to either scheme are reported in Table 1. There were no significant differences in eating disorder or other psychiatric symptom severity, HRQoL, days out of role or BMI between participants with BN, BED or OSFED/UFED/OFED diagnosed according to DSM-5 or the proposed ICD-11.

Table 1. Comparative clinical features of the study participants (N = 107).

Clinical Features	Bulimia Nervosa			Binge Eating Disorder			# Osfed/Ufed/Ofed			All
	DSM-5 (n = 15)	ICD-11 (n = 20)		DSM-5 (n = 70)	ICD-11 (n = 82)		DSM-5 (n = 22)	ICD-11 (n = 5)		N = 107
	Median (IQR)		Z (p) †	Median (IQR)		Z (p)	Median (IQR)		MWU Z (p)	
EDE global	3.59 (3.27–3.83)	3.80 (2.35–3.83)	−0.044 (0.965)	2.48 (1.95–2.88)	2.27 (1.93–2.41)	−1.233 (0.217)	2.23 (1.98–2.74)	2.60 (2.01–2.77)	−0.196 (0.845)	2.57 (2.03–3.23)
EDE restriction	3.00 (2.70–3.60)	2.20 (1.00–3.80)	−0.394 (0.694)	1.60 (0.08–2.40)	1.40 (0.50–2.20)	−0.994 (0.320)	1.60 (0.60–2.20)	1.40 (1.00–1.60)	−0.157 (0.875)	1.80 (0.80–2.40)
EDE eating concern	2.00 (1.90–2.70)	3.00 (2.60–3.20)	−1.228 (0.220)	1.20 (0.60–2.20)	0.90 (0.20–1.40)	−1.605 (0.108)	1.20 (0.20–2.40)	0.60 (0.40–2.40)	−0.197 (0.844)	1.40 (0.60–2.40)
EDE shape concern	5.00 (4.25–5.37)	4.62 (2.62–4.75)	−0.961 (0.336)	3.62 (2.62–4.50)	3.44 (3.06–4.20)	−0.230 (0.818)	3.50 (3.00–4.62)	3.62 (2.88–3.88)	−0.118 (0.906)	3.75 (2.87–4.62)
EDE weight concern	4.20 (3.30–4.70)	3.20 (3.20–3.80)	−1.488 (0.137)	3.20 (2.40–4.20)	3.20 (2.70–3.67)	−0.263 (0.793)	3.20 (2.80–3.75)	2.80 (2.60–3.60)	−0.472 (0.637)	3.20 (2.60–4.20)
Binge Eating Scale	35.00 (30.50–41.00)	32.00 (31.00–33.00)	−0.963 (0.335)	29.00 (22.00–33.00)	28.00 (21.00–32.50)	−0.677 (0.498)	28.00 (24.00–33.00)	25.00 (25.00–25.00)	−1.061 (0.289)	30.00 (23.00–35.00)
LOCES	3.67 (3.29–4.18)	3.50 (3.08–3.62)	−0.917 (0.359)	3.21 (2.79–3.50)	3.12 (2.62–3.43)	−0.564 (0.573)	3.33 (2.70–3.54)	3.45 (3.41–3.50)	−0.746 (0.456)	3.33 (2.83–3.58)
DASS depression	22.00 (16.50–33.00)	24.00 (24.00–28.00)	−0.044 (0.965)	12.00 (6.00–20.00)	14.00 (7.00–17.00)	−0.066 (0.948)	16.00 (10.00–24.00)	10.00 (8.00–12.00)	−1.178 (0.239)	14.00 (8.00–24.00)
DASS anxiety	12.00 (5.00–14.00)	22.00 (4.00–26.00)	−0.615 (0.539)	8.00 (4.00–14.00)	17.00 (2.00–20.00)	−0.896 (0.370)	18.00 (2.00–22.00)	18.00 (6.00–18.00)	−0.277 (0.782)	10.00 (4.00–16.00)
DASS stress	28.00 (20.00–34.00)	30.00 (26.00–32.00)	−0.307 (0.799)	18.00 (12.00–28.00)	21.00 (14.00–27.00)	−0.059 (0.953)	26.00 (16.00–28.00)	20.00 (18.00–22.00)	−0.511 (0.609)	20.00 (14.00–28.00)
SFMCS	30.12 (26.63–38.70)	34.35 (34.32–40.81)	−1.702 (0.089)	36.34 (26.60–42.70)	37.14 (31.24–42.94)	−0.499 (0.618)	36.70 (32.61–42.74)	42.03 (35.74–44.78)	−1.136 (0.256)	36.02 (27.42–42.71)
SFPCS	46.27 (43.51–52.98)	47.00 (46.50–55.90)	−0.567 (0.570)	50.24 (41.97–56.36)	48.77 (40.64–56.60)	−0.273 (0.785)	47.00 (41.14–55.90)	50.39 (47.13–53.58)	−0.431 (0.667)	49.82 (41.52–56.20)
Body Mass Index (kg/m^2)	32.60 (29.72–34.31)	32.70 (31.30–34.60)	−0.655 (0.513)	33.60 (31.12–35.85)	34.65 (32.63–37.02)	−0.964 (0.335)	33.80 (32.37–36.90)	33.89 (30.70–35.29)	−0.823 (0.411)	33.64 (31.08–35.90)
Days out of role/28 days	10.00 (1.00–15.00)	4.00 (2.00–10.00)	−0.482 (0.630)	5.00 (2.00–12.00)	1.00 (0–11.00)	−1.341 (0.180)	2.00 (0–10.00)	0 (0–0)	−1.466 (0.143)	5.00 (0–12.00)

Note ICD-11 has OFED as the only subthreshold category. † MWU Z = Mann Whitney U Z statistic. BED = binge eating disorder; BN = bulimia nervosa; DASS = Depression, Anxiety and Stress Scale; DSM-5 = Diagnostic and Statistical Manual of Mental Disorders 5th ed; EDE = Eating Disorder Examination; ICD-11 = International Classification of Diseases 11th ed.; IQR = Interquartile Range; LOCES = Loss of Control Over Eating Scale; OFED = Other Feeding or Eating Disorder; OSFED = Other Specified Feeding or Eating Disorder; SFMCS = Short Form Health Survey Mental Health Component Summary score; SFPCS = Short Form Health Survey Physical Health Component Summary score; UFED = Unspecified Feeding or Eating Disorder.

4. Discussion

This study compared the clinical utility and convergent validity of the two main classification systems for psychiatric disorders—the DSM-5 [1] and the provisional ICD-11 [8,9]. Threshold and subthreshold diagnoses of BN and BED were derived using the "gold standard" semi-structured interview for eating disorders—the EDE-17.0D [20]. In both systems, a majority of participants met full BN or BED criteria. This supports the improved clinical utility of both schemes over the former DSM-IV [22] and ICD-10 [2] where a larger proportion of people did not meet full criteria [6,37].

In the present study, a greater number of participants received a main diagnosis of BN or BED with the provisional ICD-11 scheme compared to the DSM-5. Despite the inclusion of some less severe cases in those diagnosed according to ICD-11, overall there were no significant differences in levels of eating disorder or general psychopathology, BMI, mental or physical HRQoL, or role impairment between diagnoses defined by either classificatory system. These data do not support the findings reported by Mitchison et al. [16] where there was less impairment in people with less severe recurrent binge eating. A possible explanation is that the Mitchison study was based on the results of a community sample and this study used a clinical sample of people with high BMIs and an eating disorder who were seeking treatment, i.e., people potentially with more severe illness. Indeed, the present study included a higher proportion of people with twice-weekly OBEs, 58.1% (50/86) compared to 40.5% (158/390) in the Mitchison sample; and in the latter study those with twice weekly binge eating had poorer mental HRQoL, whether associated or not with marked distress.

Thus, the results of this study demonstrated that regardless of the classificatory system used, significant levels of associated general psychopathology and impact on mental HRQoL were observed in people with disorders characterized by recurrent binge eating. Our findings support those of Hudson's et al. [38], in which a high association between lifetime comorbid psychiatric disorders and role impairment in people with BED and BN was reported.

Different approaches guide these two classificatory systems, in particular the fact that the proposed ICD-11 diagnostic guidelines do not provide a "check-list" for diagnostic criteria. The diagnosis is based on a description of the essential features of the conditions, i.e., symptoms and characteristics that clinicians expect to find in all cases of the disorder. Reed [37] highlights that a large number of people with mental disorders around the globe may not receive treatment as a consequence of diagnoses being restricted by over rigid criteria. We anticipate that clinicians will likely find the ICD-11 scheme more user friendly, as it allows for greater clinician judgement [3] and is more flexible than the DSM-5. More of their patients may thereby receive definitive diagnosis and also, be eligible for care that is contingent on having a main diagnosis. On the other hand, the strict criteria of the DSM-5 are more applicable to the research setting where there is a need for tight criteria for reproducibility of studies.

A strength of this study was the use of an interview considered the gold standard (the EDE) for providing eating disorders diagnoses. Limitations include the small numbers of participants with ICD-11 BN and OSFED/UFED/OFED, with a subsequent risk of TYPE II error; a sample characterized by individuals who are overweight or obese; no participants with AN or other eating disorders; and the moderate alpha level of the EDE. Further, the BES has been validated in people with obesity and this sample included a small number (13.1%) with BMI 27.5–29.9. A final limitation is that the present study reports on a secondary analysis of data from a RCT testing the efficacy of psychological interventions for overweight people with bulimic disorders and used an EDE version, which does not collect the distress criterion across both OBEs and SBEs. However, the vast majority, 77 of 82 participants, had distress associated with OBEs.

5. Conclusions

The present article found that both the DSM-5 and ICD-11 diagnostic schemes had a low proportion of participants with a poorly specified (OSFED/UFED) diagnosis. Further, those included as BN or BED in the ICD-11 were not less severe than the ones with BN or BED in the DSM-5 groupings. The increased flexibility of the proposed ICD-11 may extend the clinical utility of this scheme compared to the DSM-5. However, further research is needed in larger samples of people with BN, people who are not overweight, and in people with other eating disorders diagnoses.

Author Contributions: M.A.P. was responsible for writing the original draft and P.H. and A.C. were responsible for writing, review and editing.

Funding: This study was financed in part by the Coordenação de Aperfeiçoamento de Pessoal de Nível Superior—Brasil (CAPES)—Finance Code 001.

Acknowledgments: We thank Alexandre Giffoni, Ana Maria Roma, Bruna Boaretto, Denise Claudino, Elson Asevedo, Juliana Carvalho, Mara Maranhão, Mireille Coelho, Nara Estella, Ruth Grigolon, Sérgio Garnes, and Veruska Amigo for the valuable assistance with participant assessments.

Conflicts of Interest: P.H. and A.C. are members of the World Health Organization Working Group on Feeding and Eating Disorders for the Revision of ICD-10 Mental and Behavioral Disorders and the paper represents authors' personal views. In the past 5 years, PH has received royalties from Hogrefe and Huber, McGraw Hill Education, Blackwell Scientific Publications, Routledge, Australian Doctor, and BMJ Pubs Eating Disorder work and publications. She receives or has received honoraria from Biomed Central and PLOS Medicine for Editorial duties and has received payment from Shire for writing a commissioned report. M.A.P. has participated in a 2016 meeting of an advisory board for the treatment of Binge Eating Disorder at Shire Pharmaceuticals, São Paulo, Brazil.

Trial Registration: U.S. National Institutes of Health—clinical trial registration number NTC02464345. URL: clinicaltrials.gov/ct2/show/NCT0246434.

References

1. American Psychiatric Association (APA). *Diagnostic and Statistical Manual of Mental Disorders*, 5th ed.; American Psychiatric Publishing: Arlington, VA, USA, 2013.
2. World Health Organization (WHO). *The ICD-10 Classification of Mental and Behavioural Disorders: Clinical Descriptions and Diagnostic Guidelines*; World Health Organization: Geneva, Switzerland, 1992.
3. First, M.B.; Reed, G.M.; Hyman, S.E.; Saxena, S. The development of the ICD-11 clinical descriptions and diagnostic guidelines for mental and behavioural disorders. *World Psychiatry* **2015**, *14*, 82–90. [CrossRef] [PubMed]
4. Reed, G.M.; First, M.B.; Medina-Mora, M.E.; Gureje, O.; Pike, K.M.; Saxena, S. Draft diagnostic guidelines for ICD-11 mental and behavioural disorders available for review and comment. *World Psychiatry* **2016**, *15*, 112–113. [CrossRef] [PubMed]
5. Reed, G.M.; Correia, J.M.; Esparza, P.; Saxena, S.; Maj, M. The WPA-WHO global survey of psychiatrists' attitudes towards mental disorders classification. *World Psychiatry* **2011**, *10*, 118–131. [CrossRef] [PubMed]
6. Al-Adawi, S.; Bax, B.; Bryant-Waugh, R.; Claudino, A.M.; Hay, P.; Monteleone, P.; Norring, C.; Pike, K.M.; Pilon, D.J.; Herscovici, C.R.; et al. Revision of ICD—Status update on feeding and eating disorders. *Adv. Eat. Disord. Theory Res. Pract.* **2013**, *1*, 10–20. [CrossRef]
7. Uher, R.; Rutter, M. Classification of feeding and eating disorders: Review of evidence and proposals for ICD-11. *World Psychiatry* **2012**, *11*, 80–92. [CrossRef] [PubMed]
8. World Health Organization (WHO). *ICD-11 Diagnostic Guidelines for Internet-Based Field Study—Feeding and Eating Disorders (D), Version 6*, Unpublished work. 2015.
9. Global Clinical Practice Network WHO. ICD-11 Diagnostic Guidelines for Internet Based Field Studies. 2015. Available online: https://gcp.network/en/icd-11-guidelines (accessed on 12 October 2017).
10. Brownstone, L.M.; Bardone-Cone, A.M.; Fitzsimmons-Craft, E.E.; Printz, K.S.; Le Grange, D.; Mitchell, J.E.; Crow, S.J.; Peterson, C.B.; Crosby, R.D.; Klein, M.H.; et al. Subjective and objective binge eating in relation to eating disorder symptomatology, negative affect, and personality dimensions. *Int. J. Eat. Disord.* **2013**, *46*, 66–76. [CrossRef] [PubMed]
11. Forney, K.J.; Bodell, L.P.; Haedt-Matt, A.A.; Keel, P.K. The incremental validity of the episode size criterion in binge-eating definitions: An examination in women with purging syndromes. *Int. J. Eat. Disord.* **2016**, *49*, 651–662. [CrossRef] [PubMed]
12. Jenkins, P.E.; Conley, C.S.; Rienecke Hoste, R.; Meyer, C.; Blissett, J.M. Perception of control during episodes of eating: Relationships with quality of life and eating psychopathology. *Int. J. Eat. Disord.* **2012**, *45*, 115–119. [CrossRef] [PubMed]

13. Palavras, M.A.; Hay, P.J.; Lujic, S.; Claudino, A.M. Comparing symptomatic and functional outcomes over 5 years in two nonclinical cohorts characterized by binge eating with and without objectively large episodes. *Int. J. Eat. Disord.* **2015**, *48*, 1158–1165. [CrossRef] [PubMed]
14. Agh, T.; Kovács, G.; Supina, D.; Pawaskar, M.; Herman, B.K.; Vokó, Z.; Sheehan, D.V. A systematic review of the health-related quality of life and economic burdens of anorexia nervosa, bulimia nervosa, and binge eating disorder. *Eat. Weight Disord.* **2016**, *21*, 353–364. [CrossRef] [PubMed]
15. Hay, P.; Mitchison, D.; Collado, A.E.L.; González-Chica, D.A.; Stocks, N.; Touyz, S. Burden and health-related quality of life of eating disorders, including Avoidant/Restrictive Food Intake Disorder (ARFID), in the Australian population. *J. Eat. Disord.* **2017**, *5*, 21. [CrossRef] [PubMed]
16. Mitchison, D.; Touyz, S.; González-Chica, D.A.; Stocks, N.; Hay, P. How abnormal is binge eating? 18-Year time trends in population prevalence and burden. *Acta Psychiatry Scand.* **2017**, *136*, 147–155. [CrossRef] [PubMed]
17. Palavras, M.A.; Hay, P.; Touyz, S.; Sainsbury, A.; da Luz, F.; Swinbourne, J.; Estella, N.M.; Claudino, A. Comparing cognitive behavioural therapy for eating disorders integrated with behavioural weight loss therapy to cognitive behavioural therapy-enhanced alone in overweight or obese people with bulimia nervosa or binge eating disorder: Study protocol for a randomised controlled trial. *Trials* **2015**, *16*, 578. [CrossRef] [PubMed]
18. Lecrubier, Y.; Weiller, E.; Hergueta, T.; Amorim, P.; Bonora, L.I.; Lépine, J.P. Mini International Neuropsychiatric Interview—Brazilian Version 5.0.0. DSM-IV, 2002. Available online: www.bibliotecadigital.ufmg.br (accessed on 2 July 2015).
19. Sheehan, D.; Janavs, J.; Baker, R.; Sheehan, K.H.; Knapp, E.; Sheehan, M. Mini International Neuropsychiatric Interview—Version 7.0.0 DSM-5 2014. Available online: http://www.medical-outcomes.com (accessed on 2 July 2015).
20. Fairburn, C.G.; Cooper, Z.; O'Connor, M. *The Eating Disorder Examination*, 17th ed.; The Centre for Research on Eating Disorders at Oxford: Oxford, UK, 2014; Available online: www.credo-oxford.com/pdfs/EDE170D.pdf (accessed on 3 July 2015).
21. Sheehan, D.V.; Lecrubier, Y.; Sheehan, K.H.; Amorim, P.; Janavs, J.; Weiller, E.; Hergueta, T.; Baker, R.; Dunbar, G.C. The Mini-International Neuropsychiatric Interview (M.I.N.I.): The development and validation of a structured diagnostic psychiatric interview for DSM-IV and ICD-10. *J. Clin. Psychiatry* **1998**, *59* (Suppl. 20), 22–33. [PubMed]
22. American Psychiatric Association (APA). *Diagnostic and Statistical Manual of Mental Disorders*, 4th ed.; American Psychiatric Association: Washington, DC, USA, 1994.
23. Fairburn, C.G. Eating Disorder Examination (Edition 16.0D). In *Cognitive Behavior Therapy and Eating Disorders*; The Guilford Press: New York, NY, USA, 2008; pp. 270–308.
24. First, M.B.; Spitzer, R.L.; Gibbon, M.; Williams, J.B.W. *Structured Clinical Interview for DSM-IV Axis I Disorders-Patient Edition (SCID-I/P, Version 2.0)*; Biometric Research, New York State Psychiatric Institute: New York, NY, USA, 1996.
25. Versiani, M. *Entrevista Clínica Estruturada—DSM-IV Transtornos do Eixo I. Tradução da Structured Clinical Interview for DSM-IV Axis I/Patient*; Versão 2.1; Programa de Ansiedade e Depressão, Instituto de Psiquiatria IPUB, UFRJ: Rio de Janeiro, Brazil, 1996.
26. Gormally, J.; Black, S.; Daston, S.; Rardin, D. The assessment of binge eating severity among obese persons. *Addict. Behav.* **1982**, *7*, 47–55. [CrossRef]
27. Freitas, S.; Lopes, C.S.; Coutinho, W.; Appolinario, J.C. Tradução e adaptação para o português da escala de compulsão alimentar periódica. *Rev. Bras. Psiquiatr.* **2001**, *23*, 215–220. [CrossRef]
28. Latner, J.D.; Mond, J.M.; Kelly, M.C.; Haynes, S.N.; Hay, P.J. The Loss of Control Over Eating Scale: Development and psychometric evaluation. *Int. J. Eat. Disord.* **2014**, *47*, 647–659. [CrossRef] [PubMed]
29. Luz, F.Q.; Sainsbury, A.; Estella, N.M.; Cogo, H.; Touyz, S.W.; Palavras, M.A.; Latner, J.D.; Claudino, A.; Hay, P. An empirical evaluation of the translation to Brazilian Portuguese of the Loss of Control Over Eating Scale (LOCES). *Arch. Clin. Psychiatry* **2016**, *43*, 1–5. [CrossRef]
30. Henry, J.D.; Crawford, J.R. The short-form version of the Depression Anxiety Stress Scales (DASS-21): Construct validity and normative data in a large non-clinical sample. *Br. J. Clin. Psychol.* **2005**, *44*, 227–239. [CrossRef] [PubMed]

31. Lovibond, P.F.; Lovibond, S.H. The structure of negative emotional states: Comparison of the Depression Anxiety Stress Scales (DASS) with the Beck Depression and Anxiety Inventories. *Behav. Res. Ther.* **1995**, *33*, 335–343. [CrossRef]
32. Vignola, R.C.; Tucci, A.M. Adaptation and validation of the depression, anxiety and stress scale (DASS) to Brazilian Portuguese. *J. Affect. Disord.* **2014**, *155*, 104–109. [CrossRef] [PubMed]
33. Ware, J., Jr.; Kosinski, M.; Keller, S.D. A 12-item short-form health survey: Construction of scales and preliminary tests of reliability and validity. *Med. Care* **1996**, *34*, 220–233. [CrossRef] [PubMed]
34. Silveira, M.F.; Almeida, J.C.; Freire, R.S.; Haikal, D.S.; Martins, A.E.B.L. Propriedades psicométricas do instrumento de avaliação da qualidade de vida: 12-item health survey (SF-12). *Ciência Saúde Coletiva* **2013**, *18*, 1923–1931. [CrossRef] [PubMed]
35. Slade, T.; Johnston, A.; Oakley Browne, M.A.; Andrew, G.; Whiteford, H. 2007 National Survey of Mental Health and Wellbeing: Methods and key findings. *Aust. N. Z. J. Psychiatry* **2009**, *43*, 594–605. [CrossRef] [PubMed]
36. IBM Corp. *Released 2015. IBM SPSS Statistics for Windows*; Version 23.0; IBM Corp: Armonk, NY, USA, 2015.
37. Reed, G.M. Toward ICD-11: Improving the clinical utility of WHO's international classification of mental disorders. *Prof. Psychol. Res.* **2010**, *41*, 457–464. [CrossRef]
38. Hudson, J.I.; Hirpi, E.; Pope, H.G., Jr.; Kessler, R.C. The prevalence and correlates of eating disorders in the National Comorbidity Survey Replication. *Biol. Psychiatry* **2007**, *61*, 348–358. [CrossRef] [PubMed]

nutrients

MDPI

Review

Feedback-Based Treatments for Eating Disorders and Related Symptoms: A Systematic Review of the Literature

Claudio Imperatori [1,*], Miranda Mancini [1], Giacomo Della Marca [2], Enrico Maria Valenti [1,3] and Benedetto Farina [1]

1. Department of Human Sciences, European University of Rome, Via degli Aldobrandeschi 190, 00163 Roma, Italy; mancini.miranda@gmail.com (M.M.); enricomaria.valenti@gmail.com (E.M.V.); benfarina@gmail.com (B.F.)
2. Sleep Disorders Unit, Institute of Neurology, Catholic University, 00153 Rome, Italy; giacomodellamarca@gmail.com
3. Department of Dynamic and Clinical Psychology, Sapienza University of Rome, 00185 Rome, Italy

* Correspondence: imperatori.c@libero.it; Tel.: +06-66-54-38-73

Received: 25 October 2018; Accepted: 16 November 2018; Published: 20 November 2018

Abstract: The effectiveness of biofeedback and neurofeedback has been investigated in a range of psychiatric disorders. However, to date, there are few studies on the clinical usefulness of feedback-based techniques for eating disorders (EDs) and EDs-related symptoms (e.g., food craving). A systematic search of PubMed, Scopus and PsychINFO identified 162 articles. Among these, thirteen studies exploring the therapeutic use of biofeedback and neurofeedback in EDs or EDs-related symptoms were included. Biofeedback and neurofeedback were implemented respectively in five and eight of all reviewed articles. No studies incorporated different feedback modalities or both biofeedback and neurofeedback. The considered studies provide preliminary data of the usefulness of feedback-based techniques in the treatment of several dysfunctional eating behaviors (e.g., food craving, rumination). Although no significant effect has been reported for other important EDs-related symptoms (i.e., body image disturbance), feedback-based techniques are also associated with significant modifications of both sympathetic reaction to food-related stimuli and brain activity in several regions of the reward system (e.g., insula). Taken together the results of the present review suggest that feedback-based treatments may be useful in the treatment of several dysfunctional eating behaviors operating both on top-down and bottom-up individual coping strategies. Methodological and clinical issues are also discussed.

Keywords: biofeedback; EEG-Neurofeedback; fMRI-Neurofeedback; eating disorders; psychophysiology; eating disorders-related symptoms

1. Introduction

Eating disorders (EDs) are severe and disabling conditions caused by multiple factors (e.g., genetic and psychosocial) [1], which are associated with significant functional impairments [2], high mortality risk [3] and treatment difficulties [4]. The last edition of the Diagnostic and Statistical Manual of Mental Disorders (DSM-5) [5] includes a substantially revised section on EDs [6,7], now named "Feeding and Eating Disorders". This section includes the following diagnoses: pica, rumination disorder (RD), avoidant/restrictive food intake disorder (ARFID), anorexia nervosa (AN), bulimia nervosa (BN), binge eating disorder (BED), and other specified feeding or eating disorder (OSFED).

EDs and related symptoms are common in both children and adolescents [8,9]. In adults, the lifetime prevalence is about 0.6% for AN, 1% for BN, and 3% for BED [2,3]. Furthermore, it has been recently reported that, following the transition to DSM-5, the prevalence of OSFED has decreased, and that AN, BN and BED have increased in non-clinical samples [10]. Similarly, EDs-related symptoms, such as food craving (i.e., an intense desire to consume a specific food that is difficult to resist); Refs. [11–13] or loss of control over eating, are widely reported amongst the general population. For example, in a non-clinical sample it has been reported [14] that 28% of women and 13% of men reported food craving at least once a week during the past 6 months. This symptom is also commonly experienced in AN [15,16], BN [16–19], and BED [20,21]. Moreover, it has been reported that food craving severity is positively associated with both body mass index (BMI) [13,22–25], drop-out from weight loss programs [25–27], and a meta-analysis [28] on 3292 individuals showed that it significantly contributes to dysfunctional eating behaviours and weight gain.

Similarly, loss of control over eating is a relatively frequent experience among both adolescents from the general population (i.e., about 17%) [29], adults with obesity (i.e., BMI $\geq$ 30 kg/m^2) and patients with EDs [30]. Additionally, it was positively associated with other psychopathological symptoms (e.g., non-suicidal self-injury, body dissatisfaction, higher depressive symptoms) [31].

Multidisciplinary approaches, combining medical, dietetic and psychological interventions are generally recommended in the treatment of EDs [32]. However, it is known that current treatments for EDs are often related to treatment difficulties [4] and poor long-term efficacy [1,33,34]. For example, it has been reported that several treatments, such as nutritional rehabilitation and psychological approaches (e.g., cognitive-behavioral therapy, family-based therapy), are associated with high relapse rates in adolescents with AN [33]. Similarly, binge eating remission rates at the end of treatments are only found in 30–40% of patients with BN [1]. Therefore, the necessity of additional treatment modalities for these mental disorders has been proposed [35].

Feedback-based treatments (i.e., biofeedback and neurofeedback) have been suggested as additional treatment modalities for EDs [36]. Feedback is considered a crucial component of mental health interventions, increasing motivation, facilitating the learning process and modifying dysfunctional thoughts and behaviors [37]. Over the last thirty years there has been an increasing number of disorders, including EDs, for which biofeedback and neurofeedback have been investigated with more or less empirically supported results [38,39].

Biofeedback and neurofeedback are operant-conditioning based trainings that allow individuals to learn how to regulate neurophysiological activity in response to real-time feedback, in order to improve health and performance [38]. Biofeedback refers to an intervention that helps individuals to control or change their physiologic functioning (e.g., heart rate, electrodermal activity, respiratory rate, muscle tension and peripheral temperature) [40]. Neurofeedback refers to a form of biofeedback involving different modalities, such as electroencephalography (EEG) or real-time functional magnetic resonance imaging (rt-fMRI), that trains individuals to control or modify their brain activity [41]. Compared to other neuro-stimulation techniques (i.e., transcranial direct current stimulation), which may be associated with several mild and transient adverse effects [42], feedback-based treatments are not related with side effects [43] and seems to be easy and affordable techniques for general practices and clinicians [44,45].

During a typical feedback-based session, neurophysiological activity (e.g., brain and or electrodermal activity) is "fed back" to the individual using a brain-computer interface, providing continuously updated information about their success in regulating their neurophysiological parameters [36]. The successful self-regulation of the individuals' physiology represents an immediate and effective positive reinforcement, creating a positive loop between the machine's feedback and the patient's successful self-regulation [40]. Therefore the three necessary components for a feedback-based session are: (i) a therapist explaining the equipment and its use, (ii) a patient and (iii) a monitoring machine that provides accurate neurophysiological information [38]. Although training sessions and modalities may be different according to the individual needs and/or the diagnosis [40], general protocol guidelines are provided [38].

2. Study Rationale

The clinical efficacy of biofeedback and neurofeedback has been investigated in a range of psychiatric disorders [38,39]. However, to date, there are few studies on the clinical usefulness of feedback-based techniques for EDs or EDs-related symptoms. Therefore, the present systematic review (PRISMA checklist is reported in Table S1) was carried out to explore the current therapeutic use of biofeedback and neurofeedback in EDs and EDs-related symptoms (i.e., food craving, binge eating, loss of control over eating). Specifically, in this study we investigated: (i) the type of feedback-based protocol applied, and (ii) the usefulness of feedback-based techniques assessed through clinical scales and/or neurophysiological measures.

3. Methods

3.1. Inclusion/Exclusion Criteria

We used the P.I.C.O.S. (Population, Interventions, Comparators, Outcomes, and Study Design) criteria to identify relevant studies. This review focused on feedback-based interventions for EDs and related symptoms. Therefore, original articles reporting data from studies investigating the potential therapeutic effects of different biofeedback (i.e., heart rate, electrodermal activity, respiratory rate, muscle tension and peripheral temperature) and neurofeedback modalities (i.e., EEG, fMRI) in this field were initially considered. Studies involving children and adolescents were also taken into consideration. Book chapters, conference papers, reviews, dissertations, and case reports were not included. Articles in which either feedback-based treatments for EDs or EDs-related symptoms were not the focal point were also excluded. Moreover, feedback-based studies investigating EDs-related symptoms (i.e., food craving, binge eating, overeating) in non-clinical or subthreshold sample were initially considered. Both randomized and non-randomized controlled studies, as well as pre-/post-intervention comparison reports were considered.

According to guidelines for the evaluation of the clinical efficacy of psychophysiological interventions [46], as well as with previous systematic reviews focused of feedback-based treatments in psychiatric disorders [39,47], articles that provided the following information were included in the study: (i) feedback modality type, (ii) sample (i.e., including age, sex, medication status, BMI, recruitment), (iii) study design (including type, number and duration of protocol sessions, as well as description of study conditions), (iv) collection and analysis of neurophysiological (e.g., EEG power spectrum, electrodermal activity etc.), behavioral (e.g., number of binge episodes) and/or psychological outcomes measure (i.e., clinical scales). Furthermore, according to Schoenberg and David [39], studies that did not report 2 or more components of points (ii) and (iii), and/or articles that did not specify points (i), (iv) and (v) were excluded.

3.2. Search Strategy

Potentially relevant studies were initially identified by searching publications from the year 1970 to 5 August 2018 through the following databases: PubMed, Scopus and PsychInfo. Only English articles were taken into account. The following search terms were entered into the databases: "biofeedback" OR "neurofeedback" AND "anorexia nervosa", "bulimia nervosa", "binge eating disorder", "pica", "rumination disorder", "avoidant/restrictive food intake disorder", "food intake disorder", "food craving", "binge eating", "overeating", "eating psychopathology". Articles resulting from the search strategy were examined for relevance by screening titles and abstracts. Then, articles that appeared to meet inclusion criteria were further evaluated by two independent researchers (C.I. and M.M.) in order to assess all inclusion/exclusion criteria. In case of disagreement, a senior researcher (B.F.) resolved any discrepancies and decided whether or not the study was going to be included. A detailed flow diagram of selection of studies is reported in Figure 1.

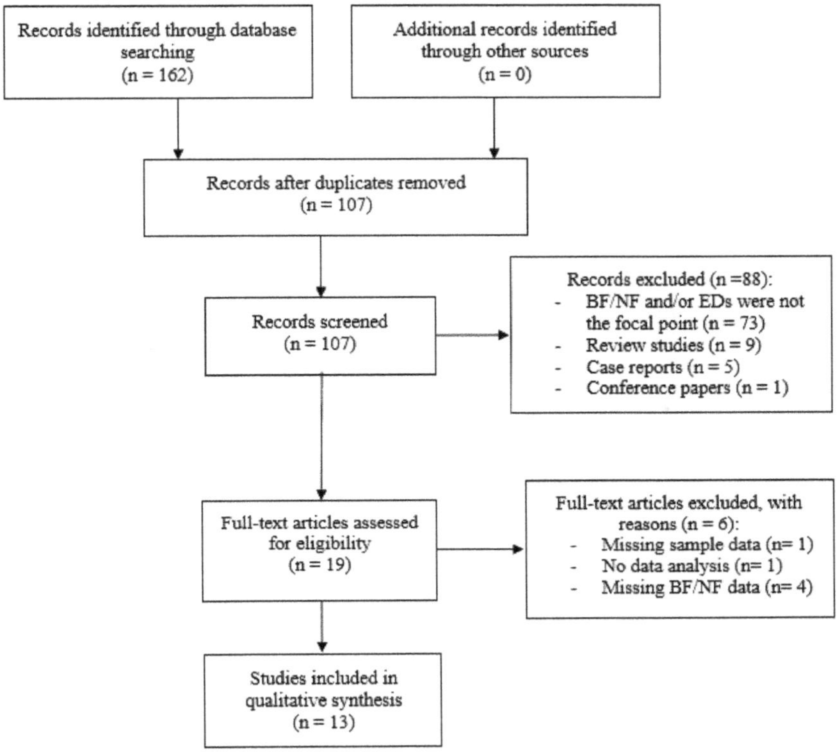

Figure 1. Flow diagram of selection of studies. Abbreviation: BF = Biofeedback; NF = Neurofeedback; EDs = Eating Disorders.

4. Results

The initial search resulted in 162 articles. Duplicate articles were eliminated, leaving 107 screened studies. Of these articles, 19 met initial inclusion criteria and were assessed for eligibility. Six articles were subsequently excluded with reasons (e.g., missing information pertaining to methods/outcome measures, no description of biofeedback modality, no statistical analysis etc.).

Thirteen articles fulfilled the quality assessment and are considered in this review (Table 1).

Table 1. Characteristics of the included studies (n = 13).

Authors	Participants	Design		Outcome Measures	Main Results
	(a) Sample (b) N (sex) (c) Age (mean ± sd. or range) (d) BMI (mean ± sd. or range) (e) Psychotropic medication (yes/no)	(a) Group (type of intervention) (b) Randomized (yes/no) (c) Blind (single/double)	(d) N of sessions (e) Duration (f) Follow-up (yes/no)	(a) Psychological/Behavioral (b) Physiological	(a) Psychological: ↑ = sign. increase; ↓ = sign. decrease; x = no change (b) Physiological: ↑ = sign. increase; ↓ = sign. decrease; x = no change (c) Stability at follow-up (yes/no)
Biofeedback Studies					
Pop-Jordanova 2000	(a) preadolescents with obesity; preadolescents with AN (b) 76 (F); 27 (F) (c) 12.75 ± 1.75; 14.25 ± 2.99 (d) bodyweight over 95th percentile; bodyweight below the 3rd percentile (e) n/a	(a) one group: ED-BF and supportive psychotherapy (b) no (c) n/a	(d) 5 (e) n/a (f) no	(a) n/a (b) EDA	(a) n/a (b)↓ of EDA in children with obesity and AN (c) n/a
Meule et al., 2012	(a) non-clinical sample (b) 56 (47 F, 9 M) (c) 24.12 ± 3.79 (d) 22.65 ± 3.19 (e) n/a	(a) 3 groups: (i) BFG (n = 14 high cravers): HRV-BF (ii) CG_1 (n = 14 high cravers): no intervention (iii) CG_2 (n = 28 low cravers): no intervention (b) pseudo-randomization * (c) single	(d) 12 (e) 20 min. (f) no	(a) FC [1]; eating disorder symptoms [2]; FA [3]; self-regulatory success in dieting; emotion regulation; locus of control (b) HR; HRV	(a) ↓ FC only in BFG; ↓ in eating and weight concerns only in BFG; x in other eating disorder symptoms, emotion regulation, FA, locus of control and self-regulatory success in dieting (b) ↓ in HRV in CG_1 (c) n/a
Teufel et al., 2013	(a) obese individuals (b) 30 (F) (c) 48.67 ± 11.93 (d) 35.5 ± 5.3 ** (e) no	(a) 3 groups: (i) BFG_1 (n = 10): ED-BF focused on food stimuli (ii) BFG_2 (n = 10): ED-BF focused on unspecific food stimuli (iii) CG (n = 10): no intervention (b) yes (c) single	(d) 8 (e) 21 min. (f) 3 months	(a) self-efficacy, stress, ability to relax, eating disorder symptoms [4]; BMI (b) EDA to food stimuli	(a) ↑ of food-related self-efficacy and perceived stress in BFGs; ↑ ability to relax in BFGs; x in BMI and, eating disorder symptoms (b) ↓ in EDA to food stimuli in BFGs (c) yes (a + b); ↓ loss of control during eating in BFG_2
Barba et al., 2015	(a) patients with RD (b) 28 (17 F, 11 M) (c) age range (14–76) (d) 22 ± 2 (e) yes (n = 4)	(a) 2 groups: (i) BFG (n = 15): EMG-BF (ii) CG (n = 4): no intervention (b) n/a (c) single	(d) 3 plus instructions for daily exercise (e) n/a (f) 1, 3, 6 months	(a) regurgitation episodes and associated abdominal symptoms. (b) EMG of abdominothoracic muscles	(a) ↓ in regurgitation episodes and associated abdominal symptoms immediately after treatment and after 6 month follow up (b) ↓ of intercostal and anterior wall muscle activity (c) yes (a + b)
Halland et al., 2016	(a) patients with RD (b) 16 (9 F, 7 M) (c) 37 ± 13 (d) 26.5 ± 5 (e) yes	(a) one group: DB-BF (b) no (c) n/a	(d) n/a (e) n/a (f) no	(a) rumination episodes (b) postprandial intragastric and esophagogastric junction pressure	(a) ↓ rumination episodes (b) ↑ of esophagogastric junction pressure; ↓postprandial intragastric pressure (c) n/a

Table 1. *Cont.*

Authors	Participants	Design		Outcome Measures	Main Results
		Neurofeedback Studies			
Schmidt & Martin 2015	(a) subthreshold sample of restrained eaters (b) 27 (F) (c) 34.54 ± 10.40 ** (d) 27.35 ± 5.24 ** (e) no	(a) 2 groups: (i) NFG (n = 14): EEG beta training NF (↓ 23–28 Hz activity at Cz) (ii) CG (n = 13): no intervention (b) yes (c) single	(d) 10 (e) 45 min. (f) 3 months	(a) overeating episodes and related distress; FC [1]; perceived dieting success; perceived stress; well-being (b) n/a	(a) ↓ overeating episodes and related distress in NFG; ↑ of perceived dieting success in NFG; x in FC, perceived stress, and well-being (b) n/a (c) yes (overeating episodes and related distress); ↓ of FC in NFG
Lackner et al., 2016	(a) adolescents with AN (b) 22 (F) (c) age range (12–18) (d) 15.41 ± 1.66 ** (e) yes (n = 1)	(a) 2 groups: (i) NFG (n = 10): EEG alpha training NF (↑ 8–12 Hz activity at Pz) and usual maintenance treatment CG (n = 12): usual maintenance treatment (b) yes (c) single	(d) 10 (e) 20 min (f) no	(a) psychological wellbeing, eating disorder symptoms [4,5,6], emotional competence, psychopathology (b) resting EEG power	(a) ↑ of disinhibition, ↑ of hunger;↓ restriction and dieting in NFG; ↓ of interpersonal sensitivity and ↑ emotional competence in NFG; x in BMI and psychopathology (b) ↑ EEG theta power (eyes closed) in NFG; x in EEG alpha power (c) n/a
Schmidt & Martin 2016	(a) subthreshold sample of binge eaters (b) 57 (F) (c) 44.77 ± 15.15 (d) 28.77 ± 5.47 (e) no	(a) 3 groups: (i) NFG (n = 18): EEG beta training NF (↓ 23–28 Hz activity at Cz) (ii) CG_1 (n = 18): mental imagery (iii) CG_2 (n = 21): no intervention (b) yes (c) single	(d) 10 (e) 45 min (f) 3 months	(a) subjective binge eating episodes and related, perceived stress, FC [7], self-efficacy (b) n/a	(a) ↓ binge eating episodes in NFG; ↓ of distress resulting from binge in NFG and CG_1; ↓ of FC in NFG and CG_1; ↓ of perceived stress and ↑ of dietary self-efficacy in NFG (b) n/a (c) yes (↓ binge eating episodes and related distress)
Ihssen et al., 2017	(a) non-clinical sample (b) 10 (F) (c) 21.4 ± 2.3 (d) 23.53 ± 2.66 (e) no	(a) one group: rt-fMRI-NF during exposure to appetitive food pictures (b) no (c) n/a	(d) 1 (e) 280 s (f) no	(a) subjective hunger, state FC [8], general FC [9], feelings of satiety (b) functional activation in brain areas	(a) ↓ of subjective hunger; ↑ of state FC; x in feelings of satiety; x in general FC (b) ↓ activation in reward brain areas (e.g., amygdala, insula, PFC) (c) n/a
Imperatori et al., 2017	(a) non-clinical sample (b) 50 (36 F, 14 M) (c) 22.90 ± 2.68 (d) 21.93 ± 3.41 (e) no	(a) 2 groups: (i) NFG (n = 25): EEG alpha/theta training NF (↓ 8–12.5 Hz and ↑ 4.5–7.5 Hz activity at Pz) (ii) CG (n = 25): no intervention (b) yes (c) single	(d) 10 (e) 27 min (f) 4 months	(a) FC [1], eating disorder symptoms [2], psychopathology (b) resting EEG power	(a) ↓ in FC in NFG; x in eating disorder symptoms and psychopathology (b) ↑ of alpha power in reward brain areas (e.g., insula, parahippocampal gyrus) (c) yes (a; b was not assessed)

Table 1. *Cont.*

Authors	Participants	Design		Outcome Measures	Main Results
Fattahi et al., 2017	(a) overweight (b) 30 (F) (c) age range (20–50) (d) n/a (e) n/a	(a) 2 groups: (i) NFG (n = 15): EEG alpha/theta training NF (↓ 8–12.5 Hz and ↑ 4.5–7.5 Hz activity at Pz) (ii) CG (n = 15): no intervention (b) yes (c) single	(d) 10 (e) 30–45 min (f) no	(a) FC [1] and mental health (b) n/a	(a) ↓ in FC and ↑ mental health in NFG (b) n/a (c) n/a
Spetter et al., 2017	(a) overweight/obese individuals (b) 8 (M) (c) 31.8 ± 4.4 (d) 29.4 ± 1.4 (e) no	(a) one group: rt-fMRI-NF during exposure to appetitive food pictures (b) n/a (c) n/a	(d) 4 (e) 9 min (f) no	(a) hunger and mood related ratings, food choice task, calorie intake (b) brain functional connectivity	(a) x in food choice task and in calorie intake assessment; x in hunger, fullness, satiety and appetite; ↓ in fear and agitation (b) ↑ functional connectivity between dlPFC and vmPFC (c) n/a
Leong et al., 2018	(a) obese individuals with FA symptoms (b) 21 (F) (c) 43.01± 13.97 ** (d) 33.5 ± 7.44 ** (e) no	(a) 2 groups: (i) NFG (n = 11): infraslow EEG-NF (modulation of slow wave activity at the PCC) (ii) CG (n = 10): placebo (b) yes (c) double	(d) 6 (e) 10 min (session #1) 20 min (other sessions) (f) 4 weeks	(a) state FC [10] (b) resting EEG power	(a) ↓ of state FC (b) ↑ in infraslow activity in the PCC (c) n/a

Abbreviations: n = number; BMI = body mass index; AN = anorexia nervosa; F = females; ED-BF = electrodermal biofeedback; n/a = not applicable; EDA = electrodermal activity; M = males: BFG = biofeedback group; HRV-BF = heart rate variability biofeedback; CG = control group; FC = food craving; FA = food addiction; HR = heart rate; HRV = heart rate variability; RD = rumination disorder; EMG-BF = electromyography biofeedback; EMG = electromyography; DB-BF = diaphragmatic breathing biofeedback; NFG = neurofeedback group; EEG = electroencephalography; rt-fMRI-NF = real-time functional magnetic resonance imaging neurofeedback; PFC = prefrontal cortex; dlPFC = dorsolateral prefrontal cortex; vmPFC = ventromedial prefrontal cortex; PCC = posterior cingulate cortex. Notes: * = 3 participants that could not participate in the study because of time constraints were then assigned to the control group; ** = pooled standard deviation; [1] = assessed with the Food Craving Questionnaire-Trait [48]; [2] = assessed with the Eating Disorder Examination Questionnaire [49]; [3] = assessed with Yale Food Addiction Scale [50]; [4] = assessed with Three Factor Eating Questionnaire [51];[5] = assessed with Eating Disorder Cognition Questionnaire [52]; [6] = assessed with Body Image Avoidance Questionnaire [53]; [7] = assessed with the Food Craving Questionnaire-Trait-reduced [24]; [8] = assessed with a single item ("How strong is your desire to eat?") rated on a five-point scale; [9] = assessed with the modified Trait and State Food Craving Questionnaire [54]; [10] = assessed with the Food Craving Questionnaire-State [48].

Biofeedback and neurofeedback were implemented respectively in five and eight of all reviewed articles. No studies incorporated different feedback modalities (e.g., electrodermal and electromyography biofeedback) or both biofeedback and neurofeedback. None of the studies investigated in this review reported relevant side effects for both biofeedback and neurofeedback training.

Mean number of sessions per study was 7.42 (range 1–12). Among reviewed article, three studies were focused on non-clinical samples [55–57], two on subthreshold samples [58,59], two on adolescents with AN [60,61], two on patients with RD [62,63] and 5 on overweight/obese individuals [61,64–67].

Eight studies were randomized [56–60,64,65,67], but only one was a double-blind trial [65]. Four studies did not have a control condition [55,61,63,66]. No treatment/waiting list was the most frequently (n = 7) control condition used [56–59,62,64,67], and only one study implemented a placebo condition (i.e., simulation protocol) [65] or an alternative treatment [59] (i.e., mental imagery).

Due to the high heterogeneity of samples, outcome measures and feedback modality, a meta-analysis was not performed.

4.1. Biofeedback Studies

Biofeedback was investigated in five of all reviewed articles. Of these, two studies implemented electrodermal biofeedback (ED-BF) [61,67], one heart rate variability biofeedback (HRV-BF) [57], one electromyography biofeedback (EMG-BF) [62], and one diaphragmatic breathing biofeedback (DB-BF) [63].

Barba et al. [62] and Halland et al., [63], investigated the usefulness of EMG-BF and DB-BF in patients with RD respectively. Both studies reported significant changes in clinical (e.g., decrease in regurgitation and rumination episodes) and physiological (e.g., decrease of intragastric pressure) outcomes.

Two studies examined the potential therapeutic effects of ED-BF in obese patients with overeating. Pop-Jordanova [61], in a pre-post study design, showed that 5 sessions of ED-BF were associated with a decrease of electrodermal activity in a sample of girls with obesity (n = 76) and AN (n = 27). In a sample of obese women (n = 30), Teufel et al. [67], through a randomized controlled study, reported that compared to a waiting list, both ED-BF focused on food stimuli and ED-BF focused on unspecific stimuli were associated with an increased ability to tolerate food-related stress (e.g., decrease of electrodermal activity and increase self-efficacy in dealing with food). Although these results remained stable after 6-months follow-up, no significant changes were observed in BMI and in ED-related symptoms (e.g., tendency to lose control of food intake).

Finally, in a study on non-clinical sample of cravers (n = 56), Meule et al., [57], reported that, compared to a waiting-list, 12 sessions of HRV-BF were associated with a decrease of food craving as well as with a decrease of eating and weight concerns. No significant changes were observed in physiological measures (e.g., HRV) and in other EDs-related symptoms (e.g., shape concern, binge frequency).

4.2. Neurofeedback Studies

Neurofeedback was investigated in eight of all reviewed articles. Of these, six studies implemented EEG [56,58–60,64,65] and two rt-fMRI [55,66].

Two randomized controlled studies investigated the usefulness of EEG beta training neurofeedback (i.e., decrease beta activity at Cz electrode) in female subthreshold samples of restrained eaters (*n* = 27) [58] and binge eaters (*n* = 57) [59]. Both studies reported that, compared to a waiting-list, 10 sessions of neurofeedback were associated with a decrease in overeating episodes and related distress. These results remained stable after 3-months follow-up.

Two randomized controlled studies investigated the effectiveness of EEG alpha/theta training neurofeedback (i.e., raise posterior theta over alpha amplitude with eyes closed without falling asleep) in reducing food craving, in a non-clinical sample (*n* = 50) [56] and in a sample of overweight women (*n* = 30) respectively [64]. It has been observed that, compared to a waiting-list, 10 sessions of neurofeedback were associated with a decrease of food craving severity [56,64] as well as with an improvement of mental health [64]. A significant increase of resting EEG alpha power in several brain areas involved in food craving (e.g., insula) and food cue reactivity (e.g., parahippocampal gyrus) was also documented [56]. Although changes in food craving persisted after 4-months follow-up, no significant modifications were reported in other EDs-related symptoms (e.g., weight and shape concerns) and in the general level of psychopathology [56].

Lackner et al. [60] examined the potential therapeutic effects of EEG alpha training neurofeedback (i.e., raise posterior alpha activity) in female adolescents with AN (*n* = 22). It has been observed that, compared to the standard treatment, 10 sessions of neurofeedback were associated with an improvement in several ED-related symptoms (e.g., decrease of restriction and dieting behavior) and with an increase of emotional competence. Although modifications of resting EEG power were also documented (i.e., increase of theta power), no significant modifications were reported in psychopathological symptoms (with the exception of interpersonal sensitivity), in BMI and in body image related symptoms.

Two studies investigated the usefulness of rt-fMRI neurofeedback during the exposure to appetitive food pictures, respectively in a non-clinical sample of women (*n* = 10) [55] and in overweight/obese men (*n* = 8) [66]. Both studies showed that rt-fMRI neurofeedback could modify brain activity [55] and brain connectivity [66] in crucial areas involved in the reward system (e.g., amygdala and prefrontal cortex). Although no significant improvement was reported in food craving or in calorie intake assessment, a decrease of subjective hunger [55] and negative mood [66] related to food stimuli was reported.

Finally, in the only double-blind, placebo-controlled neurofeedback study, Leong et al. [65], investigated the effectiveness of infraslow EEG neurofeedback (i.e., the modulation of slow wave activity (0–0.1 Hz)) in obese women with food addiction symptoms. Compared to placebo condition, it has been reported that 6 sessions of neurofeedback were associated with an increase of infraslow activity in the posterior cingulate cortex as well as with a decrease of state food craving.

4.3. Risk of Bias

Risk of bias in the reviewed articles was performed according to Cochrane standards of practice [68]. Two reviewers (CI and GDM) independently assessed the risk for bias. In case of disagreement, a senior researcher (BF) resolved any discrepancies. Risk for bias was mainly related to the lack of both blinding and control conditions. Assessment of bias in the included studies are reported in Figures 2 and 3.

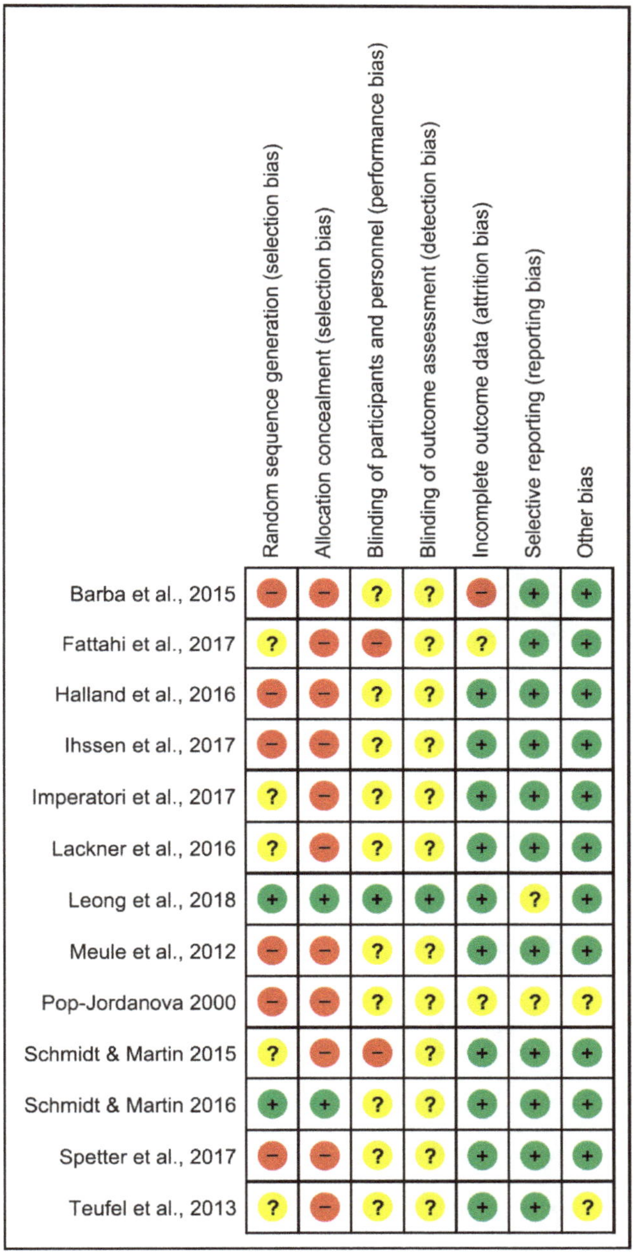

Figure 2. Risk of bias summary: review authors' judgements about each risk of bias item for each included study. Green, yellow and red circles represent low, unclear and high risk of bias respectively.

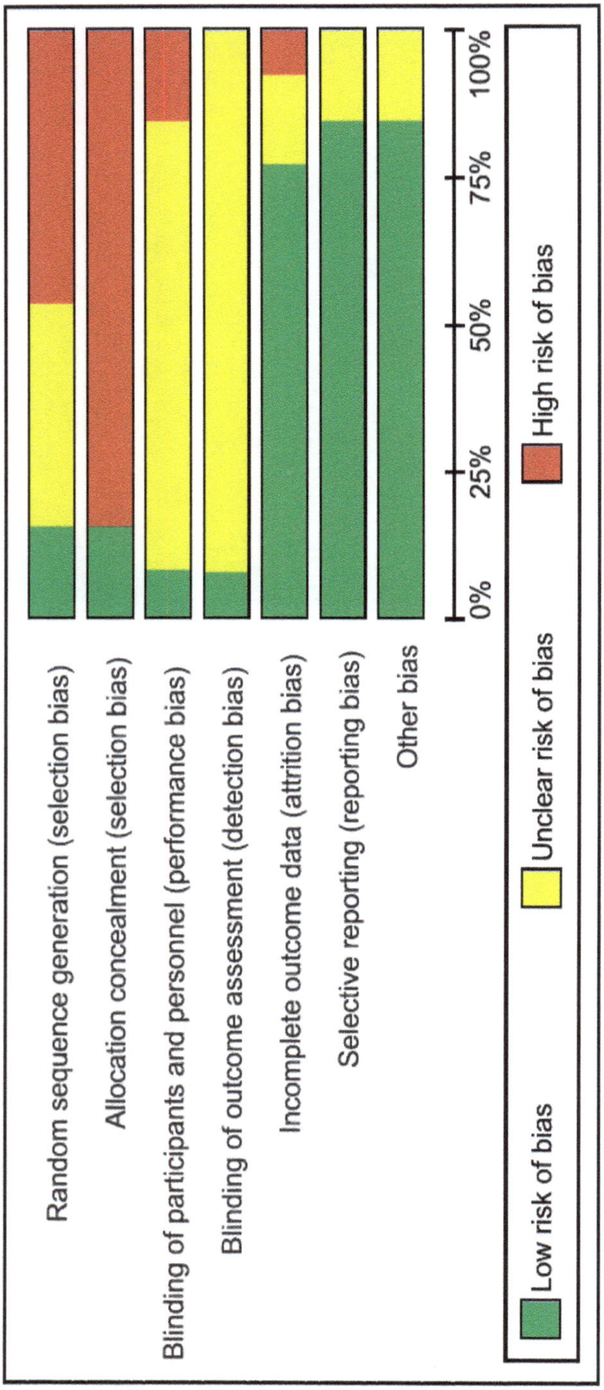

Figure 3. Risk of bias graph: review authors' judgements about each risk of bias item presented as percentages across all included studies.

5. Discussion

The main aim of the present systematic review was to report how feedback-based treatment (i.e., biofeedback and neurofeedback) have been used in the treatment of EDs and EDs-related symptoms. To the best of our knowledge, this is the first systematic review that investigates both biofeedback and neurofeedback applications in this field.

The review identified 13 articles, five focused on biofeedback and eight focused on neurofeedback, providing preliminary data of the usefulness of feedback-based techniques in the treatment of several dysfunctional eating behaviors (Table 2). Specifically, it has been reported that both neurofeedback and biofeedback training may decrease food craving severity [56–58,64,65], overeating episodes [58,59], regurgitation [62] and rumination [63] episodes, restricting behavior [60], eating and weight concerns [57]. Furthermore, this review showed that feedback-based techniques are associated with significant modifications of both sympathetic reaction to food-related stimuli [61–63,67] and brain activity in several regions of the reward system (e.g., prefrontal cortex, amygdala, insula) [55,56,60,65,66].

Table 2. Usefulness of feedback-based techniques for the treatment of dysfunctional eating behaviors.

Clinical Eating-Related Problem	Feed-Based Technique	Number of Sessions
Food craving	HRV-BF; Beta-NF; Alpha/Theta-NF; Infraslow-NF	6 to 10
Binge eating episodes	Beta-NF	10
Regurgitation episodes	EMG-BF	3
Rumination episodes	DB-BF	n/a
Restricting behavior	Alpha-NF	10
Eating and weight concerns	HRV-BF; Alpha-NF	12–10

HRV-BF = heart rate variability biofeedback; NF = Neurofeedback; EMG-BF = electromyography biofeedback; DB-BF = diaphragmatic breathing biofeedback; n/a = not applicable.

These results seem to suggest that both biofeedback and neurofeedback increased the ability to better tolerate stress and the ability to cope with situations involving food. Indeed, the most common goal of feedback-based treatments implemented for EDs and EDs-related symptoms is the reduction of stressful arousal and the increase of top-down control abilities. For example, the aim of EEG alpha training [60] is to enhance individual alpha frequency, which is usually associated with alert relaxation [69], in the parietal area (i.e., Pz electrode). Similarly, the goal of EEG beta training [58,59] is to down-regulate beta activity, which is positively associated with ruminative states of stressful arousal [70]. Consistently, the aim of alpha/theta training is to raise posterior (i.e., Pz electrode) theta over alpha amplitude in order to produce a state of deep relaxation, enhancing top-down mental functions [71], such as mentalization [72]. Finally, an rt-fMRI neurofeedback has been implemented to increase functional connectivity between brain areas (i.e., dorsolateral prefrontal cortex and ventromedial prefrontal cortex) that regulate the top-down control of appetite for high-calorie foods [66].

Interestingly, it has also been suggested that the target of neurofeedback is to increase bottom-up strategies in order to decrease the salience attached to food [65], or down-regulate brain regions activation (i.e., amygdala) during exposure to food cues [55]. Therefore, taken together these data suggest that feedback-based treatments implemented for EDs and EDs-related symptoms can operate both on top-down and bottom-up strategies in order to foster the neural mechanisms underlying successful coping during stressful food-related situations.

On the other hand, this review showed no significant effect of feedback-based techniques in improving other important EDs-related symptoms, such as body image disturbance, a crucial core of AN and BN [5], which seems to affect also BED [73]. No significant modifications associated with both biofeedback and neurofeedback were also reported for BMI in both patients with AN and overweigh/obesity. These results confirm the need of multidisciplinary approaches, combining medical, dietetic and different kind of psychological interventions in the treatment of EDs and

ED-related symptoms [32]. For example, combining EEG alpha training neurofeedback [60] with cognitive-behavioral exposure-based body image therapy [74] may be useful in the treatment of EDs.

It is also interesting to note that, compared to feedback-based interventions in other psychiatric disorders [39], no studies considered in the present review incorporated different biofeedback modalities or both biofeedback and neurofeedback. Therefore, it is possible that combining HRV-biofeedback [57] and EEG alpha/theta neurofeedback [56,64] may be more effective in reducing food craving severity in both clinical and non-clinical samples. Similarly, the combination of two neurofeedback training methods, such as EEG alpha/theta training and EEG beta training, or the combination of feedback-based techniques with other cognitive-behavioral techniques (e.g., cognitive restructuring, exposure therapy and response prevention) may be more effective in improving a wider range of ED-related symptoms (i.e., binge eating episodes, food craving).

Although the present review provided preliminary results of the usefulness of feedback-based techniques in the treatment of EDs and EDs-related symptoms, several methodological issue should be considered.

First, up to date, there are few randomized, double-blind, placebo-controlled studies investigating the effectiveness of both biofeedback and neurofeedback in large clinical samples. Indeed, among reviewed randomized trials (n = 8) the most frequent control condition implemented was the no treatment/waiting list, and only one study was double-blind. Consequently, most of the studies included in the present review had a high risk of bias, which was mostly related to the lack of both blinding and control conditions (e.g., mock feedback). This is in line with a recent systematic review investigating the potential therapeutic effects of neurofeedback training in psychiatric disorders associated with criminal offending [47]. Therefore, future studies should compare biofeedback and neurofeedback with sham procedures in order to rule out the placebo effect. Secondly, compared to feedback-based interventions in other psychiatric disorders [39], the mean number of sessions was relatively lower (i.e., 7.42). Although it has been reported that patients may benefit by undergoing 8 to 12 sessions [40], the possibility that a greater number of sessions (i.e., from 20 to 30) may maximize both biofeedback and neurofeedback results should be assessed. Furthermore, the stability of psychological/behavioral and neurophysiological (e.g., EEG power) outcomes should also be investigated taking into account long-term follow-up (i.e., at least one year). Finally, although the present review did not provide relevant differences associated with both age and gender, future studies should also investigate the relationship between feedback-based interventions outcomes (e.g., adherence to treatment, symptoms improvement) and several socio-demographic data (e.g. adolescent vs adults with EDs, and/or men vs women with EDs).

Study Limitations and Conclusions

There are several limitations of the present review that should be considered. Firstly, the search strategy was limited to articles published in English. Secondly, due to the high heterogeneity of samples, outcome measures and feedback modalities, a meta-analysis in order to quantify the effectiveness of both biofeedback and neurofeedback was not performed.

Despite these limitations, to the best of our knowledge, this is the first systematic review that investigates both biofeedback and neurofeedback applications in the treatment of EDs and EDs-related symptoms. In conclusion, the results of the present review suggest that, although future studies are needed in order to draw definitive conclusions, feedback-based techniques may be useful in the treatment of several dysfunctional eating behaviors (e.g., food craving, binge eating) operating both on top-down and bottom-up individual coping strategies.

Supplementary Materials: The following are available at http://www.mdpi.com/2072-6643/10/11/1806/s1, Table S1: Preferred Reporting Items for Systematic Reviews and Meta-Analyses (PRISMA) checklist.

Author Contributions: C.I.: study design, literature searches, data extraction, manuscript writing; M.M.: literature searches, data extraction, manuscript editing; G.D.M.: supervision, manuscript writing; E.M.V.: data extraction; B.F.: study design, supervision, manuscript writing.

Funding: This research was funded by Atena Onlus Foundation.

Acknowledgments: We thank the Atena Onlus Foundation for assistance and support.

Conflicts of Interest: The authors declare no conflicts of interest.

References

1. Treasure, J.; Claudino, A.M.; Zucker, N. Eating disorders. *Lancet* **2010**, *375*, 583–593. [CrossRef]
2. Hudson, J.I.; Hiripi, E.; Pope, H.G., Jr.; Kessler, R.C. The prevalence and correlates of eating disorders in the national comorbidity survey replication. *Biol. Psychiatry* **2007**, *61*, 348–358. [CrossRef] [PubMed]
3. Smink, F.R.; Van Hoeken, D.; Hoek, H.W. Epidemiology of eating disorders: Incidence, prevalence and mortality rates. *Curr. Psychiatry Rep.* **2012**, *14*, 406–414. [CrossRef] [PubMed]
4. Kaplan, A.S.; Garfinkel, P.E. Difficulties in treating patients with eating disorders: A review of patient and clinician variables. *Can. J. Psychiatry* **1999**, *44*, 665–670. [CrossRef] [PubMed]
5. American Psychiatric Association. *Diagnostic and Statistical Manual of Mental Disorders-DSM-5*, 5th ed.; American Psychiatric Publishing: Arlington, TX, USA, 2013.
6. Erzegovesi, S.; Bellodi, L. Eating disorders. *CNS Spectr.* **2016**, *21*, 304–309. [PubMed]
7. Hoek, H.W. Classification, epidemiology and treatment of dsm-5 feeding and eating disorders. *Curr. Opin. Psychiatry* **2013**, *26*, 529–531. [CrossRef] [PubMed]
8. Benjasuwantep, B.; Chaithirayanon, S.; Eiamudomkan, M. Feeding problems in healthy young children: Prevalence, related factors and feeding practices. *Pediatr. Rep.* **2013**, *5*, 38–42. [CrossRef] [PubMed]
9. Swanson, S.A.; Crow, S.J.; Le Grange, D.; Swendsen, J.; Merikangas, K.R. Prevalence and correlates of eating disorders in adolescents. Results from the national comorbidity survey replication adolescent supplement. *Arch. Gen. Psychiatry* **2011**, *68*, 714–723. [CrossRef] [PubMed]
10. Lindvall Dahlgren, C.; Wisting, L.; Ro, O. Feeding and eating disorders in the dsm-5 era: A systematic review of prevalence rates in non-clinical male and female samples. *J. Eat. Disord.* **2017**, *5*, 56. [CrossRef] [PubMed]
11. Weingarten, H.P.; Elston, D. The phenomenology of food cravings. *Appetite* **1990**, *15*, 231–246. [CrossRef]
12. Weingarten, H.P.; Elston, D. Food cravings in a college population. *Appetite* **1991**, *17*, 167–175. [CrossRef]
13. White, M.A.; Whisenhunt, B.L.; Williamson, D.A.; Greenway, F.L.; Netemeyer, R.G. Development and validation of the food-craving inventory. *Obes. Res.* **2002**, *10*, 107–114. [CrossRef] [PubMed]
14. Lafay, L.; Thomas, F.; Mennen, L.; Charles, M.A.; Eschwege, E.; Borys, J.M.; Basdevant, A. Gender differences in the relation between food cravings and mood in an adult community: Results from the fleurbaix laventie ville sante study. *Int. J. Eat. Disord.* **2001**, *29*, 195–204. [CrossRef]
15. Gendall, K.A.; Sullivan, P.F.; Joyce, P.R.; Bulik, C.M. Food cravings in women with a history of anorexia nervosa. *Int. J. Eat. Disord.* **1997**, *22*, 403–409. [CrossRef]
16. Moreno, S.; Rodriguez, S.; Fernandez, M.C.; Tamez, J.; Cepeda-Benito, A. Clinical validation of the trait and state versions of the food craving questionnaire. *Assessment* **2008**, *15*, 375–387. [CrossRef] [PubMed]
17. Van der Ster Wallin, G.; Norring, C.; Holmgren, S. Binge eating versus nonpurged eating in bulimics: Is there a carbohydrate craving after all? *Acta Psychiatr. Scand.* **1994**, *89*, 376–381. [CrossRef] [PubMed]
18. Waters, A.; Hill, A.; Waller, G. Bulimics' responses to food cravings: Is binge-eating a product of hunger or emotional state? *Behav. Res. Ther.* **2001**, *39*, 877–886. [CrossRef]
19. Moreno, S.; Warren, C.S.; Rodriguez, S.; Fernandez, M.C.; Cepeda-Benito, A. Food cravings discriminate between anorexia and bulimia nervosa. Implications for "success" versus "failure" in dietary restriction. *Appetite* **2009**, *52*, 588–594. [CrossRef] [PubMed]
20. White, M.A.; Grilo, C.M. Psychometric properties of the food craving inventory among obese patients with binge eating disorder. *Eat. Behav.* **2005**, *6*, 239–245. [CrossRef] [PubMed]
21. Fabbricatore, M.; Imperatori, C.; Pecchioli, C.; Micarelli, T.; Contardi, A.; Tamburello, S.; Innamorati, M.; Tamburello, A. Binge eating and bis/bas activity in obese patients with intense food craving who attend weight control programs. *Obes. Metab.* **2011**, *7*, e21–e27.
22. Delahanty, L.M.; Meigs, J.B.; Hayden, D.; Williamson, D.A.; Nathan, D.M. Diabetes Prevenion Program Research Group. Psychological and behavioral correlates of baseline bmi in the diabetes prevention program (DPP). *Diabetes Care* **2002**, *25*, 1992–1998. [CrossRef] [PubMed]
23. Franken, I.H.; Muris, P. Individual differences in reward sensitivity are related to food craving and relative body weight in healthy women. *Appetite* **2005**, *45*, 198–201. [CrossRef] [PubMed]

24. Meule, A.; Hermann, T.; Kubler, A. A short version of the food cravings questionnaire-trait: The fcq-t-reduced. *Front. Psychol.* **2014**, *5*, 190. [CrossRef] [PubMed]
25. Meule, A.; Lutz, A.; Vogele, C.; Kubler, A. Food cravings discriminate differentially between successful and unsuccessful dieters and non-dieters. Validation of the food cravings questionnaires in german. *Appetite* **2012**, *58*, 88–97. [PubMed]
26. Meule, A.; Westenhofer, J.; Kubler, A. Food cravings mediate the relationship between rigid, but not flexible control of eating behavior and dieting success. *Appetite* **2011**, *57*, 582–584. [CrossRef] [PubMed]
27. Sitton, S.C. Role of craving for carbohydrates upon completion of a protein-sparing fast. *Psychol. Rep.* **1991**, *69*, 683–686. [PubMed]
28. Boswell, R.G.; Kober, H. Food cue reactivity and craving predict eating and weight gain: A meta-analytic review. *Obes. Rev.* **2016**, *17*, 159–177. [CrossRef] [PubMed]
29. Goossens, L.; Soenens, B.; Braet, C. Prevalence and characteristics of binge eating in an adolescent community sample. *J. Clin. Child Adolesc. Psychol.* **2009**, *38*, 342–353. [CrossRef] [PubMed]
30. Heriseanu, A.I.; Hay, P.; Corbit, L.; Touyz, S. Grazing in adults with obesity and eating disorders: A systematic review of associated clinical features and meta-analysis of prevalence. *Clin. Psychol. Rev.* **2017**, *58*, 16–32. [CrossRef] [PubMed]
31. Goldschmidt, A.B.; Loth, K.A.; MacLehose, R.F.; Pisetsky, E.M.; Berge, J.M.; Neumark-Sztainer, D. Overeating with and without loss of control: Associations with weight status, weight-related characteristics, and psychosocial health. *Int. J. Eat. Disord.* **2015**, *48*, 1150–1157. [CrossRef] [PubMed]
32. Hay, P.; Chinn, D.; Forbes, D.; Madden, S.; Newton, R.; Sugenor, L.; Touyz, S.; Ward, W. Royal australian and new zealand college of psychiatrists clinical practice guidelines for the treatment of eating disorders. *Aust. N. Z. J. Psychiatry* **2014**, *48*, 977–1008. [CrossRef] [PubMed]
33. Herpertz-Dahlmann, B. Treatment of eating disorders in child and adolescent psychiatry. *Curr. Opin. Psychiatry* **2017**, *30*, 438–445. [CrossRef] [PubMed]
34. Amianto, F.; Ottone, L.; Abbate Daga, G.; Fassino, S. Binge-eating disorder diagnosis and treatment: A recap in front of dsm-5. *BMC Psychiatry* **2015**, *15*, 70. [CrossRef] [PubMed]
35. Lee, D.J.; Elias, G.J.B.; Lozano, A.M. Neuromodulation for the treatment of eating disorders and obesity. *Ther. Adv. Psychopharmacol.* **2018**, *8*, 73–92. [CrossRef] [PubMed]
36. Bartholdy, S.; Musiat, P.; Campbell, I.C.; Schmidt, U. The potential of neurofeedback in the treatment of eating disorders: A review of the literature. *Eur. Eat. Disord. Rev.* **2013**, *21*, 456–463. [CrossRef] [PubMed]
37. Musiat, P.; Hoffmann, L.; Schmidt, U. Personalised computerised feedback in e-mental health. *J. Ment. Health* **2012**, *21*, 346–354. [CrossRef] [PubMed]
38. Yucha, C.; Montgomery, D. *Evidence-Based Practice in Biofeedback and Neurofeedback*; Association for Applied Psychophysiology and Biofeedback: Wheat Ridge, CO, USA, 2008.
39. Schoenberg, P.L.; David, A.S. Biofeedback for psychiatric disorders: A. systematic review. *Appl. Psychophysiol. Biofeedback* **2014**, *39*, 109–135. [CrossRef] [PubMed]
40. McKee, M.G. Biofeedback: An overview in the context of heart-brain medicine. *Clevel. Clin. J. Med.* **2008**, *75*, S31–S34. [CrossRef]
41. Weiskopf, N. Real-time fmri and its application to neurofeedback. *Neuroimage* **2012**, *62*, 682–692. [CrossRef] [PubMed]
42. Brunoni, A.R.; Amadera, J.; Berbel, B.; Volz, M.S.; Rizzerio, B.G.; Fregni, F. A systematic review on reporting and assessment of adverse effects associated with transcranial direct current stimulation. *Int. J. Neuropsychopharmacol.* **2011**, *14*, 1133–1145. [CrossRef] [PubMed]
43. Lansbergen, M.M.; Van Dongen-Boomsma, M.; Buitelaar, J.K.; Slaats-Willemse, D. Adhd and eeg-neurofeedback: A double-blind randomized placebo-controlled feasibility study. *J. Neural Transm. (Vienna)* **2011**, *118*, 275–284. [CrossRef] [PubMed]
44. Thatcher, R.W. Advances in assessment and treatment of ADHD using network analyses. *Biofeedback* **2014**, *42*, 58–67. [CrossRef]
45. Sherlin, L.H.; Arns, M.; Lubar, J.; Heinrich, H.; Kerson, C.; Strehl, U.; Sterman, M.B. Neurofeedback and basic learning theory: Implications for research and practice. *J. Neurother.* **2011**, *15*, 292–304. [CrossRef]
46. La Vaque, T.J.; Hammond, D.C.; Trudeau, D.; Monastra, V.; Perry, J.; Lehrer, P.; Matheson, D.; Sherman, R. Template for developing guidelines for the evaluation of the clinical efficacy of psychophysiological interventions. *Appl. Psychophysiol. Biofeedback* **2002**, *27*, 273–281. [CrossRef]

47. Fielenbach, S.; Donkers, F.C.L.; Spreen, M.; Visser, H.A.; Bogaerts, S. Neurofeedback training for psychiatric disorders associated with criminal offending: A. review. *Front. Psychiatry* **2017**, *8*, 313. [CrossRef] [PubMed]
48. Cepeda-Benito, A.; Gleaves, D.H.; Williams, T.L.; Erath, S.A. The development and validation of the state and trait food-cravings questionnaires. *Behav. Ther.* **2000**, *31*, 151–173. [CrossRef]
49. Fairburn, C.G.; Beglin, S.J. Assessment of eating disorders: Interview or self-report questionnaire? *Int. J. Eat. Disord.* **1994**, *16*, 363–370. [PubMed]
50. Gearhardt, A.N.; Corbin, W.R.; Brownell, K.D. Preliminary validation of the Yale food addiction scale. *Appetite* **2009**, *52*, 430–436. [CrossRef] [PubMed]
51. Stunkard, A.J.; Messick, S. The three-factor eating questionnaire to measure dietary restraint, disinhibition and hunger. *J. Psychosom. Res.* **1985**, *29*, 71–83. [CrossRef]
52. Legenbauer, T.; Vocks, S.; Schütt-Strömel, S. Dysfunctional cognitions in eating disorders: Which contents areas can be discriminated? *J. Clin. Psychol. Psychother.* **2007**, *36*, 207–215.
53. Rosen, J.C.; Srebnik, D.; Saltzberg, E.; Wendt, S. Development of a body image avoidance questionnaire. *Psychol. Assess.* **1991**, *3*, 32–37. [CrossRef]
54. Nijs, I.M.; Franken, I.H.; Muris, P. The modified trait and state food-cravings questionnaires: Development and validation of a general index of food craving. *Appetite* **2007**, *49*, 38–46. [CrossRef] [PubMed]
55. Ihssen, N.; Sokunbi, M.O.; Lawrence, A.D.; Lawrence, N.S.; Linden, D.E.J. Neurofeedback of visual food cue reactivity: A potential avenue to alter incentive sensitization and craving. *Brain Imaging Behav.* **2017**, *11*, 915–924. [CrossRef] [PubMed]
56. Imperatori, C.; Valenti, E.M.; Della Marca, G.; Amoroso, N.; Massullo, C.; Carbone, G.A.; Maestoso, G.; Quintiliani, M.I.; Contardi, A.; Farina, B. Coping food craving with neurofeedback. Evaluation of the usefulness of alpha/theta training in a non-clinical sample. *Int. J. Psychophysiol.* **2017**, *112*, 89–97. [CrossRef] [PubMed]
57. Meule, A.; Freund, R.; Skirde, A.K.; Vogele, C.; Kubler, A. Heart rate variability biofeedback reduces food cravings in high food cravers. *Appl. Psychophysiol. Biofeedback* **2012**, *37*, 241–251. [CrossRef] [PubMed]
58. Schmidt, J.; Martin, A. Neurofeedback reduces overeating episodes in female restrained eaters: A randomized controlled pilot-study. *Appl. Psychophysiol. Biofeedback* **2015**, *40*, 283–295. [CrossRef] [PubMed]
59. Schmidt, J.; Martin, A. Neurofeedback against binge eating: A randomized controlled trial in a female subclinical threshold sample. *Eur. Eat. Disord. Rev.* **2016**, *24*, 406–416. [CrossRef] [PubMed]
60. Lackner, N.; Unterrainer, H.F.; Skliris, D.; Shaheen, S.; Dunitz-Scheer, M.; Wood, G.; Scheer, P.J.; Wallner-Liebmann, S.J.; Neuper, C. Eeg neurofeedback effects in the treatment of adolescent anorexia nervosa. *Eat. Disord.* **2016**, *24*, 354–374. [CrossRef] [PubMed]
61. Pop-Jordanova, N. Psychological characteristics and biofeedback mitigation in preadolescents with eating disorders. *Pediatr. Int.* **2000**, *42*, 76–81. [CrossRef] [PubMed]
62. Barba, E.; Burri, E.; Accarino, A.; Malagelada, C.; Rodriguez-Urrutia, A.; Soldevilla, A.; Malagelada, J.R.; Azpiroz, F. Biofeedback-guided control of abdominothoracic muscular activity reduces regurgitation episodes in patients with rumination. *Clin. Gastroenterol. Hepatol.* **2015**, *13*, 100–106.e1. [CrossRef] [PubMed]
63. Halland, M.; Parthasarathy, G.; Bharucha, A.E.; Katzka, D.A. Diaphragmatic breathing for rumination syndrome: Efficacy and mechanisms of action. *Neurogastroenterol. Motil.* **2016**, *28*, 384–391. [CrossRef] [PubMed]
64. Fattahi, S.; Naderi, F.; Asgari, P.; Ahadi, H. Neuro-feedback training for overweight women: Improvement of food craving and mental health. *NeuroQuantology* **2017**, *15*, 232–238. [CrossRef]
65. Leong, S.L.; Vanneste, S.; Lim, J.; Smith, M.; Manning, P.; De Ridder, D.A. Randomised, double-blind, placebo-controlled parallel trial of closed-loop infraslow brain training in food addiction. *Sci. Rep.* **2018**, *8*, 11659. [CrossRef] [PubMed]
66. Spetter, M.S.; Malekshahi, R.; Birbaumer, N.; Luhrs, M.; Van der Veer, A.H.; Scheffler, K.; Spuckti, S.; Preissl, H.; Veit, R.; Hallschmid, M. Volitional regulation of brain responses to food stimuli in overweight and obese subjects: A real-time fmri feedback study. *Appetite* **2017**, *112*, 188–195. [CrossRef] [PubMed]
67. Teufel, M.; Stephan, K.; Kowalski, A.; Kasberger, S.; Enck, P.; Zipfel, S.; Giel, K.E. Impact of biofeedback on self-efficacy and stress reduction in obesity: A randomized controlled pilot study. *Appl. Psychophysiol. Biofeedback* **2013**, *38*, 177–184. [CrossRef] [PubMed]

68. Higgins, J.P.T.; Altman, D.G.; Sterne, J.A.C. Chapter 8: Assessing risk of bias in included studies. In *Cochrane Handbook for Systematic Reviews of Interventions Version 5.1.0*; Higgins, J.P.T., Green, S., Eds.; The Cochrane Collaboration: London, UK, 2011.
69. Marzbani, H.; Marateb, H.R.; Mansourian, M. Neurofeedback: A comprehensive review on system design, methodology and clinical applications. *Basic Clin. Neurosci.* **2016**, *7*, 143–158. [PubMed]
70. Andersen, S.B.; Moore, R.A.; Venables, L.; Corr, P.J. Electrophysiological correlates of anxious rumination. *Int. J. Psychophysiol.* **2009**, *71*, 156–169. [CrossRef] [PubMed]
71. Gruzelier, J.H. Eeg-neurofeedback for optimising performance. Ii: Creativity, the performing arts and ecological validity. *Neurosci. Biobehav. Rev.* **2014**, *44*, 142–158. [CrossRef] [PubMed]
72. Imperatori, C.; Della Marca, G.; Amoroso, N.; Maestoso, G.; Valenti, E.M.; Massullo, C.; Carbone, G.A.; Contardi, A.; Farina, B. Alpha/theta neurofeedback increases mentalization and default mode network connectivity in a non-clinical sample. *Brain Topogr.* **2017**, *30*, 822–831. [CrossRef] [PubMed]
73. Lewer, M.; Bauer, A.; Hartmann, A.S.; Vocks, S. Different facets of body image disturbance in binge eating disorder: A review. *Nutrients* **2017**, *9*. [CrossRef] [PubMed]
74. Lewer, M.; Kosfelder, J.; Michalak, J.; Schroeder, D.; Nasrawi, N.; Vocks, S. Effects of a cognitive-behavioral exposure-based body image therapy for overweight females with binge eating disorder: A pilot study. *J. Eat. Disord.* **2017**, *5*, 43. [CrossRef] [PubMed]

nutrients

MDPI

Article

Perceived Family Functioning in Relation to Energy Intake in Adolescent Girls with Loss of Control Eating

Manuela Jaramillo [1,2], Natasha L. Burke [3], Lauren B. Shomaker [4], Sheila M. Brady [1], Merel Kozlosky [5], Jack A. Yanovski [1] and Marian Tanofsky-Kraff [1,2,*]

1 Section on Growth and Obesity, *Eunice Kennedy Shriver* National Institute of Child Health and Human Development (NICHD), National Institutes of Health (NIH), DHHS, 10 Center Drive, Bethesda, MD 20892-1103, USA; Manuela.Jaramillo@nih.gov (M.J.); BradyS@mail.nih.gov (S.M.B.); jy15i@nih.gov (J.A.Y.)

2 Department of Medical and Clinical Psychology, Uniformed Services University of the Health Sciences (USUHS), 4301 Jones Bridge Road, Bethesda, MD 20814, USA

3 Department of Psychology, Fordham University, 411 East Fordham Road, Bronx, NY 10458, USA; NBurke12@fordham.edu

4 Department of Human Development and Family Studies, Colorado State University, 303 Behavioral Sciences Building, 1570 Campus Delivery, Fort Collins, CO 80523, USA, Lauren.Shomaker@colostate.edu

5 Nutrition Department, Clinical Center, NIH, DHHS, 10 Center Drive, Bethesda, MD 20892, USA; KozloskyM@cc.nih.gov

* Correspondence: Marian.Tanofsky-Kraff@usuhs.edu; Tel.: +1-301-295-1482

Received: 1 November 2018; Accepted: 27 November 2018; Published: 2 December 2018

Abstract: Family functioning is hypothesized to influence the development, maintenance, and treatment of obesity and eating disorders. However, there are limited data examining family functioning in relation to energy intake in the laboratory among youth at high-risk for eating disorders and excess weight gain. Therefore, we examined the relationship between perceived family functioning and energy intake during a laboratory test meal designed to model a binge episode. We performed hierarchical multiple regression analyses among 108 adolescent girls in an excess weight gain prevention trial. Participants were at high-risk for eating disorders and excess weight gain due to reports of loss of control eating (LOC) and high body mass index (BMI). Participants completed the Family Adaptability and Cohesion Scale III to assess family adaptability and cohesion. Following an overnight fast, girls consumed lunch from a laboratory test meal. Poorer family adaptability, but not cohesion, was associated with lower percentage of total energy intake from protein and greater percentage of total energy intake from carbohydrates. Neither adaptability nor cohesion were significantly associated with total intake. We conclude that among girls with LOC eating and high BMI, poor reported family adaptability is associated with greater consumption of obesity-promoting macronutrients during binge episodes. Directionality and temporality of this association between unhealthy consumption and family rigidity requires further study.

Keywords: loss of control eating; obesity; BMI; adolescent; females; family functioning; energy intake

1. Introduction

Given the high prevalence of obesity among adolescents [1] and the relatively few effective treatment options for this age group [2], elucidating psychological factors that promote excess weight gain is warranted for the development of novel approaches. Loss of control eating (LOC), the subjective feeling that one cannot stop or control what or how much one consumes [3], may be one such factor. With approximately 33% of children with overweight or obesity engaging in LOC eating [4], LOC eating has been shown to be a robust predictor of excess weight and fat gain [5–7], exacerbate some components of the metabolic syndrome [8], and predict the development of partial or full-syndrome binge eating disorder [9,10]. Data have shown that, in general (for example, outside of the laboratory environment), youth with LOC eating consume more highly palatable, energy dense foods than youth without LOC eating [11–13], which may provide a mechanism for observed prospective outcomes.

The interpersonal model of binge eating disorder proposes that the link between difficulties in social functioning and LOC eating is largely mediated by negative affect resulting from relationship problems [14]. This model has been applied to adolescent girls with LOC eating [15]. While the theory focuses on any type of salient relationship, data suggest that among adolescent girls with LOC eating, family members may be most relevant to the interpersonal model [16]. Indeed, family dysfunction has been suggested to play a crucial role in child and adolescent overweight and obesity [17–19] and disordered eating [20–22].

Prior studies have operationalized family functioning as a person's perceived level of adaptability (i.e., ability of a family system to change its power structure, role relationships, and relationship rules in response to situational and developmental stress) and cohesion (i.e., emotional bonding that family members have toward one another) within their own family [23]. Research has shown that higher and/or balanced levels of perceived adaptability and/or cohesion can both relate to and predict healthy eating behaviors. Generally, it has been found that girls with diagnosed eating disorders (compared to girls without diagnosed eating disorders) report less functional levels of adaptability and/or cohesion [21,24]. For example, studies have shown that adolescents with binge-eating disorder perceive lower familial adaptability than adolescents without binge-eating disorder [25], report higher cohesion and flexibility compared to adolescent girls with anorexia nervosa or bulimia nervosa [26], and report more negative perceived maternal criticism than a control group [27]. Among non-clinical samples of adolescents with overweight, higher reports of overeating relate to lower perceived familial cohesion and adaptability [28], and mothers of adolescents with overweight also report higher psychopathology than mothers of adolescents without overweight [29].

Perceived family functioning has also been shown to relate to energy intake patterns [30,31]. For example, a cross-sectional study of youth and adults with diabetes assessing the relationships among family meal frequency, perceived familial cohesion, and reported intake found that cohesion mediated the relationship between family meal frequency and individuals' intake as measured through a food frequency questionnaire [32]. Specifically, higher levels of perceived familial cohesion were linked to a greater reported intake of several food items considered healthful, whereas lower levels of perceived familial cohesion were associated with a greater consumption of palatable and high-caloric density items like fried eggs, burgers, and chips. Similar findings were observed in a longitudinal study assessing the relationship between family cohesion and self-reported food intake in adolescents using a food diary. Perceived cohesion was positively related to healthier reported eating behaviors, such as breakfast consumption, and was negatively related to soda intake [31].

One limitation to the existing literature is the use of self-reported intake, which can be under (or over) reported [33,34], particularly among individuals with overweight and obesity [35,36] or those reporting LOC eating [37]. However, no study has examined total or macronutrient intake in relation to family functioning during actual meals, which may be more informative for understanding, and potentially preventing, obesity development. Lastly, there are no data specifically examining the family functioning and test meal intake of adolescent girls with LOC at high-risk for excess weight gain and eating disorders. We therefore related objectively measured intake at a meal designed to model a binge episode to reported familial functioning among high-risk adolescent girls. Given data showing that youth reporting LOC eating episodes tend to consume more energy from carbohydrate and fat and less energy from protein compared to youth not reporting LOC eating episodes [11,38], girls with overweight have greater overall energy consumption [13,39] and youth with LOC tend to have greater liking of foods in a test meal [40]. We hypothesized that lower levels of adaptability and cohesion would relate to greater total energy consumption, a greater percentage of energy consumed from fat and carbohydrates, and a lower percentage of energy consumed from protein.

2. Method

2.1. Participants

108 adolescent girls aged 12–17 years old and at high-risk for eating disorders and excess weight gain participated in a clinical study for the prevention of LOC eating (ClinicalTrials.gov ID#: NCT00680979). All data for the current analyses were collected at baseline prior to the initiation of any treatment. As previously described [41], inclusion criteria involved being between the 75th and 97th percentile for body mass index (BMI; kg/m^2) and having undergone at least one LOC episode in the last month. Exclusion criteria included any major medical or psychiatric diagnoses (other than binge eating disorder), regular use of medications that affect weight or appetite, current involvement in psychotherapy or a weight loss program, or weight loss in last 2 months exceeding >3% of body weight. A total of 185 participants were screened of whom 117 were eligible for the study. 108 participants completed the necessary measures for the current analysis. Signed informed consent and assent were obtained from parents and adolescents respectively. This protocol was approved by the Institutional Review Boards at the Eunice Kennedy Shriver National Institute of Child Health and Human Development and the Uniformed Services University of the Health Sciences.

2.2. Procedure

Demographic variables (e.g., age and race/ethnicity) were assessed by parent report and questionnaires and interviews were assessed by adolescent report. BMI, adiposity, and energy intake were assessed at the National Institutes of Health Clinical Research Center following an overnight fast initiated the night before at 10 p.m.

BMI and adiposity: BMI was calculated from height and weight. Weight was measured to the nearest tenth of a kilogram with a calibrated digital scale (Scale-Tronix, Wheaton, IL, USA). Height was measured in triplicate to the nearest millimeter with a calibrated electronic stadiometer (Holtain Ltd., Crymych, Wales, UK) and the average of the three heights was used. Fat mass (kg) was measured by dual energy X-ray absorptiometry (DXA) using a Hologic QDR-4500A or Discovery instrument (Bedford, MA, USA) as previously described [41].

LOC eating: The presence of LOC eating over the past month was assessed by the overeating section of the Eating Disorder Examination, Version 14 OD/C.2 (EDE; [42]). The Eating Disorder Examination is a semi-structured diagnostic clinical interview used to assess disordered attitudes and behaviors related to eating, body shape, and weight. This instrument has been shown to be reliable and valid in pediatric samples [43,44].

Family functioning: Family functioning was defined as an adolescent's perceived level of adaptability and cohesion within their own family [23]. Perceived familial adaptability and cohesion were assessed with the Family Adaptability and Cohesion Scale III (FACES III), a 20-item self-report instrument that measures perceived levels of familial adaptability (e.g., "Parent(s) and children discuss punishment together") and cohesion (e.g., "Family members like to spend free time with each other"). The FACES has been used frequently in the literature to assess family function and is based on the hypothesis that functional family systems have more balanced levels of adaptability and cohesion than do dysfunctional family systems. Items were rated on a 5-point Likert scale (i.e., almost never, once in a while, sometimes, frequently, almost always) and scales were derived by summing items. The possible subscale score ranges for adaptability and cohesion were 10–50, with higher scores indicating greater (more positive) adaptability or cohesion. The FACES III has exhibited good test–retest reliability for both subscales (adaptability Cronbach's alpha = 0.80 at the 5-week interval; cohesion Cronbach's alpha = 0.83 at the 5-week interval) and strong discriminant validity given a low correlation between adaptability and cohesion (r = 0.03) [23]. Cronbach's alpha for the current study was 0.75 for adaptability and 0.87 for cohesion. Considering that the data for the current study was collected between 2008 and 2011, the FACES version used is not the most current as of 2011. However, if adaptability and cohesion are analyzed as continuous variables (as was done in the current study) and not categorical variables, the FACES III is a valid and interpretable measure [23].

Energy intake: At 11:00 a.m., participants were presented with a 9835 kcal buffet test meal with individual items representing a wide assortment of foods that varied in macronutrient composition (12% protein, 51% carbohydrate, and 37% fat across all foods). Adolescents entered the room containing the buffet and were provided with the tape-recorded instruction stating, "let yourself go and eat as much as you want." Participants were then left alone in the room until they indicated that they were finished eating. Total consumption of each food item was assessed by weighing the food items before and after presentation to each participant. This paradigm has effectively distinguished adolescents with LOC eating from those without reported LOC eating [11]. Some of the test meal data collected at baseline have been published in previous reports [45–48].

Pre-meal hunger: A single item-assessment was used to measure pre-meal hunger. The item asked, "how hungry do you feel right now?" and individuals responded on a 1 (Not at all) to 100 (Extremely) sliding scale.

Depressive symptoms: A single item-assessment was used to measure pre-meal depressive symptoms from the Brunel Mood Scale [49]. The item asked participants to select their current level of depression on a 1 (Not at all) to 5 (Extremely) Likert scale.

Post-meal subjective evaluation of LOC eating: A single item-assessment was used to measure post-meal subjective evaluation of LOC eating. The item asked, "how much is the eating you just completed like a meal when you feel 'loss of control'?" on a 1 (Extremely) to 5 (Not at all) Likert scale.

2.3. Statistical Analyses

Analyses were performed using SPSS version 25. Hierarchical multiple regression analyses were conducted with perceived adaptability and cohesion as independent variables and macronutrients (protein, carbohydrates, and fat as a percentage of total energy consumption) and total energy intake as dependent variables. R squared values indicate the proportion of variance in the dependent variable that is explained by the model. Height, body fat (%), lean body mass (kg), age, race, depressive symptoms, pre-meal hunger, and total energy intake (kcal) were considered as covariates in the models predicting percentage of macronutrients. Age, race, depressive symptoms, and pre-meal hunger did not contribute to any model and were removed from analyses. Height was highly correlated with lean body mass ($r = 0.77$) and was not included in analyses to meet multicollinearity assumptions. Macronutrient intake percentages were arcsine square root transformed to achieve normality. All other assumptions for model testing were met. Significance was set at $\alpha = 0.05$, two-tailed. We also conducted a series of follow up analyses for participants with overweight or obesity (BMI percentile $\geq$ 85).

3. Results

Participants were 108 adolescent girls (M $\pm$ SD 14.49 $\pm$ 1.66 years) who had above-average weight with a mean BMIz of 1.54 (SD = 0.33). Racial breakdown was as follows: 58.3% White, 25.0% Black, 9.3% Multiple Races, 2.8% Asian, 0.9% American Indian or Alaskan Native, and 3.7% Other or unknown. 9.3% of the sample identified as Latina or Hispanic. (See Table 1).

Table 1. Descriptive characteristics of participants.

	N = 108
Age, year *	14.5 (1.7)
BMIz *	1.54 (0.33)
Race/Ethnicity, %	
White	58.3
Black	25.0
Asian	2.8
American Indian	0.9
Hispanic	9.3
More than one race	9.3
Other/Unknown	3.7
FACES Score *	
Adaptability	31.6 (6.2)
Cohesion	26.2 (8.1)
LOC Eating Episodes	
Episodes 1 month pre-test meal *	4.69 (6.2)
Proportion of youth reporting at least 4 episodes per month in 3 months pre-test meal	14.8%
Test Meal *	
Total kcals consumed	1,177.3 (453.7)
Kcal from protein %	12.9 (3.2)
Kcal from carbohydrates %	50.9 (8.2)
Kcal from fat %	36.2 (7.0)
Pre-meal hunger (Scale 1–100)	62.7 (18.6)
Pre-meal depressive symptoms (Scale 1–5)	0.44 (1.02)
Post-meal subjective evaluation of LOC eating (Scale 1–5)	3.94 (1.1)

* = Mean (SD).

Total and Macronutrient Intake

Total energy intake: The first step of the model (base model) included covariates and the second step (full model) added the predictors of family adaptability and cohesion. Neither the base ($F(2, 105) = 0.63$, $p = 0.534$) nor full ($F(4, 103) = 0.69$, $p = 0.598$) models significantly predicted total energy intake. The full model accounted for only 2.6% of the variance in total energy intake. Adaptability ($\beta = -0.04$, $p = 0.683$) and cohesion ($\beta = 0.13$, $p = 0.222$) were not significant contributors to the full model.

Protein: Covariates (first step) explained 5.4% of the variance in percentage protein consumed but the base model was not significant overall, $F(3, 104) = 1.98$, $p = 0.12$. Adding adaptability and cohesion to the model improved model fit and accounted for an additional 6% of the variance in percentage of protein consumed ($\Delta R^2 = 0.06$, $p = 0.038$) and the full model was significant, $F(5, 102) = 2.59$, $p = 0.030$. Percentage of body fat was a significant predictor of percentage of protein consumed ($\beta = 0.24$, $p = 0.016$) as was family adaptability ($\beta = 0.26$, $p = 0.015$), but not family cohesion ($\beta = -0.18$, $p = 0.081$) (see Table 2). Specifically, lower percentage of body fat and worse family adaptability were both significantly related to less percentage of protein consumed.

Carbohydrates: The first step of the model explained 7.2% of the variance in percentage of carbohydrates consumed and the base model was significant, $F(3, 104) = 2.70$, $p = 0.049$. Adding adaptability and cohesion to the model improved model fit and accounted for an additional 5% of the variance in percentage of carbohydrates consumed ($\Delta R^2 = 0.053$, $p = 0.049$) and the full model was significant, $F(5, 102) = 2.93$, $p = 0.016$. Total energy consumed was a significant predictor of percentage of carbohydrates consumed ($\beta = -0.24$, $p = 0.011$) as was family adaptability ($\beta = -0.26$, $p = 0.015$), but not family cohesion ($\beta = 0.12$, $p = 0.232$). Specifically, less total energy consumed and worse family adaptability were related to higher percentage of carbohydrates consumed, even when accounting for all other variables in the model.

Table 2. Hierarchical regression for total intake and macronutrients.

		Outcome Variables															
		Total Intake				Protein				Carbohydrates				Fat			
Model	Predictor Variables	β	t	p	ΔR²	β	t	p	ΔR²	β	t	p	ΔR²	β	t	p	ΔR²
1	Constant		13.0	0.00 *	0.01		3.82	0.00 *	0.05		7.87	0.00 *	0.07		1.47	0.15	0.11 †
	Total lean fat	0.06	0.61	0.54		−0.03	−0.31	0.76		−0.06	−0.62	0.54		0.08	0.82	0.42	
	Total % fat	−0.08	−0.79	0.43		0.21	2.18	0.03 *		−0.15	−1.55	0.12		0.07	0.74	0.46	
	Total intake (kcals)					−0.05	−0.53	0.60		−0.23	−2.45	0.02 *		0.32	3.39	0.00 *	
2	Constant		11.77	0.00 *	0.01		3.34	0.00 *	0.06 †		8.32	0.00 *	0.05 †		1.02	0.31	0.03
	Total lean fat	0.007	0.69	0.50		−0.07	−0.69	0.49		−0.03	−0.27	0.79		0.05	0.55	0.59	
	Total % fat	−0.08	−0.81	0.42		0.24	2.45	0.02 *		−0.17	−1.81	0.07		0.09	0.92	0.36	
	Total intake (kcals)					−0.03	−0.35	0.73		−0.24	−2.60	0.01 *		0.32	3.46	0.00 *	
	Adaptability	−0.04	−0.41	0.68		0.26	2.47	0.02 *		−0.26	−2.49	0.02 *		0.20	1.90	0.06	
	Cohesion	0.13	1.23	0.22		−0.18	−1.76	0.08		0.12	1.20	0.23		−0.07	−0.70	0.49	

† = Model significant; * = $p < 0.05$; Note: Percentages of protein, carbohydrates, and fat intake were arcsine-square root transformed for analyses.

Fat: The first step of the model explained 10.8% of the variance in percentage of fat consumed and the base model was significant, $F(3, 104) = 4.20$, $p = 0.008$. Adding adaptability and cohesion to the model did not significantly improve model fit ($\Delta R^2 = 0.031$, $p = 0.169$). The full model was significant, $F(5, 102) = 3.28$, $p = 0.009$, but adaptability and cohesion were not significant predictors. Significance was driven by total energy consumed, ($\beta = 0.32$, $p = 0.001$), with more total energy consumed related to higher percentage of fat consumed (see Table 2).

Follow-up analyses: Follow-up analyses were conducted for girls with a BMI percentile indicating overweight status (above 85th percentile) and with girls reporting four or more LOC eating episodes in the past 28 days. Follow-up analyses were conducted to assess whether results in the sub-groups would differ from the full sample. A total of 101 girls in the study had a BMI percentile above the 85th percentile and 37 girls reported four or more LOC eating episodes. Neither those with overweight nor those reporting four or more LOC eating episodes differed from the entire sample for any outcome.

4. Discussion

In this analysis of perceived family functioning and objective energy intake, we found that adolescent girls with reported LOC eating who perceived their families as being less adaptable consumed a lower percentage of energy from protein and a higher percentage from carbohydrates. Perceived level of family cohesion did not significantly relate to test meal intake measures. We found that familial adaptability was associated with degree of carbohydrate and protein intake, but not with total energy or degree of fat intake. These results are generally consistent with data comparing youth with and without LOC eating, such that those with LOC eating consume more energy from carbohydrate and less from protein [11,50,51]. Given that all participants in our sample reported LOC eating, and that poorer adaptability was specifically linked to macronutrient intake that may promote excess weight [52–55], interpersonal functioning linked to less familial flexibility may provide a more fine-grained understanding of the interpersonal model. Indeed, adolescent girls with LOC eating [15,56] and adults with binge eating [57] often describe rigidity within families. Supporting this notion, low levels of familial adaptability have been shown to correspond with high levels of stress [58] and thus, it is possible that girls consume higher amounts of carbohydrate-rich "comfort" food to cope with the stress of a relatively inflexible family environment. Likewise, protein consumption has generally been associated with healthier body weight [59,60] and eating patterns [61–63] and may thus explain how poorer family adaptability was related to adolescents' lower protein intake. Of note, the relationship between family functioning and energy intake accounted for only a small proportion of variance. This could be due to family functioning being a global construct that may be persistent whereas energy intake in the laboratory is situational (e.g., may be affected by hunger, current mood, environment, etc.). As a result, future research including a more naturalistic measure of eating behavior outside of the laboratory, such as ecological momentary assessment, is warranted.

The lack of an association between family cohesion and intake was unexpected. Previous studies have found that higher cohesion correlates with healthier food intake [30–32,64]. It is possible that the nature of our sample and test meal design may explain differences in results. Previous studies were primarily conducted in children and adolescents who were not selected for disordered eating behaviors. Moreover, studies based on self-reported intake were focused on eating in general, as opposed to a meal designed to capture a binge episode. It is possible that we would have found a significant link with family cohesion had we assessed girls' intake during a "normal" test meal. Indeed, our prior research has demonstrated that girls with overweight and reported LOC eating can distinguish between "binge" and "normal" meals in the laboratory [11]. However, this notion requires testing. Furthermore, perceived cohesion has been linked to more meals eaten as a family [31] and thus, authors of prior studies suggest that the cohesion–healthy eating relationship might be interpreted within this family-eating context, which promotes healthy food consumption [65,66]. Therefore, another possible explanation for our findings is that given that youth with LOC eating tend to consume fewer regular meals compared to those without LOC eating [67], cohesion may be less relevant with regard to intake among adolescents who report LOC eating behaviors in the context of a meal modeled to capture a binge episode. Indeed, girls ate alone during the test meal. Further, data based on self-reports tends to find that binge episodes often take place when others are not present [39,68,69].

Strengths of this investigation include the objective measure of energy intake, use of DXA to assess body composition, and the diverse sample of participants of various ethnic groups and races. Limitations of the study include that the FACES is a self-report measure, which may be vulnerable to subjective bias. Also, the cohort contained only adolescent girls of above-average weight with LOC eating, potentially limiting the generalizability of the findings. As we did not include control samples of girls with or without overweight and without LOC eating, future research should address this gap. Lastly, given the cross-sectional nature of the results, no conclusions on temporality between perceived family functioning and intake can be made.

In conclusion, we found that adolescent girls with LOC who perceived their families as being relatively less adaptable consumed significantly more carbohydrates and less protein from a test meal that modeled a LOC episode. The findings of this study underscore the importance of addressing family functioning in the clinical setting and potentially including family members in interventions involving the modification of adolescent girls' eating behaviors. Future prospective research is required to elucidate whether familial functioning plays a role in the development of adverse outcomes and intervention response.

Author Contributions: Conceptualization, M.J. and M.T.K.; designing of study, M.T.K. and J.A.Y.; data collection, M.T.K., L.B.S., S.M.B., M.K., and J.A.Y.; data analysis, M.J., N.L.B., and M.T.K.; writing-original draft preparation, M.J., M.T.K., and N.L.B.; writing-review and editing, all authors.

Funding: This research was funded by the National Institute of Diabetes and Digestive and Kidney Diseases grant 1D01DK080906 (to M.T.K.), the Uniformed Services University of the Health Sciences grant R072IC (to M.T.K.), and the Intramural Research Program, Eunice Kennedy Shriver National Institute of Child Health and Human Development, NIH, grant IZIAHD000641 (to J.A.Y.).

Conflicts of Interest: The authors declare no conflicts of interest.

References

1. Hales, C.M.; Fryar, C.D.; Carroll, M.D.; Freedman, D.S.; Ogden, C.L. Trends in obesity and severe obesity prevalence in us youth and adults by sex and age, 2007-2008 to 2015-2016. *JAMA* **2018**, *319*, 1723–1725. [CrossRef] [PubMed]
2. Ryder, J.R.; Fox, C.K.; Kelly, A.S. Treatment options for severe obesity in the pediatric population: Current limitations and future opportunities. *Obesity* **2018**, *26*, 951–960. [CrossRef] [PubMed]
3. American Psychiatric Association. *Diagnostic and Statistical Manual of Mental Disorders*, 5th ed.; American Psychiatric Association: Washington DC, USA, 2013.
4. Morgan, C.M.; Yanovski, S.Z.; Nguyen, T.T.; McDuffie, J.; Sebring, N.G.; Jorge, M.R.; Keil, M.; Yanovski, J.A. Loss of control over eating, adiposity, and psychopathology in overweight children. *Int. J. Eat. Disord.* **2002**, *31*, 430–441. [CrossRef] [PubMed]
5. Tanofsky-Kraff, M.; Cohen, M.L.; Yanovski, S.Z.; Cox, C.; Theim, K.R.; Keil, M.; Reynolds, J.C.; Yanovski, J.A. A prospective study of psychological predictors of body fat gain among children at high risk for adult obesity. *Pediatrics* **2006**, *117*, 1203–1209. [CrossRef] [PubMed]
6. Tanofsky-Kraff, M.; Yanovski, S.Z.; Schvey, N.A.; Olsen, C.H.; Gustafson, J.; Yanovski, J.A. A prospective study of loss of control eating for body weight gain in children at high risk for adult obesity. *Int. J. Eat. Disord.* **2009**, *42*, 26–30. [CrossRef] [PubMed]
7. Sonneville, K.R.; Horton, N.J.; Micali, N.; Crosby, R.D.; Swanson, S.A.; Solmi, F.; Field, A.E. Longitudinal associations between binge eating and overeating and adverse outcomes among adolescents and young adults: Does loss of control matter? *JAMA Pedatr.* **2013**, *167*, 149–155. [CrossRef] [PubMed]
8. Tanofsky-Kraff, M.; Shomaker, L.B.; Stern, E.A.; Miller, R.; Sebring, N.; DellaValle, D.; Yanovski, S.Z.; Hubbard, V.S.; Yanovski, J.A. Children's binge eating and development of metabolic syndrome. *Int. J. Obes.* **2012**, *36*, 956. [CrossRef]

9. Tanofsky-Kraff, M.; Shomaker, L.B.; Olsen, C.; Roza, C.A.; Wolkoff, L.E.; Columbo, K.M.; Raciti, G.; Zocca, J.M.; Wilfley, D.E.; Yanovski, S.Z.; Yanovski, J.A. A prospective study of pediatric loss of control eating and psychological outcomes. *J. Abnorm. Psychol.* **2011**, *120*, 108–118. [CrossRef]
10. Hilbert, A.; Hartmann, A.S.; Czaja, J.; Schoebi, D. Natural course of preadolescent loss of control eating. *J. Abnorm. Psychol.* **2013**, *122*, 684. [CrossRef]
11. Tanofsky-Kraff, M.; McDuffie, J.R.; Yanovski, S.Z.; Kozlosky, M.; Schvey, N.A.; Shomaker, L.B.; Salaita, C.; Yanovski, J.A. Laboratory assessment of the food intake of children and adolescents with loss of control eating. *Am. J. Clin. Nutr.* **2009**, *89*, 738–745. [CrossRef]
12. Mirch, M.C.; McDuffie, J.R.; Yanovski, S.Z.; Schollnberger, M.; Tanofsky-Kraff, M.; Theim, K.R.; Krakoff, J.; Yanovski, J.A. Effects of binge eating on satiation, satiety, and energy intake of overweight children. *Am. J. Clin. Nutr.* **2006**, *84*, 732–738. [CrossRef] [PubMed]
13. Theim, K.R.; Tanofsky-Kraff, M.; Salaita, C.G.; Haynos, A.F.; Mirch, M.C.; Ranzenhofer, L.M.; Yanovski, S.Z.; Wilfley, D.E.; Yanovski, J.A. Children's descriptions of the foods consumed during loss of control eating episodes. *Eat. Behav.* **2007**, *8*, 258–265. [CrossRef] [PubMed]
14. Wilfley, D.E.; Welch, R.R.; Stein, R.I.; Spurrell, E.B.; Cohen, L.R.; Saelens, B.E.; Dounchis, J.Z.; Frank, M.A.; Wiseman, C.V.; Matt, G.E. A randomized comparison of group cognitive-behavioral therapy and group interpersonal psychotherapy for the treatment of overweight individuals with binge-eating disorder. *Arch. Gen. Psychiatry* **2002**, *59*, 713–721. [CrossRef] [PubMed]
15. Tanofsky-Kraff, M.; Wilfley, D.E.; Young, J.F.; Mufson, L.; Yanovski, S.Z.; Glasofer, D.R.; Salaita, C.G. Preventing excessive weight gain in adolescents: Interpersonal psychotherapy for binge eating. *Obesity* **2007**, *15*, 1345–1355. [CrossRef] [PubMed]
16. Berger, S.S.; Elliott, C.; Ranzenhofer, L.M.; Shomaker, L.B.; Hannallah, L.; Field, S.E.; Young, J.F.; Sbrocco, T.; Wilfley, D.E.; Yanovski, J.A. Interpersonal problem areas and alexithymia in adolescent girls with loss of control eating. *Compr. Psychiatry* **2014**, *55*, 170–178. [CrossRef] [PubMed]
17. Halliday, J.A.; Palma, C.L.; Mellor, D.; Green, J.; Renzaho, A.M. The relationship between family functioning and child and adolescent overweight and obesity: A systematic review. *Int. J. Obes. (Lond).* **2014**, *38*, 480–493. [CrossRef] [PubMed]
18. Vincent, M.A.; McCabe, M.P. Gender differences among adolescents in family, and peer influences on body dissatisfaction, weight loss, and binge eating behaviors. *J. Youth Adolesc.* **2000**, *29*, 205–221. [CrossRef]
19. Tanofsky-Kraff, M.; Haynos, A.F.; Kotler, L.A.; Yanovski, S.Z.; Yanovski, J.A. Laboratory-based studies of eating among children and adolescents. *Curr. Nutr. Food Sci.* **2007**, *3*, 55–74. [CrossRef]
20. Waller, G.; Slade, P.; Calam, R. Family adaptability and cohesion: Relation to eating attitudes and disorders. *Int. J. Eat. Disord.* **1990**, *9*, 225–228. [CrossRef]
21. Vidović, V.; Jureša, V.; Begovac, I.; Mahnik, M.; Tocilj, G. Perceived family cohesion, adaptability and communication in eating disorders. *Eur. Eat. Disord. Rev.* **2005**, *13*, 19–28. [CrossRef]
22. Lundholm, J.K.; Waters, J.E. Dysfunctional family systems: Relationship to disordered eating behaviors among university women. *J. Subst. Abuse.* **1991**, *3*, 97–106. [CrossRef]
23. Olson, D.; Portner, J.; Lavee, Y. *Family Adaptability and Cohesion Evaluation Scale (faces iii)*, 1st ed.; Life Innovations: Minneapolis, MN, USA, 1985; pp. 1–17.
24. Wisotsky, W.; Dancyger, I.; Fornari, V.; Katz, J.; Wisotsky, W.L.; Swencionis, C. The relationship between eating pathology and perceived family functioning in eating disorder patients in a day treatment program. *Eat. Disord.* **2003**, *11*, 89–99. [CrossRef] [PubMed]
25. Tetzlaff, A.; Schmidt, R.; Brauhardt, A.; Hilbert, A. Family functioning in adolescents with binge-eating disorder. *Eur. Eat. Disord. Rev.* **2016**, *24*, 430–433. [CrossRef] [PubMed]
26. Cerniglia, L.; Cimino, S.; Tafà, M.; Marzilli, E.; Ballarotto, G.; Bracaglia, F. Family profiles in eating disorders: Family functioning and psychopathology. *Psychol. Res. Behav. Manag.* **2017**, *10*, 305–312. [CrossRef] [PubMed]
27. Schmidt, R.; Tetzlaff, A.; Hilbert, A. Perceived expressed emotion in adolescents with binge-eating disorder. *J. Abnorm. Child Psychol.* **2015**, *43*, 1369–1377. [CrossRef] [PubMed]
28. Cromley, T.; Neumark-Sztainer, D.; Story, M.; Boutelle, K.N. Parent and family associations with weight-related behaviors and cognitions among overweight adolescents. *J. Adolesc. Health* **2010**, *47*, 263–269. [CrossRef] [PubMed]

29. Blanco, M.; Sepulveda, A.R.; Lacruz, T.; Parks, M.; Real, B.; Martin-Peinador, Y.; Román, F.J. Examining maternal psychopathology, family functioning and coping skills in childhood obesity: A case–control study. *Eur. Eat. Disord. Rev.* **2017**, *25*, 359–365. [CrossRef]
30. Bourdeaudhuij, I.D.; Oost, P.V. Personal and family determinants of dietary behaviour in adolescents and their parents. *Psychol. Health* **2000**, *15*, 751–770. [CrossRef]
31. Franko, D.L.; Thompson, D.; Bauserman, R.; Affenito, S.G.; Striegel-Moore, R.H. What's love got to do with it? Family cohesion and healthy eating behaviors in adolescent girls. *Int. J. Eat. Disord.* **2008**, *41*, 360–367. [CrossRef]
32. Ruhee, D.; Mahomoodally, F. Relationship between family meal frequency and individual dietary intake among diabetic patients. *J. Diabetes Metab. Disord.* **2015**, *14*, 66. [CrossRef]
33. Livingstone, M.B.E.; Robson, P.; Wallace, J. Issues in dietary intake assessment of children and adolescents. *Br. J. Nutr.* **2004**, *92*, S213–S222. [CrossRef] [PubMed]
34. Gersovitz, M.; Madden, J.P.; Smiciklas-Wright, H. Validity of the 24-hr. Dietary recall and seven-day record for group comparisons. *J. Am. Diet. Assoc.* **1978**, *73*, 48–55. [PubMed]
35. Mendez, M.A.; Wynter, S.; Wilks, R.; Forrester, T. Under-and overreporting of energy is related to obesity, lifestyle factors and food group intakes in jamaican adults. *Public Health Nutr.* **2004**, *7*, 9–19. [CrossRef] [PubMed]
36. Johansson, L.; Solvoll, K.; Bjørneboe, G.-E.; Drevon, C.A. Under-and overreporting of energy intake related to weight status and lifestyle in a nationwide sample. *Am. J. Clin. Nutr.* **1998**, *68*, 266–274. [CrossRef] [PubMed]
37. Wolkoff, L.E.; Tanofsky-Kraff, M.; Shomaker, L.B.; Kozlosky, M.; Columbo, K.M.; Elliott, C.A.; Ranzenhofer, L.M.; Osborn, R.L.; Yanovski, S.Z.; Yanovski, J.A. Self-reported vs. Actual energy intake in youth with and without loss of control eating. *Eat. Behav.* **2011**, *12*, 15–20. [CrossRef] [PubMed]
38. Goldschmidt, A.B.; Tanofsky-Kraff, M.; Wilfley, D.E. A laboratory-based study of mood and binge eating behavior in overweight children. *Eat. Behav.* **2011**, *12*, 37–43. [CrossRef]
39. Tanofsky-Kraff, M.; Goossens, L.; Eddy, K.T.; Ringham, R.; Goldschmidt, A.; Yanovski, S.Z.; Braet, C.; Marcus, M.D.; Wilfley, D.E.; Olsen, C. A multisite investigation of binge eating behaviors in children and adolescents. *J. Consult. Clin. Psychol.* **2007**, *75*, 901. [CrossRef]
40. Kurz, S.; Schoebi, D.; Dremmel, D.; Kiess, W.; Munsch, S.; Hilbert, A. Satiety regulation in children with loss of control eating and attention-deficit/hyperactivity disorder: A test meal study. *Appetite* **2017**, *116*, 90–98. [CrossRef]
41. Tanofsky-Kraff, M.; Shomaker, L.B.; Wilfley, D.E.; Young, J.F.; Sbrocco, T.; Stephens, M.; Ranzenhofer, L.M.; Elliott, C.; Brady, S.; Radin, R.M.; et al. Targeted prevention of excess weight gain and eating disorders in high-risk adolescent girls: A randomized controlled trial. *Am. J. Clin. Nutr.* **2014**, *100*, 1010–1018. [CrossRef]
42. Fairburn, C.G.; Wilson, G.T.; Schleimer, K. *Binge Eating: Nature, Assessment, and Treatment*, 12th ed.; Guilford Press: New York, NY, USA, 1993; pp. 317–360.
43. Tanofsky-Kraff, M.; Shomaker, L.B.; Wilfley, D.E.; Young, J.F.; Sbrocco, T.; Stephens, M.; Brady, S.M.; Galescu, O.; Demidowich, A.; Olsen, C.H. Excess weight gain prevention in adolescents: Three-year outcome following a randomized controlled trial. *J. Consult. Clin. Psychol.* **2017**, *85*, 218. [CrossRef]
44. Tanofsky-Kraff, M.; Yanovski, S.Z.; Wilfley, D.E.; Marmarosh, C.; Morgan, C.M.; Yanovski, J.A. Eating-disordered behaviors, body fat, and psychopathology in overweight and normal-weight children. *J. Consult. Clin. Psychol.* **2004**, *72*, 53. [CrossRef] [PubMed]
45. Shank, L.M.; Crosby, R.D.; Grammer, A.C.; Shomaker, L.B.; Vannucci, A.; Burke, N.L.; Stojek, M.; Brady, S.M.; Kozlosky, M.; Reynolds, J.C. Examination of the interpersonal model of loss of control eating in the laboratory. *Compr. Psychiatry.* **2017**, *76*, 36–44. [CrossRef] [PubMed]
46. Vannucci, A.; Shomaker, L.B.; Field, S.E.; Sbrocco, T.; Stephens, M.; Kozlosky, M.; Reynolds, J.C.; Yanovski, J.A.; Tanofsky-Kraff, M. History of weight control attempts among adolescent girls with loss of control eating. *Health Psychol.* **2014**, *33*, 419. [CrossRef] [PubMed]
47. Glasofer, D.R.; Haaga, D.A.; Hannallah, L.; Field, S.E.; Kozlosky, M.; Reynolds, J.; Yanovski, J.A.; Tanofsky-Kraff, M. Self-efficacy beliefs and eating behavior in adolescent girls at-risk for excess weight gain and binge eating disorder. *Int. J. Eat. Disord.* **2013**, *46*, 663–668. [CrossRef] [PubMed]
48. Ranzenhofer, L.M.; Hannallah, L.; Field, S.E.; Shomaker, L.B.; Stephens, M.; Sbrocco, T.; Kozlosky, M.; Reynolds, J.; Yanovski, J.A.; Tanofsky-Kraff, M. Pre-meal affective state and laboratory test meal intake in adolescent girls with loss of control eating. *Appetite* **2013**, *68*, 30–37. [CrossRef] [PubMed]

49. Terry, P.C.; Lane, A.M.; Lane, H.J.; Keohane, L. Development and validation of a mood measure for adolescents. *J. Sports Sci.* **1999**, *17*, 861–872. [CrossRef] [PubMed]
50. Hilbert, A.; Tuschen-Caffier, B.; Czaja, J. Eating behavior and familial interactions of children with loss of control eating: A laboratory test meal study. *Am. J. Clin. Nutr.* **2010**, *91*, 510–518. [CrossRef]
51. Yanovski, S.Z.; Leet, M.; Yanovski, J.A.; Flood, M.N.; Gold, P.W.; Kissileff, H.R.; Walsh, B.T. Food selection and intake of obese women with binge-eating disorder. *Am. J. Clin. Nutr.* **1992**, *56*, 975–980. [CrossRef]
52. McCrory, M.A.; Fuss, P.J.; McCallum, J.E.; Yao, M.; Vinken, A.G.; Hays, N.P.; Roberts, S.B. Dietary variety within food groups: Association with energy intake and body fatness in men and women. *Am. J. Clin. Nutr.* **1999**, *69*, 440–447. [CrossRef]
53. Paddon-Jones, D.; Westman, E.; Mattes, R.D.; Wolfe, R.R.; Astrup, A.; Westerterp-Plantenga, M. Protein, weight management, and satiety. *Am. J. Clin. Nutr.* **2008**, *87*, 1558–1561. [CrossRef]
54. Schoeller, D.A.; Buchholz, A.C. Energetics of obesity and weight control: Does diet composition matter? *J. Am. Diet. Assoc.* **2005**, *105*, 24–28. [CrossRef]
55. Westerterp-Plantenga, M.S. The significance of protein in food intake and body weight regulation. *Curr. Opin. Clin. Nutr. Metab. Care* **2003**, *6*, 635–638. [CrossRef] [PubMed]
56. Berger, S.S.; Elliott, C.; Ranzenhofer, L.M.; Shomaker, L.B.; Hannallah, L.; Field, S.E.; Young, J.F.; Sbrocco, T.; Wilfley, D.E.; Yanovski, J.A.; Tanofsky-Kraff, M. Interpersonal problem areas and alexithymia in adolescent girls with loss of control eating. *Compr. Psychiatry* **2014**, *55*, 170–178. [CrossRef] [PubMed]
57. Wilfley, D.E. *Interpersonal Psychotherapy for Group*, 1st ed.; Basic Books: New York, NY, USA, 2000.
58. Glenn, S.; Cunningham, C.; Poole, H.; Reeves, D.; Weindling, M. Maternal parenting stress and its correlates in families with a young child with cerebral palsy. *Child Care Health Dev.* **2009**, *35*, 71–78. [CrossRef] [PubMed]
59. Anderson, G.H.; Moore, S.E. Dietary proteins in the regulation of food intake and body weight in humans. *J. Nutr.* **2004**, *134*, 974–979. [CrossRef] [PubMed]
60. Noakes, M.; Keogh, J.B.; Foster, P.R.; Clifton, P.M. Effect of an energy-restricted, high-protein, low-fat diet relative to a conventional high-carbohydrate, low-fat diet on weight loss, body composition, nutritional status, and markers of cardiovascular health in obese women. *Am. J. Clin. Nutr.* **2005**, *81*, 1298–1306. [CrossRef] [PubMed]
61. Xie, B.; Gilliland, F.D.; Li, Y.-F.; Rockett, H.R. Effects of ethnicity, family income, and education on dietary intake among adolescents. *Prev. Med.* **2003**, *36*, 30–40. [CrossRef]
62. Kerver, J.M.; Yang, E.J.; Obayashi, S.; Bianchi, L.; Song, W.O. Meal and snack patterns are associated with dietary intake of energy and nutrients in us adults. *J. Am. Diet. Assoc.* **2006**, *106*, 46–53. [CrossRef]
63. Neumark-Sztainer, D.; Hannan, P.J.; Story, M.; Croll, J.; Perry, C. Family meal patterns: Associations with sociodemographic characteristics and improved dietary intake among adolescents. *J. Am. Diet. Assoc.* **2003**, *103*, 317–322. [CrossRef]
64. Kintner, M.; Boss, P.G.; Johnson, N. The relationship between dysfunctional family environments and family member food intake. *J. Marriage Fam.* **1981**, 633–641. [CrossRef]
65. Videon, T.M.; Manning, C.K. Influences on adolescent eating patterns: The importance of family meals. *J. Adolesc. Health* **2003**, *32*, 365–373. [CrossRef]
66. Hammons, A.J.; Fiese, B.H. Is frequency of shared family meals related to the nutritional health of children and adolescents? *Pediatrics* **2010**. [CrossRef] [PubMed]
67. Matheson, B.E.; Camacho, C.; Peterson, C.B.; Rhee, K.E.; Rydell, S.A.; Zucker, N.L.; Boutelle, K.N. The relationship between parent feeding styles and general parenting with loss of control eating in treatment-seeking overweight and obese children. *Int. J. Eat. Disord.* **2015**, *48*, 1047–1055. [CrossRef] [PubMed]
68. Goldschmidt, A.B.; Crosby, R.D.; Cao, L.; Engel, S.G.; Durkin, N.; Beach, H.M.; Berg, K.C.; Wonderlich, S.A.; Crow, S.J.; Peterson, C.B. Ecological momentary assessment of eating episodes in obese adults. *Psychosom. Med.* **2014**, *76*, 747. [CrossRef] [PubMed]
69. Hilbert, A.; Rief, W.; Tuschen-Caffier, B.; de Zwaan, M.; Czaja, J. Loss of control eating and psychological maintenance in children: An ecological momentary assessment study. *Behav. Res. Ther.* **2009**, *47*, 26–33. [CrossRef] [PubMed]

nutrients

Article

Managing Risk of Non-Communicable Diseases in Women with Bulimia Nervosa or Binge Eating Disorders: A Randomized Trial with 12 Months Follow-Up

Therese Fostervold Mathisen [1,*], Jorunn Sundgot-Borgen [1], Jan H. Rosenvinge [2] and Solfrid Bratland-Sanda [3]

1 Department of Sports Medicine, Norwegian School of Sport Sciences; Sognsvegen 220, 0806 Oslo, Norway; jorunn.sundgot-borgen@nih.no

2 Department of Psychology, Faculty of Health Sciences, UiT- the Arctic University of Norway, N-9037 Tromsø, Norway; jan.rosenvinge@uit.no

3 Department of Sports and Physical Education and Outdoor Sciences, University of South-Eastern Norway, N-3800 Bø in Telemark, Norway; solfrid.bratland-sanda@usn.no

* Correspondence: t.f.mathisen@nih.no; Tel.: +47-9575-2818

Received: 14 November 2018; Accepted: 28 November 2018; Published: 3 December 2018

Abstract: Persons with bulimia nervosa (BN) or binge eating disorder (BED) have an elevated risk of non-communicable diseases (NCDs). However, lowering this risk is rarely addressed in standard cognitive-behavioral treatment (CBT). We aimed to compare CBT with an intervention combining physical exercise and dietary therapy (PED-t), and hypothesized that the PED-t would do better than CBT in lowering the risk of NCD both initially and longitudinally. In this study, 164 women with bulimia nervosa or binge eating disorder were randomly assigned to 16-weeks of outpatient group therapy with either PED-t or CBT. Body composition (BC) was measured by dual-energy X-ray absorptiometry. Measures of physical fitness (VO_2peak and one repetition maximum (1RM) in squats, bench press, and seated row) were also recorded. All measurements were completed baseline, post-treatment, and at 6- and 12-month follow-ups, respectively. Our results showed that PED-t improved more than CBT on mean (99% CI) absolute Vo2peak; 57,2 (84.4, 198.8) mL ($g = 0.22$, $p < 0.001$) post-treatment. There were small to medium long-term differences in 1RM after PED-t compared to CBT. BC deteriorated in both groups during follow-up. Neither the PED-t nor the CBT lowered the risk for NCDs. Clearly, other approaches need to be considered to promote physical fitness and lower the risk of NCDs among individuals with BN and BED.

Keywords: physical fitness; visceral adipose tissue; obesity; eating disorders; nutrition; physical activity; exercise; bulimia; binge eating disorder

1. Introduction

Poor physical fitness is a major public health challenge, and it has been found to be prevalent among those suffering from bulimia nervosa (BN) or binge eating disorders (BED) [1,2]. Poor physical fitness may in return increase the risk of non-communicable diseases (NCDs) such as type 2 diabetes, obesity, and cardiovascular symptoms [3]: risk profiles previously identified in BN and BED [4–9].

It is well documented that lifestyle interventions focusing on diet and physical activity may reduce the risk of obesity and many NCDs [10]. However, in the treatment of BN, and notably, anorexia nervosa, there is a reluctance to focus on physical activity because of fear of triggering or exacerbating dieting, compulsive exercise, and other eating disorder symptoms (ED-symptoms) [11,12]. Further, with respect to BN, and BED in particular, a need to focus on physical activity due to a risk of obesity is hampered by the fact that many treatment guidelines recommend postponing such a focus until eating disorder symptoms have been successfully treated [12,13]. Another problem regarding the limited attention to somatic comorbidity during treatment of BN and BED is the poor specificity of body mass index (BMI) categories and the waist-circumference ratio to detect overweight problems. Thus, "masked obesity" in terms of a morbid body composition may occur in cases of a high body fat percentage [2,14] and a high level of visceral adipose tissue despite normal BMI [2]. For these reasons, physical fitness is understudied and poorly addressed in the treatment of BN and BED. As a consequence, many treatment guidelines related to physical health are somewhat skewed towards the management and treatment of severe anorexia nervosa [12].

Cognitive-behavioral therapy (CBT) is recognized as a gold standard treatment for eating disorders due to its capacity to reduce concern for body weight and shape, to improve self-esteem, self-efficacy, and self-compassion, and to affect regulation [15,16]. Such cognitive-affective changes lead to behavioral changes like reduced bingeing and increased health-related physical activity [17,18]. However, in a previous clinical study on eating disorders, we showed that a CBT-based treatment approach, in fact, did not produce changes in physical fitness and body composition [19]. A possible explanation of such findings is that CBT for eating disorders lacks a specific focus on weight loss and physical fitness and how to improve it [20]. On the other hand, several studies as well as a systematic review have reported that including physical activity in treatment may reduce BN and BED symptoms [21–28]. However, these studies have not reported data on changes in physical fitness, body composition, and other variables related to NCDs. In sum then, with a lack of focus on addressing physical fitness in the CBT manuals, one may hypothesize that a CBT treatment for BN and BED may not lower the risk of NCDs. Consequently, it is reasonable to hypothesize that a treatment of BN and BED that has an explicit focus on physical activity and that has been found to reduce compulsive exercise [27] and to match CBT in overall treatment efficiency [28] may be more effective than a CBT treatment in terms of lowering the risk of NCDs.

In addition to investigating the effect of a new treatment program for BN and BED on ED-symptoms, i.e., bingeing/purging, and an overvaluation on the need to control food intake, body weight and shape (previously reported) [27,28], we also wanted to investigate the acute and long-term effects of physical exercise and dietary therapy (PED-t) or CBT on physical fitness, body composition (BC), and risk of NCDs. We hypothesized that PED-t improves physical fitness and BC more than CBT, hence resulting in a more favorable risk profile for NCDs.

2. Materials and Methods

2.1. Subjects

We recruited females with BN or a BED to a 16-week outpatient group treatment, arranged at the Norwegian School of Sport Sciences (NSSS) during 2014–2016 [28]. The recruitment was directed through general practitioners, national and regional media, and social media.

All interested were interviewed by telephone using the Eating Disorder Examination questionnaire (EDE-q) [29] and the mini international neuropsychiatric interview (MINI) [30]. To optimize group heterogeneity, only women aged 18–40 years with BN or a BED were eligible. Participation in the study was restricted to women who were not currently pregnant and who had a BMI to 17.5–35 in order to reduce the risk of injuries and other complications if being randomized to the PED-t, as women who do not meet these criteria may not be able to follow a standardized exercise and dietary treatment protocol or to follow group exercise with minor room for individual adjustments. The study also excluded competitive athletes, those with comorbid mental disorders in need of other treatments, or those living distances to the study site that prevented regular attendance.

As previously reported [31], power analysis indicted a need for a minimum of 144 (72 per group) participants. We randomized 164 of those 419 who initially responded to recruitment to either PED-t (n = 76) or CBT (n = 73) (Figure 1). A randomization list with block size of eight was produced by www.randomizer.org by a statistician not connected to the study, and a fellow worker with no involvement in the trial randomized participants to either CBT or PED-t. All participants were informed about the outcome of the randomization after they had completed all baseline measures.

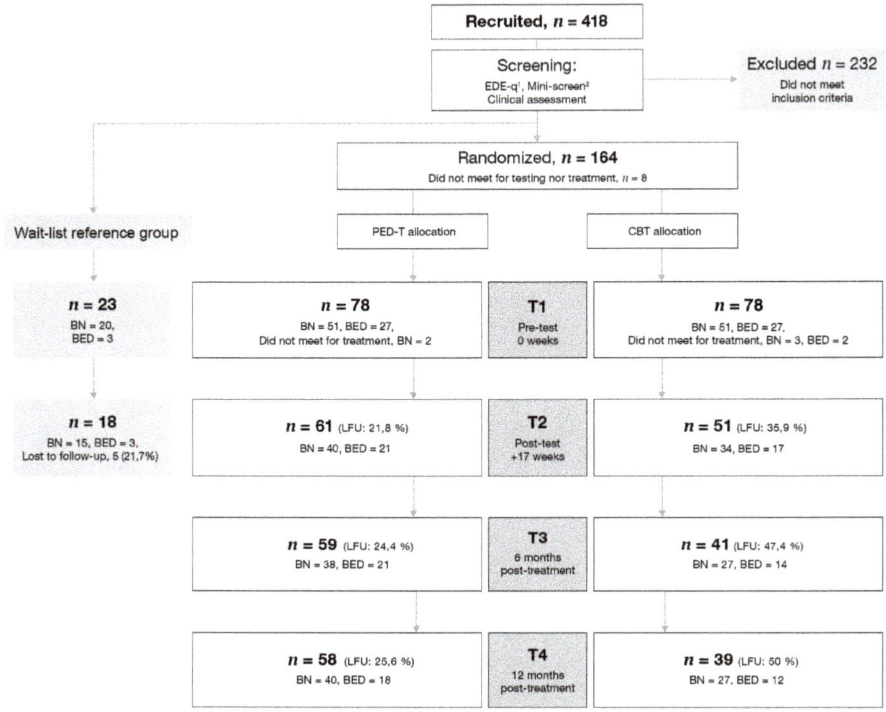

Figure 1. Recruitment, retention, and attrition during test periods. Overview of recruitment, screening, randomization, and attendance to the baseline (T1), post-treatment (T2), and follow-up measures (T3–T4). PED-t: physical exercise and dietary therapy; CBT: cognitive behavior therapy; BN: bulimia nervosa; BED: binge-eating disorder; EDE-q: eating disorder examination questionnaire; LFU: lost to follow up; [1] Fairburn and Beglin, 2008 [29]; [2] Sheehan, Lecrubier, Sheehan, et al., 1998 [30].

2.2. Treatments

The 16-week CBT and PED-t group-based therapies consisted of 20 sessions, each of 90 min duration, with five to eight participants in each group. A detailed account of the therapies and design are described elsewhere [31].

The manual-based CBT rests on a transdiagnostic model positing generic characteristics across ED-diagnoses [32]. Psychologists certified in CBT, with at least 10 years of experience, were conducting this therapy. The therapists were supervised by one senior therapist (PhD, psychologist and scientist) with more than 20 years of experience in CBT.

The PED-t consisted of a combination of dietary therapy and progressive resistance training (RET) and high intensity interval running (HIIT) [31]. The dietary manual focused on education on nutrition, group discussions, and practical skills in overcoming challenges in establishing regular daily eating patterns. We designed the whole-body, progressive resistance exercise program with two sessions per week arranged in three modules across the 16 weeks following basic principles for increases in maximal muscle strength (Table 1) [33]. The HIIT was designed with session intensity according to a pyramid structure, with progressive exercise load throughout the 16 weeks, following general recommendation for cardio respiratory fitness (CRF) improvement [34].

Table 1. Overview of the exercise module of the PED-t treatment. Resistance load is given as number of repetition maximum (RM).

		Supervised Exercise	Unsupervised Exercise	
Week	**Micro Cycle**	**Resistance Exercise**	**Interval Running**	**Resistance Exercise**
1–3	1	10RM	Pyramid interval (1–3 min intervals)	10RM
4–7	2	8RM	Pyramid interval (1–3 min intervals)	10RM
8–11	3	6RM	Pyramid interval (1–3 min intervals)	10RM
12–14	4	4RM	Pyramid interval (1–4 min intervals)	10RM
15–16	5	2RM	Pyramid interval (1–4 min intervals)	10RM

Specialists in physical exercise and in dietetics (MSc), all of whom were instructed by one experienced therapist (dietitian and exercise physiologist), were responsible for this therapy.

Participants were requested to complete training diaries throughout the treatment period in order to analyze adherence rate to training intervention.

2.3. Outcomes and Procedures

We measured body composition, physical activity, cardiorespiratory fitness (CRF), and maximal muscle strength during baseline and all follow-up test periods. Before all measure points, participants had to fast and to use passive transportation to the laboratories at the NSSS from 7:30 to 10:00 AM.

2.3.1. Body Composition

Participants were weighed in their underwear, and their height was measured with a fixed stadiometer (Seca scale, Mod: 8777021094, S/N: 5877248124885, Seca Deutschland, Hamburg, Germany). A dual-energy X-ray absorptiometry (Lunar iDXA, enCORE Software, version 14.10.022; GE Healthcare, Madison, WI, USA) performing a three-site scan was used to measure body composition (fat mass, percent body fat (%BF), lean body mass, visceral adipose tissue (VAT), android-to-gynoid fat mass ratio (AG ratio), and bone mineral density (lumbar area (L2–L4); femoral neck, trochanter, and shaft (proximal femur); whole body). All data were analyzed according to previously established guidelines [35].

We evaluated visceral adipose tissue (VAT) according to a cut-off for healthy VAT level of $\leq$300 g, based on previous findings of increased risk for high levels of triglycerides and fasting insulin levels with VAT above this threshold [36]. An optimal level of body fat percentage was defined as <33% [2,37], and masked obesity was defined as having a normal body weight according to the BMI scale (i.e., <25) but with high levels of body fat percentage (i.e., $\geq$33%) [2].

2.3.2. Cardio Respiratory Fitness (CRF)

After a breakfast meal, CRF was measured by performing a cardiopulmonary exercise test on a treadmill (ELG 90/200 Sports; Woodway, Weil am Rhein, Germany) with an incremental modified Balke protocol until exhaustion [38]. Gas exchange was measured using a breath-by-breath gas analysis system (OxyconPro analyzer; Jaeger, Würtzburg, Germany) with a Hans Rudolph two-way breathing mask (2700 series; Hans Rudolph, Kansas City, KS, USA). Measures of respiratory exchange ratio (RER) $\geq$ 1.10, and lactate concentration $\geq$ 7.0 mmol/L measured 1 min after test termination and analyzed immediately in a 1500-Sport-lactate analyzer (YSI, Yellow Springs Instruments, Yellow Springs, OH), were required to ensure a valid measure of peak oxygen uptake (VO_2 peak) [39]. A Borg scale rating $\geq$17 was additionally required to approve the test result [40,41].

We evaluated CRF as low according to the suggestion from a previous publication that found an increased risk of having a cluster of risk factors for cardiovascular diseases if VO2peak $\leq$ 35.1 mL$\times$kg BW$\times$min [42].

2.3.3. Maximal Muscle Strength

Maximal strength tests (one repetition maximum, 1RM) followed the cardiopulmonary exercise test in the following order: squats in Smith machine, bench press, and seated cable row. These three tests were performed according to predefined performance criteria and initiated with standardized warm-up sets of 10, 8, 6, and 4 repetitions.

2.3.4. NCD Risk Profile

We categorized participants into high-risk groups for NCD if they matched at least two out of three categories for high-risk evaluation: (1) having (either/or) high BMI, high body fat percentage, or masked obesity; (2) having high VAT levels; and/or (3) having low VO2peak.

2.4. Ethics

Active informed consent was required, and participants needed a conformation from their general practitioner that entering the study was medically safe. The study was approved by the Norwegian Regional Committee for Medical and Health Research Ethics (ID: 2013/1871) and registered in Clinical Trials (ID: NCT02079935).

2.5. Statistics

All analyses were conducted in SPSS version 24 (IBM, Armonk, NY, USA). Linear mixed regression models were built to estimate the between-group differences (PED-t vs. CBT) and the within-group changes (baseline vs. any of the three post-test measures). This analysis yields relatively unbiased estimates despite drop out (i.e., in the event that data are missing completely at random or missing at random). Moreover, it can be safely used without conducting multiple imputations beforehand [43]. Standard errors were estimated with the restricted maximum likelihood function, and type III *F*-tests were preferred. Dependency in the repeated outcome measures was accounted for by including a random intercept factor. The fixed factors were: *Group* (0-PED-t, 1-CBT), representing the overall treatment difference; *Time* (repeated measures), representing change across measurements; and the *Group*$\times$*Time* interaction, which was used in order to detect treatment differences at certain time points only. The between-group analyses used the baseline values as a covariate to increase the statistical power [44]. Differences between the treatment arms were examined with planned comparisons at each time point (least square difference tests). The within-group analyses included all four measurements in the *Time* factor. Due to the number of tests, differences with p-values < 0.01 were considered to be significant. A comparable statistical approach was used for the dichotomous outcome variables, replacing the analysis with a generalized linear model using a binominal distribution and logit link function (reference coded 0). Degrees of freedom were computed using Satterthwaite approximation. The outcome data are presented as estimated means including 99% confidence intervals.

Standardized Hedge's g effect sizes for continuous data were calculated as a ratio of the estimated means (extracted from the mixed model) to the observed pooled standard deviations (SDs). Values around 0.2, 0.5, and 0.8 were interpreted as weak, medium, and strong effect sizes, respectively [45].

Attrition rates were analyzed separately for each time (T2–T4) with independent t-test or chi-square analyses, as appropriate. A significance level of $p < 0.05$ were used for all t-tests or Mann-Whitney tests.

3. Results

3.1. Attrition Analysis

Drop-outs were less physically active (lower number of counts per minute in moderate-to-vigorous intensity of physical activity, MVPA, (p = 0.02)) and significantly more drop-outs had low femur bone mineral density (BMD) values (p = 0.02). Significantly more CBT-participants were lost to follow-up both at T3 (PED-t = 19 (24.4%), CBT = 37 (47.4%), p = 0.005) and T4 (PED-t = 20 (25.6%), CBT = 39 (50.0%), p = 0.006).

3.2. Demographics

Demographic information is presented in Table 2. The two treatment groups did not differ in any of the demographic variables. The mean (SD) attendance rate to therapist-lead PED-t sessions was 80.6% (11.4) and 82.1% (45.7) (p = 0.79) in CBT. In PED-t, the adherence rate to exercise sessions (supervised in therapy + unsupervised used for homework) was 69.8% for resistance exercise and 56.7% for HIIT.

Table 2. Demographic description of participants in therapy groups. Results are mean (SD).

	PED-t	CBT
Age, years	28.3 (6.2)	27.8 (5.3)
BMI, kg × height^{-1}	25.3 (5.1)	25.4 (4.6)
EDE-q, total score	3.7 (0.9)	3.7 (1.0)
Duration of illness, years	12.9 (7.5)	11.9 (6.7)
Bulimia nervosa, *n* (%)	51 (65.4)	50 (66.7)
Binge eating disorder, *n* (%)	27 (34.6)	25 (33.3)

Note: PED-t: Physical Exercise and Dietary therapy; CBT: Cognitive Behavior Therapy; BMI: Body Mass Index; EDE-q: Eating Disorder Examination questionnaire.

3.3. Body Composition

Changes in body composition are presented in Figures 2 and 3.

Mean BMI (99% CI) in PED-t increased to 25.64 (24.1, 27.1) at T2, 26.0 (24.5, 27.5) at T3, and 26.0 (24.5, 27.6) at T4. Only T3 ($g = -0.39$, p = 0.001) and T4 ($g = -0.4$, p = 0.002) were statistical different from baseline. There were corresponding findings in CBT, with levels of 25.2 (23.7, 26.8), 25.8 (24.3, 27.4), and 26.2 (24.6, 27.8), respectively, with only T4 different from baseline ($g = -0.36$, p = 0.004).

The within-group change in total body fat was significant at T3 ($g = -0.38$, p = 0.003) and T4 ($g = -0.31$, p = 0.003) in PED-t, and in CBT ($g = -0.34$, p = 0.006, and $g = -0.36$, p = 0.002, respectively). The numbers with masked obesity were 6.5% (99% CI: 2.0, 1.9) in PED-t and 5.3% (99% CI: 1.4, 1.8) in CBT, with no change by time in either group.

The within-group change in lean body mass (LBM) was significant at T2 ($g = -0.98$, $p < 0.001$) and T4 ($g = -0.47$, p = 0.01) in PED-t, while no change was found in CBT.

The within-group change in total VAT was significant at T4 in PED-t ($g = -0.29$, p = 0.004), with no significant change in CBT at any time. The numbers with VAT above recommended levels at T1 were 35.1% (99% CI: 22.4, 50.3) in PED-t and 36.0% (99% CI: 23.0, 51.5) in CBT, with no change by time in either group.

There were no between-group differences at any time in soft tissue body composition.

PED-t improved mean spine BMD at T3 ($g = -0.45$, p = 0.004) and T4 ($g = -0.31$, p = 0.01), and mean proximal femur BMD at T4 ($g = -0.37$, p = 0.01) (Figure 3). There were no changes in mean spine or proximal femur BMD after CBT. The occurrence of low proximal femur BMD at baseline was 1.3% (99% CI: 0.0, 55.7) in PED-t and 1.3% (99% CI: 0.2, 9.0) in CBT, with no change by time (T2–T4) in either group. There were corresponding findings for low spine BMD, with 5.2% (99% CI: 1.5, 16.8) in PED-t and 6.7% (99% CI: 2.2, 18.8) in CBT at T1, respectively.

No differences between groups were found at any time, other than a better score in proximal femur BMD ($g = 0.19$, $p = 0.01$) and proximal femur BMD Z-score ($g = 0.19$, $p = 0.007$) in PED-t compared to CBT at T4.

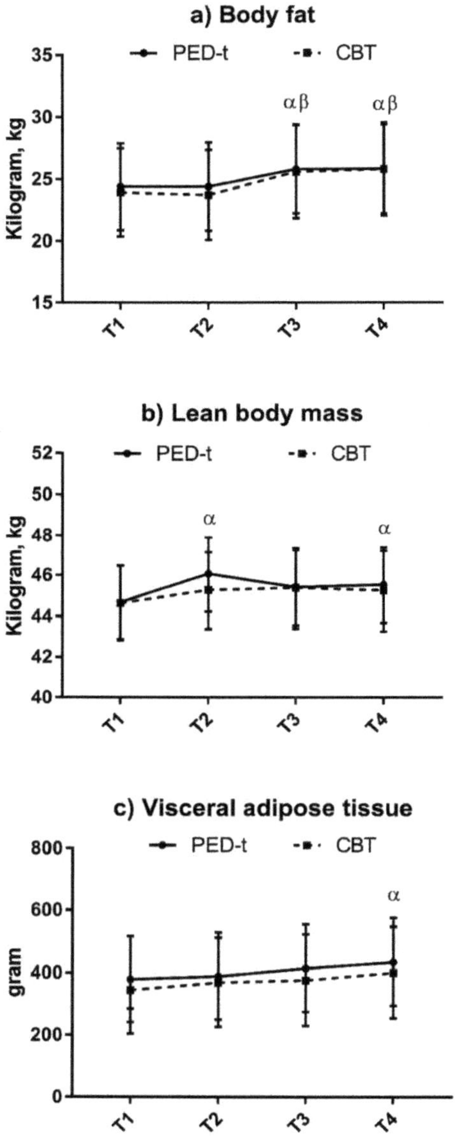

Figure 2. Changes in soft tissue body composition after PED-t or CBT. Results are estimated means (99% CI). (**a**) Changes in total body fat (kg); (**b**) changes in lean body mass (kg); (**c**) changes in visceral adipose tissue (gram). PED-t: Physical Exercise and Dietary therapy; CBT: Cognitive Behavior Therapy; 99% CI: 99% confidence interval; T1: baseline; T2: post-treatment; T3: 6 months post-treatment; T4: 12 months post-treatment; α: significant within-group change from T1 in PED-t ($p < 0.01$); β: significant within-group change from T1 in CBT ($p < 0.01$).

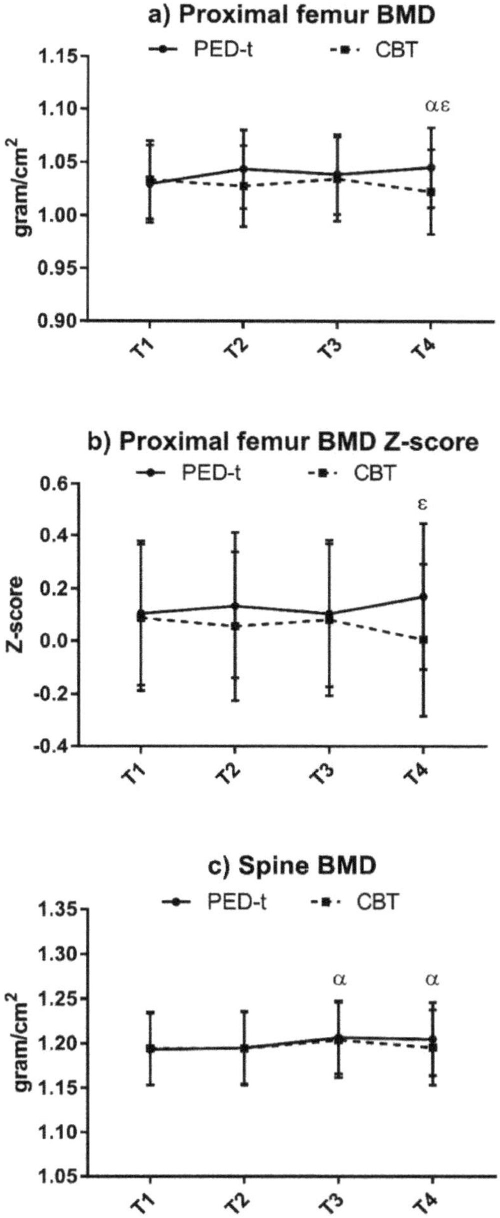

Figure 3. Changes in proximal femur bone mineral density (BMD), proximal femur BMD Z-score, and spine BMD after PED-t or CBT. Results are estimated means (99% CI). (**a**) Changes in proximal femur BMD (gram/cm^2); (**b**) changes in proximal femur BMD Z-score; (**c**) changes in spine BMD (gram/cm^2). PED-t: Physical Exercise and Dietary therapy; CBT: Cognitive Behavior Therapy; 99% CI: 99% confidence interval; BMD: bone mineral density; T1: baseline; T2: post-treatment; T3: 6 months post-treatment; T4: 12 months post-treatment; α: significant within-group change from T1 in PED-t ($p < 0.01$); ε: significant between-group difference ($p < 0.01$).

3.4. Physical Fitness

Effects from the two therapies on physical fitness are presented in Table 3.

3.4.1. 1RM

PED-t improved 1RM in squat, bench press, and seated row at all time points, with medium-to-large effect sizes. CBT improved in 1RM squat at all time points with small effect sizes, but resulted in no other observed 1RM improvements.

There were small-to-medium between-group differences for all strength tests at all time points, except no difference for 1RM squat at T3.

3.4.2. CRF

There was a small but significant within-group increase in CRF (in absolute terms; L $\times$ min)) after PED-t, but with no further effect from the PED-t during follow-up (T3–T4) (Table 3). No change in CRF after CBT occurred, and there were no between-group differences at any time.

Table 3. VO_2peak absolute, VO_2peak relative to BW, and maximal strength (1RM) in squats, bench press, and seated row at T1–T4. Results are estimated means (99% CI), and significant within-group changes are marked with asterisks.

	T1	T2	T3	T4	Between Effects, *p*-Value, Effect Size (g) T2	T3	T4
VO_2peak $_{absolute}$ ($L \times min^{-1}$)							
PED-t	2.67 (2.53, 2.81)	2.78 * (2.63, 2.93) $g = 0.22$	2.72 (2.57, 2.87)	2.77 (2.61, 2.92)			
CBT	2.73 (2.59, 2.88)	2.77 (2.61, 2.93)	2.78 (2.59, 2.96)	2.80 (2.62, 2.98)	*n.s.*	*n.s.*	*n.s.*
VO_2peak $_{relative}$ ($mL \times kg^{-1} \times min^{-1}$)							
PED-t	38.25 (35.87, 40.63)	39.47 (36.92, 42.02)	38.35 (35.70, 41.00)	39.01 (36.30, 41.72)			
CBT	39.01 (36.49, 41.54)	40.35 (37.63, 43.08)	39.13 (35.95, 42.32)	39.24 (36.14, 42.33)	*n.s.*	*n.s.*	*n.s.*
Squat, 1RM (kg)							
PED-t	63.95 (58.33, 69.56)	78.60 * (72.81, 84.39) $g = -0.83$	73.89 * (67.94, 79.85) $g = -0.56$	74.98 * (68.96, 81.00) $g = -0.71$			
CBT	64.21 (58.37, 70.06)	67.15 * (61.06, 73.24) $g = -0.15$	70.07 ** (63.41, 76.72) $g = -0.30$	69.31 * (62.65, 75.97) $g = -0.26$	11.78 (7.42, 16.12) $g = 0.65$ $p < 0.001$	*n.s.*	6.10 (0.84, 11.36) $g = 0.31$ $p = 0.003$
Bench press, 1RM (kg)							
PED-t	37.02 (34.07, 39.97)	45.22 * (42.18, 48.26) $g = -0.86$	42.68 * (39.56, 45.79) $g = -0.62$	43.77 * (40.62, 46.93) $g = -0.74$			
CBT	38.32 (35.28, 41.37)	38.99 (35.80, 42.18)	39.81 (36.37, 43.26)	39.35 (35.90, 42.79)	7.28 (4.92, 9.63) $g = 0.63$ $p < 0.001$	4.12 (1.41, 6.84) $g = 0.30$ $p < 0.001$	5.60 (2.85, 8.35) $g = 0.43$ $p < 0.001$

Table 3. *Cont.*

					Between Effects, p-Value, Effect Size (g)		
Seated row, 1RM (kg)							
PED-t	34.38 (32.41, 36.34)	38.41 * (36.36, 40.46) $g = -0.65$	37.50 * (35.36, 39.64) $g = -0.52$	37.22 * (35.05, 39.40) $g = -0.46$			
CBT	34.56 (32.54, 36.58)	35.20 (33.06, 37.34)	35.03 (32.66, 37.41)	34.73 (32.31, 37.14)	3.39 (1.45, 5.34) $g = 0.52$ $p < 0.001$	2.58 (0.35, 4.81) $g = 0.41$ $p = 0.003$	2.74 (0.45, 5.02) $g = 0.40$ $p = 0.002$

PED-t: Physical Exercise and Dietary therapy; CBT: Cognitive Behavior Therapy; BW: Body Weight; 1RM: one repetition maximum; VO_2peak: peak maximal oxygen uptake; 99% CI: 99% confidence interval; g: Hedges g (effect size); T1: baseline; T2: post-treatment; T3: 6 months post-treatment; T4: 12 months post-treatment; n.s., non-significant; * $p < 0.001$; ** $p = 0.01$.

3.5. Risk of NCDs

In the evaluation of NCD risk, two participants impaired their risk profile during the treatment period in PED-t, while five participants improved. In total, 33 participants in PED-t remained without any high-risk NCD profile during treatment, while 19 participants remained in the high-risk group. The corresponding findings in CBT were one impairment, three improvements, 28 without any risk profile during treatment, and 17 remaining in the high-risk group.

4. Discussion

The aim of this study was to examine the immediate and long-term effects of CBT versus a physical exercise and dietary therapy (PED-t) on physical fitness, body composition, and the risk of NCDs. We found improvements in BMD, long-term increased maximal muscle strength, and short-term increased peak oxygen uptake after a treatment period with PED-t, while CBT did not result in comparable results. The overall study findings could not support the hypothesis that the PED-t provided sufficient improvements in physical fitness that actually lowered the risk of NCDs.

No improvement after CBT was expected. Here, healthy living was addressed, but the treatment did not consist of practical elements to help participants to improve nutrition and establish or maintain physical activity. It was unexpected, however, to observe no changes in soft BC and risk of NCDs after the PED-t; these results require some further considerations. First, it needs to be emphasized that the main aim of the PED-t was not to lower the risk of NCD, but to reduce eating disorder symptoms like irregular eating patterns and concerns about body and weight. Thus, learning how to achieve healthy living (i.e., adequate physical activity and a healthy diet composition) may be considered as positive side effects. To some extent, such side effects have been achieved through a shift of focus from overvaluation of the need to control body figure and weight towards attaining health and fitness [28]. In retrospect, however, given the low baseline values on parameters indicating an elevated risk of NCDs, it may have been overly optimistic to expect a change in physical activity and nutrition that really would lower this risk. Hence, findings that the PED-t may bring about a relaxation of dietary restrictions and compulsive physical exercise [27,28] may have counteracted any potential effect from PED-t on weight reduction and risk of NCDs. Secondly, the negative findings may, to some extent, also be explained by suboptimal treatment compliance. Thus, the participants in the PED-t, following an exercise program designed to affect BC (resistance exercise), as well as CRF and VAT (HIIT), reported unsatisfactory compliance to the program (i.e., ~70% of the RET and ~57% of the HIIT).

The deterioration of soft tissue BC, with increases in VAT, body fat, and BMI above recommendations [2,36,46] at the follow-ups, raises concern for the health of females under and after any kind of treatment for BN and BED, and the PED-t approach included herein. Such a concern highlights that the need to improve physical fitness and BC should be focused upon in the treatment of BN and BED. In a previous PED-t publication we showed that such a focus does not initiate or maintain excessive and obsessive physical exercise frequently observed in BN and BED [27]. Hence, there is empirical evidence refuting a main clinical reluctance to incorporate guided physical activity in the treatment of eating disorders.

An important limitation to our findings and conclusions is the skewed and high attrition rate during follow-up, with more participants being lost to follow-up in CBT compared to PED-t. The strengths of the study are the randomized design, the follow-up period, and the inclusion of participants from a real-life setting. As our findings show, maintaining lifestyle changes necessary for improvement of health is difficult in such real-life settings for persons suffering from BN or BED.

An important implication from the present study is that implementing guided physical exercise and dietary therapy is not sufficient to improve physical health in these patient groups. A recent systematic review of population-based studies on overweight has reported small but significant effects of combining CBT with a motivating interview (MI) [47]. Within the theoretical realm of self-determination theory, MI serves the purpose of internalizing treatment goals, while CBT may be effective in combating dysfunctional cognitions [48]. Such cognitions may comprise beliefs about not being able to reach treatment goals (i.e., low self-efficacy) as well as undue concerns about body, weight, and shape and the need to control eating as well as ambivalence towards change. The behavioral components of CBT serve the overall purpose of promoting self-regulation, a purpose that has been reported as being useful in the treatment of obesity [49]. However, future studies should examine if a combination of cognitive and behavioral approaches to lifestyle change improves long-term adherence to health-related exercise and eating behavior, and thus reduces risk of NCDs in persons with BN or BED to a greater extent than single-component interventions. A task for future randomized controlled studies may then be to explore the efficacy of various combinations of MI, CBT, and PED-t in the treatment of eating disorders as well as other disorders where poor physical fitness and a risk of NCDs is an issue of concern.

Author Contributions: Conceptualization, J.S.B., J.H.R., T.F.M. and S.B.S.; Methodology, J.S.B., J.H.R., T.F.M. and S.B.S.; Formal Analysis, T.F.M.; Investigation, T.F.M. and J.S.B.; Resources, T.F.M.; Writing-Original Draft Preparation, T.F.M. and S.B.S.; Writing-Review & Editing, J.S.B., J.H.R., T.F.M. and S.B.S.; Visualization, T.F.M.; Supervision, J.S.B. and J.H.R.; Project Administration, T.F.M.; Funding Acquisition, J.S.B., J.H.R., T.F.M. and S.B.S.

Funding: TFM's PhD position in this project was funded by the Norwegian Women's Public Health Association. This research was partly funded by the Norwegian School of Sport Sciences, the UiT (The Arctic University of Norway), by the Norwegian Osteoporosis society, and by an assigned fund from the Research Council of Norway. Dairy sports recovery products were supplied by Tine Dairy Producer (Norway) as part of their charity funding activity.

Acknowledgments: We would like to thank our master students in exercise is medicine for lab, exercise, and test services. We further would like to thank the head of the Sport Medicine department, Solveig Sunde, for taking care of concealed randomization.

Conflicts of Interest: The authors declare no conflict of interest. The funders had no role in the design of the study; in the collection, analyses, or interpretation of data; in the writing of the manuscript, or in the decision to publish the results.

References

1. Kaminsky, L.A.; Arena, R.; Myers, J. Reference Standards for Cardiorespiratory Fitness Measured with Cardiopulmonary Exercise Testing: Data From the Fitness Registry and the Importance of Exercise National Database. *Mayo. Clin. Proc.* **2015**, *90*, 1515–1523. [CrossRef] [PubMed]
2. Mathisen, T.F.; Rosenvinge, J.H.; Friborg, O.; Pettersen, G.; Stensrud, T.; Hansen, B.H.; Underhaug, K.E.; Teinung, E.; Vrabel, K.; Svendsen, M.; et al. Body composition and physical fitness in women with bulimia nervosa or binge-eating disorder. *Int. J. Eat. Disord.* **2018**, *51*, 331–342. [CrossRef] [PubMed]
3. Myers, J.; McAuley, P.; Lavie, C.J.; Despres, J.P.; Arena, R.; Kokkinos, P. Physical activity and cardiorespiratory fitness as major markers of cardiovascular risk: Their independent and interwoven importance to health status. *Prog. Cardiovasc. Dis.* **2015**, *57*, 306–314. [CrossRef] [PubMed]
4. Raevuori, A.; Suokas, J.; Haukka, J.; Gissler, M.; Linna, M.; Grainger, M.; Suvisaari, J. Highly increased risk of type 2 diabetes in patients with binge eating disorder and bulimia nervosa. *Int. J. Eat. Disord.* **2015**, *48*, 555–562. [CrossRef] [PubMed]
5. Hudson, J.I.; Lalonde, J.K.; Coit, C.E.; Tsuang, M.T.; McElroy, S.L.; Crow, S.J. Longitudinal study of the diagnosis of components of the metabolic syndrome in individuals with binge-eating disorder. *Am. J. Clin. Nutr.* **2010**, *91*, 1568–1573. [CrossRef] [PubMed]
6. Nieto-Martinez, R.; González-Rivas, J.P.; Medina-Inojosa, J.R.; Florez, H. Are Eating Disorders Risk Factors for Type 2 Diabetes? A Systematic Review and Meta-analysis. *Curr. Diab. Rep.* **2017**, *17*, 138. [CrossRef] [PubMed]
7. Villarejo, C.; Fernández-Aranda, F.; Jiménez-Murcia, S.; Peñas-Lledó, E.; Granero, R.; Penelo, E. Lifetime obesity in patients with eating disorders: Increasing prevalence, clinical and personality correlates. *Eur. Eat. Disord. Rev.* **2012**, *20*, 250–254. [CrossRef] [PubMed]
8. Nakai, Y.; Noma, S.I.; Fukusima, M.; Taniguchi, A.; Teramukai, S. Serum Lipid Levels in Patients with Eating Disorders. *Intern. Med.* **2016**, *55*, 1853–1857. [CrossRef]

9. Olguin, P.; Fuentes, M.; Gabler, G.; Guerdjikova, A.I.; Keck, P.E.; McElroy, S.L. Medical comorbidity of binge eating disorder. *Eat. Weight Disord. Stud. Anorex. Bulim. Obes.* **2017**, *22*, 13–26. [CrossRef]
10. Pedersen, B.K.; Saltin, B. Exercise as medicine—Evidence for prescribing exercise as therapy in 26 different chronic diseases. *Scand. J. Med. Sci. Sports* **2015**, *25*, 1–72. [CrossRef]
11. da Luz, F.Q.; Hay, P.; Touyz, S.; Sainsbury, A. Obesity with Comorbid Eating Disorders: Associated Health Risks and Treatment Approaches. *Nutrients* **2018**, *10*, 829. [CrossRef] [PubMed]
12. Hilbert, A.; Hoek, H.W.; Schmidt, R. Evidence-based clinical guidelines for eating disorders: International comparison. *Curr. Opin. Psychiatry* **2017**, *30*, 423–437. [CrossRef] [PubMed]
13. Norwegian Directorate of Health. *National Guidlines for Early Detection, Progress and Treatment of Eating Disorders*; Dahle, K.A., Ed.; Norwegian Directorate of Health: Oslo, Norway, 2016.
14. Davidson, L.E.; Hunt, S.C.; Adams, T.D. Fitness versus adiposity in cardiovascular disease risk. *Eur. J. Clin. Nutr.* 2018. [CrossRef]
15. Linardon, J.; Fairburn, C.G.; Fitzsimmons-Craft, E.E.; Wilfley, D.E.; Brennan, L. The empirical status of the third-wave behaviour therapies for the treatment of eating disorders: A systematic review. *Clin. Psychol. Rev.* **2017**, *58*, 125–140. [CrossRef] [PubMed]
16. de Jong, M.; Schoorl, M.; Hoek, H.W. Enhanced cognitive behavioural therapy for patients with eating disorders: A systematic review. *Curr. Opin. Psychiatry* **2018**, *31*, 436–444. [CrossRef] [PubMed]
17. Beck, A.T. Cognitive Therapy: Nature and Relation to Behavior Therapy—Republished Article. *Behav. Ther.* **2016**, *47*, 776–784. [CrossRef] [PubMed]
18. Denison, E.; Underland, V.; Mosdøl, A.; Vist, G.E. NIPH Systematic Reviews. In *Cognitive Therapies for Increasing Physical Activity*; The Norwegian Institute of Public Health (NIPH): Oslo, Norway, 2016.
19. Bratland-Sanda, S.; Martinsen, E.W.; Sundgot-Borgen, J. Changes in physical fitness, bone mineral density and body composition during inpatient treatment of underweight and normal weight females with longstanding eating disorders. *Int. J. Environ. Res. Public Health* **2012**, *9*, 315–330. [CrossRef]
20. Castelnuovo, G.; Pietrabissa, G.; Manzoni, G.M.; Cattivelli, R.; Rossi, A.; Novelli, M. Cognitive behavioral therapy to aid weight loss in obese patients: Current perspectives. *Psychol. Res. Behav. Manag.* **2017**, *10*, 165–173. [CrossRef] [PubMed]
21. Vancampfort, D.; Vanderlinden, J.; De Hert, M.; Adamkova, M.; Skjaerven, L.H.; Catalán-Matamoros, D. A systematic review on physical therapy interventions for patients with binge eating disorder. *Disabil. Rehabil.* **2013**, *35*, 2191–2196. [CrossRef] [PubMed]
22. Fossati, M.; Amati, F.; Painot, D.; Reiner, M.; Haenni, C.; Golay, A. Cognitive-behavioral therapy with simultaneous nutritional and physical activity education in obese patients with binge eating disorder. *Eat. Weight. Disord.* **2004**, *9*, 134–138. [CrossRef] [PubMed]
23. Levine, M.D.; Marcus, M.D.; Moulton, P. Exercise in the treatment of binge eating disorder. *Int. J. Eat. Disord.* **1996**, *19*, 171–177. [CrossRef]
24. Vancampfort, D.; Vanderlinden, J.; De Hert, M.; Soundy, A.; Adámkova, M.; Skjaerven, L.H. A systematic review of physical therapy interventions for patients with anorexia and bulemia nervosa. *Disabil. Rehabil.* **2014**, *36*, 628–634. [CrossRef] [PubMed]
25. Sundgot-Borgen, J.; Rosenvinge, J.H.; Bahr, R.; Schneider, L.S. The effect of exercise, cognitive therapy, and nutritional counseling in treating bulimia nervosa. *Med. Sci. Sports Exerc.* **2002**, *34*, 190–195. [CrossRef] [PubMed]
26. Hoie, L.H.; Myking, E.; Reine, E.C.; Bruusgaard, D. Diet and exercise in addition to psychotherapy, in the treatment of patients suffering from eating disorders with obesity. *Eat. Weight Disord.* **1997**, *2*, 207–210. [CrossRef] [PubMed]
27. Mathisen, T.F.; Bratland-Sanda, S.; Rosenvinge, J.H.; Friborg, O.; Pettersen, G.; Vrabel, K.A.; Sundgot-Borgen, J. Treatment effects on compulsive exercise and physical activity in eating disorders. *J. Eat. Disord.* **2018**, in press.
28. Mathisen, T.F. A randomized controlled trial of physical exercise- and dietary therapy versus cognitive behavior therapy: Treatment effects for women with bulimia nervosa or binge eating disorder. Ph.D. Thesis, Norwegian School of Sport Science, Oslo, Norway, September 2018. Available online: https://brage.bibsys.no/xmlui/handle/11250/2562679 (accessed on 28 November 2018).
29. Fairburn, C.; Beglin, S. Eating Disorder Examination Questionnaire (EDE-Q 6.0). In *Cognitive Behavior Therapy and Eating Disorders*; Fairburn, C., Ed.; Guilford Press: New York, NY, USA, 2008.

30. Sheehan, D.V.; Baker, R.; Dunbar, G.C. The Mini-International Neuropsychiatric Interview (M.I.N.I.): The development and validation of a structured diagnostic psychiatric interview for DSM-IV and ICD-10. *J. Clin. Psychiatry* **1998**, *59*, 34–57.
31. Mathisen, T.F.; Rosenvinge, J.H.; Pettersen, G.; Friborg, O.; Vrabel, K.; Bratland-Sanda, S. The PED-t trial protocol: The effect of physical exercise –and dietary therapy compared with cognitive behavior therapy in treatment of bulimia nervosa and binge eating disorder. *BMC Psychiatry* **2017**, *17*, 180. [CrossRef]
32. Fairburn, C.G.; Cooper, Z.; Doll, H.A.; O'connor, M.E.; Bohn, K.; Hawker, D.M. Transdiagnostic Cognitive-Behavioral Therapy for Patients with Eating Disorders: A Two-Site Trial with 60-Week Follow-Up. *Am. J. Psychiatry* **2009**, *166*, 311–319. [CrossRef]
33. Ratamess, N.; Alvar, B.; Evetoch, T.; Housh, T.; Kibler, W.; Kraemer, W. Progression Models in Resistance Training for Healthy Adults. *Med. Sci. Sports Exerc.* **2009**, *41*, 687–708.
34. Garber, C.E.; Blissmer, B.; Deschenes, M.R.; Franklin, B.A.; Lamonte, M.J.; Lee, I.M. Quantity and Quality of Exercise for Developing and Maintaining Cardiorespiratory, Musculoskeletal, and Neuromotor Fitness in Apparently Healthy Adults: Guidance for Prescribing Exercise. *Med. Sci. Sports Exerc.* **2011**, *43*, 1334–1359.
35. Nana, A.; Slater, G.J.; Stewart, A.D.; Burke, L.M. Methodology Review: Using Dual-Energy X-Ray Absorptiometry (DXA) for the Assessment of Body Composition in Athletes and Active People. *Int. J. Sport Nutr. Exerc. Metab.* **2015**, *25*, 198–215. [CrossRef] [PubMed]
36. Bosch, T.A.; Steinberger, J.; Sinaiko, A.R.; Moran, A.; Jacobs Jr, D.R.; Kelly, A.S.; Dengel, D.R. Identification of sex-specific thresholds for accumulation of visceral adipose tissue in adults. *Obesity* **2015**, *23*, 375–382. [CrossRef] [PubMed]
37. Imboden, M.T.; Welch, W.A.; Swartz, A.M.; Montoye, A.H.; Finch, H.W.; Harber, M.P.; Kaminsky, L.A. Reference standards for body fat measures using GE dual energy x-ray absorptiometry in Caucasian adults. *PLoS ONE* **2017**, *12*, e0175110. [CrossRef]
38. Edvardsen, E.; Hansen, B.H.; Holme, I.M.; Dyrstad, S.M.; Anderssen, S.A. Reference Values for Cardiorespiratory Response and Fitness on the Treadmill in a 20- to 85-Year-Old Population. *Chest* **2013**, *144*, 241–248. [CrossRef] [PubMed]
39. Edvardsen, E.; Hem, E.; Anderssen, S.A. End Criteria for Reaching Maximal Oxygen Uptake Must Be Strict and Adjusted to Sex and Age: A Cross-Sectional Study. *PLoS ONE* **2014**, *9*, e85276. [CrossRef]
40. Borg, G. Psychophysical bases of perceived exertion. *Med. Sci. Sports Exerc.* **1982**, *14*, 377–381.
41. Haff, G.; Dumke, C. *Laboratory Manual for Exercise Physiology*, 2nd ed.; Human Kinetics: Champaign, IL, USA, 2012.
42. Aspenes, S.T.; Nilsen, T.I.; Skaug, E.A.; Bertheussen, G.F.; Ellingsen, Ø.; Vatten, L.; Wisløff, U. Peak Oxygen Uptake and Cardiovascular Risk Factors in 4631 Healthy Women and Men. *Med. Sci. Sports Exerc.* **2011**, *43*, 1465–1473.
43. Twisk, J.; de Boer, M.; de Vente, W.; Heymans, M. Multiple imputation of missing values was not necessary before performing a longitudinal mixed-model analysis. *J. Clin. Epidemiol.* **2013**, *66*, 1022–1028. [CrossRef]
44. Egbewale, B.E.; Lewis, M.; Sim, J. Bias, precision and statistical power of analysis of covariance in the analysis of randomized trials with baseline imbalance: A simulation study. *BMC Med. Res. Methodol.* **2014**, *14*, 49. [CrossRef]
45. Hedges, G.; Olkin, I. *Statistical Methods in Meta-Analysis*; Academic Press: Cambridge, MA, USA, 1985.
46. World Health Organization. Physical status: Theuse and interpretation of anthropometry. In *Technical Report Series*; World Health Organization: Geneva, Switherland, 1995; pp. 427–438.
47. Barrett, S.; Begg, S.; O'Halloran, P.; Kingsley, M. Integrated motivational interviewing and cognitive behaviour therapy for lifestyle mediators of overweight and obesity in community-dwelling adults: A systematic review and meta-analyses. *BMC Public Health* **2018**, *18*, 1160. [CrossRef]
48. Ryan, R.M.; Deci, E.L. Self-determination theory and the facilitation of intrinsic motivation, social development, and well-being. *Am. Psychol.* **2000**, *55*, 68. [CrossRef] [PubMed]
49. Samdal, G.B.; Eide, G.E.; Barth, T.; Williams, G.; Meland, E. Effective behaviour change techniques for physical activity and healthy eating in overweight and obese adults; systematic review and meta-regression analyses. *Int. J. Behav. Nutr. Phys. Act.* **2017**, *14*, 42. [CrossRef] [PubMed]

nutrients

Article

Disordered Eating Attitudes and Behavioral and Neuroelectric Indices of Cognitive Flexibility in Individuals with Overweight and Obesity

Caitlyn G. Edwards [1], Anne M. Walk [2], Sharon V. Thompson [1], Sean P. Mullen [2], Hannah D. Holscher [1,2,3] and Naiman A. Khan [1,2,4,*]

1 Division of Nutritional Sciences, University of Illinois, Urbana, IL 61801, USA; cgedwar2@illinois.edu (C.G.E.); svthomp2@illinois.edu (S.V.T.); hholsche@illinois.edu (H.D.H.)
2 Department of Kinesiology and Community Health, University of Illinois, Urbana, IL 61801, USA; amcclur3@illinois.edu (A.M.W.); spmullen@illinois.edu (S.P.M.)
3 Department of Food Science and Human Nutrition, University of Illinois, Urbana, IL 61801, USA
4 Neuroscience Program, University of Illinois, Urbana, IL 61801, USA
* Correspondence: nakhan2@illinois.edu; Tel.: +1-217-300-2197

Received: 12 October 2018; Accepted: 30 November 2018; Published: 4 December 2018

Abstract: Impairment in cognitive flexibility is a trait characteristic among individuals with diagnosed eating disorders. However, the extent to which these relationships exist in individuals with overweight or obesity remains unclear. Furthermore, there is a lack of knowledge characterizing the neural underpinnings of these relationships. The current study aimed to investigate disordered eating attitudes and cognitive flexibility among adults with overweight and obesity. The Eating Attitudes Test (EAT-26) and a task-switching paradigm were collected from 132 adults (50 males, Body Mass Index (BMI) = 32.0 ± 5.8 kg/m^2). Behavioral measures (accuracy and reaction time (RT)) and neuroelectric indices (amplitude and latency) of the P3 component were assessed. Hierarchical linear regressions, following adjustment of age, sex, intelligence quotient (IQ), weight status, and diet quality were developed using summative and subscale scores of the EAT-26. Higher EAT-26 summative scores, and the Dieting subscale, were related to longer RT. Only the Bulimia and Food Preoccupation subscale was related to longer P3 latency. The relationship between disordered eating attitudes and cognitive flexibility extends to individuals with overweight and obesity and is independent of age, sex, IQ, weight status, and diet quality. These findings are important, as differences in cognitive flexibility can lead to behavioral rigidity. Future work should aim to examine other neuroelectric components to identify where differences driving behavioral latencies may be occurring.

Keywords: feeding behavior; cognition; obesity; event-related potential; P3

---

1. Introduction

Despite many large-scale public health efforts targeted towards reducing excess energy intake and improving diet quality, many Americans fail to meet federally recommended dietary guidelines [1]. While there are many gaps in current knowledge concerning how to overcome the barriers to improving diet quality, there is limited research on the relationship between the mental or cognitive processes surrounding dietary regulation. Understanding these relationships is increasingly important, as our environment is inundated by aggressively advertised and hedonically rewarding high-fat/high-sugar foods, thus requiring constant control of the drive to consume foods beyond hunger and metabolic needs [2].

Exploration of cognitive flexibility, one of many interrelated, yet dissociable, components of cognitive control, may hold particular promise to understanding modulation of eating attitudes and behaviors. Cognitive control allows for the initiation, planning, regulation, and achievement of goal-oriented behavior [3]. Cognitive flexibility, as a component of cognitive control, can be thought of as the ability to appropriately adjust one's behavior according to a changing environment [4]. In our increasingly obesogenic environment, one where we are constantly barraged by images and marketing strategies aimed at overconsumption, cognitive flexibility becomes increasingly pertinent [5]. For some individuals, particularly those with obesity or disordered eating attitudes, adequately employing cognitive flexibility can be challenging in obesogenic settings that may require choosing less appealing food options in the name of health, in the face of more immediately rewarding options [6,7].

Although much work has been dedicated towards behavior change promotion, many individuals perpetually struggle to maintain healthful eating behaviors. Cognitive inflexibility potentially contributes to this lack of success. Previous work has indicated that impairment in cognitive flexibility is a trait characteristic among patients with diagnosed eating disorders [8–10]. This research is becoming increasingly relevant as 30 million adults in the United States report suffering from clinically significant disordered eating attitudes at some point in their lives [11]. Infrequently studied is the relationship between disordered eating attitudes and cognitive control among individuals who suffer from sub-clinical disordered eating thought patterns. Indeed, in a lifetime prevalence study of eating disorders, both males and females were more likely to suffer from a "subthreshold binge eating disorder" than either anorexia nervosa or bulimia nervosa [11]. While these subthreshold disordered eating attitudes have been briefly studied, the literature is sparse and particularly lacking in individuals with overweight and obesity [12]. It is possible, and probable, that individuals with these subthreshold disorders will similarly have difficulty adequately regulating their eating behaviors, potentially due to poor cognitive flexibility.

Cognitive flexibility is commonly assessed using behavioral measures (i.e., accuracy and reaction time (RT)) in task-switching paradigms, but previous literature relating these behavioral measures to disordered eating attitudes lacks proposed mechanisms of action. The use of the electroencephalography and the event-related potential (ERP) technique allows for examination of stimuli response with millisecond precision, allowing for examination of not only the behavioral responses but also the neural underpinnings of said responses. Specifically, the P300 (P3, P3b), a positive-going component occurring roughly 300–700 milliseconds (ms) post-stimulus onset, signifies the resources required for stimulus context updating and resource allocation [13]. In a task-switching paradigm, the P3 is largely thought to reflect how well one can activate currently relevant stimulus-response rules and deactivate previously relevant rules [14]. The P3 amplitude refers to the magnitude to which attentional resources are reconfigured to adapt to the change in stimulus-response rules, while the latency references the speed of this information processing [15]. Captured in these measures is an attentional (changes in stimuli that then require rule-set adaptation) as well as an intentional (changes in the rule-set then requiring selection of motor responses) switch [16]. Examining the P3 component in relation to disordered eating attitudes in a task-switching paradigm may provide novel insights into the potential neural mechanism by which disordered eating attitudes may contribute to poorer cognitive flexibility, or vise-versa.

An additionally important factor to consider when studying the relationship between eating attitudes and cognitive control is weight status. Individuals with overweight or obesity have been previously shown to exhibit poorer performance on cognitive control tasks [17,18]. Given the frequency of co-morbidity between disordered eating attitudes and obesity, poor dietary choices may be a consequence of cognitive flexibility decrements among individuals with overweight and obesity and disordered eating attitudes. This is additionally problematic given the emergence of recent evidence that individuals with a BMI ≥ 25 kg/m^2 may have greater than two-fold risk for disordered eating [19]. Disordered eating attitudes and behaviors have also been shown to be prevalent across both sexes [11]. However, there is a paucity of data linking disordered eating attitudes to specific aspects of cognitive control, particularly among adults with overweight and obesity. Accordingly, the aim of this study was to elucidate the relationship between eating attitudes and cognitive flexibility in a non-clinical group of men and women with overweight and obesity. We hypothesized that we would observe evidence of disordered eating attitudes in our non-clinical sample. We also hypothesized that higher disordered eating attitudes would be related to lower accuracy and longer RT in a task-switching paradigm. We further aimed to explain these increased RT's through the examination of the P3 component. We hypothesized that for this component, increased disordered eating attitudes would be related to lower amplitudes and longer latencies.

2. Materials and Methods

2.1. Participants and Procedures

Participant characteristics are described in Table 1. Data were collected from 132 adults (50 male), with BMIs ranging from 25.0 to 57.7 kg/m^2. As an ethnic breakdown of our sample, 1.5% of participants identified as American Indian or Alaskan, 10% identified as of Asian descent, 70% identified as white or Caucasian, 5% identified as Black or African American, and 4% identified as mixed or other. In terms of Social-economic status, 16% of our sample reported an annual household income between 0–$30,000, 56% reported between $30,000–$90,000, and 20% reported greater than $90,000. To qualify for the study, participants had to have a BMI $\geq$ 25.0 kg/m^2, be between 25–45 years of age, be free of diagnosed neurological disorders, and free of clinician-diagnosed depression and anxiety disorders. Participants were recruited using flyers posted in community settings, e-mails sent to University employees, as well as word-of-mouth recruitment. To ensure recruitment reached a wide variety of participants, recruitment focused on pursuing individuals outside of the University setting through bus advertisements, postcard mailing in rural neighborhoods, and school flyers in surrounding neighborhoods. Participants were compensated with gift cards upon completion of all study procedures. During the first laboratory visit, participants provided demographic data, completed the EAT-26, as well as height and weight measurements for BMI assessment. The Kaufman Brief Intelligence Test was administered to assess IQ [20]. Participants also completed the National Cancer Institute's Diet History Questionnaire II to assess overall diet quality [21]. During the second laboratory visit, cognitive testing was conducted following a 10-hour fast in the morning hours to reduce the potentially confounding effects of acute meal consumption on cognitive performance [22]. All participants provided verbal and written consent in accordance with the University of Illinois' Institutional Review Board and the Declaration of Helsinki.

Table 1. Demographic characteristics, weight status, and EAT-26 variables [1].

Variable	Group	Female	Male
N	132	82	50
Age, years	33.88 ± 6.00	34.28 ± 5.98	33.22 ± 6.06
IQ	108.48 ± 12.22	107.18 ± 11.67	110.60 ± 12.91
BMI, kg/m [2]	32.03 ± 5.81 *	33.18 ± 5.39	30.14 ± 6.05
HEI-2015 [3]	54.33 ± 13.71	53.49 ± 13.56	55.72 ± 13.96
EAT-26 Summative Score	6.73 ± 5.82 *	7.72 ± 7.26	5.12 ± 4.55
Dieting Subscale	4.69 ± 4.38	5.22 ± 4.94	3.82 ± 3.10
Bulimia and Food Preoccupation Subscale	1.45 ± 2.75	1.56 ± 3.20	1.56 ± 3.20
Oral Control Subscale	1.26 ± 1.65	1.37 ± 1.76	1.08 ± 1.44

[1] Values are means ± standard deviation unless otherwise stated; [2] Determined by the Center for Disease Control Body Mass Index (BMI) classifications; [3] Calculated using National Cancer Institute Healthy Index (HEI) 2015 Assessment; * Independent *t*-tests revealed significant differences between sex ($p < 0.05$).

2.2. Intelligence Quotient

KBIT-2 is a test of general intellectual abilities that has been nationally normed for ages 4–90 years [23]. The test is comprised of three subtests: Verbal Knowledge, Riddles, and Matrices. A composite score of the three subtests is then used as a measure of general intellectual abilities.

2.3. *Habitual Diet Quality*

The Healthy Eating Index-2015 (HEI-2015) was calculated using the Dietary History Questionnaire II with portion sizes to assess diet quality. Data were analyzed using National Cancer Institute's Diet*Calc (Diet*Calc Analysis Program, Version 1.5.0., National Cancer Institute, Epidemiology and Genomics Research Program, Bethesda, MD, USA) software and HEI-2015 scores were generated using HEI-2015 macros in Statistical Analysis System (SAS version 9.4; SAS Institute, Inc., Cary, NC, USA.). HEI scores range from 0–100, based on compliance to 2015–2020 Dietary Guidelines for Americans recommendations. The Healthy Eating Index contains 13 components, including nine adequacy (minimum standard) and four moderation (maximum allowed) components. The component scores were summed to calculate the total HEI score, which was used for analysis. HEI-2015 was calculated to account for the possibility that disordered eating attitudes may influence overall diet quality, which in turn may affect cognitive control processes [24,25].

2.4. *Anthropometric Measures*

Height and weight measurements were completed to calculate BMI (weight (kg)/height (m^2)). Height and weight were assessed using a stadiometer (model 240; SECA, Hamburg, Germany) and a digital scale (WB-300 Plus; Tanita, Tokyo, Japan). Participant height and weight were assessed while wearing light clothing and no shoes.

2.5. *Eating Attitudes Test-26*

Disordered eating attitudes were assessed using the self-report 26 question EAT-26 [26]. The EAT-26 has been validated for use in both populations with and without diagnosed eating disorders [27]. The composite EAT-26 score is a continuous variable summative of three subscales: A Dieting subscale, a Bulimia and Food Preoccupation subscale, and an Oral Control subscale. The three subscales tap into different aspects of disordered eating attitudes. The Dieting subscale assesses behaviors related to over concern with weight and calorie content of foods, the Bulimia and Food Preoccupation subscale assesses preoccupations with food and bulimic tendencies, and the Oral Control subscale assesses aspects of self-control [27]. A score on the summative score, as well as the subscales scores, indicates a larger degree of disordered eating attitudes.

2.6. *Switch Task*

Cognitive Flexibility was assessed using a Switch task [14,16]. The Switch task is comprised of three blocks, two homogenous and one heterogeneous. To emulate a real-world scenario where individuals may be forced to switch between rule-sets, the purpose of the homogeneous block is to learn an association, or rule, on certain stimuli (Figure 1). The first homogeneous block is entitled "Less than/greater than" and participants viewed a series of numbers between 1 and 10 inside of a solid box. Participants responded with a right button press if the number was less than 5, and a left button press if the number was greater than 5, thus associating a solid box with the less than/greater than rule-set. The second homogenous block is entitled "Odd/even" and participants viewed a series of numbers between 1 and 10 inside of a dashed box. Participants responded with a right button press if the number was even, and a left button press if the number was odd, thus associating a dashed box with the odd/even rule-set. A test block of 90 trials with jittered inter-stimulus interval (ISI) of either 1600, 1800, or 2000 ms was administered for both homogeneous blocks. In the heterogeneous condition, participants are shown numbers in both solid and dashed boxes. After a practice block of 50 trials, 200 trials of randomized less than/greater than and odd/even stimuli (i.e., randomized homogeneous blocks) were presented and participants were required to switch back and forth between the previously learned mental rule-sets. A Switch trial in the heterogeneous block is defined as a trial in which the previous stimuli belonged to a different mental set than the one presented, or a number was presented inside of a dashed box and followed by a number in a solid box. A NonSwitch trial is defined as a trial in which the previous stimuli belonged to the same mental set as the stimuli presented, or a number was presented inside of a dashed box and followed by another number inside a dashed box. Measures of accuracy and RT for homogeneous and heterogeneous blocks, and for both Switch and NonSwitch trials of the heterogeneous block, were assessed. Global Switch Cost for accuracy was calculated as overall accuracy of the homogenous trials—overall accuracy of the heterogeneous trials, and for RT as overall RT of the heterogeneous trials—overall RT of the homogenous trials.

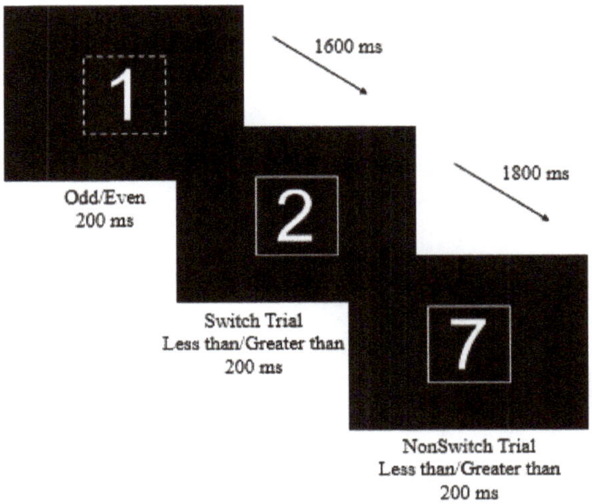

Figure 1. Task stimuli and parameters for the Switch task. Participants completed three task blocks, two homogeneous (within rule-set and dashed/solid boxes) and one heterogeneous (between rule-set and dashed/solid boxes).

2.7. ERP Assessment

Electroencephalographic (EEG) activity was recorded via a Neuro-scan Quik-cap (Compumedics, Neuroscan, Charlotte, NC, USA) with 64 scalp electrodes arranged in the international 10-10 system. Electrooculographic (EOG) activity was recorded with a set of four electrodes placed at the outer canthus of each eye and above and below the left orbit. A midline sensor placed between Cz and CPz served as a reference and AFz served as the ground. Using a Neuroscan SynampsRT amplifier (Compumedics, Neuroscan, Charlotte, NC, USA), the continuous EEG signal was digitized at a sampling rate of 500 Hz, amplified 500 times to an online low-pass 70-Hz filter with a direct current and a 60-Hz notch filter. Impedance values for all electrodes were maintained $\leq$10 kohms.

Offline, continuous data were re-referenced to averaged mastoids and merged with behavioral data. An independent components analysis (ICA) was used to systematically reject eye-blink artifacts from the data. Data were submitted to a 0.1-Hz high-pass filter before being submitted to the ICA. ICA and vertical EOG channel correlations greater than 0.35 were considered eye-blinks and were thus rejected. The ICA-corrected EEG data were segmented for each trial beginning −200 ms prior to stimulus onset and continuing 1200 ms post onset. The −200 ms to stimulus onset was used for baseline correction. Data were filtered using a 30-Hz zero phase shift low-pass filter.

Based on evidence observed from post-hoc topographic images, a 6-sensor region of interest (ROI) comprised of C1, CZ, C2, CPZ, CP1, and CP2 electrodes was used for P3 assessment. Topographic grand average plots were constructed using a stylized topographic map plugin for EEGLAB/ERPLAB [28]. Only correct trials from individuals who reported >50 usable trials in both homogenous and heterogeneous trial types were used for analyses. The P3 component was defined as the localized peak and corresponding latency occurring between 300–600 ms post-stimulus onset. Amplitude was measured as a change score from the pre-stimulus baseline and peak latency was defined as the time point of the maximum amplitude.

2.8. Statistical Analysis

Statistical analyses were performed with SPSS Statistics version 24 (IBM, Armonk, New York). Internal consistency for the EAT-26 instrument was assessed using Cronbach's Alpha. Pearson product-moment correlations were conducted to examine bivariate relationships between demographic factors (age, IQ, and sex (females coded as 0 and males coded as 1)), HEI-2015, BMI, EAT-26, and cognitive control variables. Due to non-normality as assessed via Shapiro-Wilk $p < 0.05$, log transformations of all EAT-26 variables were used for all analyses. Hierarchical linear regression analyses were used to determine the contribution of the summative EAT-26 score and each subscale to the cognitive control outcomes. Factors correlated with any one of the cognitive control outcomes were included in step 1 of the regression model. Overall model fit was assessed using ANOVA significance ($p < 0.05$) and tests for multicollinearity were conducted for each subscale. Based on published research demonstrating large effect sizes among clinical samples [9,29], we conducted an a priori power calculation. Specifically, we applied a moderate effect size ($r = 0.30$), two-sided α of 0.05, and 80% power resulting in a minimum sample size target of 81 participants to conduct the multiple regression analyses. For ERP waveform illustrative purposes in Figure 2, participants with "low" (<11) and "high" (>11) EAT-26 responses. An independent t-test was conducted among these groups with a significance threshold of $p < 0.05$, and they were plotted for comparison purposes in Figure 2.

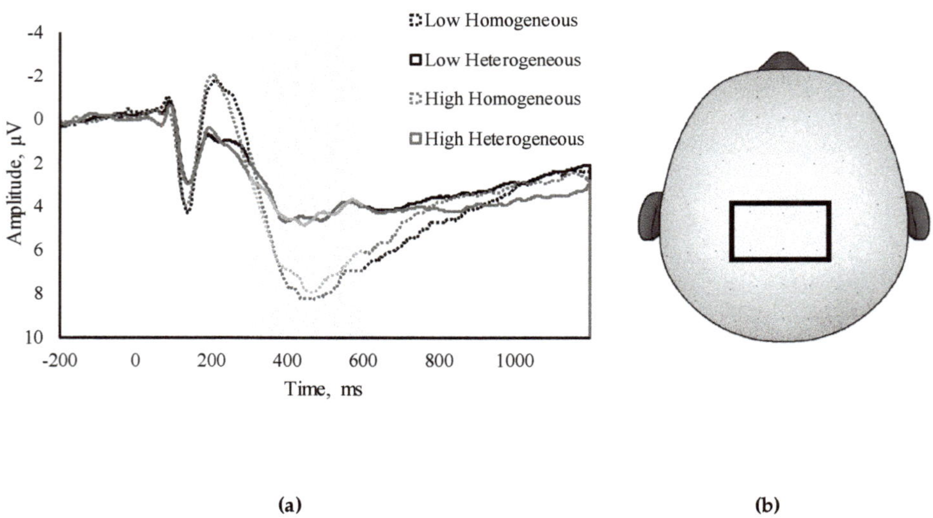

Figure 2. (**a**) Waveform depictions of "low" (n = 105) and "high" (n = 29) EAT-26 scores of the homogenous and heterogeneous Switch task trials, and (**b**) a topographic representation of the 6 electrode sites (C1, CZ, C2, CPZ, CP1, and CP2) used in the P3 region of interest (ROI).

3. Results

3.1. EAT-26

Mean scores from all participants for summative scores and subscales are reported in Table 1. Only 13% of study participants reported a summative EAT-26 score of 0, therefore, 87% of our sample reported some degree of disordered eating attitudes. Three percent of individuals reported scores of 20 or above (the score at which clinician referral is recommended) and 20% of individuals scored above an 11 (the score at which a doctor referral has been proposed for individuals belonging to non-clinical populations) [23,24]. While the EAT-26 score cannot be used to diagnose an eating disorder without also being coupled with an evaluation by a physician, these results indicate that our sample may be largely comprised of individuals who display subthreshold disordered eating attitudes, or disordered eating attitudes at levels that do not qualify for clinical diagnosis. Cronbach's alpha conducted on the Dieting, Bulimia and Food Preoccupation, and Oral Control subscales yielded scores of 0.79, 0.73, and 0.50, respectively.

3.2. Bivariate Correlations

Negative relationships were observed between age and the Bulimia and Food Preoccupation subscale ($r = -0.26$, $p = 0.003$) and between IQ and the Dieting subscale ($r = -0.18$, $p = 0.04$). EAT-26 variables were unrelated to BMI, sex, and HEI-2015 scores ($p > 0.05$).

Regarding the behavioral Switch task outcomes, sex was related to RT of the NonSwitch ($r = 0.30$, $p = 0.001$) and Switch trials ($r = 0.20$, $p = 0.02$), indicating that males took longer to respond on these trials. IQ was related to accuracy of both the NonSwitch ($r = 0.38$, $p < 0.001$) and Switch trials ($r = 0.30$, $p = 0.001$). No relationships were observed between BMI, age, or HEI-2015 scores and behavioral Switch task outcomes of accuracy nor RT. The correlations between EAT-26 variables and Switch task variables are described in Table 2.

Table 2. Bivariate Correlations between EAT-26 variables and Switch task behavioral variables.

	Summative EAT-26	Dieting Subscale	Bulimia and Food Preoccupation Subscale	Oral Control Subscale
		Homogeneous		
Overall Accuracy	−0.09	−0.08	−0.10	0.06
Overall RT	0.25 **	0.26 **	−0.10	0.16
		Heterogeneous		
NonSwitch Accuracy	−0.17	−0.22 *	0.04	0.03
NonSwitch RT	0.16	0.19 *	−0.12	0.03
Switch Accuracy	−0.19 *	−0.22 **	0.00	−0.02
Switch RT	0.15	0.20 *	−0.04	0.10
		Switch Cost		
Global Accuracy	0.16	0.21 *	−0.07	0.01
Local Accuracy	0.04	0.03	0.05	0.07
Global RT	−0.01	0.03	−0.02	−0.05
Local RT	0.05	0.10	0.07	0.13

RT—Reaction Time; ** Correlation is significant at the 0.01 level (2-tailed). * Correlation is significant at the 0.05 level (2-tailed).

Regarding the ERP Switch task outcomes and EAT-26 variables, the EAT-26 summative score was not correlated with any of the ERP variables (all p's > 0.05). The Dieting subscale was positively associated with the Global Switch Cost calculation for accuracy ($r = 0.17$, $p = 0.05$). An inverse trend was also observed between the Dieting subscale and peak P3 amplitude in the homogeneous trials ($r = -0.17$, $p = 0.06$). The Bulimia and Food Preoccupation subscale was negatively correlated with peak P3 latency in the homogenous trials ($r = -0.23$, $p < 0.01$) and trending in its relationships with the NonSwitch ($r = -0.17$, $p = 0.06$) and Switch ($r = -0.15$, $p = 0.09$) trials. The Oral Control subscale was not correlated with any of the ERP variables. In terms of demographic variables, IQ was associated with peak P3 latency in the homogenous trials ($r = -0.18$, $p = 0.04$) and HEI-2015 scores were positively associated with peak P3 amplitude of the Switch trials ($r = 0.18$, $p = 0.04$). Sex, BMI, and age were not correlated with any of the ERP variables. Complete correlations between ERP outcomes and EAT-26 variables are reported in Table 3.

Table 3. Bivariate Correlations between EAT-26 variables and Switch task ERP variables.

	Summative EAT-26	Dieting Subscale	Bulimia and Food Preoccupation Subscale	Oral Control Subscale
		Homogeneous		
Amplitude	−0.09	−0.17 †	0.05	0.01
Latency	0.01	0.03	−0.23 **	0.11
		Heterogeneous		
NonSwitch Amplitude	0.08	0.03	0.09	0.04
NonSwitch Latency	0.01	−0.01	−0.17 †	−0.02
Switch Amplitude	0.10	0.06	0.06	0.05
Switch Latency	0.40	0.01	−0.15	0.06
		Switch Cost		
Global Amplitude	0.13	0.17 *	0.12	−0.01
Local Amplitude	0.00	0.02	−0.09	−0.07
Global Latency	−0.10	−0.08	0.00	−0.16
Local Latency	0.07	0.10	0.04	0.11

** Correlation is significant at the 0.01 level (2-tailed). * Correlation is significant at the 0.05 level (2-tailed). † Correlation is trending at $p < 0.07$ (2-tailed).

3.3. *Regression Analyses*

Age, sex, BMI, IQ, and HEI-2015 scores were entered into step 1 for each model, as they were shown to be associated with cognitive control outcomes at the bivariate level. Sex was pertinent to the aim of our study, and BMI, age and IQ have been previously associated with cognitive control tasks [3]. For each dependent variable, a standardized step 1 was used, followed by 4 different step 2 regression analyses. The summative EAT-26 and each subscale were therefore entered as separate step 2 variables. Tests for multicollinearity indicated that a low level of multicollinearity was present between the Summative EAT-26 and subscales (variance inflation factor (VIF) Dieting subscale = 1.37, Bulimia and Food Preoccupation subscale = 1.13, Oral Control subscale = 1.31).

Full behavioral regression values are reported in Table 4. For the behavioral Switch task variables, no step 2 variable was associated with accuracy in the homogeneous trials (all $p > 0.05$), indicating that disordered eating attitudes are not associated with accuracy in these trial types. The model for RT in the homogenous trials was significantly improved with the addition of EAT-26 summative score ($\Delta R^2 = 0.06$, $\beta = 0.25$) as well as with the Dieting subscale ($\Delta R^2 = 0.06$, $\beta = 0.26$). The addition of the Dieting subscale was associated with an improved model for overall heterogeneous accuracy ($\Delta R^2 = 0.3$, $\beta = -0.17$) as well as Switch accuracy ($\Delta R^2 = 0.3$, $\beta = -0.17$) and trending for the NonSwitch accuracy ($\Delta R^2 = 0.02$, $\beta = -0.15$). These results indicate that individuals with higher Dietary subscale scores took longer to respond on both homogeneous and heterogeneous trial types and performed worse on measures of heterogeneous accuracy. Similarly, the model for RT of the NonSwitch trials was significantly improved with the addition of EAT-26 summative scores ($\Delta R^2 = 0.04$, $\beta = 0.20$) and with the addition of the Dieting subscale ($\Delta R^2 = 0.04$, $\beta = 0.19$). RT of the Switch trials was significantly improved following the inclusion of the summative EAT-26 ($\Delta R^2 = 0.03$, $\beta = 0.18$) and the Dieting subscale ($\Delta R^2 = 0.04$, $\beta = 0.20$). These results indicate that individuals with higher summative EAT-26 scores took longer to respond on these trial types, and that the Dieting subscale was even further associated with an increased RT, as indicated by the significant ΔR^2. The Dieting subscale was trending with Global Accuracy Cost ($\Delta R^2 = 0.02$, $\beta = 0.16$), though no relationships were observed for Global RT Cost, nor Local Switch Costs.

Table 4. Hierarchical Regression between pertinent variables and Switch task cognitive outcomes.

Step and Variable	Homogeneous RT			NonSwitch RT			Switch RT		
	β	ΔR^2	Model p	β	ΔR^2	Model p	β	ΔR^2	Model p
Step 1									
Sex	0.07			0.30 **			0.20 *		
BMI	−0.03			−0.05			−0.11		
IQ	−0.10	0.02	0.68	−0.12	0.14	$p < 0.01$	−0.10	0.08	0.05
Age	0.09			0.18 *			0.12		
HEI-2015	0.05			0.02			−0.01		
Step 2									
Summative EAT-26	0.25 **	0.06 **	0.08	0.20 *	0.04 *	$p < 0.001$	0.18*	0.03 *	0.02
Dieting Subscale	0.26 **	0.06 **	0.07	0.20 *	0.04 *	$p < 0.001$	0.20 *	0.04 *	0.01
Bulimia and Food Preoccupation Subscale	−0.08	0.01	0.69	−0.10	0.01	$p < 0.001$	−0.01	0.00	0.09
Oral Control Subscale	0.15	0.02	0.41	0.03	0.00	$p < 0.001$	0.09	0.01	0.06

RT—Reaction Time. ** Correlation is significant at the 0.01 level (2-tailed). * Correlation is significant at the 0.05 level (2-tailed).

The model for latency of the homogeneous P3 trials was significantly improved by the addition of the Bulimia and Food Preoccupation subscale ($\Delta R^2 = 0.04$, $\beta = -0.20$). Intriguingly, apart from this, no models were predictive of Switch task ERP variables in either the homogenous or heterogeneous task conditions, nor in terms of Global or Local Switch Costs (all $p > 0.05$). Therefore, while relationships were observed between disordered eating attitudes and behavioral accuracy and RT, relationships were largely not seen regarding the P3, indicating that these behavioral decrements may not be driven by differences in P3 amplitude or latency. Waveform depictions are presented in Figure 2.

4. Discussion

We aimed to elucidate relationships between disordered eating attitudes and cognitive flexibility in a non-clinical sample of adults with overweight and obesity. As hypothesized, behavioral latencies in a cognitive flexibility task were correlated with higher disordered eating attitudes, specifically the EAT-26 Dieting subscale. Furthermore, the contribution of disordered eating attitudes was generalized such that it was evident for both the homogenous and heterogeneous task conditions. Importantly, this relationship occurred even after controlling for potential confounding factors such as sex, age, BMI, diet quality, and intellectual abilities. However, the only statistically significant relationship observed between measures of disordered eating attitudes and ERP P3 variables was with the Bulimia and Food Preoccupation subscale. These results suggest that the neural mechanisms by which disordered eating attitudes influence cognitive flexibility may be evident without decrements captured by the P3 ERP component, and that future work should examine possible alternative neurophysiological mechanisms of this relationship.

Our findings are consistent with previous literature indicating that individuals with eating disorders and with overweight or obesity exhibit differential patterns during cognitive flexibility task performance [30,31]. Both homogenous and heterogeneous trial types of the Switch task were related with disordered eating attitudes, as indicated by longer RTs and lower accuracies among individuals with higher Dieting subscale scores. These results also extend previous work relating eating attitudes to cognitive flexibility by demonstrating that cognitive impairment related to disordered eating risk is not limited to clinical populations but is also present among otherwise healthy individuals with overweight and obesity [30]. Interestingly, the relationship between RT and disordered eating attitudes was observed across both the EAT-26 summative score as well as the Dieting subscale for all trial types, suggesting both a generalized and specific negative influence of disordered eating attitudes on processing speed.

While the EAT-26 is a widely used eating disorder screening tool, there is substantially less work evaluating the independent subscales. Evidence in support of the specificity between the Dieting subscale and cognitive flexibility reinforces the theory of functional differences across disordered eating symptoms. The Dieting subscale is thought to reflect "negative body image and avoidance of fattening foods" [32]. Orbitello et al. reported that, in a sample of non-clinical individuals with overweight and obesity, a high Dieting subscale score was a risk factor for eating disorders not otherwise specified (previously EDNOS, now other specified feeding or eating disorder (OSFED)) [27]. Our results reveal that participants with higher Dieting subscale scores took longer to respond in both homogenous and heterogeneous task conditions. Our results indicate that, not only do a large number of participants identify with the Dieting subscale, but also that they exhibit cognitive rigidity patterns similarly evident in clinical studies of patients with eating disorder diagnoses. These results point to a need for more studies examining cognitive barriers to behavior change among community populations.

Intriguingly, in contrast to our hypothesis, the only relationships between EAT-26 variables and P3 outcomes that maintained significance after controlling for pertinent demographic and body composition variables were between the Bulimia and Food Preoccupation subscale and latency in the homogenous task trials. Yet, no relationships were observed between the Bulimia and Food Preoccupation subscale and behavioral variables. This is interesting, as bivariate relationships were observed between the Dieting subscale and the peak amplitude during homogeneous trials, yet this relationship did not persist in regression modeling. To the authors this implies that there may be some relationship between these variables, albeit not very strong. The homogeneous trials are also thought of as the "easier" task trials, in that you are staying within one rule-set, and thus it is intriguing that results were observed here.

The P3 component is largely thought to reflect contextual updating of task-set configurations, or how well one can activate currently relevant stimulus-response rules and deactivate previously relevant rules (in this case the difference prompted by the solid or dashed boxes) [14]. As outlined below, various explanations may explain these relationships. In the present task, motor responses were held constant across conditions, meaning that our task was better able to capture an attentional switch rather than an intentional switch. The lack of associations indicates that decrements in behavioral performance are perhaps not reliant on stimulus evaluation or contextual updating and may instead draw mechanistic foundations from measures of an *intentional* switch, including task-specific motor response remapping, or inhibition of response alternatives. Support for this explanation can also be drawn from the correlations between RT and P3 latency variables. While RT is an index of both duration of stimulus evaluation process as well as response selection, the P3 latency is only reflective of stimulus evaluation [16]. Our results revealed correlations between RT and P3 latency in the homogenous conditions ($r = -0.31$, $p < 0.01$), but no relationships between RT and P3 latency in the Switch and NonSwitch conditions ($r = 0.12$, $p = 0.18$; $r = 0.07$, $p = 0.43$). While interpretations of this result may vary, one can view these relationships as another indication that an individual's eating attitudes do not have bearing on the stimulus evaluation component of the P3, indicating a need for investigation of disordered eating attitudes using tasks designed to evaluate intentional switches involved in behavior. Another explanation for a lack of a relationship between disordered eating attitudes and P3 outcomes may be that, in this task, while we observed global switch effects we did not observe local switch effects (Figure 1). Further tasks using the ERP technique in conjunction with task-switching paradigms are thus warranted.

While this study draws its strength from the novel use of the ERP technique in conjunction with eating attitude assessment in a large non-clinical sample of individuals with overweight and obesity, our study was not without limitations. Primarily, our study was cross-sectional, and thus any conclusions drawn are correlational, rather than causational. Thus, cognitive flexibility could have been driven by the disordered eating attitudes, or disordered eating attitudes could be maintained due to cognitive rigidity. Further longitudinal work is thus needed to elucidate these relationships. Nevertheless, we were able to shed light on a relatively concordant relationship between eating attitudes and behavioral measures of cognitive flexibility in a non-clinical group of men and women with overweight or obesity.

5. Conclusions

We observed statistically significant relationships between disordered eating attitudes and behavioral RT, yet not neuroelectric indices, on a cognitive flexibility task in a sample of men and women with overweight and obesity. Importantly, these relationships were independent of age, sex, BMI, IQ, and overall dietary quality. More experimental work is necessary to explore the relationship between eating attitudes and cognitive flexibility to determine the cognitive underpinnings of eating behavior regulation and inform future therapeutic approaches to improving adherence to healthful diet habits in the general population with overweight and obesity.

Author Contributions: C.G.E. and N.A.K. wrote the manuscript. C.G.E. and S.V.T. collected the data. A.M.W., S.P.M., and H.D.H. reviewed and commented on subsequent drafts of the manuscript.

Funding: This work was supported by funds provided by the Department of Kinesiology and Community Health at the University of Illinois and the United States Department of Agriculture's National Institute of Food and Agriculture, Hatch project 1009249. Partial support was also provided by the Hass Avocado Board.

Acknowledgments: We would like to thank the undergraduate research team of the Body Composition and Nutritional Neuroscience laboratory.

Conflicts of Interest: The authors declare no conflict of interest.

References

1. Krebs-Smith, S.M.; Guenther, P.M.; Subar, A.F.; Kirkpatrick, S.I.; Dodd, K.W. Americans do not meet Federal Dietary Recommendations. *J. Nutr.* **2010**, *140*, 1832–1838. [CrossRef]
2. Hofmann, J.; Ardelt-Gattinger, E.; Paulmichl, K.; Weghuber, D.; Blechert, J. Dietary restraint and impulsivity modulate neural responses to food in adolescents with obesity and healthy adolescents. *Obesity* **2015**, *23*, 2183–2189. [CrossRef] [PubMed]
3. Diamond, A. Executive Functions. *Annu. Rev. Clin. Psychol.* **2013**, *64*, 135–168. [CrossRef] [PubMed]
4. Dajani, D.R.; Uddin, L.Q. Demystifying cognitive flexibility: Implications for clinical and developmental neuroscience. *Anal Chem.* **2015**, *25*, 368–379. [CrossRef] [PubMed]
5. Ziauddeen, H.; Alonso-Alonso, M.; Hill, J.O.; Kelley, M.; Khan, N.A. Obesity and the neurocognitive basis of food reward and the control of intake. *Adv. Nutr.* **2015**, *6*. [CrossRef] [PubMed]
6. Mobbs, O.; Van der Linden, M.; d'Acremont, M.; Perroud, A. Cognitive deficits and biases for food and body in bulimia: Investigation using an affective shifting task. *Eat. Behav.* **2008**, *9*, 455–461. [CrossRef] [PubMed]
7. Hendrikse, J.J.; Cachia, R.L.; Kothe, E.J.; Mcphie, S.; Skouteris, H.; Hayden, M.J. Attentional biases for food cues in overweight and individuals with obesity: A systematic review of the literature. *Obes. Rev.* **2015**, *16*, 424–432. [CrossRef]
8. Roberts, M.E.; Tchanturia, K.; Stahl, D.; Southgate, L.; Treasure, J. A systematic review and meta-analysis of set-shifting ability in eating disorders. *Psychol. Med.* **2007**, *37*, 1075–1084. [CrossRef] [PubMed]
9. Rosval, L.; Steiger, H.; Bruce, K.; Israël, M.; Richardson, J.; Aubut, M. Impulsivity in women with eating disorders: Problem of response inhibition, planning, or attention? *Int. J. Eat. Disord.* **2006**, *39*, 590–593. [CrossRef] [PubMed]
10. Perpiñá, C.; Segura, M.; Sánchez-Reales, S. Cognitive flexibility and decision-making in eating disorders and obesity. *Eat. Weight Disord. Stud. Anorexia Bulim. Obes.* **2016**, *22*, 435–444. [CrossRef]
11. Hudson, J.I.; Hiripi, E.; Pope, H.G.; Kessler, R.C. The Prevalence and Correlates of Eating Disorders in the National Comorbidity Survey Replication. *Biol. Psychiatry* **2007**, *61*, 348–358. [CrossRef] [PubMed]
12. Wolz, I.; Fagundo, A.B.; Treasure, J.; Fernandez-Aranda, F. The processing of food stimuli in abnormal eating: A systematic review of electrophysiology. *Eur. Eat. Disord. Rev.* **2015**, *23*, 251–261. [CrossRef] [PubMed]
13. Polich, J.; Kok, A. Cognitive and biological determinants of P300: An integrative review. *Biol. Psychol.* **1995**, *41*, 103–146. [CrossRef]
14. Kray, J.; Li, K.Z.H.; Lindenberger, U. Age-related changes in task-switching components: The role of task uncertainty. *Brain Cogn.* **2002**, *49*, 363–381. [CrossRef] [PubMed]
15. Hillman, C.H.; Kramer, A.F.; Belopolsky, A.V.; Smith, D.P. A cross-sectional examination of age and physical activity on performance and event-related brain potentials in a task switching paradigm. *Int. J. Psychophysiol.* **2006**, *59*, 30–39. [CrossRef] [PubMed]
16. Kieffaber, P.D.; Hetrick, W.P. Event-related potential correlates of task switching and switch costs. *Psychophysiology* **2005**, *42*, 56–71. [CrossRef] [PubMed]
17. Sellaro, R.; Colzato, L.S. High body mass index is associated with impaired cognitive control. *Appetite* **2017**, *113*, 301–309. [CrossRef] [PubMed]
18. Yang, Y.; Shields, G.S.; Guo, C.; Liu, Y. Executive function performance in obesity and overweight individuals: A meta-analysis and review. *Neurosci. Biobehav. Rev.* **2018**, *84*, 225–244. [CrossRef] [PubMed]
19. Waaddegaard, M.; Davidsen, M.; Kjøller, M. Obesity and prevalence of risk behaviour for eating disorders among young Danish women. *Scand. J. Public Health* **2009**, *37*, 736–743. [CrossRef] [PubMed]
20. Kaufman, A.S.; Kaufman, N.L. *K-BIT: Kaufman Brief Intelligence Test*; American Guidance Service: Circle Pines, MN, USA, 1990.
21. *Diet History Questionnaire, Version 2.00*; National Cancer Institute: Bethesda, MD, USA, 2010.
22. Hoyland, A.; Lawton, C.L.; Dye, L. Acute effects of macronutrient manipulations on cognitive test performance in healthy young adults: A systematic research review. *Neurosci. Biobehav. Rev.* **2008**, *32*, 72–85. [CrossRef] [PubMed]
23. Naugle, R.I.; Chelune, G.J.; Tucker, G.D. Validity of the kaufman brief intelligence test. *Psychol. Assess.* **1993**, *5*, 182–186. [CrossRef]

24. Walk, A.M.; Edwards, C.G.; Baumgartner, N.W.; Chojnacki, M.R.; Covello, A.R.; Reeser, G.E.; Hammond, B.R.; Renzi-Hammond, L.M.; Khan, N.A. The role of retinal carotenoids and age on neuroelectric indices of attentional control among early to middle-aged adults. *Front. Aging Neurosci.* **2017**, *9*, 1–13. [CrossRef] [PubMed]
25. Khan, N.A.; Raine, L.B.; Drollette, E.S.; Scudder, M.R.; Hillman, C.H. The relation of saturated fats and dietary cholesterol to childhood cognitive flexibility. *Appetite* **2015**, *93*, 51–56. [CrossRef] [PubMed]
26. Garner, D.M.; Olmsted, M.P.; Bohr, Y.; Garfinkel, P.E. The Eating Attitudes Test: Psychometric features and clinical correlates. *Psychol. Med.* **1982**, *12*, 871–878. [CrossRef] [PubMed]
27. Orbitello, B.; Ciano, R.; Corsaro, M.; Rocco, P.L.; Taboga, C.; Tonutti, L.; Armellini, M.; Balestrieri, M. The EAT-26 as screening instrument for clinical nutrition unit attenders. *Int. J. Obes.* **2006**, *30*, 977–981. [CrossRef]
28. Pontifex, M.B. Stylized Topographic Map Plugin for EEGLAB/ERPLAB. Available online: http://education.msu.edu/kin/hbcl/software.html (accessed on 22 September 2018).
29. Tchanturia, K.; Davies, H.; Roberts, M.; Harrison, A.; Nakazato, M.; Schmidt, U.; Treasure, J.; Morris, R. Poor Cognitive Flexibility in Eating Disorders: Examining the Evidence using the Wisconsin Card Sorting Task. *PLoS ONE* **2012**, *7*, 1–5. [CrossRef]
30. Zastrow, A.; Kaiser, S.; Stippich, C.; Walther, S.; Herzog, W.; Tchanturia, K.; Belger, A.; Weisbrod, M.; Treasure, J.; Friederich, H.-C. Neural correlates of impaired cognitive-behavioral flexibility in anorexia nervosa. *Am. J. Psychiatry* **2009**, *166*, 608–616. [CrossRef] [PubMed]
31. Wu, M.; Brockmeyer, T.; Hartmann, M.; Skunde, M.; Herzog, W.; Friederich, H.-C. Set-shifting ability across the spectrum of eating disorders and in overweight and obesity: A systematic review and meta-analysis. *Psychol. Med.* **2014**, *44*, 3365–3385. [CrossRef]
32. Masuda, A.; Latzman, R.D. Psychological flexibility and self-concealment as predictors of disordered eating symptoms. *J. Context. Behav. Sci.* **2012**, *1*, 49–54. [CrossRef]

nutrients

Review

Food Parenting Practices among Parents with Overweight and Obesity: A Systematic Review

Chloe Patel [1,*], Eleni Karasouli [2], Emma Shuttlewood [3] and Caroline Meyer [1,2,3]

1 Applied Psychology, International Digital Laboratory, Warwick Manufacturing Group, University of Warwick, Coventry CV4 7AL, UK; c.meyer@warwick.ac.uk
2 Warwick Clinical Trials Unit, Warwick Medical School, University of Warwick, Coventry CV4 7AL, UK; e.karasouli@warwick.ac.uk
3 Weight Management Services, Specialist Surgery, University Hospitals Coventry and Warwickshire NHS Trust, Coventry CV2 2DX, UK; Emma.Shuttlewood@uhcw.nhs.uk
* Correspondence: c.patel.2@warwick.ac.uk; Tel.: +44-2476-523-535

Received: 15 November 2018; Accepted: 10 December 2018; Published: 12 December 2018

Abstract: Given the links between parental obesity and eating psychopathology in their children, it is important to understand the mechanisms via which unhealthy relationships with eating are passed from generation to generation. The aim was to review research focusing on food-related parenting practices (FPPs) used by parents with overweight/obesity. Web of Science, PubMed and PsycINFO were searched. Studies that included a measure of FPPs were considered eligible and were required to have examined FPPs by parental weight status. Twenty studies were included. Single studies suggest differences between parents with healthy-weight vs. overweight/obesity with respect to; food accessibility, food availability and modelling. Multiple studies suggest that several parenting strategies do not differ according to parental weight status (child involvement, praise, use of food to control negative emotions, use of food-based threats and bribes, pressure, restriction, meal and snack routines, monitoring, and rules and limits). There was inconclusive evidence with respect to differences in parental control, encouragement and use of unstructured FPPs among parents with healthy-weight vs. overweight/obesity. The findings of this review imply some differences between parents with overweight/obesity and healthy-weight and the use of some food-related parenting practices, however, they should be interpreted with caution since research remains limited and is generally methodologically weak. The review highlights opportunities for further research, and suggests improvements to current measures of FPPs.

Keywords: children; eating disorders; eating behavior; feeding practices; obesity

1. Introduction

A child is ten to twelve times more likely to have obesity when they have two parents with obesity when compared to having two parents with healthy weight [1,2]. In addition, children are developing obesity earlier [3], increasing the risk of developing adiposity-related conditions later in life including type II diabetes mellitus, cardiovascular diseases, sleep apnoea, problems with physical function, and some cancers [4–7]. Not only is parental obesity linked to obesity in their children, it has also been implicated in the aetiology of eating disorders (EDs), such as bulimia nervosa [8], binge-eating disorder (BED) [9], and anorexia nervosa [10]. For example, patients with anorexia nervosa have cited that living with a family member with obesity was one of the causes of the development of their ED [11].

Both obesity and eating disorders present in a significant proportion of young people. For instance, in 2016, 41 million infants and young children were overweight or obese globally [12]. In the UK, approximately one third of 2–15 year old children have overweight or obesity [13,14]. ED prevalence is also high, approximately five percent of children aged thirteen to eighteen will suffer from anorexia nervosa, bulimia, or binge eating disorder, with lifetime prevalence rates of 0.9%, 1.5%, and 3.5% among women, and 0.3%, 0.5%, and 2.0% among men [9]. BED is the most prevalent eating disorder associated with obesity among adults and adolescents [9,15] where the transmission of disordered eating has been illustrated in research. Parents with obesity, reporting binge-eating disorder (BED) behaviours, are significantly more likely to also report overeating, and binge-eating behaviours in their children than parents without BED behaviours [16]. Furthermore, children of mothers with overweight and obesity exhibit higher levels of emotional eating than children of healthy-weight mothers [17].

Research suggests that a child's diet and preferences for food are usually influenced by food environments, including the eating behaviours of their parents [18,19]. This influence is strongest in early childhood, where parents act as gatekeepers and role models around food [20,21]. One important approach to tackling obesity in childhood and prevent the development of disordered eating behaviours is to understand and positively influence the modifiable determinants of healthy eating behaviours early in life [18,22]. Food parenting practices (FPPs) have been found to be one of the environmental factors associated with the development of overweight and obesity in childhood [22], and encompass the behaviours used by parents to influence their child's behaviours, attitudes, or beliefs around food and eating [23]. FPPs are defined as active techniques or behaviours used by parents to influence a child's food intake [24–26]. Although the relationship between FPPs, child weight and dietary intake is complex and bidirectional [27], one known predictor of children's Body Mass Index (BMI)/weight is parental BMI [28–30]. This association can be attributed to genetic predisposition and environmental factors [31,32], including FPPs. Indeed, parents have a vital role in modelling food choices and shaping their children's food preferences [33,34].

Due to recognised inconsistencies in the terminology and definitions on parents' food-related behaviours, a working group of experts critically appraised the FPP literature and devised a content map to guide future research and to assist with study comparisons [23]. The appraisal resulted in three higher-order FPP constructs: coercive control, structure, and autonomy support/promotion [23]. Coercive control involves FFPs such as restriction, pressure to eat, threats and bribes, and use of food to control negative emotions [23]. Structure involves FPPs such as rules and limits around food, limiting/guiding food choices, monitoring, meal and snack routines, modelling, food availability, food accessibility, food preparation, and unstructured practices [23]. Autonomy support or promotion involves FPPs, such as nutrition education, child involvement, encouragement, praise, reasoning, and negotiation [23]. For the purpose of this review the FPP map was adopted to guide the description of results.

FPPs that support autonomy are non-directive, for example, encouraging balance and variety around food and providing nutritional education [35]. Such FPPs are believed to stimulate healthy food intake, and prevent consumption of unhealthy foods [25]. Conversely, coercive FPPs are directive, for example, pressuring a child to eat, restricting unhealthy or snack foods and use of food-based threats and bribes [36].

The latter type of FPPs, although well intended to prevent overeating [26], have been found to be associated with increased childhood weight and obesogenic eating behaviours, such as emotional eating and overeating [37]. For example, the use of food-based threats has been shown to affect BMI in adulthood [38]. This is because the reward status placed on the restricted food(s) increases the food's affective value [39] and desirability [40], thus making them more likely to be eaten in excessive amounts [41]. Retrospective research conducted among adults indicates a heightened preference for foods that were restricted in childhood and higher levels of emotional overeating in adulthood [38,42], increasing the risk of binge-eating and bulimia [43,44].

Additionally, the use of food to control negative emotions is another coercive FPP that has been found to be associated with increased child BMI [45] and eating in the absence of hunger [46]. Adults recalling their own parents' use of food to control their behaviours as a child via reward or punishment have also reported higher levels of binge-eating and dietary restraint [38]. Further, pressure to eat beyond satiety is detrimental to a child's ability to acknowledge and react appropriately to hunger and fullness cues which in turn influences food intake [47]. Loth and colleagues identified that pressure to eat and food restriction were both significantly and positively associated with disordered eating among adolescent boys [48].

Extensive research has also shown that parents who are concerned with their own weight and eating behaviours are likely to exert coercive FPPs when feeding their children [49,50]. However, later in life, the use of such FPPs are associated with children's less healthy eating behaviours, and disordered eating [48,51,52]. Studies such as these suggest that parents may, unknowingly, be promoting disordered eating and subsequent excessive weight gain in their child/ren via the use of unhelpful FPPs and eating behaviours [53]. Furthermore, since the risk of obesity is greater for children with one or more parents with obesity, identifying the particular FPPs used by parents with overweight/obesity could be helpful in informing the development of family based interventions.

In order to understand the determinants of FPPs, Birch and Davison's model of multiple interactions proposes that there are numerous familial influences on the use of FPPs [54]. The influences described in the model are: parental weight status, parental eating behaviours, child weight status, and child eating behaviours [54]. Although the model does not acknowledge all the environmental factors associated with the development of childhood obesity [54], the model is appropriate for exploring the influences at the parental level, such as parental weight, on the use of FPPs.

In summary, the FPPs currently being used by parents with overweight and obesity are yet to be identified despite parental BMI being associated with eating disorders and the strongest predictor of child weight/BMI. Therefore, the aim of this review is to systematically identify and review the types of parental FPPs used by parents with overweight and obesity (defined by a BMI $\geq$ 25.0 [55]). To aid cross-study comparisons, minimise conflicting findings and move towards consensus in measurement, the results are presented under Vaughn and Colleagues' three higher-order food parenting constructs of the content map [23].

2. Methods

2.1. Search Strategy

Potential studies were identified from three relevant electronic databases: Web of Science, PubMed, and PsycINFO. Published, peer-reviewed articles that examined FPPs were included. The reference lists of all relevant articles were hand-searched to further identify any additional studies that may have not been captured by the searches [56]. There was no limit placed on the publication date. Database searches were initially conducted in January 2017 and updated on 7 September 2018. Search strategies for each database can be found in Supplementary File 1.

2.2. Selection Criteria

The inclusion of studies was based on the PRISMA checklist's PICOS (Participants; Interventions; Comparators; Outcome and Study design) taxonomy [57]. Participants: Studies were eligible if they were conducted with participants who identified themselves as parents, primary caregivers, or legal guardians. Participants had to have been grouped by BMI status or equivalent (e.g., healthy-weight, overweight, or obese). Studies focussing on infant feeding and studies including participants with medical conditions or disabilities that may influence FPPs and/or weight (e.g., Prada-Willi syndrome, Anorexia Nervosa, Binge Eating Disorder, Type I Diabetes Mellitus) were excluded. Interventions: Studies needed to have used a measure of FPPs, e.g., the Child Feeding Questionnaire. Comparators: Studies were eligible where there was a comparison group of parents with healthy-weight. Outcome: Studies needed to have considered a relationship between parental BMI and FPPs. Study design: Studies conducted quantitatively (cross-sectional, laboratory-based observation, longitudinal) were included. Peer reviewed studies that were written in English were considered eligible. Individual case studies, prospective and protocol articles were excluded. Studies involving FPP intervention or manipulation were also excluded as these studies do not capture naturalistic FPPs. Furthermore, participating in an intervention study can raise awareness of participants' unhealthy behaviours [58].

2.3. Article Screening

The most recent studies identified from the search were published in 2018 and the oldest study was published in 1969. The titles and abstracts were screened for potential inclusion by one author (CP). A second reviewer (DM) also independently assessed each potential article for inclusion to determine whether it could be excluded on the basis of the inclusion/exclusion criteria. Disagreements were discussed and resolved by consensus [59]. A third reviewer (CM) was consulted where there was uncertainty. Full texts of potentially eligible studies were then screened by one reviewer (CP) and verified by the second (DM).

2.4. Data Extraction and Synthesis

Data from each article were extracted and tabulated to present the study information. A data extraction form was developed according to the Centre for Reviews and Dissemination guidance [59]. The review and narrative synthesis was guided by the PRISMA statement for systematic reviews (http://prisma-statement.org/prismastatement/Checklist.aspx) (Supplementary File 2) [57], and was registered on the PROSPERO database (CRD42018108891). A meta-analysis was not appropriate due to the heterogeneity between studies.

2.5. Quality Assessment

Articles were scored on their methodological quality, internal and external validity using the NICE quality appraisal for quantitative studies checklist [60]. It has been used in previous systematic reviews [61,62] and was adapted for the purposes of this review. The scoring for each criterion in the checklist ranged from ++ (when all or the majority of criteria were fulfilled), + (the criteria have been partially fulfilled), to - (few or none of the criteria have been fulfilled). Due to the limited number of studies revealed by the review, no publications were excluded from the review based on quality scoring. Study quality was also independently assessed by the second reviewer (DM) to examine possible risks of study bias, as suggested by Moher and colleagues [57]. Publication bias was not assessed due to heterogeneity among studies. Inter-rater reliability was in the acceptable range, intraclass correlation coefficient (ICC) = 0.87, and was assessed using a two-way mixed, consistency, average-measures ICC to examine the degree of agreement in study ratings between the two reviewers (CP and DM).

3. Results

3.1. Summary of Included Studies

The initial search yielded 5599 abstracts (Figure 1). A proportion of articles (n = 197) were removed due to duplication, and 5402 abstracts were screened. The majority of abstracts (n = 5356) were excluded upon review as they did not meet the inclusion criteria. Forty-seven full-text articles were retrieved and read, however, a further twenty-seven were excluded from this review for the following reasons: not reporting FPPs by parental weight status (n = 10), no demographic data on the number/percentage of parents per BMI category (n = 11), the article presented the results of an intervention (n = 4), the sample included parents with healthy-weight only (n = 1), and measured perception of hunger (n = 1). One additional study was identified from a systematic review article [63] that was not identified in the search. Twenty studies were included in this review [64–84].

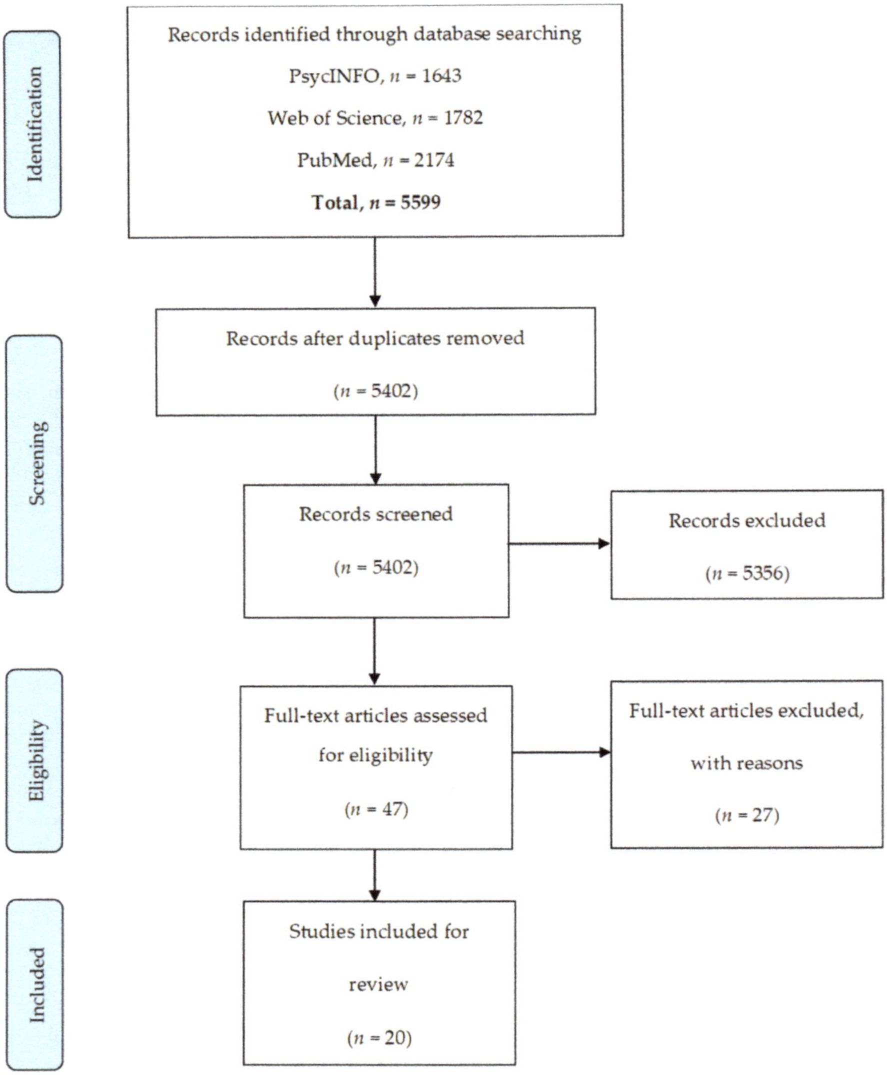

Figure 1. PRISMA Flowchart.

Apart from one study, 19 of the 20 included studies used widely-accepted BMI cut-offs for overweight and obesity (≥25). Lipowska and colleagues [75] used body-fat status measured by a body composition analyser and grouped parents into either overfat, healthy or underfat categories according to societal norms proposed by Gallagher and colleagues [84].

The oldest studies included in the review were published in 2001 [64,69] and the most recent studies were published in 2018 [75,79] (Table 1: Study results). Of the 20 relevant studies, 16 were cross-sectional [64,66–69,71–73,77,78,81,85], three were observational [74,76,82], and one longitudinal [70]. Research was conducted in the USA (n = 9), the UK (n = 2), Germany (n = 2), Turkey (n = 1), Australia (n = 1), Australia and New Zealand (n = 1), Brazil (n = 1), The Netherlands

(n = 1), Poland (n = 1), and China (n = 1). Mothers comprised the participants in the majority of the studies (n = 13).

Table 1. Quality rating by study.

Study	Quality Rating
Baughcum et al., 2001 [64]	+
Cebeci and Guven, 2015 [66]	+
Corsini et al., 2010 [67]	-
Costa et al., 2011 [68]	-
Francis et al., 2001 [69]	+
Francis and Birch, 2005 [70]	+
Haycraft, Karasouli, and Meyer, 2017 [71]	+
Jingxiong et al., 2008 [72]	+
Kröller and Warschburger, 2008 [73]	+
Lewis and Worobey, 2011 [74]	-
Lipowska et al., 2018 [75]	+
Lumeng and Burke, 2006 [76]	-
Powers et al., 2006 [77]	+
Raaijmakers et al., 2014 [78]	+
Roberts, Goodman, and Musher-Eizenmann, 2018 [79]	++
Russell et al., 2018 [80]	+
Wardle et al., 2002 [81]	+
Wendt et al., 2015 [82]	+
Williams et al., 2017 [83]	+
Berge et al., 2015 [85]	++

(-) indicates poor, (+) indicates reasonable in quality, (++) indicates good.

All 20 studies used nonclinical samples. The sample sizes varied where the largest sample was over 3000 parents [85], the smallest sample size was 20 mothers [74] (Table 1). FPPs were measured using questionnaires (n = 17), observations (n = 2), and a conjunction of both (n = 1). The questionnaires used in studies varied, however, the Child Feeding Questionnaire (CFQ) and CFQ subscales appeared to be used most frequently [66–70,73,74,77,85]. Other measures used to collect FPP data included the Pre-Schooler Feeding Questionnaire (PFQ) [64], the Chatoor Feeding Scale (CFS) [86], the Parental Feeding Style Questionnaire (PFSQ) [75,81], the Toddler Snack Food Feeding Questionnaire (TSFFQ) [67], the Comprehensive Feeding Practices Questionnaire (CFPQ) [35,79,80], the Caregiver's Feeding Styles Questionnaire (CFSQ) [87], the Feeding Strategies Questionnaire (FSQ) [79], the Parenting Strategies for Eating and Activity Scale (PSEAS) [83], and the Meals in our Household (MioH) [79] measure.

3.2. Study Quality

Using the National Institute for Health and Care Excellence (NICE) rating system, four studies were rated as poor (-), fourteen were rated reasonable in quality (+), and two studies were rated good (++). The majority of research examined (14 studies) was rated as reasonable in quality (Table 1). This means that the criteria for internal and external validity were partially met to a standard whereby any criteria that were not fulfilled, would be unlikely to change the study conclusions [60]. Four studies were rated as poor in quality. This means that the design of the study contained sources of bias, such as little consideration for confounding variables [68,74], small sample sizes [74], and little or unclear information about the study sample [67,68,76].

3.3. FPP Results

A summary of the studies can be found in Table 2.

Table 2. Study results.

Author(s), Study Country	Design	Aim(s)	Sample	BMI	*n*	Age of Children	FPP Measures	Relevant FPP Findings	Relevant Conclusions
Baughcum et al. (2001), USA [64]	Cross-sectional	To develop the Pre-schooler Feeding Questionnaire (PFQ).	634 mothers	18.5–29.9	488	23 months–5 year olds	PFQ	Significantly higher degree of age-inappropriate feeding (p = 0.004) (no longer true after adjusting for family income), concern about child overeating or being overweight (p = 0.001) regardless of child overweight and family income. Significantly lower degree of structure during feeding interactions (p = 0.001) (no longer true after adjusting for family income) among mothers with obesity vs. mothers without obesity. No significant differences on child control of feeding interactions (p = 0.070), using food to calm the child, concern about the child being underweight, difficulty in child feeding, and pushing the child to eat more (p values not reported) among mothers with obesity vs. mothers without obesity.	There is no specific feeding style associated with overweight young children.
				≥30	146				
Cebeci and Guven (2014), Turkey [66]	Cross-sectional	To examine the influence of maternal obesity on FPPs with their children with obesity.	491 mothers	18–24.9	41	6–18.5 year olds	Turkish CFQ	Other than perceived parent weight (p < 0.001), there were no significant differences in any CFQ subscales (concern over perceived responsibility (p = 0.494), perceived child weight (p = 0.093), concern over child's weight (p = 0.152), restriction (p = 0.234), pressure to eat (p = 0.072), and monitoring (p = 0.782)) among mothers with obesity vs. mothers without obesity.	Maternal BMI does not appear to have a significant influence on FPPs.
				25–29.9	134				
				≥30	316				
Corsini et al. (2010), Australia [67]	Cross-sectional	To develop and validate the Toddler Snack Food Feeding Questionnaire (TSFFQ).	Sample 2: 216 mothers	≤18.5	2	4–5 year olds	TFSSQ and CFQ subscales: Restriction, Pressure to Eat and Monitoring	*Sample 2 (pre-schoolers, past practices)* Mothers without obesity allowed access to snack foods significantly less (p = 0.001), and implemented rules around snacking more (approaching statistical significance, p = 0.022) compared to mothers with obesity. No significant differences were found on any other constructs (p values not reported).	The TSFFQ is a useful measure that could be used in addition to other measures of parental feeding control.
				18.5–24.9	120				
				25–29.9	45				
				≥30	37				
				NR	12				
Costa et al. (2011), Brazil [68]	Cross-sectional	To examine parents feeding attitudes, parent BMI, and children's weight status.	105 Parents/Care-givers	<25	68	6–10 year olds	Portuguese CFQ	Significant differences in perceived parent weight (p = 0.001), concern about child weight (p = 0.006), and restriction (p = 0.023) between parents with healthy-weight vs. parents with overweight/obesity. No significant differences in perceived responsibility (p = 0.861), perceived child weight (p = 0.844), pressure to eat (p = 0.233), and monitoring (p = 0.21) between parents with healthy-weight and parents with overweight/obesity.	Perceptions and attitudes of parents may independently be associated with overweight in children aged 6–10.
				>25	37				
Francis et al. (2001), USA [69]	Cross-sectional	To explore the predictors of the use of maternal restriction and pressure FPPs.	196 mothers	<25	92	5 year olds	CFQ subscales: Perceived child overweight, Child overweight, Restriction, and Pressure to Eat	There were no significant differences in the level of CFQ restriction and CFQ pressure to eat between mothers with healthy-weight and mothers with overweight. Among mothers with overweight, the use of restriction was significantly predicted by concern for daughters' weight ($p \leq 0.05$); pressure to eat was significantly predicted by daughters' adiposity ($p \leq 0.05$) and mothers' concern for daughters' weight ($p \leq 0.05$).	Maternal weight status does not influence FPPs.
				≥25	104				

Table 2. *Cont.*

Author(s), Study Country	Design	Aim(s)	Sample	BMI	*n*	Age of Children	FPP Measures	Relevant FPP Findings	Relevant Conclusions
Francis and Birch (2005), USA [70]	Longitudinal	To explore restriction on food intake, the influence of eating in the absence of hunger on BMI, and maternal weight status as a mediator on these relationships.	171 mothers	≤24.9	80	5–9 year olds	CFQ subscale: Restriction	Overall, there was no significant difference in the amount of restriction used by mothers with overweight vs. mothers with healthy weight. Among mothers with overweight, use of restrictive FPPs significantly predicted daughters' eating in the absence of hunger ($p < 0.05$).	There is no specific feeding style associated with mothers with overweight and obesity.
				≥25	91				
Haycraft, Karasouli and Meyer (2017), UK [71]	Cross-sectional	To compare maternal FPPs by maternal weight status.	437 mothers	19–24.9	249	2–6 year olds	CFPQ	Significantly higher reports of child control ($p < 0.001$) and lower reports of encouraging balance and variety ($p = 0.029$), environment ($p = 0.021$) and modelling ($p < 0.001$) among mothers with overweight/obesity vs. mothers with healthy-weight. There were no significant differences between mothers with healthy-weight/overweight and obesity on any other CFPQ subscales (involvement, monitoring, pressure to eat, restriction for health, restrictions for weight control, food as a reward, emotion regulation).	Mothers with overweight and obesity engage in fewer healthy FPPs when compared to a healthy weight sample of mothers.
				≥25	188				
Jingxiong et al. (2008), China [72]	Cross-sectional	To examine the relationship between FPPs and parental characteristics.	430 mothers	≤24	323	1–3 year olds	An interview to obtain information on: parent education level, family income, and FPPs (including a 24-h dietary recall)	In comparison to mothers with healthy-weight, mothers with overweight/obesity worry significantly more about their child overeating ($p = 0.004$) and that their child would develop obesity ($p = 0.003$). Significantly more mothers with overweight/obesity controlled feeding with a regular schedule in comparison to healthy-weight mothers ($p = 0.017$) and used food to soothe the child significantly less than healthy-weight mothers ($p = 0.008$).	Mothers with overweight report controlling child feeding with a regular feeding schedule and soothed children using food less often than mothers with healthy-weight.
				≥24	107				
Kröller and Warschburger (2008), Germany [73]	Cross-sectional	To explore the impact of various FPPs on child's food intake and the influence of socio-economic status and weight on the use of different types of FPPs.	219 mothers	≤24.9	104	3–6 year olds	Items from the CFQ, CFSQ and newly developed questions from interviews with mothers and experts	No significant differences in FPPs between mothers with healthy weight and overweight/obesity. Maternal weight (underweight/healthy weight/overweight/obesity) had no significant effect on the use of FPPs ($p = 0.60$).	Maternal weight does not influence the use of FPPs.
				≥25	111				
Lewis and Worobey (2011), USA [74]	Laboratory observation	To explore maternal control and whether feeding style is different between healthy and overweight mothers.	20 mothers	<25	10	2 year olds	CFQ, food record, observed behaviours and video recordings.	No significant differences in pressure ($p = 0.56$) and restriction ($p = 0.28$), observed feeding style pressure ($p = 0.49$), and observed feeding style restriction ($p = 0.28$) between mothers with healthy weight and mothers with overweight/obesity. Mothers with overweight/obesity demonstrated significantly more concern about their own weight ($p = 0.05$) than mothers with healthy weight. Maternal BMI was not correlated with reported or observed feeding styles.	Lack of association between reported and observed feeding styles.
				≥25	10				
Lipowska et al. (2018), Poland [75]	Cross-sectional	To explore nutritional knowledge, eating habits, and appetite traits among children with and without excess body fat in the context of FPPs and body-fat status.	315 mothers; 276 fathers	Healthy * Mothers Fathers	190 109	5 year olds	PFSQ	Mothers with healthy body fat use encouragement to eat significantly less than mothers with an overfat body status ($p < 0.05$). Fathers with healthy body fat use control over eating significantly more than fathers with an overfat body status ($p < 0.05$). There were no significant findings on food as a reward and emotional feeding and parental body fat status (p values not reported).	Mothers with an overfat body status do not necessarily transmit unhealthy eating behaviours to their children.
				Overfat * Mothers Fathers	125 167				

Table 2. *Cont.*

Author(s), Study Country	Design	Aim(s)	Sample	BMI	*n*	Age of Children	FPP Measures	Relevant FPP Findings	Relevant Conclusions
Lumeng and Burke (2006), USA [76]	Laboratory observation	To explore if there is an association between maternal prompting to eat, child compliance and mother and child weight status.	71 mothers	<30	45	3–6 year olds	Parental prompting and child compliance	There was no significant difference found in prompting child to eat ($p = 0.55$) between mothers with and without obesity.	Greater maternal prompting was predicted by a younger child age, a novel food, more bites of food taken by the mother and low maternal education.
				≥30	26				
Powers et al. (2006), USA [77]	Cross-sectional	To explore the association of maternal feeding practices with maternal BMI and child eating behaviours.	290 mothers	<24.9	77	2–4.9 year olds	CFQ subscales: Restriction and Pressure to eat, PFSQ subscale: Control	There were no significant differences found with between maternal BMI and maternal FPPs: restriction ($p = 0.63$), pressure to eat ($p = 0.33$), and control ($p = 0.62$).	There is no particular feeding style shared among mothers with overweight or obesity.
				25–29.9	86				
				30–39.9	97				
				≥40.0	30				
Raaijmakers et al. (2014), The Netherlands [78]	Cross-sectional	To explore the use of instrumental and emotional feeding practices between main meals.	359 mothers	≤18.49	11	4–12 year olds	Self-constructed instrument developed from interviews with mothers and health promotion experts	Using food as a reward (26.8% of mothers with obesity) was reported more than use of food as a punishment (18.3% of mothers with obesity) and as a comfort (16.9% of mothers with obesity) with their child. No significant association between emotional and instrumental child feeding practices and maternal BMI.	Mothers offered energy dense and nutrient poor food items in emotional and instrumental child feeding practices.
				18.5–24.9	175				
				25–29.9	101				
				≥30	71				
				Over-weight (≥25)	5				
				Obese	10				
Roberts, Goodman and Musher-Eizenmann (2018), USA [79]	Cross-sectional	To investigate socioeconomic status, parental BMI and dieting status on the use of FPPs.	376 mothers; 118 fathers	18.5–24.9	223	2.5–7.5 year olds	CFPQ, FSQ, MioH, and newly developed questions	Post-hoc analysis revealed that in comparison to parents with healthy-weight and overweight, parents with obesity use significantly less structure FPPs. There was no significant difference between parents with healthy-weight and overweight. There was no significant post-hoc differences between parents with healthy-weight, overweight, and obesity and autonomy promotion (irrespective of a significant main effect) and coercive control.	When compared to other parental characteristics such as parental BMI, socioeconomic status has a small influence on the use of FPPs.
				25–29.9	149				
				≥ 30	120				
Russell et al. (2018), Australia and New Zealand [80]	Cross-sectional (secondary data analysis)	To explore FPPs among parents of toddlers and pre-schoolers and to examine the how FPPs differ by parent and child demographic data.	751 mothers	≤25	383	4–6 year olds	CFPQ	Among pre-schoolers (and adjusted for receiving a nutrition intervention before the measurement of FPPs), the odds of mothers with obesity using CFPQ food as a reward and CFPQ child control were higher compared to mothers with healthy-weight (OR = 1.13, 95% CI 0.94, 1.36; OR = 1.22, 95% CI 0.71, 2.09). The odds of mothers with obesity using CFPQ restriction for health and pressure to eat were lower compared to mothers with healthy-weight (OR = 0.86, 95% CI 0.72, 1.02; OR = 0.82, 95% CI 0.73, 0.91).	Nutrition interventions are unlikely to detect change in targeted FPPs since parents already report best practices, such as modelling and a healthy food environment.
				25 ≤ 30	186				
				≥30	152				
				NR	30				
Wardle et al. (2001), UK [81]	Cross-sectional	To identify any differences in feeding styles among mothers with obesity and normal weight.	Families with healthy-weight, over-weight and obesity	≤25	114	4–5 year olds	PFSQ	Mothers with obesity reported significantly less control over their children's eating ($p = 0.01$) than mothers with healthy-weight. There were no significant differences in reports of emotional feeding, instrumental feeding, and prompting/encouragement to eat.	No difference in use of emotional, instrumental, and prompting/encouragement to eat parental feeding styles among mothers with healthy-weight, and obesity.
				Mothers ≥28.5 Fathers ≥25	100				

Table 2. *Cont.*

Author(s), Study Country	Design	Aim(s)	Sample	BMI	*n*	Age of Children	FPP Measures	Relevant FPP Findings	Relevant Conclusions
Wendt et al. (2015), Germany [82]	Laboratory observation	To explore parent-child interactions during feeding or joint eating and investigate the differences between mothers and fathers and parental weight.	148 mothers; 148 fathers	≤18.5 Mothers Fathers	 4 2	7 months–3.9 year olds	Observation rated using the CFS	No significant differences found in CFS subscales: dyadic reciprocity, dyadic conflict, talk/distraction, struggle for control, and non-contingency among mothers with healthy-weight, overweight, and obesity. There were also no significant differences found among fathers with healthy-weight, overweight, and obesity apart from struggle for control. Fathers with overweight demonstrated a significantly higher amount of struggle for control than fathers with healthy-weight and obesity ($p = 0.003$).	Parents with healthy-weight, overweight, and obesity parents show the same ability to show relatedness, interpret child cues, and affective engagement during feeding and joint eating.
				18.5–24.9 Mothers Fathers	 83 77				
				25–29.9 Mothers Fathers	 17 32				
				≥30 Mothers Fathers	 44 37				
Williams et al. (2017), USA [83]	Cross-sectional	To explore parental BMI and family behaviours associated with childhood obesity in a community sample.	143 parents	≤25	70	9–10 year olds	PSEAS	Underweight and healthy-weight parents monitor their child's diet significantly more than parents with overweight and obesity ($p < 0.000$). There were no significant differences among parental BMI and discipline (children are disciplined for unhealthy eating), control, limit setting (boundaries with unhealthy eating), and reinforcement (praise for eating healthy foods).	Lower parental BMI is associated with a healthier home food environment.
				≥25	73				
Berge et al. (2015), USA [85]	Cross-sectional	To explore food restriction and pressure to eat by parent and adolescent weight concordance and discordance.	3252 parents	≤25	1444	Adoles-cents (mean age 14.4 years old)	CFQ subscales: Pressure to eat and Restriction	Parents with healthy-weight reported significantly higher levels of pressure to eat, compared to parents with overweight and obesity ($p < 0.05$). Parents with overweight/obesity reported significantly more food restriction compared to parent with healthy-weight ($p < 0.05$).	Use of FPPs are as a result of parental weight status and their adolescent's weight status.
				≥25	2108				

* Determined using a segmental body composition monitor. Parental body fat percentage was calculated individually due to the differences in age. FPP: Food Parenting Practice, NR: Not Reported, BMI, Body Mass Index, PFQ: Pre-schooler Feeding Questionnaire, CFQ: Child Feeding Questionnaire, CFS: Chatoor Feeding Scale, PFSQ: Parental Feeding Style Questionnaire, TSFFQ: Toddler Snack Food Feeding Questionnaire, CFPQ: Comprehensive Feeding Practices Questionnaire, CFSQ: Caregiver's Feeding Styles Questionnaire, PSEAS: Parenting Strategies for Eating and Activity Scale, FSQ: Feeding Strategies Questionnaire, MioH: Meals in our Household, OR: Odds Ratio, CI: Confidence Interval.

3.3.1. Coercive Control

The term "coercive control" is a distinct type of control that reflects parental attempts to dominate, pressure, or impose parental will on the child [88]. FPPs that are coercive have been described as parent-centred strategies with the aim to meet parental goals and desires [23]. Such FPPs that have been identified by the review are the following:

Parental control

The measures that assessed parental control over their child's eating were heterogeneous. This, in turn, revealed an inconclusive relationship between parental weight and use of parental control. There is some evidence to suggest that mothers with overweight/obesity have less control over their child's intake and, therefore, their child has more control around their own intake of food [81]. Specifically, Wardle and colleagues [81] found that mothers with overweight/obesity reported significantly less control over their child's food intake on the PFSQ when compared to mothers with healthy-weight. Similarly Haycraft and colleagues [71] found significantly higher reports of mothers with overweight/obesity giving their child more control around eating, as assessed by the CFPQ, in comparison to mothers with healthy-weight. In contrast, two cross-sectional studies reported no significant differences between parents with healthy-weight, overweight and obesity and CFQ control [77] and PSEAS control [83].

In one laboratory-based observational study, fathers with overweight demonstrated significantly more struggle for control (efforts by parent or child to control feeding) than fathers with healthy-weight and obesity [82]. The authors suggested that fathers with overweight attempt to try and control feeding due to concern about their child's weight. This finding was not observed among the mothers in the sample.

Using food to control negative emotions

Using food to control negative emotions [23] is a behaviour used by parents in response to their child's emotional state [35,89], and is suggested to influence emotional eating in adulthood [90]. In the reviewed studies, the use of food to control negative emotions was measured using the PFSQ emotional feeding, e.g., "I give my child something to eat to make him feel better when he is upset" [81], the PFQ using food to calm a child, e.g., "Gave something to eat/drink if the child was upset" [64], the CFPQ emotion regulation, e.g., "Do you give this child something to eat/drink if s/he is upset even if you think s/he is not hungry?" [71] and by newly-developed questions, e.g., "Do you use foods to comfort your child?" [78].

There were five studies that reported no significant difference between parents with healthy-weight, overweight and obesity and the use of food to control negative emotions. Raaijmakers and colleagues [78] also reported no significant difference between use of food to control negative emotions and maternal healthy-weight, overweight, and obesity. However, this assessment was dichotomous, and consequently the frequency of the use of this FPP is unknown [78]. Another study reported that mothers with overweight/obesity use food to soothe their child significantly less than mothers with healthy-weight [72].

Threats and bribes

Five of the twenty identified studies explored the use of food-based threats and bribes. The majority of evidence identified appears to show no significant difference between parents with healthy-weight, overweight and obesity and the use of food-based threats and bribes in exchange for a favourable outcome (e.g., good behaviour from the child [37]), despite the varied measurement of this FPP. Wardle and colleagues [81] reported no significant differences between parents with healthy-weight, overweight, and obesity and PFSQ instrumental feeding. Haycraft and colleagues study also reported non-significant findings among maternal healthy-weight, overweight, and obesity using the CFPQ food as a reward subscale where their data was collected from a large sample of mothers with healthy-weight, overweight, and obesity in a community setting [71]. Two further studies also concluded that maternal weight had no significant effect on the use of food based threats and bribes [73,78]. In contrast, however, one study reported that the odds of mothers with obesity using CFPQ food as a reward was higher than compared to mothers with healthy-weight [80].

Discipline

One study examined the use of discipline among parents with their children via the PSEAS, which asks parents whether they discipline their child for unhealthy eating [83]. There were no significant differences between parents with healthy-weight, overweight and obese and the use of discipline for eating unhealthy foods [83].

Pressure to eat

Pressure to eat is a controlling, directive feeding practice that aims to increase a child's food intake [91]. There appears to be no difference between parents with healthy-weight, overweight, and obesity and pressuring a child to eat. No significant difference was found on the PFQ pushing the child to eat more [64], CFQ pressure to eat [66,68,69,73,74,77], PFSQ prompting/encouragement to eat [81] CFPQ pressure [71], and laboratory observational prompting a child to eat [76]. One study however, reported that parents with healthy-weight used significantly higher levels of CFQ pressure to eat when compared to parents with overweight and obesity, suggesting that parents with overweight/obesity use pressure to eat less [85]. Francis and colleagues [69] reported that pressure to eat by mothers with overweight/obesity was significantly predicted by daughters' adiposity, and mothers' concern for daughters' weight. Pressure to eat by mothers with healthy-weight on the other hand was significantly predicted by mothers' perception of daughters as underweight [69].

Restriction

Restriction involves controlling a child's intake of unhealthy foods [91]. Parents might control a child's intake with the intention to limit unhealthy foods or to decrease or maintain a child's weight [35]. Ten identified studies included the assessment of restriction which used the CFQ and the CFPQ [66,68–71,73,74,77,80,85]. The evidence suggests that there is no difference between parents with healthy-weight, overweight, and obesity and the use of restrictive FPPs. Five studies found no significant difference in CFQ restriction [66,69,70,74,77] among mothers with healthy-weight, overweight, and obesity. Additionally, there was no significant difference between mothers with healthy-weight and overweight/obesity on CFPQ subscales: restriction for health and restriction for weight [71]. It has also been reported that the odds of mothers with obesity using CFPQ restriction for health were lower compared to mothers of healthy-weight [80].

Contrary to the aforementioned findings, two studies did report a significant difference in CFQ restriction between mothers, caregivers and parents with healthy-weight and overweight/obesity [68, 85]. Francis and colleagues [69] conducted a five-year longitudinal study that reported among mothers with overweight/obesity, restriction could be significantly predicted by maternal concern for their daughters' weight regardless of their daughters' actual weight status, maternal perception of daughters as overweight, and maternal investment in weight and eating issues.

One study combined multiple subscales from the CFPQ, FSQ, and the MioH [79] measure, and analysed the three overarching food parenting constructs outlined by Vaughn and colleagues [23]: coercive control, structure, and autonomy. Roberts and colleagues reported that there was no significant difference between parents with healthy-weight, overweight and obesity, and use of coercive FPPs [79].

3.3.2. Structure

Meal and snack routines

Meal and snack routines are created by parents and includes the "location, timing, presence of family members, atmosphere or mood, and presence or absence of distractions during meals and snacks" [92] (p. 106). With regards to mealtime structure, the evidence remains inconclusive as this was explored in only one identified study [64]. Specifically, Baughcum and colleagues [64] included a domain in the PFQ that assessed structure during feeding interactions. This domain asks about whether the child watched television during meals, whether the child had a set mealtime and snack routine and whether the mother sat down with the child during mealtimes. A significantly lower degree of structure during mealtimes was reported by mothers with obesity than mothers without obesity [64].

Only one study examined mealtime atmosphere which reported no significant difference in dyadic reciprocity (affective engagement and quality of relatedness between mother and child), dyadic conflict (conflicts between mother and child over eating), talk and distraction during feeding (mother or child attempts to engage or control each other by talking or distracting), and maternal non-contingency (parental inability to interpret and respond to child cues) among mothers and fathers with healthy-weight, overweight and obesity [82]. More research is needed to examine meal and snack routines and parental BMI.

Monitoring

Parental monitoring involves the degree to which the parent keeps track of a child's food consumption [36]. The small amount of evidence identified appears to suggest no difference between parents with healthy-weight, overweight and obesity and monitoring. Four studies found no significant difference in CFQ monitoring and CFPQ monitoring [66,68,71,73] and parent weight. Costa and colleagues [68] suggested that rather than parental weight, parental concern about their child's weight, i.e., where the child is at risk of developing overweight or is already overweight, is related to parental monitoring of their child's eating which questions the direction of this relationship. In contrast, another study using the PSEAS, reported that underweight and healthy-weight parents monitor their child's diet significantly more than parents with overweight and obesity [83], suggesting that parents with overweight and obesity monitor their child's diet less.

Food accessibility

Food accessibility involves how easy or difficult it is for a child to access food independently or with assistance [23]. Access to such foods was assessed using the TFSSQ, and only one study used this measure [67]. Compared to mothers with obesity, mothers with healthy-weight and overweight recall previously allowing access to sweets and snack foods significantly less [67], suggesting that mothers with obesity allow access to sweets and snack foods more frequently than mothers with healthy-weight/overweight. In this particular study, mothers were asked to recall their previous and current FPPs. The recollection of CFPs may have, however, been influenced by mothers' current CFPs or weight status and therefore this non-significant finding should be interpreted with caution.

Rules and limits

Parents may set rules and limits to clarify what, how much, when and where their child/ren should eat [23]. Rules around snack foods was assessed in two studies via the TFSSQ [67] and PSEAS [83]. There was no significant difference between mothers with obesity and without obesity regarding their implemented rules around snack foods (TFSSQ), however, this did approach significance [67]. Also measured in this study was mothers' flexibility around snack foods (TFSSQ), where there was also no significant difference between maternal BMI and this FPP [67]. Limit setting is assessed on the PSEAS, and asks parents about their use of boundaries around the consumption of unhealthy foods [83]. In this study there were no significant difference among parents with healthy-weight and overweight/obesity and limit setting [83].

Food availability

The types of food available and unavailable in the home is described as food availability [23]. Parental encouragement of balance and variety around food and the home food environment was assessed by one study [71]. This study utilized the CFPQ [35] where there were significantly lower reports of encouraging balance and variety among mothers with overweight/obesity in comparison to mothers with healthy-weight. Further, mothers with overweight/obesity reported having a significantly less healthy home food environment [71]. However, the sample in this study lacked heterogeneity as the majority were identified as white (76%).

Modelling

One study with a rather large sample (n = 437) explored maternal BMI and food modelling using the CFPQ [71]. Mothers with overweight/obesity reported significantly less modelling of healthy eating in comparison to mothers with healthy-weight [71].

Unstructured practices

FPPs that are "unstructured" involve the absence of parental control or structure around child eating, examples include meeting the child's demands, allowing the child to make inappropriate food-related decisions, and providing little guidance or direction [23].

Child control of feeding interactions is a domain in the PFQ and the CFPQ and asks mothers whether they let their child choose their food from what is being served, whether mothers make something different if their child did not like what was being served, and whether mothers allowed their child to eat snacks whenever their child wanted [35,64]. Three studies explored child control around eating and reported contradictory findings. Specifically, Baughcum and colleagues reported no significant difference in PFQ child control around eating between mothers with obesity and mothers without obesity [64]. However, Haycraft and colleagues reported that mothers with overweight and obesity gave their child significantly more control around eating when compared to mothers with healthy-weight [71]. Russell and colleagues also reported that the odds of mothers with obesity allowing child control (CFPQ child control) is higher when compared to mothers with healthy-weight [80].

Age inappropriate feeding is a domain assessed by the PFQ and asks mothers to report; for example, if they gave the child a bottle during the day and whether they fed the child themselves if they did not eat enough [64]. Only one study found that mothers with obesity used significantly more age-inappropriate feeding in comparison to mothers without obesity. However, this difference was no longer significant after adjusting for family income [64].

One study combined multiple subscales from the CFPQ, FSQ, and the MioH [79], and analysed the three overarching food parenting constructs outlined by Vaughn and colleagues [23]: coercive control, structure and autonomy. Roberts and colleagues concluded that in comparison to parents with healthy-weight, parents with obesity use significantly less structure FPPs (there was no significant difference between parents with healthy-weight and overweight).

3.3.3. Autonomy Support/Promotion

Child involvement

There was no significant difference between mothers with healthy-weight, overweight, and obesity, and involving their child in planning and preparing meals and encouraging participation in food shopping. This is based on just a single study examining maternal BMI and involvement using the CFPQ [71].

Encouragement

In contrast to pressure to eat, whereby parents demand that their child eats more, encouragement involves parental use of positive, gentle, and supportive behaviours that are non-coercive [23]. Parental encouragement aims for children to build habits around healthy eating [23].

Two studies assessed parental encouragement using the PSFQ [75,81] which presented contradictory results. Lipowska and colleagues [75] reported that, among a Polish sample of parents, mothers with healthy body fat (body fat composition was measured rather than BMI) reported PSFQ encouragement FPPs significantly less than mothers with an overfat body status, suggesting that mothers with overfat use more encouraging FPPs than mothers with a healthy body fat status. Wardle and colleagues [81] on the other hand, reported that there are no significant differences in the PSFQ encouragement among mothers with healthy-weight, overweight, and obesity.

Praise

Vaughn and colleagues define praise as a form of positive reinforcement where parents provide verbal feedback to the child [23]. One study assessed praise in the PSEAS which asks parents whether they use praise when their child eats healthy snacks [83], which found no significant differences between parental BMI and use of praise.

One study combined multiple subscales from the CFPQ, FSQ, and the MioH [79], and analysed the three overarching food parenting constructs outlined by Vaughn and colleagues [23]: coercive control, structure, and autonomy. Roberts and colleagues reported that there was no significant differences between parents with healthy-weight, overweight and obesity, and use of autonomy support FPPs [79].

Nutrition education

Teaching about nutrition involves parents providing information and skills to their children to aid their decision making about the foods they eat, thus supporting the child's autonomy since this information guides volition, and eating behaviours. One study included the assessment of teaching about nutrition using the subscale from the CFPQ [71], however, due to subscale reliability in the study was excluded from the analyses. More research is warranted to explore this FPP further.

4. Discussion

The aim of this review was to systematically identify the types of food-related parenting practices used by parents with overweight/obesity in comparison to parents with healthy weight. This is important since extensive research indicates an increased presence of EDs among individuals who have parents with overweight and/or increased BMIs [9,93–95].

With regards to coercive food parenting practices, there is evidence (based on eleven studies) suggesting that there is no difference among parents with healthy-weight, overweight and obesity in their use of food to control negative emotions, use of food-based threats and bribes, pressure to eat and restriction [64,66,68–71,73,74,76–78,81]. The evidence examining parental control was inconclusive due to contradictory study findings [71,77,81,83]. These results are of interest as previous research suggests that parental weight status is a predictor of the use of coercive FPPs [54]. Parents who struggle with their own eating and weight are more likely to use coercive FPPs with their children [69,96,97] and adolescents [85]. However, the results in the current review, that there appears to be no difference between parental weight and use of coercive FPPs, suggests otherwise. The use of such FPPs could rather, be more driven by other parental cognitions such as concern about their child's weight rather than their own weight. This was evident in one of the identified studies that reported restriction and pressure to eat was significantly predicted by maternal concern for their daughters' weight [69].

With regards to parenting practices involving structure, there also appears to be no difference between parents with healthy-weight, overweight and obesity and: meal and snack routines, monitoring, or rules and limits [64,66–68,71,73,82,83]. However, the available research indicates that there are significant differences between parents with overweight and obesity versus parents with healthy-weight with respect to food accessibility, food availability, and modelling [67,71]. The research suggests that parents with overweight and obesity have a less healthy home food environment and model healthy eating less than parents with healthy-weight. Such findings shed light on the types of food environments children may be exposed to in families with overweight and obesity, which is one of the determinants of child weight [98]. Access and availability of healthy foods alongside parental modelling are all important FPPs in developing children's healthy eating behaviours. For example, parental modelling of fruit and vegetable intake has been found to be positively associated with children's fruit and vegetable intake [99] and lower availability of high-fat foods and sweet snacks [100]. Further, access to healthy foods might reduce the need for parents to exert coercive FPPs such as restriction. It should however, be highlighted that apart from rules and limits which was assessed in two studies, the structure FPPs described above were all examined in single, unreplicated studies. With regards to unstructured FPPs, the evidence was inconclusive due to contradictory study results [64,71,79,80]. FPPs that are unstructured include the absence of parental control [23], while this is an important for the development of child autonomy, having too much freedom with food choices and eating in addition to a less healthy home food environment, could result in less healthier selections of foods. It is important that unstructured FPPs are further researched particularly as eating behaviours in childhood can be tracked into adulthood [101], which emphasises the importance of the development of healthy eating behaviours in early life.

Finally the results examining autonomy support FPPs, indicated that there are no significant differences between parents with healthy-weight, overweight and obesity and child involvement and praise which is also based on single, unreplicated studies [71,83]. Encouragement was examined in two studies, however, due to contradictory results, the evidence is inconclusive [75,81]. Although there was little evidence identified on autonomy support FPPs, they should be the focus of further research, since they provide parents the opportunity to convey information about healthy eating, subsequently allowing the child to internalise healthy norms and make informed decisions through the fostering of their autonomy [102].

The findings from this review should be interpreted with caution, since some FPPs in relation to parental BMI were examined in single studies, particularly where the research involved structure and autonomy support FPPs. In addition, it is unknown whether the research indicating that there is no relationship between parental BMI and FPPs is due to a real effect, the absence of methodological rigour (only two studies received ++ in this review) or the use of inadequate measures to capture FPPs. There may be value in conducting a review of measures using the COSMIN (Consensus-based Standards for the selection of health Measurement Instruments) checklist to aid the selection of the most appropriate measure for the FPP research at hand [103].

The current review identified numerous and inconsistent measures that are available to measure FPPs. Although the CFQ was the most frequently used measure to capture self-reported FPPs, many more feeding practices have been identified [23]. The CFQ does not capture the wider range of FPPs, such as parental modelling and teaching about nutrition [35], and so it is possible that there were additional FPPs used by parents that were not captured. It has been suggested that the inconsistent results between parental BMI and FPPs may be due to other variables, for example, parents own weight concerns, child age, and child weight [79]. On the other hand, it is possible that some of the inconclusive findings described above between parental BMI and FPPs are due to a lack of well-defined concepts being measured [92], subsequently resulting in a number of FPP measures that include similar subscales, but assessing different behaviours [92]. For example, the CFQ's restriction subscale covers items about regulating the child's intake such as limiting the amount of sweets and high fat foods consumed [36] and items such as, "I offer my child her favourite foods in exchange for good behaviour". However, this is an item that others measures (such as the CFPQ Food as a reward subscale [35] and PSFQ Instrumental feeding subscale [81]) regard as food-based threats and bribes to behave [35].

Often only the minimal stages are used to design measures rather than what is required for rigorous measure development [92]. For example, seventy-one FPP measures have been identified in another systematic review, however, just less than half of these involved clear identification and definition of concepts to be measured during the development stage [92]. For the review this was problematic since there were limitations when comparing and evaluating the relationships between parental weight and subsequent use of FPPs among the studies included in the review. One of the strengths of the current review, however, is that the study findings were grouped and guided by Vaughn and Colleagues' FPPs content map [23] that will help researchers plan future studies.

Study Limitations and Future Research

Several limitations have been identified. The samples in some of the studies may have introduced bias to the data identified in the review. For instance, Kröller and Warschburger [73] recruited mothers from clinics where they were receiving psychoeducation about their weight. Thus, their conclusion that maternal weight does not influence the use of FPPs might have been due to the mothers' newly-acquired knowledge about the potential relationship between the use of certain FPPs and their children's weight [73]. Two studies also reported there are no particular FPPs shared among mothers with overweight/obesity [64,77], however, this may have been due to mothers being recruited from the Special Supplemental Nutrition Programme for Women, Infants and Children where they may have been more attuned to eating behaviours before participating.

Participants were predominantly white across the studies, so the generalisability of findings is restricted to other ethnicities. Two of the identified studies are applicable to white mothers and their daughters only [69,70]. Future research should seek to include more diverse ethnic samples, particularly as South Asian and Black Afro-Caribbean parents have reported greater pressure to eat [104], higher levels of restrictive FPPs and lower levels of monitoring [105] in comparison to White British and White German parents.

Furthermore, household income is another sociodemographic characteristic that has been extensively associated with weight status [106–108] and so it is important that future research endeavours to collect this information. A small number of studies identified in the review did not collect this data [71,74,76,81].

In addition to the inclusion of family characteristics, the current evidence could be strengthened by larger sample sizes in future studies. Although Stevens suggests that "power is not an issue" when there is sample of 100 or more [109], none of the included studies presented a power calculation. Therefore, the results of those studies that included less than 100 parents with healthy-weight, overweight and obesity suggesting that there is little or no difference in the use of FPPs between parents with healthy-weight, overweight or obesity may have been due to studies being insufficiently powered [70,74,76,83], resulting in different statistical outcomes.

With regards to study design, the current review identified only one longitudinal study [70]. The majority of studies were cross-sectional, which is an appropriate design for capturing the prevalence of behaviours without the risk of losing participants to follow-up (e.g., in longitudinal studies) [110]. However, neither the causality nor long-term impact of specific FPPs on child weight can be determined in cross-sectional studies. More longitudinal studies are required to further explore the relationship between parental BMI, FPPs, and childhood weight and eating behaviours.

More research is also needed to help determine inconclusive and limited findings. Future research aiming to develop or improve measures of FPPs should do so using the appropriate steps for questionnaire development. Additionally, the bidirectional relationships that exists between parental FPPs and child eating behaviours should also be explored that includes parental BMI. It is also important for research to acknowledge that other adult caregivers may be influential on a child's diet and eating behaviours. Parents are not only influential on their children, but also react, respond, and modify their FPPs to children's behaviours and own parental feeding goals [111].

Although infant feeding was outside of the current review's scope, it would be interesting to explore whether there is any relationship between parental weight and pressure (e.g., encouraging bottle emptying) with infants whom are bottle-fed. One of the concerns with the encouragement of bottle emptying is the interference with the infant's ability to self-regulate their intake, and in combination with the parent's potential to be unresponsiveness to the infant's cues of satiety, can lead to unhealthy FPPs used with their child later in life. For example, frequent encouragement of bottle emptying has been found to increase the likelihood of the use of pressure-related FPPs in later childhood [112].

5. Conclusions

In conclusion, the findings of the review showed that studies with an improved methodological quality is required. A better understanding is required around the potential influence parental BMI has on the use of FPPs which may contribute to the parent-child BMI and eating behaviour relationship, particularly as FPPs are deeply influential on children's eating behaviours and relationships with food later in life. This could be achieved by replication and extending of existing research including more longitudinal research with repeated use of the same or improved measures to capture FPPs [23]. Despite the mixed findings in the review, it is important that healthcare professionals working in weight management address disordered eating if successful weight-loss is the desired outcome. Similarly, it is important that healthcare professionals working with patients with EDs address weight management. Although more research is required, there may also be value in incorporating education around creating healthier home food environments within family-based interventions delivering nutrition education.

Supplementary Materials: The following are available online at http://www.mdpi.com/2072-6643/10/12/1966/s1, S1: Database Search Strategies; S2: PRISMA Checklist.

Author Contributions: C.P., E.K., E.S., and C.M. contributed to the design of the review and interpretation of findings. C.P. performed the literature search, data extraction and quality assessment. All authors read, revised, and approved the final manuscript.

Funding: This research is supported by a WMG, University of Warwick and University Hospitals Coventry and Warwickshire NHS Trust PhD studentship (to C.P.).

Acknowledgments: We would like to thank Duncan McCaig (DM) for his assistance during the quality assessment process.

Conflicts of Interest: The authors declare no conflict of interest.

References

1. Reilly, J.J.; Armstrong, J.; Dorosty, A.R.; Emmett, P.M.; Ness, A.; Rogers, I.; Steer, C.; Sherriff, A. Early life risk factors for obesity in childhood: Cohort study. *BMJ* **2005**, *330*, 1357. [CrossRef] [PubMed]
2. Whitaker, K.L.; Jarvis, M.J.; Beeken, R.J.; Boniface, D.; Wardle, J. Comparing maternal and paternal intergenerational transmission of obesity risk in a large population-based sample. *Am. J. Clin. Nutr.* **2010**, *91*, 1560–1567. [CrossRef] [PubMed]
3. Johnson, W.; Li, L.; Kuh, D.; Hardy, R. How has the age-related process of overweight or obesity development changed over time? co-ordinated analyses of individual participant data from five united kingdom birth cohorts. *PLoS Med.* **2015**, *12*, e1001828. [CrossRef] [PubMed]
4. Guh, D.P.; Zhang, W.; Bansback, N.; Amarsi, Z.; Birmingham, C.L.; Anis, A.H. The incidence of co-morbidities related to obesity and overweight: A systematic review and meta-analysis. *BMC Public Health* **2009**, *9*, 88. [CrossRef] [PubMed]
5. Lang, I.A.; Llewellyn, D.J.; Alexander, K.; Melzer, D. Obesity, physical function, and mortality in older adults. *J. Am. Geriatr. Soc.* **2008**, *56*, 1474–1478. [CrossRef]
6. Hemminki, K.; Li, X.; Sundquist, J.; Sundquist, K. Obesity and familial obesity and risk of cancer. *Eur. J. Cancer Prev.* **2011**, *20*, 438–443. [CrossRef]

7. Resta, O.; Foschino-Barbaro, M.P.; Legari, G.; Talamo, S.; Bonfitto, P.; Palumbo, A.; Minenna, A.; Giorgino, R.; De Pergola, G. Sleep-related breathing disorders, loud snoring and excessive daytime sleepiness in obese subjects. *Int. J. Obes. Relat. Metab. Disord.* **2001**, *25*, 669–675. [CrossRef]
8. Fairburn, C.G.; Welch, S.L.; Doll, H.A.; Davies, B.A.; O'Connor, M.E. Risk factors for bulimia nervosa. A community-based case-control study. *Arch. Gen. Psychiatry* **1997**, *54*, 509–517. [CrossRef]
9. Hudson, J.I.; Hiripi, E.; Pope, H.G., Jr.; Kessler, R.C. The prevalence and correlates of eating disorders in the National Comorbidity Survey Replication. *Biol. Psychiatry* **2007**, *61*, 348–358. [CrossRef]
10. Moskowitz, L.; Weiselberg, E. Anorexia Nervosa/Atypical Anorexia Nervosa. *Curr. Probl. Pediatr. Adolesc. Health Care* **2017**, *47*, 70–84. [CrossRef]
11. Tozzi, F.; Sullivan, P.F.; Fear, J.L.; McKenzie, J.; Bulik, C.M. Causes and recovery in anorexia nervosa: The patient's perspective. *Int. J. Eat. Disord.* **2003**, *33*, 143–154. [CrossRef] [PubMed]
12. WHO. Facts and Figures on Childhood Obesity. Available online: http://www.who.int/end-childhood-obesity/facts/en/ (accessed on 30 August 2018).
13. England, P.H. Childhood Obesity: Applying All Our Health. Available online: https://www.gov.uk/government/publications/childhood-obesity-applying-all-our-health/childhood-obesity-applying-all-our-health (accessed on 24 August 2017).
14. Health and Social Care Information Centre. Health Survey for England-2014. Available online: https://www.gov.uk/government/statistics/health-survey-for-england-2014 (accessed on 14 December 2017).
15. Swanson, S.A.; Crow, S.J.; Le Grange, D.; Swendsen, J.; Merikangas, K.R. Prevalence and correlates of eating disorders in adolescents. Results from the national comorbidity survey replication adolescent supplement. *Arch. Gen. Psychiatry* **2011**, *68*, 714–723. [CrossRef] [PubMed]
16. Lydecker, J.A.; Grilo, C.M. Children of parents with BED have more eating behavior disturbance than children of parents with obesity or healthy weight. *Int. J. Eat. Disord.* **2017**, *50*, 648–656. [CrossRef] [PubMed]
17. Jahnke, D.L.; Warschburger, P.A. Familial transmission of eating behaviors in preschool-aged children. *Obesity (Silver Spring)* **2008**, *16*, 1821–1825. [CrossRef] [PubMed]
18. Savage, J.S.; Fisher, J.O.; Birch, L.L. Parental influence on eating behavior: Conception to adolescence. *J. Law Med. Ethics.* **2007**, *35*, 22–34. [CrossRef] [PubMed]
19. Vereecken, C.A.; Keukelier, E.; Maes, L. Influence of mother's educational level on food parenting practices and food habits of young children. *Appetite* **2004**, *43*, 93–103. [CrossRef] [PubMed]
20. McCaffree, J. Childhood eating patterns: The roles parents play. *J. Am. Diet. Assoc.* **2003**, *103*, 1587. [CrossRef] [PubMed]
21. Wardle, J.; Carnell, S.; Cooke, L. Parental control over feeding and children's fruit and vegetable intake: How are they related? *J. Am. Diet. Assoc.* **2005**, *105*, 227–232. [CrossRef]
22. Skouteris, H.; McCabe, M.; Ricciardelli, L.A.; Milgrom, J.; Baur, L.A.; Aksan, N.; Dell'Aquila, D. Parent–child interactions and obesity prevention: A systematic review of the literature. *Early Child. Dev. Care* **2012**, *182*, 153–174. [CrossRef]
23. Vaughn, A.E.; Ward, D.S.; Fisher, J.O.; Faith, M.S.; Hughes, S.O.; Kremers, S.P.; Musher-Eizenman, D.R.; O'Connor, T.M.; Patrick, H.; Power, T.G. Fundamental constructs in food parenting practices: A content map to guide future research. *Nutr. Rev.* **2016**, *74*, 98–117. [CrossRef]
24. Blissett, J. Relationships between parenting style, feeding style and feeding practices and fruit and vegetable consumption in early childhood. *Appetite* **2011**, *57*, 826–831. [CrossRef] [PubMed]
25. Larsen, J.K.; Hermans, R.C.; Sleddens, E.F.; Engels, R.C.; Fisher, J.O.; Kremers, S.P. How parental dietary behavior and food parenting practices affect children's dietary behavior. Interacting sources of influence? *Appetite* **2015**, *89*, 246–257. [CrossRef] [PubMed]
26. Shloim, N.; Edelson, L.R.; Martin, N.; Hetherington, M.M. Parenting styles, feeding styles, feeding practices, and weight status in 4–12 year-old children: A systematic review of the literature. *Front. Psychol.* **2015**, *6*, 1849. [CrossRef] [PubMed]
27. Jansen, P.W.; Tharner, A.; van der Ende, J.; Wake, M.; Raat, H.; Hofman, A.; Verhulst, F.C.; van Ijzendoorn, M.H.; Jaddoe, V.W.; Tiemeier, H. Feeding practices and child weight: Is the association bidirectional in preschool children? *Am. J. Clin. Nutr.* **2014**, *100*, 1329–1336. [CrossRef] [PubMed]
28. Strauss, R.S.; Knight, J. Influence of the home environment on the development of obesity in children. *Pediatrics* **1999**, *103*, e85. [CrossRef] [PubMed]

29. Danielzik, S.; Langnäse, K.; Mast, M.; Spethmann, C.; Müller, M.J. Impact of parental BMI on the manifestation of overweight 5–7 year old children. *Eur. J. Nutr.* **2002**, *41*, 132–138. [CrossRef] [PubMed]
30. Maffeis, C.; Talamini, G.; Tatò, L. Influence of diet, physical activity and parents' obesity on children's adiposity: A four-year longitudinal study. *Int. J. Obes.* **1998**, *22*, 758. [CrossRef]
31. Birbilis, M.; Moschonis, G.; Mougios, V.; Manios, Y. Obesity in adolescence is associated with perinatal risk factors, parental BMI and sociodemographic characteristics. *Eur. J. Clin. Nutr.* **2013**, *67*, 115–121. [CrossRef]
32. Laitinen, J.; Power, C.; Jarvelin, M.R. Family social class, maternal body mass index, childhood body mass index, and age at menarche as predictors of adult obesity. *Am. J. Clin. Nutr.* **2001**, *74*, 287–294. [CrossRef]
33. Anzman, S.L.; Rollins, B.Y.; Birch, L.L. Parental influence on children's early eating environments and obesity risk: Implications for prevention. *Int. J. Obes.* **2010**, *34*, 1116–1124. [CrossRef]
34. Scaglioni, S.; Arrizza, C.; Vecchi, F.; Tedeschi, S. Determinants of children's eating behavior. *Am. J. Clin. Nutr.* **2011**, *94*, S2006–S2011. [CrossRef] [PubMed]
35. Musher-Eizenman, D.; Holub, S. Comprehensive feeding practices questionnaire: Validation of a new measure of parental feeding practices. *J. Pediatr. Psychol.* **2007**, *32*, 960–972. [CrossRef] [PubMed]
36. Birch, L.L.; Fisher, J.O.; Grimm-Thomas, K.; Markey, C.N.; Sawyer, R.; Johnson, S.L. Confirmatory factor analysis of the Child Feeding Questionnaire: A measure of parental attitudes, beliefs and practices about child feeding and obesity proneness. *Appetite* **2001**, *36*, 201–210. [CrossRef] [PubMed]
37. Rodgers, R.F.; Paxton, S.J.; Massey, R.; Campbell, K.J.; Wertheim, E.H.; Skouteris, H.; Gibbons, K. Maternal feeding practices predict weight gain and obesogenic eating behaviors in young children: A prospective study. *Int. J. Behav. Nutr. Phys. Act.* **2013**, *10*, 24. [CrossRef] [PubMed]
38. Puhl, R.M.; Schwartz, M.B. If you are good you can have a cookie: How memories of childhood food rules link to adult eating behaviors. *Eat. Behav.* **2003**, *4*, 283–293. [CrossRef]
39. Birch, L.L.; Zimmerman, S.I.; Hind, H. The Influence of social-affective context on the formation of children's food preferences. *Child Dev.* **1980**, *51*, 856–861. [CrossRef]
40. Ventura, A.K.; Worobey, J. Early influences on the development of food preferences. *Curr. Biol.* **2013**, *23*, R401–R408. [CrossRef]
41. Baughcum, A.E.; Burklow, K.A.; Deeks, C.M.; Powers, S.W.; Whitaker, R.C. Maternal feeding practices and childhood obesity: A focus group study of low-income mothers. *Arch. Pediatr. Adolesc. Med.* **1998**, *152*, 1010–1014. [CrossRef]
42. Tan, C.C.; Ruhl, H.; Chow, C.M.; Ellis, L. Retrospective reports of parental feeding practices and emotional eating in adulthood: The role of food preoccupation. *Appetite* **2016**, *105*, 410–415. [CrossRef]
43. Allen, K.L.; Byrne, S.M.; La Puma, M.; McLean, N.; Davis, E.A. The onset and course of binge eating in 8- to 13-year-old healthy weight, overweight and obese children. *Eat. Behave.* **2008**, *9*, 438–446. [CrossRef]
44. Waller, G.; Osman, S. Emotional eating and eating psychopathology among non-eating-disordered women. *Int. J. Eat. Disord.* **1998**, *23*, 419–424. [CrossRef]
45. Stifter, C.A.; Anzman-Frasca, S.; Birch, L.L.; Voegtline, K. Parent use of food to soothe infant/toddler distress and child weight status. An exploratory study. *Appetite* **2011**, *57*, 693–699. [CrossRef] [PubMed]
46. Blissett, J.; Haycraft, E.; Farrow, C. Inducing preschool children's emotional eating: Relations with parental feeding practices. *Am. J. Clin. Nutr.* **2010**, *92*, 359–365. [CrossRef] [PubMed]
47. Carper, J.L.; Orlet Fisher, J.; Birch, L.L. Young girls' emerging dietary restraint and disinhibition are related to parental control in child feeding. *Appetite* **2000**, *35*, 121–129. [CrossRef] [PubMed]
48. Loth, K.A.; MacLehose, R.F.; Fulkerson, J.A.; Crow, S.; Neumark-Sztainer, D. Are food restriction and pressure-to-eat parenting practices associated with adolescent disordered eating behaviors? *Int. J. Eat. Disord.* **2014**, *47*, 310–314. [CrossRef] [PubMed]
49. Blissett, J.; Haycraft, E. Parental eating disorder symptoms and observations of mealtime interactions with children. *J. Psychosom. Res.* **2011**, *70*, 368–371. [CrossRef] [PubMed]
50. Blissett, J.; Meyer, C.; Haycraft, E. Maternal and paternal controlling feeding practices with male and female children. *Appetite* **2006**, *47*, 212–219. [CrossRef]
51. Galloway, A.T.; Fiorito, L.M.; Francis, L.A.; Birch, L.L. 'Finish your soup': Counterproductive effects of pressuring children to eat on intake and affect. *Appetite* **2006**, *46*, 318–323. [CrossRef]
52. Kröller, K.; Jahnke, D.; Warschburger, P. Are maternal weight, eating and feeding practices associated with emotional eating in childhood? *Appetite* **2013**, *65*, 25–30. [CrossRef]

53. Clark, H.R.; Goyder, E.; Bissell, P.; Blank, L.; Peters, J. How do parents' child-feeding behaviours influence child weight? Implications for childhood obesity policy. *J. Public Health* **2007**, *29*, 132–141. [CrossRef]
54. Birch, L.; Davison, K. Family environmental factors influencing the developing behavioral controls of food intake and childhood overweight. *Pediatr. Clin. North Am.* **2001**, *48*, 893–907. [CrossRef]
55. WHO. 10 Facts on Obesity. Available online: http://www.who.int/features/factfiles/obesity/en/ (accessed on 16 December 2016).
56. Horsley, T.; Dingwall, O.; Sampson, M. Checking reference lists to find additional studies for systematic reviews. *Cochrane Database Syst. Rev.* **2011**. [CrossRef] [PubMed]
57. Moher, D.; Liberati, A.; Tetzlaff, J.; Altman, D.G. Preferred reporting items for systematic reviews and meta-analyses: The PRISMA statement. *Ann. Intern. Med.* **2009**, *151*, 264–269. [CrossRef] [PubMed]
58. MacNeill, V.; Foley, M.; Quirk, A.; McCambridge, J. Shedding light on research participation effects in behaviour change trials: A qualitative study examining research participant experiences. *BMC Public Health* **2016**, *16*, 91. [CrossRef] [PubMed]
59. Tacconelli, E. Systematic reviews: CRD's guidance for undertaking reviews in health care. *Lancet Infect. Dis.* **2010**, *10*, 226. [CrossRef]
60. NICE. Guidelines Manual. Appendix G: Quality Appraisal Checklist-Quantitative Studies Reporting Correlations and Associations. Available online: https://www.nice.org.uk/process/pmg4/chapter/appendix-g-quality-appraisal-checklist-quantitative-studies-reporting-correlations-and (accessed on 10 January 2017).
61. Kelly, S.; Martin, S.; Kuhn, I.; Cowan, A.; Brayne, C.; Lafortune, L. Barriers and facilitators to the uptake and maintenance of healthy behaviours by people at mid-life: A rapid systematic review. *PLoS ONE* **2016**, *11*, e0145074. [CrossRef]
62. Windle, G.; Hughes, D.; Linck, P.; Russell, I.; Woods, B. Is exercise effective in promoting mental well-being in older age? A systematic review. *Aging Ment. Health* **2010**, *14*, 652–669. [CrossRef]
63. McPhie, S.; Skouteris, H.; Daniels, L.; Jansen, E. Maternal correlates of maternal child feeding practices: A systematic review. *Matern. Child Nutr.* **2014**, *10*, 18–43. [CrossRef]
64. Baughcum, A.E.; Powers, S.W.; Johnson, S.B.; Chamberlin, L.A.; Deeks, C.M.; Jain, A.; Whitaker, R.C. Maternal feeding practices and beliefs and their relationships to overweight in early childhood. *JDBP* **2001**, *22*, 391–408. [CrossRef]
65. Van Strien, T.; Frijters, J.E.R.; Bergers, G.P.A.; Defares, P.B. The Dutch Eating Behavior Questionnaire (DEBQ) for assessment of restrained, emotional, and external eating behavior. *Int. J. Eat. Disords.* **1986**, *5*, 295–315. [CrossRef]
66. Cebeci, A.N.; Guven, A. Does maternal obesity have an influence on feeding behavior of obese children? *Minerva Pediatr.* **2015**, *67*, 481–487. [PubMed]
67. Corsini, N.; Wilson, C.; Kettler, L.; Danthiir, V. Development and preliminary validation of the Toddler Snack Food Feeding Questionnaire. *Appetite* **2010**, *54*, 570–578. [CrossRef] [PubMed]
68. Costa, F.S.; Pino, D.L.; Friedman, R. Caregivers' attitudes and practices: Influence on childhood body weight. *J. Biosoc. Sci.* **2011**, *43*, 369–378. [CrossRef] [PubMed]
69. Francis, L.A.; Hofer, S.M.; Birch, L.L. Predictors of maternal child-feeding style: Maternal and child characteristics. *Appetite* **2001**, *37*, 231–243. [CrossRef] [PubMed]
70. Francis, L.A.; Birch, L.L. Maternal weight status modulates the effects of restriction on daughters' eating and weight. *Int. J. Obes.* **2005**, *29*, 942–949. [CrossRef] [PubMed]
71. Haycraft, E.; Karasouli, E.; Meyer, C. Maternal feeding practices and children's eating behaviours: A comparison of mothers with healthy weight versus overweight/obesity. *Appetite* **2017**, *116*, 395–400. [CrossRef] [PubMed]
72. Jingxiong, J.; Rosenqvist, U.; Huishan, W.; Koletzko, B.; Guangli, L.; Jing, H.; Greiner, T. Relationship of parental characteristics and feeding practices to overweight in infants and young children in Beijing, China. *Public Health Nutr.* **2009**, *12*, 973–978. [CrossRef] [PubMed]
73. Kröller, K.; Warschburger, P. Associations between maternal feeding style and food intake of children with a higher risk for overweight. *Appetite* **2008**, *51*, 166–172. [CrossRef]
74. Lewis, M.; Worobey, J. Mothers and toddlers lunch together. The relation between observed and reported behavior. *Appetite* **2011**, *56*, 732–736. [CrossRef]

75. Lipowska, M.; Lipowski, M.; Jurek, P.; Jankowska, A.M.; Pawlicka, P. Gender and body-fat status as predictors of parental feeding styles and children's nutritional knowledge, eating habits and behaviours. *Int. J. Environ. Res. Public Health* **2018**. [CrossRef]
76. Lumeng, J.C.; Burke, L.M. Maternal prompts to eat, child compliance, and mother and child weight status. *J. Pediatr.* **2006**, *149*, 330–335. [CrossRef] [PubMed]
77. Powers, S.W.; Chamberlin, L.A.; van Schaick, K.B.; Sherman, S.N.; Whitaker, R.C. Maternal feeding strategies, child eating behaviors, and child BMI in low-income African-American preschoolers. *Obesity* **2006**, *14*, 2026–2033. [CrossRef] [PubMed]
78. Raaijmakers, L.G.; Gevers, D.W.; Teuscher, D.; Kremers, S.P.; van Assema, P. Emotional and instrumental feeding practices of Dutch mothers regarding foods eaten between main meals. *BMC Public Health* **2014**, *14*, 171. [CrossRef] [PubMed]
79. Roberts, L.T.; Goodman, L.C.; Musher-Eizenman, D.R. Parental correlates of food parenting practices: Socioeconomic status, weight, and dieting status. *Ecol. Food Nutr.* **2018**, *57*, 330–345. [CrossRef] [PubMed]
80. Russell, C.G.; Haszard, J.J.; Taylor, R.W.; Heath, A.M.; Taylor, B.; Campbell, K.J. Parental feeding practices associated with children's eating and weight: What are parents of toddlers and preschool children doing? *Appetite* **2018**, *128*, 120–128. [CrossRef] [PubMed]
81. Wardle, J.; Sanderson, S.; Guthrie, C.A.; Rapoport, L.; Plomin, R. Parental feeding style and the inter-generational transmission of obesity risk. *Obesity* **2002**, *10*, 453–462. [CrossRef] [PubMed]
82. Wendt, V.; Bergmann, S.; Herfurth-Majstorovic, K.; Keitel-Korndorfer, A.; von Klitzing, K.; Klein, A.M. Parent-child interaction during feeding or joint eating in parents of different weights. *Eat. Behave.* **2015**, *18*, 131–136. [CrossRef]
83. Williams, J.E.; Helsel, B.; Griffin, S.F.; Liang, J. Associations between parental bmi and the family nutrition and physical activity environment in a community sample. *J. Community Health* **2017**, *42*, 1233–1239. [CrossRef]
84. Gallagher, D.; Heymsfield, S.B.; Heo, M.; Jebb, S.A.; Murgatroyd, P.R.; Sakamoto, Y. Healthy percentage body fat ranges: An approach for developing guidelines based on body mass index. *Am. J. Clin. Nutr.* **2000**, *72*, 694–701. [CrossRef]
85. Berge, J.M.; Meyer, C.S.; Loth, K.; MacLehose, R.; Neumark-Sztainer, D. Parent/adolescent weight status concordance and parent feeding practices. *Pediatrics* **2015**, *136*, e591–e598. [CrossRef]
86. Chatoor, I.; Getson, P.; Menvielle, E.; Brasseaux, C.; O'Donnell, R.; Rivera, Y.; Mrazek, D.A. A feeding scale for research and clinical practice to assess mother—infant interactions in the first three years of life. *Infant Ment. Health J.* **1997**, *18*, 76–91. [CrossRef]
87. Hughes, S.O.; Power, T.G.; Orlet Fisher, J.; Mueller, S.; Nicklas, T.A. Revisiting a neglected construct: Parenting styles in a child-feeding context. *Appetite* **2005**, *44*, 83–92. [CrossRef] [PubMed]
88. Grolnick, W.S.; Pomerantz, E.M. Issues and challenges in studying parental control: Toward a new conceptualization. *Child Dev. Perspect.* **2009**, *3*, 165–170. [CrossRef]
89. Snoek, H.M.; Engels, R.C.M.E.; Janssens, J.M.A.M.; van Strien, T. Parental behaviour and adolescents' emotional eating. *Appetite* **2007**, *49*, 223–230. [CrossRef] [PubMed]
90. Gibson, E.L. The psychobiology of comfort eating: Implications for neuropharmacological interventions. *Behav. Pharmacol.* **2012**, *23*, 442–460. [CrossRef] [PubMed]
91. Gregory, J.E.; Paxton, S.J.; Brozovic, A.M. Maternal feeding practices, child eating behaviour and body mass index in preschool-aged children: A prospective analysis. *Int. J. Behav. Nutr. Phys. Act.* **2010**, *7*, 55. [CrossRef]
92. Vaughn, A.E.; Tabak, R.G.; Bryant, M.J.; Ward, D.S. Measuring parent food practices: A systematic review of existing measures and examination of instruments. *Int. J. Behav. Nutr. Phys. Act.* **2013**, *10*, 61. [CrossRef] [PubMed]
93. Palavras, M.A.; Kaio, G.H.; Mari Jde, J.; Claudino, A.M. A review of Latin American studies on binge eating disorder. *Braz. J. Psychiatr.* **2011**, *33*, S81–S108. [CrossRef]
94. Udo, T.; Grilo, C.M. Prevalence and correlates of DSM-5–Defined eating disorders in a nationally representative sample of U.S. adults. *Biol. Psychiatry* **2018**, *84*, 345–354. [CrossRef]
95. Villarejo, C.; Fernández-Aranda, F.; Jiménez-Murcia, S.; Peñas-Lledó, E.; Granero, R.; Penelo, E.; Tinahones, F.J.; Sancho, C.; Vilarrasa, N.; Montserrat-Gil de Bernabé, M.; et al. Lifetime obesity in patients with eating disorders: Increasing prevalence, clinical and personality correlates. *Eur. Eat. Disord. Rev.* **2012**, *20*, 250–254. [CrossRef]

96. Tiggemann, M.; Lowes, J. Predictors of maternal control over children's eating behaviour. *Appetite* **2002**, *39*, 1–7. [CrossRef] [PubMed]
97. Haines, J.; Downing, K.L.; Tang, L.; Campbell, K.J.; Hesketh, K.D. Associations between maternal concern about child's weight and related behaviours and maternal weight-related parenting practices: A cross-sectional study. *Int. J. Behav. Nutr. Phys. Act.* **2018**, *15*, 104. [CrossRef] [PubMed]
98. Rosenkranz, R.R.; Dzewaltowski, D.A. Model of the home food environment pertaining to childhood obesity. *Nutr. Res.* **2008**, *66*, 123–140. [CrossRef] [PubMed]
99. Pearson, N.; Biddle, S.J.H.; Gorely, T. Family correlates of fruit and vegetable consumption in children and adolescents: A systematic review. *Public Health Nutr.* **2009**, *12*, 267–283. [CrossRef] [PubMed]
100. Watts, A.W.; Barr, S.I.; Hanning, R.M.; Lovato, C.Y.; Mâsse, L.C. The home food environment and associations with dietary intake among adolescents presenting for a lifestyle modification intervention. *BMC Nutrition* **2018**, *4*, 3. [CrossRef]
101. Emmett, P.M.; Jones, L.R.; Northstone, K. Dietary patterns in the avon longitudinal study of parents and children. *Nutr. Res.* **2015**, *73*, 207–230. [CrossRef] [PubMed]
102. Di Pasquale, R.; Rivolta, A. A conceptual analysis of food parenting practices in the light of self-determination theory: Relatedness-enhancing, competence-enhancing and autonomy-enhancing food parenting practices. *Front. Psychol.* **2018**. [CrossRef]
103. Prinsen, C.A.C.; Mokkink, L.B.; Bouter, L.M.; Alonso, J.; Patrick, D.L.; de Vet, H.C.W.; Terwee, C.B. COSMIN guideline for systematic reviews of patient-reported outcome measures. *Qual. Life Res.* **2018**, *27*, 1147–1157. [CrossRef]
104. Gu, C.; Warkentin, S.; Mais, L.A.; Carnell, S. Ethnic differences in parental feeding behaviors in UK parents of preschoolers. *Appetite* **2017**, *113*, 398–404. [CrossRef]
105. Blissett, J.; Bennett, C. Cultural differences in parental feeding practices and children's eating behaviours and their relationships with child BMI: A comparison of Black Afro-Caribbean, White British and White German samples. *Eur. J. Clin. Nutr.* **2013**, *67*, 180–184. [CrossRef]
106. Cardel, M.; Willig, A.L.; Dulin-Keita, A.; Casazza, K.; Mark Beasley, T.; Fernández, J.R. Parental feeding practices and socioeconomic status are associated with child adiposity in a multi-ethnic sample of children. *Appetite* **2012**, *58*, 347–353. [CrossRef] [PubMed]
107. Loth, K.A.; MacLehose, R.F.; Fulkerson, J.A.; Crow, S.; Neumark-Sztainer, D. Eat this, not that! Parental demographic correlates of food-related parenting practices. *Appetite* **2013**, *60*, 140–147. [CrossRef] [PubMed]
108. Wehrly, S.E.; Bonilla, C.; Perez, M.; Liew, J. Controlling parental feeding practices and child body composition in ethnically and economically diverse preschool children. *Appetite* **2014**, *73*, 163–171. [CrossRef] [PubMed]
109. Stevens, J. *Applied Multivariate Statistics for the Social Sciences*; Lawrence Erlbaum Associates: Mahwah, NJ, USA, 1996.
110. Sedgwick, P. Cross sectional studies: Advantages and disadvantages. *BMJ* **2014**. [CrossRef]
111. Ventura, A.K.; Birch, L.L. Does parenting affect children's eating and weight status? *Int. J. Behav. Nutr. Phys. Act.* **2008**, *5*, 15. [CrossRef] [PubMed]
112. Li, R.; Scanlon, K.S.; May, A.; Rose, C.; Birch, L. Bottle-feeding practices during early infancy and eating behaviors at 6 years of age. *Pediatrics* **2014**, *134*, S70–S77. [CrossRef] [PubMed]

nutrients

MDPI

Article

Neuropsychological and Neurophysiological Indicators of General and Food-Specific Impulsivity in Children with Overweight and Obesity: A Pilot Study

Ricarda Schmidt [1,*], Caroline Sebert [1], Christine Kösling [1], Martin Grunwald [2], Anja Hilbert [1], Claudia Hübner [1,†] and Lisa Schäfer [1,†]

1 Integrated Research and Treatment Center Adiposity Diseases, Department of Medical Psychology and Medical Sociology and Psychosomatic Medicine and Psychotherapy, Leipzig University Medical Center, 04103 Leipzig, Germany; Caroline.Sebert@medizin.uni-leipzig.de (C.S.); Christine.Koesling@medizin.uni-leipzig.de (C.K.); Anja.Hilbert@medizin.uni-leipzig.de (A.H.); Claudia.Huebner@medizin.uni-leipzig.de (C.H.); Lisa.Schaefer@medizin.uni-leipzig.de (L.S.)

2 Haptic-Research Laboratory, Paul-Flechsig-Institute for Brain Research, University of Leipzig, 04103 Leipzig, Germany; mgrun@medizin.uni-leipzig.de

* Correspondence: ricarda.schmidt@medizin.uni-leipzig.de; Tel.: +49-341-9715366

† These authors contributed equally to this work.

Received: 6 November 2018; Accepted: 11 December 2018; Published: 15 December 2018

Abstract: Impulsivity, particularly towards food, is a potential risk factor for increased energy intake and the development and maintenance of obesity in children. However, neuropsychological and neurophysiological indicators of general and food-specific impulsivity and their association with children's weight status are poorly understood. This pilot study examined electroencephalography (EEG) frequency band profiles during eyes-closed and eyes-open resting state in n = 12 children with overweight or obesity versus n = 22 normal-weight controls and their link to child- and parent-reported and experimentally assessed impulsivity of children (e.g., risk-taking behavior, approach-avoidance behavior towards food). The main results indicated that children with overweight/obesity versus normal weight showed significantly increased delta and decreased alpha band activity during eyes-closed resting state. Across the total sample, EEG slow-wave band activity was particularly linked to self- and parent-reported impulsivity and greater risk-taking behavior, but not to approach behavior towards food, after controlling for children's age and weight status. The identification of specific EEG patterns in children with excess weight may provide a new basis for developing neurophysiological diagnostic and treatment approaches for childhood obesity. Future studies with larger samples and longitudinal designs are needed to replicate the present findings and test their stability over time.

Keywords: EEG; frequency bands; obesity; brain activity; impulsivity; children

1. Introduction

During the last decades, an increasing number of studies focused on the neuronal basis of obesity, mostly based on functional magnet resonance imaging or electroencephalography (EEG, for reviews see References [1–3]). Consistently, neuroimaging studies revealed altered neurophysiological processes in the orbitofrontal cortex [4–6], a region crucial for reward and reinforcement processes [7], and the dorsolateral prefrontal cortex, which is known to be involved in cognitive control [8–10], particularly in the processing of food cues [11]. Processes of both reward and cognitive control are major determinants of human approach and avoidance behaviors and can be termed as facets of impulsivity, defined as spontaneous, unplanned behavior with lack of regard or diminished sensitivity towards negative or long-term consequences [12]. In line with neuronal measures, neuropsychological measures of impulsivity indicated abnormalities in a number of facets of impulsivity in individuals with overweight and obesity across the age range compared to normal-weight controls [13].

In the general population, longitudinal studies indicated poor inhibitory control to predict higher body mass index (BMI, kg/m^2) in children [14,15]. Recent research suggested that the association between impulsivity and weight status is driven by increased food intake [16,17]. In fact, experimental evidence revealed that children and adults with overweight and obesity were characterized by food-specific inhibition and interference deficits compared to normal-weight controls as measured by food-specific neuropsychological tasks (e.g., References [18–22]). However, while most evidence on impulsivity in children with obesity focused on the facets of inhibition or delay of gratification, there is little evidence on other dimensions of impulsivity, particularly decision-making, including risk-taking behavior [23] and automatic approach-avoidance tendencies towards food stimuli. Based on the Iowa Gambling Task (IGT) [24], an ecologically valid measure of decision-making under uncertainty in a context of punishment and reward, there is inconclusive evidence whether children and adolescents with excess weight show a general preference for disadvantageous, risky decisions compared to normal-weight controls [25,26] or not [27–29]. Similarly, studies applying other tasks than the IGT provided inconsistent findings on deviant decision-making in children and adolescents with excess versus normal weight [30,31]. As only two previous studies [25,30] used child-adapted tasks to examine decision-making in children and adolescents with excess weight, it is not clear whether methodological aspects accounted for the heterogeneity of findings.

Apart from behavioral measures, EEG profiles provide a more objective evaluation of pathological impulsivity across the age range [32]. The brain's functional states as measured by resting-state EEG are relatively stable over time and may be used as an indicator of arousal, cognitive activation, and psychopathology [32,33]. Based on spectral power analysis, the EEG waveform can be classified within different bands spanning the frequency spectrum, ranging from slow-wave frequencies (delta, theta) to moderate (alpha) and high frequency activity (beta). A vast number of studies found increased slow-wave EEG activity to be associated with behavioral impulsivity, including reduced inhibition [34] and increased risk-taking behavior in adults with attention-deficit/hyperactivity disorder (ADHD) or healthy university students [35–37]. Clinically, children with spectral elevations of resting-state slow-wave frequencies, mainly theta, and/or reduced alpha and beta activity were likely to have a diagnosis of externalizing behavior, including ADHD or antisocial symptomatology [34,38,39], which are common comorbidities in childhood obesity [40]. In contrast, the preponderance of fast-wave activity during resting-state EEG was found to be related to slower reaction times during a neuropsychological task in adults with ADHD [41]. In a sample of adults with a gambling disorder, frontal and central alpha band activity during eyes-closed resting state was negatively associated with self-reported impulsivity [42]. Thus, conditions characterized by increased impulsivity were found to show an EEG profile with increased slow-wave and decreased fast-wave band activity, suggesting cortical hypoarousal or a maturational lag in these individuals, respectively.

Despite the evidence that resting-state EEG brain activity is a marker of behavioral impulsivity, EEG studies in children did not explicitly consider child weight status so far, leaving the question whether the neurophysiological profile in children with obesity is actually deviant. EEG studies focusing on early, event-related information processing in children and adolescents with overweight and obesity versus normal weight found general and food-specific reductions in inhibitory processing during task performance [43,44], but nothing is known about the continuous brain activity at rest. Following the assumption of a proposed neuronal overlap between childhood obesity and ADHD [45], the EEG profile of children with obesity should be expected to resemble that of children with ADHD, at least to a certain extent. The only two studies analyzing EEG spectral power in relation to child's weight status revealed increased frontal beta in adolescent girls with overweight or obesity during a working memory task [46] and increased functional connectivity in the delta and beta band at eyes-closed rest [47] compared to normal-weight peers, but nothing is known about EEG spectral power at resting-state activity. Simultaneously, there is very little evidence on the EEG power spectrum and its associations with impulsivity in adults with obesity available [3]. Based on evidence from only two studies on the sources of resting-state EEG, adults with overweight and obesity showed lower parieto-occipital alpha oscillations during eyes-closed resting-state EEG [48], as well as posterior alpha desynchronization during eyes-open resting state compared to normal-weight adults [49] reflecting abnormal arousal/vigilance processes in these individuals.

Thus, the present pilot study sought to examine neuropsychological and neurophysiological indicators of impulsivity and their relation in children with overweight and obesity versus normal-weight controls. Specifically, this study aimed at investigating associations between eyes-closed and eyes-open resting-state EEG indices and neuropsychological, as well as questionnaire-based measures of general and food-specific impulsivity in children aged 8 to 13 years for the first time. Given the exploratory design of this study and the few available findings on EEG resting state activity in individuals with overweight and obesity, especially in children, both eyes-closed and eyes-open resting state were examined. It was hypothesized that children with overweight or obesity will exhibit greater slow-wave EEG band activity and lower fast-wave band activity during resting state than children with normal weight. According to previous findings in adults with ADHD [41] and the hypoarousal model of ADHD [50], it was expected that group differences would be more pronounced during eyes-closed resting-state, assuming that children with overweight and obesity are cortically under-aroused during eyes-closed resting condition and seeking for external stimulation. In order to assess children's impulsivity as detailed as possible and to reduce age-related biases in the context of self-report questionnaires, parent-report measures were used as well. Since EEG frequency band activity was evidenced to be a general indicator of impulsivity both in clinical child and non-clinical adult samples [36,41], the study aimed to evaluate the association between EEG resting-state activity and multiple indicators of impulsivity in a non-clinical child sample using the total sample. Specifically, it was expected that EEG resting-state slow-wave band activity would be positively and fast-wave band activity would be negatively related to experimentally assessed decision-making and automatic approach-avoidance tendencies towards foods, as well as self- and parent-reported general and food-specific impulsivity, respectively.

2. Materials and Methods

2.1. Participants

Eligible participants were German-speaking children aged 8 to 13 years with overweight or obesity, and normal weight, respectively, who were recruited from the population (e.g., via advertisements on the Internet, supermarkets) and clinical institutions (e.g., University Medical Center, outpatient weight reduction programs). Inclusion in the experimental group (EG) required objectively measured overweight or obesity based on age- and sex-specific German reference data [51]. Overweight and obesity were defined via BMI-standard deviation scores (SDS) ≥ 1.28 and ≥ 1.88, respectively. Children were assigned to the control group (CG) if they had normal weight ($-1.28 \leq$ BMI-SDS < 1.28). Exclusion criteria for both groups included parent-reported left-handedness, mental, neurological, or serious physical disorders (e.g., ADHD), medication intake affecting executive functions or brain activity, or mental retardation of the child. The pilot study was approved by the local Ethics Committee of the University of Leipzig.

The EG was comprised of $n = 5$ children with overweight and $n = 7$ children with obesity. The CG consisted of $n = 22$ children with normal weight, stratified to the EG for age and sex. By design, the groups significantly differed in their weight status, with the EG having a higher BMI-SDS than the CG ($p < 0.001$), but also in their socioeconomic status [52], with children of the EG having a lower socioeconomic status ($p < 0.01$) than the CG (Table 1).

Table 1. Sociodemographic description of the experimental group (EG) and control group (CG).

	EG (n = 12)	**CG (n = 22)**			
	n (%)	*n* (%)	χ^2	*df*	*p*
Sociodemographics					
Sex (female)	8 (66.7)	10 (45.5)	1.40	1	0.236
	M (*SD*)	*M* (*SD*)	*t*	*df*	*p*
Age (years)	10.9 (1.9)	10.1 (1.6)	1.26	1, 32	0.217
BMI percentile (0–100)	96.5 (3.3)	54.8 (20.7)	9.25	1, 22.9	<0.001
BMI-SDS	2.09 (0.49)	0.14 (0.60)	9.60	1, 32	<0.001
SES Winkler index (0–21)	12.3 (3.8)	15.8 (3.2)	−2.82	1, 32	0.008
Intelligence					
Matrix reasoning (1–19)	11.2 (2.8)	12.6 (1.8)	−1.55	1, 16.1	0.141

Note: BMI body mass index; CG control group; EG experimental group; *M* mean; *SD* standard deviation; SDS standard deviation score; SES socioeconomic status.

2.2. Procedure

The standardized experimental sessions were conducted by two highly trained PhD and MD students. In the beginning, written informed consent and assent were obtained from the parent and child, respectively, followed by children's intelligence assessment. During the subsequent EEG preparation, children completed self-report questionnaires, while parents were asked to do so at home beforehand. After EEG recordings and a 5-min break, neuropsychological tests were conducted. Subsequently, children's eating disorder psychopathology and mental comorbidities were assessed via separate clinical interviews with the child and one parent, respectively (Eating Disorder Examination adapted for Children [53,54], K-DIPS [55]). The experimental session ended with the objective assessment of children's weight and height. Altogether, the experimental session took approximately 3 h. Children and their parents received a financial compensation of 15€ for participation.

2.3. EEG Recording and Analysis

EEG recordings took place in an acoustically and electromagnetically shielded cabin with video control and were conducted using a 32 channel QuickAmp amplifier and Brain Vision Analyzer 2.1 software (Brain Products, Gilching, Germany). For all recordings, participants were grounded peripherally following the standard 10–20 International system with linked ear referencing to obtain EEG activity from 19 scalp sites (Fp1, Fp2, F3, F4, F7, F8, Fz, C3, C4, Cz, T3, T4, T5, T6, P3, P4, Pz, O1, and O2) at a sampling rate of 250 Hz. Eye movements and blinks were measured with two bipolar EOG electrodes placed 1 cm beyond the outer edge of both eyes and 1 cm below and above the right eye. EEG resting state was recorded for 300 s with eyes-open (EO) while looking at a fixation cross on the display and for 300 s with eyes-closed (EC). The order of EEG resting state with EO and EC was randomized.

A band-pass filter of 0.53–70 Hz and a notch filter of 50 Hz were used to filter EEG data. The continuous EEG was segmented in 2-s intervals and ocular artifact correction was conducted in accordance with Gratton et al. [56]. Further, automatic artifact rejection was applied to segments with voltage steps greater than 50 µV/ms and amplitudes exceeding ±100 µV. Subsequent to these automated procedures, two extensively trained researchers visually scanned all data in order to identify and remove residual contaminants (e.g., artifacts, focal abnormalities, drowsiness). At least 30 artifact-free segments (not necessarily consecutive) of the filtered EEG data were required for EO and EC to be included in the analysis. As a consequence, n = 10 children of the EG (*Mean [M]* = 57.8 segments; *Standard Deviation [SD]* = 19.8; range 36–88) and n = 19 children of the CG (*M* = 78.32 segments; *SD* = 28.1; range 39–127) were included in further analyses in the EO condition. Regarding EC, n = 11 children of the EG (*M* = 108.3 segments; *SD* = 38.0; range 41–150) and n = 22 children of the CG (*M* = 89.4 segments; *SD* = 30.9; range 40–156) were included in the subsequent analyses.

The filtered EEG data were Fourier transformed with a Hanning window length of 20% extracting delta (δ, 1.0–3.5 Hz), theta (θ, 3.5–7.5 Hz), alpha (α, 7.5–12.5 Hz), and beta (β, 12.5–30 Hz) frequency bands. The extracted absolute power for each frequency band was grouped for frontal (Fp1, Fp2, F3, F4, F7, F8, Fz), central (C3, C4, Cz), temporal (T3, T4, T5, T6), parietal (P3, P4, Pz), and occipital (O1, O2) regions, converted to relative band power (%), and ln-transformed before statistical hypotheses testing to obtain normally distributed data.

2.4. Neuropsychological Tasks

Approach-Avoidance Task (AAT). The study-specific AAT was adapted from Wiers et al. [57] and is a computerized measure for assessing approach and avoidance tendencies towards food in children. Following the principle of the AAT, children had to move the computer mouse as quickly and as accurately as possible in dependence of the format of pictures presented on a computer screen (portrait or landscape): By pulling the computer mouse to the bottom of the computer screen, the picture grows bigger (approach), while by pushing the computer mouse to the top of the screen, the picture size decreases (avoidance). After successful completion of a test run, including 10 grey rectangles, 40 pictures were presented in both landscape and portrait format in a randomized order, summing up to 80 trials. Specifically, there are four picture categories with 10 pictures each presenting high-calorie foods (e.g., burger), low-calorie foods (e.g., banana), pleasant neutral stimuli (e.g., smartphone), as well as boring neutral stimuli (e.g., ladder) to evaluate automatic responses depending on stimulus content. Boring neutral pictures and food pictures were pre-selected from a large, validated picture data base [58] based on the highest ratings of perceptibility and high familiarity. Finally, food pictures and pleasant neutral pictures were selected based on the criteria of high liking and perceptibility derived from a previous independent rating of food and pleasant neutral pictures in 38 children of two elementary schools aged between 8 and 12 years. In accordance to Wiers et al. [57], one child with overweight and two children with normal weight had to be excluded based on error percentages greater than 25%. Per each picture category, difference scores were computed based on mean reaction times in ms for the onset of correct responses to approach and avoidance trials, for example, "high calorie food/push—high calorie food/pull." Positive scores indicate relatively faster reaction times for approach responses compared to avoidance, hence an approach behavior. In the present study, only approach-avoidance tendencies for low-calorie and high-calorie food pictures were analyzed.

Youth Version of the Balloon Analogue Risk Task (BART-Y). The BART-Y [59] is a computerized task for the assessment of risk-taking behavior through balancing reward versus loss of points. Children were instructed to pump up 30 computer-generated balloons by clicking a button. With each click, the balloon was inflated further, and points were added to a counter up to a certain threshold at which the balloon explodes. If the child decided to cash-out before the balloon explodes, the accumulated points for that trial were added to the counter. However, if the balloon exploded, the child lost the points earned so far for that trial. Children were not informed about the balloons' break point that varied across each of the 30 trials. Thus, each pump confers greater risk, but also greater potential reward. After balloon explosion or saving of points, a new balloon appeared. At the end of the task, collected points were exchanged to differently sized prizes (small, medium, large, and bonus toy). Risk-taking behavior was measured by the average number of pumps on balloons that did not explode, with higher scores indicating higher risk-taking behavior.

2.5. Self-Report Questionnaires

To assess children's eating behavior and food-specific approach-behaviors, the subscales 'enjoyment of food' (α = Cronbach's α in this study's sample = 0.81) and 'food responsiveness' ($\alpha = 0.91$) of the Children's Eating Behavior Questionnaire (CEBQ) [60] were administrated to parents and mean scores were computed for each subscale. Sum scores of the subscale 'hyperactivity' from the parent version of the Strength and Difficulties Questionnaire (SDQ; $\alpha = 0.72$, [61]) were used to determine children's general impulsivity. Additionally, children's self-reported general impulsivity was measured using the sum score of the subscale 'impulsivity' of the Inventory for the Assessment of Impulsivity, Venturesomeness and Empathy in 9–14 years old children (IVE, $\alpha = 0.62$, [62]) which is an adapted German version of the Impulsivity Questionnaire I6 by Eysenck and Eysenck [63].

2.6. Intelligence

Children's intelligence was estimated using the 'matrix reasoning subtest' of the Wechsler Intelligence Scale for Children—Fourth edition (WISC-IV; [64,65]) which nonverbally assesses abstract-logical reasoning. Subtest scores were converted into age-specific standard values ranging between 1 and 19, with higher scores indicating higher levels of intelligence.

2.7. Data Analytic Plan

Statistical analyses were performed using IBM SPSS Statistics version 23 (IBM Corp. Released 2015. IBM SPSS Statistics for Windows, Version 23.0. Armonk, NY: IBM Corp) and consisted of two steps. First, group differences between the EG and CG regarding impulsivity measures and resting-state EEG activity measured during EC and EO were examined using two-tailed independent sample t tests. In order to correct for possible inflations of the Type I error rate due to multiple testing, an adjusted significance level of $p < 0.05/20 = 0.0025$ was considered to indicate statistical significance. In terms of violation of normality and homogeneity of variances, non-parametric tests were used and reported if results differed from the parametric tests. Effect sizes of group differences were reported by Cohen's d, whereby values ≥ 0.20 refer to small, ≥ 0.50 to medium, and ≥ 0.80 to large effects [66].

Second, associations between children's EEG activity and various impulsivity indicators (AAT, BART-Y, CEBQ, SDQ, IVE) over and above group status (EG vs. CG) were examined via partial correlations (Pearson) with children's weight status (BMI-SDS) and age serving as control variables to exclude weight- and development-related effects on measured EEG activity [67]. Effect sizes of correlations were interpreted according to Cohen with values $r \geq 0.10$ referring to small, $r \geq 0.30$ to medium, and $r \geq 0.50$ to large effects [66]. Statistical significance for correlation analyses was set at $\alpha < 0.05$. Post-hoc power analyses revealed adequate power ($1 - \beta = 0.80$) for detecting large-sized group differences ($d > 1$) in EEG resting state and medium-to-large-sized effects ($r > 0.40$) in correlation analyses.

3. Results

3.1. Neuropsychological Tasks

While the EG showed an avoidance behavior and the CG an approach behavior of medium effect size regarding high-calorie foods, an approach behavior to low-calorie foods was found in both groups; however, biases were not significantly different from 0 ($p > 0.05$). The EG and CG did not significantly differ in approach or avoidance behaviors to high- or low-calorie foods in the AAT ($p > 0.05$, Table 2).

A non-significant ($p > 0.05$), but medium-sized group difference was found for the number of pumps in the BART-Y, with the EG presenting a lower average number of pumps than the CG, indicating lower risk-taking behavior.

3.2. Self-Report Questionnaires

Parents of children of the EG reported significantly higher levels of 'food responsiveness' ($p < 0.01$, large effect) and marginally significantly higher levels on the subscale 'enjoyment of food' ($p < 0.100$, medium effect) of the CEBQ compared to the CG.

For general self- and parent-reported impulsivity, small-to-medium-sized, but non-significant group differences were revealed ($p > 0.05$) indicating descriptively higher levels of impulsivity in the EG than the CG.

Table 2. Self-reported and neuropsychological measures of general and food-specific impulsivity as a function of weight status.

	EG	CG				
Neuropsychological Tasks	*M (SD)*	*M (SD)*	*t*	*df*	*p*	*d*
AAT (ms)						
High-calorie food	−12.2 (134.5)	70.6 (171.3)	−1.38	1, 29	0.177	−0.52
Low-calorie food	39.2 (272.1)	82.2 (230.6)	−0.46	1, 28	0.649	−0.18
BART-Y						
N pumps	17.9 (9.0)	24.0 (10.8)	−1.66	1, 31	0.108	−0.60
Self-report questionnaires	*M (SD)*	*M (SD)*	*t*	*df*	*p*	*d*
CEBQ						
Enjoyment of Food	3.2 (0.7)	2.9 (0.5)	1.79	1, 32	0.083	0.52
Food Responsiveness	2.2 (1.2)	0.9 (0.5)	3.54	1, 13.2	0.004	1.60
IVE						
Impulsivity	8.1 (3.2)	6.7 (2.8)	1.35	1, 32	0.188	0.48
SDQ						
Hyperactivity	3.3 (2.1)	2.6 (1.9)	0.94	1, 32	0.357	0.36

Note. AAT Approach Avoidance Task; BART-Y Youth Version of the Balloon Analogue Risk Task; CEBQ Children's Eating Behavior Questionnaire; CG control group; EG experimental group; IVE Inventory for the Assessment of Impulsivity, Venturesomeness and Empathy in 9–14 years old children; *M* mean; *SD* standard deviation; SDQ Strengths and Difficulties Questionnaire. Negative *d* values indicate that the EG scored lower in the respective measure than the CG.

3.3. Resting-State EEG Activity

As depicted in Table 3, the EG showed significantly higher delta band activity than the CG during EC resting state with large-sized effects for parietal and occipital regions ($p \leq 0.003$), while greater delta band activity in the EG versus CG did not reach significance for other regions ($0.022 \leq ps \leq 0.149$). Although non-significant, large-sized group effects were found for greater occipital theta band activity and lower alpha band activity in all brain regions in the EG versus CG ($0.007 \leq ps \leq 0.036$). Descriptively higher theta and beta band activity in the EG versus CG did not reach significance ($ps \geq 0.027$).

Table 3. Eyes-closed resting-state electroencephalography (EEG) activity as a function of weight status.

	EG	CG				
	M (SD)	*M (SD)*	*t*	*df*	*p*	*d*
Delta (μV^2)						
Frontal	−1.07 (0.18)	−1.18 (0.21)	1.48	1, 31	0.149	0.55
Central	−1.19 (0.15)	−1.34 (0.19)	2.41	1, 31	0.022	0.84
Parietal	−1.25 (0.19)	−1.51 (0.23)	3.26	1, 31	0.003	1.19
Temporal	−1.22 (0.17)	−1.35 (0.17)	2.13	1, 31	0.041	0.77
Occipital	−1.29 (0.23)	−1.71 (0.38)	3.31	1, 31	0.002	1.24
Theta (μV^2)						
Frontal	−1.27 (0.16)	−1.37 (0.26)	1.21	1, 31	0.235	0.43
Central	−1.16 (0.12)	−1.30 (0.25)	1.84	1, 31	0.975	0.65
Parietal	−1.31 (0.15)	−1.51 (0.32)	1.96	1, 31	0.059	0.72
Temporal	−1.23 (0.13)	−1.38 (0.24)	1.88	1, 31	0.069	0.71
Occipital	−1.48 (0.23)	−1.83 (0.46)	2.33	1, 31	0.027	0.87
Alpha (μV^2)						
Frontal	−1.54 (0.32)	−1.26 (0.34)	−2.29	1, 31	0.029	−0.84
Central	−1.41 (0.34)	−1.06 (0.36)	−2.73	1, 31	0.010	−0.99
Parietal	−1.26 (0.30)	−0.94 (0.30)	−2.88	1, 31	0.007	−1.07
Temporal	−1.33 (0.31)	−1.09 (0.30)	−2.19	1, 31	0.036	−0.79
Occipital	−1.00 (0.33)	−0.69 (0.36)	−2.36	1, 31	0.025	−0.88
Beta (μV^2)						
Frontal	−1.95 (0.22)	−2.11 (0.34)	1.41	1, 31	0.167	0.52
Central	−2.06 (0.12)	−2.19 (0.34)	1.27	1, 31	0.214	0.45
Parietal	−2.25 (0.26)	−2.36 (0.33)	0.93	1, 31	0.360	0.36
Temporal	−2.05 (0.19)	−2.12 (0.34)	0.62	1, 31	0.538	0.23
Occipital	−2.37 (0.37)	−2.43 (0.43)	0.39	1, 31	0.703	0.15

Note: Percentage EEG activity at a particular location increases as the mean of the ln-transformed data becomes less negative. Negative *d* values indicate that the EG scored lower in the respective measure than the CG. *M* mean; *SD* standard deviation.

For resting-state EEG activity measured during EO, no significant group differences were found for any frequency band and any brain region ($0.333 \leq ps \leq 0.998$).

3.4. Associations between Resting-State EEG Activity and Impulsivity Measures

Eyes-open. Results of the correlation analyses between frequency band activities measured during EO resting-state EEG and neuropsychological indices of impulsivity are presented in Figure 1. After controlling for children's age and weight status, increased slow-wave band activity (i.e., delta and theta) found in frontal, central, parietal, and temporal regions was significantly associated with higher scores in the CEBQ subscale 'enjoyment of food' with medium-to-large-sized effects ($0.002 \leq ps \leq 0.043$). Additionally, significant positive correlations of medium effect size were detected between frontal, central, and temporal theta band activity and average numbers of pumps in the BART-Y ($0.038 \leq ps \leq 0.046$).

Regarding fast-wave band activity (i.e., alpha and beta), increased frontal and central alpha band activity was significantly associated with lower scores in the CEBQ subscale 'enjoyment of food' with medium-to-large-sized effects ($0.004 \leq ps \leq 0.005$). Increased central and temporal beta band activity was significantly associated with approach behavior for low-calorie food in the AAT with medium-to-large-sized effects ($0.023 \leq ps \leq 0.024$). Medium-sized significant positive correlations were revealed between occipital beta band activity and the SDQ subscale 'hyperactivity' ($p = 0.044$). No other significant correlations were found during EO.

Eyes-closed. After controlling for children's age and weight status, occipital delta band activity and average numbers of pumps in the BART-Y were negatively correlated with medium-sized effects ($p = 0.028$).

Regarding fast-wave band activity, increased beta band activity in frontal regions was associated with lower scores on the IVE subscale 'impulsivity' ($p = 0.021$, medium-to-large-sized effect). Other correlations between EC resting-state EEG and impulsivity indices were not significant.

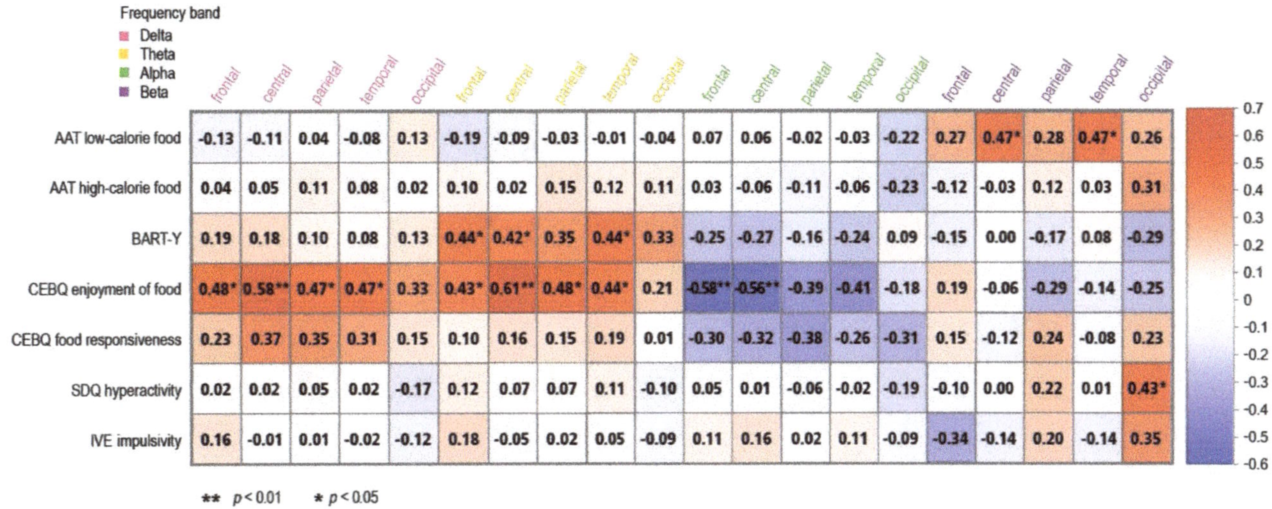

Figure 1. Matrix of correlations between eyes-open EEG resting-state activity, Approach-Avoidance-Task (AAT), the Youth Version of the Balloon Analogue Risk Task (BART-Y), parent-reported Child Eating Behavior Questionnaire (CEBQ), Strengths and Difficulties Questionnaire (SDQ), and child-reported Inventory of Venturesomeness and Empathy in 9–14 years old children (IVE) across the total sample with valid EEG data ($n = 29$), while controlling for child age and weight status.

4. Discussion

To our knowledge, this is the first study that investigated both eyes-closed (EC) and eyes-open (EO) resting-state EEG activity in 8-to-13-year-old children with overweight and obesity versus normal weight and its associations with general and food-specific impulsivity measured experimentally and via self- and parent-report. The results revealed an obesity-specific EEG profile characterized by greater slow-wave and decreased alpha band activity during EC resting-state EEG, congruent with EEG patterns found in other conditions marked by increased impulsivity, such as ADHD (e.g., References [68,69]). Independent of children's weight status, increased slow-wave and decreased alpha band activity during EO resting state were associated with higher impulsivity, characterized by greater risk-taking behavior during a neuropsychological task and parent-reported food-approach behaviors, mirroring findings in youth with ADHD [70] and healthy individuals [35,36].

The preponderance of slow-wave band activity and reductions of alpha band activity during EC resting state in children with overweight and obesity suggested neuronal similarities with ADHD, a highly comorbid disorder to obesity across the age range [40]. Because a concurrent diagnosis of ADHD was an exclusion criterion for the present sample, the results were not contaminated by underlying neuronal abnormalities due to the presence of this neurodevelopmental disorder. Notably, disorder-specific symptoms in individuals with deviant EEG patterns are considered to reflect compensatory mechanisms to counter-regulate the vigilance level, either via withdrawal and sensation avoidance (depression) or inattention, hyperactivity/impulsivity [71]. Thus, general deficiencies in self-control in children with obesity might be attributable to cortical hypoarousal, as in those with ADHD or other externalizing behavior [39]. Although there are no studies available addressing the particular aspect of the association between cortical arousal and self-regulation neither in adults nor in children with overweight and obesity, preliminary evidence in adults with obesity indicated that stimulant treatment, such as methylphenidate, may have an effect on the reduction of food intake, at least in some individuals [72] proposing that there might be an EEG phenotype of slow-wave preponderance in individuals with obesity. According to Knyazev (2012) [73], delta band activity represents the most basic evolutionary old oscillatory mode in animals and humans and is especially associated with motivational processes and biological rewards, including food, suggesting that children with overweight and obesity may be neurophysiologically characterized by persistent states of attention to motivationally rewarding stimuli.

Existing evidence on resting-state EEG activity in individuals with obesity was based on two studies in adults with obesity and comorbid binge-eating disorder (BED) [74,75]. Consistently, these studies revealed increased beta band activity and functional connectivity, respectively, in adults with obesity with versus without BED, while there were no group differences for other frequency bands [74,75]. However, the present study did not reveal significant differences in the beta band in either resting-state condition between children with overweight and obesity versus normal weight suggesting that increased beta band activity has a crucial role for individuals with obesity and high levels of food-specific impulsivity characterizing those with comorbid BED, but not children with obesity only. Notably, none of these previous studies on EEG resting-state activity included a control group of normal-weight individuals so far, making specific comparisons to these previous studies difficult [74,75]. It therefore remains to be further examined whether there are EEG subtypes in individuals with obesity and/or BED, possibly reflecting the heterogeneity in eating disorder and general psychopathology, including impulsivity in this population [76,77], in accordance with findings in ADHD research [78,79].

The fact that children with overweight and obesity versus those with normal weight did not show greater approach behavior towards high-calorie foods during the AAT is contrary to expectations, but fits into the inconsistent findings of previous studies in child and adult samples (e.g., References [80,81]). Within an intervention study in 276 8–16 years old youth, baseline AAT data already indicated avoidance tendencies for snack foods in children with obesity, much like in the present study; however, there were no data of a normal-weight control group available [82]. Similarly, the only study investigating adults with obesity did not find an approach bias towards high- or low-calorie foods [81], while university students with high levels of food cravings showed greater approach behavior towards food cues than adults with low levels of food craving [83]. The lack of effects may mirror conditioned responses towards high-calorie foods, the anticipation of punishment, or repeated reminders to avoid high-calorie foods, because children with obesity were mainly recruited via weight loss facilities. As the AAT is a reaction time task, socially desirable response behavior can be ruled out. In contrast, the BART-Y does not include any time component, but reflexive decision-making. The results of the BART-Y were unexpected as well, because children with overweight and obesity were not found to decide highly risky and did not strive for a large reward. Thus, the present results add to the inconsistent evidence on decision-making and risk-taking behavior in children with obesity (e.g., References [25,28]). Compared to the IGT or its age-adapted versions, such as the Hungry Donkey Task [25], the component of punishment in the BART-Y is more emotionally intensive as it is presented by an annoying tone when the balloon explodes. Thus, the results obtained from the BART-Y may rather mirror sensitivity to punishment or increased levels of anxiety (e.g., Reference [84]) than risk-taking behavior in children with obesity. Importantly, the questionnaire-based measures indicated higher levels of food-specific and general impulsivity in children with overweight and obesity versus normal-weight controls, consistent with recent findings [85].

Given that EEG resting-state frequency band activity serves as an electrophysiological signature for a range of impulsivity facets [32], correlational analyses between these measures were conducted across the total sample of children with normal weight, overweight, and obesity. In line with expectations and previous findings [34–37], delta and theta band activity during EO was positively related to parent-reported levels of enjoyment of food, describing strong approach behaviors towards foods. In contrast, but as expected [42], the direction of the association between alpha band activity and parent-reported food approach tendencies was the opposite (i.e., negative). After controlling for children's weight status and age, children's theta band activity and risk-taking behavior in the BART-Y were positively associated, as found in previous studies using the IGT in university student samples [35–37]. Notably, these associations were consistently found across many brain regions underlying the strength and connectivity of findings. For fast-wave band activity, positive relations between occipital beta band activity and children's level of hyperactivity were revealed, which goes in line with studies in adult and adolescent samples with obesity, although these findings were particularly relevant for frontal brain regions (for a review, see Reference [3]).

Compared to the associations found between EO resting-state frequency band activity and impulsivity measures the results on EC resting-state correlates were more selective regarding brain region and the direction of the association. For example, occipital delta band activity was negatively associated with risk-taking decisions during the BART-Y. These localized changes in the direction and topography of effects might be related to task-specific activation processes or the differential cortical processing of visual input, as EO and EC conditions generally produce differences in power and topography levels in children and adults [86,87].

A major strength of this pilot study is the standardized record of children's resting-state EEG activity in an acoustically and electromagnetically shielded cabin with video control. To increase the validity of the present results, EEG data were cleaned from artifacts by two independent experts. Furthermore, behavioral parameters of impulsivity were multimodally assessed via neuropsychological tasks with child-adapted food-specific and neutral stimuli and state-of-the-art questionnaires. For the first time, children's weight status was considered to describe specific EEG patterns in children with overweight and obesity under exclusion of ADHD and eating disorders.

However, some limitations must be considered when interpreting the results. Only large effects could be detected with sufficient power, due to the small sample size. For this reason, non-parametric tests were used where necessary and the corresponding effect sizes were reported. In addition to children with obesity, children with overweight were included in the EG, possibly attenuating between-group differences in EEG profiles related to obesity only. Due to the cross-sectional design, no conclusions can be drawn about the predictive value of EEG profiles on children's eating behavior and weight status.

Clinically, the identification of EEG profiles specific to childhood overweight and obesity may allow for taking a neurophysiological approach to target insufficient self-regulation in obesity, for example via EEG neurofeedback. Recent studies revealed promising effects of a specific EEG frequency band training for reducing the number of binge-eating episodes in women with obesity [88]. From a research point of view, this study implicates the need for further EEG studies in childhood obesity using larger sample sizes for detecting small-to-medium-sized group differences and longitudinal designs to evaluate the stability of EEG profiles over time. In this context, future studies should consider using alternative measures of impulsivity to cover its multifaceted nature, for example, via the stop signal task [89], a measure of response inhibition. Finally, research is warranted to determine the presence of EEG subtypes in children with obesity in order to account for the expected neurophysiological heterogeneity similar to that in ADHD (e.g., Reference [90]).

Author Contributions: Conceptualization, R.S. and C.H.; methodology, R.S., C.H., M.G., and L.S.; formal analysis, L.S. and C.H.; investigation, C.S., C.K., C.H.; resources, M.G. and A.H.; writing—original draft preparation, R.S., C.H. and L.S.; writing—review and editing, all authors; supervision, M.G.; funding acquisition, R.S. and A.H.

Funding: This research was funded by the junior research grant of the Medical Faculty, University of Leipzig. R.S. and A.H. were funded by the Integrated Research and Treatment Center Adiposity Diseases by the German Federal Ministry of Education and Research (grant 01EO1501).

Acknowledgments: We are grateful to all children and their families for participating in the study and to Sabine Schäfer for her help in data visualization.

Conflicts of Interest: The authors declare no conflict of interest.

References

1. Carnell, S.; Gibson, C.; Benson, L.; Ochner, C.N.; Geliebter, A. Neuroimaging and obesity: Current knowledge and future directions. *Obes. Rev.* **2012**, *13*, 43–56. [CrossRef] [PubMed]
2. Makaronidis, J.M.; Batterham, R.L. Obesity, body weight regulation and the brain: Insights from fMRI. *Br. J. Radiol.* **2018**. [CrossRef] [PubMed]
3. Blume, M.; Schmidt, R.; Hilbert, A. Abnormalities in the EEG power spectrum in bulimia nervosa, binge-eating disorder, and obesity: A systematic review. *Eur. Eat. Disord. Rev.* **2018**. [CrossRef] [PubMed]
4. Tang, D.W.; Fellows, L.K.; Small, D.M.; Dagher, A. Food and drug cues activate similar brain regions: A meta-analysis of functional MRI studies. *Physiol. Behav.* **2012**, *106*, 317–324. [CrossRef] [PubMed]
5. Bruce, A.S.; Holsen, L.M.; Chambers, R.J.; Martin, L.E.; Brooks, W.M.; Zarcone, J.R.; Butler, M.G.; Savage, C.R. Obese children show hyperactivation to food pictures in brain networks linked to motivation, reward and cognitive control. *Int. J. Obes. (Lond.)* **2010**, *34*, 1494–1500. [CrossRef] [PubMed]
6. Pursey, K.M.; Stanwell, P.; Callister, R.J.; Brain, K.; Collins, C.E.; Burrows, T.L. Neuronal responses to visual food cues according to weight status: A systematic review of functional magnetic resonance imaging studies. *Front. Nutr.* **2014**, *1*, 7. [CrossRef] [PubMed]
7. Volkow, N.D.; Baler, R.D. Now vs. later brain circuits: Implications for obesity and addiction. *Trends Neurosci.* **2015**, *38*, 345–352. [CrossRef]
8. Aron, A.R.; Robbins, T.W.; Poldrack, R.A. Inhibition and the right inferior frontal cortex. *Trends Cogn. Sci.* **2004**, *8*, 170–177. [CrossRef]
9. Aron, A.R.; Robbins, T.W.; Poldrack, R.A. Inhibition and the right inferior frontal cortex: One decade on. *Trends Cogn. Sci.* **2014**, *18*, 177–185. [CrossRef]
10. Ridderinkhof, K.R.; van den Wildenberg, W.P.; Segalowitz, S.J.; Carter, C.S. Neurocognitive mechanisms of cognitive control: The role of prefrontal cortex on action selection, response inhibition, performance monitoring, and reward-based learning. *Brain Cogn.* **2004**, *56*, 129–140. [CrossRef]
11. Burger, K.S.; Berner, L.A. A functional neuroimaging review of obesity, appetitive hormones and ingestive behavior. *Physiol. Behav.* **2014**, *136*, 121–127. [CrossRef] [PubMed]
12. Moeller, F.G.; Barratt, E.S.; Dougherty, D.M.; Schmitz, J.M.; Swann, A.C. Psychiatric aspects of impulsivity. *Am. J. Psychiatry* **2001**, *158*, 1783–1793. [CrossRef] [PubMed]

13. Yang, Y.; Shields, G.S.; Guo, C.; Liu, Y. Executive function performance in obesity and overweight individuals: A meta-analysis and review. *Neurosci. Biobehav. Rev.* **2018**, *84*, 225–244. [CrossRef] [PubMed]
14. Graziano, P.A.; Kelleher, R.; Calkins, S.D.; Keane, S.P.; Brien, M.O. Predicting weight outcomes in preadolescence: The role of toddlers' self-regulation skills and the temperament dimension of pleasure. *Int. J. Obes.* **2013**, *37*, 937–942. [CrossRef] [PubMed]
15. Francis, L.A.; Susman, E.J. Self-regulation and rapid weight gain in children from age 3 to 12 years. *Arch. Pediatr. Adolesc. Med.* **2009**, *163*, 297–302. [CrossRef] [PubMed]
16. Nederkoorn, C.; Dassen, F.C.; Franken, L.; Resch, C.; Hauben, K. Impulsivity and overeating in children in the absence and presence of hunger. *Appetite* **2015**, *93*, 57–61. [CrossRef] [PubMed]
17. Van den Berg, L.; Pieterse, K.; Malik, J.A.; Luman, M.; Willems van Dijk, K.; Oosterlaan, J.; Delemarre-van de Waal, H.A. Association between impulsivity, reward responsiveness and body mass index in children. *Int. J. Obes.* **2011**, *35*, 1301–1307. [CrossRef]
18. Batterink, L.; Yokum, S.; Stice, E. Body mass correlates inversely with inhibitory control in response to food among adolescent girls: An fMRI study. *Neuroimage* **2010**, *52*, 1696–1703. [CrossRef]
19. Houben, K.; Nederkoorn, C.; Jansen, A. Eating on impulse: The relation between overweight and food-specific inhibitory control. *Obesity (Silver Spring)* **2014**, *22*, E6–E8. [CrossRef]
20. Nederkoorn, C.; Coelho, J.S.; Guerrieri, R.; Houben, K.; Jansen, A. Specificity of the failure to inhibit responses in overweight children. *Appetite* **2012**, *59*, 409–413. [CrossRef]
21. Braet, C.; Crombez, G. Cognitive interference due to food cues in childhood obesity. *J. Clin. Child Adolesc. Psychol.* **2003**, *32*, 32–39. [CrossRef] [PubMed]
22. Koch, A.; Matthias, E.; Pollatos, O. Increased attentional bias towards food pictures in overweight and obese children. *J. Child Adolesc. Behav.* **2014**, *2*, 130. [CrossRef]
23. Liang, J.; Matheson, B.E.; Kaye, W.H.; Boutelle, K.N. Neurocognitive correlates of obesity and obesity-related behaviors in children and adolescents. *Int. J. Obes. (Lond.)* **2014**, *38*, 494–506. [CrossRef] [PubMed]
24. Bechara, A.; Damasio, A.R.; Damasio, H.; Anderson, S.W. Insensitivity to future consequences following damage to human prefrontal cortex. *Cognition* **1994**, *50*, 7–15. [CrossRef]
25. Verbeken, S.; Braet, C.; Bosmans, G.; Goossens, L. Comparing decision making in average and overweight children and adolescents. *Int. J. Obes. (Lond.)* **2014**, *38*, 547–551. [CrossRef] [PubMed]
26. Verdejo-García, A.; Pérez-Expósito, M.; Schmidt-Río-Valle, J.; Fernández-Serrano, M.J.; Cruz, F.; Pérez-García, M.; López-Belmonte, G.; Martín-Matillas, M.; Martín-Lagos, J.A.; Marcos, A.; et al. Selective alterations within executive functions in adolescents with excess weight. *Obesity (Silver Spring)* **2010**, *18*, 1572–1578. [CrossRef] [PubMed]
27. Delgado-Rico, E.; Río-Valle, J.S.; González-Jiménez, E.; Campoy, C.; Verdejo-García, A. BMI predicts emotion-driven impulsivity and cognitive inflexibility in adolescents with excess weight. *Obesity* **2012**, *20*, 1604–1610. [CrossRef]
28. Goldschmidt, A.B.; O'Brien, S.; Lavender, J.M.; Pearson, C.M.; Le Grange, D.; Hunter, S.J. Executive functioning in a racially diverse sample of children who are overweight and at risk for eating disorders. *Appetite* **2018**, *124*, 43–49. [CrossRef]
29. Kittel, R.; Schmidt, R.; Hilbert, A. Executive functions in adolescents with binge-eating disorder and obesity. *Int. J. Eat. Disord.* **2017**, *50*, 933–941. [CrossRef]
30. Nederkoorn, C.; Braet, C.; Van Eijs, Y.; Tanghe, A.; Jansen, A. Why obese children cannot resist food: The role of impulsivity. *Eat. Behav.* **2006**, *7*, 315–322. [CrossRef]
31. Mata, F.; Verdejo-Roman, J.; Soriano-Mas, C.; Verdejo-Garcia, A. Insula tuning towards external eating versus interoceptive input in adolescents with overweight and obesity. *Appetite* **2015**, *93*, 24–30. [CrossRef] [PubMed]
32. Andreassi, J.L. *Psychophysiology: Human Behavior and Physiological Response*, 5th ed.; Taylor & Francis Inc.: New York, NY, USA, 2006.
33. Loo, S.K.; Lenartowicz, A.; Makeig, S. Use of EEG biomarkers in child psychiatry research: Current state and future directions. *J. Child Psychol. Psychiatry* **2016**, *57*, 4–17. [CrossRef] [PubMed]
34. Loo, S.K.; McGough, J.J.; McCracken, J.T.; Smalley, S.L. Parsing heterogeneity in attention-deficit hyperactivity disorder using EEG-based subgroups. *J. Child Psychol. Psychiatry* **2018**, *59*, 223–231. [CrossRef]

35. Massar, S.A.A.; Rossi, V.; Schutter, D.J.L.G.; Kenemans, J.L. Baseline EEG theta/beta ratio and punishment sensitivity as biomarkers for feedback-related negativity (FRN) and risk-taking. *Clin. Neurophysiol.* **2012**, *10*, 1958–1965. [CrossRef] [PubMed]
36. Massar, S.A.A.; Kenemans, J.L.; Schutter, D.J.L.G. Resting-state EEG theta activity and risk learning: Sensitivity to reward or punishment? *Int. J. Psychophysiol.* **2014**, *3*, 172–177. [CrossRef] [PubMed]
37. Schutter, D.J.L.G.; Van Honk, J. Electrophysiological ratio markers for the balance between reward and punishment. *Brain Res. Cogn. Brain Res.* **2005**, *24*, 685–690. [CrossRef] [PubMed]
38. Ogrim, G.; Kropotov, J.; Hestad, K. The quantitative EEG theta/beta ratio in attention deficit/hyperactivity disorder and normal controls: Sensitivity, specificity, and behavioral correlates. *Psychiatry Res.* **2012**, *198*, 482–488. [CrossRef]
39. Rudo-Hutt, A.S. Electroencephalography and externalizing behavior: A meta-analysis. *Biol. Psychol.* **2015**, *105*, 1–19. [CrossRef]
40. Cortese, S.; Moreira-Maia, C.R.; St Fleur, D.; Morcillo-Peñalver, C.; Rohde, L.A.; Faraone, S.V. Associations between ADHD and obesity: A systematic review and meta-analysis. *Am. J. Psychiatry* **2016**, *173*, 34–43. [CrossRef]
41. Van Dongen-Boomsma, M.; Lansbergen, M.M.; Bekker, E.M.; Kooij, J.J.; van der Molen, M.; Kenemans, J.L.; Buitelaar, J.K. Relation between resting EEG to cognitive performance and clinical symptoms in adults with attention-deficit/hyperactivity disorder. *Neurosci. Lett.* **2010**, *469*, 102–106. [CrossRef]
42. Lee, J.Y.; Park, S.M.; Kim, Y.J.; Kim, D.J.; Choi, S.W.; Kwon, J.S.; Choi, J.S. Resting-state EEG activity related to impulsivity in gambling disorder. *J. Behav. Addict.* **2017**, *6*, 387–395. [CrossRef] [PubMed]
43. Chen, S.; Jia, Y.; Woltering, S. Neural differences of inhibitory control between adolescents with obesity and their peers. *Int. J. Obes.* **2018**, *42*, 1753–1761. [CrossRef] [PubMed]
44. Hill, C.; Wu, J.; Crowley, M.J.; Fearon, P. Restrictive feeding practices and adiposity are differentially related to P3b cortical responses to food stimuli in children. *Appetite* **2013**, *63*, 7–17. [CrossRef] [PubMed]
45. Seymour, K.E.; Reinblatt, S.P.; Benson, L.; Carnell, S. Overlapping neurobehavioral circuits in ADHD, obesity, and binge eating: Evidence from neuroimaging research. *CNS Spectr.* **2015**, *20*, 401–411. [CrossRef] [PubMed]
46. Bauer, L.O.; Manning, K.J. Challenges in the detection of working memory and attention decrements among overweight adolescent girls. *Neuropsychobiology* **2016**, *73*, 43–51. [CrossRef] [PubMed]
47. Olde Dubbelink, K.T.E.; Felius, A.; Verbunt, J.P.A.; van Dijk, B.W.; Berendse, H.W.; Stam, C.J.; Delemarre-van de Waal, H. Increased resting-state functional connectivity in obese adolescents: A magnetoencephalographic pilot study. *PLoS ONE* **2008**, *3*, e2827. [CrossRef] [PubMed]
48. Babiloni, C.; Marzano, N.; Lizio, R.; Valenzano, A.; Triggiani, A.I.; Petito, A.; Bellomo, A.; Lecce, B.; Mundi, C.; Soricelli, A.; et al. Resting state cortical electroencephalographic rhythms in subjects with normal and abnormal body weight. *Neuroimage* **2011**, *58*, 698–707. [CrossRef] [PubMed]
49. Del Percio, C.; Triggiani, A.I.; Marzano, N.; Valenzano, A.; De Rosas, M.; Petito, A.; Bellomo, A.; Lecce, B.; Muni, C.; Infarinato, F.; et al. Poor desynchronisation of resting-state eyes-open cortical alpha rhythms in obese subjects without eating disorders. *Clin. Neurophysiol.* **2013**, *124*, 1095–1105. [CrossRef]
50. Satterfield, J.H.; Cantwell, D.P.; Satterfield, B.T. Pathophysiology of the hyperactive child syndrome. *Arch. Gen. Psychiatry* **1974**, *31*, 839–844. [CrossRef]
51. Kurth, B.M.; Schaffrath Rosario, A. Overweight and obesity in children and adolescents in Germany. *Bundesgesundheitsblatt Gesundheitsforschung Gesundheitsschutz* **2010**, *53*, 643–652. [CrossRef]
52. Lange, M.; Kamtsiuris, P.; Lange, C.; Schaffrath Rosario, A.; Stolzenberg, H.; Lampert, T. Sociodemographic characteristics in the German health interview and examination survey for children and adolescents (KiGGS)—Operationalization and public health significance, taking as an example the assessment of general state of health. *Bundesgesundheitsblatt Gesundheitsforschung Gesundheitsschutz* **2007**, *50*, 578–589. [CrossRef] [PubMed]
53. Bryant-Waugh, R.J.; Cooper, P.J.; Taylor, C.L.; Lask, B.D. The use of the eating disorder examination with children: A pilot study. *Int. J. Eat. Disord.* **1996**, *19*, 391–397. [CrossRef]
54. Hilbert, A. *Eating Disorder Examination für Kinder: Deutschsprachige Übersetzung [Eating Disorder Examination for Children: German translation]*; DGVT-Verlag: Tübingen, Germany, 2016; ISBN 978-3-87159-413-7.
55. Schneider, S.; Unnewehr, S.; Margraf, J. *Kinder-DIPS: Diagnostisches Interview bei Psychischen Störungen im Kindes- und Jugendalter [Diagnostic Interview for Mental Disorders in Childhood and Adolescence]*, 2nd ed.; Springer: Berlin, Germany, 2009; ISBN 978-3540782100.

56. Gratton, G.; Coles, M.G.; Donchin, E. A new method for off-line removal of ocular artifact. *Electroencephalogr. Clin. Neurophysiol.* **1983**, *55*, 468–484. [CrossRef]
57. Wiers, R.W.; Rinck, M.; Dictus, M.; van den Wildenberg, E. Relatively strong automatic appetitive action-tendencies in male carriers of the OPRM1 G-allele. *Genes Brain Behav.* **2009**, *8*, 101–106. [CrossRef] [PubMed]
58. Blechert, J.; Meule, A.; Busch, N.A.; Ohla, K. Food-pics: An image database for experimental research on eating and appetite. *Front. Psychol.* **2014**, *5*, 617. [CrossRef] [PubMed]
59. Lejuez, C.; Aklin, W.; Daughters, S.; Zvolensky, M.; Kahler, C.; Gwadz, M. Reliability and validity of the youth version of the Balloon Analogue Risk Task (BART-Y) in the assessment of risk-taking behavior among inner-city adolescents. *J. Clin. Child Adolesc. Psychol.* **2007**, *36*, 106–111. [CrossRef] [PubMed]
60. Wardle, J.; Guthrie, C.A.; Sanderson, S.; Rapoport, L. Development of the Children's Eating Behavior Questionnaire. *J. Child Psychol. Psychiatry* **2001**, *42*, 963–970. [CrossRef]
61. Klasen, H.; Woerner, W.; Rothenberger, A.; Goodman, R. The German version of the Strengths and Difficulties Questionnaire (SDQ-Deu)—Overview over first validation and normative studies. *Prax. Kinderpsychol. Kinderpsychiat.* **2003**, *52*, 491–502.
62. Stadler, C.; Janke, W.; Schmeck, K. *Inventar zur Erfassung von Impulsivität, Risikoverhalten und Empathie bei 9-bis 14-Jährigen Kindern [Inventory for Assessing Impulsivity, Risk Behavior, and Empathy]*; Hogrefe: Göttingen, Germany, 2004.
63. Eysenck, S.B.G.; Eysenck, H.J. Impulsiveness and venturesomeness in children. *Personal. Individ. Differ.* **1980**, *1*, 73–78. [CrossRef]
64. Wechsler, D. *The Wechsler Intelligence Scale for Children-Fourth Edition*; Pearson: London, UK, 2003.
65. Petermann, F.; Petermann, U. *Wechsler Intelligence Scale for Children—Fourth Edition (WISC-IV)*; Pearson: Frankfurt, Germany, 2011; ISBN 978-3-943274-00-4.
66. Cohen, J. *Statistical Power Analysis for the Behavioral Sciences*, 2nd ed.; Erlbaum: Hillsdale, NJ, USA, 1988; ISBN 9780805802832.
67. Clarke, A.R.; Barry, R.J.; McCarthy, R.; Selikowitz, M. Age and sex effects in the EEG: Development of the normal child. *Clin. Neurophysiol.* **2001**, *112*, 806–814. [CrossRef]
68. Clarke, A.R.; Barry, R.J.; McCarthy, R.; Selikowitz, M. EEG-defined subtypes of children with attention-deficit/hyperactivity disorder. *Clin. Neurophysiol.* **2001**, *112*, 2098–2105. [CrossRef]
69. Markovska-Simoska, S.; Pop-Jordanova, N. Quantitative EEG in children and adults with attention deficit hyperactivity disorder: Comparison of absolute and relative power spectra and theta/beta ratio. *Clin. EEG Neurosci.* **2017**, *48*, 20–32. [CrossRef] [PubMed]
70. Rommel, A.-S.; James, S.-N.; McLoughlin, G.; Brandeis, D.; Banaschewski, T.; Asherson, P.; Kuntsi, J. Altered EEG spectral power during rest and cognitive performance: A comparison of preterm-born adolescents to adolescents with ADHD. *Eur. Child Adolesc. Psychiatry* **2017**, *26*, 1511–1522. [CrossRef]
71. Hegerl, U.; Hensch, T. The vigilance reduction model of affective disorders and ADHD. *Neurosci. Biobehav. Rev.* **2014**, *44*, 45–57. [CrossRef]
72. Leddy, J.J.; Epstein, L.H.; Jaroni, J.L.; Roemmich, J.N.; Paluch, R.A.; Goldfield, G.S.; Lerman, C. Influence of methylphenidate on eating in obese men. *Obes. Res.* **2004**, *12*, 224–232. [CrossRef] [PubMed]
73. Knyazev, G.G. EEG delta oscillations as a correlate of basic homeostatic and motivational processes. *Neurosci. Biobehav. Rev.* **2012**, *36*, 677–695. [CrossRef] [PubMed]
74. Imperatori, C.; Fabbricatore, M.; Farina, M.; Innamorati, M.; Quintiliani, M.I.; Lamis, D.A.; Contardi, A.; Della Marca, G.; Speranza, A.M. Alterations of EEG functional connectivity in resting state obese and overweight patients with binge eating disorder: A preliminary report. *Neurosci. Lett.* **2015**, *607*, 120–124. [CrossRef]
75. Tammela, L.I.; Pääkkönen, A.; Karhunen, L.J.; Karhu, J.; Uusitupa, I.J.; Kuikka, J.T. Brain electrical activity during food presentation in obese binge-eating women. *Clin. Physiol. Funct. Imaging* **2010**, *30*, 135–140. [CrossRef]
76. Braet, C.; Beyers, W.; Goossens, L.; Verbeken, S.; Moens, E. Subtyping children and adolescents who are overweight based on eating pathology and psychopathology. *Eur. Eat. Disord. Rev.* **2012**, *20*, 279–286. [CrossRef]

77. Sysko, R.; Blake Zakarin, E.B.; Devlin, M.J.; Bush, J.; Walsh, B.T. A latent class analysis of psychiatric symptoms among 125 adolescents in a bariatric surgery program. *Int. J. Pediatr. Obes.* **2011**, *6*, 289–297. [CrossRef]
78. Sander, C.; Arns, M.; Olbrich, S.; Hegerl, U. EEG-vigilance and response to stimulants in paediatric patients with attention deficit/hyperactivity disorder. *Clin. Neurophysiol.* **2010**, *121*, 1511–1518. [CrossRef] [PubMed]
79. Arns, M.; Gunkelman, J.; Breteler, M.; Spronk, D. EEG phenotypes predict treatment outcome to stimulants in children with ADHD. *J. Integr. Neurosci.* **2008**, *7*, 421–438. [CrossRef] [PubMed]
80. Becker, D.; Jostmann, N.B.; Wiers, R.W.; Holland, R.W. Approach avoidance training in the eating domain: Testing the effectiveness across three single session studies. *Appetite* **2015**, *85*, 58–65. [CrossRef] [PubMed]
81. Paslakis, G.; Kühn, S.; Grunert, S.; Erim, Y. Explicit and implicit approach vs. avoidance tendencies towards high vs. low calorie food cues in patients with obesity and active binge eating disorder. *Nutrients* **2017**, *9*, 1068. [CrossRef] [PubMed]
82. Warschburger, P.; Gmeiner, M.; Morawietz, M.; Rinck, M. Battle of plates: A pilot study of an approch-avoidance training for overweight children and adolescents. *Public Health Nutr.* **2018**, *21*, 426–434. [CrossRef] [PubMed]
83. Brockmeyer, T.; Hahn, C.; Reetz, C.; Schmidt, U.; Friederich, H.-C. Approach bias and cue reactivity towards food in people with high versus low levels of food craving. *Appetite* **2015**, *95*, 197–202. [CrossRef]
84. Esposito, M.; Gallai, B.; Roccella, M.; Marotta, R.; Lavano, F.; Lavano, S.M.; Mazzotta, G.; Bove, D.; Sorrentino, M.; Precenzano, F.; et al. Anxiety and depression levels in prepubertal obese children: A case-control study. *Neuropsychiatr. Dis. Treat.* **2014**, *10*, 1897–1902. [CrossRef]
85. Webber, L.; Hill, C.; Saxton, J.; Van Jaarsveld, C.H.; Wardle, J. Eating behaviour and weight in children. *Int. J. Obes. (Lond.)* **2009**, *33*, 21–28. [CrossRef]
86. Barry, R.J.; Clarke, A.R.; Johnstone, S.J.; Magee, C.A.; Rushby, J.A. EEG differences between eyes-closed and eyes-open resting conditions. *Clin. Neurophysiol.* **2007**, *118*, 2765–2773. [CrossRef]
87. Barry, R.J.; Clarke, A.R.; Johnstone, S.J.; Brown, C.R. EEG differences in children between eyes-closed and eyes-open resting conditions. *Clin. Neurophysiol.* **2009**, 1806–1811. [CrossRef]
88. Schmidt, J.; Martin, A. Neurofeedback against binge eating: A randomized controlled trial in a female subclinical threshold sample. *Eur. Eat. Disord. Rev.* **2016**, *24*, 406–416. [CrossRef] [PubMed]
89. Logan, G.D.; Dagenbach, D.; Carr, T.H. On the ability to inhibit thought and action. A users' guide to the stop signal paradigm. In *Inhibitory Processes in Attention, Memory and Language*, 1st ed.; Dagenbach, D., Carr, T.H., Eds.; Academic Press: San Diego, CA, USA, 1994; pp. 189–236, ISBN 9780122004100.
90. Barth, B.; Mayer-Carius, K.; Strehl, U.; Kelava, A.; Häußinger, F.B.; Fallgatter, A.J.; Ehlis, A.C. Identification of neurophysiological biotypes in attention deficit hyperactivity disorder. *Psychiatry Clin. Neurosci.* **2018**, *72*, 836–848. [CrossRef] [PubMed]

nutrients

MDPI

Commentary

Shared Concerns and Opportunity for Joint Action in Creating a Food Environment That Supports Health

Kendrin R. Sonneville [1,*] and Rachel F. Rodgers [2]

1 Department of Nutritional Sciences, University of Michigan School of Public Health, Ann Arbor, MI 48109, USA

2 Department of Applied Psychology, Bouve College of Health Sciences, Northeastern University, Boston, MA 02115, USA; R.Rodgers@northeastern.edu

* Correspondence: kendrins@umich.edu; Tel.: +1-734-763-8789

Received: 15 November 2018; Accepted: 21 December 2018; Published: 25 December 2018

Abstract: The food industry is a for-profit industry with high relevance to universal eating disorders prevention. To date, policy which targets the food industry and food environment has been underutilized in efforts to decrease the incidence of eating disorders and associated risk factors. In contrast, food policy has been extensively leveraged with the aim of reducing the incidence of obesity. While philosophical misalignments with these later efforts may have constituted an obstacle to identifying the food environment as a key target for eating disorders prevention, food policy is an area where shared interests can be found. Specifically, a shared goal of obesity and eating disorders prevention efforts is creating a food environment that supports health, while minimizing the influence of the food industry that profits from the sale of highly palatable, processed foods and "diet" foods and from increasing portions of foods served and eaten.

Keywords: eating disorders; obesity; prevention; food industry; food environment; food policy

1. Introduction

Eating disorders are a significant public health issue and affect people of all backgrounds [1–4]. Approximately 5% of individuals in the U.S. will have an eating disorder at some point in their lives [2] and many more will struggle with sub-threshold symptoms [5–7], putting them at risk for substantial psychiatric comorbidities [8] and serious medical complications [9]. As evidence emerges for sociocultural drivers of eating disorder risk, recognition of the need to identify population-level approaches to eating disorders prevention has increased [10]. For-profit industries that benefit when people have an unhealthy relationship with food and their bodies (e.g., the diet, fashion, and beauty industries) have been implicated as important targets for macro-level intervention for eating disorders prevention [11,12]. The food industry, which includes food and beverage companies and quick-serve restaurants, is another such for-profit industry with high relevance to universal eating disorders prevention. To date, however, it has been neglected in efforts to decrease the incidence of eating disorders and associated risk factors [13]. In contrast, policy related to the food industry has been leveraged with the aim of reducing the incidence of obesity [14–16]. In this way, food policy is an area where shared interests can be found with the goal of creating a food environment that supports health. While food policy encompasses a heterogeneous set of policies involving many sectors that impact how food is produced, processed, distributed, marketed, purchased, and consumed [17], we will specifically focus on policy which targets practices of the food industry related to the processing, distribution, and marketing of foods. The aim here is to outline the rationale for leveraging food policy as an approach to eating disorders prevention. We will examine ways in which this lens would benefit ongoing efforts to regulate the food environment that largely aim to reduce individuals' intake and will reflect upon the challenges to finding common ground in working towards informing food policy.

2. The Relevance of the Food Industry to Universal Eating Disorders Prevention Efforts

Eating disorders are characterized by an intense preoccupation with weight and shape, engagement in behaviors that aim to alter weight and shape, and/or the experience of loss of control while eating. In particular, restrictive-type eating disorders include efforts to eat less often, consume smaller quantities, and choose foods that are lower in caloric density [18]. These efforts frequently result in strict food rules and certain foods being thought of as permitted, while others are forbidden. In addition, binge-type eating disorders are characterized by the consumption of large amounts of food in a short amount of time, with an accompanying experience of loss of control [19]. These episodes may be followed by compensatory behaviors, including self-induced vomiting, fasting, over-exercise, or the use or diuretics and laxatives in an effort to offset or eliminate the calories consumed. Individuals who experience binge-eating behaviors have reported experiencing strong cravings for certain foods that may precipitate the eating episode [20]. Furthermore, avoidance of certain foods (i.e., restriction) has been shown to increase the risk for binge-eating behaviors [21]. We will discuss how practices, including the processing, distribution, and marketing of foods, employed by the food industry may be related to eating disorder symptoms, such as preoccupation with weight and shape, dietary restriction, binge-eating behaviors, and cravings. These practices include the ways in which products are developed, ("engineering" of foods), packaged (serving size and portion), and marketed ("diet" foods and "health halo") (Figure 1). This suggests that it is important to consider the food environment as a context that could increase the risk for eating disorders.

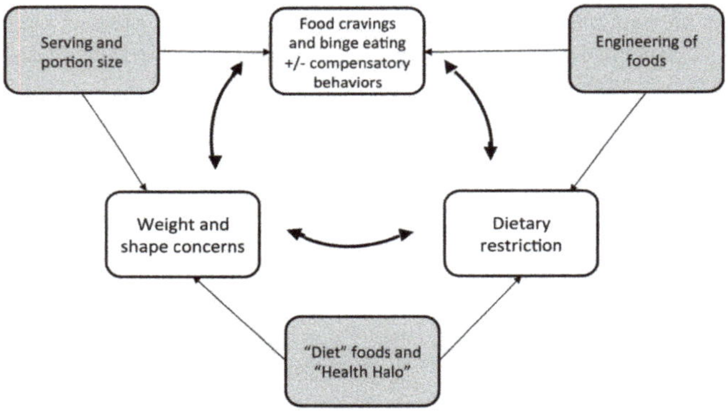

Figure 1. Food industry practices and eating disorder risk.

3. *"Engineering"* of Foods

In recent decades, the food industry has focused its resources on developing highly palatable, processed foods that are engineered to be as rewarding as possible to their target audience by combining levels of sugar, fat, and salt [22–24]. This has included research on the non-linear relationships between sweetness and the appeal of a food to identify the optimal sweetness for different foods. In particular, foods marketed specifically to children, such as children's breakfast foods, have been developed on the basis of their preference for markedly sweeter foods [25]. In addition, the food industry has paid increasing attention to developing foods that minimize satiety, such as liquids that possess a lower satiating capacity compared to solid foods [26]. The result of these practices is a range of foods that have been perfected in their capacity not only to appeal but also to fail to be satiating, so as to maximize consumption.

The engineering of foods in this manner is relevant to eating disorders prevention efforts in several ways and emerging data confirm the association between the consumption of these foods and eating disorder risk. Firstly, foods that are "engineered in ways that appear to surpass the rewarding properties of traditional foods" [24] may disturb the processes of appetite regulation. [27] Consistent with this, highly-processed foods, containing refined sugars and added fats, have been identified as being most associated with loss of control eating [28–30]. Furthermore, evidence from animal models of binge eating has supported the role of highly palatable, processed foods in triggering binge eating [31–34]. Relatedly, the capacity for these foods to disrupt the development of self-regulated eating processes in children has also been questioned. The role of reward in driving these eating behaviors has led researchers to draw parallels between the effects of these foods and those of addictive substances [35–37].

4. Serving and Portion Size

The contemporary Western food environment, through practices related to the presentation, packaging, and selling of food, has been linked to increasingly large serving and portion sizes of foods (e.g., [38,39]). Examples of these practices include normalizing large portion sizes through servings in restaurants, pricing scales designed to sell larger portions, displaying foods in stores in ways that increase purchasing, and selling foods in portions or packaging that exceed a typical serving size [40,41]. These practices could increase consumption [42–44] and thus potentiate profits, which may explain their perpetuation. Larger serving and portion sizes could also theoretically increase the risk for binge eating. Consistent with this, preliminary evidence supports the fact that the effects of large portion sizes on increased consumption are strongest among youth who experience loss of control eating or binge eating [45,46]. In addition, a food-rich environment, in conjunction with social appearance ideals of thinness/leanness and the stigmatization of larger bodies, may place some individuals under increased pressure to restrict their intake [47]. Thus, large serving and portion sizes may be associated with either binge-type eating pathology, or restriction, through different pathways and thus increase risk for eating disorders.

5. The Creation of "Diet" Foods and the "Health Halo"

The rising preoccupation with weight control and discourse identifying individual eating behaviors as determinants of health has been accompanied by the creation of numerous "diet" foods (e.g., reduced-calorie or "light" food products). These products have been developed to contain low-calorie artificial sweeteners in place of sugar, reduced levels of fat, or other reformulations of nutrients. For example, the food industry profited from dietary guidelines that emphasized reducing total fat in the diet by creating numerous low-fat, high-carbohydrate, high-sugar products [48,49]. In addition, the food industry has been described as manipulating perceptions of the health benefits of their products through the use of various claims about foods [50]. Importantly, while these claims may assist individuals in their food choices, they may also be misleading [51].

The increasing availability and marketing of "diet" foods may be relevant to eating disorders through a number of pathways. These products may be marketed as assisting in weight control and therefore attractive to individuals with weight concerns. Meta-analytic findings have confirmed that health-related claims on foods have a substantial effect on food choices and increased purchasing [50,52], which may particularly affect those with weight and shape concerns. However, consumption of "diet" or "health" products is unlikely to alleviate weight and shape concerns, or be helpful in terms of establishing eating patterns that are regulated by internal cues. Instead, consuming artificially-sweetened beverages rather than sugar-sweetened ones has been shown to be associated with increased levels of restrained and emotional eating [53,54]. Furthermore, consuming these products may increase cravings and loss of control eating through the process of cognitive restraint [55]. In addition, "diet' and "health" foods might substitute consumption of less processed foods, that are more helpful to appetite regulation [28]. Finally, at the macro-level, the proliferation of such foods and their intense marketing serves to increase weight-related pressures and contributes to the sociocultural discourse that promotes disordered eating [56]. In summary, the food environment may increase risk for eating disorders via multiple pathways and is therefore an important target for universal prevention efforts, particularly through policy and regulation.

6. Food Policy for the Prevention of Obesity

Efforts to leverage policy for the prevention of obesity are widespread and largely aim to reduce individuals' overall intake. Public policy strategies related to obesity prevention in the U.S. and abroad have focused on a wide range of environments, including those related to child care, health care, and schools, [14] and are designed to increase the availability, affordability, and acceptability of healthy food and beverage choices in various settings (e.g., schools, workplace, community), while decreasing the availability of less healthy options in these settings [15]. While many of these policy efforts could have relevance to eating disorders and their prevention, these potential intersections have been underexplored.

Policy efforts aimed at limiting portion sizes are an example of a food policy for obesity prevention that also has relevance for eating disorders prevention. Based on the body of research linking portion size to greater consumption [57], a number of initiatives have been undertaken, ranging from voluntary pledges to regulations [58]. In the U.S., the Food and Drug Administration (USDA) already requires a statement regarding portion sizes on the labels of foods. Furthermore, the USDA is currently in the process of implementing changes to the description of portion sizes to better reflect the amount generally consumed in the nutritional information included on the labels. These changes intend to ensure that food package labels provide a more easily interpretable estimation of the energy and nutrition provided by foods. However, because portion size signals a norm about what should be consumed, these changes could ultimately influence food consumption [43,59,60]. How such practices and the resultant policies affect eating disorders and associated risk factors warrants further investigation.

An additional example within the U.S. is regulation that requires calorie labeling in restaurants in an effort to guide consumers towards lower-calorie options [61]. While such policies are viewed positively for increasing food industry transparency, the impact of such policies on calorie consumption has been limited [62–64]. Moreover, a number of concerns have been expressed regarding the ways in which such labeling might impact individuals with eating concerns, who experience high levels of preoccupation around calorie content. Indeed, recent data suggest that individuals with disordered eating behaviors [65] and those with eating disorders [66] may be particularly vulnerable to unintended negative effects of calorie labels on menus. Given the limited efficacy of these policies and their potential for unintended negative effects, greater involvement from those with expertise in eating disorders prevention during the development of such policies is warranted.

A final example of a food policy related to obesity prevention involves the levying of sugar-taxes and the regulation of serving sizes, particularly in the context of sugar-sweetened beverages [67]. It has been suggested that the increase of sugar-related taxes would have a significant positive public health impact, as well as a number of economic benefits [68]. Similarly, unsuccessful efforts made by the New York City Board of Health to regulate the size of sugar-sweetened beverages sold in that state were considered to have a strong potential for positive impact on public health [69]. However, concern regarding other unintended harmful effects, such as increases in alcohol consumption and the disproportionate impact on low-income groups, have been voiced [70]. Furthermore, in the context of eating disorders, such policies may contribute to maintaining the focus on weight as opposed to health and thus perpetuate appearance-related pressures [56]. Thus, again, the inclusion of eating disorders prevention perspectives in the development of such policies is critical.

Broadly, efforts to regulate the food environment that have aimed to prevent obesity have targeted aspects of the food environment that are of relevance to the prevention of eating disorders, namely, the lack of transparency of the industry with regard to the nutritional content of foods, as well as the selling and marketing practices that aim to increase profit. As described above, these practices are those through which the food environment may increase risk for eating disorders. Therefore, policies that are capable of altering these practices could serve eating disorders prevention efforts.

7. Challenges to Integrating Eating Disorders and Obesity Prevention Policy

Common to obesity prevention and eating disorders prevention efforts is the desire to improve public health and reduce factors that drive disparities in health. As such, a shared goal of these prevention efforts would include access to a food environment that promotes health, while minimizing the influence of the food industry that profits from the sale of highly palatable, processed foods and "diet" foods, and from increasing portions sizes. Several challenges to targeting the food industry exist that relate to philosophical misalignments between the perspectives of eating disorders and obesity prevention efforts, however.

The first challenge relates to the extent to which weight is a primary indicator of health and as the primary rationale for changing food policy. Obesity prevention efforts are designed to reduce the prevalence of obesity using a definition based on body mass index (BMI). Using this framing to justify policy changes implies that weight gain is inherently unhealthy and crudely categorizes smaller bodies as "healthy" and larger bodies and "unhealthy" or "diseased." Weight stigma scholars and fat advocates generally reject the term obesity for this reason—that it pathologizes fat bodies, ignores natural size diversity, and, by relying solely on BMI, fails to measure health more holistically [71,72]. Within eating disorders prevention, experts generally reject the idea that weight gain is unhealthy (indeed, weight gain is a necessary and healthy part of recovery for many people with eating disorders, irrespective of weight), yet the erratic and disordered eating habits and/or binge eating behavior that may be associated with weight gain should be considered problematic. To the extent that the food industry contributes to and profits from this type of eating, eating disorders prevention must target their practices, while also advocating for weight-neutral approaches and advocating against weight bias.

A second challenge relates to the types of policy changes that are proposed. Many obesity prevention policy efforts focus on specific foods (e.g., sugar sweetened beverages, fast food, etc.). This approach is seemingly incompatible with evidence-based eating disorders frameworks based on moderation and trusting one's own internal cues of hunger, taste, and fullness (e.g., Health at Every Size®, intuitive eating, mindful eating, etc.) [73–75]. Many individuals with eating disorders assign "good" or "bad" labels to foods or have "forbidden foods" that they avoid eating out of fear or guilt. Learning to eat these in moderation has been shown to be a key element of successful treatment [76]. As such, eating disorders prevention messaging often adopts a "no good/bad foods" mantra. This perspective represents a substantial barrier to joining efforts to limit access to or penalize certain foods. Importantly, the food environment has changed considerably in the last few decades. Accordingly, a more nuanced perspective on food quality may better reflect the current reality of the food environment, and may need to be incorporated into approaches for the prevention of eating disorders. Individuals who are at risk for developing eating disorders may be particularly vulnerable to the presence in the food environment of foods that are designed to appeal to hedonic drives and override homeostatic drives. As such, the prevention of eating disorders includes the criticism of tactics used by the food industry that may capitalize on this vulnerability.

Philosophical differences and key concerns with messaging underlying obesity prevention policies do present an obstacle to integrating eating disorders prevention perspectives into existing efforts that target the food industry. These differences have contributed to the absence of efforts to leverage food policy as a means of the universal prevention of eating disorders. By steering clear of these efforts, however, the considerations that are unique and critical to efforts to prevent eating disorders are left out of the larger conversation related to the regulation of the food environment. Thus, the food industry benefits from minimal oversight related to their contribution to eating disorder risk.

8. Conclusions

The food industry is a key player in the creation of a food environment, characterized by the over-abundance and aggressive marketing of engineered foods that may increase risk for eating disorders or negatively impact their remission. Developing and implementing effective policy approaches to limit the food industry's capacity to continue shaping the food environment in this way is emerging as a critical goal for universal prevention efforts. However, the capacity for these efforts to pathologize larger bodies or vilify specific foods has constituted an obstacle to considering how the broader goal of obesity prevention efforts (i.e., creating a food environment that supports health) may also serve eating disorders prevention. An unintended consequence of this position may be the proliferation of food industry practices that might increase eating disorder risk. Meanwhile, those who are highly susceptible to the presence of these foods or food industry practices may suffer. Eating disorders experts have a crucial part to play in informing policies targeting the food industry to ensure that such policies do no harm. Furthermore, policy efforts targeting the food industry should be considered as a means of improving universal prevention and decreasing an important environmental risk for eating disorders.

Author Contributions: K.R.S. and R.F.R. conceived of the presented idea and contributed to the writing of the manuscript.

Funding: This research received no external funding.

Financial Disclosure: The authors have no financial relationships relevant to this article to disclose.

Conflicts of Interest: The authors declare no conflict of interest.

References

1. Swanson, S.A.; Crow, S.J.; Le Grange, D.; Swendsen, J.; Merikangas, K.R. Prevalence and correlates of eating disorders in adolescents: Results from the national comorbidity survey replication adolescent supplement. *Arch. Gen. Psychiatry* **2011**, *68*, 714–723. [CrossRef] [PubMed]
2. Hudson, J.I.; Hiripi, E.; Pope, H.G., Jr.; Kessler, R.C. The prevalence and correlates of eating disorders in the national comorbidity survey replication. *Biol. Psychiatry* **2007**, *61*, 348–358. [CrossRef]
3. Lipson, S.K.; Sonneville, K.R. Eating disorder symptoms among undergraduate and graduate students at 12 U.S. Colleges and universities. *Eat. Behav.* **2017**, *24*, 81–88. [CrossRef] [PubMed]
4. Sonneville, K.R.; Lipson, S.K. Disparities in eating disorder diagnosis and treatment according to weight status, race/ethnicity, socioeconomic background, and sex among college students. *Int. J. Eat. Disord.* **2018**, *51*, 518–526. [CrossRef] [PubMed]
5. Field, A.E.; Sonneville, K.R.; Micali, N.; Crosby, R.D.; Swanson, S.A.; Laird, N.M.; Treasure, J.; Solmi, F.; Horton, N.J. Prospective association of common eating disorders and adverse outcomes. *Pediatrics* **2012**, *130*, e289–e295. [CrossRef] [PubMed]
6. Field, A.E.; Sonneville, K.R.; Crosby, R.D.; Swanson, S.A.; Eddy, K.T.; Camargo, C.A.; Horton, N.J.; Micali, N. Prospective associations of concerns about physique and the development of obesity, binge drinking, and drug use among adolescent boys and young adult men. *JAMA Pediatrics* **2014**, *168*, 34–39. [CrossRef] [PubMed]
7. Haines, J.; Hannan, P.J.; van den Berg, P.; Eisenberg, M.E.; Neumark-Sztainer, D. Weight-related teasing from adolescence to young adulthood: Longitudinal and secular trends between 1999 and 2010. *Obesity* **2013**, *21*, E428–E434. [CrossRef] [PubMed]
8. Chamay-Weber, C.; Narring, F.; Michaud, P.-A. Partial eating disorders among adolescents: A review. *J. Adolesc. Health* **2005**, *37*, 416–426. [CrossRef]
9. Rosen, D. Identification and management of eating disorders in children and adolescents. *Pediatrics* **2010**, *126*, 1240–1253. [CrossRef]
10. Austin, S.B. A public health approach to eating disorders prevention: It's time for public health professionals to take a seat at the table. *BMC Public Health* **2012**, *12*. [CrossRef]
11. Bell, M.J.; Rodgers, R.F.; Paxton, S.J. Towards successful evidence-based universal eating disorders prevention: The importance of zooming out. *Eat. Behav.* **2017**, *25*, 89–92. [CrossRef]

12. Austin, S.B. Accelerating progress in eating disorders prevention: A call for policy translation research and training. *Eat. Disord.* **2016**, *24*, 6–19. [CrossRef] [PubMed]
13. Rodgers, R.; Sonneville, K. Research for leveraging food policy in universal eating disorder prevention. *Int. J. Eat. Disord.* **2018**, *51*, 503–506. [CrossRef] [PubMed]
14. Chriqui, J.F. Obesity prevention policies in u.S. States and localities: Lessons from the field. *Curr. Obes. Rep.* **2013**, *2*, 200–210. [CrossRef]
15. Zhang, Q.; Liu, S.; Liu, R.; Xue, H.; Wang, Y. Food policy approaches to obesity prevention: An international perspective. *Curr. Obes. Rep.* **2014**, *3*, 171–182. [CrossRef] [PubMed]
16. Hawkes, C.; Smith, T.G.; Jewell, J.; Wardle, J.; Hammond, R.A.; Friel, S.; Thow, A.M.; Kain, J. Smart food policies for obesity prevention. *Lancet* **2015**, *385*, 2410–2421. [CrossRef]
17. Duncan, J.; Lambek, N. *Why We Need to Talk about Food Policy*; Committee on World Food Security: Rome, Italy, 2016.
18. Williamson, D.A.; White, M.A.; York-Crowe, E.; Stewart, T.M. Cognitive-behavioral theories of eating disorders. *Behav. Modif.* **2004**, *28*, 711–738. [CrossRef]
19. Corwin, R.L.; Buda-Levin, A. Behavioral models of binge-type eating. *Physiol. Behav.* **2004**, *82*, 123–130. [CrossRef]
20. Ng, L.; Davis, C. Cravings and food consumption in binge eating disorder. *Eat. Behav.* **2013**, *14*, 472–475. [CrossRef]
21. Stice, E.; Agras, W.S.; Telch, C.F.; Halmi, K.A.; Mitchell, J.E.; Wilson, T. Subtyping binge eating-disordered women along dieting and negative affect dimensions. *Int. J. Eat. Disord.* **2001**, *30*, 11–27. [CrossRef]
22. Martínez Steele, E.; Raubenheimer, D.; Simpson, S.J.; Baraldi, L.G.; Monteiro, C.A. Ultra-processed foods, protein leverage and energy intake in the USA. *Public Health Nutr.* **2017**, *21*, 114–124. [CrossRef] [PubMed]
23. Gearhardt, A.N.; Davis, C.; Kuschner, R.; Brownell, K.D. The addiction potential of hyperpalatable foods. *Curr. Drug Abus. Rev.* **2011**, *4*, 140–145. [CrossRef] [PubMed]
24. Gearhardt, A.N.; Grilo, C.M.; DiLeone, R.J.; Brownell, K.D.; Potenza, M.N. Can food be addictive? Public health and policy implications. *Addiction* **2011**, *106*, 1208–1212. [CrossRef] [PubMed]
25. Moskowitz, H.R. Relative importance of perceptual factors to consumer acceptance: Linear vs quadratic analysis. *J. Food Sci.* **1981**, *46*, 244–248. [CrossRef]
26. De Graaf, C.; Kok, F.J. Slow food, fast food and the control of food intake. *Nat. Rev. Endocrinol.* **2010**, *6*, 290–293. [CrossRef] [PubMed]
27. Erlanson-Albertsson, C. How palatable food disrupts appetite regulation. *Basic Clin. Pharmacol. Toxicol.* **2005**, *97*, 61–73. [CrossRef] [PubMed]
28. Schulte, E.M.; Avena, N.M.; Gearhardt, A.N. Which foods may be addictive? The roles of processing, fat content, and glycemic load. *PLoS ONE* **2015**, *10*, e0117959. [CrossRef]
29. Yanovski, S.Z.; Leet, M.; Yanovski, J.A.; Flood, M.; Gold, P.W.; Kissileff, H.R.; Walsh, B.T. Food selection and intake of obese women with binge-eating disorder. *Am. J. Clin. Nutr.* **1992**, *56*, 975–980. [CrossRef]
30. Rosen, J.C.; Leitenberg, H.; Fisher, C.; Khazam, C. Binge-eating episodes in bulimia nervosa: The amount and type of food consumed. *Int. J. Eat. Disord.* **1986**, *5*, 255–267. [CrossRef]
31. Hagan, M.M.; Chandler, P.C.; Wauford, P.K.; Rybak, R.J.; Oswald, K.D. The role of palatable food and hunger as trigger factors in an animal model of stress induced binge eating. *Int. J. Eat. Disord.* **2003**, *34*, 183–197. [CrossRef]
32. Boggiano, M.M.; Artiga, A.I.; Pritchett, C.E.; Chandler-Laney, P.C.; Smith, M.L.; Eldridge, A.J. High intake of palatable food predicts binge-eating independent of susceptibility to obesity: An animal model of lean vs obese binge-eating and obesity with and without binge-eating. *Int. J. Obes.* **2007**, *31*, 1357–1367. [CrossRef] [PubMed]
33. Corwin, R.L.; Avena, N.M.; Boggiano, M.M. Feeding and reward: Perspectives from three rat models of binge eating. *Physiol. Behav.* **2011**, *104*, 87–97. [CrossRef] [PubMed]
34. Oswald, K.D.; Murdaugh, D.L.; King, V.L.; Boggiano, M.M. Motivation for palatable food despite consequences in an animal model of binge eating. *Int. J. Eat. Disord.* **2011**, *44*, 203–211. [CrossRef] [PubMed]
35. Gearhardt, A.N.; Corbin, W.R.; Brownell, K.D. Food addiction: An examination of the diagnostic criteria for dependence. *J. Addict. Med.* **2009**, *3*, 1–7. [CrossRef] [PubMed]
36. Schulte, E.M.; Joyner, M.A.; Schiestl, E.T.; Gearhardt, A.N. Future directions in "food addiction": Next steps and treatment implications. *Curr. Addict. Rep.* **2017**, *4*, 165–171. [CrossRef]

37. Ahmed, S.H.; Guillem, K.; Vandaele, Y. Sugar addiction: Pushing the drug-sugar analogy to the limit. *Curr. Opin. Clin. Nutr. Metab. Care* **2013**, *16*, 434–439. [CrossRef] [PubMed]
38. Hill, J.O.; Peters, J.C. Environmental contributions to the obesity epidemic. *Science* **1998**, *280*, 1371–1374. [CrossRef]
39. Economos, C.D.; Hatfield, D.P.; King, A.C.; Ayala, G.X.; Pentz, M.A. Food and physical activity environments: An energy balance approach for research and practice. *Am. J. Prev. Med.* **2015**, *48*, 620–629. [CrossRef]
40. Benton, D. Portion size: What we know and what we need to know. *Crit. Rev. Food Sci. Nutr.* **2015**, *55*, 988–1004. [CrossRef]
41. Nestle, M. Increasing portion sizes in american diets: More calories, more obesity. *J. Am. Diet. Assoc.* **2003**, *103*, 39–40. [CrossRef]
42. Birch, L.L.; Savage, J.S.; Fisher, J.O. Right sizing prevention. Food portion size effects on children's eating and weight. *Appetite* **2015**, *88*, 11–16. [CrossRef] [PubMed]
43. Herman, C.P.; Polivy, J.; Pliner, P.; Vartanian, L.R. Mechanisms underlying the portion-size effect. *Physiol. Behav.* **2015**, *144*, 129–136. [CrossRef] [PubMed]
44. Steenhuis, I.; Poelman, M. Portion size: Latest developments and interventions. *Curr. Obes. Rep.* **2017**, *6*, 10–17. [CrossRef] [PubMed]
45. English, L.; Lasschuijt, M.; Keller, K.L. Mechanisms of the portion size effect. What is known and where do we go from here? *Appetite* **2015**, *88*, 39–49. [CrossRef] [PubMed]
46. Mirch, M.C.; McDuffie, J.R.; Yanovski, S.Z.; Schollnberger, M.; Tanofsky-Kraff, M.; Theim, K.R.; Krakoff, J.; Yanovski, J.A. Effects of binge eating on satiation, satiety, and energy intake of overweight children. *Am. J. Clin. Nutr.* **2006**, *84*, 732–738. [CrossRef] [PubMed]
47. Harriger, J.A.; Thompson, J.K. Psychological consequences of obesity: Weight bias and body image in overweight and obese youth. *Int. Rev. Psychiatry* **2012**, *24*, 247–253. [CrossRef] [PubMed]
48. La Berge, A.F. How the ideology of low fat conquered america. *J. Hist. Med. Allied Sci.* **2008**, *63*, 139–177. [CrossRef] [PubMed]
49. Willett, W. *Eat, Drink, and be Healthy: The Harvard Medical School Guide to Healthy Eating*; Simon and Schuster: New York, NY, USA, 2001.
50. Chandon, P.; Wansink, B. The biasing health halos of fast-food restaurant health claims: Lower calorie estimates and higher side-dish consumption intentions. *J. Consum. Res.* **2007**, *34*, 301–314. [CrossRef]
51. Mariotti, F.; Kalonji, E.; Huneau, J.F.; Margaritis, I. Potential pitfalls of health claims from a public health nutrition perspective. *Nutr. Rev.* **2010**, *68*, 624–638. [CrossRef]
52. Kaur, A.; Scarborough, P.; Rayner, M. A systematic review, and meta-analyses, of the impact of health-related claims on dietary choices. *Int. J. Behav. Nutr. Phys. Act.* **2017**, *14*, 93. [CrossRef]
53. Elfhag, K.; Tynelius, P.; Rasmussen, F. Sugar-sweetened and artificially sweetened soft drinks in association to restrained, external and emotional eating. *Physiol. Behav.* **2007**, *91*, 191–195. [CrossRef]
54. Lavin, J.; French, S.; Read, N. The effect of sucrose-and aspartame-sweetened drinks on energy intake, hunger and food choice of female, moderately restrained eaters. *Int. J. Obes.* **1997**, *21*, 37–42. [CrossRef]
55. Yang, Q. Gain weight by "going diet?" artificial sweeteners and the neurobiology of sugar cravings: Neuroscience 2010. *Yale J. Biol. Med.* **2010**, *83*, 101–108. [PubMed]
56. Rodgers, R.F. The role of the "healthy weight" discourse in body image and eating concerns: An extension of sociocultural theory. *Eat. Behav.* **2016**, *22*, 194–198. [CrossRef] [PubMed]
57. Vermeer, W.M.; Steenhuis, I.H.M.; Poelman, M.P. Small, medium, large or supersize? The development and evaluation of interventions targeted at portion size. *Int. J. Obes.* **2014**, *38*, S13–S18. [CrossRef] [PubMed]
58. Crino, M.; Sacks, G.; Wu, J.H. A review of population-level actions targeting reductions in food portion sizes to address obesity and related non-communicable diseases. *Curr. Nutr. Rep.* **2016**, *5*, 323–332. [CrossRef]
59. Kerameas, K.; Vartanian, L.R.; Herman, C.P.; Polivy, J. The effect of portion size and unit size on food intake: Unit bias or segmentation effect? *Health Psychol.* **2015**, *34*, 670–676. [CrossRef]
60. Marchiori, D.; Papies, E.K.; Klein, O. The portion size effect on food intake. An anchoring and adjustment process? *Appetite* **2014**, *81*, 108–115. [CrossRef]
61. Burton, S.; Kees, J. Flies in the ointment? Addressing potential impediments to population-based health benefits of restaurant menu labeling initiatives. *J. Public Policy Mark.* **2012**, *31*, 232–239. [CrossRef]
62. Swartz, J.J.; Braxton, D.; Viera, A.J. Calorie menu labeling on quick-service restaurant menus: An updated systematic review of the literature. *Int. J. Behav. Nutr. Phys. Act.* **2011**, *8*, 135. [CrossRef]

63. Sinclair, S.E.; Cooper, M.; Mansfield, E.D. The influence of menu labeling on calories selected or consumed: A systematic review and meta-analysis. *J. Acad. Nutr. Diet.* **2014**, *114*, 1375–1388. [CrossRef] [PubMed]
64. Long, M.W.; Tobias, D.K.; Cradock, A.L.; Batchelder, H.; Gortmaker, S.L. Systematic review and meta-analysis of the impact of restaurant menu calorie labeling. *Am. J. Public Health* **2015**, *105*, e11–e24. [CrossRef] [PubMed]
65. Larson, N.; Haynos, A.F.; Roberto, C.A.; Loth, K.A.; Neumark-Sztainer, D. Calorie labels on the restaurant menu: Is the use of weight-control behaviors related to ordering decisions? *J. Acad. Nutr. Diet.* **2018**, *118*, 399–408. [CrossRef] [PubMed]
66. Haynos, A.F.; Roberto, C.A. The effects of restaurant menu calorie labeling on hypothetical meal choices of females with disordered eating. *Int. J. Eat. Disord.* **2017**, *50*, 275–283. [CrossRef] [PubMed]
67. Brownell, K.D.; Frieden, T.R. Ounces of prevention—The public policy case for taxes on sugared beverages. *N. Engl. J. Med.* **2009**, *360*, 1805–1808. [CrossRef] [PubMed]
68. Andreyeva, T.; Chaloupka, F.J.; Brownell, K.D. Estimating the potential of taxes on sugar-sweetened beverages to reduce consumption and generate revenue. *Prev. Med.* **2011**, *52*, 413–416. [CrossRef] [PubMed]
69. Pomeranz, J.L.; Brownell, K.D. Can government regulate portion sizes? *N. Engl. J. Med.* **2014**, *371*, 1956–1958. [CrossRef] [PubMed]
70. Brown, A.W.; Allison, D.B. Unintended consequences of obesity-targeted health policy. *Virtual Mentor* **2013**, *15*, 339–346.
71. Tylka, T.L.; Annunziato, R.A.; Burgard, D.; Danielsdottir, S.; Shuman, E.; Davis, C.; Calogero, R.M. The weight-inclusive versus weight-normative approach to health: Evaluating the evidence for prioritizing well-being over weight loss. *J. Obes.* **2014**, *2014*, 983495. [CrossRef]
72. Meadows, A.; Daníelsdóttir, S. What's in a word? On weight stigma and terminology. *Front. Psychol.* **2016**, *7*. [CrossRef]
73. Tylka, T.L.; Kroon Van Diest, A.M. The intuitive eating scale–2: Item refinement and psychometric evaluation with college women and men. *J. Couns. Psychol.* **2013**, *60*, 137–153. [CrossRef] [PubMed]
74. Tylka, T.L.; Calogero, R.M.; Daníelsdóttir, S. Is intuitive eating the same as flexible dietary control? Their links to each other and well-being could provide an answer. *Appetite* **2015**, *95*, 166–175. [CrossRef]
75. Hepworth, N.S. A mindful eating group as an adjunct to individual treatment for eating disorders: A pilot study. *Eat. Disord.* **2010**, *19*, 6–16. [CrossRef] [PubMed]
76. Coelho, J.S.; Wilson, S.; Winslade, A.; Thaler, L.; Israel, M.; Steiger, H. Over-evaluation of thoughts about food: Differences across eating-disorder subtypes and a preliminary examination of treatment effects. *Int. J. Eat. Disord.* **2014**, *47*, 302–309. [CrossRef]

nutrients

MDPI

Article

Executive Functioning in Obesity, Food Addiction, and Binge-Eating Disorder

Marie Blume *, Ricarda Schmidt and Anja Hilbert

Integrated Research and Treatment Center Adiposity Diseases, Departments of Medical Psychology and Medical Sociology and Psychosomatic Medicine and Psychotherapy, University of Leipzig Medical Center, 04103 Leipzig, Germany; ricarda.schmidt@medizin.uni-leipzig.de (R.S.); anja.hilbert@medizin.uni-leipzig.de (A.H.)

* Correspondence: marie.blume@medizin.uni-leipzig.de; Tel.: +49-341-9715380

Received: 14 November 2018; Accepted: 21 December 2018; Published: 28 December 2018

Abstract: This study aimed to investigate food addiction (FA) and binge-eating disorder (BED) in their association to executive dysfunctions in adults with obesity. Data on response inhibition, attention, decision-making, and impulsivity were derived from four groups of adults with obesity: obesity and FA (n = 23), obesity and BED (n = 19), obesity and FA plus BED (FA/BED, n = 23), and a body mass index-, age-, and sex-stratified control group of otherwise healthy individuals with obesity (n = 23, OB), using established computerized neuropsychological tasks. Overall, there were few group differences in neuropsychological profiles. Individuals of the FA group did not differ from the OB group regarding executive functioning. Individuals with BED presented with significantly higher variability in their reaction times and a deficient processing of feedback for performance improvement compared to individuals of the OB group. Strikingly, individuals with FA/BED did not present neuropsychological impairments, but higher levels of depression than all other groups. The results indicated the presence of a BED-specific neuropsychological profile in the obesity spectrum. The additional trait FA was not related to altered executive functioning compared to the OB or BED groups. Future research is needed to discriminate FA and BED further using food-specific tasks.

Keywords: executive function; obesity; binge-eating disorder; food addiction; addictive-like eating

1. Introduction

Obesity, defined as an excessive accumulation of body fat (body mass index (BMI) $\geq$ 30.0 kg/m ^{2}) [1], presents one of the most prevalent health conditions in the Western world [2]. During the last decade, research on the causal and maintaining factors of obesity has focused on executive functioning and neural characteristics [3–5]. Executive functions represent a range of higher cognitive capacities enabling goal-directed behavior including inhibition, cognitive flexibility, planning, or decision-making [6,7]. Importantly, impairments in general executive functions in individuals with obesity, for example, reduced inhibition and planning, were linked to unsuccessful weight-loss related behavior, such as poor dietary quality and less success in weight loss therapies [8,9]. In order to provide targeted treatment options for executive dysfunctions, the specification of neuropsychological profiles in the obesity spectrum is warranted [10].

In this context, a recent review showed substantial similarities between executive functions in obesity and substance use disorder, including increased impulsive decision-making and an attentional bias towards disorder-related stimuli in both conditions [11]. In addition to these neuropsychological abnormalities, several neuroimaging studies documented a considerable overlap between obesity and substance use disorder regarding functional alterations in frontal brain regions and meso-corticolimbic circuits, which are involved in reward processing and decision-making [11–13].

Recent research hypothesized that certain foods, especially high-fat and high-sugar foods, elicit addictive-like behavioral responses in vulnerable individuals characterized by high impulsivity and reward sensitivity through the activation of reward-related brain circuits [12,14–16]. This so-called food addiction (FA) hypothesis has been controversially discussed [15,17–20], since certain aspects of substance use symptomatology, including symptoms of withdrawal or tolerance, have not been demonstrated regarding food [21]. FA is mainly operationalized as a trait based on a self-report questionnaire to assess food-related addictive behavior, the *Yale Food Addiction Scale 2.0* (YFAS 2.0) [22]. Although FA was found in individuals across the weight range, it was often described in the context of obesity, with highly varying prevalence of 6.7–56.8% in samples of treatment-seeking individuals who were overweight or obese [14]. Two recent studies specifically investigated alterations in executive functioning in individuals with obesity and trait FA, showing that higher versus lower FA severity in obesity was related to poorer decision-making, greater attentional impairments [23], significantly poorer inhibition and cognitive flexibility assessed via self-report questionnaires and a computerized neuropsychological test battery [24]. Individuals with obesity and trait FA, may therefore present with a specific neuropsychological profile in the obesity spectrum.

Likewise, the clinical eating disorder diagnosis of binge-eating disorder (BED) [25] has been associated with addictive-like eating behavior [26,27]. According to the 5th edition of the Diagnostic and Statistical Manual of Mental Disorders (DSM-5) [25], the core feature of BED is represented by recurrent episodes of objective binge eating, which are characterized by a feeling of loss of control over eating while consuming an unambiguously large amount of food in a discrete period of time. BED is not associated with regular inappropriate compensatory behaviors, such as vomiting or excessive exercising [25]. Among treatment-seeking individuals with overweight and obesity, 23.9% presented with comorbid BED [28]. Individuals with BED were repeatedly found to show impairments in executive functioning exceeding those observed in obesity only, including increased impulsivity, reward sensitivity, rash spontaneous behavior, risky decision-making, and reduced inhibition [29–34]. These alterations were found in general executive functioning tasks [30,35,36] as well as in food-related tasks [30,37,38], strengthening the assumption of a specific neuropsychological profile of individuals with obesity and comorbid BED.

Even though trait FA and the diagnosis of BED have a significant number of behavioral symptoms in common (e.g., consumption of large amounts of food, loss of control, continued use despite negative consequences, cravings) and show a comorbidity of 57.0–72.2% in treatment-seeking and population-based samples with obesity [39], no study has yet compared the neuropsychological profiles of individuals with obesity presenting with or without FA and BED.

In the context of executive functions in obesity as described above, we therefore aimed to investigate general executive functions, specifically decision-making, reward sensitivity, cognitive flexibility, inhibition, and cognitive control in four distinct groups of individuals with obesity: those with FA, BED, FA plus BED (FA/BED), and a control group of otherwise healthy individuals with obesity (OB) stratified to the other groups based on age, sex, and BMI. Among the four groups, we assumed that individuals with OB would show the highest levels of executive functioning. For those with FA, we particularly expected poorer decision-making, cognitive control, inhibition, and flexibility than for OB. Furthermore, we assumed that individuals with BED would perform significantly worse than individuals with OB in tasks investigating impulsivity, reward sensitivity, and inhibition. Due to a lack of evidence, no evidence-based hypothesis was derived regarding possible differences on executive functioning between individuals with trait FA and those with BED. However, based on a recent finding that individuals with FA plus BED displayed greater eating disorder and general psychopathology than individuals with BED only [40], we suggested cumulative adverse effects on executive functioning. Thus, individuals with FA/BED were expected to show lower levels of executive functioning than individuals with OB, FA, and BED only.

2. Materials and Methods

2.1. Participants

Adults with obesity were recruited at the time of admission of two outpatient brain-directed psychological treatment studies at the Integrated Research and Treatment Center Adiposity Diseases in Leipzig, Germany (Cognitive remediation therapy for adults with obesity [41]; electroencephalographic neurofeedback training for adults with BED [42]), and were tested prior to the beginning of either intervention. Inclusion and exclusion criteria for both studies were similar. Relatedly, participants included in this study were required to be between 18 and 60 years of age, present with a BMI $\geq$ 35.0 kg/m^2, display sufficient German language skills, and provide informed consent. Exclusion criteria were (1) serious somatic conditions (e.g., neurological disorders, stroke, head injury); (2) serious mental conditions (e.g., psychotic disorder, suicidality, substance use disorder, developmental or intellectual disability); (3) physical, mental, or other inability to participate in assessments (e.g., impediment in hearing, vision, or language); (4) previous or planned bariatric surgery; (5) use of medication that impacts weight or executive functioning (e.g., antipsychotics, sedatives, hypnotics); (6) current psychotherapy regarding weight or eating behavior; (7) current participation in other interventional studies; (8) lack of compliance; and (9) pregnancy or lactation. Individuals eligible for the OB group were required not to display any FA symptoms according to the YFAS 2.0 [22,43] and not to report any objective binge-eating episode during the last three months as determined via clinical interview [44,45]. Individuals eligible for the FA group needed to present with trait FA, according to the YFAS 2.0 [22,43], and were required not to report any objective binge-eating episode during the last three months as determined via clinical interview [44,45]. Individuals eligible for the BED group were required to present with the DSM-5 diagnosis of BED assessed with a clinical interview [44,45] and not to present with trait FA according to the YFAS 2.0 [22,43]. Individuals eligible for the FA/BED group had to present with trait FA, according to the YFAS 2.0 [22,43], and with the DSM-5 diagnosis of BED assessed with a clinical interview [44,45].

2.2. Ethics and Procedure

Both studies were approved by the Ethical Committee of Leipzig University Medical Center (256-15-13072015, 143-15-20042015) and carried out in accordance with the Declaration of Helsinki. Within the two mentioned treatment studies, all participants were screened for eligibility using a standardized telephone interview. All eligible participants were invited to a baseline in-person diagnostic session. At the beginning of the diagnostic session, informed consent was obtained, followed by a series of neuropsychological tasks (see below). BMI was calculated based on participants' weight (in kg) and height (in cm) which were objectively measured using calibrated instruments at the end of the diagnostic session. The diagnostic sessions were standardized and conducted by trained staff. All participants were asked to refrain from eating at least 2 h prior to testing, in order to avoid any uncontrolled confounding effects of hunger or satiety on executive functioning.

2.3. Sample

Between November 2015 and April 2018, a total of n = 1082 individuals registered with an interest in one of the two brain-directed treatment studies, of whom a total of n = 258 were eligible and included in one of these brain-directed treatment studies. All n = 258 individuals participated in the baseline diagnostic session. For the present study, a convenience sample out of this study population was used, consisting of n = 23 individuals with trait FA based on the YFAS 2.0 [22,43], n = 19 with the DSM-5 diagnosis of BED based on clinical interview [44,45], and n = 23 individuals characterized by trait FA and BED (FA/BED). Out of n = 85 individuals eligible for the OB group, a total of n = 23 otherwise healthy individuals with obesity were stratified to the mean scores of the other groups regarding age, BMI, sex, and education.

2.4. Measures

2.4.1. Eating Disorder Examination

The diagnosis of BED according to DSM-5 [25] was derived from the diagnostic items of the validated German version of the Eating Disorder Examination interview (EDE 17.0D) [44,45]. According to DSM-5, the following severity levels of BED were determined: mild (1–3 objective binge-eating episodes per week), moderate (4–7 objective binge-eating episodes per week), severe (8–13 objective binge-eating episodes per week), and extreme (≥14 objective binge-eating episodes per week). The EDE has high interrater reliability ($r \geq 0.90$) [46].

2.4.2. Yale Food Addiction Scale

The validated German version of the 35-item self-report Yale Food Addiction Scale 2.0 (YFAS 2.0; $\alpha = 0.914$) [22,43] was used to determine FA. Participants were instructed to indicate how often they experienced addictive-like behavior towards food over the last year, with responses ranging from 0 (never) to 7 (every day). A total score was calculated by adding up all DSM-5 symptoms for addiction, ranging from 0 to 11. Scores ≥ 2 in combination with clinically significant distress indicate the presence of FA, with higher scores representing more severe FA: mild (2–3 symptom scores), moderate (4–5 symptom scores), and severe (≥6 symptom scores).

2.4.3. Eating Disorder Examination-Questionnaire

The validated German version of the short 8-item version of the Eating Disorder Examination-Questionnaire (EDE-Q8; $\alpha = 0.766$) [47] was used to evaluate participants' global eating disorder psychopathology. A mean score, ranging from 0 to 6, was calculated, with higher scores indicating greater eating disorder psychopathology.

2.4.4. Patient Health Questionnaire-Depression Scale

The validated German version of the 9-item Patient Health Questionnaire-Depression Scale (PHQ-9; $\alpha = 0.813$) [48,49] was administered to assess the level of depression based on the DSM-5 criteria for depression. Items were scored on a 0 (not at all) to 3 (almost every day) scale. Participants' sum scores were computed, ranging from 0 to 27, with higher scores representing more severe depression. Scores < 5 indicate no depressive symptoms, scores between 5 and 10 a mild depression, and scores > 10 a major depression [48,49].

2.5. Neuropsychological Assessment

2.5.1. Iowa Gambling Task

The computerized version of the Iowa Gambling Task (IGT) [50] was used to assess decision-making under uncertainty and complexity. The IGT requires participants to choose 100 times from four possible card decks (A, B, C, and D), aiming at winning the highest possible amount of virtual money. Each card deck contains profits and losses of different amounts. In the long term, choosing from card decks A and B will result in overall long-term loss (disadvantageous decks), whereas choosing cards from card decks C and D will result in overall long-term gain (advantageous decks). Performance in the IGT was determined by the total net score, calculated by subtracting the total number of disadvantageous choices from the total number of advantageous choices. Additionally, a learning effect across the net score of the five consecutive blocks of 20 cards was considered.

2.5.2. Delay Discounting Task

The computerized version of the Delay Discounting Task (DDT) [51], provided by the test software Millisecond [52] was used to determine the individual discounting rate of delayed rewards, which represents a measure of impulsive decision-making [51]. In this paradigm participants were instructed to choose between a standard amount of money (10 EUR) with different temporal delays (0, 2, 30, 180, and 365 days) or a variable amount (0–10 EUR) with no delay, until an indifference point for each delay was found or until the maximum number of trials (30) has been run for each delay. Five indifference points were calculated, where the immediate reward and delayed reward were equal in terms of subjective value. To determine performance in the DDT, the five indifference points were used to calculate the area under the curve (AUC) [53]. The AUC may range from 0 to 1 with greater AUC values being associated with less discounting of delayed rewards, i.e., less impulsivity [53].

2.5.3. Go/No Go

The computerized version of the visual Go/No Go paradigm [54], provided by the Vienna Test System [55], was used to assess inhibitory control. The visual Go/No Go paradigm required participants to determine whether a stimulus required a reaction or an inhibition. Therefore, 202 triangles were shown on the screen, which required a fast response, while a total of 48 circles appeared randomly in-between, indicating that no response should be given. Performance in the Go/No Go paradigm was determined by the number of commission errors (false positive responses towards a No Go trial), with more commission errors suggesting diminished inhibitory control [56].

2.5.4. Wisconsin Card Sorting Test

The computerized version of the Wisconsin Card Sorting Test (WCST) [57] was used as a measure of cognitive flexibility. The WCST required participants to sort each of maximally 128 cards according to three possible principles or rules (e.g., shape, color, or number), which were unknown to the participant, but would become apparent via feedback during the trials. After 10 consecutively and correctly sorted cards the rule changed suddenly and without warning. The participant then had to generate solutions and use the feedback to adapt to the new rule. Performance on the WCST was measured with the percentage of perseverative errors, which represent a tendency to perseverate on the previous rule, and the learning to learn score, which represents the average growth of conceptual efficiency during the test (average difference in percent errors between successive categories). The learning to learn score can only be calculated if participants have completed at least three categories or completed two categories and attempted a third. The learning to learn score can obtain positive and negative values, with positive scores indicating enhanced efficiency across consecutive categories, presumably because of learning [57].

2.5.5. Alertness

Alertness and the variability in early attentional processes was assessed with a computerized perception and attention functions battery (WAFA) [58], provided by the Vienna Test System [55]. To assess visual intrinsic alertness, participants were required to look at a fixation cross at the center of the screen and press a button as fast as possible when a target stimulus, a circle, appeared. For the assessment of phasic alertness, an auditory cue appeared shortly before the visual stimulus, preparing the participant for next execution of the reaction. Performance in intrinsic and phasic alertness was reported as log-transformed mean reaction time, with higher scores indicating longer reaction times and therefore less alertness [58]. Variability in performance in intrinsic and phasic alertness was reported as a measure of dispersion, with higher scores indicating greater variability in intrinsic or phasic alertness.

2.6. Statistical Procedure

Statistical analyses were performed using IBM SPSS Statistics version 24 (IBM Corp. Released 2016. IBM SPSS Statistics for Windows, Version 24.0. Armonk, NY: IBM Corp). All tests were two-tailed and considered significant when p values were <0.05. Since the domains of executive functioning are distinct and based on single measures, adjusting for multiple testing was not necessary, except for the computerized alertness task (WAFA) where four outcome measures were used. The p value for testing group differences in the WAFA was therefore adjusted to $p = 0.05/4 = 0.0125$. For the comparison of groups regarding socio-demographic and clinical variables, univariate analyses of variance (ANOVAs) were calculated for continuous variables and Chi-square tests (X^2) for categorical variables. The prerequisites for performing the tests (normal distribution and homogeneity of variance) were tested with the Shapiro-Wilk and Levene tests. When prerequisites were not met, Welch ANOVA was used, because of its robustness against violations of the assumption of homogeneity of variances [59]. In case of significance and homogeneity of variances, the Bonferroni post-hoc test was used to determine pair-wise differences; in case of violation of homogeneity of variances the Games-Howell post-hoc test was used. For Welch ANOVA, estimated omega squared (est. ω^2) was calculated for which $\omega^2 \geq 0.01$ is considered a small effect, $\omega^2 \geq 0.06$ a moderate, and $\omega^2 \geq 0.14$ a large effect [60]. For mean differences in post-hoc tests Cohen's d was calculated, with $d \geq 0.2$ being considered a small effect, $d \geq 0.5$ a moderate, and $d \geq 0.8$ a large effect [61]. In the present study, a power of ≥ 0.75 was observed to detect moderate and ≥ 0.95 to detect large group differences in ANOVAs (two-tailed $p < 0.05$).

3. Results

3.1. Sample

As depicted in Table 1, groups did not differ in socio-demographic characteristics. Significant differences between groups were found in eating disorder psychopathology and depression. For eating disorder psychopathology, post-hoc tests did not reach significance. The FA/BED group showed significantly more depressive symptoms compared to the OB group (5.17, 95% Confidence interval (CI) (1.86, 8.49), $p \leq 0.001$). Significantly more individuals of the FA/BED group presented with severe FA compared to the FA group, where there were more cases of mild FA. The FA/BED group did not differ significantly regarding BED severity from the BED group.

Table 1. Sociodemographic characteristics.

Variable	Obesity Only $n = 23$	Food Addiction $n = 23$	Binge-Eating Disorder $n = 19$	Food Addiction Plus Binge-Eating Disorder $n = 23$	Test			Effect Size
	M (SD)	*M (SD)*	*M (SD)*	*M (SD)*	*F*	*df*	*p*	*Est.* ω^2
Age (years)	40.48 (10.85)	43.39 (10.35)	38.84 (9.43)	37.53 (10.12)	1.38	3, 84	0.254	0.013
Body mass index (kg/m^2)	42.84 (4.76)	44.14 (6.59)	41.92 (5.25)	42.23 (6.13)	0.64	3, 84	0.589	−0.012
	n	*n*	*n*	*n*	χ^2	*df*	*p*	
Sex (female/male)	17/6	18/5	14/5	16/7	0.45	3	0.930	
Education (low/middle/high) [1]	3/11/9	3/16/4	1/7/11	4/10/9	8.50	6	0.203	
	M (SD)	*M (SD)*	*M (SD)*	*M (SD)*	*F*	*df*	*p*	*Est.* ω^2
Eating disorder psychopathology (EDE-Q8)	3.59 (0.98) ^{a}	4.20 (0.80) ^{a}	3.55 (1.03) ^{a}	4.36 (1.20) ^{a}	3.92	3, 84	0.011	0.091
Depression (PHQ-D)	5.00 (3.47) ^{a}	7.71 (3.80) $^{a, b}$	7.99 (5.27) $^{a, b}$	10.17 (4.10) ^{b}	5.98	3, 84	0.001	0.145
	n	*n*	*n*	*n*	χ^2	*df*	*p*	
FA severity (mild/moderate/severe)	-	9/10/4	-	0/6/17	18.05	2	<0.001	
BED severity (mild/moderate/severe)	-	-	14/5/0	16/4/3	2.89	2	0.236	

Note. M: mean, SD: standard deviation, df: degrees of freedom, FA: food addiction, BED: binge-eating disorder, BMI: body mass index, PHQ-D: Patient Health Questionnaire-Depression Scale, EDE-Q8: short version of the Eating Disorder Examination-Questionnaire ^{a,b} Different superscripts denote significant differences in post-hoc comparisons with Bonferroni corrections. [1] In Germany, secondary school is subdivided into three tracks: lower $\leq$ 9 years of education, middle = 10 years of education, high $\geq$ 12 years of education.

3.2. Neuropsychological Assessment

In the WAFA, groups differed significantly in the variability to react to a cued target (measure of dispersion phasic alertness), see Table 2, with individuals with BED showing significantly more variability in reaction times than individuals with OB (0.88, 95% CI [0.13, 1.63], $p = 0.018$, $d = 1.12$). Significant group differences were furthermore observed in the growth of conceptual efficiency in the WCST (learning to learn score), indicating that individuals with BED showed significantly less growth of conceptual efficiency in learning compared to individuals with OB (−3.47, 95% CI [−6.92, −0.01], $p = 0.049$, $d = -0.85$). Regarding decision-making, all groups improved their net score over the five consecutive blocks of the IGT, as depicted in Figure 1. Although descriptive data of the IGT net score seem to differ substantially, no significant group differences were found and only a small effect size was observed (see Table 2), suggesting that trait FA and BED diagnosis were not associated with altered decision-making in individuals with obesity. In addition, groups did not differ in their mean reaction time (intrinsic and phasic) and variability to react to un-cued visual targets (measure of dispersion intrinsic alertness) in the WAFA, the amount of perseverative errors in the WCST, and the amount of commission errors in the Go/No Go task (see Table 2), indicating that trait FA and BED were not associated with altered attention, cognitive flexibility, and inhibition in individuals with obesity.

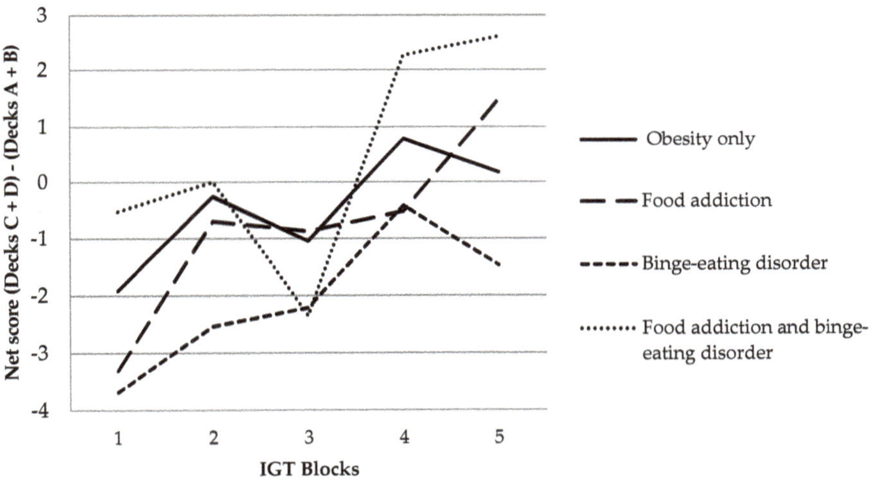

Figure 1. Iowa Gambling Task (IGT) learning effect across five consecutive blocks.

Table 2. Performance on neuropsychological assessments.

Variable		Obesity Only $n = 23$	Food Addiction $n = 23$	Binge-Eating-Disorder $n = 19$	Food Addiction plus Binge-Eating Disorder $n = 23$	Welch ANOVA			Effect Size
		M (SD)	M (SD)	M (SD)	M (SD)	F	df	p	Est. ω^2
IGT	Net score	−2.26 (32.78)	−3.91 (32.18)	−10.32 (39.36)	2.00 (35.17)	0.37	3, 46	0.773	−0.022
DDT	Area under the curve	0.47 (0.32)	0.31 (0.26)	0.54 (0.26)	0.46 (0.24)	2.80	3, 46	0.050	0.058
Go/No Go	Commission errors	11.61 (5.98)	11.39 (7.88)	9.74 (6.06)	12.52 (7.22)	0.64	3, 46	0.591	−0.012
WCST	Perseverative errors	17.70 (6.67)	17.40 (8.38)	14.31 (4.75)	18.38 (8.28)	2.02	3, 46	0.125	0.034
	Learning to learn [1]	2.01 (4.22) [a]	0.88 (6.60) [a, b]	−1.45 (3.90) [b]	3.70 (10.08) [a, b]	2.94	3, 40	0.045	0.069
WAFA	Mean reaction time intrinsic in ms	254.22 (45.69)	264.61 (45.02)	265.37 (43.22)	266.00 (72.05)	0.30	3, 46	0.824	−0.024
	Mean reaction time phasic in ms	253.78 (57.09)	242.04 (61.98)	223.63 (88.57)	249.00 (95.92)	0.56	3, 45	0.642	−0.015
	Measure of dispersion intrinsic	1.18 (0.67)	1.24 (0.11)	1.18 (0.06)	1.28 (0.39)	2.53	3, 45	0.069	0.050
	Measure of dispersion phasic	1.41 (0.18) [a]	1.56 (0.50) [a, b]	2.29 (1.15) [b]	1.79 (1.02) [a, b]	4.80	3, 37	0.006	0.115

Note. M: mean, SD: standard deviation, df: degrees of freedom, IGT: Iowa Gambling Task, DDT: Delay Discounting Task, WAFA: Perception and attention functions battery alertness, WCST: Wisconsin Card Sorting Task, ms: milliseconds. [a,b] Different superscripts denote significant differences in post-hoc comparisons with Games-Howell corrections. [1] Sample size for learning to learn score $n = 79$ ($n = 22$ obesity only, $n = 19$ food addiction, $n = 18$ binge-eating disorder, $n = 20$ food addiction plus binge-eating disorder).

4. Discussion

The present study aimed at investigating the associations of trait FA and the DSM-5 diagnosis of BED regarding executive functions in adults with obesity. It was found that individuals with BED showed lower executive functioning, characterized by a higher variability in reaction times and less feedback integration, compared to otherwise healthy individuals with obesity. Contrary to expectations, there were no differences in executive functioning among individuals with FA, FA/BED, and obesity only. The results thus suggest a BED-specific, but not a FA-specific, neuropsychological profile in individuals with obesity. The combined presentation of trait FA and BED was not associated with greater impairments in executive functioning compared to their single presentations.

The fact that individuals with obesity and BED displayed a significantly higher variability in their reaction times compared to the OB group is similar to findings showing a high variability in reaction times in ADHD [62]. ADHD is highly comorbid to obesity and BED and is associated with comparable neuronal processes [62–64]. In ADHD, it is usually believed that the variability of response times reflects occasional gaps in attention [62], which could be related to high distractibility, making an attentional shift and the detection of task-irrelevant stimuli, for example, food cues, more likely. Another result was the significant and medium-sized difference between the BED and the OB group in the learning to learn score in the WCST, in accordance with recent research [37]. The negative learning to learn score indicated that individuals with BED became less rather than more efficient on consecutive trials of the WCST [57]. Hypothetically, this could be caused by an inability to appropriately integrate the feedback in order to improve performance, as previously evidenced in BED [29]. Transferred into everyday life, the deficient processing of feedback to improve performance could be related to a lack of feedback integration in daily learning, such as feedback given by one's own body after an objective binge-eating episode in order to prevent such an episode from occurring again, leaving an individual without control [65]. In this context, it is worth noting that the BED group did not display heightened depressive symptoms compared to the OB and FA group. Observed differences between the BED and OB group can therefore not be attributed to increased general psychopathology, but were related to BED diagnosis.

Contrary to the two previous studies investigating executive functions in individuals with trait FA [23,24], demonstrating that higher versus lower FA severity in obesity was related to poorer decision-making, inhibition, and cognitive flexibility, no other performance score reached significance in the present study. The hypothesis that individuals with obesity and FA may present with a specific neuropsychological profile in the obesity spectrum was therefore not supported in this clinical treatment-seeking sample. It is of note, however, that the FA group mostly presented with mild and moderate FA symptomatology only, allowing to speculate that FA severity was not high enough to be accompanied by cognitive impairments in this sample. On the other hand, this result could also reflect the assumption that BED, as a clinical eating disorder diagnosis, is associated with more cognitive impairments than subjective trait FA.

The hypothesis of cumulative effects on executive dysfunctions in individuals with FA plus BED was not confirmed in the present study, since the FA/BED group did not display lower performance compared to the OB, FA, or BED group in any of the tasks under investigation. Notably, the FA/BED group reported considerably more depressive symptoms compared to the OB group, with an average in the range of a major depression [48,49], and thus contradicts neuropsychological evidence of impaired executive functioning in individuals with depression [66]. However, the underlying mechanisms of this finding cannot currently be identified. Therefore, this result needs replication in larger, independent samples of individuals with FA/BED.

4.1. Methodological Considerations

When interpreting the results several strength and limitations have to be mentioned. First, using well-established measures, the diagnosis of BED was derived from an expert interview, the EDE 17.0D [44,45], and trait FA was assessed via the established self-questionnaire YFAS 2.0 [22,43]. Second, the OB group was stratified to the other groups and groups were mutually exclusive regarding trait FA and objective binge-eating episodes. Third, executive functioning was measured with established, standardized, and computerized tasks. Critically, the relatively small group sizes have to be mentioned, as only medium-to-large-sized effects could be detected with adequate power. Additionally, there might be an assessment bias across diagnostic groups, as FA was assessed with a self-administered questionnaire, while BED diagnosis was made by clinical expert interview, suggesting that trait FA and BED mirror different levels of clinical severity. Furthermore, no food-specific tasks were used. Various studies have shown a stronger association between executive functions in food-related tasks in relation to binge-eating behavior [30,38]. Lastly it is important to note that the design of this study was cross-sectional; therefore, causal conclusions about the direction of observed effects are not indicated.

4.2. Implications and Future Directions

The current study identified greater executive dysfunctions in individuals with obesity and comorbid BED compared to those with obesity only. Clinically, the assessment of eating disorder symptomatology, specifically a diagnosis of BED, seems therefore indicated in individuals with obesity. In these individuals, an increase in neuropsychological impairments is likely to interfere with standard treatment options [8,9] and may thus constitute a specific target for intervention, for example, via cognitive remediation therapy [41]. Based on this study's results, an in-depth investigation in the variability of reaction times (alertness tasks) is indicated, especially considering the effects of food stimuli, as current research points to an increased attentional bias towards food cues in individuals with BED e.g., [66,67].

Regarding trait FA, this study revealed no impairments in executive functioning other than a tendency towards higher choice-impulsivity, which could be related to the high proportion of individuals characterized by low FA severity in the FA group. Studies investigating executive functions in individuals with obesity and more severe FA are therefore needed. Alternatively, it could be argued that similarities in executive functioning between individuals with obesity plus trait FA and individuals with substance use disorder as recently shown [12] only manifest on a neurobiological [12] and not on a neuropsychological level. To further differentiate these aspects of addictive-like eating behavior, future research is warranted to specifically investigate neuronal and neuropsychological overlaps and distinctive features between trait FA and substance use disorder, especially in the context of disorder-related stimuli (e.g., food stimuli).

It was surprising that the observed large differences in attentional variability and conceptual learning between the BED and OB group did not manifest in the FA/BED group, particularly as this group presented as the most impaired group concerning mental health, with more depressive symptoms than the OB group. The assessment of trait FA in individuals with versus without BED may therefore be helpful to determine identify individuals at risk for greater mental health impairment and in need of more intensive treatment. Further research into the neuropsychological characteristics of individuals with FA plus BED is however warranted, preferably using larger samples and a longitudinal study design in order to evaluate the effects of trait FA plus BED on weight trajectories and treatment outcome in individuals with obesity.

Author Contributions: Conceptualization, M.B., R.S. and A.H.; methodology, M.B., R.S. and A.H.; software, M.B. and A.H.; formal analysis, M.B. investigation, M.B.; resources, A.H.; data curation, M.B.; writing—original draft preparation, M.B.; writing—review and editing, M.B., R.S. and A.H.; visualization, M.B.; supervision, R.S. and A.H.; project administration, M.B. and A.H.; funding acquisition, A.H.

Funding: This study was supported by the Federal Ministry of Education and Research, Germany (Grant 01EO1501).

Acknowledgments: The authors would like to thank Claudia Hübner, Helen Eißner, Ronja Runge, Annika Kleinschmitt, Robert Kratzer, Fabrice Sigleur, Eva Stenger, Johanna Müller, Eileen Lashani, Nikolas Verfuß, Anne-Sophie Pelzl, Anna-Maria Hoffmann, Sabrina Höft, Jenny Kaiser-Baumgärtner and Sarah-Verena Schmieger for their assistance in data collection.

Conflicts of Interest: The authors declare no conflict of interest.

References

1. World Health Organization [WHO]. Obesity and Overweight: Fact Sheet. Available online: http://www.who.int/mediacentre/factsheets/fs311/en/ (accessed on 30 July 2017).
2. NCD Risk Factor Collaboration (NCD-RisC). Worldwide trends in body-mass index, underweight, overweight, and obesity from 1975 to 2016: A pooled analysis of 2416 population-based measurement studies in 128·9 million children, adolescents, and adults. *Lancet* **2017**, *390*, 2627–2642. [CrossRef]
3. Horstmann, A. It wasn't me; it was my brain-Obesity-associated characteristics of brain circuits governing decision-making. *Physiol. Behav.* **2017**, *176*, 125–133. [CrossRef] [PubMed]
4. Makaronidis, J.M.; Batterham, R.L. Obesity, body weight regulation and the brain: Insights from fMRI. *Br. J. Radiol.* **2018**. [CrossRef] [PubMed]
5. Yang, Y.; Shields, G.S.; Guo, C.; Liu, Y. Executive function performance in obesity and overweight individuals: A meta-analysis and review. *Neurosci. Biobehav. Rev.* **2018**, *84*, 225–244. [CrossRef] [PubMed]
6. Shallice, T. *From Neuropsychology to Mental Structure*, 1st ed.; Cambridge University Press: Cambridge, England, 1988; ISBN 978-0-521-31360-5.
7. Stuss, D.T.; Benson, D.F. *The Frontal Lobes*; Raven Press: New York, NY, USA, 1986; ISBN 978-0-88167-153-7.
8. Wyckoff, E.P.; Evans, B.C.; Manasse, S.M.; Butryn, M.L.; Forman, E.M. Executive functioning and dietary intake: Neurocognitive correlates of fruit, vegetable, and saturated fat intake in adults with obesity. *Appetite* **2017**, *111*, 79–85. [CrossRef] [PubMed]
9. Brockmeyer, T.; Hamze Sinno, M.; Skunde, M.; Wu, M.; Woehning, A.; Rudofsky, G.; Friederich, H.-C. Inhibitory control and hedonic response towards food interactively predict success in a weight loss programme for adults with obesity. *Obes. Facts* **2016**, *9*, 299–309. [CrossRef] [PubMed]
10. Jones, A.; Hardman, C.A.; Lawrence, N.; Field, M. Cognitive training as a potential treatment for overweight and obesity: A critical review of the evidence. *Appetite* **2017**, *124*, 50–67. [CrossRef] [PubMed]
11. Michaud, A.; Vainik, U.; Garcia-Garcia, I.; Dagher, A. Overlapping neural endophenotypes in addiction and obesity. *Front. Endocrinol.* **2017**, *8*, 127. [CrossRef]
12. Lindgren, E.; Gray, K.; Miller, G.; Tyler, R.; Wiers, C.E.; Volkow, N.D.; Wang, G.-J. Food addiction: A common neurobiological mechanism with drug abuse. *Front. Biosci. Landmark Ed.* **2018**, *23*, 811–836.
13. Jauch-Chara, K.; Oltmanns, K.M. Obesity—A neuropsychological disease? Systematic review and neuropsychological model. *Prog. Neurobiol.* **2014**, *114*, 84–101. [CrossRef]
14. Burrows, T.; Kay-Lambkin, F.; Pursey, K.; Skinner, J.; Dayas, C. Food addiction and associations with mental health symptoms: A systematic review with meta-analysis. *J. Hum. Nutr. Diet.* **2018**, *31*, 544–572. [CrossRef] [PubMed]
15. Gordon, E.L.; Ariel-Donges, A.H.; Bauman, V.; Merlo, L.J. What is the evidence for "food addiction?" a systematic review. *Nutrients* **2018**, *10*, 477. [CrossRef] [PubMed]
16. Smith, D.G.; Robbins, T.W. The neurobiological underpinnings of obesity and binge eating: A rationale for adopting the food addiction model. *Biol. Psychiatry* **2013**, *73*, 804–810. [CrossRef] [PubMed]
17. Davis, C. A commentary on the associations among "food addiction", binge eating disorder, and obesity: Overlapping conditions with idiosyncratic clinical features. *Appetite* **2017**, *115*, 3–8. [CrossRef] [PubMed]
18. Gearhardt, A.N.; Corbin, W.R.; Brownell, K.D. Preliminary validation of the yale food addiction scale. *Appetite* **2009**, *52*, 430–436. [CrossRef] [PubMed]
19. Lacroix, E.; Tavares, H.; von Ranson, K.M. Moving beyond the "eating addiction" versus "food addiction" debate: Comment on Schulte et al. (2017). *Appetite* **2018**, *130*, 286–292. [CrossRef] [PubMed]
20. Schulte, E.M.; Potenza, M.N.; Gearhardt, A.N. A commentary on the "eating addiction" versus "food addiction" perspectives on addictive-like food consumption. *Appetite* **2017**, *115*, 9–15. [CrossRef] [PubMed]
21. Hilbert, A. *Binge-Eating Disorder*; Psychiatric Clinics of North America in Press: Amsterdam, The Netherlands, 2002.
22. Gearhardt, A.N.; Corbin, W.R.; Brownell, K.D. Development of the yale food addiction scale version 2.0. *Psychol. Addict. Behav.* **2016**, *30*, 113–121. [CrossRef]
23. American Psychiatric Association. *DSM-5: Diagnostic and Statistical Manual of Mental Disorders*, 5th ed.; American Psychiatric Publishing: Arlington, VA, USA, 2013.

24. Steward, T.; Mestre-Bach, G.; Vintró-Alcaraz, C.; Lozano-Madrid, M.; Agüera, Z.; Fernández-Formoso, J.A.; Granero, R.; Jiménez-Murcia, S.; Vilarrasa, N.; García-Ruiz-de-Gordejuela, A.; et al. Food addiction and impaired executive functions in women with obesity. *Eur. Eat. Disord. Rev.* **2018**, *26*, 574–584. [CrossRef]
25. Rodrigue, C.; Ouellette, A.-S.; Lemieux, S.; Tchernof, A.; Biertho, L.; Bégin, C. Executive functioning and psychological symptoms in food addiction: A study among individuals with severe obesity. *Eat. Weight Disord.* **2018**, *23*, 469–478. [CrossRef]
26. Cassin, S.E.; von Ranson, K.M. Is binge eating experienced as an addiction? *Appetite* **2007**, *49*, 687–690. [CrossRef] [PubMed]
27. Davis, C.; Mackew, L.; Levitan, R.D.; Kaplan, A.S.; Carter, J.C.; Kennedy, J.L. Binge eating disorder (BED) in relation to addictive behaviors and personality risk factors. *Front. Psychol.* **2017**, *8*, 579. [CrossRef] [PubMed]
28. Ricca, V.; Castellini, G.; Lo Sauro, C.; Ravaldi, C.; Lapi, F.; Mannucci, E.; Rotella, C.M.; Faravelli, C. Correlations between binge eating and emotional eating in a sample of overweight subjects. *Appetite* **2009**, *53*, 418–421. [CrossRef] [PubMed]
29. Córdova, M.E.; Schiavon, C.C.; Busnello, F.M.; Reppold, C.T. Nutritional and neuropsychological profile of the executive functions on binge eating disorder in obese adults. *Nutr. Hosp.* **2017**, *34*, 1448–1454. [CrossRef] [PubMed]
30. Giel, K.E.; Teufel, M.; Junne, F.; Zipfel, S.; Schag, K. Food-related impulsivity in obesity and binge eating disorder—A Systematic update of the evidence. *Nutrients* **2017**, *9*, 1170. [CrossRef] [PubMed]
31. Kollei, I.; Rustemeier, M.; Schroeder, S.; Jongen, S.; Herpertz, S.; Loeber, S. Cognitive control functions in individuals with obesity with and without binge-eating disorder. *Int. J. Eat. Disord.* **2018**, *51*, 233–240. [CrossRef] [PubMed]
32. Leehr, E.J.; Schag, K.; Dresler, T.; Grosse-Wentrup, M.; Hautzinger, M.; Fallgatter, A.J.; Zipfel, S.; Giel, K.E.; Ehlis, A.-C. Food specific inhibitory control under negative mood in binge-eating disorder: Evidence from a multimethod approach. *Int. J. Eat. Disord.* **2018**, *51*, 112–123. [CrossRef]
33. Manasse, S.M.; Forman, E.M.; Ruocco, A.C.; Butryn, M.L.; Juarascio, A.S.; Fitzpatrick, K.K. Do executive functioning deficits underpin binge eating disorder? A comparison of overweight women with and without binge eating pathology. *Int. J. Eat. Disord.* **2015**, *48*, 677–683. [CrossRef]
34. Svaldi, J.; Naumann, E.; Biehl, S.; Schmitz, F. Impaired early-response inhibition in overweight females with and without binge eating disorder. *PLoS ONE* **2015**, *10*, e0133534. [CrossRef]
35. Kessler, R.M.; Hutson, P.H.; Herman, B.K.; Potenza, M.N. The neurobiological basis of binge-eating disorder. *Neurosci. Biobehav. Rev.* **2016**, *63*, 223–238. [CrossRef]
36. Schag, K.; Schönleber, J.; Teufel, M.; Zipfel, S.; Giel, K.E. Food-related impulsivity in obesity and binge eating disorder—A systematic review: Food-related impulsivity. *Obes. Rev.* **2013**, *14*, 477–495. [CrossRef]
37. Balodis, I.M.; Grilo, C.M.; Potenza, M.N. Neurobiological features of binge eating disorder. *CNS Spectr.* **2015**, *20*, 557–565. [CrossRef] [PubMed]
38. Kittel, R.; Brauhardt, A.; Hilbert, A. Cognitive and emotional functioning in binge-eating disorder: A systematic review. *Int. J. Eat. Disord.* **2015**, *48*, 535–554. [CrossRef] [PubMed]
39. Davis, C.; Curtis, C.; Levitan, R.D.; Carter, J.C.; Kaplan, A.S.; Kennedy, J.L. Evidence that "food addiction" is a valid phenotype of obesity. *Appetite* **2011**, *57*, 711–717. [CrossRef] [PubMed]
40. Gearhardt, A.N.; White, M.A.; Masheb, R.M.; Morgan, P.T.; Crosby, R.D.; Grilo, C.M. An examination of the food addiction construct in obese patients with binge eating disorder. *Int. J. Eat. Disord.* **2012**, *45*, 657–663. [CrossRef] [PubMed]
41. Hilbert, A.; Blume, M.; Petroff, D.; Neuhaus, P.; Smith, E.; Hay, P.J.; Hübner, C. Group cognitive remediation therapy for adults with obesity prior to behavioural weight loss treatment: Study protocol for a randomised controlled superiority study (CRT study). *BMJ Open* **2018**, *8*, e022616. [CrossRef] [PubMed]
42. Blume, M.; Schmidt, R.; Schmidt, J.; Martin, A.; Hilbert, A. German Clinical Trials Register: EEG Neurofeedback for Adults with Binge-Eating Disorder. Available online: https://www.drks.de/drks_web/navigate.do?navigationId=trial.HTML&TRIAL_ID=DRKS00010496 (accessed on 7 August 2018).
43. Meule, A.; Müller, A.; Gearhardt, A.N.; Blechert, J. German version of the Yale Food Addiction Scale 2.0: Prevalence and correlates of "food addiction" in students and obese individuals. *Appetite* **2017**, *115*, 54–61. [CrossRef] [PubMed]
44. Fairburn, C.G.; Cooper, Z.; O'Connor, M. *Eating Disorder Examination (17.0D)*; Guilford Press: New York, NY, USA, 2014.

45. Hilbert, A.; Tuschen-Caffier, B. *Eating Disorder Examination. Deutschsprachige Übersetzung*, 2nd ed.; Deutsche Gesellschaft für Verhaltensterapie: Tübingen, Germany, 2016; ISBN 978-3-87159-411-3.
46. Berg, K.C.; Peterson, C.B.; Frazier, P.; Crow, S.J. Psychometric evaluation of the eating disorder examination and eating disorder examination-questionnaire: A systematic review of the literature. *Int. J. Eat. Disord.* **2012**, *45*, 428–438. [CrossRef]
47. Kliem, S.; Mößle, T.; Zenger, M.; Strauß, B.; Brähler, E.; Hilbert, A. The eating disorder examination-questionnaire 8: A brief measure of eating disorder psychopathology (EDE-Q8). *Int. J. Eat. Disord.* **2016**, *49*, 613–616. [CrossRef]
48. Gräfe, K.; Zipfel, S.; Herzog, W.; Löwe, B. Screening psychischer Störungen mit dem "Gesundheitsfragebogen für Patienten (PHQ-D)". *Diagnostica* **2004**, *50*, 171–181. [CrossRef]
49. Spitzer, R.L.; Kroenke, K.; Williams, J.B. Validation and utility of a self-report version of PRIME-MD: The PHQ primary care study. Primary Care Evaluation of Mental Disorders. Patient Health Questionnaire. *JAMA* **1999**, *282*, 1737–1744. [CrossRef] [PubMed]
50. Bechara, A.; Damasio, A.R.; Damasio, H.; Anderson, S.W. Insensitivity to future consequences following damage to human prefrontal cortex. *Cognition* **1994**, *50*, 7–15. [CrossRef]
51. Richards, J.B.; Zhang, L.; Mitchell, S.H.; de Wit, H. Delay or probability discounting in a model of impulsive behavior: Effect of alcohol. *J. Exp. Anal. Behav.* **1999**, *71*, 121–143. [CrossRef] [PubMed]
52. Millisecond. *Inquisit (Version 4)*, Windows; Millisecond Software: San Francisco, CA, USA, 2015.
53. Myerson, J.; Green, L.; Warusawitharana, M. Area under the curve as a measure of discounting. *J. Exp. Anal. Behav.* **2001**, *76*, 235–243. [CrossRef] [PubMed]
54. Kaiser, S.; Aschenbrenner, S.; Pfüller, U.; Roesch-Ely, D.; Weisbrod, M. *Wiener Testsystem: Response Inhibition*, Schuhfried: Mödling, Germany, 2015.
55. Schuhfried Gmbh. *Vienna Test System*, Windows; Schuhfried Gmbh: Mödling, Austria, 2015.
56. Lezak, M.D.; Howieson, D.B.; Bigler, E.D.; Tranel, D. *Neuropsychological Assessment*; Oxford University Press: Oxford, NY, USA, 2012; ISBN 978-0-19-539552-5.
57. Heaton, R.K.; Chelune, G.J.; Talley, J.L.; Kay, G.G.; Curtiss, G. *Wisconsin Card Sorting Test Manual*; Psychological Assessment Resources, Inc.: Odessa, FL, USA, 1993.
58. Sturm, W. *Wiener Testsystem: Wahrnehmungs- und Aufmerksamkeitsfunktionen*, Schuhfried: Mödling, Austria, 2015.
59. Lix, L.M.; Keselman, J.C.; Keselman, H.J. Consequences of assumption violations revisited: A quantitative review of alternatives to the one-way analysis of variance f test. *Rev. Educ. Res.* **1996**, *66*, 579–619. [CrossRef]
60. Keppel, G. *Design and Analysis: A Researcher's Handbook*, 3rd ed.; Prentice Hall: Upper Saddle River, NJ, USA, 1991.
61. Cohen, J. *Statistical Power Analysis for the Behavioral Sciences*, 2nd ed.; Lawrence Erlbaum Associates: New York, NY, USA, 1988.
62. Tamm, L.; Narad, M.E.; Antonini, T.N.; O'Brien, K.M.; Hawk, L.W.; Epstein, J.N. Reaction time variability in ADHD: A review. *Neurotherapeutics* **2012**, *9*, 500–508. [CrossRef]
63. Cortese, S.; Bernardina, B.D.; Mouren, M.-C. Attention-deficit/hyperactivity disorder (adhd) and binge eating. *Nutr. Rev.* **2007**, *65*, 404–411. [CrossRef]
64. Voon, V. Cognitive biases in binge eating disorder: The hijacking of decision making. *CNS Spectr.* **2015**, *20*, 566–573. [CrossRef]
65. Restivo, M.R.; McKinnon, M.C.; Frey, B.N.; Hall, G.B.; Syed, W.; Taylor, V.H. The impact of obesity on neuropsychological functioning in adults with and without major depressive disorder. *PLoS ONE* **2017**, *12*, e0176898. [CrossRef]
66. Schmidt, R.; Lüthold, P.; Kittel, R.; Tetzlaff, A.; Hilbert, A. Visual attentional bias for food in adolescents with binge-eating disorder. *J. Psychiatr. Res.* **2016**, *80*, 22–29. [CrossRef] [PubMed]
67. Sperling, I.; Baldofski, S.; Lüthold, P.; Hilbert, A. Cognitive food processing in binge-eating disorder: An eye-tracking study. *Nutrients* **2017**, *9*, 903. [CrossRef] [PubMed]

nutrients

MDPI

Article

Orthorexic Tendency in Polish Students: Exploring Association with Dietary Patterns, Body Satisfaction and Weight

Marta Plichta *, Marzena Jezewska-Zychowicz and Jerzy Gębski

Department of Organization and Consumption Economics, Faculty of Human Nutrition and Consumer Sciences, Warsaw University of Life Sciences (SGGW-WULS), 159C Nowoursynowska Street, 02-787 Warsaw, Poland; marzena_jezewska_zychowicz@sggw.pl (M.J.-Z.); jerzy_gebski@sggw.pl (J.G.)

* Correspondence: marta_plichta@sggw.pl

Received: 15 November 2018; Accepted: 30 December 2018; Published: 5 January 2019

Abstract: Body dissatisfaction is central to clinically diagnosed eating disorders (ED) and seems to be important in causing other non-clinical disorders, including orthorexia nervosa (ON). It can also affect eating behaviors. The aim of this study was to assess the associations of ON tendency with dietary patterns (DPs) and body satisfaction. The data were collected in 2017 through questionnaire survey among 1120 students of health-oriented and other academic programs from seven universities in Poland. Principal components analysis (PCA) was conducted to derive DPs and body satisfaction factors. Six DPs, such as, 'High-sugar products & snacks', 'Fresh products & nuts', 'Fatty products & dressings', 'Oils & potatoes', 'Dairy products & whole-meal bread', 'Meat', and two body satisfaction factors, such as, 'Bottom body & weight', and 'Upper body' were identified. ON tendency was measured using ORTO-15 questionnaire with both cut-offs, i.e., 35 and 40. Logistic regression analysis was used to verify associations between ON tendency, body satisfaction factors, and DPs. More students of health related majors were characterized by ON tendency in comparison to students of other majors (35.9 vs. 37.2; $p < 0.001$). More women were dissatisfied with 'Bottom body & weight compared to men (<0.001). The higher the body mass index (BMI), the more people were dissatisfied with 'Bottom body & weight' ($p < 0.001$). More students with ON tendency were satisfied with their 'Upper body' than those without ON tendency, but there were no differences in ON tendency in regard to 'Bottom body & weight' satisfaction. ON tendency was associated with more frequent consumption of vegetables, fruits, nuts and seeds, and less frequent consumption of products high in sugar, snacks, fatty products and dressings. Using cut-off at 35 in ORTO-15 seems to be more appropriate than cut-off at 40 to identify external variables describing ON. Future research on orthorexia nervosa should use other research tools than ORTO-15 to better identify individuals with ON and to confirm our findings.

Keywords: dietary patterns; body satisfaction; orthorexia nervosa; students

1. Introduction

Dissatisfaction with one's body, distorted body image perception and obsession with thinness are central to clinically diagnosed eating disorders (ED) such as anorexia nervosa (AN), bulimia nervosa (BN), binge eating disorder (BED) and eating disorders not otherwise specified (EDNOS) [1]. It can be assumed, that these factors may also contribute to other non-clinical types of disorders including orthorexia nervosa (ON). ON expresses a pathological interest in healthy food. The healthy behavior and ON are placed as extreme poles on the continuum scale of states differing in the intensity of orthorexic symptoms [2].

ON was used to define an unhealthy obsession with healthy eating [3]. Individuals with ON eliminate certain food products that are perceived by them as unhealthy and impure. They avoid foods with high content of salt, sugar and fat, foods containing genetically-modified ingredients, herbicides, pesticides and artificial substances and also non-organic foods. Each meal is prepared with great concern and attention, often with repetitive activities which are to ensure the safety of food intake. This obsession is driven by a desire to optimize own health and well-being [4]. Individuals with ON may be on alternative diets (e.g., vegetarianism, veganism, raw foods, macrobiotics, fruitarianism) [5–7]. Recently, Dunn and Bratman [8] proposed the new criteria of classification of ON containing extreme preoccupation with healthy eating, restrictive eating behaviors, malnutrition, severe weight loss as a results of food choices as well as feeling guilt or self-loathing if diet is not followed correctly. However, no standardized tool for diagnosis currently exists [9–13].

To assess ON, ORTO-15 questionnaire [14] based on Bratman Orthorexia Test (BOT) [4] is widely used, despite criticism regarding this research tool [7]. Some researchers suggested that ORTO-15 questionnaire may not be able to distinguish pathological behaviors and is not clinically relevant [15]. However, the recent review of the studies using ORTO-15 showed that Cronbach's alpha coefficients were ranging from 0.83 to 0.91 [16]. The Italian version of ORTO-15 was translated into several languages, usually with the use of complicated multistep methods, and then administered to different samples. The results of confirmatory analysis and other methods allowed researchers to shorten original ORTO-15 [7]. In this way, the Turkish version of ORTO-11 [10] and ORTO-11-Hu, Hungarian adaptation of the ORTO-15 [12], were developed. In the original version of ORTO-15, to distinguish the orthorexic tendency it is recommended to use the cut-off point below 40 [17], and some researchers followed this recommendation [18,19]. Nevertheless, there are also suggestions to lower the cut-off point in this test to 35 [11,18]. Lowering the cut-off point would allow distinguishing a group of people in which the ON symptoms can be clearly identified. Thus, it enables a more effective search for the ON symptoms, its causes and consequences.

ON reveals several similarities with other eating disorders, such as avoidant/restrictive food intake disorder (AFRID) [20] and AN [21]. AFRID is characterized by the lack of interest in food, avoiding food products with specific shapes or colors, or anxiety about the aversive consequences of eating [22]. Nevertheless, the anxiety about eating results from a response to a preceding traumatic event (e.g., choking) or an aversive experience (e.g., repeated vomiting) [22,23] and not from excessive concerns for health as in ON. In contrast, AN and ON share traits of perfectionism, cognitive rigidity, high co-morbid anxiety, and need for control of life transferred to eating [5,21]. Both patients with AN and patients with ON perceive their behaviors as ego-syntonic [24]. Nonetheless, patients with ON are concerned about food quality rather than food quantity in contrast to patients with AN [25]. In addition to AN characteristics, individuals with ON may evince obsessive-compulsive disorders (OCD) [26] due to burdensome obsessions (e.g., intensive meal planning, intrusive thoughts of food) and compulsions (e.g., exact measuring and weighing of food). However, the obsessions in OCD are described as ego-dystonic [6].

ON may lead to severe physical and psychological complications such as, caloric deficit, lack of vitamins and minerals, gastrointestinal problems, stomach inflammation, anemia, osteopenia, hyponatremia, pancytopenia, heart failure, significant distress, and social isolation [2,5,27,28]. However, ON is still not diagnosed well and not recognized in the Diagnostic and Statistical Manual of Mental Disorders DSM-5 [1]. Thus, further research is needed to better understand the symptoms of ON [27,29].

Despite certain similarities between AN and ON, some researchers suppose that ON is not associated with weight control [24,30]. Nevertheless, young people are often dissatisfied with their bodies [31,32], and such negative body image may put them at severe health risk because it strongly predicts the development of disordered eating [33]. It has been showed that females with ON were characterized by striving for thinness, lower body satisfaction, and lower body acceptance [34]. Previous studies have shown that increased ON symptomatology was associated with calorie restriction and preoccupation with weight [10,13,18,35–39]. Nevertheless, the relationship of ON and body satisfaction requires further research.

Orthorexic individuals represented very specific eating habits, among others they avoid foods that may include genetically modified ingredients or pesticides, foods high in salt or sugar, and foods high in fat [24,40]. Previous research has shown that individuals eating whole wheat cereals, as well as fruits and vegetables more frequently were characterized by higher ON tendency compared to others [41]. However, despite the fact that ON is characterized by very specific eating behaviors, still little is known about food intake frequency in relation to this disorder [12,41]. To the best of our knowledge, the relationship between dietary patterns (DPs), body satisfaction and ON tendency was not examined. Therefore the aim of our study was first, to estimate the orthorexic tendency among students of different college majors, and second, to find the associations between ON tendency, body satisfaction, and dietary patterns in students taking into account gender, body mass index (BMI) and college majors, and third to recognize the usefulness of both cut-offs used to identify orthorexic tendency (at 35, and 40 points in ORTO-15) in the determination of external variables describing ON symptoms including dietary patterns and body satisfaction.

2. Materials and Methods

2.1. Ethical Approval

The study protocol was approved by the Ethics Committee of Faculty of Human Nutrition and Consumer Science, Warsaw University of Life Sciences (Resolution number 45/2017). Informed consent to participate in the study was collected from all participants.

2.2. Participants and Procedure

The study sample was selected in seven universities from Poland. The survey was conducted during lectures by a trained person. The teacher left the room after consenting to the survey among students. The persons participating in the study were informed about the purpose, course and duration of the study, as well as about the possibility of resigning from the study at any stage without bearing any legal liability. Participation in the study was voluntary. The questionnaire took approximately 15 min to complete. In total, 1300 students of health-oriented and other academic programs were invited to participate in the study. Male and female students at the age from 18 to 35 years old were included in the sample. As a result of incomplete questionnaires, 162 participants were excluded from the sample. Moreover, 18 students were excluded from the sample as they were older than 35 years old. Finally, the sample consisted of 1120 students who completed questionnaires correctly. The data were collected in 2017.

2.3. Questionnaire

The ORTO-15 questionnaire [19] was used to identify the ON tendency. The Polish version used in our study was adapted from the original Italian ORTO-15 [14], and has good repeatability and satisfactory reliability (Cronbach's alpha 0.70–0.90) [19]. The ORTO-15 is a validated measure consisting of 15 items that assesses beliefs about the perceived effects of eating healthy food, attitudes conditioning food selection, habits regarding food consumption, and the extent to which food concerns affect daily life [24]. Responses expressing the obsessive attitude of the individuals in choosing, buying, preparing and consuming food are scored on a 4-point scale (always, often, sometimes, never). Responses indicating ON symptoms were scored 1, while responses describing adequate eating behaviors were scored 4. The sum of scores was calculated for each participant with a minimum of 15 and a maximum of 60.

The Questionnaire of Body Particular Parts and Parameters Satisfaction [42] was used to measure body satisfaction. This tool was developed and then validated in the Polish population. The obtained reliability index for the entire scale was considered satisfactory (Cronbach's alpha

0.86) [42]. Respondents defined the satisfaction level with particular body parts on a nine-point scale, where: 1—totally dissatisfied; 5—neither dissatisfied nor satisfied; 9—totally satisfied. The following parts of the body were included in the questionnaire: face; shoulders; breast/chest; waist/midsection; abdomen; hips; thighs; legs; weight and height of body.

The Food Frequency Questionnaire (FFQ-6) was applied to determine respondents' dietary habits [43]. The FFQ-6 was validated in females aged 13–21 years old [43] and in both men and women aged 21–26 years old [44]. The FFQ-6 covered the diet thoroughly, including many of the most popular dishes consumed in Poland. The FFQ contained a list of 165 products and dishes which represented such food groups as: sweets and snacks; dairy products and eggs; cereal products; fats; fruits; vegetables and grains; meat and fish products; beverages. The frequency of food consumption throughout the year preceding the study was assessed. For this analysis, 26 products and dishes were chosen, including: sugar; chocolate, chocolate candies and chocolate bars; non-chocolate candies; biscuits and cookies; salty snacks; milk and natural milk drinks; sweetened milk drinks; cheese; whole-meal bread; refined bread; oils; butter; margarine; sour cream and sweet cream; other animal fats; mayonnaise and dressings; fresh fruits; processed fruit products; fresh vegetables; potatoes; nuts; grains and wheat germ; red meat; poultry meat and rabbit meat; fatty fish; sweetened fizzy drinks. When selecting 26 products, the results of other studies on the relationship between body dissatisfaction and consumed foods were taken into account [45,46]. In addition, the choice of items resulted from their importance in diet of individuals with ON tendency. FFQ-6 included six categories of food intake frequency: never or almost never (1 points); once a month or less frequently (2 points); several times per month (3 points); several times per week (4 points); every day (5 points); and several times per day (6 points).

Socioeconomic profile of participants was assessed based on questions regarding gender, age (in years), place of residence, and college major. Body Mass Index (BMI) was calculated using self-reported weight and height and categorized accordingly World Health Organization [47] into four groups: underweight (BMI < 18.5 kg/m^2), normal weight (18.5 $\leq$ BMI $\leq$ 24.9 kg/m^2), overweight (25.0 $\leq$ BMI $\leq$ 29.9 kg/m^2) and obesity (BMI $\geq$ 30.0 kg/m^2).

2.4. The Sample Characteristics

The characteristics of the sample are presented in Table 1. The sample included 1120 college students, of which 70.4% were female and 29.6% were male. The highest number of participants were younger than 20 years old (36.1%). Majority of the students lived in cities (71.6%). More participants were enrolled in bachelor or engineering studies (88.7%) than in master studies (11.3%). Almost a half of the sample (48.8%) represented health related majors (Food Technology and Human Nutrition, Dietetics, Physiotherapy, Physical Education and Wellness) and 51.2% were students of other majors. The majority of participants had normal weight (72.9%).

Table 1. Sociodemographic characteristics of the study sample.

Variables		*N* = 1120	%
Gender	Female	789	70.4
	Male	331	29.6
Age	18–19	404	36.1
	20–22	388	34.6
	23–25	253	22.6
	26–35	75	6.7
Place of residence	Village	318	28.4
	City ≤ 100.000 citizens	319	28.5
	City > 100.000 citizens	483	43.1
Level of studies	Bachelor or engineering studies	994	88.7
	Master studies	126	11.3

Table 1. *Cont.*

Variables		N = 1120	%
College major	Health related	547	48.8
	Non health related	573	51.2
BMI categories	Underweight	123	11.0
	Normal weight	817	72.9
	Overweight	154	13.8
	Obesity	26	2.3

N—number of participants, BMI—body mass index.

2.5. Data Analysis

Descriptive statistics including frequency distributions and cross-tabulations were carried out. The Principal Component Analysis (PCA) was applied to identify body satisfaction factors and dietary patterns (DPs), separately. The factors were orthogonally rotated (the varimax option) to maintain uncorrelated factor variables. The number of factors was based on the following criteria: components with an eigenvalue of 0.1, scree plot test and the interpretability of the factors. The factorability of data was confirmed with Kaiser–Meyer–Olkin (KMO) measure of sampling adequacy and Bartlett's test of sphericity achieving statistical significance. Bartlett's tests have a significance of $p < 0.001$ for both data. KMO value for body satisfaction data was 0.862 and for dietary data was 0.842. Factor loadings higher than 0.4 assure that the variables extracted are shown through a specific factor, therefore both food items and body parts with factor-loadings of at least 0.50 have been taken into consideration and used to label the dietary patterns and body satisfaction factors, respectively [48].

Two body satisfaction factors were identified: 'Bottom body & weight' and 'Upper body'. Total variance explained was 57.6%. The factor-loading matrix for the body satisfaction identified by principal component analysis (PCA) is presented in detail in Table 2.

Table 2. Factor-loading matrix for the body satisfaction factors identified by principal component analysis (PCA).

Variables	Bottom Body & Weight	Upper Body
Waist/midsection	**0.617**	0.438
Abdomen	**0.692**	0.321
Hips	**0.800**	0.261
Thighs	**0.853**	0.137
Legs	**0.795**	0.141
Weight	**0.758**	0.436
Face	0.186	**0.715**
Shoulders	0.282	**0.666**
Breasts/chest	0.064	**0.750**
Variance Explained (%)	46.0	11.6
Total Variance Explained (%)	57.6	
Kaiser's Measure of Sampling Adequacy	0.862	

Bolded values are marked for the main components of PCA-derived body satisfaction factors with absolute loadings ≥ 0.5.

Six dietary patterns were identified: 'High-sugar products & snacks', 'Fresh products & nuts', 'Fatty products & dressings', 'Oils & potatoes', 'Dairy products & whole-meal bread', and 'Meat'. Total variance explained was 51.3%. For each factor the explained variance was: 19.1%, 10.9%, 6.7%, 5.4%, 4.8%, and 4.4%, respectively. The factor-loading matrix for the DPs identified by principal component analysis (PCA) is presented in detail in Table 3.

Table 3. Factor-loading matrix for the DPs identified by principal component analysis (PCA).

Variables	High-Sugar Products & Snacks	Fresh Products & Nuts	Fatty Products & Dressings	Oils & Potatoes	Dairy Products & Whole-Meal Bread	Meat
Chocolate, chocolate candies and chocolate bars	**0.722**	−0.094	−0.020	0.090	0.084	0.016
Biscuits and cookies	**0.709**	−0.023	0.028	0.115	0.195	0.032
Non chocolate candies	**0.757**	0.024	0.103	−0.046	0.006	0.125
Salty snacks	**0.580**	−0.093	0.251	0.121	−0.075	0.045
Sweetened milk drinks	**0.506**	−0.083	0.243	−0.017	0.461	0.022
Milk and natural milk drinks	0.095	0.073	−0.001	0.007	**0.785**	0.034
Cheese, blue cheese, melted cheese, spread cheese	0.111	−0.075	0.250	0.159	**0.616**	0.034
Whole-meal bread	−0.085	0.249	−0.225	0.054	**0.525**	−0.058
Margarine	0.190	−0.028	**0.561**	0.064	0.012	−0.187
Sour cream and sweet cream	0.178	−0.001	**0.537**	0.312	0.312	0.073
Other animal fats	0.048	0.139	**0.640**	0.047	−0.051	0.381
Mayonnaise and dressings	0.229	−0.066	**0.502**	0.298	0.166	0.141
Fresh fruits	−0.006	**0.640**	−0.372	0.304	0.134	−0.088
Fresh vegetables	−0.207	**0.594**	−0.328	0.311	0.106	0.013
Nuts	−0.099	**0.728**	0.084	−0.058	−0.037	0.093
Seeds (e.g., pumpkin, sesame, sunflower, wheat germ)	−0.068	**0.738**	0.104	−0.111	0.018	−0.047
Red meat (e.g., pork, beef, veal)	0.065	−0.010	0.233	0.139	−0.018	**0.770**
Poultry meat and rabbit meat	0.115	−0.039	−0.095	0.123	0.030	**0.764**
Oils	−0.008	0.172	−0.008	0.658	0.082	0.068
Potatoes	0.258	−0.017	0.159	0.631	−0.053	0.129
Variance Explained (%)	19.1	10.9	6.7	5.4	4.8	4.4
Total Variance Explained (%)	51.3					
Kaiser's Measure of Sampling Adequacy			0.842			

Bolded values are marked for the main components of PCA-derived dietary patterns factors with absolute loadings ≥ 0.5.

Respondents allocated to each of the dietary patterns were divided into three groups based on tertile distribution: bottom, middle and upper tertile. Participants in the upper tertile had the strongest adherence to the pattern.

Two categories within each body satisfaction factors, such as, satisfaction and dissatisfaction, were created using factor scores obtained with regression approach. The factor scores of 0 and below is interpreted as 'dissatisfaction', whereas the value above 0 as 'satisfaction' with body.

According to Donini et al. [14], a score lower than or equal to 40 indicates ON tendency, while higher scores inform about adequate eating behaviors. Whereas according to Ramacciotti et al. [11], a cut-off at 35 provides a lower and more accurate estimate of ON tendency, than the cut-off at 40. Both cut-offs were included in our study. Cronbach's alpha for ORTO-15 was 0.7.

The differences between groups were verified by Chi-square test (the ON tendency groups versus sociodemographic characteristics, including gender, age bracket, place of residence, level of studies, college major and BMI categories); student's *t*-test (mean score of ORTO-15 versus gender and college majors); the one-way analysis of variance ANOVA (mean score of ORTO-15 versus BMI categories).

A simple logistic regression analysis was applied to the models verifying associations between ON tendency, body satisfaction, and DPs. The odds ratio (OR) and 95% confidence interval (95% CI) were calculated. Such dichotomous variables as ON tendency, 'Bottom body & weight' and 'Upper body' have been introduced into models as dependent variables. The independent variables in the models were dietary patterns. The OR calculated for each independent variable represents the odds ratio between a given variable level (the upper tertile of each dietary pattern), and the adopted level of reference (the bottom tertile—OR = 1.00) while the remaining explanatory (independent) variables remain constant. The adjusted models were developed for the potential confounders, such as, gender (categorical, female/men), age (continuous, years), place of residence (categorical, village/city $\leq$ 100.000 citizens/city > 100.000 citizens), level of studies (categorical, bachelor or engineering studies/master studies), college major (categorical, health related/non health related), and BMI (continuous, kg/m^2). The level of significance of the odds ratio was assessed with a Wald test. A p-value ≤ 0.05 was considered statistically significant for all tests. All analyses were carried out applying sample weights to adjust for non-response and missing data. All analyses were performed using SAS 9.4. software (SAS Institute, Cary, NC, USA).

3. Results

3.1. Orthorexia Nervosa Tendency and Body Satisfaction across Gender, BMI and College Major

The ON tendency was observed among 75.0% of the sample when the cut-off at 40 was used. However, only 28.3% of students showed ON tendency when the cut-off at 35 was implemented. Mean value of ORTO-15 was 36.6 (standard deviation 4.2). More than a half of participants were satisfied with both 'Bottom body & weight' (52.9%) and 'Upper body' (51.4%). Twice more females than males were dissatisfied with 'Bottom body & weight' ($p < 0.001$). There were no significant differences in ON tendency and 'Upper body' satisfaction between gender groups (Table 4).

The differences between BMI categories regarding 'Bottom body & weight' satisfaction were observed (<0.001). The higher the BMI, the more people were dissatisfied with 'Bottom body & weight'. No significant differences were observed between BMI categories in regard to the ON tendency (regardless of the cut-off point) and 'Upper body' satisfaction (Table 5).

Students of health related majors (35.9 $\pm$ 4.1) scored significantly lower in ORTO-15 than students of other majors (37.2 $\pm$ 4.2). More students of health related majors (79.3%) than students of other majors (70.9%) displayed ON tendency (cut-off at 40). Similarly, such difference was observed with the cut-off at 30 (32.9 and 23.9%, respectively). There were no significant differences both in 'Bottom body & weight' and 'Upper body' satisfaction across the college majors (Table 6).

Table 4. Orthorexia nervosa tendency and body satisfaction in the total sample and gender groups.

Variables	Total Sample	Female	Male	Chi-Squared Test/Student's *t*-Test	*p*-Value
	N = 1120	*N* = 789	*N* = 331		
Orthorexia nervosa *n* (%)					
ON tendency (<40)	840 (75.0)	595 (75.4)	245 (74.0)	0.24 *	0.623
Without ON tendency (<40)	280 (25.0)	194 (24.6)	86 (26.0)		
ON tendency (<35)	317 (28.3)	219 (27.8)	98 (29.6)	0.39 *	0.530
Without ON tendency (<35)	803 (71.7)	570 (72.2)	233 (70.4)		
ORTO-15 score (M ± SD)	36.6 ± 4.2	36.6 ± 4.1	36.6 ± 4.4	0.03 **	0.973
'Bottom body & weight' *n* (%)					
Dissatisfaction	527 (47.1)	437 (55.4)	90 (27.2)	74.41 *	<0.001
Satisfaction	593 (52.9)	352 (44.6)	241 (72.8)		
'Upper body' *n* (%)					
Dissatisfaction	544 (48.6)	372 (47.2)	172 (52.0)	2.16 *	0.141
Satisfaction	576 (51.4)	417 (52.8	159 (58.0)		

* Chi-squared test; ** Student's *t*-test (t); ON—orthorexia nervosa; M—mean; SD—standard deviation.

Table 5. Orthorexia nervosa tendency and body satisfaction according to BMI categories.

Variables	Underweight	Normal Weight	Overweight	Obesity	Chi-Squared Test/ANOVA	*p*-Value
	N = 123	*N* = 817	*N* = 154	*N* = 26		
Orthorexia nervosa *n* (%)						
ON tendency (<40)	91 (74.0)	620 (75.9)	111 (72.1)	18 (69.2)	1.57 *	0.665
Without ON tendency (<40)	32 (26.0)	197 (24.1)	43 (27.9)	8 (30.8)		
ON tendency (<35)	38 (30.9)	230 (28.2)	43 (27.9)	6 (23.1)	0.78 *	0.855
Without ON tendency (<35)	85 (69.1)	587 (71.9)	111 (72.1)	20 (76.9)		
ORTO-15 score (M ± SD)	36.5 ± 4.4	36.6 ± 4.1	36.6 ± 4.6	37.7 ± 3.6	1.23 **	0.197
'Bottom body & weight' *n* (%)						
Dissatisfaction	32 (26.0)	382 (46.8)	93 (60.4)	20 (76.9)	42.18 *	<0.001
Satisfaction	91 (74.0)	435 (53.2)	61 (39.6)	6 (23.1)		
'Upper body' *n* (%)						
Dissatisfaction	70 (56.9)	389 (47.6)	69 (44.8)	16 (61.5)	6.35 *	0.096
Satisfaction	53 (43.1)	428 (52.4)	85 (55.2)	10 (38.5)		

* Chi squared test; ** one-way analysis of variance ANOVA (F).

Table 6. Orthorexia nervosa tendency and body satisfaction according to majors of the study.

Variables	Health Related Majors	Non Health Related Majors	Chi-Squared Test/Student's *t*-Test	*p*-Value
	N = 547	*N* = 573		
Orthorexia nervosa *n* (%)				
ON tendency (<40)	434 (79.3)	406 (70.9)	10.75 *	0.001
Without ON tendency (<40)	113 (20.7)	167 (29.1)		
ON tendency (<35)	180 (32.9)	137 (23.9)	11.16 *	<0.001
Without ON tendency (<35)	367 (67.1)	436 (76.1)		
ORTO-15 score (M ± SD)	35.9 ± 4.1	37.2 ± 4.2	4.95 **	<0.001
'Bottom body & weight' *n* (%)				
Dissatisfaction	270 (49.4)	257 (44.9)	2.28 *	0.131
Satisfaction	277 (50.6)	316 (55.2)		
'Upper body' *n* (%)				
Dissatisfaction	269 (49.2)	275 (48.0)	0.16 *	0.692
Satisfaction	278 (50.8)	298 (52.0)		

* Chi squared test; ** Student's *t*-test (t).

3.2. Orthorexia Nervosa Tendency and Body Satisfaction

More students with ON tendency were satisfied with their 'Upper body' in comparison with students without ON tendency. There was not a significant difference in 'Bottom body & weight' satisfaction in respect to ON tendency. Such relationships were demonstrated for categories identified using both cut-offs ($p = 0.027$ and $p = 0.005$, respectively at 40 and 35) (Table 7).

3.3. Associations between Orthorexia Nervosa Tendency, Body Satisfaction and Dietary Patterns

The results from the adjusted model have demonstrated that students who consumed high-sugar products and snacks most often (the upper tertile of DP) were less likely to display ON tendency, regardless of the cut-off point. Odds Ratio (OR) was higher at the cut-off at 35 points compared to the cut-off at 40 points (0.32 and 0.34, respectively). In addition, students in the upper tertile of 'Fatty products & dressings' pattern were less likely to display ON tendency compared to those in the bottom tertile of this DP. However, Odds Ratio (OR) was lower at the cut-off at 35 compared to the cut-off at 40 (0.52 and 0.59, respectively). In contrast, students in the upper tertile of 'Fresh products & nuts' were more than twice as likely to have ON tendency compared to those in the bottom tertile of this DP. Odds Ratio (OR) was higher at the cut-off at 35 compared to the cut-off at 40 (2.49 and 2.30, respectively) (Table 8).

Table 7. Orthorexia nervosa tendency and body satisfaction in the total sample.

Variables	ON Tendency (<40)	Without ON Tendency (<40)	Chi-Squared Test	*p*-Value	ON Tendency (<35)	Without ON Tendency (<35)	Chi-Squared Test	*p*-Value
	N = 840	*N* = 280			*N* = 317	*N* = 803		
'Bottom body & weight' *n* (%)								
Dissatisfaction	392 (46.7)	135 (48.2)	0.20	0.653	139 (43.9)	388 (48.3)	1.82	0.177
Satisfaction	448 (53.3)	145 (51.8)			171 (56.1)	415 (51.7)		
'Upper body' *n* (%)								
Dissatisfaction	392 (46.7)	152 (54.3)	4.88	0.027	133 (42.0)	411 (51.2)	7.75	0.005
Satisfaction	448 (53.3)	128 (45.7)			184 (58.0)	392 (48.8)		

Table 8. Dietary patterns by orthorexia nervosa tendency and body satisfaction: adjusted logistic regression model (odds ratios with 95% confidence interval).

ON Tendency/Body Satisfaction	Dietary Patterns											
	High-Sugar Products & Snacks [c] (Ref. Bottom Tertile)		Fresh Products & Nuts [c] (Ref. Bottom Tertile)		Fatty Products & Dressings [c] (Ref. Bottom Tertile)		Oils & Potatoes [c] (Ref. Bottom Tertile)		Dairy Products & Whole-Meal Bread [c] (Ref. Bottom Tertile)		Meat [c] (Ref. Bottom Tertile)	
	Upper Tertile	*p*	Upper Tertile	*p*	Upper Tertile	*p*	Upper Tertile	*p*	Upper Tertile	*p*	Upper Tertile	*p*
Orthorexia nervosa [a] (ON tendency <40) [b]	0.32 [d] (0.22; 0.46) [e]	<0.001	2.30 (1.59; 3.32)	<0.001	0.59 (0.41; 0.85)	0.004	0.93 (0.65; 1.32)	0.690	1.06 (0.74; 1.51)	0.771	1.15 (0.79; 1.68)	0.471
Orthorexia nervosa [a] (ON tendency <35) [b]	0.33 (0.24; 0.48)	<0.001	2.46 (1.72; 3.52)	<0.001	0.52 (0.36; 0.75)	<0.001	0.75 (0.53; 1.05)	0.094	0.93 (0.66; 1.32)	0.687	1.00 (0.70; 1.43)	0.994
'Bottom body & weight' [a] (dissatisfaction) [b]	0.92 (0.66; 1.28)	0.606	0.82 (0.59; 1.15)	0.248	0.94 (0.66; 1.32)	0.714	0.81 (0.59; 1.13)	0.217	1.00 (0.72; 1.39)	0.992	0.78 (0.55; 1.11)	0.163
'Upper body' [a] (dissatisfaction) [b]	1.75 (1.29; 2.37)	<0.001	0.65 (0.48; 0.88)	0.005	1.03 (0.76; 1.41)	0.832	0.76 (0.57; 1.03)	0.073	1.02 (0.75; 1.37)	0.922	1.07 (0.78; 1.47)	0.669

[a] dependent variable; [b] predicted level of dependent variable; [c] independent variables; [d] OR point estimate (e^{β}) upper tertile vs. lower tertile; [e] 95% Wald Confidence Intervals. All data adjusted for sample weights. ORs were adjusted for: gender (categorical, female/men), age (continuous, years), place of residence (categorical, village/city ≤ 100.000 citizens/city > 100.000 citizens), level of studies (categorical, bachelor or engineering studies/master studies), college major (categorical, health related/non health related), BMI (continuous, kg/m^2); $p < 0.05$ (Wald's test).

Students in the upper tertile of 'High-sugar products & snacks' were more likely to be dissatisfied with their 'Upper body' ((OR) 1.75, 95% CI: 1.29–2.37) compared to those in the bottom tertile. Students who consumed fresh products and nuts most often (the upper tertile of 'Fresh products & nuts') were less likely to be dissatisfied with their 'Upper body' ((OR) 0.65, 95% CI: 0.48–0.88) than those in the bottom tertile. No significant associations between 'Bottom body & weight' satisfaction and DPs were revealed (Table 8).

4. Discussion

In our study we attempted to assess the occurrence of the ON tendency amongst students, who, due to their young age, are prone to developing incorrect eating behaviors [49]. Our results obtained in the ORTO-15 test for the cut-off of 40 are in accordance with other studies [12,38,50,51]. After reducing the cut-off limit to 35 points, there was almost a three-fold decrease in the number of people with ON tendency (from 75.0% to 28.3%). Other researchers also pointed out the validity of lowering the cut-off below 35 points in the ORTO-15 test [11,18].

Previous research indicate that the occurrence of ON is more common among students of medicine [10], exercise science [52], dietetics [53] and majors related to nutrition [9]. Our results also confirm these observations in relation to health-related majors. Both the percentage of people with ON symptoms and the mean value of ORTO-15 indicate differences between students of majors related to health and the rest of participants, but these differences were not of clinical significance. However, they can be used in the development of education programs. Students of health-related majors acquire knowledge about the principles of adequate nutrition and health consequences resulting from their non-observance. In addition, they use other sources of information (e.g., Internet sources) about food and its impact on health [54]. This may result in the application of strict nutritional rules aimed at maintaining health or normal body weight, however this can also lead to the development of eating disorders [55,56].

Our study did not reveal differences in the occurrence of ON tendency between the categories identified due to BMI, both for the cut-off limit at 35, and at 40 points in the ORTO-15 test. Previous research did not confirm the association between ON and BMI as well [36,57,58], which indicates the distinctiveness of ON from AN in terms of this index [21,24,59,60]. Excessive concentration of people with the ON tendency on the quality of food [24] does not have to be combined with control of the amount of food consumed. In studies on stereotypical thinking about healthy food, it was shown that when people assessed its impact on weight gain mainly the health-related properties of the food consumed were taken into account and not its quantity [61,62]. The lack of association between orthorexic symptoms and BMI, but also stereotypical thinking of healthy food as good for body could therefore suggest that encouraging the choice of healthy food is not sufficient to limit overweight and obesity. The recommendation to choose healthy food has to be supplemented with the recommendation to control the amount in which healthy food is consumed.

The results of our study revealed the relationship of BMI with the student's satisfaction with 'Bottom body & weight', with the highest number of underweight individuals being satisfied with 'Bottom body & weight'. Likewise Goswami et al. [63] we observed a higher level of body satisfaction among the respondents with BMI < 18.5 kg/m^2 in comparison to people with higher BMI (>25 kg/m^2). The majority of obese people were dissatisfied with their 'Bottom body & weight', which may result from excess of body fat deposited especially in the lower body parts, as well as excessive body weight. The overweight or obese individuals may experience strong stigma and discrimination due to weight and size of their body, leading them to focus increasingly and obsessively on dieting for weight loss and body dissatisfaction [64]. Low body satisfaction may lead to development of an ED, as well as to sadness, low self-esteem and depression [49]. However, it is alarming that among people with a normal body weight, almost half were dissatisfied with 'Bottom body & weight', which may lead them to implementing dietary restrictions. An important factor causing the lack of satisfaction with one's own body is the internalization of information provided by parents, peers and mass media [65]. Interestingly, the messages addressed to men and women significantly differ from each other [66]. In the case of women, the information transmit the pressure of having a slim figure. For men, the pressure concentrates on having an athletic and muscular body. Dissatisfaction with one's own body may stem from the inability to meet the imposed ideals [67]. Women internalize messages regarding the body image more often and they tend to be more severe judges of their looks in comparison to men [68–70]. This tendency occurs alike among children [71], adolescents [72], and grown-ups [73]. The lack of associations between body satisfaction and BMI demonstrated in our study can be used in the development of messages aimed at reducing obesity. In order to encourage people to maintain or reduce weight, both health and body satisfaction should be emphasized as resulting from controlling one's diet. Body satisfaction would be presented as a result of the action undertaken, and at the same time a reward for the effort made, which may increase the effectiveness of the process of behaviors' change.

Although more women than men experience ED [74–77], our results did not confirm the relationship between gender and ON tendency regardless of the cut-off point used in the ORTO-15 test. Previous studies also did not show any definite relationship between gender and ON. Some research papers have pointed to a higher incidence of ON among men [10,14,78], whereas others observed it more often in women [26,36,79]. Considerable number of publications, like our study, did not indicate any significant relationship between gender and ON [80,81]. The discrepancies in results may be related to the specificity of ON. An unhealthy obsession with proper nutrition resulting from the preoccupation with one's health is the main characteristic of ON [3,4]. The increasing awareness of the relationship between nutrition and health induces growing interest in this issue [82], which may favor the application of strict nutrition rules regardless of gender. Their use can reach the pathological level and turn into ON, also regardless of gender. In the case of ED, such as AN or BN, dissatisfaction with body image, fear of obesity and distorted assessment of body dimensions are the main factors affecting the formation of these disorders [1]. Thus, women who are generally less satisfied with the image of their own body constitute a group that is particularly vulnerable to this type of disorders.

Previous studies did not indicate a connection between the negative image of one's body and ON [30,83], but the fact that the perception of one's own body is a frequent cause of changing one's eating behaviors has prompted us to include this variable in our study. The obtained results indicate the lack of relationship between ON tendency (both cut-offs in ORTO-15 test) and satisfaction with own body, but only in regard to 'Bottom body & weight'. In ED, concerns about the body image refer primarily to those parts of the body (i.e., abdomen, hip, thighs and buttocks) in which fatty tissue accumulates [42]. The lack of this relationship could confirm the differences between ON and BN, due to the lack of a characteristic symptom of AN and BN (i.e., body dissatisfaction). Nevertheless, our results indicate a relationship of satisfaction with the upper body with ON tendency. Higher satisfaction with the upper body of people with ON tendency may result from the fact that they eliminate products with a high sugar content and processed food from their diet [3,4], which may affect skin condition adversely [84]. Our results confirm that the respondents from the upper tertile of 'High-sugar products & snacks' pattern were more likely to be dissatisfied with upper body and those in the upper tertile of 'Fresh products & nuts' pattern were less likely to be dissatisfied with upper body. Thus, the restrictions introduced by people with ON tendency can positively affect the skin condition of these parts of the body, and thus increase the satisfaction with their body.

Our research has pointed to the lower risk of ON tendency (regardless of the cut-off limit in ORTO-15) among the respondents in the upper tertile of 'High-sugar products & snacks' and 'Fatty products & dressings' patterns. People with ON avoid foods rich in sugar, fat and salt [13,24,41], which is confirmed by our results. In addition, in our study greater ON tendency (for both cut-offs in ORTO-15 test) in people from the upper tertile of 'Fresh products & nuts' pattern was observed. An earlier study also showed higher intake of vegetables and fruits among people with ON [12]. Our results did not confirm the relationship between 'Meat' DP and ON tendency, regardless of the cut-offs used in ORTO-15. Some researchers suggest that vegetarian diet does not lead directly to ED, however, the prevalence of ON among vegans and vegetarians is higher than among people who eat meat [85–88]. It seems that only the complete elimination of meat from the diet, and not the varied frequency of its consumption may be the reason for the more frequent occurrence of ON tendency among vegans and vegetarians. However, further research into ON should be carried out in the context of the use of alternative diets.

The use of both cut-off points in our analysis (at 35 and at 40 points in ORTO-15) in the determination of ON tendency has not provided us with findings which we expected. There were no major differences in the results after applying both cut-offs, except for the estimation of the occurrence of ON tendency. The differences shown in the dietary patterns after taking into account both cut-off points in ORTO-15 were only minimal. However, slightly higher chances of representing the upper tertile of 'Fresh products & nuts' and lower chances of representing the upper tertile of 'Fatty products & dressing' were observed in people with higher symptoms of ON when the cut-off at 35 was used, which is also confirmed in other studies [12,13,24,41]. Although the use of cut-off at 35 in ORTO-15 seems more appropriate to diagnose external variables describing ON, further studies are needed to confirm our results.

Strengths and Limitations

The strength of our results is a relatively large sample of Polish students. Although our findings are specific to Polish cultural background and should not be generalized to populations of students of various nationalities, the findings could be of potential use in further research on ON tendency and its symptoms, especially when methodological issues are concerned. We believe that including body satisfaction and dietary patterns in the study brought a wider perspective on symptoms of ON tendency.

Nevertheless, there are several limitations within the study. The first limitation of the current study is carrying out the survey in lectures, which limited the anonymity of the respondents. The literature suggests that anonymity may enhance the accuracy of disclosure among college students for questions of a sensitive nature [89]. Secondly, the self-reported weight and height could have led to an inaccurate body mass index classification. The ability to self-report weight and height data may be influenced by sociodemographic features such as age, gender and economic status [90]. Next, the three identified dietary patterns explained only 5.4% or less of the total variance in the dietary intake data, which is lower compared to another studies undertaking similar type of analyses [91,92]. This value may be a results of the inclusion of a high numbers of variables in the PCA [93]. Finally, the cross-sectional design of the present study and data collection at a single point in time did not allow conclusions to be drawn about causality, but only on the associations of ON tendency with both dietary patterns and body satisfaction. Moreover, using the ORTO-15 for examining ON tendencies can be questioned due to its limitations [94,95].

5. Conclusions

The results of our study indicate that there was no body dissatisfaction among people with ON tendency. What's more, people with ON tendency were more satisfied with their upper body in comparison to people with no orthorexic characteristics. In addition, there was no relationship between ON tendency and BMI. The obtained results do not confirm the suggested relationship between ON and AN due to the lack of ON relationship with dissatisfaction with one's body and BMI. However, further research in this area is needed in order to confirm the relationship between the one's body satisfaction and ON in different populations, including youth that does not attend college, adults and people with ED. Moreover, the assessment of the relationship of ON tendency with dietary patterns allowed characterizing dietary behaviors of people with ON tendency, which may be important in the development of educational programs and nutritional interventions directed to people with ON.

The use of both cut-off points for results obtained in ORTO-15, and then their inclusion in the analyses suggests the legitimacy of using the cut-off point 35, because it results in a decrease in the number of people with ON tendency. However, in the diagnosis of ON symptoms such as body satisfaction and dietary patterns, there were no major differences from the cut-off point at 40. This can confirm the limitations of the ORTO-15 demonstrated by other researchers. Future research on ON should use other research tools than ORTO-15 to identify individuals with ON and to confirm our findings. Simultaneously, research should be intensified in order to create a new tool for better identification of ON and its symptoms, both behavioral and related to psychological characteristics.

Author Contributions: M.P. made substantial contributions to the study conception, design, and data acquisition; J.G. and M.P. analyzed the data; M.P. and M.J.-Z. interpreted the data and wrote the manuscript; M.J.-Z., and J.G. were involved in critically revising the manuscript, and have given their approval to the manuscript submitted.

Funding: This research was funded by Polish Ministry of Science and Higher Education within funds of Faculty of Human Nutrition and Consumer Sciences, Warsaw University of Life Sciences (WULS), for scientific research, grant number 505-10-102500-Q00306-99.

Acknowledgments: Thanks are expressed to the participants for their contributions to the study.

Conflicts of Interest: The authors declare that they have no competing interests. The founders played no role in the design of the study; in the collection, analyses, or interpretation of data; in the writing of the manuscript, and in the decision to publish the results.

References

1. American Psychiatric Associaton. *Diagnostic and Statistical Manual of Mental Disorders DSM-5*; American Psychiatric Publishing: Arlington, VA, USA, 2013.
2. Varga, M.; Dukay-Szabó, S.; Túry, F.; Van Furth, E.F. Evidence and gaps in the literature on orthorexia nervosa. *Eat. Weight Disord.* **2013**, *18*, 103–111. [CrossRef]
3. Bratman, S. Health Food Junkie. *Yoga J.* **1997**, 42–50.
4. Bratman, S.; Knight, D. *Healthy Food Junkies: Overcoming the Obsession with Healthful Eating*; Broadway Books: New York, NY, USA, 2000.
5. Catalina Zamora, M.L.; Bonaechea, B.; Sánchez, G.; Rial, R. Orthorexia nervosa. A new eating behavior disorder? *Actas Esp. Psiquiatr.* **2005**, *33*, 66–68. [PubMed]
6. Dell'Osso, L.; Abelli, M.; Carpita, B.; Massimetti, G.; Pini, S.; Rivetti, L.; Gorrasi, F.; Tognetti, R.; Ricca, V.; Carmassi, C. Orthorexia nervosa in a sample of Italian university population. *Riv. Psichiatr.* **2016**, *51*, 190–196. [CrossRef] [PubMed]
7. Missbach, B.; Dunn, T.M.; König, J.S. We need new tools to assess Orthorexia Nervosa. A commentary on "Prevalence of Orthorexia Nervosa among College Students Based on Bratman's Test and Associated Tendencies". *Appetite* **2017**, *108*, 521–524. [CrossRef]
8. Dunn, T.M.; Bratman, S. On orthorexia nervosa: A review of the literature and proposed diagnostic criteria. *Eat. Behav.* **2016**, *21*, 11–17. [CrossRef] [PubMed]
9. Bo, S.; Zoccali, R.; Ponzo, V.; Soldati, L.; De Carli, L.; Benso, A.; Fea, E.; Rainoldi, A.; Durazzo, M.; Fassino, S.; et al. University courses, eating problems and muscle dysmorphia: Are there any associations? *J. Transl. Med.* **2014**, *12*, 221. [CrossRef]
10. Fidan, T.; Ertekin, V.; Işikay, S.; Kirpinar, I. Prevalence of orthorexia among medical students in Erzurum, Turkey. *Compr. Psychiatry* **2010**, *51*, 49–54. [CrossRef]
11. Ramacciotti, C.E.; Perrone, P.; Coli, E.; Burgalassi, A.; Conversano, C.; Massimetti, G.; Dell'Osso, L. Orthorexia nervosa in the general population: A preliminary screening using a self-administered questionnaire (ORTO-15). *Eat. Weight Disord.* **2011**, *16*, e127–e130. [CrossRef]
12. Varga, M.; Thege, B.K.; Dukay-Szabó, S.; Túry, F.; van Furth, E.F. When eating healthy is not healthy: Orthorexia nervosa and its measurement with the ORTO-15 in Hungary. *BMC Psychiatry* **2014**, *14*, 59. [CrossRef]
13. Bundros, J.; Clifford, D.; Silliman, K.; Neyman Morris, M. Prevalence of Orthorexia nervosa among college students based on Bratman's test and associated tendencies. *Appetite* **2016**, *101*, 86–94. [CrossRef] [PubMed]
14. Donini, L.M.; Marsili, D.; Graziani, M.P.; Imbriale, M.; Cannella, C. Orthorexia nervosa: Validation of a diagnosis questionnaire. *Eat. Weight Disord.* **2005**, *10*, e28–e32. [CrossRef] [PubMed]
15. Dunn, T.M.; Gibbs, J.; Whitney, N.; Starosta, A. Prevalence of orthorexia nervosa is less than 1%: Data from a US sample. *Eat. Weight Disord.* **2017**, *22*, 185–192. [CrossRef] [PubMed]

16. Costa, C.B.; Hardan-Khalil, K.; Gibbs, K. Orthorexia Nervosa: A Review of the Literature. *Issues Ment. Health Nurs.* **2017**, *38*, 980–988. [CrossRef] [PubMed]
17. Clifford, T.; Blyth, C. A pilot study comparing the prevalence of orthorexia nervosa in regular students and those in University sports teams. *Eat. Weight Disord.* **2018**. [CrossRef] [PubMed]
18. Segura-García, C.; Papaianni, M.C.; Caglioti, F.; Procopio, L.; Nisticò, C.G.; Bombardiere, L.; Ammendolia, A.; Rizza, P.; De Fazio, P.; Capranica, L. Orthorexia nervosa: A frequent eating disordered behavior in athletes. *Eat. Weight Disord.* **2012**, *17*, 226–233. [CrossRef]
19. Stochel, M.; Janas-Kozik, M.; Zejda, J.E.; Hyrnik, J.; Jelonek, I.; Siwiec, A. Validation of ORTO-15 Questionnaire in the group of urban youth aged 15–21. *Psychiatr. Pol.* **2015**, *49*, 119–134. [CrossRef] [PubMed]
20. Brytek-Matera, A.; Rogoza, R.; Gramaglia, C.; Zeppegno, P. Predictors of orthorexic behaviours in patients with eating disorders: A preliminary study. *BMC Psychiatry* **2015**, *15*, 252. [CrossRef]
21. Koven, N.S.; Abry, A. The clinical basis of orthorexia nervosa: Emerging perspectives. *Neuropsychiatr. Dis. Treat.* **2015**, *11*, 385–394. [CrossRef]
22. Kreipe, R.E.; Palomaki, A. Beyond picky eating: Avoidant/restrictive food intake disorder. *Curr. Psychiatry Rep.* **2012**, *14*, 421–431. [CrossRef]
23. Bryant-Waugh, R.; Kreipe, R.E. Avoidant/Restrictive Food Intake Disorder in *DSM-5*. *Psychiatr. Ann.* **2012**, *42*, 402–405. [CrossRef]
24. Brytek-Matera, A. Orthorexia nervosa—An eating disorder, obsessive-compulsive disorder or disturbed eating habit? *Arch. Psychiatry Psychother.* **2012**, *14*, 55–60. [CrossRef]
25. Turner, P.G.; Lefevre, C.E. Instagram use is linked to increased symptoms of orthorexia nervosa. *Eat. Weight Disord.* **2017**, *22*, 277–284. [CrossRef] [PubMed]
26. Koven, N.S.; Senbonmatsu, R. A neuropsychological evaluation of orthorexia nervosa. *Open J. Psychiatry* **2013**, *3*, 214–222. [CrossRef]
27. Moroze, R.M.; Dunn, T.M.; Craig Holland, J.; Yager, J.; Weintraub, P. Microthinking About Micronutrients: A Case of Transition From Obsessions About Healthy Eating to Near-Fatal "Orthorexia Nervosa" and Proposed Diagnostic Criteria. *Psychosomatics* **2015**, *56*, 397–403. [CrossRef]
28. Park, S.W.; Kim, J.Y.; Go, G.J.; Jeon, E.S.; Pyo, H.J.; Kwon, Y.J. Orthorexia nervosa with hyponatremia, subcutaneous emphysema, pneumomediastinum, pneumothorax, and pancytopenia. *Electrolyte Blood Press.* **2011**, *9*, 32–37. [CrossRef]
29. Frances, A. *Saving Normal: An Insider's Revolt Against Out-Of-Control Psychiatric Diagnosis, DSM-5, Big Pharma, and the Medicalization of Ordinary Life*, 3rd ed.; Sage Publications: New York, NY, USA, 2013.
30. Brytek-Matera, A.; Fonte, M.L.; Poggiogalle, E.; Donini, L.M.; Cena, H. Orthorexia nervosa: Relationship with obsessive-compulsive symptoms, disordered eating patterns and body uneasiness among Italian university students. *Eat. Weight Disord.* **2017**, *22*, 609–617. [CrossRef]
31. Grabe, S.; Hyde, J.S. Ethnicity and body dissatisfaction among women in the United States: A meta-analysis. *Psychol. Bull.* **2006**, *132*, 622–640. [CrossRef]
32. Olivardia, R.; Pope, H.G.; Borowiecki, J.J.; Cohane, G.H. Biceps and body image: The relationship between muscularity and self-esteem, depression, and eating disorder symptoms. *Psychol. Men Masc.* **2004**, *5*, 112–120. [CrossRef]
33. Harrison, K.; Cantor, J. The Relationship Between Media Consumption and Eating Disorders. *J. Commun.* **1997**, *47*, 40–67. [CrossRef]
34. Barthels, F.; Meyer, F.; Pietrowsky, R. Orthorektisches Ernährungsverhalten. *Ernahrungs Umschau* **2015**, *62*, 156–161. [CrossRef]
35. Segura-Garcia, C.; Ramacciotti, C.; Rania, M.; Aloi, M.; Caroleo, M.; Bruni, A.; Gazzarrini, D.; Sinopoli, F.; De Fazio, P. The prevalence of orthorexia nervosa among eating disorder patients after treatment. *Eat. Weight Disord.* **2015**, *20*, 161–166. [CrossRef] [PubMed]
36. Arusoğlu, G.; Kabakçi, E.; Köksal, G.; Merdol, T.K. Orthorexia Nervosa and Adapta on of ORTO-11 into Turkish. *Türk Psikiyatr. Derg. Turkish J. Psychiatry* **2008**, *19*, 283–291.
37. Brytek-Matera, A.; Krupa, M.; Poggiogalle, E.; Donini, L.M. Adaptation of the ORTHO-15 test to Polish women and men. *Eat. Weight Disord.* **2014**, *19*, 69–76. [CrossRef] [PubMed]

38. Sanlier, N.; Yassibas, E.; Bilici, S.; Sahin, G.; Celik, B. Does the rise in eating disorders lead to increasing risk of orthorexia nervosa? Correlations with gender, education, and body mass index. *Ecol. Food Nutr.* **2016**, *55*, 266–278. [CrossRef] [PubMed]
39. Asil, E.; Sürücüoğlu, M.S. Orthorexia Nervosa in Turkish Dietitians. *Ecol. Food Nutr.* **2015**, *54*, 303–313. [CrossRef]
40. Sellin, J. Dietary Dilemmas, Delusions, and Decisions. *Clin. Gastroenterol. Hepatol.* **2014**, *12*, 1601–1604. [CrossRef]
41. Kaźmierczak, N.; Łukasiewicz, K.; Niedzielski, A. The outlook, behavior and eating habits occurring in the course of orthorexia nervosa. *Nurs. Public Heal.* **2017**, *7*, 125–133. [CrossRef]
42. Głębocka, A. *Niezadowolenie z Wyglądu a Rozpaczliwa Kontrola Wagi*; Oficyna Wydawnicza "Impuls": Kraków, Poland, 2009.
43. Wadolowska, L.; Niedzwiedzka, E.; Kowalkowska, J. Kwestionariusz Częstotliwości Spożycia Żywności FFQ-6 [Food Frequency Questionnaire FFQ-6]. Available online: http://www.uwm.edu.pl/edu/lidiawadolowska/ (accessed on 15 October 2018).
44. Wądołowska, L. Validation of food frequency questionaire–FFQ. Rreproducibility assessment. *Bromatol. Chem. Toksykol.* **2005**, *38*, 27–33.
45. Ribeiro-Silva, R.C.; Fiaccone, R.L.; Conceição-Machado, M.E.P.D.; Ruiz, A.S.; Barreto, M.L.; Santana, M.L.P. Body image dissatisfaction and dietary patterns according to nutritional status in adolescents. *J. Pediatr.* **2018**, *94*, 155–161. [CrossRef]
46. Bibiloni, M.D.M.; Pich, J.; Pons, A.; Tur, J.A. Body image and eating patterns among adolescents. *BMC Public Health* **2013**, *13*, 1104. [CrossRef] [PubMed]
47. World Health Organization. Body Mass Index—BMI. Available online: http://www.euro.who.int/en/health-topics/disease-prevention/nutrition/a-healthy-lifestyle/body-mass-index-bmi (accessed on 15 September 2018).
48. Field, A. *Discovering Statistics Using SPSS*, 3rd ed.; Sage Publications: London, UK, 2009.
49. Wong, Y.; Lin, J.S.; Chang, Y.J. Body satisfaction, emotional intelligence, and the development of disturbed eating: A survey of Taiwanese students. *Asia Pac. J. Clin. Nutr.* **2014**, *23*, 651–659. [CrossRef] [PubMed]
50. Ab Hamid, M.R.; Azman, N.N.; Said, N.; Rahman, A.N.A. Orthorexia Nervosa and the Quality of Life among Health Sciences Students in Universiti Teknologi MARA, Selangor. *Environ. Proc. J.* **2018**, *3*, 121. [CrossRef]
51. De Souza, Q.J.O.V.; Rodrigues, A.M. Comportamento de risco para ortorexia nervosa em estudantes de nutrição. *J. Bras. Psiquiatr.* **2014**, *63*, 201–204. [CrossRef]
52. Malmborg, J.; Bremander, A.; Olsson, M.C.; Bergman, S. Health status, physical activity, and orthorexia nervosa: A comparison between exercise science students and business students. *Appetite* **2017**, *109*, 137–143. [CrossRef] [PubMed]
53. Grammatikopoulou, M.G.; Gkiouras, K.; Markaki, A.; Theodoridis, X.; Tsakiri, V.; Mavridis, P.; Dardavessis, T.; Chourdakis, M. Food addiction, orthorexia, and food-related stress among dietetics students. *Eat. Weight Disord.* **2018**, *23*, 459–467. [CrossRef] [PubMed]
54. Gubiec, E.; Stetkiewicz-Lewandowicz, A.; Rasmus, P.; Sobów, T. Orthorexia in a group of dietetics students. *Medycyna Ogólna i Nauki o Zdrowiu* **2015**, *21*, 95–100. [CrossRef]
55. Borzekowski, D.L.G.; Schenk, S.; Wilson, J.L.; Peebles, R. E-Ana and e-Mia: A content analysis of pro-eating disorder web sites. *Am. J. Public Health* **2010**, *100*, 1526–1534. [CrossRef]
56. Norris, M.L.; Boydell, K.M.; Pinhas, L.; Katzman, D.K. Ana and the Internet: A review of pro-anorexia websites. *Int. J. Eat. Disord.* **2006**, *39*, 443–447. [CrossRef]
57. Aksoydan, E.; Camci, N. Prevalence of orthorexia nervosa among Turkish performance artists. *Eat. Weight Disord.* **2009**, *14*, 33–37. [CrossRef]
58. Kinzl, J.F.; Hauer, K.; Traweger, C.; Kiefer, I. Orthorexia nervosa in dieticians. *Psychother. Psychosom.* **2006**, *75*, 395–396. [CrossRef] [PubMed]
59. Dell'Osso, L.; Abelli, M.; Carpita, B.; Pini, S.; Castellini, G.; Carmassi, C.; Ricca, V. Historical evolution of the concept of anorexia nervosa and relationships with orthorexia nervosa, autism, and obsessive-compulsive spectrum. *Neuropsychiatr. Dis. Treat.* **2016**, *12*, 1651–1660. [CrossRef] [PubMed]
60. Zipfel, S.; Giel, K.E.; Bulik, C.M.; Hay, P.; Schmidt, U. Anorexia nervosa: Aetiology, assessment, and treatment. *Lancet Psychiatry* **2015**, *2*, 1099–1111. [CrossRef]

61. Oakes, M.E. Differences in judgments of food healthfulness by young and elderly women. *Food Qual. Prefer.* **2003**, *14*, 227–236. [CrossRef]
62. Jeżewska-Zychowicz, M. Stereotypical thinking about food in the context of promoting weight gain. *Ann. Natl. Inst. Hyg.* **2007**, *58*, 437–444.
63. Goswami, S.; Sachdeva, S.; Sachdeva, R. Body image satisfaction among female college students. *Ind. Psychiatry J.* **2012**, *21*, 168–172.
64. Szyszkowska, B.; Łepecka-Klusek, C.; Kozłowicz, K. The change of the image of women in the modern world and eating disorders. *Arch. Physiother. Glob. Res.* **2014**, *18*, 11–16. [CrossRef]
65. Goncalves, J.D.A.; Moreira, E.A.M.; Trindade, E.B.S.D.M.; Fiates, G.M.R. Eating disorders in childhood and adolescence. *Rev. Paul. Pediatr.* **2013**, *31*, 96–103. [CrossRef]
66. Tiggemann, M. Sociocultural perspectives on human appearance and body image. In *Body Image: A Handbook od Science, Practice and Prevention*; Cash, T.F., Smolak, L., Eds.; Guilford Press: New York, NY, USA, 2011.
67. Czepczor, K.; Kościcka, K.; Brytek-Matera, A. The sociocultural attitudes towards appearance and body dissatisfaction among late adolescence: A pilot study. *Pol. Forum Psychol.* **2016**, *21*, 364–377.
68. Brechan, I.; Kvalem, I.L. Relationship between body dissatisfaction and disordered eating: Mediating role of self-esteem and depression. *Eat. Behav.* **2015**, *17*, 49–58. [CrossRef]
69. Ferguson, C.J. In the eye of the beholder: Thin-ideal media affects some, but not most, viewers in a meta-analytic review of body dissatisfaction in women and men. *Psychol. Pop. Media Cult.* **2013**, *2*, 20–37. [CrossRef]
70. Mitchell, S.H.; Petrie, T.A.; Greenleaf, C.A.; Martin, S.B. Moderators of the internalization-body dissatisfaction relationship in middle school girls. *Body Image* **2012**, *9*, 431–440. [CrossRef] [PubMed]
71. Heron, K.E.; Smyth, J.M.; Akano, E.; Wonderlich, S.A. Assessing body image in young children: A preliminary study of racial and developmental differences. *SAGE Open* **2013**, *3*, 1–7. [CrossRef]
72. Bucchianeri, M.; Arikian, A.; Hannan, P.; Eisenberg, M. Body Dissatisfaction from Adolescence to Young Adulthood: Findings from a 10-Year Longitudinal Study. *Body Image* **2013**, *10*, 1–15. [CrossRef] [PubMed]
73. Blake, C.E.; Hébert, J.R.; Lee, D.C.; Adams, S.A.; Steck, S.E.; Sui, X.; Kuk, J.L.; Baruth, M.; Blair, S.N. Adults with greater weight satisfaction report more positive health behaviors and have better health status regardless of BMI. *J. Obes.* **2013**, *2013*, 291371. [CrossRef] [PubMed]
74. Afifi, T.O.; Sareen, J.; Fortier, J.; Taillieu, T.; Turner, S.; Cheung, K.; Henriksen, C.A. Child maltreatment and eating disorders among men and women in adulthood: Results from a nationally representative United States sample. *Int. J. Eat. Disord.* **2017**, *50*, 1281–1296. [CrossRef] [PubMed]
75. Brown, K.L.; LaRose, J.G.; Mezuk, B. The relationship between body mass index, binge eating disorder and suicidality. *BMC Psychiatry* **2018**, *18*, 196. [CrossRef]
76. Fisher, M.M.; Rosen, D.S.; Ornstein, R.M.; Mammel, K.A.; Katzman, D.K.; Rome, E.S.; Callahan, S.T.; Malizio, J.; Kearney, S.; Walsh, B.T. Characteristics of Avoidant/Restrictive Food Intake Disorder in Children and Adolescents: A "new disorder" in DSM-5. *J. Adolesc. Health* **2014**, *55*, 49–52. [CrossRef]
77. Norris, M.L.; Robinson, A.; Obeid, N.; Harrison, M.; Spettigue, W.; Henderson, K. Exploring avoidant/restrictive food intake disorder in eating disordered patients: A descriptive study. *Int. J. Eat. Disord.* **2014**, *47*, 495–499. [CrossRef]
78. Donini, L.M.; Marsili, D.; Graziani, M.P.; Imbriale, M.; Cannella, C. Orthorexia nervosa: A preliminary study with a proposal for diagnosis and an attempt to measure the dimension of the phenomenon. *Eat. Weight Disord.* **2004**, *9*, 151–157. [CrossRef]
79. Eriksson, L.; Baigi, A.; Marklund, B.; Lindgren, E.C. Social physique anxiety and sociocultural attitudes toward appearance impact on orthorexia test in fitness participants. *Scand. J. Med. Sci. Sport.* **2008**, *18*, 389–394. [CrossRef] [PubMed]
80. Bağci Bosi, A.T.; Çamur, D.; Güler, Ç. Prevalence of orthorexia nervosa in resident medical doctors in the faculty of medicine (Ankara, Turkey). *Appetite* **2007**, *49*, 661–666. [CrossRef] [PubMed]
81. Korinth, A.; Schiess, S.; Westenhoefer, J. Eating behaviour and eating disorders in students of nutrition sciences. *Public Health Nutr.* **2010**, *13*, 32–37. [CrossRef] [PubMed]
82. Kiss-Leizer, M.; Rigó, A. People behind unhealthy obsession to healthy food: The personality profile of tendency to orthorexia nervosa. *Eat. Weight Disord.* **2018**. [CrossRef] [PubMed]
83. Brytek-Matera, A.; Donini, L.M.; Krupa, M.; Poggiogalle, E.; Hay, P. Orthorexia nervosa and self-attitudinal aspects of body image in female and male university students. *J. Eat. Disord.* **2015**, *3*, 2. [CrossRef] [PubMed]

84. Katta, R.; Desai, S.P. Diet and Dermatology. *Clin. Aesthet. Dermatol.* **2014**, *7*, 46–51. [CrossRef]
85. Barnett, M.J.; Dripps, W.R.; Blomquist, K.K. Organivore or organorexic? Examining the relationship between alternative food network engagement, disordered eating, and special diets. *Appetite* **2016**, *105*, 713–720. [CrossRef] [PubMed]
86. Barthels, F.; Meyer, F.; Pietrowsky, R. Orthorexic and restrained eating behaviour in vegans, vegetarians, and individuals on a diet. *Eat. Weight Disord.* **2018**, *23*, 159–166. [CrossRef] [PubMed]
87. Brytek-Matera, A.; Czepczor-Bernat, K.; Jurzak, H.; Kornacka, M.; Kołodziejczyk, N. Strict health-oriented eating patterns (orthorexic eating behaviours) and their connection with a vegetarian and vegan diet. *Eat. Weight Disord.* **2018**. [CrossRef]
88. Luck-Sikorski, C.; Jung, F.; Schlosser, K.; Riedel-Heller, S.G. Is orthorexic behavior common in the general public? A large representative study in Germany. *Eat. Weight Disord.* **2018**. [CrossRef]
89. Kays, K.; Gathercoal, K.; Buhrow, W. Does survey format influence self-disclosure on sensitive question items? *Comput. Hum. Behav.* **2012**, *28*, 251–256. [CrossRef]
90. Johansson, G.; Wikman, Å.; Åhrén, A.-M.; Hallmans, G.; Johansson, I. Underreporting of energy intake in repeated 24-hour recalls related to gender, age, weight status, day of interview, educational level, reported food intake, smoking habits and area of living. *Public Health Nutr.* **2001**, *4*, 919–927. [CrossRef] [PubMed]
91. Hamer, M.; Mishra, G.D. Dietary patterns and cardiovascular risk markers in the UK Low Income Diet and Nutrition Survey. *Nutr. Metab. Cardiovasc. Dis.* **2010**, *20*, 491–497. [CrossRef] [PubMed]
92. McCourt, H.J.; Draffin, C.R.; Woodside, J.V.; Cardwell, C.R.; Young, I.S.; Hunter, S.J.; Murray, L.J.; Boreham, C.A.; Gallagher, A.M.; Neville, C.E.; et al. Dietary patterns and cardiovascular risk factors in adolescents and young adults: The Northern Ireland Young Hearts Project. *Br. J. Nutr.* **2014**, *112*, 1685–1698. [CrossRef] [PubMed]
93. Roberts, K.; Cade, J.; Dawson, J.; Holdsworth, M. Empirically derived dietary patterns in uk adults are associated with sociodemographic characteristics, lifestyle, and diet quality. *Nutrients* **2018**, *10*, 177. [CrossRef] [PubMed]
94. Roncero, M.; Barrada, J.R.; Perpiñá, C. Measuring Orthorexia Nervosa: Psychometric Limitations of the ORTO-15. *Span. J. Psychol.* **2017**, *20*, E41. [CrossRef] [PubMed]
95. Missbach, B.; Hinterbuchinger, B.; Dreiseitl, V.; Zellhofer, S.; Kurz, C.; König, J. When eating right, is measured wrong! A validation and critical examination of the ORTO-15 questionnaire in German. *PLoS ONE* **2015**, *10*, e0235772. [CrossRef]

nutrients

MDPI

Article

Binge-Type Eating in Rats is Facilitated by Neuromedin U Receptor 2 in the Nucleus Accumbens and Ventral Tegmental Area

Ashley E. Smith [1,2], James M. Kasper [1,3], Ara 13 [1], Noelle C. Anastasio [1,3] and Jonathan D. Hommel [1,2,3,*]

1 Center for Addiction Research, University of Texas Medical Branch, Galveston, TX 77555, USA; aesmith@utmb.edu (A.E.S.); jakasper@utmb.edu (J.M.K.); ara13c@gmail.com (Ara 13); ncanasta@utmb.edu (N.C.A.)

2 Department of Neuroscience, Cell Biology and Anatomy, University of Texas Medical Branch, Galveston, TX 77555, USA

3 Department of Pharmacology and Toxicology, University of Texas Medical Branch, Galveston, TX 77555, USA

* Correspondence: jdhommel@utmb.edu; Tel.: +1-409-747-7057

Received: 20 December 2018; Accepted: 30 January 2019; Published: 2 February 2019

Abstract: Binge-eating disorder (BED) is the most common eating disorder, characterized by rapid, recurrent overconsumption of highly palatable food in a short time frame. BED shares an overlapping behavioral phenotype with obesity, which is also linked to the overconsumption of highly palatable foods. The reinforcing properties of highly palatable foods are mediated by the nucleus accumbens (NAc) and the ventral tegmental area (VTA), which have been implicated in the overconsumption behavior observed in BED and obesity. A potential regulator of binge-type eating behavior is the G protein-coupled receptor neuromedin U receptor 2 (NMUR2). Previous research demonstrated that NMUR2 knockdown potentiates binge-type consumption of high-fat food. We correlated binge-type consumption across a spectrum of fat and carbohydrate mixtures with synaptosomal NMUR2 protein expression in the NAc and VTA of rats. Synaptosomal NMUR2 protein in the NAc demonstrated a strong positive correlation with binge intake of a "lower"-fat (higher carbohydrate) mixture, whereas synaptosomal NMUR2 protein in the VTA demonstrated a strong negative correlation with binge intake of an "extreme" high-fat (0% carbohydrate) mixture. Taken together, these data suggest that NMUR2 may differentially regulate binge-type eating within the NAc and the VTA.

Keywords: binge-eating disorder; BED; obesity; binge-type eating; neuromedin U receptor 2; NMUR2; nucleus accumbens; ventral tegmental area

1. Introduction

Binge-eating disorder (BED) is an under-recognized public health problem that is prevalent worldwide [1,2]. In the US, BED affects 3.5% of adult women and 2% of adult men, with a combined lifetime prevalence of 1.4% [1,2]. Although BED is the most common eating disorder, it remains both under-diagnosed and understudied [2]. Therefore, a more mechanistic appreciation of feeding behaviors that contribute to BED is critical to understanding disease etiology, and for identifying potential pharmacotherapeutic targets.

BED is characterized by binge episodes when an individual overconsumes highly-palatable food in a discrete period of time ($\leq$2 h) [3–5]. The frequency of these binge episodes is a hallmark of BED and is used to determine the disease's severity [3–5]. BED is partially attributed to the increased availability of highly palatable food, and also shares physiological, psychological, and epidemiological overlaps with obesity [1,4,6–10].

Obesity is an alarming health crisis that affects 39.8% of adults within the US alone [11]. Obese individuals present a challenging public health problem due to the increased risk of life-threatening co-morbidities [12]. Thus, the health burden of obesity is immense and demands an improved understanding of the feeding behaviors that contribute to obesity. Similar to BED, one of the feeding behaviors that contributes to obesity is the overconsumption of highly palatable food.

Highly palatable food, including high-fat food, is both energy dense and highly reinforcing in humans and rodents [13]. These reinforcing properties promote overconsumption behavior that is potentiated by dysregulation in portion control [14–17]. In fact, individuals with BED ascribe higher reinforcement value to high-fat food than individuals without BED [18]. The reinforcing properties of food are largely encoded by brain regions within the mesolimbic "reward" pathway, which includes the nucleus accumbens (NAc) and the ventral tegmental area (VTA) [19,20]. Both the NAc and the VTA have been implicated in BED and obesity [2,9,19–25]. Reinforcement value is mediated by the NAc—a key neuroanatomical region that regulates hedonic feeding, or food intake in the absence of a caloric deficit [9,19,20]. The VTA is also linked to reinforcement value, and affects obesogenic diet consumption [26].

Overall, BED and obesity share multifaceted feeding behaviors involving multiple brain circuits that regulate a complex interplay of emotions, food intake, and food reinforcement. These feeding behaviors can be probed using animal models designed for quantifying specific aspects of these diseases. Models of binge-type eating have been validated in rodents, demonstrating success in studying the overconsumption behavior characteristic of both BED and obesity [27–35]. The intermittent access model provides ad libitum access to regular chow and water, with limited presentation of a highly palatable food, which simulates a binge episode, similar to that observed in BED and obesity [27,29,30,32,33,35]. While this model can recreate and quantify food intake during a binge episode, it does not replicate the psychological aspects of BED, such as feelings of loss of control and feelings of shame and guilt [2–5]. Nonetheless, this model is helpful in understanding neural mechanisms underlying binge-type consumption and identifying potential regulators of this specific maladaptive feeding behavior.

Here, we investigate a novel mediator of binge-type eating, the neuropeptide receptor neuromedin U receptor 2 (NMUR2). NMUR2 is a G protein-coupled receptor predominantly expressed throughout the mammalian central nervous system. This receptor is known to regulate food intake and body weight [36–40]. For example, NMUR2-knockout mice are hyperphagic and demonstrate increased food intake patterns [41]. Additionally, deletion of hypothalamic NMUR2 via viral-mediated RNAi resulted in increased motivation for high-fat food and potentiated binge-type eating [32,42]. These studies indicate that NMUR2 regulates food intake—a process that is dysregulated in BED and obesity. Interestingly, the role of NMUR2 in reinforcement brain centers such as the NAc and VTA in binge-type eating has not been explored.

Importantly, the endogenous expression of NMUR2 is highly variable among individuals and among various brain regions [41,43,44]. Neuroanatomical variability and individual differences in NMUR2 expression may underlie aspects of individual differences observed in BED and obesity [45]. The purpose of the current study was to explore relationships between synaptosomal NMUR2 expression in the NAc and the VTA—key brain regions associated with reinforcement—in a rodent model of binge-type eating across a spectrum of dietary fat and carbohydrate contents. Our findings revealed a strong positive correlation between the intake of "lower"-fat (i.e., higher carbohydrate) food and synaptosomal NMUR2 protein expression in the NAc, and a strong negative correlation between the intake of "extreme" high-fat (0% carbohydrate) food and synaptosomal NMUR2 protein expression in the VTA.

2. Materials and Methods

2.1. Animals

Male Sprague-Dawley rats (Harlan, Houston, TX, USA) weighing 225–250 g were used in all experiments. Animals were housed individually in a temperature (i.e., 21–23 °C) and humidity (40%–50%) controlled environment with a standard 12 h light–dark cycle (lights on between 06:00 and 18:00 h). All animals were given ad libitum access to normal chow (17% fat by kcal; Teklad LM-485 Mouse/Rat Sterilizable Diet; Teklad Diets, Madison, WI, USA) and water in their home cages, including during binge sessions. Upon arrival, animals were allowed to acclimate to the room for seven days prior to handling and experimental procedures. All experiments were conducted in accordance with the NIH Guide for Use and Care of Laboratory Animals (2011), and with approval from the Institutional Animal Use and Care Committee at the University of Texas Medical Branch.

2.2. NMUR2 Immunohistochemistry

Rats (n = 4) were anesthetized with 1%–5% isoflurane, perfused with phosphate buffered saline for 5 min, followed by 4% paraformaldehyde (PFA) for 15 min. Brains were removed and sliced into 40 micronsections using a cryostat. NAc and VTA sections were stained as described in previous studies [33,43,46]. Briefly, sections were washed twice in 1× PBS, and then antigen-unmasked with 1% SDS for 5 min. Next, sections were blocked in donkey serum and incubated in 1:150 primary antibody rabbit αNMUR2 (NBP1-02351, Novus Biologicals, Littleton, CO, USA) overnight. The following day, sections were washed three times in 1X PBS, then incubated with 1:200 donkey αrabbit IgG Alexa Fluor 568 (A10042, Invitrogen, Carlsbad, CA, USA). Images were acquired using Leica True Confocal Scanner SPE in confocal mode and Leica Application Suite × software (Leica Microsystems, Wetzlar, Germany).

2.3. Binge Study Design

Our binge-type eating protocol was based on previously published models [27,29,32,33,35]. Briefly, male Sprague-Dawley rats (n = 10) were maintained on a diet of normal chow (17% fat by kcal) and water. Rats were not restricted from feeding prior to the binge period, and had ad libitum access to normal chow and water throughout the study, including during the binge period. Two days prior to experiments, animals were exposed to a mixture of 60% fat by kcal and 40% carbohydrate by kcal to minimize food neophobia. Fat–carbohydrate mixtures were prepared and weighed immediately before the binge period. Vegetable shortening (Crisco, Orrville, OH, USA) comprised of 100% fat by energy (110 kcal/12 g serving with 110 kcal from fat; 9.16 kcal/g) was mixed with marshmallow creme (Kraft, Chicago, IL, USA), containing 100% carbohydrate by energy (45 kcal/13 g serving with 0 kcal from fat; 3.46 kcal/g) to create a total of five fat mixtures of varying fat–carbohydrate content. The fat–carbohydrate mixtures were prepared as follows: 2.18 g fat and 23.12 g carbohydrate were mixed for 20% fat/80% carbohydrate/0% protein by energy, 4.36 g fat and 17.34 g carbohydrate were mixed for 40% fat/60% carbohydrate/0% protein by energy, 6.55 g fat and 11.56 g carbohydrate were mixed for 60% fat/40% carbohydrate/0% protein by energy, 8.73 g fat and 5.78 g carbohydrate were mixed for 80% fat/20% carbohydrate/0% protein by energy, and 10 g fat and 0 g carbohydrate was used for 100% fat/0% carbohydrate/0% protein by energy. One limitation is that the marshmallow creme does contain any flavoring. However, the consistency and texture of the marshmallow creme were required to promote homogeneity among the mixtures.

Rats were randomized into five groups using a Latin square design, with each animal receiving all fat–carbohydrate mixtures in a randomized order. Each group was presented with mixtures of 20% fat (80% carbohydrate), 40% fat (60% carbohydrate), 60% fat (40% carbohydrate), 80% fat (20% carbohydrate), and 100% fat (0% carbohydrate) for a period of 5 days. Exposure to fat–carbohydrate mixtures occurred during binge 1 at the first 2-h of the dark cycle (18:00–20:00) and binge 2 at 2-h near the end of the light cycle (14:00–16:00). For all exposures, fat–carbohydrate mixtures were weighed prior to presentation and then immediately after the 2-h binge period. Differences in food weight were interpreted as total grams consumed or total calories consumed during the binge period.

2.4. NAc and VTA Protein Extraction

After the completion of binge studies, rats (n = 10) were anesthetized with 1%–5% isoflurane, and brains were removed. Both NAc and VTA were microdissected from each rat, using guidance from a rat brain atlas [26,44,47], then stored at −80 °C until protein extraction. The crude synaptosomal protein fraction was isolated as previously published to identify long-term changes in protein expression [48]. NAc and VTA tissue were homogenized in ice-cold Krebs-sucrose buffer containing protease inhibitors (P8340, Millipore Sigma, St. Louis, MO, USA) and phosphatase inhibitors (P5726, P0044 Millipore Sigma, St. Louis, MO, USA). The crude synaptosomal protein fractionation protocol enriches samples for pre- and postsynaptic proteins (i.e., presynaptic terminals, postsynaptic membranes, etc.) [49]. Samples were centrifuged for 10 min at 100 g at 4 °C to pellet the nuclear protein fraction. The supernatant was centrifuged for 20 min at 16,000 g at 4 °C to separate the crude synaptosomal protein fraction (pellet). The NAc and VTA synaptosomal protein fractions were used for all further analyses. After extraction, total protein concentration was determined using a Pierce BCA Protein Assay Kit (23225, Thermo Fisher, Waltham, MA, USA).

2.5. NAc and VTA NMUR2 Protein Expression

NAc (n = 10) and VTA (n = 10) samples were assayed for NMUR2 protein expression using the Wes™ (ProteinSimple, San Jose, CA, USA) automated Western blotting system. Wes™ is a capillary electrophoresis-based immunoblotting instrument, and was optimized for receptor quantification in brain tissues [48,50]. Wes™ reagents (biotinylated molecular weight marker, streptavidin-HRP fluorescent standards, luminol-S, hydrogen peroxide, sample buffer, DTT, stacking matrix, separation matrix, running buffer, wash buffer, matrix removal buffer, secondary antibodies, antibody diluent, and capillaries) were obtained from the manufacturer (ProteinSimple) and used according to the manufacturer's specifications with minor modifications. NMUR2 polyclonal antibody (NBP1-02351, Novus Biologicals, Littleton, CO, USA) was diluted 1:50 in antibody diluent.

Samples were prepared and subjected to capillary electrophoresis-based immunoblotting as described previously [49]. Briefly, 2 µg of protein was denatured in 0.1× sample buffer and 5× master mix at 95 °C for 5 min. Then, samples and primary antibody were dispensed into a prefilled microplate (ProteinSimple). Capillary electrophoresis (375 V, 25 min, 25 °C) and immunodetection were completed using the following settings: separation matrix load, 200 s; stacking matrix load, 15 s; sample load, 9 s; antibody diluent, 30 min; primary antibody incubation, 60 min; secondary antibody incubation, 30 min; and chemiluminescent signal exposure for 15, 30, 120, 240, and 480 s. Data were analyzed using Compass Software (ProteinSimple). The Western blot analysis signal was defined as the area under the curve (AUC) for the NMUR2 peak at 48 kDa and representative "virtual blot" electrophoretic images for NMUR2 were automatically generated by the Compass Software (ProteinSimple).

2.6. Statistical Analysis

Binge-type eating across a spectrum of fat–carbohydrate contents in binge 1 and binge 2 was analyzed by repeated measures one-way ANOVA and Bonferroni's multiple comparisons. All comparisons were made to the intake of a 20% fat mixture. Correlations between binge-type eating across a spectrum of fat–carbohydrate contents and NMUR2 protein expression in the NAc and the VTA were analyzed by linear regression. All statistical analyses were performed in GraphPad Prism 7.0a (GraphPad Software Inc., La Jolla, CA, USA) with an experiment-wise error rate of $\alpha = 0.05$.

3. Results

3.1. NMUR2 is Expressed Presynaptically in the NAc and the VTA

Previous work demonstrated that NMUR2 is expressed postsynaptically in the hypothalamus and presynaptically in the NAc [32,46]. We confirmed NAc and VTA localization of NMUR2 with immunohistochemistry. We observed a "beads on a string" staining pattern indicative of presynaptic NMUR2 expression in the NAc and in the VTA (Figure 1).

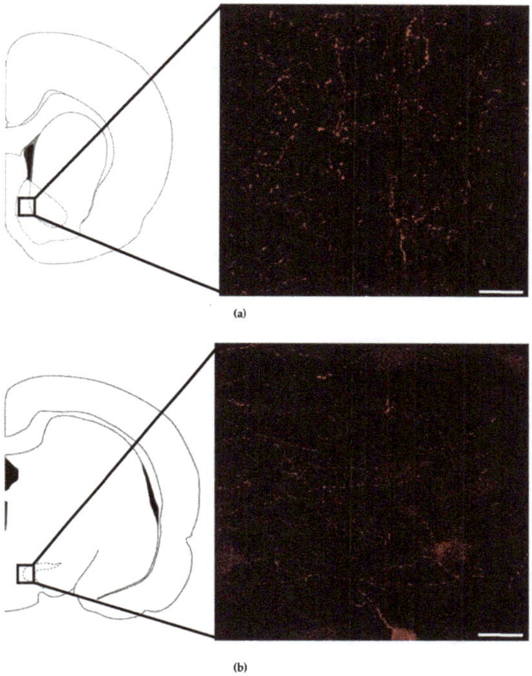

Figure 1. Neuropeptide receptor neuromedin U receptor 2 (NMUR2)immunostaining in the nucleus accumbens (NAc) and the ventral tegmental area (VTA). (**a**) Representative image of NMUR2 immunostaining in the NAc (bregma +1.92); (**b**) Representative image of NMUR2 immunostaining in the VTA (bregma −4.80). Images were acquired from the regions indicated at in confocal mode, scale bar = 25 μm.

3.2. Fat Content and Binge-Type Eating

Using our binge-type eating paradigm, we quantified how much rats would consume during a 2-h binge period (Figure 2). Figure 2 illustrates binge intake across a spectrum of fat–carbohydrate contents during binge 1 and binge 2. Comparisons were made within each binge to the intake of a 20% fat (80% carbohydrate) mixture. In binge 1, rats consumed significantly fewer grams of the 100% fat (0% carbohydrate) mixture ($p = 0.0003$) compared to the 20% fat (80% carbohydrate) mixture (Figure 2). In binge 2, rats consumed significantly more grams of the 60% fat (40% carbohydrate) mixture ($p = 0.010$) compared to the 20% fat (80% carbohydrate) mixture (Figure 2). Notably, common Western diet foods contain percentages of fat that fall at the peak of the curve, including French fries (42% fat), potato chips (56% fat), cheesecake (63% fat), and peanut butter (78% fat), which gives context for the percentages of fat used in our rodent studies.

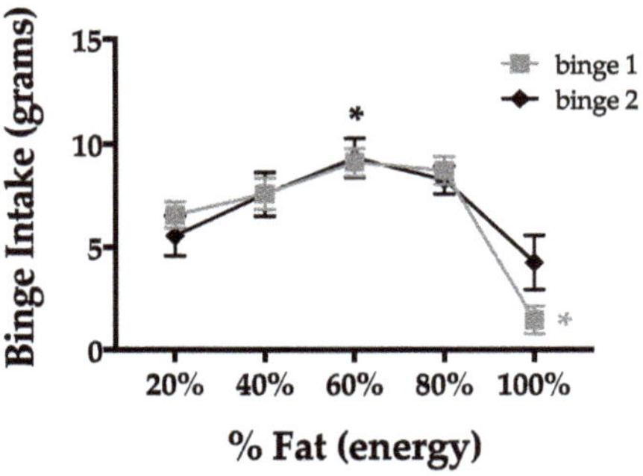

Figure 2. Rat binge-type eating across a spectrum of fat–carbohydrate contents. Binge-type eating in rats was highest at 60% fat (40% carbohydrate) and lowest at 80% fat (20% carbohydrate) compared to 20% fat (80% carbohydrate). * $p < 0.05$.

3.3. Binge-Type Intake and NAc NMUR2 Protein Expression

To determine the relationship between binge-type intake and NMUR2 expression in the NAc, we quantified NAc NMUR2 synaptosomal protein (Figure 3a), and correlated it to fat intake during the binge period (Figure 3b–f). Interestingly, NAc NMUR2 expression demonstrated a strong positive correlation with binge intake of a "lower"-fat (higher carbohydrate) mixture, specifically 20% fat (80% carbohydrate) ($p = 0.047$) and 40% fat (60% carbohydrate) ($p < 0.001$) (Figure 3b–c). As fat content increased and carbohydrate content decreased, the relationship diminished. However, no significant correlation was observed when NAc NMUR2 was correlated to total calories consumed to account for energy density. In addition, we found no significant correlation between NAc NMUR2 and binge intake of a 60% (40%) ($p = 0.86$), 80% (20%) ($p = 0.084$), or 100% (0%) ($p = 0.86$) fat (carbohydrate) mixture (Figure 3d–f).

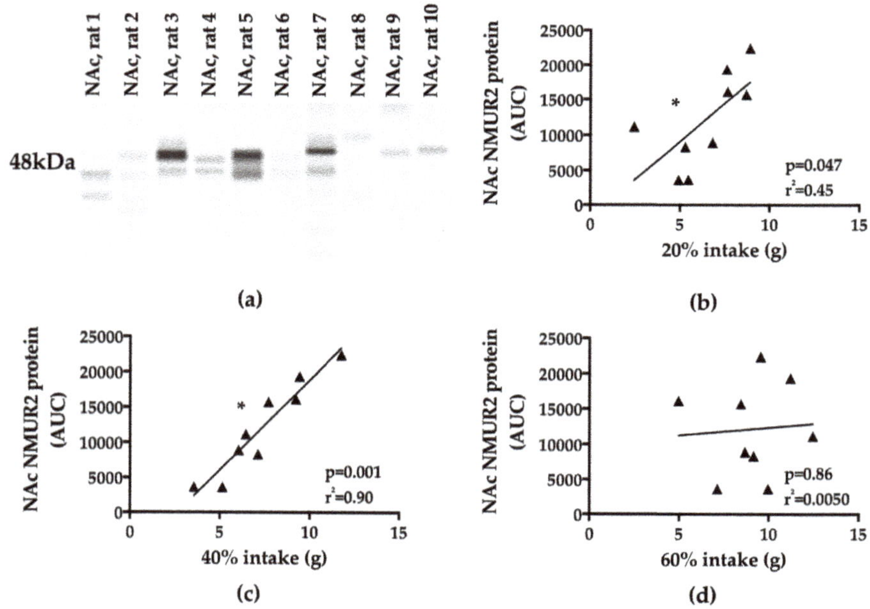

Figure 3. *Cont.*

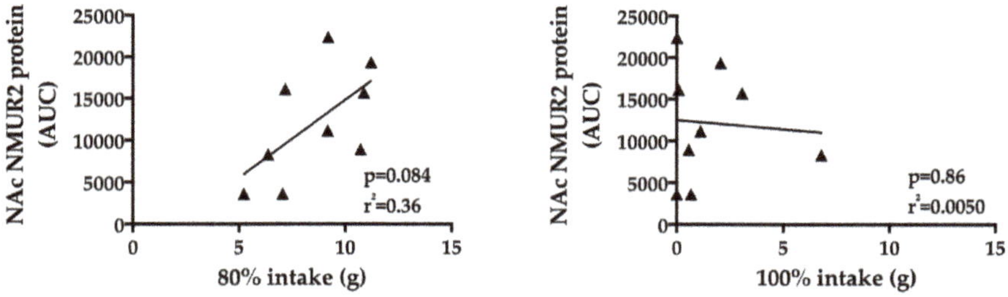

(e) (f)

Figure 3. NAc NMUR2 protein expression was positively correlated with binge-type eating. (**a**) representative Western blot image for NMUR2 synaptosomal protein from NAc samples; (**b**) NAc NMUR2 expression was positively correlated with intake of a 20% fat (80% carbohydrate) mixture; (**c**) NAc NMUR2 expression was positively correlated with intake of a 40% fat (60% carbohydrate) mixture; (**e**) NAc NMUR2 expression was not correlated with intake of a 60% fat (40% carbohydrate) mixture; (**f**) NAc NMUR2 expression was not correlated with intake of an 80% fat (20% carbohydrate) mixture; (**g**) NAc NMUR2 protein expression was not correlated with intake of a 100% fat (0% carbohydrate) mixture. AUC: area under the curve. * $p < 0.05$.

3.4. Binge-Type Intake and VTA NMUR2 Protein Expression

Next, we quantified VTA NMUR2 synaptosomal protein (Figure 4a). We correlated VTA NMUR2 synaptosomal protein to fat intake during the binge period (Figure 4b–f). No significant correlation was observed between VTA NMUR2 and binge intake of a 20% (80%) ($p = 0.11$), 40% (60%) ($p = 0.37$), 60% (40%) ($p = 0.95$), or 80% (20%) ($p = 0.26$) fat (carbohydrate) mixture (Figure 4b–e). VTA NMUR2 demonstrated a strong negative correlation with binge intake of an "extreme" high-fat mixture of 100% fat (0% carbohydrate) ($p = 0.034$) (Figure 4f). Interestingly, the slope of the trend line transitioned from a positive slope value for the lower-fat mixtures (higher carbohydrate) to a negative slope for the higher-fat mixtures (lower carbohydrate).

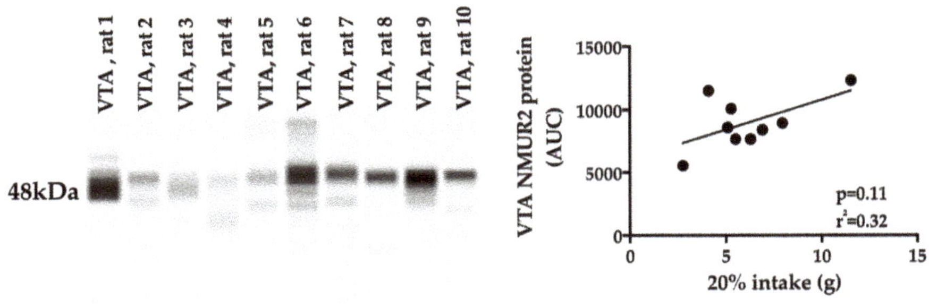

(a) (b)

Figure 4. *Cont.*

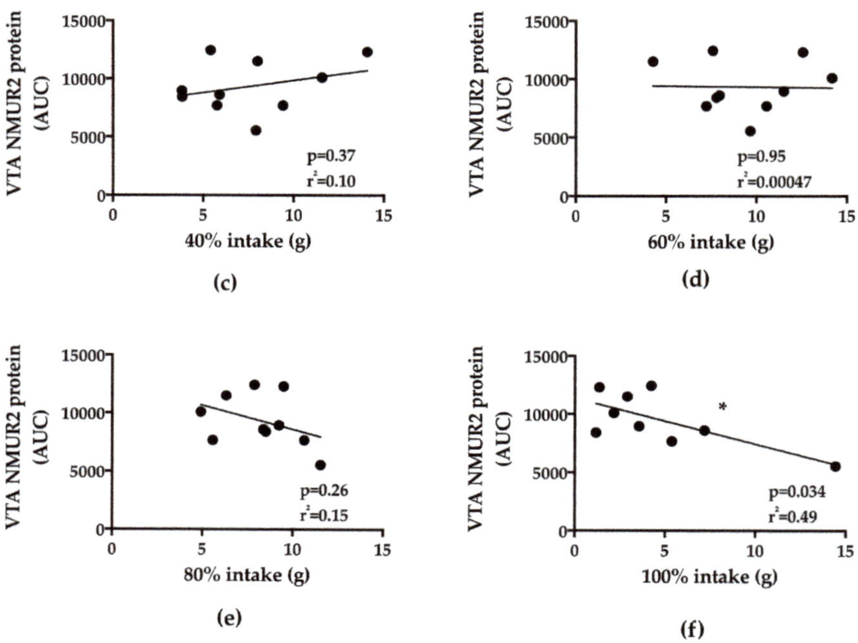

Figure 4. VTA NMUR2 protein expression was negatively correlated with binge-type eating. (**a**) representative Western blot image for NMUR2 synaptosomal protein from VTA samples; (**b**) VTA NMUR2 expression was not correlated with intake of a 20% fat (80% carbohydrate) mixture; (**c**) VTA NMUR2 expression was not correlated with intake of a 40% fat (60% carbohydrate) mixture; (**d**) VTA NMUR2 expression was not correlated with intake of a 60% fat (40% carbohydrate) mixture; (**e**) VTA NMUR2 expression was not correlated with intake of an 80% fat (20% carbohydrate) mixture; (**f**) VTA NMUR2 expression was negatively correlated with intake of a 100% fat (0% carbohydrate) mixture. * $p < 0.05$.

4. Discussion

In the present study, we assessed the synaptic localization of NMUR2 in the NAc and the VTA. Our results support previous studies indicating synaptic NMUR2 expression in the NAc. Additionally, these results extend our knowledge by demonstrating Western blot staining of NMUR2 in synaptosomal VTA fractions, and by visualizing punctate staining patterns for NMUR2 in the VTA, consistent with synaptic localization [46]. Our NMUR2 antibody has previously been shown to stain NMUR2-expressing cell bodies in the PVN, suggesting that the staining pattern is not an antibody limitation [32]. In the NAc, NMUR2 is localized to synapses that express a neuronal marker of GABAergic signaling, which supports a role for NMUR2 in inhibitory signaling [46]. Additional studies are needed to determine the functional role of NMUR2 in the mesoaccumbens circuit, including its effects on BED and obesity.

We used an animal model of binge-type eating to quantify binge intake in rats. This model only simulated a binge episode, similar to that observed in BED and obesity [27,29,30,32,33,35]. One of the major limitations of our study is the inability of our model to replicate all clinical aspects of BED. While our model can quantify food intake during a binge episode, it does not replicate the psychological aspects of BED, such as feelings of loss of control and feelings of shame and guilt [2–5]. Nonetheless, this model is helpful in understanding neural mechanisms underlying binge-type consumption and identifying potential regulators of this specific overconsumption behavior. During our studies, animals were maintained on their normal chow consisting of 17% fat by kcal which does not promote overconsumption and maintains a healthy energy balance. However, energy-dense diets are reinforcing and are significantly preferred by rodents. The fat–carbohydrate mixtures were designed to contain the preferred higher energy density, which promotes overeating and improves the translational relevance in which humans binge on energy-dense foods [13,35,51–53].

Using this model, we quantified binge-type consumption across a spectrum of fat–carbohydrate mixtures and correlated it to synaptosomal NMUR2 protein expression in the NAc and the VTA in rats. To our knowledge, we are the first to quantify synaptosomal NMUR2 protein in the NAc and VTA and the first to explore relationships between NMUR2 expression and binge intake. Our results demonstrated a strong positive correlation between synaptosomal NMUR2 protein expression in the NAc and binge intake of a "lower"-fat (higher carbohydrate) mixture of 20% fat (80% carbohydrate) and 40% fat (60% carbohydrate). This region-specific effect of NAc NMUR2 facilitated the binge-type intake of a "lower"-fat (higher carbohydrate) mixture, especially food around 40% fat (60% carbohydrate), which is commonly overconsumed in humans [13,51–54]. Synaptosomal VTA NMUR2 protein expression demonstrated a strong negative correlation with the binge intake of an "extreme" high fat mixture, particularly 100% fat (0% carbohydrate). Contrary to NAc NMUR2, this finding implicates VTA NMUR2 as an inhibitor of binge intake of "extreme" high-fat, low-carbohydrate food. Thus, VTA NMUR2 may act as a "behavioral brake" on the binge intake of high-fat, low-carbohydrate food.

Overall, our findings demonstrate key relationships and brain-region-specific differences in synaptosomal NMUR2 protein expression, and establish NMUR2 as a regulator of binge-type intake in rats in the NAc and the VTA. Binge-type eating changes based on fat–carbohydrate content and NMUR2 expression varies not only across animals, but across brain regions. Interestingly, binge-type intake could be based on fat content, carbohydrate content, or fat-to-carbohydrate ratio, and future studies should delineate the role of NMUR2 in fat and carbohydrate preference. Thus, endogenous NMUR2 may be a driver of individual differences in binge-type eating. Although the observed high degree of inter-animal variability and inter-brain region variability of NMUR2 can limit data interpretation based on averaged differences in NMUR2, it also raises the possibility that NMUR2 protein contributes to individual differences for binge-type food intake in humans.

The clinical implications of our findings establish NMUR2 as a novel regulator of binge-type eating and therefore as a potential druggable candidate for the overconsumption behavior observed in BED and obesity. Recently, we showed that small-molecule NMUR2 agonists successfully suppressed high-fat food intake in rats, which supports NMUR2 as a viable therapeutic target [55]. Future studies will continue to investigate the contribution of NMUR2 in the NAc and the VTA at molecular, neural, and pharmacological levels, including investigating the effects of these small-molecule NMUR2 agonists on binge-type eating.

5. Conclusions

The overconsumption behavior observed in BED and obesity is poorly understood, and demands more mechanistic and molecular studies. NMUR2 facilitates binge-type eating in rats by promoting the binge intake of "lower"-fat diets via the NAc while suppressing the intake of "extreme" higher fat diets via the VTA. Therefore, NMUR2 represents a promising druggable target, and has already been shown to successfully alter feeding behavior [55–57]. The current study demonstrates key relationships between NMUR2 expression in "reward" centers of the brain and binge-type behavior that will contextualize the interpretation of future research determining the therapeutic potential of NMUR2 to regulate overconsumption behavior.

Author Contributions: Conceptualization, A.E.S., J.M.K., and J.D.H.; Methodology, A.E.S. and N.C.A.; Formal analysis, A.E.S. and J.D.H.; Investigation, A.E.S. and J.M.K; Visualization, A.E.S.; Writing—original draft preparation, A.E.S.; Writing—review and editing, A.E.S., J.M.K., Ara 13, N.C.A., and J.D.H.; Supervision, J.D.H.; Funding acquisition, J.D.H.

Funding: This research was funded by the National Institute of Diabetes and Digestive and Kidney Diseases (R01DK106229); the National Institute on Drug Abuse (T32DA07287); the Clinical and Translational Science Award (UL1TR001439, KL2TR001441); and the UTMB Center for Addiction Research.

Acknowledgments: We acknowledge Erica D. Holliday, for assistance with statistical analysis, Reyna Collura for assistance with graphical design.

Conflicts of Interest: The authors declare no conflict of interest. The funders had no role in the design of the study; in the collection, analyses, or interpretation of data; in the writing of the manuscript, or in the decision to publish the results.

References

1. Kessler, R.C.; Berglund, P.A.; Chiu, W.T.; Deitz, A.C.; Hudson, J.I.; Shahly, V.; Aguilar-Gaxiola, S.; Alonso, J.; Angermeyer, M.C.; Benjet, C.; et al. The prevalence and correlates of binge eating disorder in the world health organization world mental health surveys. *Biol. Psychiatry* **2013**, *73*, 904–914. [CrossRef] [PubMed]
2. Guerdjikova, A.I.; Mori, N.; Casuto, L.S.; McElroy, S.L. Binge eating disorder. *Psychiatr. Clin. N. Am.* **2017**, *40*, 255–266. [CrossRef] [PubMed]
3. American Psychiatric Association. *Feeding and Eating Disorders*; American Psychiatric Publishing: Washington, DC, USA, 2013.
4. *Eating Disorders and Obesity a Comprehensive Handbook*, 3rd ed.; The Guilford Press: New York, NY, USA, 2017.
5. American Psychiatric Association. *Diagnostic and Statistical Manual of Mental Disorders*; American Psychiatric Publishing: Washington, DC, USA, 2013.
6. De Zwaan, M. Binge eating disorder and obesity. *Int. J. Obes. Relat. Metab. Disord.* **2001**, *25*, S51–S55. [CrossRef] [PubMed]
7. Berridge, K.C. 'Liking' and 'wanting' food rewards: Brain substrates and roles in eating disorders. *Physiol. Behav.* **2009**, *97*, 537–550. [CrossRef] [PubMed]
8. Berridge, K.C.; Ho, C.Y.; Richard, J.M.; DiFeliceantonio, A.G. The tempted brain eats: Pleasure and desire circuits in obesity and eating disorders. *Brain Res.* **2010**, *1350*, 43–64. [CrossRef] [PubMed]
9. Volkow, N.D.; Wang, G.J.; Tomasi, D.; Baler, R.D. The addictive dimensionality of obesity. *Biol. Psychiatry* **2013**, *73*, 811–818. [CrossRef] [PubMed]
10. Rancourt, D.; McCullough, M.B. Overlap in eating disorders and obesity in adolescence. *Curr. Diab. Rep.* **2015**, *15*, 78. [CrossRef]
11. Hales, C.M.; Carroll, M.D.; Fryar, C.D.; Ogden, C.L. Prevalence of obesity among adults and youth: United States, 2015–2016. *NCHS Data Brief.* **2017**, *219*, 1–8.
12. National Institutes of Health, National Heart, Lung, and Blood Institute. Managing Overweight and Obesity in Adults, Systematic Evidence Review from the Obesity Expert Panel. Available online: https://www.nhlbi.nih.gov/sites/default/files/media/docs/obesity-evidence-review.pdf (accessed on 1 December 2018).
13. Drewnowski, A.; Almiron-Roig, E. Human perceptions and preferences for fat-rich foods. In *Fat Detection: Taste, Texture, and Post Ingestive Effects*; Montmayeur, J., le Coutre, J., Eds.; CRC Press/Taylor & Francis: Boca Raton, FL, USA, 2010.
14. Rippin, H.L.; Hutchinson, J.; Jewell, J.; Breda, J.J.; Cade, J.E. Portion size of energy-dense foods among french and uk adults by bmi status. *Nutrients* **2018**. [CrossRef]
15. Lyons, J.; Walton, J.; Flynn, A. Larger food portion sizes are associated with both positive and negative markers of dietary quality in irish adults. *Nutrients* **2018**, *10*, 1929. [CrossRef]
16. Carstairs, S.A.; Caton, S.J.; Blundell-Birtill, P.; Rolls, B.J.; Hetherington, M.M.; Cecil, J.E. Can reduced intake associated with downsizing a high energy dense meal item be offset by increased vegetable variety in 3–5-year-old children? *Nutrients* **2018**. [CrossRef] [PubMed]
17. Reale, S.; Kearney, C.M.; Hetherington, M.M.; Croden, F.; Cecil, J.E.; Carstairs, S.A.; Rolls, B.J.; Caton, S.J. The feasibility and acceptability of two methods of snack portion control in United Kingdom (UK) preschool children: Reduction and replacement. *Nutrients* **2018**. [CrossRef] [PubMed]
18. Schebendach, J.; Broft, A.; Foltin, R.W.; Walsh, B.T. Can the reinforcing value of food be measured in bulimia nervosa? *Appetite* **2013**, *62*, 70–75. [CrossRef] [PubMed]
19. Volkow, N.D.; Wang, G.J.; Tomasi, D.; Baler, R.D. Obesity and addiction: Neurobiological overlaps. *Obes. Rev.* **2013**, *14*, 2–18. [CrossRef] [PubMed]

20. Volkow, N.D.; Wise, R.A. How can drug addiction help us understand obesity? *Nat. Neurosci.* **2005**, *8*, 555–560. [CrossRef] [PubMed]
21. Davis, C.; Carter, J.C. Compulsive overeating as an addiction disorder. A review of theory and evidence. *Appetite* **2009**, *53*, 1–8. [CrossRef]
22. Dichter, G.S.; Damiano, C.A.; Allen, J.A. Reward circuitry dysfunction in psychiatric and neurodevelopmental disorders and genetic syndromes: Animal models and clinical findings. *J. Neurodev. Disord.* **2012**, *4*, 19.
23. Witt, A.A.; Lowe, M.R. Hedonic hunger and binge eating among women with eating disorders. *Int. J. Eat. Disord.* **2014**, *47*, 273–280. [CrossRef]
24. Satta, V.; Scherma, M.; Piscitelli, F.; Usai, P.; Castelli, M.P.; Bisogno, T.; Fratta, W.; Fadda, P. Limited access to a high fat diet alters endocannabinoid tone in female rats. *Front. Neurosci.* **2018**, *12*, 40. [CrossRef]
25. Corwin, R.L.; Wojnicki, F.H.; Zimmer, D.J.; Babbs, R.K.; McGrath, L.E.; Olivos, D.R.; Mietlicki-Baase, E.G.; Hayes, M.R. Binge-type eating disrupts dopaminergic and gabaergic signaling in the prefrontal cortex and ventral tegmental area. *Obesity* **2016**, *24*, 2118–2125. [CrossRef]
26. Hommel, J.D.; Trinko, R.; Sears, R.M.; Georgescu, D.; Liu, Z.W.; Gao, X.B.; Thurmon, J.J.; Marinelli, M.; DiLeone, R.J. Leptin receptor signaling in midbrain dopamine neurons regulates feeding. *Neuron* **2006**, *51*, 801–810. [CrossRef] [PubMed]
27. Corwin, R.L.; Wojnicki, F.H. Binge eating in rats with limited access to vegetable shortening. *Curr. Protoc. Neurosci.* **2006**. [CrossRef]
28. Wojnicki, F.H.; Babbs, R.K.; Corwin, R.L. Reinforcing efficacy of fat, as assessed by progressive ratio responding, depends upon availability not amount consumed. *Physiol. Behav.* **2010**, *100*, 316–321. [CrossRef] [PubMed]
29. Corwin, R.L.; Avena, N.M.; Boggiano, M.M. Feeding and reward: Perspectives from three rat models of binge eating. *Physiol. Behav.* **2011**, *104*, 87–97. [CrossRef] [PubMed]
30. Corwin, R.L.; Babbs, R.K. Rodent models of binge eating: Are they models of addiction? *ILAR J.* **2012**, *53*, 23–34. [CrossRef] [PubMed]
31. Babbs, R.K.; Wojnicki, F.H.; Corwin, R.L. Assessing binge eating. An analysis of data previously collected in bingeing rats. *Appetite* **2012**, *59*, 478–482. [CrossRef] [PubMed]
32. Benzon, C.R.; Johnson, S.B.; McCue, D.L.; Li, D.; Green, T.A.; Hommel, J.D. Neuromedin u receptor 2 knockdown in the paraventricular nucleus modifies behavioral responses to obesogenic high-fat food and leads to increased body weight. *Neuroscience* **2014**, *258*, 270–279. [CrossRef]
33. Price, A.E.; Stutz, S.J.; Hommel, J.D.; Anastasio, N.C.; Cunningham, K.A. Anterior insula activity regulates the associated behaviors of high fat food binge intake and cue reactivity in male rats. *Appetite* **2018**, *133*, 231–239. [CrossRef]
34. Price, A.E.; Anastasio, N.C.; Stutz, S.J.; Hommel, J.D.; Cunningham, K.A. Serotonin 5-ht2c receptor activation suppresses binge intake and the reinforcing and motivational properties of high-fat food. *Front. Pharmacol.* **2018**, *9*, 821. [CrossRef]
35. Kasper, J.M.; Johnson, S.B.; Hommel, J.D. Fat preference: A novel model of eating behavior in rats. *J. Vis. Exp.* **2014**, e51575. [CrossRef]
36. Howard, A.D.; Wang, R.; Pong, S.S.; Mellin, T.N.; Strack, A.; Guan, X.M.; Zeng, Z.; Williams, D.L.; Feighner, S.D.; Nunes, C.N.; et al. Identification of receptors for neuromedin u and its role in feeding. *Nature* **2000**, *406*, 70–74. [CrossRef] [PubMed]
37. Shan, L.; Qiao, X.; Crona, J.H.; Behan, J.; Wang, S.; Laz, T.; Bayne, M.; Gustafson, E.L.; Monsma, F.J.; Hedrick, J.A. Identification of a novel neuromedin u receptor subtype expressed in the central nervous system. *J. Biol. Chem.* **2000**, *275*, 39482–39486. [CrossRef] [PubMed]
38. Hosoya, M.; Moriya, T.; Kawamata, Y.; Ohkubo, S.; Fujii, R.; Matsui, H.; Shintani, Y.; Fukusumi, S.; Habata, Y.; Hinuma, S.; et al. Identification and functional characterization of a novel subtype of neuromedin u receptor. *J. Biol. Chem.* **2000**, *275*, 29528–29532. [CrossRef] [PubMed]
39. Raddatz, R.; Wilson, A.E.; Artymyshyn, R.; Bonini, J.A.; Borowsky, B.; Boteju, L.W.; Zhou, S.; Kouranova, E.V.; Nagorny, R.; Guevarra, M.S.; et al. Identification and characterization of two neuromedin u receptors differentially expressed in peripheral tissues and the central nervous system. *J. Biol. Chem.* **2000**, *275*, 32452–32459. [CrossRef] [PubMed]
40. Brighton, P.J.; Szekeres, P.G.; Willars, G.B. Neuromedin u and its receptors: Structure, function, and physiological roles. *Pharmacol. Rev.* **2004**, *56*, 231–248. [CrossRef] [PubMed]

41. Egecioglu, E.; Ploj, K.; Xu, X.; Bjursell, M.; Salomé, N.; Andersson, N.; Ohlsson, C.; Taube, M.; Hansson, C.; Bohlooly-Y, M.; et al. Central nmu signaling in body weight and energy balance regulation: Evidence from nmur2 deletion and chronic central nmu treatment in mice. *Am. J. Physiol. Endocrinol. Metab.* **2009**, *297*, E708–E716. [CrossRef] [PubMed]
42. McCue, D.L.; Kasper, J.M.; Hommel, J.D. Regulation of motivation for food by neuromedin u in the paraventricular nucleus and the dorsal raphe nucleus. *Int. J. Obes.* **2017**, *41*, 120–128. [CrossRef] [PubMed]
43. Gartlon, J.; Szekeres, P.; Pullen, M.; Sarau, H.M.; Aiyar, N.; Shabon, U.; Michalovich, D.; Steplewski, K.; Ellis, C.; Elshourbagy, N.; et al. Localisation of nmu1r and nmu2r in human and rat central nervous system and effects of neuromedin-u following central administration in rats. *Psychopharmacology* **2004**, *177*, 1–14. [CrossRef] [PubMed]
44. Kasper, J.; Smith, A.; Hommel, J. Cocaine-evoked locomotor activity correlates with the expression of neuromedin-u receptor 2 in the nucleus accumbens. *Front. Behav. Neurosci.* **2018**. In press. [CrossRef]
45. Zander, M.E.; De Young, K.P. Individual differences in negative affect and weekly variability in binge eating frequency. *Int. J. Eat. Disord.* **2014**, *47*, 296–301. [CrossRef]
46. Kasper, J.M.; McCue, D.L.; Milton, A.J.; Szwed, A.; Sampson, C.M.; Huang, M.; Carlton, S.; Meltzer, H.Y.; Cunningham, K.A.; Hommel, J.D. Gamma-aminobutyric acidergic projections from the dorsal raphe to the nucleus accumbens are regulated by neuromedin u. *Biol. Psychiatry* **2016**, *80*, 878–887. [CrossRef] [PubMed]
47. Paxinos, G.; Watson, C. *The Rat Brain in Stereotaxic Coordinates*, 6th ed.; Elsevier: Amsterdam, The Netherlands, 2007.
48. Anastasio, N.C.; Stutz, S.J.; Fink, L.H.; Swinford-Jackson, S.E.; Sears, R.M.; DiLeone, R.J.; Rice, K.C.; Moeller, F.G.; Cunningham, K.A. Serotonin (5-ht) 5-ht2a receptor (5-ht2ar):5-ht2cr imbalance in medial prefrontal cortex associates with motor impulsivity. *ACS Chem. Neurosci.* **2015**, *6*, 1248–1258. [CrossRef] [PubMed]
49. Breukel, A.I.; Besselsen, E.; Ghijsen, W.E. Synaptosomes. A model system to study release of multiple classes of neurotransmitters. *Methods Mol. Biol.* **1997**, *72*, 33–47. [PubMed]
50. Fink, L.H.; Anastasio, N.C.; Fox, R.G.; Rice, K.C.; Moeller, F.G.; Cunningham, K.A. Individual differences in impulsive action reflect variation in the cortical serotonin 5-ht2a receptor system. *Neuropsychopharmacology* **2015**, *40*, 1957–1968. [CrossRef] [PubMed]
51. Drewnowski, A.; Grinker, J.A.; Hirsch, J. Obesity and flavor perception: Multidimensional scaling of soft drinks. *Appetite* **1982**, *3*, 361–368. [CrossRef]
52. Drewnowski, A.; Greenwood, M.R. Cream and sugar: Human preferences for high-fat foods. *Physiol. Behav.* **1983**, *30*, 629–633. [CrossRef]
53. Drewnowski, A. Taste preferences and food intake. *Annu. Rev. Nutr.* **1997**, *17*, 237–253. [CrossRef]
54. Yanovski, S.Z.; Leet, M.; Yanovski, J.A.; Flood, M.; Gold, P.W.; Kissileff, H.R.; Walsh, B.T. Food selection and intake of obese women with binge-eating disorder. *Am. J. Clin. Nutr.* **1992**, *56*, 975–980. [CrossRef]
55. Sampson, C.M.; Kasper, J.M.; Felsing, D.E.; Raval, S.R.; Ye, N.; Wang, P.; Patrikeev, I.; Rytting, E.; Zhou, J.; Allen, J.A.; et al. Small-molecule neuromedin u receptor 2 agonists suppress food intake and decrease visceral fat in animal models. *Pharmacol. Res. Perspect.* **2018**, *6*, e00425. [CrossRef]
56. Kaisho, T.; Nagai, H.; Asakawa, T.; Suzuki, N.; Fujita, H.; Matsumiya, K.; Nishizawa, N.; Kanematsu-Yamaki, Y.; Dote, K.; Sakamoto, J.I.; et al. Effects of peripheral administration of a neuromedin u receptor 2-selective agonist on food intake and body weight in obese mice. *Int. J. Obes.* **2017**, *41*, 1790–1797. [CrossRef]
57. Kanematsu-Yamaki, Y.; Nishizawa, N.; Kaisho, T.; Nagai, H.; Mochida, T.; Asakawa, T.; Inooka, H.; Dote, K.; Fujita, H.; Matsumiya, K.; et al. Potent body weight-lowering effect of a neuromedin u receptor 2-selective pegylated peptide. *J. Med. Chem.* **2017**, *60*, 6089–6097. [CrossRef] [PubMed]

nutrients

MDPI

Article

Usability and Engagement Evaluation of an Unguided Online Program for Promoting a Healthy Lifestyle and Reducing the Risk for Eating Disorders and Obesity in the School Setting

Martina Nitsch [1,†], Tanja Adamcik [1,†], Stefanie Kuso [1], Michael Zeiler [2] and Karin Waldherr [1,*]

1 FernFH Distance Learning University of Applied Sciences, Ferdinand Porsche Ring 3, 2700 Wiener Neustadt, Austria; martina.nitsch@fernfh.ac.at (M.N.); tanja.adamcik@fernfh.ac.at (T.A.); stefanie.kuso@fernfh.ac.at (S.K.)

2 Department for Child and Adolescent Psychiatry, Medical University of Vienna, Waehringer Guertel 18-20, 1090 Vienna, Austria; michael.zeiler@meduniwien.ac.at

* Correspondence: karin.waldherr@fernfh.ac.at; Tel.: +43-2622-32600-260

† Both authors contributed equally to this work.

Received: 17 February 2019; Accepted: 24 March 2019; Published: 27 March 2019

Abstract: Implementing integrated online prevention to reduce the risk of both obesity and eating disorders, in the school setting, is a promising approach. The challenge is to develop highly user-friendly and motivating programs, to foster adherence and effectiveness. The purpose of this study was to evaluate the usability of such a universal prevention program for students aged 14–19 years, and to address engagement issues. A mixed-methods approach was chosen, consisting of a think-aloud task, a semi-structured interview, and a questionnaire including items on sociodemographic characteristics and the System Usability Scale (SUS). Usability tests were conducted in two rounds, with five adolescents participating per round. Mean score in the SUS was 92.5 of 100 points (range 85–100), in the second round, after some adaptations from the participants' feedback. In the course of the think-aloud tasks and interviews, five major themes emerged—visual design, navigation, mode of transfer, content, and engagement conditions. Interesting headlines, gamification, and monitoring tools are crucial for engagement. Apart from the importance of using the program during school hours, the study showed that problems currently perceived as important by the target group, need to be considered and addressed, prior to offering them prevention programs, which highlights the importance of a user-centered design.

Keywords: usability study; online health intervention; adolescents; school setting; eating disorders; overweight; prevention; engagement; E-Mental Health

1. Introduction

Prevalence rates of overweight and obesity, worldwide, have increased drastically [1,2]; consequently, the World Health Organization has labeled obesity as a "global epidemic" [3]. Over-evaluation of weight and shape, restricted eating and dieting are also on the rise [4], and are amongst the strongest risk factors for full and sub-threshold eating disorders (EDs) [5]. Whereas, EDs like anorexia nervosa and bulimia nervosa especially affect girls and young women, health implications of problematic eating and exercise habits affect both women and men, at all ages [4,6,7]. Recurring episodes of unhealthy dieting, binge eating, and purging behavior are also common in adolescents suffering from overweight and obesity [7–9], influenced by the social pressure on overweight people to reduce their weight. However, a couple of longitudinal studies have shown an association between dieting and weight gain, among adolescents [10–13].

Given the shared risk factors for eating disorders and being overweight, researchers have called for integrated approaches to prevention [14]. Such approaches are also considered to reduce the risk of unintentionally causing eating disorders with obesity prevention programs [14], and they have the potential to reduce stigma. There already exists a number of effective prevention programs addressing the full range between anorexia nervosa and obesity [15].

Due to their scalability, their potential to reach a large number of people, and relatively low costs, online programs seem to have a high potential to tackle this public health challenge [16]. Especially in group settings, like school classes, online programs offer the possibility to provide different program parts for different participants, simultaneously, within the same school class, thus allowing to tailor program content to participants' characteristics, like gender, and risk status [17]. Furthermore, it is assumed that adolescents, especially, can benefit from Internet-based interventions [18].

More than 95% of European adolescents and young adults between 16 and 24 years, are using the Internet regularly, therefore, Internet-based or mobile phone applications/platforms could be a key resource in providing health information to adolescents [19]. As for interventions promoting mental health, there is evidence of positive effects on young people's mental health, especially when implemented in the school setting [20–22]. However, the challenges of such intervention programs are poor adherence and high dropout rates [23,24]. Since these factors limit the effectiveness of Internet-based interventions, further insights into user technology interaction are urgently needed. Traditional approaches like randomized controlled trials (RCT) are not appropriate for investigating those complex phenomena, including many contextual and confounding factors. Thus, several authors suggest the application of a mixed-methods design, focusing on process variables like dropout and usage, and outcome variables like costs, health condition, or adherence [25].

Accordingly, this study aimed to evaluate the usability of a school-based online intervention program for adolescents, as well as to address engagement issues, to reduce dropout rates in the "Healthy Teens @ School" study, a multi-country cluster RCT [26]. The intervention was adapted from an evidence-based program developed in the USA, called "Staying Fit" [17,27]. The unguided online intervention program "Healthy Teens @ School" aims to promote a healthy lifestyle and reduce problematic eating behavior, eating disorder risk, and obesity risk, among adolescents aged 14 to 19 years. Prior to the conduction of the main study on "Healthy Teens @ School" in Austria, we conducted three focus groups with representatives of the target group [28], and a subsequent usability study. For the usability study we used a mixed-methods approach suggested by Nitsch et al., [29] which proved to be an appropriate design, in order to get detailed insights into users' needs and to learn more about the challenges regarding engagement at the same time. In this context, especially the evaluation of the first program modules and the users' first interaction with the program, are crucial elements for determining future engagement and adherence patterns, since most participants drop out from online interventions at this very early stage of a program [23,30,31]. This paper will present the results of the usability study and highlight the importance of investigating engagement issues, prior to the program start.

2. Materials and Methods

2.1. Recruitment

Potential participants were recruited via social media (Facebook). Girls and boys aged between 14 and 18 years, from different schools in Vienna, were invited to take part in a study aiming to test the prototype of an online program for promoting healthy habits in pupils. The inclusion criteria for this usability study reflected the target population of the "Healthy Teens @ School" program that was designed for students between 14 and 19 years. Participants were offered gift cards of € 20 for their participation.

Following the principles of usability evaluation, we conducted usability tests in two rounds, with five participants per round. A sample size of five participants per round was regarded as sufficient to detect more than 85% of usability problems. Including more participants would have required more resources in terms of time and money, while only producing repetitive information [32,33]. In the first round, five participants tested the prototype of the program on the computer. Based on the results of the first round, the program was modified and tested by another five participants in the second round.

2.2. Program/Intervention

"Healthy Teens @ School" is a ten-week online program (one online-module per week) designed to promote a healthy lifestyle and reduce eating disorder risk and obesity risk. Based on a screening questionnaire, which includes the assessment of eating behaviors, eating disorder risk, weight status, weight/shape concerns, physical activity habits, stress coping, depression, anxiety, self-esteem, and quality of life, the participants get access to the online program and are assigned to either one of two program tracks. Adolescents with normal weight (with and without eating disorder risk) are assigned to the "Healthy habits" track, overweight adolescents (>85th sex-age-specific BMI percentile) are assigned to the "Weight management" track. In ten modules, the students learn about building a healthy lifestyle, about balanced nutrition and physical activity habits, about ways of improving their body image and body satisfaction, as well as ways of improving media literacy. Whereas the content in the "Healthy habits" track is framed towards building a healthy lifestyle, the content in the "Weight management track" is framed more towards maintaining a healthy weight. In the course of the three preceding focus groups, especially stress in school turned out to be a major issue for the students [28]. As a result, we adapted the program and added elements about how to deal with difficult and challenging situations, emotions, and stress, in order to prevent mental health problems. Details on the program content are published elsewhere [26]. The program is based on principles of Cognitive Behavioral Therapy (e.g., goal setting, behavior monitoring, practical exercises to be tried out between online modules). The users are encouraged to use a "diary"-function that can be accessed via PC or an app, to monitor their habits on a daily, or at least weekly basis. Furthermore, the users receive feedback on their strengths and weaknesses, based on the results of the screening questionnaire.

The program is provided on an online platform hosted by Minddistrict GmbH. The users log on the platform via an e-mail address and a self-chosen password. From the user's dashboard, the screening questionnaire and program modules can be accessed; students can see new tasks assigned and they have the possibility to contact the study team via a messaging function. Screenshots of the user's dashboard and the program module including the app-diary are provided in Figures 1 and 2.

The program can be accessed within and outside school lessons, via different devices, like computers, tablets, and smartphones [26]. For this usability study, we used a shortened version of the screening questionnaire and feedback, the first two online modules, as well as the diary function. We decided to test those parts that are scheduled at the beginning of the program, as they may be crucial for subsequent adherence [23,29–31]. The screening questionnaire used in the usability study included about 60 items, covering sociodemographic questions (including height and weight) and standardized questionnaires, to assess stress coping, intuitive eating, self-esteem, and health-related quality of life. The KIDCOPE [34] assesses the frequency and perceived effectiveness of ten different coping strategies for a defined problem. Coping strategies are divided into active strategies (e.g., cognitive restructuring), avoiding strategies (e.g., social withdrawal) and negative strategies (e.g., self-blame). Prior to rating the frequency and effectiveness of the used coping strategies on a 4-point scale, participants were asked to define a situation or problem that has stressed them often. Coping is conceptualized as a dynamic process and not a stable personality trait, resulting in a rather limited re-test reliability, after 10 weeks ($r = 0.15–0.43$). The Intuitive Eating Scale (IES, [35]) measures the individuals' tendency to follow their physical hunger and satiety cues, by determining when, what, and how much to eat. The 23 items are rated on a five-point scale and are summed up to a total score and four subscales ("Unconditional Permission to Eat", "Eating for Physical Rather than Emotional Reasons", "Reliance on Hunger and Satiety Cues", and "Body-Food Choice Congruence"). Good internal consistencies of the total score (Cronbach Alpha 0.91 for females and 0.82 for males) and subscales (Cronbach Alphas

>0.72) were reported [36]. The Rosenberg Self-Esteem Scale [37] is a standard measure for self-esteem, consisting of ten items rated on a five-point scale. Internal consistencies are high (Cronbach Alpha = 0.88) [38]. Finally, we also used the Inventory of Life Quality for Children and Adolescents [39], which measures subjective well-being and satisfaction in seven different domains, including school, family, peers, leisure activities, physical health, psychological health, and overall health-related quality of life. The seven items are rated on a five-point scale and calculated to an overall score. The re-test reliabilities for the total score reported by the authors range from r = 0.60 to r = 0.80.

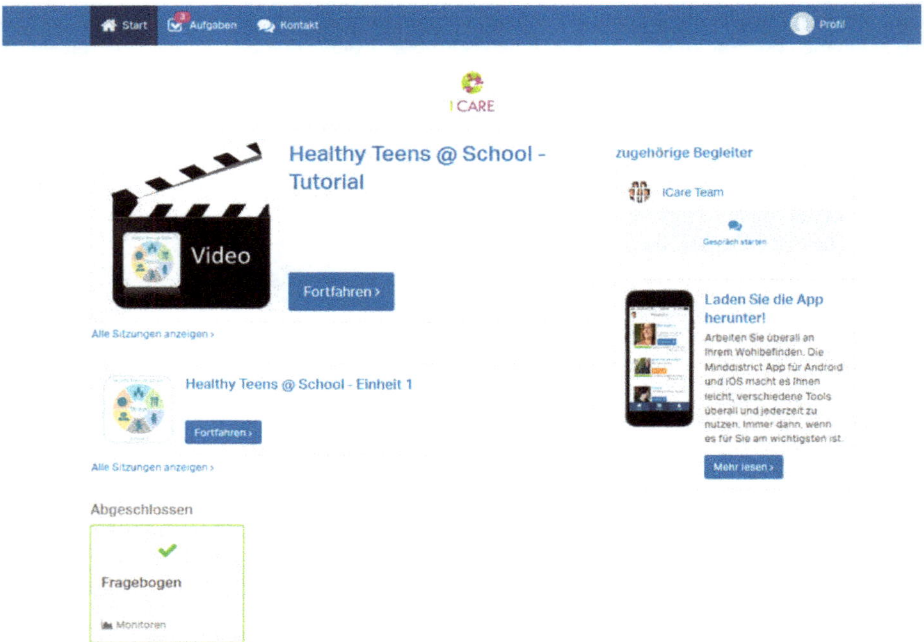

Figure 1. Screenshot of the user's dashboard on the online platform.

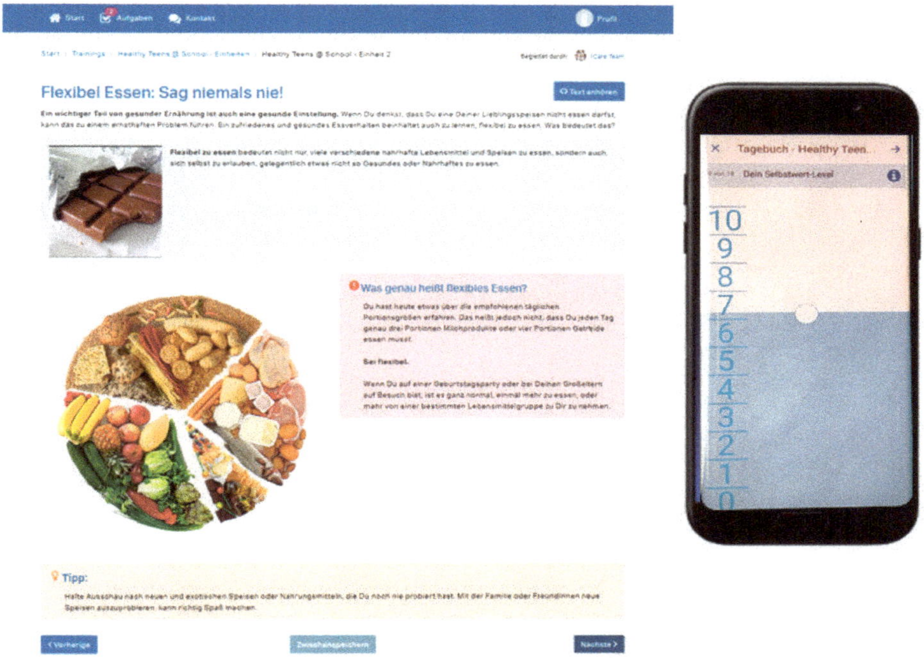

Figure 2. Screenshot of one page in module 2 of the Healthy Teens @ School program and the app-diary.

2.3. Procedure

We conducted an evaluation study focusing on aspects of usability and engagement, following the study protocol of Nitsch et al. [29].

Prior to testing, informed consents of the participants and legal representatives were obtained, and the researcher explained the procedure. The usability testing sessions consisted of three parts, (a) program use while performing the think-aloud technique, (b) a semi-structured interview, and (c) completion of a questionnaire, including sociodemographic questions and the System Usability Scale (SUS, [40]). The think-aloud process involved four tasks. First, registration on the platform and setting a password; second, completion of the online assessment and reading the feedback; third, completion of the first and the second module of the "Healthy Teens @ School" program; and fourth, to make a diary entry on the PC and via the app. Before starting the think-aloud task, the students practiced the technique by completing an Internet-based task (searching for a DVD on Amazon), which was unrelated to the "Healthy Teens @ School" program. The moderator of the test presented the different think-aloud tasks to the participant. However, participants were instructed to act as if they were alone, talking to themselves. Participants were encouraged to express anything that came into their mind, including positive and negative thoughts about the program, as the researchers on-site were not involved in the development of the original program but are only interested in improving it. There was little interaction with the researchers, only in case the participant stopped thinking aloud, the moderator motivated the student to try again. All comments and problems during the think-aloud task were recorded and protocolled by an observer. In addition, the computer screen was recorded (©Microsoft Expression Encoder 4 Screen Capture SP2), in order to capture verbal and non-verbal reactions of the participants.

Following the think-aloud task, a semi-structured interview was conducted. The interview guide included questions about expectations towards the program, impressions of the program, questions about program content, the diary, motivation for completing the program, and if the participant would recommend the program to others.

Subsequent to the semi-structured interview, the participants were asked to complete questions on sociodemographic characteristics, their current Internet use, as well as the SUS questionnaire [40]. The SUS is a method for measuring the usability of an application. It is a standardized 10-item questionnaire. The items are rated on a five-point Likert scale. A high reliability (Cronbach Alpha = 0.91) was reported for the total SUS score [41].

The usability testing sessions took 55 to 90 min, in which participants had the possibility to familiarize themselves with the program and answer the questions. The testing sessions were conducted from January till February 2017, and took place at the FernFH Distance Learning University of Applied Sciences in Vienna and at the Medical University of Vienna.

The study protocol was approved by the Ethics Commission of the Medical University of Vienna (Austria, Record Number: 2209/2015).

2.4. Analysis

Both, the think-aloud task and the interviews, were videotaped and audiotaped, then transcribed verbatim, including the non-verbal reactions of the participants, based on the video recordings and the observer notes. The transcripts were coded and analyzed, using NVivo 11. Thematic analysis [42] was used to identify new aspects and relations between the themes and to combine data from the think-aloud task and the semi-structured interviews. The themes and categories were discussed, reviewed, and interpreted by the research team. The SUS questionnaire was analyzed in © Microsoft Excel, as follows. After recoding the inverted items, item codings were summed up and the sum score was multiplied by 2.5. This resulted in a total SUS score that ranged from 0 (no usability) to 100 (perfect usability). Finally, we calculated an average score for each usability round. A SUS-score of higher than 70 points is regarded as an acceptable usability (representing the average SUS scores found in other usability studies) and scores higher than 85 points are regarded as excellent usability [41].

3. Results

3.1. Participants

All ten participants were students between 14 and 18 years old (mean age = 16.2 years, standard deviation (SD) = 1.2), attending different high schools in Vienna. In the first usability test round, four male students and one female student took part, and in the second round, four female students and one male student participated. Their BMI ranged from 18.8 to 24.2 (mean = 21.67, SD = 1.73). None of the participants had a diagnosed psychiatric disorder or received psychotherapeutic treatment. In the IES which was defined as the main outcome of the intervention, eight participants had average scores and two participants had above-average scores (mean score = 3.76, SD = 0.45).

3.2. SUS-Questionnaire

Regarding the SUS-questionnaire, the usability of the program was in the acceptable range (SUS-Score > 70) in the first round, and in the excellent range (SUS-Score > 85) in the second round. The average SUS score was 84 (range from 67.5 to 97.5), in the first round, and improved to an average SUS score of 92.5 (range from 85 to 100) of 100 points, in the second usability test round.

3.3. Think-Aloud Task and Semi-Structured Interview

By using the think-aloud tasks and the semi-structured interviews, we were able to identify five central themes, referring to visual design, navigation, mode of transfer, content, and engagement conditions.

3.3.1. Visual Design

Most of the students liked the visual design of the "Healthy Teens @ School" program, especially the pictures and graphics were highlighted as positive. The layout of the program was perceived as *"youthful"*, *"cool"*, *"pretty"*, *"appealing"*, and *"clearly arranged"* and reminded some participants of social media platforms and search engines: *"The landing page looks up-to-date, similar to social media and Facebook and instant messaging design, appealing to teenagers (...) I also liked the layout and pictures"* (male#5). The program's color design was rated ambivalent by the participants. Some liked the variation, others recommended a reduction in colors or a more targeted use of colors. *"Maybe, there should be less red, because I know, especially on a bright website, red indicates that there is something very important or wrong"* (male#7). Some students observed, that the font size was too small in some areas. All participants mentioned, that they like the layout of the diary, regardless of using it on the computer or via the app. They were also motivated to complete the diary because they liked the visualization of their improvement in healthy habits over time. Furthermore, participants liked the absence of advertising elements in the program.

3.3.2. Navigation

The majority of the students described the navigation of the program as *"easy"* and *"self-explanatory"*. However, it seemed to be a challenge to create a secure password. Only one of ten participants managed to include all demanded aspects (minimum 12 characters and one special character) at the first attempt.

In the think-aloud sessions we observed some challenges finding the next module or the diary function. Some asked for help, others found the next module or the diary after repeatedly trying. Consequently, we produced and included a tutorial video lasting five minutes for the second usability test round. This video included a short introduction to the navigation and the functions of the program and the platform. Most participants liked the tutorial video, they described it as *"helpful"*, *"reasonable for orientation"*, and *"well-illustrated"*. Others said, that they would not need such a video, stating young people prefer to try out programs and do not want to watch videos about the navigation: *"I think, it is self-explanatory (...). And I think, most teenagers would prefer to simply try it out instead of watching some explanation for a long time. Okay, actually, it's not so long, but I think, that most people would just try it out"* (female#6). After showing the tutorial video in the second usability round we could monitor more targeted approaches to find the diary, the different modules and an overall improvement in the platform navigation. A participant even mentioned that *"you will instantly find your way"* (male#7) in the program.

3.3.3. Mode of Transfer

This theme refers to the way the content and information is communicated to the user. After completing the screening questionnaire, some participants were irritated by certain questions of the IES, which sounded similar and felt like a repetition to them.

During the first test round, participants had to scroll to the top several times, as due to its length, the response options of the IES questionnaire did not fit on one screen, after a certain number of items. Therefore, prior to the second test round, we divided a long block of questions into two smaller parts, in order to ensure that the response options were visible at all times. Negated questions were harder to understand for some students. One person said that sometimes the wording in the IES questionnaire was unclear (e.g., "substantial food") or students indicated questions that appeared strange to them. Furthermore, some participants mentioned that the open question asking to describe a personal stress inducing problem (out of the KIDCOPE-questionnaire), was somewhat confusing, since the subsequent set of questions, directly referring to the mentioned problem, were not always fitting.

In the interviews, participants criticized the long text passages, very detailed information and suggested shorter texts and sentences: *"There was a bit too much written text, but the texts were not always the same, and addressed you directly"* (male#3). An aversion for long texts became also apparent in the think-aloud sessions, where many participants only skimmed or even skipped longer texts. On the contrary, interactive tools like quizzes and questions were always noticed and used and rated as positive: *"It is better than just reading tips, (...) that you can fill out things and instantly get feedback"* (male#1). Accordingly, the students underlined the importance of the "gamification" of the program; they liked to do quizzes to repeat the content or knowledge games, instead of reading long texts with detailed information and complex wording. For example, one girl argued that interactive tools might also be helpful with regard to concentration: *"You can't finish it [the program] in five minutes; instead you really have to take your time, sit down and read it in detail. Maybe it should be a bit shorter, so that you don't have to read that much, yeah, more quizzes, and just make it simpler, so you don't have to concentrate so hard"* (female#2). Furthermore, the participants said that they liked to explore new things in the program and that they like being addressed personally with "you" or "your". Since text passages without interesting headlines were partially only skimmed and students stated that significant headlines motivated them to read text passages, we added more headings after the first round.

The diary tool was considered as interesting and useful, especially regarding the possibility to visualize habits over time. In the second round, the diary function was available on the computer and additionally on the app. Both modes were rated as positive, but two advantages of the app were highlighted—the app appeared more game-like and chances of using the app more frequently were rated higher, since it is more convenient to use the program on the smartphone: *"It is done real quick, it takes less time than a normal diary entry. Well, on the smartphone it is quick, you can do it on the subway or on the way home, that's fine, that's convenient"* (male#7).

3.3.4. Content

In general, the students denoted the information delivered in the different parts of the "Healthy Teens @ School" program as *"helpful"*, *"informative"*, *"diversified"*, *"good to read"* and *"meaningful"*. One participant said that the program *"is cool"* because *"it is not counseling, not like at the psychologist or the doctor, you don't feel sick (...) it is a kind of help but not in an uncomfortable way (...) not bad for your self-worth"* (female#8).

The explanation and the outcome of the feedback were described as fitting to the person and very informative: *"I think, it fits me well, and it came across very personal and that I find really cool, I mean that was really cool. And for me personally, it is real fun to fill out quizzes and to get such feedback. That is fun, that is cool"* (female#6).

The provided information in the modules was described as meaningful and interesting. Some students expressed that they have already heard about some of the information, but it was also nice to hear familiar content again. Some parts of the content were new to them. For example, most participants stated that they already knew about the food pyramid or learned about it in school. The information on how many portion sizes a day is recommended for the different food groups, and how portion sizes can be measured, was perceived as new and interesting: *"I didn't know much yet, for example the daily food requirement, how many snacks you should eat, what and how much food you should eat to be balanced, in school and at home"*(male#5).

3.3.5. Engagement Conditions

The participants stated that they would use the program in their daily routine, if they feel that they need it and would recommend the program to colleagues and friends, if they had psychological or health problems or if they think the content would be interesting for them. Some students indicated that they like the program because it was informative, exciting, easy and fast to use. The motivation to complete the program was the desire for a change in daily lifestyle and the personal feedback received. For example, one participant stated that *"if you do that (the program), then you want that something changes. If you wouldn't want to change something, then you would not do it"* (male#3). The possibility to use the program, including the diary, on different devices like computer, smartphone, and tablet was very attractive for the users and might also improve the adherence of participants. Especially, the smartphone version of the program was described as *"user friendly"*, *"comfortable"* and *"always within reach"*. For example, one participant said that she would use the program *"more likely on the smartphone as it's always in reach. And I do not have to turn on the computer, enter the password and so on (...) but your smartphone is always there. You can also do it on the way"* (female#9). Another participant found that he personally would prefer doing the program *"on the computer because there is a keyboard and I prefer that, but for many others at my age the smartphone is the number one and they would prefer doing it on their smartphone"* (male#5).

Since a lack of time also seemed to be an important aspect for students, they positively highlighted the length of the program modules. The majority of the participants indicated that over the course of 10 weeks, investing 20 to 30 min once a week, seems to be feasible.

The possibility of using the program within school lessons turned out to be an important factor in terms of engagement. On the one hand, all participants stated, that if they had the chance to do the program in class, they would use it regularly. However, in most cases the program simply turned out to be a better alternative than regular school lessons: *"I would do it, I'm not sure if the other students would do it as well, but when it takes place in school instead of a regular class, then I think they would. It depends on how the first five modules are, if I would do it at home as well"* (female#10). On the other hand, although the school was generally described as an adequate setting for using the program, the school setting itself raised many issues in connection with the topic of stress. For example, in the course of the usability session, students were asked to describe a recent problem that bothered them and nine out of ten participants gave an example of school-related stress, including *"work overload"*, *"exam stress"*, stress related to bad grades and interpersonal problems with classmates. During the think-aloud task, many participants emphasized consequences of school stress, for example influencing their overall well-being: *"I'm not feeling well at the moment, because I have school stress"* (female#10). Another participant highlighted that stress has a negative effect on his leisure activities: *"I have too much schoolwork and don't have much free time to do anything else"* (male#3). This finding is especially important, since it validates and highlights the results of the pre-study, in which focus groups with students were conducted and stress turned out to be a major issue as well [28]. One participant emphasized that she *"would recommend [the program] to students experiencing stress or health problems; but rather not to others"* (female#10).

4. Discussion

The aim of this usability study was to evaluate and advance the usability and engagement aspects of an unguided online intervention program for promoting a healthy lifestyle and to reduce the risk for eating disorders and obesity among adolescents. Additionally, we aimed to validate the results of preceding focus groups with representatives of the target group. The application of a mixed methods research design not only allowed us to gain deeper insights regarding the students' perception of online health promotion and prevention programs and their media usage, but also to improve and test the program in a very effective way. In this usability study, we found five major themes—visual design, navigation, mode of transfer, content, and engagement conditions.

Especially, the findings of the current study regarding the design, navigation, and the mode of transfer of online interventions are comparable to other studies. For example, one major finding was the fact that the participants disliked reading long texts and preferred multimedia content, which was also a result in similar studies [29,43,44]. This implies that the transfer of content on prevention, via multimedia elements, might increase engagement and, therefore, is preferable to text-based information [43,45]. Furthermore, instead of presenting participants an introductory text about navigation and functions of the program, we produced a short tutorial video, in order to reduce the amount of text. Although some participants doubted the need of the tutorial video for program navigation, we observed an overall improvement regarding the navigation of the different tools, after its implementation.

Since some participants tended to skim or skip long texts, it is crucial to visually distinguish important from less important text parts [44]. We tried to highlight important information, concerning content and navigation, by putting it into boxes with prominent colors, like red and yellow. Informative headings facilitate orientation and let users choose what to read. In general, this might be a more realistic approach regarding the needs and usage habits of adolescents, than to expect them to read everything.

Similar to the study of Nitsch et al. [29], some participants expressed objections about the length of the assessments and particular questions. As a result of the standardized instruments used, a change of the questions was not possible. Based on present and previous research, there is clearly a lack of user-friendly research assessment, which have been developed to use within online programs, by considering adequate wording and format. However, a very positive mentioned tool, in conjunction with the assessment, was the subsequent personalized feedback, which all participants regarded as suitable for their needs and as very informative. Especially, the prospect of receiving a feedback turned out to be an important motivational factor to complete the assessment.

Furthermore, especially for adolescents, the integration of interactive and gamification elements seems to be an essential prerequisite [46]. Changes in the layout, navigation, and content showed improvements in the second usability round.

We observed that time was a crucial factor for using the program or recommending it to others. The length of the weekly modules was described as suitable and the daily diary was evaluated as very good and realistic, regarding regular program use. Accordingly, the participants mentioned the importance of different user devices. The possibility to use the online intervention program, including the diary, on the computer, smartphone, and the tablet increases the accessibility.

Another motivating point was that the program addressed the users personally with "you". In the diary the participants liked the possibility to visualize habits over time and mentioned this as a factor for using the diary regularly or daily.

A crucial factor in terms of engagement and regular program use was the possibility of working with the program in the school setting, and not in the free time. This result can also be confirmed by various other studies, for example Neil et al. [47] highlighted that participation in an online prevention program in the school setting, yields higher adherence than not participating in the school. Additionally, the majority of youth can be reached through the school setting and since schools are familiar settings for students, stigma, for example, associated with mental health interventions can be reduced [48]. Generally, evidence also suggests that the school is an important setting for universal prevention interventions [49,50].

However, when implementing interventions in particular settings, confounding or contextual factors concerning the setting itself need to be considered as well. The present study showed that the school setting raised various issues related to the topic of stress. For example, when students were asked about a recent problem, the majority of the participants mentioned a school-related problem. Accordingly, the problems currently perceived as important by the target group, need to be considered and addressed, prior to offering them programs for health-related issues, which they might not even think of, or are interested in. The results of this study, as well as our previous research on engagement issues, suggest that framing a program, primarily designed to reduce eating disorder and obesity risk, towards stress and stress reduction, might help to improve engagement. Stress turned out to be a major issue for adolescents who participated in our study, and this might also motivate them to use the program. Furthermore, program content covering a balanced nutrition, physical activity, and body image, can easily be linked to the topic of stress, for example, by highlighting the association between high levels of stress and fast eating or the benefits of regular physical activity for stress reduction. On the other hand, providing adolescents with helpful coping strategies, might prevent them from resorting to negative behavioral patterns, like self-blame or emotional eating. Furthermore, participating in a program labeled as a stress-reduction program might also be less stigmatizing than participating in a program for preventing eating disorders and obesity, since almost every adolescent experiences stress in some way or another. This was also an issue in another study where adolescents said that the terms describing mental disorders sounded daunting. They recommended that the program title and content should be framed positively (e.g., "improving healthy habits" instead of "reducing risk for eating disorders and obesity") [28]. Generally, we suggest evaluating the potential users' needs, prior to the program start, since addressing their needs might contribute to adherence and engagement. However, for students in a different context, other topics might be more relevant.

In this context, the value of user-centered design needs to be highlighted, since it does not only allow us to tailor interventions to the users' needs, but also offers a high potential to improve the translation of evidence-based health research into particular settings [51]. Moreover, the design of online (mental) health programs affects their uptake and use [25,52–54]. Accordingly, future research needs to address this gap, by highlighting the value of integrating aspects from different interdisciplinary fields. In this context, especially a combination of different methods from the broader field of implementation science and human computer-interaction, is suggested [52,53].

Besides the usability and engagement issues, which were addressed in the present study, further steps are necessary to ensure a successful and sustainable implementation of online prevention programs in school settings. Strong evidence for the effectiveness and cost-effectiveness of such programs are an important prerequisite for long-term implementation, not only according to various stakeholders in the school setting, but also from an ethical point of view [28]. Therefore, the "Healthy Teens @ School" program is currently being tested for its effectiveness and cost-effectiveness, as part of a cluster RCT, involving more than 800 adolescents in two European countries [26,55]. Since adherence to an online prevention program and consequently its effectiveness are not only affected by usability issues but also by other contextual factors, such as participant, setting, and intervention characteristics, we also aim to investigate a variety of moderators and mediators potentially influencing outcome [56]. Furthermore, we aim to evaluate the potential public health impact of this program by applying the Reach-Effectiveness-Adoption-Implementation-Maintenance (RE-AIM) framework [57]. RE-AIM encourages the researcher not only to focus on effectiveness but also to obtain a number of indicators—reach of adolescents, adoption (willingness of schools to offer the intervention to their students), implementation (e.g., adherence, adaptations to be made), and maintenance (both on the individual and organizational level). Overall, these research steps will help us to develop an online prevention program for EDs and obesity, which is well-accepted by schools and adolescents and which can be further disseminated to a wide range of schools.

Limitations

The participants completed only the first part of the assessments and the program modules. Therefore, results can only partly be generalized to the other assessment questionnaires or modules. However, the evaluation of engagement and usability issues of the users' first interaction with the program proved to be a suitable method, in order to determine future participant behavior [29]. Moreover, most participants drop-out during the very early stage of an online program, which indicates that the first impression is crucial for future adherence [23,30,31]. Furthermore, since the usability testing took place in a lab, it is possible, that the students were influenced by the situation itself. However, we addressed this issue and gave the participants the opportunity to test the think-aloud method, before we started with the actual study.

Not all of the feedback of the participants could be implemented in the second round and subsequently for the actual clinical trial, due to multiple reasons. Although much of the criticism about some questions seemed legitimate, the used questionnaires were standardized questionnaires that could not be changed, simplified, or shortened. Some problems or barriers were related to the navigation which was not intuitive in some aspects and led to the need to try out a few times. Since our possibilities to change these aspects, which were linked to the functions of the Minddistrict platform, were limited, we tried to tackle these issues by providing the tutorial video and additional information on the navigation in the text.

Another major limitation might be the gender imbalance of the test rounds. In the first round, four boys and one girl participated and in the second round four girls and one boy took part. We tried to reach a balance of gender per round, but due to time collisions and short-term illness of two participants, this was not feasible.

5. Conclusions

This usability and engagement study was conducted in preparation for a randomized controlled trial of the unguided online program "Healthy Teens @ School", taking place in the school setting. This study helped us to improve the usability of our online program, prior to the program start, in five major areas—visual design, navigation, mode of transfer, content, and engagement conditions. Furthermore, the results of this study contribute towards a wider research base, showing that usability and engagement issues in this first phase of the users' interaction with the program is not only inextricably linked, but is essential for identifying future engagement and adherence issues. Especially, the users' current needs have to be evaluated and addressed. As the results of this study showed, the engagement issues of this particular target group were closely linked to specific setting-related issues, such as stress in school or the possibility to use the program during school hours. This implies that the involvement and participation of the target group in the development of online interventions, should be an essential part in future research designs. Especially for prevention interventions, intrinsic motivation plays a major role, since members of the potential target group usually do not feel a certain urge or level of suffering that motivates them to use an online program. Additionally, from a public health perspective, it is important to point out the benefits of such programs for the target group. In this context, user centered-designs do not only help to improve the usability and adherence of online programs but also their overall effectiveness.

Author Contributions: Conceptualization, M.N., K.W.; methodology, M.N., T.A., and M.Z.; software, M.Z. and S.K.; formal analysis, T.A. and S.K.; investigation, T.A., M.Z., and S.K.; resources, Medical University of Vienna, FernFH Distance Learning University of Applied Sciences.; writing—original draft preparation, T.A. and M.N.; writing—review and editing, M.N., T.A., K.W., M.Z., and S.K.; visualization, M.Z and T.A.; supervision, K.W.; project administration, M.Z. and S.K.; funding acquisition, ICare Consortium.

Funding: This project has received funding from the European Union's Horizon 2020 research and innovation program, under grant agreement No. 634757.

Acknowledgments: We would like to thank the participants, without whom this study would not be possible and Ursula Fitsch for transcribing the interviews.

Conflicts of Interest: The authors declare no conflict of interest and the funders had no role in the study design, data collection and analyses, decision to publish, or the preparation of the manuscript.

References

1. Hales, C.M.; Carroll, M.D.; Fryar, C.D.; Ogden, C.L. Prevalence of obesity among adults and youth: United States, 2015-2016. *NCHS Data Brief* **2017**, *288*.
2. Ahluwalia, N.; Dalmasso, P.; Rasmussen, M.; Lipsky, L.; Currie, C.; Haug, E.; Kelly, C.; Damsgaard, M.T.; Due, P.; Tabak, I.; et al. Trends in overweight prevalence among 11-, 13- and 15-year-olds in 25 countries in Europe, Canada and USA from 2002 to 2010. *Eur. J. Public Health* **2015**, *25* (Suppl. 2), 28–32. [CrossRef] [PubMed]
3. World Health Organization. *Obesity: Preventing and Managing the Global Epidemic*; 2000. Available online: https://www.who.int/nutrition/publications/obesity/WHO_TRS_894/en/ (accessed on 14 February 2019).
4. Hay, P.J.; Mond, J.; Buttner, P.; Darby, A. Eating disorder behaviors are increasing: Findings from two sequential community surveys in South Australia. *PLoS ONE* **2008**, *3*, e1541. [CrossRef] [PubMed]
5. Jacobi, C.; Hütter, K.; Fittig, E. Psychosocial risk factors for eating disorders. In *The Oxford Handbook of Eating Disorders*, 2nd ed.; Agras, W.S., Robinson, A., Eds.; Oxford University Press: New York, NY, USA, 2017.
6. Shisslak, C.M.; Crago, M.; Estes, L.S. The spectrum of eating disturbances. *Int. J. Eat. Disord.* **1995**, *18*, 209–219. [CrossRef]

7. Zeiler, M.; Waldherr, K.; Philipp, J.; Nitsch, M.; Dür, W.; Karwautz, A.; Wagner, G. Prevalence of eating disorder risk and associations with health-related quality of life: results from a large school-based population screening. *Eur. Eat. Disord. Rev.* **2016**, *24*, 9–18. [CrossRef]
8. French, S.A.; Jeffery, R.W.; Sherwood, N.E.; Neumark-Sztainer, D. Prevalence and correlates of binge eating in a nonclinical sample of women enrolled in a weight gain prevention program. *Int. J. Obes. Relat. Metab. Disord. J. Int. Assoc. Study Obes.* **1999**, *23*, 576–585. [CrossRef]
9. Boutelle, K.; Neumark-Sztainer, D.; Story, M.; Resnick, M. Weight control behaviors among obese, overweight, and nonoverweight adolescents. *J. Pediatr. Psychol.* **2002**, *27*, 531–540. [CrossRef]
10. Field, A.E.; Austin, S.B.; Taylor, C.B.; Malspeis, S.; Rosner, B.; Rockett, H.R.; Gillman, M.W.; Colditz, G.A. Relation between dieting and weight change among preadolescents and adolescents. *Pediatrics* **2003**, *112*, 900–906. [CrossRef] [PubMed]
11. Stice, E.; Cameron, R.P.; Killen, J.D.; Hayward, C.; Taylor, C.B. Naturalistic weight-reduction efforts prospectively predict growth in relative weight and onset of obesity among female adolescents. *J. Consult. Clin. Psychol.* **1999**, *67*, 967–974. [CrossRef]
12. Neumark-Sztainer, D.; Wall, M.; Guo, J.; Story, M.; Haines, J.; Eisenberg, M. Obesity, disordered eating, and eating disorders in a longitudinal study of adolescents: How do dieters fare 5 years later? *J. Am. Diet. Assoc.* **2006**, *106*, 559–568. [CrossRef] [PubMed]
13. Neumark-Sztainer, D.; Wall, M.; Story, M.; Standish, A.R. Dieting and unhealthy weight control behaviors during adolescence: associations with 10-year changes in body mass index. *J. Adolesc. Health* **2012**, *50*, 80–86. [CrossRef]
14. Haines, J.; Neumark-Sztainer, D. Prevention of obesity and eating disorders: A consideration of shared risk factors. *Health Educ. Res.* **2006**, *21*, 770–782. [CrossRef] [PubMed]
15. Sánchez-Carracedo, D.; Neumark-Sztainer, D.; López-Guimerà, G. Integrated prevention of obesity and eating disorders: Barriers, developments and opportunities. *Public Health Nutr.* **2012**, *15*, 2295–2309. [CrossRef]
16. Kazdin, A.E.; Fitzsimmons-Craft, E.E.; Wilfley, D.E. Addressing critical gaps in the treatment of eating disorders. *Int. J. Eat. Disord.* **2017**, *50*, 170–189. [CrossRef] [PubMed]
17. Jones, M.; Taylor Lynch, K.; Kass, A.E.; Burrows, A.; Williams, J.; Wilfley, D.E.; Taylor, C.B. Healthy weight regulation and eating disorder prevention in high school students: A universal and targeted Web-based intervention. *J. Med. Internet Res.* **2014**, *16*, e57. [CrossRef] [PubMed]
18. Hollis, C.; Falconer, C.J.; Martin, J.L.; Whittington, C.; Stockton, S.; Glazebrook, C.; Davies, E.B. Annual Research Review: Digital health interventions for children and young people with mental health problems—A systematic and meta-review. *J. Child Psychol. Psychiatry* **2017**, *58*, 474–503. [CrossRef]
19. European Commission Internet Access and Use Statistics—Households and Individuals 2017. Available online: https://ec.europa.eu/eurostat/statistics-explained/index.php?title=Internet_access_and_use_statistics_-_households_and_individuals&oldid=324579#Internet_use_by_individuals (accessed on 14 February 2019).
20. Lee, Y.Y.; Barendregt, J.J.; Stockings, E.A.; Ferrari, A.J.; Whiteford, H.A.; Patton, G.A.; Mihalopoulos, C. The population cost-effectiveness of delivering universal and indicated school-based interventions to prevent the onset of major depression among youth in Australia. *Epidemiol. Psychiatr. Sci.* **2017**, *26*, 545–564. [CrossRef]
21. Werner-Seidler, A.; Perry, Y.; Calear, A.L.; Newby, J.M.; Christensen, H. School-based depression and anxiety prevention programs for young people: A systematic review and meta-analysis. *Clin. Psychol. Rev.* **2017**, *51*, 30–47. [CrossRef]
22. Dray, J.; Bowman, J.; Campbell, E.; Freund, M.; Wolfenden, L.; Hodder, R.K.; McElwaine, K.; Tremain, D.; Bartlem, K.; Bailey, J.; et al. Systematic review of universal resilience-focused interventions targeting child and adolescent mental health in the school setting. *J. Am. Acad. Child Adolesc. Psychiatry* **2017**, *56*, 813–824. [CrossRef]
23. Eysenbach, G. The law of attrition. *J. Med. Internet Res.* **2005**, *7*, e11. [CrossRef]
24. Kelders, S.M.; Kok, R.N.; Ossebaard, H.C.; Gemert-Pijnen, J.E.V. Persuasive system design does matter: A systematic review of adherence to web-based interventions. *J. Med. Internet Res.* **2012**, *14*, e152. [CrossRef] [PubMed]

25. Van Gemert-Pijnen, J.E.; Nijland, N.; van Limburg, M.; Ossebaard, H.C.; Kelders, S.M.; Eysenbach, G.; Seydel, E.R. A holistic framework to improve the uptake and impact of ehealth technologies. *J. Med. Internet Res.* **2011**, *13*, e111. [CrossRef]
26. Jones Bell, M.; Zeiler, M.; Herrero, R.; Kuso, S.; Nitsch, M.; Etchemendy, E.; Fonseca-Baeza, S.; Oliver, E.; Adamcik, T.; Karwautz, A.; et al. Healthy Teens @ School: Evaluating and disseminating transdiagnostic preventive interventions for eating disorders and obesity for adolescents in school settings. *Internet Interv.* **2019**, *16*, 65–75. [CrossRef]
27. Taylor, C.B.; Taylor, K.; Jones, M.; Shorter, A.; Yee, M.; Genkin, B.; Burrows, A.; Kass, A.E.; Rizk, M.; Redman, M.; et al. Obesity prevention in defined (high school) populations. *Int. J. Obes. Suppl.* **2012**, *2*, S30–S32. [CrossRef]
28. Zeiler, M.; Kuso, S.; Nitsch, M.; Simek, M.; Adamcik, T.; Herrero, R.; Etchemendy, E.; Mira, A.; Oliver, E.; Jones Bell, M.; et al. Online Interventions to prevent mental health problems implemented in school settings: The perspectives from key stakeholders in Austria and Spain. *Eur. J. Public Health* **2019**, in press.
29. Nitsch, M.; Dimopoulos, C.N.; Flaschberger, E.; Saffran, K.; Kruger, J.F.; Garlock, L.; Wilfley, D.E.; Taylor, C.B.; Jones, M. A Guided online and mobile self-help program for individuals with eating disorders: An iterative engagement and usability study. *J. Med. Internet Res.* **2016**, *18*, e7. [CrossRef]
30. Wangberg, S.C.; Bergmo, T.S.; Johnsen, J.-A.K. Adherence in Internet-based interventions. *Patient Prefer. Adherence* **2008**, *2*, 57–65.
31. Wanner, M.; Martin-Diener, E.; Bauer, G.; Braun-Fahrländer, C.; Martin, B.W. Comparison of trial participants and open access users of a web-based physical activity intervention regarding adherence, attrition, and repeated participation. *J. Med. Internet Res.* **2010**, *12*, e3. [CrossRef] [PubMed]
32. Nielsen, J. Iterative user-interface design. *Computer* **1993**, *26*, 32–41. [CrossRef]
33. Nielsen, J.; Landauer, T.K. A Mathematical Model of the Finding of Usability Problems. In Proceedings of the INTERACT '93 and CHI '93 Conference on Human Factors in Computing Systems, Amsterdam, The Netherlands, 24–29 April 1993; ACM: New York, NY, USA, 1993; pp. 206–213.
34. Spirito, A.; Stark, L.J.; Williams, C. Development of a brief coping checklist for use with pediatric populations. *J. Pediatr. Psychol.* **1988**, *13*, 555–574. [CrossRef]
35. Tylka, T.L.; Kroon Van Diest, A.M. The Intuitive Eating Scale-2: Item refinement and psychometric evaluation with college women and men. *J. Couns. Psychol.* **2013**, *60*, 137–153. [CrossRef] [PubMed]
36. Van Dyck, Z.; Herbert, B.M.; Happ, C.; Kleveman, G.V.; Vögele, C. German version of the intuitive eating scale: Psychometric evaluation and application to an eating disordered population. *Appetite* **2016**, *105*, 798–807. [CrossRef] [PubMed]
37. Rosenberg, M. *Society and the Adolescent Self-Image*; Princeton University Press: Princeton, NJ, USA, 1965.
38. Roth, M.; Decker, O.; Herzberg, P.Y.; Brähler, E. Dimensionality and Norms of the Rosenberg Self-esteem Scale in a German General Population Sample. *Eur. J. Psychol. Assess.* **2008**, *24*, 190–197. [CrossRef]
39. Mattejat, F.; Remschmidt, H. *ILK-Inventar zur Erfassung der Lebensqualität bei Kindern und Jugendlichen: Ratingbogen für Kinder, Jugendliche und Eltern: Manual*; Huber: Bern, Switzerland, 2006.
40. Brooke, J. System usability scale (SUS): A quick-and-dirty method of system evaluation user information. *Read. UK Digit. Equip. Co Ltd.* **1986**, 43.
41. Bangor, A.; Kortum, P.T.; Miller, J.T. An empirical evaluation of the system usability scale. *Int. J. Hum. Comput. Interact.* **2008**, *24*, 574–594. [CrossRef]
42. Froschauer, U.; Lueger, M. *Das Qualitative Interview*, 1st ed.; Facultas: Vienna, Austria, 1993.
43. Grieben, C.; Stassen, G.; Froböse, I. How should web-based physical activity and healthy eating interventions be designed for young office workers? A Qualitative Approach. *J. Healthc. Commun.* **2018**, *3*, 1–15.
44. Schaarup, C.; Hartvigsen, G.; Larsen, L.B.; Tan, Z.-H.; Årsand, E.; Hejlesen, O.K. Assessing the potential use of eye-tracking triangulation for evaluating the usability of an online diabetes exercise system. *Stud. Health Technol. Inform.* **2015**, *216*, 84–88. [PubMed]
45. Ludden, G.D.S.; van Rompay, T.J.L.; Kelders, S.M.; van Gemert-Pijnen, J.E.W.C. How to increase reach and adherence of web-based interventions: A design research viewpoint. *J. Med. Internet Res.* **2015**, *17*, e172. [CrossRef] [PubMed]
46. Kuosmanen, T.; Fleming, T.M.; Barry, M.M. Using computerized mental health programs in alternative education: Understanding the requirements of students and staff. *Health Commun.* **2018**, *33*, 753–761. [CrossRef]

47. Neil, A.L.; Batterham, P.; Christensen, H.; Bennett, K.; Griffiths, K.M. Predictors of adherence by adolescents to a cognitive behavior therapy website in school and community-based settings. *J. Med. Internet Res.* **2009**, *11*, e6. [CrossRef]
48. Masia-Warner, C.; Nangle, D.W.; Hansen, D.J. Bringing evidence-based child mental health services to the schools: General issues and specific populations. *Educ. Treat. Child.* **2006**, *29*, 165–172.
49. Kern, L.; Mathur, S.R.; Albrecht, S.F.; Poland, S.; Rozalski, M.; Skiba, R.J. The need for school-based mental health services and recommendations for implementation. *School Ment. Health* **2017**, *9*, 205–217. [CrossRef]
50. Arango, C.; Díaz-Caneja, C.M.; McGorry, P.D.; Rapoport, J.; Sommer, I.E.; Vorstman, J.A.; McDaid, D.; Marín, O.; Serrano-Drozdowskyj, E.; Freedman, R.; et al. Preventive strategies for mental health. *Lancet Psychiatry* **2018**, *5*, 591–604. [CrossRef]
51. Dopp, A.R.; Parisi, K.E.; Munson, S.A.; Lyon, A.R. A glossary of user-centered design strategies for implementation experts. *Transl. Behav. Med.* **2018**, in press. [CrossRef] [PubMed]
52. Mohr, D.C.; Lyon, A.R.; Lattie, E.G.; Reddy, M.; Schueller, S.M. Accelerating digital mental health research from early design and creation to successful implementation and sustainment. *J. Med. Internet Res.* **2017**, *19*, e153. [CrossRef] [PubMed]
53. Dopp, A.R.; Parisi, K.E.; Munson, S.A.; Lyon, A.R. Integrating implementation and user-centred design strategies to enhance the impact of health services: Protocol from a concept mapping study. *Health Res. Policy Syst.* **2019**, *17*, 1. [CrossRef] [PubMed]
54. Lyon, A.R.; Koerner, K. User-Centered Design for Psychosocial Intervention Development and Implementation. *Clin. Psychol. Publ. Div. Clin. Psychol. Am. Psychol. Assoc.* **2016**, *23*, 180–200. [CrossRef] [PubMed]
55. Beecham, J.; Bonin, E.-M.; Görlich, D.; Baños, R.; Beintner, I.; Buntrock, C.; Bolinski, F.; Botella, C.; Ebert, D.D.; Herrero, R.; et al. Assessing the costs and cost-effectiveness of ICare internet-based interventions (protocol). *Internet Interv.* **2019**, *16*, 12–19. [CrossRef]
56. Beintner, I.; Görlich, D.; Berger, T.; Ebert, D.D.; Zeiler, M.; Herrero Camarano, R.; Waldherr, K.; Jacobi, C. Interrelations between participant and intervention characteristics, process variables and outcomes in online interventions: A protocol for overarching analyses within and across seven clinical trials in ICare. *Internet Interv.* **2019**, *16*, 86–97. [CrossRef] [PubMed]
57. Glasgow, R.E.; Vogt, T.M.; Boles, S.M. Evaluating the public health impact of health promotion interventions: The RE-AIM framework. *Am. J. Public Health* **1999**, *89*, 1322–1327. [CrossRef]

MDPI
St. Alban-Anlage 66
4052 Basel
Switzerland
Tel. +41 61 683 77 34
Fax +41 61 302 89 18
www.mdpi.com

Nutrients Editorial Office
E-mail: nutrients@mdpi.com
www.mdpi.com/journal/nutrients

www.ingramcontent.com/pod-product-compliance
Lightning Source LLC
Chambersburg PA
CBHW041753220926
51847CB00014B/187
9783038979982